BUILDINGS
ACROSS TIME

AN INTRODUCTION
TO WORLD
ARCHITECTURE

BUILDINGS ACROSS TIME

AN INTRODUCTION TO WORLD ARCHITECTURE

Marian Moffett
The University of Tennessee

Michael Fazio
Mississippi State University

Lawrence Wodehouse
The University of Tennessee

Boston   Burr Ridge, IL   Dubuque, IA   Madison, WI   New York   San Francisco
St. Louis   Bangkok   Bogotá   Caracas   Lisbon   London   Madrid   Mexico City
Milan   New Delhi   Seoul   Singapore   Sydney   Taipei   Toronto

McGraw-Hill Higher Education

A Division of The **McGraw-Hill** *Companies*

Copyright © 2004 by the McGraw-Hill Companies, Inc. Printed in
Singapore. Except as permitted under the United States Copyright
Act of 1976, no part of this publication may be reproduced or
distributed in any form or by any means, or stored in a data base or
retrieval system, without the prior written permission of the publisher.

This book is printed on acid-free paper.

7 8 9 0   2 1 0 9 8 7 6 5 4 3

ISBN 0-7674-0511-0

Library of Congress Cataloging-in-Publication Data
Moffett, Marian.
  Buildings across time : an introduction to world architecture.
    p. cm.
  Includes bibliographical references and index.
  ISBN 0-7674-0511-0
  1. Architecture — History. I. Fazio, Michael. II. Title.
NA200.W64 2004
720'9—dc21   2003044458

Publisher: Chris Freitag
Senior Sponsoring Editor: Joe Hanson
Editorial Assistant: Torrii Yamada
Marketing Manager: Lisa Berry
Media Producer: Shannon Gattens

This book was designed and produced by
Laurence King Publishing Ltd
71 Great Russell Street, London WC1B 3BP
www.laurenceking.co.uk

Every effort has been made to contact copyright holders, but should
there be any errors or omissions, Laurence King Publishing Ltd
would be pleased to insert the appropriate acknowledgment in any
subsequent printing of this publication.

Senior Managing Editor: Richard Mason
Designer: Newton Harris
Cover Designer: Price Watkins
Picture Researcher: Peter Kent
Typesetter: Fakenham Photosetting
Maps by Advanced Illustration
Printed in Singapore

Frontispiece: Interior of the nave, Vézelay, France, 1120–40. © Paul
M.R. Maeyaert.
Frontcover: Cesar Pelli, Petronas Towers, Kuala Lumpur, Malaysia,
1998.
Backcover: Guarino Guarini, Intrados of the Dome, S. Lorenzo,
Turin, 1668–80.

CONTENTS

PREFACE   x

MAPS   xi–xvi

INTRODUCTION   1

A Word about Drawings and Images   5

CHAPTER 1

THE BEGINNINGS OF ARCHITECTURE   9

Prehistoric Settlements and Megalith Constructions   9
   Eastern Europe   9
   Western Europe   10
Ancient Mesopotamia   14
   Sumerians, Akkadians, and Neo-Sumerians   15
   Babylonians, Hittites, and Assyrians   18
   Neo-Babylonians and Persians   20
Ancient Egypt   22
   Essay: "Hydraulic" Civilizations   23
   The Early Dynastic Period and Old Kingdom   24
   The First Pyramids   24
   Fourth-Dynasty Pyramids at Giza   27
   The Middle Kingdom   30
   The New Kingdom   31

CHAPTER 2

THE GREEK WORLD   39

The Minoans   39
The Mycenaeans   42
   Mycenae   42
Greece: The Archaic Period   47
Greece: The Classical Period   50
   The Parthenon, Athens   51
   Other Buildings on the Acropolis   53
   Essay: Celebrating Athena's Birthday   54
Greece: The Hellenistic Period   57
Greek City Planning   60
   The Athenian Agora   60
   Hellenistic Cities   62

CHAPTER 3

THE ARCHITECTURE OF ANCIENT INDIA
AND SOUTHEAST ASIA   67

Religions of India   69
Early Buddhist Shrines   70
   Essay: Bamiyan and the Colossal Buddha   74
The Spread of Buddhist Influence   75
Hindu Temples   76
   Early Buildings   76
   Later Temples   77
   Angkor Wat   83

CHAPTER 4

TRADITIONAL ARCHITECTURE OF CHINA
AND JAPAN   87

Chinese Architectural Principles   90
Principles of City Planning   93
Houses and Gardens   96
   Essay: Elder Brother Rock   97
Japanese Temple Architecture   99
   Buddhist Temples   99
   Shinto Shrines   102
Japanese Cities, Houses, and Castles   103
Zen Buddhist Architecture: Katsura   107

CHAPTER 5

THE ROMAN WORLD   111

Etruscan Imprints   111
Roman Architecture   113
Building Techniques and Materials   114
City Planning   116
   Essay: The Engineering Might of the Romans   122
Temples   123
Public Buildings   126
   Basilicas   126
   Public Baths   127
   Theaters and Amphitheaters   129
Residences   132
   Urban Housing   132
   Rural Villas and Urban Palaces   135

CHAPTER 6
EARLY CHRISTIAN AND BYZANTINE
ARCHITECTURE 141

Early Christian Basilicas 142
Martyria, Baptisteries, and Mausolea 143
   Essay: Eusebius and Constantine 146
Byzantine Basilicas and Domed Basilicas 148
Centrally Planned Byzantine Churches 152
Byzantine Churches in Russia 155
   Masonry Churches 155
   Wooden Churches 159

CHAPTER 7
ISLAMIC ARCHITECTURE 165

Early Shrines and Palaces 165
Development of the Mosque 169
Regional Variations in Mosque Design 170
   Columnar Hall Designs 170
   Iwan Designs 172
   Courtyard Designs 174
   Pavilion Designs 179
   Domed Prayer Hall Designs 180
Houses, Palaces, and Urban Patterns 184

CHAPTER 8
EARLY MEDIEVAL AND ROMANESQUE
ARCHITECTURE 191

Carolingian Architecture 191
   The Revival of Masonry Construction 192
   Monasteries 195
Anglo-Saxon and Viking Architecture 198
   English Churches 198
   Norwegian Stave Churches 199
Early Romanesque Architecture 202
Romanesque Architecture of the Holy Roman Empire
   205
Pilgrimage Roads 210
The Order of Cluny 213
   Essay: The Mystic Mill from Vézelay 215
Aquitaine and Provence 217
Cistercian Monasteries 221
Norman Architecture 224

CHAPTER 9
GOTHIC ARCHITECTURE 229

Early Gothic 230
   The Abbey Church of St. Denis 230
   Early Gothic Cathedrals 232
High Gothic 236
   Chartres and Bourges 237
   Beauvais and Ste. Chapelle 241
English Gothic 245
   Essay: A Wool Church 246
   Early English 247
   Decorated and Perpendicular 250
German and Italian Gothic 255
   German Hall Churches 255
   Italian Gothic Variations 257
Medieval Construction 262
Medieval Houses and Castles 263
   Housing 263
   Castles 265
Medieval Cities 268

CHAPTER 10
INDIGENOUS ARCHITECTURE IN THE
PRE-COLUMBIAN AMERICAS 275

Tribes of the Great Plains and the Great Lakes 275
Tribes of the Northeast 276
Tribes of the Mississippi River Basin 277
   Essay: The Birthplace of the Choctaws 278
Arctic and Subarctic Tribes 279
Tribes of the Northwest and Northern California 280
Tribes of the Southwest 281
Mexico, Central America, and South America 283
   The Olmecs of the Eastern Mexican Coast 283
   Teotihuacán in the Valley of Mexico 283
   The Zapotecs and Mixtecs at Monte Albán, Oaxaca 285
   The Maya 286
   Tikal 287
   Copán and Palenque 288
   Uxmal and Chichén-Itzá 289
   The Toltecs in the Valley of Mexico 291
   The Aztecs at Tenochtitlán 292
   The Incas in the Andes 292

CHAPTER 11
RENAISSANCE ARCHITECTURE   295

Filippo Brunelleschi   296
   Florence Cathedral   296
   Other Florentine Buildings   299
Michelozzo Bartolomeo and the Palazzo Medici   302
Leon Battista Alberti   303
   Writings   303
   The Palazzo Rucellai, Florence   305
   Churches in Rimini and Mantua   305
   Essay: Pius's Resolutions   307
   The Ideal City   308
Other Renaissance City Plans   308
The Spread of the Renaissance   310
   Urbino   310
   Milan   311
   Moscow   312
Leonardo Da Vinci   313
Donato Bramante   314
   The Tempietto, Rome   316
   St. Peter's, Rome   317
   The Belvedere Courtyard and the House of Raphael,
      Rome   318
The Late Renaissance, Mannerism   319
   The Villa Madama, Rome   320
   The Uffizi, Florence   321
   The Palazzo del Te, Mantua   322
Michelangelo   323
   S. Lorenzo, Florence   323
   The Campidoglio, Rome   325
   The Palazzo Farnese, Rome   326
   St. Peter's, Rome   326
   Porta Pia, Rome   328
   Sforza Chapel, Rome   329
Andrea Palladio   330
   Buildings in Vicenza   331
   Villa Designs in the Veneto   331
   Churches in Venice   335
   The Teatro Olimpico   336
Palladio's Venice   336
Garden Design   338
   Boboli Gardens, Florence   340
The Renaissance in France   341
   Châteaux in the Loire Valley   341
   Sebastiano Serlio and Philibert de l'Orme   343
   The Louvre, the French Place and Hôtel, Paris   344
The Renaissance in England   346
   Elizabethan Country Houses   347
   Inigo Jones   349

CHAPTER 12
BAROQUE ARCHITECTURE   353

The Reformation and Counter-Reformation   353
   Il Gesù, Rome   353
Pope Sixtus V and the Replanning of Rome   355
   St. Peter's   357
Gianlorenzo Bernini   358
   The Completion of St. Peter's   358
   S. Andrea al Quirinale, Rome   361
Francesco Borromini   362
   S. Carlo alle Quattro Fontane, Rome   362
   S. Ivo della Sapienza   363
Urban Open Spaces in Baroque Rome   365
   The Piazza Navona   365
   Essay: Piazza Navona—A Space for Spectacle   367
   The Piazza del Popolo   368
The Spread of Baroque Architecture to Northern Italy
      370
   Guarino Guarini   370
   Bernardo Vittone   372
   Filippo Juvarra   372
The Baroque in Central Europe   373
   Die Wies, Bavaria   376
The Baroque in France   381
   The Louvre, Paris   381
   François Mansart   382
   The Châteaux of Vaux-le-Vicomte and Versailles   384
   Jules-Hardouin Mansart   387
Christopher Wren and the Baroque in England   388
   The City Churches   389
   St. Paul's   390
   Housing in the Manner of Wren   392
Nicholas Hawksmoor, Sir John Vanbrugh, and James
      Gibbs   393

CHAPTER 13
THE EIGHTEENTH CENTURY   397

The English Neo-Palladians   398
The Return to Antiquity   400
   Essay: Piranesi's View of Rome   401
Robert Adam and William Chambers   402
Etienne-Louis Boullée and Claude-Nicolas Ledoux   405
French Architects and the Aggrandizement of the State
      409
French Architectural Education and the Ecole des
      Beaux-Arts   413
The Challenge of the Industrial Revolution   413
Romanticism and the Picturesque   415
The Romantic Landscape   416
Picturesque Buildings   417

CHAPTER 14
NINETEENTH-CENTURY
DEVELOPMENTS 419

Neo-Classicism 420
    Karl Friedrich Schinkel 420
    Sir John Soane 423
    Benjamin Henry Latrobe and Thomas Jefferson 424
The Gothic Revival 429
    A.W.N. Pugin 429
    The Ecclesiological Movement in England and America
      430
    Eugène-Emmanuel Viollet-le-Duc 431
The Ecole des Beaux-Arts 432
    Richard Morris Hunt and the World's Columbian
      Exposition 433
    McKim, Mead, and White 434
Progress in Iron Fabrication 437
    Iron Bridges 437
    Developments in Steel 438
    Essay: The Coming of the Railroad 439
Architectural Applications of Iron and Steel Construction
    440
    Joseph Paxton 441
    Henri Labrouste 442
    Gustave Eiffel 444
    The First Skyscrapers 445
Skeletal Construction in Concrete and Wood 448
The Arts and Crafts Movement 448
    John Ruskin 448
    William Morris 449
    Richard Norman Shaw, C.F.A. Voysey, and Herman
      Muthesius 450
Art Nouveau 452
    Victor Horta and Hector Guimard 453
    Antonio Gaudí 454
    Charles Rennie Mackintosh 457
The Viennese Secession 460
The Search for an American Style 462
    Henry Hobson Richardson 462
    Louis Henri Sullivan 467

CHAPTER 15
THE TWENTIETH CENTURY
AND MODERNISM 475

The Idea of a Modern Architecture 475
    The War of Words 475
Adolf Loos 477
    Ornament and Crime 477
    The Raumplan and Loos's Buildings 478
Frank Lloyd Wright 480
    Developing the Prairie House 480
    Early Public Buildings 484
    The Flight from America 486
Peter Behrens and the Deutscher Werkbund 487
Futurism and Constructivism 488
Dutch and German Expressionism 490
Art Deco 495
De Stijl 501
Exploiting the Potential of Concrete 503
Tony Garnier and the Industrial City 506
Le Corbusier 508
    The Dom-ino and Citrohan Houses 508
    The Villa Stein and the Villa Savoye 509
    The Cité Universitaire and Le Corbusier's "Five Points"
      511
Walter Gropius 511
    Building Designs 511
    The Bauhaus in Weimar and Dessau 512
    Essay: A Russian Painter at the Bauhaus 513
Ludwig Mies van der Rohe 515
    The Barcelona Pavilion and the Tugendhat House 516
The Weissenhof Siedlung and the International Style
    518
Later Work of Mies van der Rohe 520
    Planning and Building at I.I.T. 521
Later Work of Frank Lloyd Wright 523
    Broadacre City 523
    Fallingwater 523
    The Johnson Wax Company 525
    The Guggenheim Museum and Taliesin West 526
Later Work of Le Corbusier 528
    Ronchamp and Ste-Marie-de-la-Tourette 529
    Chandigarh 530
The Decline of Modernism 531

CHAPTER 16
MODERNISMS IN THE MID- AND LATE
TWENTIETH CENTURY   533

Alvar Aalto   533
Eero Saarinen   537
Louis I. Kahn   538
Robert Venturi's Radical Counter-Proposal to Modernism
    541
Intellectual Inspirations for Post-Modernism   543
Philip Johnson   544
Charles Moore   545
Michael Graves   547
Robert A.M. Stern   549
Richard Meier   550
The Exploitation of Technology by James Stirling and
    Others   551
Deconstruction   557
Peter Eisenman   557
    Essay: M.C. Escher and the Paradoxical Staircases of
    Post-Modernism   558
Frank Gehry   560
Glenn Murcutt   563

GLOSSARY   568

BIBLIOGRAPHY   572

PICTURE CREDITS   576

INDEX   577

PREFACE

We have written this survey of world architecture not only for students taking introductory courses, but also for the general reader interested in the story that buildings have to tell, the people who built them, and those who used them. We begin with the prehistoric era and end in the late twentieth century, covering the Western tradition together with a consideration of buildings in the pre-Columbian Americas, India, China and Southeast Asia, Russia, Japan, and the Islamic world.

Our aim has been to present this diverse sampling of the built environment in a straightforward but lively writing style that is meaty without becoming dense, so as to create a useful book for all those who have a passion for architectural history but who are not specialists in the field. Architectural terms are set off in boldface type when they first appear and are collected in a glossary at the end of the book.

Because architecture is at once a functional and a visual art, the text and illustrations are inseparable. This book contains 270 black-and-white photographs, 300 color photographs, and 350 line drawings, most of which have discursive captions that can be read separately or in conjunction with the text. Each chapter (except chapter 7) includes a short essay based upon a single image, a device intended to introduce the reader both to the spirit and content of that chapter. An annotated bibliography at the end of the book provides suggestions for further reading.

In writing this book, we have received assistance from many sources. Our colleagues Lynn Barker, Robert Craig, Jack Elliott, Jay Henry, David Lewis, Daniel MacGilvray, Charles Mack, Mark Reinberger, C. Murray Smart, Jr., and Julia Smyth-Pinney contributed essays. The following reviewers read portions of the manuscript at various times and made comments that assisted us in clarifying and improving the text: Martha Bradley, University of Utah; Roger T. Dunn, Bridgewater State College; Fil Hearn, University of Pittsburgh; Lisa Reilly, University of Virginia; Mark Reinberger, University of Georgia; Pamela H. Simpson, Washington and Lee University; Murray Smart, Jr., University of Arkansas; Robert L. Vann, University of Maryland; and Craig Zabel, Penn State University. Two graduate students in the School of Architecture at Mississippi State University, Yan Huang and Kai Pan, used their exceptional talents with graphics software to produce the line drawings.

At McGraw-Hill, Chris Freitag, Joe Hanson, Torrii Yamada, Lisa Berry, and Shannon Gattens provided important support. At Laurence King Publishing all editorial, design, illustrative, and scheduling issues were expertly managed by Richard Mason. Nick Newton and Randell Harris designed the book with great skill, and Peter Kent researched most of the fine photographs. To these people and to our families we express our gratitude.

Photographs are acknowledged in the photo credits. In addition to taking some photographs ourselves, we would also like to thank the following colleagues who supplied some of them: Gerald Anderson, Robert Craig, Mark DeKay, Jeff Elder, Jason Labutka, David Lewis, Dan MacGilvray, Rachel McCann, Alison Moffett, Kenneth Moffett, R. Bruce Moffett, Max Robinson, J. William Rudd, Brenda Sartoris, Pamela Scott, Raiford Scott, Ronald Scott, C. Murray Smart, Jr., Patrick Snadon, and Lawrence Wodehouse.

Using the CD-ROM

This book is complemented by an interactive CD-ROM on which you will find, by chapter, photos and line art of many of the buildings covered in the text and their descriptive captions, with additional line art that could not be accommodated within the book. For each chapter, there are also one or more buildings presented in greater depth, a timeline, and review exercises to test your mastery of fundamentals presented in the text. You may also construct a comprehensive review of your choice of chapters. Review exercises are randomly generated, so you will have a different set of questions each time you go through them. Links to related websites can be accessed if you work from a computer connected to the Internet. We recommend that you study the book first, then turn to the CD.

Finally, we would like to hear from you. Send your comments or suggestions to Art and Humanities Editor, McGraw-Hill Higher Education, 20th floor, Two Penn Plaza, New York, NY 10121-2298.

Marian Moffett
Michael Fazio
May 2003

Map 1: Central and Eastern Europe and the Middle East

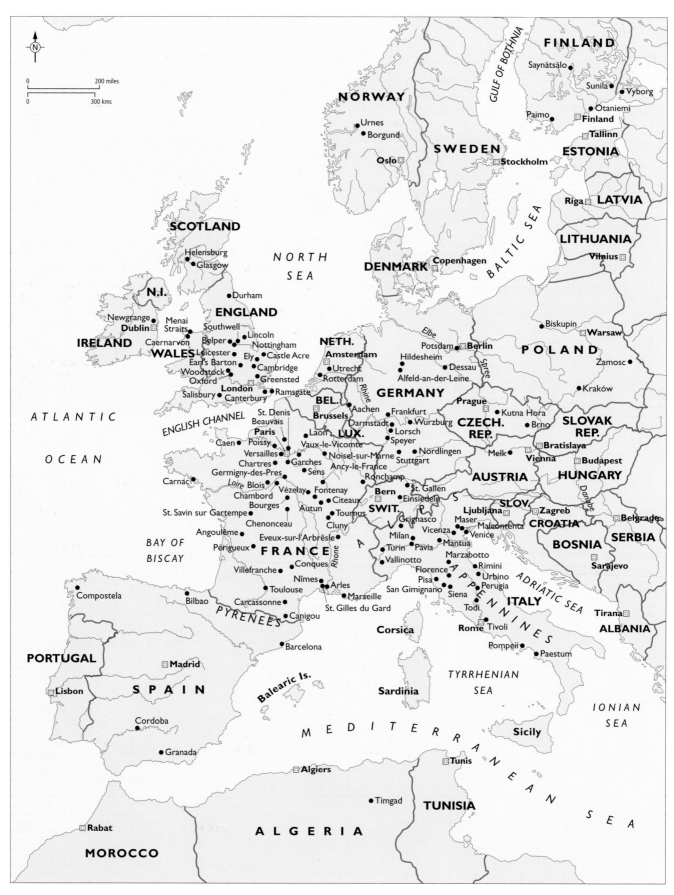

Map 2: Europe and North Africa

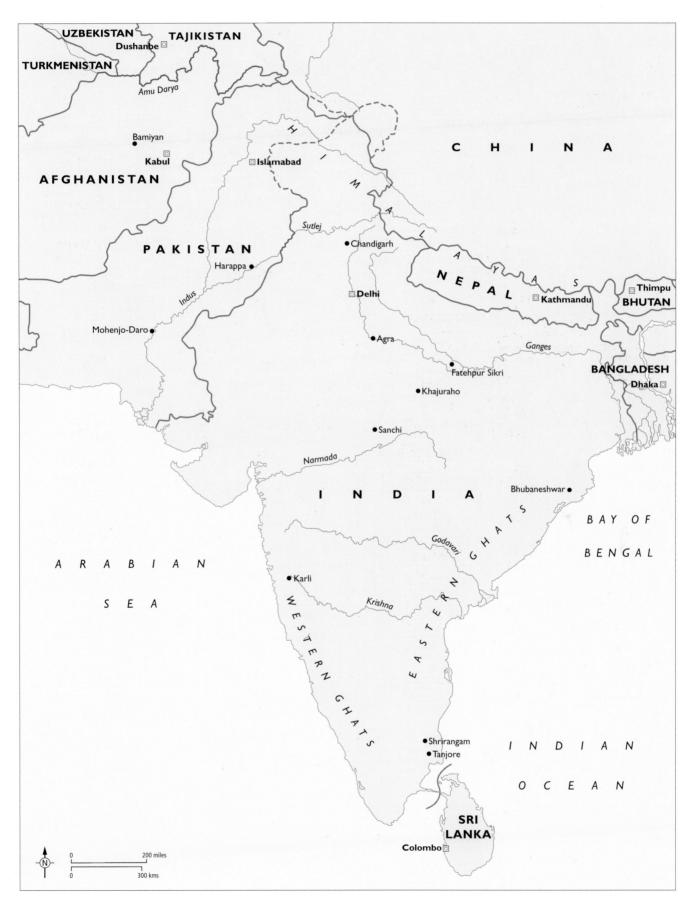

Map 3: Western Asia and India

Map 4: North America

MEXICO
• Tula
Tenochtitlán
Teotihuacán
• • La Venta
Mexico City
• Uxmal • Chichén-Itzá
• Monte
Albán
• Palenque
Tikal • Belmopan
GUAT. BELIZE
Guatemala City • Copán HONDURAS
San Salvador Tegucigalpa
EL NICARAGUA
SALV. • Managua
• San José
COSTA Panama City
RICA PANAMA

GULF OF
MEXICO

CUBA
HAITI DOM.
REP.
JAMAICA PUERTO
RICO
GREATER ANTILLES
LESSER ANTILLES

CARIBBEAN SEA

ATLANTIC

OCEAN

Caracas
VENEZUELA Georgetown SURINAM Paramaribo
Orinoco GUYANA Cayenne
Bogotá FRENCH
COLOMBIA GUIANA

Negro
Quito
ECUADOR Amazon

B R A Z I L
PERU São Francisco
Marañón

Lima Machu Picchu
Cuzco BRAZILIAN HIGHLANDS
Saqsaywaman
La Paz Brasília
BOLIVIA

PARAGUAY

PACIFIC Asunción

OCEAN
Paraná

C URUGUAY
Santiago Buenos Aires Montevideo
H A ARGENTINA
I N
L D Colorado
E E
S S

ATLANTIC

OCEAN

FALKLAND
ISLANDS (U.K.)

N

0   400 miles

0   600 kms

Map 5: Central and South America

Map 6: Eastern Asia and Australia

xvi

INTRODUCTION

You, the reader, are the reason for this book. We, the authors, have drawn on our cumulative experience in teaching and writing about architectural history to convey in words and images information about some of the world's most interesting and important buildings. This book surveys Western architecture in some depth and offers an introduction to non-Western architecture in India, China, Southeast Asia, and Japan, and many Islamic settings. Together the text and illustrations encourage discussion, thought, and analysis. In this introduction, we offer a guide to the effective use of this book.

Architectural history begins with buildings. In order really to see these buildings, one needs to use precise descriptive language. Hence we have tried throughout to present clear, understandable, but provocative text, and to define basic terminology when it is first introduced. Still, if left at the level of pure information, these words produce little true insight. We have therefore written this book in a way that encourages looking, but more than that, *seeing*; and the difference between the two is considerable. Seeing requires proceeding beyond the image projected on the retina to a process of analysis and the making of critical judgments. This, in turn, calls for placing buildings in their various contexts—social, political, economic, artistic, technological, and environmental—and determining whether they fulfill their obligations to their clients, to other users, and to society at large. To do this, it is necessary to enter the mind of the architect and to suspend modern biases so that we can evaluate the work as the product of a particular time and place.

What is architecture? Certainly it is shelter, but it can be much more. The phrase "frozen music" is often used, but such a description seems to imply that architecture has only an esthetic component. The "shaping of space for human use" seems more obviously useful, but it hardly explains the fascination of the Egyptian pyramids or the symbolism of a state capitol building. The Roman architect and engineer Vitruvius, active around 40 BCE, considered the essentials of architecture to be *firmitas*, *utilitas*, and *venustas*, commonly translated as firmness, commodity, and delight. Here firmness is structural stability, commodity is the meeting of functional requirements, and delight is beauty. One can hardly disagree with the need for firmness and commodity: any building that collapses or does not provide the right kind of space for the client's purposes must be considered a failure. Delight, or beauty, however, is a more elusive term, one with standards that have changed over time. Some have argued that beauty arises naturally from the fulfillment of functional requirements. Others have seen it as an inevitable result of the logical use of building materials and structural systems. Still others have found it in applied ornamentation.

Let us consider the first two terms in Vitruvius's triad in a slightly different way by asking, why and how is architecture produced? In order to erect buildings, people must have a motive—a will to build; materials and a knowledge of how to use them—a means to build; and systems of construction—an ability to build. The will to build certainly includes responses to functional requirements, but often goes well beyond these to address spiritual, psychological, and emotional needs. For some building types, such as industrial buildings, practical concerns naturally predominate. In others, such as civic or religious buildings, meanings may be dramatically revealed through symbolic forms. To most people, for example, the interior of a religious building should elevate the human spirit, while a warehouse must only protect material goods. However, utilitarian high-rise office buildings are usually designed to reflect the corporate image that the CEO and board of directors wish to project, and homeowners commonly modify their houses both inside and out, not only to accommodate changing functional demands but also to express their own personalities and values. All architecture reflects such values, and the best of it expresses the tastes and aspirations of the entire society. More money, finer workmanship and materials, and (often) better design have typically been expended on buildings that shelter activities important to large segments of society. Thus, for many periods, religious buildings have been the principal laboratories for architectural experimentation and have

0.1 Library of Celsus, Ephesus, Asia Minor, 114–17.
Constructed by the Romans, this is an example of post-and-lintel (column-and-beam) construction.

been built to endure, while residential architecture and even commercial buildings have been more transitory, which explains the abundance of religious buildings in a text such as this one.

At the beginning of an architectural project, the client and architect develop a program, or statement, of projected spatial uses, sizes, qualities, and relationships. The program for an apartment building, say, would itemize the number of apartments and their sizes, the common spaces such as lobbies, the service spaces such as mechanical rooms and storage, and also include an allowance for horizontal and vertical circulation (corridors, stairs, ramps, and elevators). Because many designs can satisfy such a program, it is the architect's responsibility to develop alternatives, to select the best ideas from among them, and to present the results in the form of drawings and models from which the building can be erected.

No matter how strong the will to build, people must also have the resources with which to build, which historically has meant local building materials. In turn, materials have strongly influenced architectural character. One of the most fascinating aspects of studying everyday buildings from the past is noticing how the simplest materials, such as wood, clay, thatch, and stone, have been employed to create architecture. If clay alone was available in abundance, people used tamped earth or made bricks. If people lived in areas that were heavily forested, they built in wood. The ancient Greeks were among the most skilled carvers of stone, but they would hardly have become so

without the abundant local marble that could be chiseled with extremely fine detail.

People must also have the ability to build. That is, they must be able to assemble materials into stable systems of construction. Structural materials can be classified according to the way they accept loads: in tension or compression, or a combination of the two. When in compression, the fibers of a material are pressed together; when in tension the fibers are pulled apart. Stone, brick, and concrete are all strong in compression but not in tension. Wood is strong in both tension and compression, as is iron; but iron is also brittle. In the nineteenth and twentieth centuries, metallurgists refined iron into steel, a material to which small amounts of other metals have been added to form alloys that are highly malleable. Because it combines the compressive strength of concrete with the tensile strength of embedded steel, reinforced concrete is also strong in both tension and compression.

All structures respond to the vertical pull of gravity in the form of live and dead loads, and to side loads or lateral forces created by the wind and earthquakes. Live loads are the people (and/or animals) that inhabit a structure. Dead loads are the weight of the building itself and of its inanimate contents such as furniture. Wind loads are accommodated primarily by diagonal bracing, and seismic loads through flexible connections.

Only in the past 150 years has it become possible to quantify the direction and magnitude of loads and to measure the ability of specific building materials to resist external forces, providing designers with the basis for producing mathematical models that predict structural behavior. For the vast majority of buildings considered in this

0.2 Arch, Kabah, Mexico, 850–900.
Built by the Maya of Central America, this is an example of corbeled construction. Note that the stones forming the triangular arch are laid in horizontal courses.

0.3 Barn, Cades Cove, Great Smoky Mountains National Park, Tennessee, 19th century.

This is an example of cantilevered construction. The second-floor loft overhangs the log cribs of the base, supported on long wooden cantilevers extending to the sides and front-to-back across the width of the barn.

book, however, achieving a stable structure was a matter of trial and error, based upon modifications of what had been done in the past.

Structural systems can be classified into five categories according to the geometric configuration of their members and the way in which loads are resisted: (1) post and lintel (or column and beam); (2) corbel and cantilever; (3) arch and vault; (4) truss and space frame; and (5) tensile. Post-and-lintel systems, formed by vertical and horizontal members, are perhaps the most common type, sometimes known as trabeated systems (Fig. 0.1). The possible distance between posts is primarily determined by the spanning capability of the beams. Under loading, the beams bend or deflect downward, stretching (or placing in tension) the fibers in the lower half of the member and pressing together (or placing in compression) the fibers in the upper half. Materials such as stone tend to fail quickly if placed in tension, so one can hardly imagine a wire made of stone. Since materials for lintels should be equally strong in tension and compression, wood, steel, and reinforced concrete are widely used.

Stone was the most durable building material available to early societies. These civilizations found ways to overcome stone's inherent weakness in tension and at the same time used it to span greater distances than were possible in post-and-lintel construction. The earliest method was through corbeling (Fig. 0.2). Stones were laid in horizontal courses, with the last stone in each course projecting slightly beyond the one below it to form a corbeled arch. A corbeled dome is made up of rings of stones (or even wood), with each succeeding ring smaller and, therefore, projecting beyond the one below it. This same principle has been used in cantilever construction, where a beam or beams (often of wood) project beyond their

supports to form an overhang, such as an eave below a roof or an overhanging second floor or jetty (Fig. 0.3).

Masonry arches and vaults are composed of wedge-shaped stones called **voussoirs** that must be supported on a temporary framework, called **centering**, until the arch or vault is completed, at which time the stones press tightly against one another and become self-supporting (Fig. 0.4). Such construction requires firm lateral bracing, as an arch or vault exerts not only a downward thrust but also a lateral thrust, which is an outward, overturning force that must be counteracted if the arch or vault is to remain in equilibrium. While all arches behave in a similar manner structurally, their profiles vary considerably. Semicircular (or Roman), pointed, horseshoe, and segmental arches are among the most important historically. Domes may also

0.4 Street in Rhodes, 1100–1300.

Buildings here have been braced with arches as a result of earthquakes. Several different arch profiles can be seen, all constructed of wedge-shaped voussoirs.

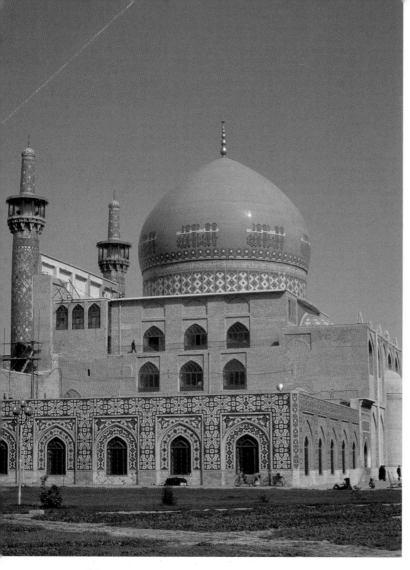

vary in profile, from shallow saucer shapes to semicircular or hemispherical to steeply pitched; the steeper the arch or dome's profile, the less the lateral thrust (Fig. 0.5).

The trussing method of spanning space calls for short wooden or metal elements to be connected in triangular configurations (Fig. 0.6). The Romans developed this technique for wooden bridges, but their experiments were not continued by subsequent societies. In the medieval period, trusses in church roofs depended on having one member, the bottom chord, equal in length to the span being covered. Early in the nineteenth century, bridge-builders reinvented the art of constructing trusses using short members, employing first wood and then iron and steel in various triangulated configurations, many of which were patented. The Warren Truss, named for its designer and composed of equilateral triangles, is probably the most common today. A truss repeated in three dimensions is known as a space frame, a twentieth-century structural development that is particularly useful for long, clear-span roofs.

Some structures are based largely on tension. Fabric tents with upright posts are examples of tensile structures, as are suspension bridges (Fig. 0.7). In both cases, the load is partly carried by fibers or cables woven or spun together. Builders in China and the Andes of Peru used animal or vegetable fibers such as hair, vines, and sisal to build tension structures, but these were limited in durability by the inherent weakness of the fibers and their tendency to decay. Great progress has been made in the development of tensile construction in the nineteenth and twentieth centuries as engineers have used iron bars or spun thin strands of steel into cables to support the world's longest bridges. Cables have also been used to suspend floors of

0.5 Goharshad Mosque, Mashhad, Iran, 1419.
This mosque shows typical Islamic arch profiles and a handsome blue-tiled dome.

0.6 Railroad bridge, Tennessee river, Knoxville, Tennessee, ca. 1906.
This bridge over the Tennessee river is composed of Warren trusses.

0.7 Seventh Street Bridge, Pittsburgh, Pennsylvania, 1925–28.

This is an example of a suspension structure where loads are carried primarily in tension.

multi-story buildings. Pneumatic structures, like balloons, have lightweight membranes supported by pressurized air, and thus are also based on tension.

The possibilities of these structural systems are vast. In addition, there are hybrid systems such as cantilevered and arched trusses. The selection of any one of them for a particular building depends on available materials, economics, spatial requirements, and the esthetic sensibilities of the architect and client.

Finally, a few words about styles and precedents. During the eighteenth and nineteenth centuries, historians developed taxonomies classifying the architectural work of various periods according to perceived common characteristics. Today, we recognize that the story is often much more complex and that the lines between the chronological classifications are blurred. The reader should take this into account when studying a chapter on, say, the "Renaissance" or the "Baroque." These are convenient terms, but they should be seen as no more than that, conveniences, and should not obscure the diversity and complexity of the historical built environment. Likewise, the buildings discussed here have been carefully chosen. In most cases, they are the so-called "canonical" buildings, that is, the ones that have been recognized by many scholars over time as best representing a time and place or the work of an individual. The canon has changed and will continue to change, particularly for buildings outside the European context and those of the more recent past. Furthermore, not only historians but also architects themselves have participated in establishing the canon. Throughout history, architects have learned from those who preceded them. The buildings that they admired, studied, and emulated became design precedents. For instance, the exterior of McKim, Mead, and White's Boston Public Library (1887–93) (see Fig. 14.31) owes much to the principal façade of Henri Labrouste's Bibliothèque Ste. Geneviève in Paris (1844–50) (see Fig. 14.38), which, in turn, was

based upon the side elevation of Leon Battista Alberti's church of S. Francesco in Rimini (begun ca. 1450) (see Fig. 11.15). At S. Francesco, Alberti was inspired by the arches of the Tomb of Theodoric in nearby Ravenna (ca. 526). A similar backward trajectory can be established for the dome of the U.S. Capitol (1851–67), designed by Thomas U. Walter, who was inspired by Sir Christopher Wren's design for St. Paul's Cathedral in London (1675–1710) (see Fig. 12.55). Wren's probable precedent was François Mansart's dome of Val-de-Grâce in Paris (see Fig. 12.42), which was in turn inspired by Michelangelo's dome for St. Peter's in Rome (see Fig. 11.46), which was itself based on Brunelleschi's dome for Florence Cathedral (see Fig. 11.3). Brunelleschi had looked for his inspiration to the Pantheon in Rome (see Fig. 5.17), erected about 125 CE for the Emperor Hadrian. Where Hadrian's architects got their ideas, we leave for you to discover. Throughout the ages, then, architects have been influenced by the works of their predecessors. We hope that you, our readers, whether you are concerned with history or design or both, will be equally informed and inspired by what is presented in the pages that follow.

A WORD ABOUT DRAWINGS AND IMAGES

In this book, there are many drawings as well as photographs of interior and exterior views. Architects have long relied on the convention of orthographic projections—plans, elevations, and sections—to describe buildings. A plan represents a building as seen from above once a horizontal cutting plane has been passed through it, usually just above the height of the window sills, with everything above this cutting plane removed and the lines of the plan cast onto the cutting plane (Fig. 0.8). Elements that have been cut are usually defined by the darkest lines in the drawing or are blackened in completely. Elements below the cutting plane are drawn with thinner lines, and doors may appear as arcs showing the direction of their swings. Dotted lines in plan usually indicate ceiling elements above the cutting plane, such as vaults and coffers. Thus, in a single, economical drawing, a plan can

08 Plans, elevations, and sections.

This diagram explains the basis of orthographic projection of plan, elevation, and section.

indicate spatial distribution and dimensions on a particular floor and even give some idea of the structure above.

Elevations are obtained by passing a vertical cutting plane down through the ground a few feet in front of one exterior face of a building, with the image of the building then projected onto the cutting plane. Sections also result from a vertical cutting plane, but in this case one passed down inside a building with its image cast upon the plane. By convention, these cutting planes in elevation and section are placed parallel to the building's principal walls. In an elevation, the only line that is intersected by the cutting plane is the ground line, so this line is shown as the darkest in the drawing. In a section, as in a plan, all the building elements that have been cut are usually defined by the darkest lines on the drawing or are blackened in completely, and elements beyond the cutting plane are seen in elevation and, therefore, are drawn with thinner

lines. While it may take some experience to "read" orthographic drawings, they are very useful in the building process because dimensions can be scaled directly from them.

Let us see how drawings work by considering the pair of two-story houses shown in Figs. 0.9 and 0.10. They represent a common type built by early colonists in Connecticut, and both were enlarged by a one-story addition at the rear that was covered by extending the existing roof slope. The resulting form was dubbed a "saltbox" because it resembled the bulk salt containers found in nineteenth-century general stores. In Fig. 0.11, we see the plan and two elevations of another saltbox house as documented by the Historic American Buildings Survey, a national record of buildings begun in the 1930s and archived in the Library of Congress. From the plan it is easier to see the rear addition and to understand how the interior of the house was arranged. A perspective drawing, Fig. 0.12a, more closely resembles the photographs in Figs. 0.9 and 0.10, because perspective drawings show all three dimensions through foreshortening, as photography does, with elements that are farther away (the front-left and back-right corners of

0.9, 0.10 (left) John Graves House, Madison, Connecticut, 1675; (right) Samuel Daggett House, 1750, Connecticut.

Although these colonial houses are not identical, they share a similar form and massing around a central chimney.

0.11 Plan and two elevations of Ogden House, Fairfield, Connecticut, ca. 1700.

Fine lines on this drawing indicate dimensions taken from the building when it was measured for the Historic American Buildings Survey.

the house, in this case) diminishing in size. We know that in fact both front corners of the house are the same height, but in a perspective the one closer to the viewer will be taller. Because most of us understand perspective drawing readily, this drawing type provides architects with a powerful tool for communicating the appearance of buildings

not yet constructed in a way that non-architects can understand. An axonometric drawing, as in Fig. 0.12b, also depicts all three dimensions, but does so without distorting these dimensions as measured along the axes of height, width, and depth. Something must be distorted to capture a three-dimensional object in two dimensions, however, and in this case it is some of the angles at which these axes intersect. At the front- and right-side elevations, some 90° angles, like those at the right front corner, have become acute angles, while others are now obtuse angles.

One of the important uses of drawings is to show conditions that may not be visible in the finished building. Fig. 0.12c shows a perspective view of the structure of a saltbox house, allowing us to see the heavy timber frame that is covered by the exterior siding and also to understand how the massive stone chimney fits into the core. Images of buildings, no matter how detailed, are inevitably abstractions of reality. Even photographs do not show everything "as it really is." Therefore, having multiple images, drawings as well as photographs, aids in understanding a building's structure and space.

0.12a Perspective drawing of Ogden House.

This is based on the dimensions of a house measured by the Historic American Buildings Survey.

0.12b Axonometric drawing of Ogden House.

This is based on the dimensions of a house measured by the Historic American Buildings Survey. Compare this view with the perspective drawing (see Fig. 0.12a) to see how these drawing types differ from one another.

0.12c Analytic perspective of a saltbox house.

With the exterior siding, doors, and windows removed, one can see the heavy timber frame and masonry chimney that distinguish the structure of this building.

CHAPTER 1

THE BEGINNINGS OF ARCHITECTURE

Architecture is an ancient and necessary art, for people have always sought shelter from the elements, and thus the beginnings of architecture are part of prehistory, the period before the development of written language. Prehistory begins as early as 35,000 BCE and extends to about 3000 BCE in the lands of the eastern Mediterranean, and until well after 2000 BCE in parts of western Europe. On the timescale of humankind, these dates correspond to the earliest years of "modern" human evolution from cooperative hunting-and-gathering societies into agricultural civilizations with a fixed settlement area and a ruling class. In the absence of written records, archaeologists and historians must interpret the fragmentary evidence of ancient people—pottery, household implements and rubbish, burials, tombs, and building remains—found in locations scattered across Europe, Africa, and Asia. New technologies have assisted the dating of artifacts through the use of radioactive carbon 14, thermoluminescence, and dendrochronological analysis, but both the methods and the hypotheses derived from them are subject to continual revision as researchers discover new evidence and reexamine old ideas. Reconstructions based on post-holes or masonry foundations help us visualize the simple buildings erected by early societies and provide clues to the more elaborate structures that come later. The study of prehistory is still a very young discipline with many unanswered questions.

Hypostyle Hall, Great Temple of Amun, Karnak, Egypt, ca. 1390–1224 BCE.

This vast roofed hall composed of closely spaced columns of large diameter was illuminated by sunlight filtered through clerestory grilles, one of which is seen here. Mysterious gloom inside the hypostyle hall contrasted with brilliant sunlight in the temple's open courts.

PREHISTORIC SETTLEMENTS AND MEGALITH CONSTRUCTIONS

EASTERN EUROPE

Human settlement seems to have originated at the small clan or family level, with a sufficient number of people living together to provide mutual assistance in hunting and food gathering and joint protection against enemies. Among the earliest huts to be discovered are those at sites in the central Russian Plain (today's Ukraine), dated to about 14,000 BCE. Constructed of mammoth bones and pine poles, with a lining of animal skins and a central hearth, the largest dome-shaped hut incorporated skeleton parts from nearly a hundred mammoths in its framework. Archaeologists have also found clusters of skin-covered huts dated to about 12,000 BCE between Moscow and Novgorod. The largest of these huts, measuring about thirty-nine by thirteen feet in plan, had an irregular shape formed by three interlocking cones of inclined branches and was open at the top to allow smoke to escape from the three hearths.

Excavations of town sites suggest that larger communities were a much later development. The existence of urban settlements depends on an agricultural surplus that enables some people to assume specialized roles (priest, ruler, merchant, craftworker) not directly tied to the production of food. Two of the earliest known urban communities were Jericho, Israel (ca. 8000 BCE) and the trading town of Çatal Hüyük (6500–5700 BCE) in Anatolia, part of present-day Turkey. Jericho was a fortified settlement, with a stone wall up to twenty-seven feet thick enclosing an area of about ten acres. Its earliest dwellings consisted of circular mud huts that may have had conical roofs. The inhabitants were farmers and hunters who buried their dead below the hut floors. Although by contrast Çatal Hüyük appears to have been unfortified, the town was a dense package of dwellings without streets (Figs. 1.1a,b). Residents gained access to the dwellings across roofs, while high openings in the walls were for ventilation. Mud-brick walls and a post-and-lintel timber

1.1a Reconstruction view of buildings, Çatal Hüyük, Anatolia, ca. 6500–5700 BCE.

Notice how buildings abut one another, forming a continuous grouping broken occasionally by open courtyards. The buildings represent a mixture of dwelling houses, workshops, and shrines, all of which were accessed from the rooftops.

1.1b Reconstruction of shrine room, Çatal Hüyük, Anatolia, ca. 6500–5700 BCE.

The central figure on the left-hand wall represents a female figure giving birth, while the horned bull skulls suggest masculine properties. Without written documentation, it is difficult to understand completely the significance of other architectural features, such as the stepped floor levels.

framework enclosed rectangular spaces that abutted the neighboring houses so that together they established a perimeter town wall. Interspersed with the houses were windowless shrines containing decorative motifs of bulls and cult statuettes of deities. These seem to indicate that the themes of prehistoric cave art—hunting and fecundity—had not been discarded by this early urban society. The settlement at Çatal Hüyük is the precursor of more sophisticated communities that developed in the fertile valleys of the Tigris and Euphrates rivers at the beginning of the fourth millennium.

WESTERN EUROPE

In western Europe the transition to urban communities was slower in coming, although the shift from hunting-and-gathering societies to larger agricultural groups under the direction of a priest-king was similar to the experience of societies on the eastern rim of the Mediterranean Sea.

The significant prehistoric architectural achievements of western Europe were megalith constructions, composed of large stones or boulders (**megalith** literally means "great stone"), many of which were erected for astronomical observatories or communal tombs for the privileged classes. Before 4000 BCE, chambered tombs of dry-wall masonry (stones laid without mortar) with corbeled roofs were constructed in Spain and France. One of the earliest of the megalith tombs, dated to 4200 BCE, is at Er-Mané, Carnac, in Brittany (Fig. 1.2). As with many other chambered tombs, this one was stabilized by a covering of earth.

Ireland is particularly rich in megalith tombs, having over 500 documented sites. Constructing these communal graves for cremated or skeletal remains seems to have been not only an expression of reverence for ancestors but also a means of establishing claims to land, and megalith tombs are frequently located on prominent sites. Among the most impressive is the passage grave at Newgrange, County Meath, built about 3100 BCE on the crest of a hill overlooking the Boyne river. An earthen mound nearly 300 feet in diameter and thirty-six feet high covers the tomb, with the weight of the soil providing stability for the megaliths below. Decorated boulders surround the perimeter of the mound. (The white quartz facing is a modern reconstruction based on excavations, providing visibility from a distance.) The south-facing entry leads to a sixty-two-foot-long, upward-sloping passage covered by stone lintels terminating in a cruciform chamber covered by a beehive corbeled ceiling twenty feet high. Parts of the stonework in the passage and chamber are decorated with incised patterns, including diamond shapes and spirals, whose meanings are unknown (Figs. 1.3–1.4). The whole construction is carefully oriented so that, in the five days around the winter solstice, light from the rising sun enters through the doorway and a transom-like light box,

1.2 Megalithic tomb, Er-Mané, Carnac, Brittany, France, ca. 4200 BCE.

This structure presents an early example of corbeled construction, in which stones are laid without mortar in layers, with each course projecting slightly beyond the previous one, to enclose space. In the neighborhood are other prehistoric tomb chambers and nearly 3000 standing and fallen megaliths set in rows aligned to indicate the direction of sunrise at the solstices and equinox.

The ability to work large stones and to observe fundamental astronomical phenomena merged in the most celebrated of megalith constructions, Stonehenge, located on Salisbury Plain in southwestern England (Figs. 1.5–1.7). At least three distinct building phases can be observed. The first phase began about 2900 BCE with excavation of two concentric circular ditches. Inside the perimeter, fifty-six evenly spaced holes (the Aubrey holes) were dug and filled with chalk, while a northeasterly line of sight to the horizon was established from the center across a pointed upright (the heel stone) outside the ditches. About 2400 BCE eighty-two coffin-sized stones of gray-blue dolerite, weighing about two tons each, were transported from quarries in the Pressely mountains of Wales and erected in a double ring of thirty-eight pairs, with six extra stones defining the northeast approach axis. At some point, perhaps before this second stage was completed, the bluestones were removed (their sockets are the so-called Q and R holes). The third and final stage involved transporting thirty-five lintels and forty sarcen stones (a form of

1.4 Entranceway, Newgrange passage grave, County Meath, Ireland, ca. 3100 BCE.

This shows the stone façade as reconstructed by archaeologists. Note the rectangular opening that serves as a "transom light" over the portal, providing the path for sunlight on the winter solstice. Spiral designs on the stone that blocks direct entry may represent sun signs. The old stone door is visible on the right of the opening.

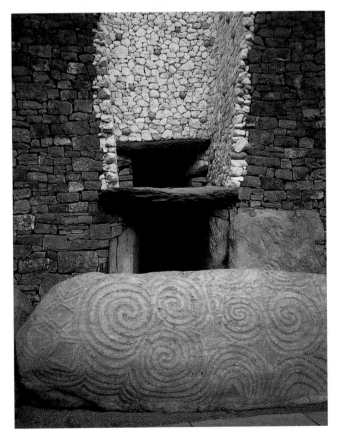

1.3 Plans and section, Newgrange passage grave, County Meath, Ireland, ca. 3100 BCE.

The cruciform chamber of this communal grave is approached through a long passage created by upright stones. The near-horizontal shaded area represents the path of early morning sunlight on the winter solstice, which illuminates the passage and chamber floor, establishing a connection between the human and celestial worlds.

creeping along the passage to illuminate the chamber within for about fifteen minutes (Fig. 1.4). To those fortunate enough to witness this annual event (the only time there is any light in the interior), the effect is magical and very moving. Constructing such a massive tomb (and there are two others on the same scale nearby) would have required sustained effort over many years. Available technology provided nothing harder than copper or bronze tools for shaping stone, and there were no wheeled vehicles or draft animals to assist with transport. Nonetheless, these ancient builders made the necessary astronomical observations and organized a work force sufficient to maneuver stones weighing up to five tons.

1.5 Stonehenge, Salisbury Plain, England, ca. 2900–1400 BCE.

Perhaps the most famous monument from prehistoric times, Stonehenge exemplifies the ability of early civilizations to organize workers and materials to create evocative ceremonial places. The heel stone is to the right beyond the circle.

sandstone) weighing up to twenty tons each. These were erected in a circle of thirty uprights enclosing five trilithons (two uprights capped by a single lintel) arranged in a U shape to focus on the Avenue, the axis toward the heel stone. Knobs (tenons) cut on the tops of the uprights fit into socket holes (mortises) carved on the undersides of the lintels, so that the stones lock together in a mortise-and-tenon joint when correctly positioned.

To the first visitors coming on Stonehenge in more recent times, the sophisticated design and massive construction of the site seemed beyond the capacities of pre-historic people. The site has been interpreted variously as the work of giants, magicians, people imported from the Aegean, or even extra-terrestrials. The truth is more

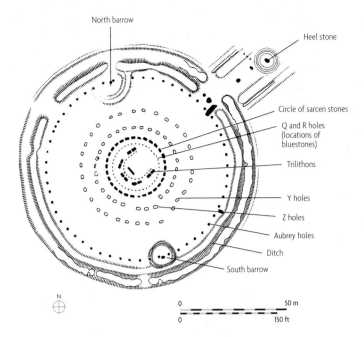

North barrow

Heel stone

Circle of sarcen stones

Q and R holes (locations of bluestones)

Trilithons

Y holes

Z holes

Aubrey holes

Ditch

South barrow

N

0   50 m

0   150 ft

1.6   Plan, Stonehenge, Salisbury Plain, England, ca. 2900–1400 BCE.

This plan includes the original earthworks. The central axis through the trilithons set in a U shape in the center passes between perimeter stones to align with the heel stone set outside the circle. On the summer solstice, the sun rose precisely over the heel stone, when viewed from the center of Stonehenge.

prosaic: archaeo-astronomer Gerald Hawkins demonstrated that Stonehenge was a great observatory for determining the solstices (thus establishing the annual calendar) and predicting lunar and solar eclipses, knowledge that could prove very useful in a society without almanacs. Its circular layout may well reflect a symbolic tie to the heavens, a link between human and celestial realms.

Stonehenge represents the culmination of construction skill and scientific observation in the prehistoric era. Its builders met the challenge of moving and shaping massive stones. Bluestones from Wales were transported, largely by water, over 190 miles to the site, being dragged overland for the last leg of the journey. The larger sarcen uprights

came from the Marlborough Downs, about fifteen miles from Stonehenge, and were probably dragged to the site. Modern experiments to move and erect a trilithon on the scale of Stonehenge show that assembly could be done with simple machines (lever and inclined plane), a sledge and greased track, wooden scaffolds, stout ropes, and about 130 people working together. Experience gained in the construction and orientation of megalith tombs enabled early inhabitants of the British Isles to erect one of the most haunting architectural works of all time.

While the most substantial remains from prehistory are built in stone, there is no doubt that timber was widely used in most early European settlements. Wood was plentiful and relatively easy to work, but its perishable nature means that wooden buildings are only incidentally preserved. At Biskupin in northern Poland, an entire prehistoric village from ca. 1000 to 500 BCE was preserved under water until it came to the attention of archaeologists during a drought in 1938. Careful investigation revealed a trading community established on an island in a small lake, with houses, streets, and fortifications constructed of wood (Fig. 1.8). The approximately oval-plan village wall enclosed just over 100 identical dwellings arranged in attached rows, all oriented to face south. An open square just inside the entrance gate functioned as communal open space (Fig. 1.9). House walls were constructed of horizontal wooden members inset into vertical posts, while roofs were of thatch. Each dwelling was preceded by an antechamber, probably used as a stable for animals, while the house had a central stone hearth (Fig. 1.10). Streets between rows of houses were paved with split logs laid side by side. The perimeter wall was built of

1.7   Stonehenge, Salisbury Plain, England, ca. 2900–1400 BCE.

This shows the present-day configuration of stones. Where the lintels are gone, the knobs (tenons) that held the horizontal stones in place can be seen on top of the uprights.

1.8 Fortifications and houses, Biskupin, Poland, ca. 1000–500 BCE.

The original timber, preserved under water until 1938, provided evidence for this partial reconstruction of a prehistoric settlement in northern Europe. At the left is the gatehouse guarding the only entrance through the enclosing wall.

1.9 Plan of Biskupin, Poland, ca. 1000–500 BCE.

The community derived its basic protection from being located on an island in a lake. All houses follow a similar plan, with their doors facing toward the south. The black dots indicate the location of hearths. The only public open space is just inside the entrance to the enclosure.

Street

Houses

Enclosing wall

Open square

Fortified entrance gate

N   0   50 m
    0   150 ft

1.10 Reconstruction of a house, Biskupin, Poland, ca. 1000–500 BCE.

The windowless dwelling was entered off streets paved with split logs, and similar materials were used for floors surrounding the central hearth. Walls were logs anchored in upright posts, and roofs were thatch. Stalls for domestic animals were located just inside the entrance, with living space for the family centered around the hearth.

rectangular sections of notched horizontal logs filled with earth. Portions of the site have been reconstructed, while others have been left unexplored for future archaeological study. Biskupin was able to use its island location to good defensive advantage. It is likely that other prehistoric settlements congregated around similar natural features, such as hilltops, from which all traces of their existence have since disappeared.

ANCIENT MESOPOTAMIA

The distinction between the prehistoric world and historic times involves the development of written language, which was achieved by about 3500 BCE by the Sumerians in the Middle Eastern lands of present-day Iraq and Iran. There, in the fertile lands between the Tigris and Euphrates rivers (named Mesopotamia or "between the rivers" by the ancient Greeks), the earliest literate civilizations developed in independent urban communities called city-states. Writing first developed as a means of documenting governmental transactions and was only later employed for what might be called literary purposes, reflecting the legends, glorious deeds, hopes, and fears of the people. In about 3000 BCE, perhaps as a result of contacts with Mesopotamia, another center of civilization emerged in northeast Africa, along the banks of the Nile river in Egypt. These two regions, Egypt and Mesopotamia, are considered the cradles of Western history and architecture.

Mesopotamia encompasses an area about 500 miles long by no more than 300 miles wide. Its southern boundary is the Persian Gulf, the shore of which was about 130 miles farther north during the third millennium than it is today. In addition, shifts in the river channels, climatic changes, and increased salinity of formerly irrigated lands have combined to bring about profound changes in the environment since antiquity. The Tigris and Euphrates rivers flow separately into the gulf. The Euphrates originates in the mountains of eastern Turkey and meanders across the plains in its lower reaches. The more easterly Tigris rises in the same mountains, but develops into a more swiftly flowing stream because of its numerous tributaries in the Zagros mountains. As a result, the Tigris was less navigable and did not have as great a unifying effect on settlements along its banks as did the Euphrates.

SUMERIANS, AKKADIANS, AND NEO-SUMERIANS

Sometime around 4000 BCE, a nomadic people called the Al Ubaid, Indo-Europeans from the steppes of central Asia, migrated into southern Mesopotamia from the region east of the Caspian Sea. They settled in the fertile valley, mastered the arts of agriculture, and developed systems of irrigation to use the flood waters of the Euphrates. Their civilization, which lasted until about 2350 BCE, is known as Sumerian, and the typical form of their settlements was the city-state, a political and religious center devoted to serving gods based on natural elements. These deities included the divine triad of Anu, god of the sky; Enlil, god of the earth; and Ea, god of water; supplemented by Nannar, god of the moon; Utu, god of the sun; and Inanna, goddess of fertility. The Sumerians believed that the sky and earth were two disks that had been blown apart and that all existence was governed by the gods, who represented the unpredictable elements affecting human life. They believed that human beings were created from the alluvial silt deposits in the river valleys to serve the gods and to relieve them of toil. Because the gods benefited from human praise, they had to remain in human favor. Thus there was a balance in the creative and destructive forces of the gods and a mutual inter-dependence between people and gods.

Urban communities developed around religious shrines, the dwelling places of the gods and the repositories for surplus food stores, and thus there were monumental temple complexes at the heart of Sumerian cities. The earliest level of Eridu, the oldest city, had a small shrine with a brick altar in front of a wall niche, probably constructed to contain a cult statue. The elements of altar and niche were found in all later Sumerian temples. Rebuildings of this temple at Eridu successively enlarged the relatively modest original shrine, and by about 3800 BCE the temple stood on a platform. Its rectangular buttressed walls enclosed a long shrine room flanked by smaller side chambers. At about the same time Tepe

1.11 Reconstruction of the temple, Tepe Gawra, Sumer (Iraq), ca. 3800 BCE.

This temple was associated with a more complex urban community than was the case with prehistoric societies. The importance of its priestly class is indicated by the scale of the building erected on a high point in the city. Mud-brick walls were reinforced by pilasters.

Gawra, nearly 500 miles to the north, featured an acropolis with two temples, a shrine, and dwelling houses. Its major buildings formed a U-shaped open court around the North Temple, which measured forty by twenty feet. The temple had a central hall with side chambers, and its brick façade was articulated by buttresses and pilasters (Fig. 1.11), motifs that are found also in early Egyptian architecture.

Most Sumerian buildings were executed in sun-baked brick, a material easily obtained by shaping mud in molds and leaving it to dry for several weeks in the sun, but the resulting brick is not particularly resistant to weathering. As a result, much of Sumerian architecture is known only from foundations and lower sections of walls. Roofs were fabricated from lightweight wooden members or reeds that could not span great distances, so there were no large interior spaces. In both Sumerian and later Mesopotamian architecture, important buildings were given additional durability by having weather-resistant casings for the brick, and greater dignity by being raised on a platform.

Such was the case at Uruk, where the so-called White Temple was built (ca. 3500–3000 BCE) on a forty-foot-high base of rubble from earlier buildings and provided with a protective coat of whitewash over its sun-dried brick which was laid in panels between sloping buttresses (Fig. 1.12). Entrance to the temple was through a chamber in the long side, so that a "bent axis" led from the outside into the courtyard and sanctuary. Contemporary structures excavated in the nearby precinct of Eanna (dedicated to Inanna) include two groups of temples flanking a courtyard ornamented by a mosaic of thousands of small terracotta cones. The base of each cone was dipped in black, white, or red glaze, and then its apex was inserted into the clay of the wall to form a polychromatic zigzag pattern with circular elements.

1.12 View and plan of the White Temple, Uruk, Mesopotamia (Iraq), ca. 3500–3000 BCE.

Many temples in Mesopotamia were erected on raised platforms. The base of this temple was made in part with the rubble from previous buildings on the site, buttressed in a regular pattern and protected by layers of whitewash, hence the temple's name.

1.13 Ziggurat at Ur, Mesopotamia (Iraq), ca. 2100 BCE.

One of the best preserved of the massive temple mounds that once dominated every major Mesopotamian city, this ziggurat served to elevate a temple closer to the gods. Its core is sun-dried brick, overlaid with an outer layer of kiln-fired brick and bitumen as protection against weathering.

The settlements of the Sumerians were disrupted about 2350 BCE by the arrival of a new group of Semitic people from the steppes of central Asia. These immigrants established cities in Sippar and Akkad, and the people take their name, the Akkadians, from the latter. Surviving evidence indicates that the Akkadians were a fierce people, governed not only by a priestly class but also by a warrior-king. Many aspects of Sumerian culture were adopted by the Akkadians, but their decision to retain a king instead of copying the Sumerians' form of city-state leadership was later instrumental in forging imperial states composed of many urban settlements.

The Akkadian Empire was in turn overthrown in about 2150 BCE by the Guti, a group of savage tribes from the mountain regions of Iran. The military influence of the Guti weakened within a century, and political allegiances reminiscent of the first Sumerian city-states returned in what is termed the Neo-Sumerian period (ca. 2150–2000 BCE). This period witnessed the development of urban temple forms, particularly the temple elevated on an artificial mound, or **ziggurat.** Commonly constructed of sun-dried brick bonded with bitumen, reed matting, or rope, ziggurats were finished with a weather-resistant exterior layer of kiln-fired brick. From a rectangular base, the ziggurat rose with battered or inward-sloping walls in a series of stepped platforms, culminating in a high temple at the top. A flight of stairs set in the center of one side connected the temple to the ground. (Elements so placed in the center of a symmetrical form and aligned toward a terminus are said to be axial.) Ziggurats were essentially stepped platforms designed to elevate the temples to the gods so that the latter might descend from the heavens and ensure the prosperity of the community. Symbolically, the ziggurat may have represented the mountains whence the Sumerians came. To make their gods feel at home in the lowlands of the river valley, the Sumerians and their successors in Mesopotamia may have aspired to re-create their highland dwelling place. Raising the temple well above the elevation of the valley may also have reflected a

1.14 Reconstruction of the ziggurat at Ur, Mesopotamia (Iraq), ca. 2100 BCE.

This drawing shows the original details that are now lost. Priestly processions up the successive flights of stairs to the temple on the uppermost platform could be observed by the populace from below.

desire to protect the sacred precinct from flood waters; it certainly gave it visual prominence in the city.

Little remains of the ziggurats constructed during the brief Neo-Sumerian interlude. Sun-dried brick is not sufficiently durable to withstand the weather, and once this outer casing was removed by scavengers, the earthen core of ziggurats eroded considerably. Of those lofty artificial mountains that towered over Mesopotamian cities, only the ziggurat at Ur (ca. 2100 BCE) remains with some of its features intact (Figs. 1.13–1.14). One can still distinguish the three long stairways that converged on a tower gate at the level of the first platform. Shorter flights led to the second and third terraces, to which only the priests were allowed to ascend. These upper levels, together with the crowning temple, have been reduced to crumbled heaps, but archaeologists who worked on the site calculate that the original height was about seventy feet, with a base of

1.15b Plan of a residential quarter, Ur, Mesopotamia (Iraq), ca. 2100 BCE.

Surviving foundations indicate houses laid out on right-angled plans with living spaces organized around courtyards, a design that promoted urban density while also providing privacy and fresh air to each dwelling. Later versions of this house type can be found in Mohenjo-Daro, Priene, and in Islamic cities in the Middle East and North Africa.

1.15a Plan of Ur, Mesopotamia (Iraq), ca. 2100 BCE.

This shows the walled center with the ziggurat and the enclosing city wall. A portion of the residential section that has been excavated is indicated to the southeast of the city center. Note the maze-like arrangement of houses, contrasting sharply to the larger open spaces of the administrative and ceremonial center.

about 200 by 150 feet. In contrast to the grand temple complexes, the houses of the ordinary population were set in densely packed neighborhoods. Plans were roughly orthogonal, and houses were constructed around open courtyards that provided light and fresh air to all rooms (Figs. 1.15a,b). To the street, the houses presented a blank wall, thereby ensuring privacy. Courtyard houses continue to the present day to be typical of Mediterranean and Middle Eastern communities.

BABYLONIANS, HITTITES, AND ASSYRIANS

Dominance in the turbulent Mesopotamian region passed to the Amorite Dynasty in the city-state of Babylon from about 1800 to 1600 BCE. There, an exceptionally able king, Hammurabi (1728–1686 BCE), restored the Akkadian tradition of a central government leading diverse city-states. Babylon developed as a major city, with a great temple to Marduk, who was considered the king of the gods. About 1530 BCE the Hittites, a vigorous Indo-European people from Anatolia, overran the First Dynasty of

Babylon. After bringing down the city-states of Mesopotamia, the Hittites ruled northern Mesopotamia and Syria from their homeland capital, Hattusas (now Bogazköy in Turkey). At the height of the Hittite Empire (ca. 1400–1200 BCE), the rambling, asymmetrically built city of Hattusas covered some 300 acres enclosed in a four-mile stone-based fortification wall (Fig. 1.16a). Upper wall sections were made from sun-dried brick that has since disappeared. Corbeled vaults were used for gates in the town wall, and two of these gates were flanked by sculptures of sphinxes or lions. On a rocky outcrop within the enclosure was a separately fortified palace complex containing audience halls, a library, archives, and granaries. The stone construction employed for its storage rooms made extensive use of parabolic corbeled vaults to enclose long, narrow rooms. Within the town, five temples dedicated to the weather gods were constructed around central courtyards surrounded by storage rooms and well-lit ritual chambers (Fig. 1.16b).

At their peak, the Hittites rivaled the Egyptians for control of the eastern Mediterranean coast, and at the

1.16a Plan of Hattusas, Turkey, ca. 1400–1200 BCE.

The capital of the Hittite Empire, this 300-acre city developed to the west and south of the fortified palace (center right). The great temple to the weather gods is located northwest of the palace. Defensive walls took advantage of topography, hence the irregular layout.

1.16b (inset) Plan of the Temple of the Weather Gods, Hattusas, Turkey, ca. 1400–1200 BCE.

The temple itself is a series of small chambers constructed around an open central court. Long storage rooms are grouped in the irregular quadrangle enclosing the temple. Some of these chambers contained a library and archives.

1.17a Reconstruction of the palace, Khorsabad, Assyria, ca. 720 BCE.

Fortified walls enclose the palace. The royal audience hall was accessed by a route that turned through a sequence of courtyards and smaller chambers. Compare this to the axial layouts typically found in Egyptian architecture.

ziggurat

temple buildings

throne room

state court

entrance court

1.17b Plan of the palace, Khorsabad, Assyria, ca. 720 BCE.

This shows the complex layout that contained the ceremonial route. The stepped ziggurat is a dwindled version of forms found in earlier cities in Mesopotamia.

0   250 m

0   750 ft

battle of Qadesh (ca. 1285 BCE) they were able to defend their claims to Syria against the armies of Ramesses II, leading to the signing of a peace treaty in ca. 1269 BCE. Hittite archives include numerous exchanges with the Egyptians, including an urgent communication from Queen Ankhesenamun, the widow of Tutankhamun, seeking a Hittite prince to marry and install as pharaoh. (The prince was intercepted and murdered before reaching Egypt.) Invasions by other Indo-European tribes, notably the Thracians, Phrygians, and Assyrians, broke up the Hittite Empire about 1200 BCE, although its artistic influence continued in later Assyrian art and in the fortified gates carved with beasts, especially lions, found in the Aegean settlements of the Mycenaeans.

While the Hittites were ruling much of the west from their capital at Hattusas, the relatively ineffective Kassites and Mitanni dominated the traditional southeastern centers around Babylon. The weakness of these rulers gave the Assyrians, a fierce people of northern Mesopotamia,

an opportunity to gain a foothold in the fertile plains to the south. By 900 BCE, their military might had established an empire, with capitals sequentially at Calah (present-day Nimrud), Dur-Sharrukin (Khorsabad), and Nineveh (Kuyunjik). Strongly fortified citadels built for each capital reflect the Assyrians' relentless warring as well as the ruthless character of their kings.

Khorsabad, the royal city built by Sargon II in ca. 720 BCE, illustrates the main characteristics of Assyrian architecture and planning (Figs. 1.17a,b). At the center of the city the twenty-five-acre palace occupied a plateau fifty feet above the level of the town. Orthogonal geometry governed buildings in the palace area, which was bordered by a sturdy wall heavily reinforced by watchtowers. Rising near the central axis was a seven-stage ziggurat, 143 feet square at the base, representing the cosmic order of the seven planets. (Despite the fact that they treated captive populations cruelly, the Assyrians adopted many of the religious and cultural practices of Sumeria and Babylon.)

The palace was organized around large courtyards surrounded by rectangular rooms, including the great hall and throne room, while the approach sequence was circuitous, perhaps to confuse visitors and to heighten the sense of grandeur. Winged bulls with human heads carved in high relief from thirteen-foot-tall stone blocks guard the entrances to the palace. Bone and muscle are realistically represented, while feathers, hair, and beard are stylized, forcefully conveying the strength of the monarch: as man, the lord of creation; as eagle, king of the sky; and as bull, fecundator of the herd. Other relief carvings within the palace depict marching armies burning, killing, and pillaging to emphasize the folly of resisting Assyrian power. Without subtlety, Sargon II had the art and architecture of his palace communicate the overwhelming power residing in his person.

NEO-BABYLONIANS AND PERSIANS

After first losing the more remote portions of their empire, the Assyrians finally fell in 612 BCE to the combined assaults of Babylonians, Scythians, Persians, and Medes. Their successor in southern Mesopotamia was the Neo-Babylonian Empire (ca. 612–539 BCE), which was distinguished architecturally by the rebuilding and enlargement of Babylon (Fig. 1.18) under Nebuchadnezzar II (604–562 BCE). The city's processional way passed

through the Ishtar Gate, a fortified portal clad in blue-glazed brick. Animals were modeled in shallow relief on the surface of the bricks, which were glazed separately and then assembled as the covering was laid in horizontal courses. The gate's front face, now in Berlin's Pergamon Museum (Fig. 1.19), recalls the colorful splendor of ancient Babylon. Contemporary visitors marveled at the "Hanging Gardens," designated one of the Seven Wonders of the World. In all likelihood these gardens consisted of planted terraces not unlike modern conservatories, irrigated by water brought in buckets on an endless chain from a subterranean well. The ziggurat at Babylon, now a crumbled ruin, is remembered in the Old Testament as the Tower of Babel.

Babylon's greatness was eclipsed in 539 BCE when it became part of the Persian Empire of Cyrus II. The Persians had previously overthrown the Medes, and they continued to expand outward from their capital at Susa (in present-day Iran) to conquer all of Mesopotamia, Asia Minor, and even Egypt by 525 BCE. Within a century they controlled territory from the Danube to the Indus, and from the Jaxartes to the Nile, failing to subjugate only the Greek peninsula. The greatest surviving architectural contribution of the Persians is an impressive ruin at Persepolis (Fig. 1.20), the city founded in 518 BCE by Darius as a ceremonial capital to supplement Susa, the administrative capital, and Pasargadae as centers of court life. Lacking strong artistic traditions of their own, the Persians borrowed freely from the cultures they conquered. At Persepolis, there are echoes of Egyptian temple gates and

1.18 Plan of Babylon, Mesopotamia (Iraq), ca. 612–539 BCE.

As reconstructed by Nebuchadnezzar II, Babylon was surrounded by a rectangular wall and moat, with two fortress complexes on the northern side. The Ishtar Gate was the principal entrance from the north, and the ziggurat set near the Euphrates river was the biblical Tower of Babel.

1.19 The Ishtar Gate, Babylon, Mesopotamia (Iraq), ca. 612–539 BCE, as reerected in the Pergamon Museum in Berlin.

The dignity and power of these low-relief carvings conveys a sense of royal might. Blue-glazed bricks provided both decoration and weather-resistance. Note the use of an arch with voussoirs.

hypostyle halls, Hittite audience chambers, and Mesopotamian sculpted animal motifs. The great palace, used primarily for ceremonies at the New Year and the beginning of spring, occupied a terrace 1500 by 900 feet; it contained reception courts, banquet rooms, and audience halls in a loosely organized orthogonal layout. King Xerxes's throne room was known as the Hall of a Hundred Columns, and this audience hall, completed by Artaxerxes, was the largest enclosed space in the palace, able to contain 10,000 people within its 250-foot square plan. Most of the construction was in stone. Stone columns supported wooden roof beams resting on the unique double-headed capitals carved in the form of bulls and lions (Fig. 1.21). Access to the terrace was gained via a flight of stairs flanked by relief sculptures representing delegations from twenty-three nations bringing tribute to the sovereign (Fig. 1.22). These stone figures, shown engaged in the same kind of activities as real-life visitors, provided a foretaste of the pageantry and banquets waiting in the palace above.

The conquests of Alexander the Great ended Persian dominance in 331 BCE. Alexander's armies eventually reached India, where Persian craftsmen appear to have accompanied them and then

Inner gatehouse

Stairs to terrace

Gateway of All Nations

Apadana of Darius

Tripylon

Small Palace of Darius

Palace of Xerxes

Hall of 100 Columns (Apadana of Xerxes)

Treasury (administration and storage)

Women's quarters

1.20 Plan of the palace, Persepolis, Iran, begun ca. 518 BCE.

This great complex was created by at least three Persian monarchs as one of the capitals of the Persian Empire. Its ruins reveal architectural influences from other cultures in Mesopotamia, notably the Hittites and Assyrians, as well as the Egyptians.

0   100 m
0   300 ft

1.21 View of the ruins of the palace, Persepolis, Iran, ca. 518 BCE.

Persepolis was destroyed by Alexander the Great. Two columns with intact capitals are seen here framed by carved stone doorways from the palace ruins.

1.22 Staircase to the upper terrace, Persepolis, Iran, ca. 518 BCE.

Isolated columns from the Apadana of Darius are visible, with doorways from Darius's palace in the background.

remained. They helped build the capital at Pataliputra (now Patna) for Chandragupta, where the many-columned halls and animal capitals recall the palace at Persepolis. Persian architecture is one of the major influences for the early stone architecture of India.

ANCIENT EGYPT

The geography of Egypt is dominated by one great river, the Nile, which originates in the highlands of Uganda and passes through the Sudan and Ethiopia as it traverses more than 2000 miles before flowing out into the Mediterranean Sea to the north. Within the 600 lower miles of the river valley, agriculture is facilitated by the warm climate and the annual flood deposits of organic silt, which renew the fertility of the fields. On the margins of the valley in dynastic times there were marshes and open lands rich in

game. (Today the desert encroaches on these areas.) Outside the rather narrow fertile band bordering the Nile, great expanses of inhospitable desert provided security from outside invasion, just as the Mediterranean served as a barrier for settlements on the Nile Delta. The culture that developed along the banks of the river was thus predominantly agricultural, in contrast to urban-oriented settlements in turbulent Mesopotamia. Egyptian life was organized around the annual flooding of the river, and the cyclical rhythm of the seasons fostered a civilization that remained remarkably unchanging and stable for more than 2000 years. Two centers of Egyptian civilization, with differing cultural practices, arose in prehistoric times: Lower Egypt in the broad Nile Delta, and Upper Egypt in the more narrow southern river valley. At a very early stage, Egyptians also developed writing in the form of hiero-glyphs, a system using both pictorial and phonetic symbols to record information.

"HYDRAULIC" CIVILIZATIONS

by Dan MacGilvray

There is but little rain in Assyria. It is this which nourishes the roots of the corn; but it is irrigation from the river that ripens the crop and brings the grain to fullness: it is not as in Egypt, where the river itself rises and floods the fields: in Assyria they are watered by hand and by swinging beams. For the whole land of Babylon, like Egypt, is cut across by canals. The greatest of these is navigable: it runs . . . from the Euphrates to the Tigris . . .

. . . all the land . . . watered by the Nile in its course was Egypt, and all who dwelt lower down than the city Elephantine (Aswan) and drank of that river's water were Egyptians.

. . . there are no men, neither in the rest of Egypt, nor in the whole world, who gain from the soil with so little labour; they have not the toil of breaking up the land with the plough, nor of hoeing . . . the river rises of itself, waters the fields, and then sinks back again; thereupon each man sows his field and sends swine into it to tread down the seed, and waits for the harvest . . .

1A Obelisk in a quarry, Aswan, Egypt.

The Greek historian Herodotus (484–425 BCE) traveled extensively throughout the ancient world and wrote the first narrative history. He was a keen observer of culture, and these quotations define one of the essential characteristics of Mesopotamian and Egyptian civilizations: their dependence on the rivers that were their life-blood. Water is an essential ingredient of all life, and flowing water is required for the development of civilization, not only for drinking and irrigation, but also to remove the human waste that accumulates in areas of dense population. Thus, all of the early civilizations from that of the Indus to the Mayans were founded on rivers. We refer to these as "hydraulic" civilizations.

Of necessity, a hydraulic civilization is a cooperative federation, in contrast to, say, a group of squabbling city-states. In a given watershed, strong centralized control is required for the construction of an inter-dependent system of canals to divert water for irrigation and drain swamps for cultivation, or dams and levees for flood control and water retention. Early hydraulic engineers learned the techniques of surveying and developed the skills to manage large-scale construction projects as they struggled to control the waters that brought both abundance and destruction. As Herodotus notes, the nation of Egypt defined itself by the Nile, and there is no doubt that the engineers of the pyramids learned to survey, to level, and to organize large work forces on the banks of the Nile. It has also been speculated that, because the farmers were inactive during flood times, they were available for conscription onto construction work gangs for massive projects like the pyramids.

The Tigris, Euphrates and Nile rivers also served as the primary transportation arteries for the movement of goods between the various communities that lined them. Even today, in the age of jet travel, by far the cheapest means of moving freight per ton-mile is the river barge. In medieval times it was ten times cheaper to move cargo by boat than by ox-cart. And, because of the Nile, the ancient Egyptians had no use for wheeled vehicles or even paved roads; the chariot was a foreign import that arrived late to the water-borne Egyptians, who, in contrast, developed sophisticated construction techniques for boats of all sizes. In tomb paintings the largest are shown laden with two granite obelisks (Fig. 1A), a cargo of up to 1000 tons.

The history of Egypt begins in about 3000 BCE with the union of Upper and Lower Egypt by Menes, the pharaoh king of Upper Egypt, who established his capital at Memphis, near the junction of the two lands. (Please note that dates in Egyptian history, especially for individual pharaohs in the early dynasties, are still matters of scholarly debate. All dates given here should therefore be treated as approximations.) Menes, like all his successors, was both a temporal ruler and a manifestation of the falcon-headed god Horus, the god of pharaohs. When the pharaoh died, he became identified with Osiris, father of Horus and lord of the underworld, and his successor as pharaoh assumed the Horus role. Egyptian theology linked both Osiris and Horus with the sun god Ra, whose symbol in the ancient temple at Heliopolis was the phallic, cone-shaped ben-ben stone, later stylized as a pyramid. The use of pyramid shapes at the top of stone shafts (obelisks) or as the building form itself (as in the pyramids) was thus a visual symbol of the connection between the ruler and the sun god.

THE EARLY DYNASTIC PERIOD AND OLD KINGDOM (FIRST–EIGHTH DYNASTIES, ca. 2920–2134 BCE)

Egyptian history is divided into thirty dynasties, encompassing the period from Pharaoh Narmer's accession (ca. 3000 BCE) to the conquest of Egypt by Alexander the Great in 332 BCE. What we know of this early period comes largely from funerary monuments and inscriptions, where the focus is on the transition from the world of the living to that of the dead. Egyptians believed strongly in an afterlife. Their religion taught that earthly existence was followed by an afterlife in which the *ka*, or life-force, was reunited with the *ba*, or physical manifestation, to become an *akh*, or spirit. Elaborate rituals were developed inside tomb chambers to ensure that the transformation from life to death was successful. Preservation of the physical body (or at least a temporary forestalling of its putrefaction) after death was of great importance, as was the provision of household furnishings, surrogate servants, food, drink, and a suitable permanent chamber. The *ka* of an important person, especially the pharaoh, who was inadequately prepared for the afterlife might wander unsatisfied about the world and cause mischief for the living. It was therefore in society's interest to ensure that the pharaoh's body and spirit were well served. This goal led to the construction of enduring tombs for royalty and the development of mummification to preserve the body. Tombs, rather than temples or palaces, became the most lasting religious structures.

Mastabas, the earliest tombs, were built as eternal houses for the departed and were in all likelihood based on the design of the dwellings of the living. Ordinary houses were constructed of reed, thatch, and wood, materials wholly unsuited for a permanent residence, so the builders of mastaba tombs sought greater durability by

1.23 Drawing of mastaba tombs.

This shows the burial chamber beneath the structure and the small chambers provided at ground level for offerings to the spirit of the deceased. It is thought that these tombs, constructed of sun-dried brick or stone, were based on the designs of actual dwellings constructed of less durable materials.

using brick while retaining characteristic details provided by the customary bundled reeds and wooden supports. The basic mastaba (Fig. 1.23) was a blocklike structure above ground containing a small room for offerings and another chamber for the body and a statue of the deceased. Worldly goods entombed with the dead soon attracted thieves, so an early revision of mastaba design added a deep shaft under the building. The body was placed at its base, and the shaft was then filled with stone and rubble to deter would-be robbers. In the *serdab*, a chamber above ground, a statue of the deceased would receive offerings. A later change toward increasing permanence involved using stone in the construction of the mastaba.

THE FIRST PYRAMIDS

As the religious ritual prescribed by the priesthood changed to enhance the significance of the pharaoh, the mastaba was likewise enlarged to form a pyramid. At death the pharaoh accompanied the sun god on his daily journey across the sky, and he would therefore need to be lifted skyward in his eternal home. The pyramid, an upward-stepping form whose peak caught the first rays of morning light, was the emblem of the sun god as worshiped at Heliopolis. The shape also makes symbolic reference to the annual rebirth of nature, for as floods recede, the first signs of plant life appear on the small hillocks. Thus the pyramid's form represented both daily and yearly rebirth throughout eternity.

Imhotep, architect to the Third-Dynasty pharaoh Djoser (2630–2611 BCE), is credited with designing the first pyramid, for Djoser's funerary complex at Saqqara, outside Memphis (Fig. 1.24). This was also Egypt's first monumental construction in stone, no small factor in its survival through 4600 years. The complex is a large rectangle in plan, covering thirty-five acres, surrounded by a wall thirty-three feet high and a mile long (Figs. 1.25a,b). There is only one entrance, a small door in the southeast

1.24 The step pyramid, Saqqara, Egypt, ca. 2630 BCE.

As the first monumental stone construction in Egypt, this building set the precedent for later pyramids of the pharaohs. Its architect, Imhotep, was remembered for his genius and later revered as a deity.

1.25a (right) Plan of Djoser's funerary complex, Saqqara, Egypt, ca. 2630 BCE.

The step pyramid is the rectangular element in the center, dominating a great court accessed through the narrow corridor passage at the lower left. Smaller courtyards to the south were formed by buildings thought to resemble the actual palace in which Djoser lived. A mile-long perimeter wall enclosed all the buildings.

Chapel · altar · Great Altar · a · B · Great Court · Entrance · Court of the Southern Palace · Pyramid · Mortuary Temple · N · Heb-Sed court · Court of the Northern Palace · 0 — 100 m · 0 — 300 ft

A Original entrance
B Second entrance
C Robber's entrance
★ Blue chambers

N · 0 — 50 m · 0 — 150 ft

corner that leads into a narrow colonnaded processional hall. At the end of the corridor, one enters a main courtyard dominated by Djoser's stepped pyramid, which rises 197 feet above its 397-by-358-foot base. Begun as a mastaba, the pyramid was built up in several stages to attain its present shape, a mass rising in six steps. The exterior of the pyramid was faced with dressed limestone, while the courtyards and surrounding buildings are thought to be representations of Djoser's earthly palace in Memphis, rebuilt here to last for eternity. The appearance and typical details of the original materials are imitated in stone: reed-bundle and papyrus-stalk columns, log ceilings, even a

1.25b Section and plan of the step pyramid, Saqqara, Egypt, ca. 2630 BCE.

The section drawing shows the successive stages of construction, through which the original mastaba form was enlarged to become a pyramid. It preserves the burial chamber under the center. The plan drawing shows the industry of later tomb robbers who tunneled in to recover treasure buried with Djoser.

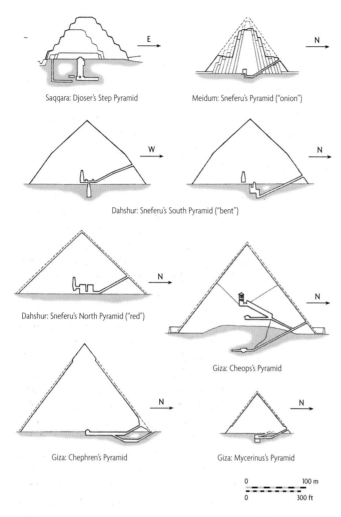

Saqqara: Djoser's Step Pyramid

Meidum: Sneferu's Pyramid ("onion")

Dahshur: Sneferu's South Pyramid ("bent")

Dahshur: Sneferu's North Pyramid ("red")

Giza: Cheops's Pyramid

Giza: Chephren's Pyramid

Giza: Mycerinus's Pyramid

| 0 | 100 m |
| 0 | 300 ft |

1.26 Sections through pyramids at Saqqara, Meidum, Dahshur, and Giza, Egypt, ca. 2550–2460 BCE.

These drawings indicate the relative sizes of the major pyramids from the Third and Fourth dynasties. That of Cheops remains the largest pile of stones ever assembled, and it also has the most complex array of interior passages and chambers.

stone hinge for an immobile stone door. North of the pyramid is the temple in which the pre-burial ritual was performed. A statue of Djoser looking outward sits in the serdab, with a small aperture cut in the wall being the only access to the outside world.

Djoser's complex includes areas for the practice of rituals that are not completely understood today, but that were apparently important symbols of the bond between Upper and Lower Egypt. The main courtyard was the scene of the Heb-Sed race, run annually by the pharaoh to ensure fertility of the fields. The course consisted of four circuits of the court in each direction, clockwise for half of the kingdom and counterclockwise for the other half. Djoser had two burial chambers to symbolize his power and paternity over Upper and Lower Egypt. One chamber, located beneath the pyramid, contained his mummy in an alabaster coffin. The access passage was blocked by a stone plug six feet in diameter and weighing six tons, but this was inadequate protection against robbers, who nonetheless gained access to the tomb in antiquity. In 1928 excavators discovered the second chamber in the south side of

the perimeter wall. Although it too had been plundered, the chamber originally contained the embalmed internal organs of the pharaoh, emblematic of his fertility and his protection of Lower Egypt. Grave robbers did not steal the handsome blue faïence wall decorations, which are now all that remains of the interior. These tiles are set into horizontal and vertical stone members to represent rush matting between wooden slats attached to larger wooden supports. On one wall is a relief carving depicting Djoser running the Heb-Sed race. Wearing the white crown of Upper Egypt, Djoser is portrayed in the manner peculiar to Egyptian art, with head, legs, and feet shown in profile and the torso shown frontally. In this one view Egyptian artists captured the essential features of the human body with great exactitude, even though the pose is not a "realistic" or natural one.

From its beginnings at Saqqara, the evolution of what we now think of as the "true" pyramid proceeds through at least three major projects before its culmination in the Fourth-Dynasty tombs at Giza, outside Cairo (Fig. 1.26). All three of these developmental pyramids were built or modified for one of the first pharaohs of the Fourth Dynasty, Sneferu (2575–2551 BCE), whose cult remained active for over 2000 years after his death. At Meidum, six miles south of Saqqara, Sneferu added an outer layer to the pyramid that may have been begun for Huni, the last pharaoh of the Third Dynasty. It began with a stepped core of seven stages, which was transformed into a true pyramid with the addition of two overbuildings. As the third and final outer casing of limestone was being installed, there is evidence that the upper portions of the work collapsed because the pyramid's stonework was insufficiently supported, given the relatively steep angle of inclination (51° 50′ 35″). Had it been completed as planned, the pyramid would have reached nearly 302 feet in height. As it stands, with its stepped core rising above the rubble, it has been given the descriptive name of an "onion" pyramid. Entrance was through a sloping corridor opening off the north side, descending below ground, and then rising a short distance vertically to the burial chamber at the center of the pyramid's base. Corbeled construction in the vault of this chamber marks the first time this technique was employed in stone by the Egyptians, although it had been used earlier in brick.

The collapse of the Meidum pyramid had an impact on another of Sneferu's pyramids under construction at the same time at Dahshur, about twenty-eight miles south of Meidum. There, a partially finished structure was transformed to create the so-called "bent" pyramid that began with a 616-foot-square base and sides inclined at 54° 27′ 44″. Observing the collapse at Meidum, the builders at Dahshur changed to a lower inclination angle of 41° 22′ when the pyramid was half-built. Eventually reaching a height of 344 feet, the bent pyramid gains added stability from its firm limestone foundation and core, large stone casing blocks that are slightly inclined to the center, and the reduced angle of inclination. These stabilizing design features were incorporated from the beginning in the third pyramid of Sneferu, the north or "red" pyramid, also at Dahshur. (The color name derives from oxidation of the limestone used for its core, exposed after stone scavengers removed the white limestone casing.) From a base 722 feet square, the north pyramid rises at a constant 43° 22' angle to its apex 344 feet above the ground. Its profile is thus relatively low, a testimony to the conservative attitudes of its designers.

FOURTH-DYNASTY PYRAMIDS AT GIZA

The trio of large pyramids at Giza (2550–2460 BCE) are the work of Sneferu's descendants, the Fourth-Dynasty pharaohs known as Khufu, Khafre, and Menkaure (or Cheops, Chephren, and Mycerinus in Greek transliteration) (Figs. 1.27–1.28). The largest pyramid, that of Khufu, who reigned 2551–2528 BCE, was built first and planned from the start to be a true pyramid of unprecedented proportions. The 755-by-755-foot base covers over thirteen acres; the sides rise at an angle of 51° 50' 40" to an apex at 481 feet. Most of the stone in the pyramid is limestone, although the large pharaoh's chamber in the center is made of granite. Nothing built in stone before or since has rivaled the Great Pyramid of Khufu for sheer size.

Khufu's pyramid is not completely solid, however. Three burial chambers are built within it, one excavated out of foundation bedrock and the other two constructed as the stone mountain was erected. Although once these were thought to represent changes made in design as work progressed, they are now interpreted as deliberate accommodations. The roughly finished lowest chamber is thought to represent the underworld. The middle chamber, the so-called Queen's Chamber, probably contained an over-life-sized statue of Khafre and served as his spirit chamber, or serdab. The top, or King's Chamber, beautifully constructed of red granite, contains a granite sarcophagus in which Khufu was in fact buried. To transfer the tremendous weight of the pyramid around the ceiling of the King's Chamber, eleven pairs of granite beams were set as a gabled brace or saddle roof extending into the mass of the pyramid above the chamber. Five massive sets of horizontal granite slabs form relieving chambers stacked between the saddle roof and the flat ceiling of the crypt as a means of reducing weight and pressure from above. The corbeled gallery leading to this chamber is also a construction marvel, rising twenty-six feet in height, a splendid contrast to a four-foot-high ascending passage to which it connects.

Both the King's and Queen's chambers have pairs of small shafts angling upwards through the mass of the pyramid that may have been intended for ventilation. Their particular orientation implies connection to the pole star (north side) and Orion (south side), although the precise function and symbolic meaning of these ventilation shafts are unclear.

Next in sequence of construction (and only slightly smaller in size) is the pyramid of Khafre, a son of Khufu, who reigned 2520–2494 BCE. Khafre's pyramid is 705 feet square at the base and rises at an angle of 53° 20' to an ultimate elevation of 471 feet. In many photographs of the Giza pyramids, this one seems the tallest of the three, but this is only because it stands on higher ground than that of Khufu. Khafre's monument is readily distinguished by the substantial fragment of the original smooth limestone casing that survives at the apex. On the inside there is a single tomb chamber in the center of the pyramid at the base level. A passageway in the north side provides access to the room, which, like all the tomb chambers in pyramids, was pillaged in ancient times.

The smallest of the Giza trio of major pyramids belonged to Menkaure, a son of Khafre who reigned 2490–2472 BCE. Containing less than one-tenth of the amount of stone of Khufu's pyramid, Menkaure's tomb seems to have been erected hurriedly and with less care than those of his predecessors. We know that it was not finished before Menkaure died. Its dimensions—335 by 343 feet at the base, a slope of 51° 20' 25", and 213 feet high—maintain the general proportions established by the neighboring tombs. Menkaure's successor, Shepseskaf, the last pharaoh in the Fourth Dynasty, chose not to have a pyramid burial, and although pyramids continued to be built by later rulers, the quality and scale of the Giza trio were never exceeded.

Associated with each of the pyramids were ancillary temples that are now largely ruins. Alongside the Nile was a lower or valley temple, where the boat bearing the pharaoh's body would land to disembark its royal cargo. The valley temple may have been where the process of mummification took place, although the evidence is not entirely clear on this point. A causeway connected the river temple to the upper or mortuary temple at the base of the pyramid itself. Here the corpse would receive a final ritual cleansing prior to entombment.

Of all the Giza valley temples, the lower temple of Khafre remains in the best state of preservation. Essentially square in plan, with thick limestone walls encased in red granite, its central hall is an inverted T-shape. Red granite piers supported a roof with a clerestory; the windows were set so that sunlight coming through them illuminated the twenty-three statues of the pharaoh placed around the edges of the wall. Two levels of narrow storage rooms extended into the solid wall mass. Today the temple stands without a roof or its outer stone facing beside the Sphinx, a man-headed lion 187 feet long and sixty-six feet high, carved in situ out of a natural rock ledge (Fig. 1.29). (It has long been presumed that the head on the Sphinx was a likeness of Khafre, but this cannot be proven. Recent speculation that the Sphinx may be significantly older than the pyramids is not generally accepted by Egyptologists.) Khafre's mortuary temple at the base of the pyramid is connected to the valley temple by a causeway running at

1.27 Pyramids, Giza, Egypt, ca. 2550–2460 BCE.

Khufu's pyramid is the farthest back, to the right of Khafre's pyramid (distinguished by its remnant of outer casing stones at the peak). In front of Khafre's pyramid is that of Menkaure, while three much smaller pyramids in the foreground belonged to queens of Menkaure.

1.28 Plan of the pyramids at Giza, Egypt, ca. 2550–2460 BCE.

In order from top to bottom, these belonged to Khufu, Khafre, and Menkaure. Khufu's pyramid in particular has a large number of subsidiary tombs, including smaller pyramids and mastabas for members of the court. Khufu's pyramid has the best preserved valley temple and causeway. Note the position of the Sphinx to the north of the causeway leading to Khafre's pyramid.

Mastaba tombs

Pyramid of Khufu (Cheops)

Causeway to mortuary temple

Pyramid of Khafre (Chephren)

Sphinx

Valley temple with causeway to mortuary temple

Valley temple with causeway to mortuary temple

Pyramid of Menkaure (Mycerinus)

small pyramids for queens of Menkaure

0   500 m

0   1500 ft

an oblique angle to the river. The mortuary temple is rectangular in plan, with a series of axially disposed interior spaces. Its limestone structure was probably cased with a finer material, and the floor was alabaster. At the center of the temple was a large courtyard surrounded by enormous pillars, in front of which stood twelve large statues of the pharaoh.

Pyramids, especially the impressive Giza group, have long provoked two questions: How could ancient peoples, working with simple technologies, have built such enormous structures, and why would they have built them? The answer to the first question can be reasonably surmised, although this is still an area of study. Even though the Egyptians lacked metals harder than copper and made no use of the wheel for transport, they were not primitive. Their knowledge of surveying, necessary for reestablishing field boundaries after the annual flood, enabled them to lay out the pyramid's base accurately and to orient the square plan to the cardinal directions. Khufu's pyramid deviates only 5½ minutes of arc from true north; its summit is only one foot off the center of the base; and there is only an eight-inch error in the length of one side of the base. The absence of wheeled vehicles was not a serious handicap, as much of the stone transport would have been over water or across sand, where wheels would provide no real advantage over the boats and sledges actually used. Quarrying was accomplished with metal saws for the softer limestones or sandstones, and by repeatedly pounding balls of very hard rock (dolerite) along seams in the harder stones such as granite. The finishing of cut surfaces could be accomplished with stone hammers, chisels, axes, and sand or grindstones. By any method, quarry work was tedious, and it was probably assigned to prisoners or conscripts. Much of the limestone in the core of the Giza pyramids was quarried on-site. Finer display stone and granite was transported by water from more distant locations.

Construction of the pyramids was probably done by large teams of laborers during the flood season when agricultural work was impossible. The muscle power of men hauled blocks into place. Studies of ruined or incomplete pyramids have revealed that there was no single construction method used on all these monuments; least of all is known about the most complete monuments, the Giza trio, because their interiors cannot be inspected closely. In some cases, ramps were erected along with the masonry mountain to provide an inclined plane for dragging stone on sledges. It is also possible that the rising stepped core of the Giza pyramids served as a construction staircase that was used to pull and lever the blocks onto the upper levels, as the volume of material needed for ramps on these enormous buildings and the difficulty of hauling stone around corners would make inclined planes impractical. While the number of men and length of time required to see a major pyramid through to completion are still subject to debate, the ability to organize labor forces and quarrymen

in seasonal building campaigns remains a tribute to the abilities of Egyptian engineers.

The question of why the pyramids were built has inspired more speculation and nonsense than the how question. Theories ranging from embodiments of standard measures (as defined in English units) to apocalyptic predictions of the end of the world have been offered to explain the configuration of Khufu's pyramid, but Egyptologists are convinced that the pyramids were first and foremost tombs for the pharaohs. Why people should devote so much effort to what we might regard as a fundamentally useless project is harder to answer unless the Egyptian world view is first understood. Perhaps no other society before or since has invested so much time and labor to ensure survival after death for its most important personages. Virtually all Egyptian art and architecture was very practical: to assist one's passage to the next world and ensure comfort and pleasant living once one arrived. The evidence that peasants, not slaves or prisoners, composed the work crews has led some scholars to propose that pyramid-building was devised to keep agricultural workers busy during the flood season, thus preventing tribal bickering and at the same time forging national unity. Since the beginning of the Fifth Dynasty coincides with the ascendancy of priests of the cult of Ra, the sun god whose shrine was capped by a pyramid, some have proposed that the form may have been exploited for pharaonic tombs to reflect the ruler's divinity. In terms of architecture, the Fourth-Dynasty tombs represent a high point in Egyptian building during the Old Kingdom.

1.29 Khafre's pyramid and the Sphinx, Giza, Egypt, ca. 2550–2460 BCE.

Remains of the entrance to Khafre's valley temple are visible to the left.

1.31 Plans and section of rock-cut tombs, Beni Hasan, Egypt, ca. 2000–1900 BCE.

Even when working amorphous rock, the builders chose to replicate rectangular geometries and to carve details reflecting the wooden and plastered reed construction that doubtless characterized houses.

1.30 Reconstruction and plan of Mentuhotep's mortuary temple, Deir-el-Bahari, Egypt, ca. 2061–2010 BCE.

This Middle-Kingdom temple represents an interesting synthesis of an axial temple, hypostyle hall, and burial chamber into a single composition. Its ramps and stepped terraces would be echoed in the New-Kingdom temple of Hatshepsut built about 400 years later on an adjoining site.

THE MIDDLE KINGDOM (ELEVENTH–THIRTEENTH DYNASTIES, ca. 2040–1640 BCE)

The first eight Egyptian dynasties gave way to a period of upheaval when local feudal lords upset the unity achieved by Menes. This era of inter-regional strife is designated the First Intermediate period, and it was followed by a second phase of centralized government called the Middle Kingdom. During this period, the royal capital was relocated from Memphis to Thebes, and the pharaoh's position was more that of a feudal lord over local vassals than an absolute and divine ruler in the Old-Kingdom tradition. Royal tombs were still of major architectural importance, but Middle-Kingdom tombs generally neither endured nor intimidated grave robbers.

The tomb of Mentuhotep II at Deir-el-Bahari (ca. 2061–2010 BCE) (Fig. 1.30) is an exceptional work of architectural innovation, combining temple and tomb chamber in a single composition. The complex, approached by an axial route from the Nile, had two levels of colonnaded terraces surrounding a masonry mass, long thought to have been a pyramid but more recently interpreted as a flat-roofed hall. (The building is a ruin today, so one cannot be sure of the initial design. The case for a flat-roofed hall is based on there being insufficient foundation to support even a modest pyramid.) The central axis continues beyond this reception temple through a courtyard and hypostyle hall to Mentuhotep's actual burial vault carved in the rock cliff. This integration of previously disparate elements into a compact group was a rare innovation in Egyptian architecture, and Mentuhotep's tomb would serve as a prototype for the more elaborate adjoining funerary complex built by the New-Kingdom pharaoh Hatshepsut.

More typical of Middle-Kingdom tombs are those at Beni Hasan, which are cut into rock cliffs and provided with sheltering porticoes (Fig. 1.31). Reflecting the political importance of their builders, these tombs were constructed for minor nobles and court officials, who evidently enjoyed considerable influence and wealth. Most of the architectural character was created by excavation, and the builders replicated spaces and details associated with ordinary dwellings, that is, wooden and plastered reed structures with slightly arched roofs composed of mats laid on the frame. As was the case at Djoser's complex at Saqqara, the stone has been carved in imitation of non-stone materials, including palm trunks, bundled reeds, lotus flowers, and binding cords.

THE NEW KINGDOM (EIGHTEENTH–TWENTIETH DYNASTIES, ca. 1550–1070 BCE)

The Middle Kingdom was terminated by the arrival of the Hyksos, shepherd-kings who may have come from Asia. Whatever their origins, the Hyksos were the first successful invaders of Egypt in centuries, and they ruled for about 100 years in what is known as the Second Intermediate period. They introduced metallurgy, the two-person chariot, new deities, and new weapons to Egyptian culture, but their rule produced no lasting artistic innovations. With the expulsion of the Hyksos came the New Kingdom, which was characterized by an invigorated dynastic line of pharaohs and an increasingly powerful hereditary priesthood who brought Egypt to new heights of political and cultural brilliance.

The Eighteenth Dynasty, the first of the New Kingdom, continued the Middle-Kingdom tradition of burial in rock-cut tombs, going a stage further by eliminating all suggestions of monumentality. It had escaped no one's notice that all the dynastic tombs had been successfully penetrated by grave robbers. The Giza pyramids were probably plundered during the First Intermediate period.

1.32 Mortuary temple of Queen Hatshepsut, Deir-el-Bahari, Egypt, ca. 1473–1458 BCE.

In its day, this great temple, with planted terraces and dignified carved colonnades framed by the cliff face, must have been a restful oasis in the dry landscape, a fitting monument to the peaceful reign of Hatshepsut, one of the rare woman rulers in antiquity.

1.33 View and plan of Hatshepsut's mortuary temple, Deir-el-Bahari, Egypt, ca. 1473–1458 BCE.

To thwart thieves, New-Kingdom pharaohs arranged for their bodies to be buried in concealed tombs in the Valley of the Kings (behind these cliffs), where priests guarded against robbers. Mentuhotep's earlier tomb is seen just beyond Hatshepsut's monument.

To preserve the worldly remains of the pharaoh and thwart the thieves, Eighteenth-Dynasty builders relied on concealment and improved policing of the royal necropolis. New-Kingdom pharaohs were interred secretly in the desert wilderness beyond Deir-el-Bahari, a region known as the Valley of the Kings, where very modest chambers were hewn out of the cliffs, and the entrances were hidden by dirt and sand. Spiritual nourishment for the deceased was provided at increasingly elaborate separately erected funerary temples.

Among the most splendid of the Eighteenth-Dynasty temples is the funerary complex of Queen Hatshepsut (1473–1458 BCE) at Deir-el-Bahari (Fig. 1.32), notable both for its architecture and for the fact that its patron was a woman. Succession to the throne passed through the female line, but the pharaoh was almost always male. Hatshepsut was the daughter of Thutmose I, and she married her half-brother, who became Pharaoh Thutmose II. During his reign she relegated him to a subsidiary role, and after his death she ruled independently, though ostensibly as regent for Thutmose II's son by a concubine, Thutmose III. Her court favorite was a commoner, Senmut, who was also responsible (perhaps as architect) for her

funerary temple. Hatshepsut was buried on the other side of the mountain range in the Valley of the Kings, so the temple complex was a mortuary chapel dedicated to the god Amun, the sun god with whom the pharaoh was associated. Ramps lead up from the valley to three broad terraces, each defined by colonnades, which also serve as retaining walls for the next level (Fig. 1.33). The overall design was doubtless inspired by the neighboring temple of Mentuhotep, although Hatshepsut's temple is considerably larger and grander. Columns in the north colonnade of the second terrace are faceted in a manner suggesting the flutes of later Doric columns (Fig. 1.34). Relief carvings and wall paintings within the sanctuary spaces and in the great hall depict Hatshepsut's divine birth as the child of Amun and the activities of her peaceful reign, including trading expeditions to Punt (perhaps the Somali coast) bearing gold, ivory, baboons, and botanical specimens. Hatshepsut herself is usually depicted as a man, sometimes as the god Osiris, wearing the apron and headdress of a pharaoh.

Today they are sand-covered and barren, but in the Eighteenth Dynasty the terraces of Hatshepsut's temple were embellished with incense trees planted in earth-filled pits to create a garden for Amun's promenades. Buried irrigation pipes supplied water to sustain the plants, and priests placed tributes to the god in the shade beneath the branches. The entire setting of the temple, from the axial-ramp approach to the termination of the processional way at a false door painted on the wall of the final rock-hewn sanctuary, is a masterful blending of architecture into a dramatic landscape including rugged hillsides. Although Hatshepsut reigned and died peacefully, her successors did everything possible to eradicate her memory, erasing her name from inscriptions, smashing almost all of her sculptural representations, and desecrating the burial site of Senmut.

In the course of the Eighteenth Dynasty, temple complexes built to honor both gods and pharaohs became more extensive and elaborate, aided by the establishment of Amun as the main "state" god and the increased power and influence of his priesthood. Successive rulers would add new portions or renovate older temples, creating designs whose chief attribute was overbearing grandeur, not coherence or esthetic delight. The temple at Karnak, across the Nile from Deir-el-Bahari, is an example of this process (Fig. 1.35). Begun about 1550 BCE, it was enlarged by Thutmose I, enriched by obelisks given by his daughter, Hatshepsut, and again expanded with a hypostyle jubilee festival hall constructed by Thutmose III for his own glorification. Yet another hypostyle hall, the largest of all, was built by Ramesses II.

Hypostyle halls are large chambers created by rows of large columns placed closely together. The tight spacing was necessary to support the stone lintels of the roof, while the large column diameter reflected the substantial height of the stone cylinders. The net effect was a dim

1.34 Upper colonnade (detail), Hatshepsut's mortuary temple, Deir-el-Bahari, Egypt, ca. 1473–1458 BCE.

Behind the rectangular piers are cylindrical columns with fluting that has led to their being called proto-Doric. Certainly they are evidence of Egyptian precedent for what in Greek hands would become an aspect of the orders of architecture.

1.35 Plan of the Great Temple of Amun, Karnak, Egypt, begun ca. 1550 BCE.

This temple is celebrated more for its sheer size than for its architectural coherence. Dedicated to the sun god Amun, whose priesthood was powerful during the New Kingdom, the temple maintained a strong sense of axiality and monumental procession through all its additions.

interior without a sense of spatial expanse. Daylight admitted through slits in the stone clerestory grilles filtered through the incense smoke and the upper volume of the hypostyle columns to create a sense of mystery, the desired effect for religious ritual (page 8 & Fig. 1.36). The temple was the habitation of the god, who was sheltered, clothed, and fed by the priests, by now a powerful and largely hereditary group. Each day the priests performed purification rites in the sacred lake within the temple precinct, dressed the statue of the deity in rich garments, and presented it offerings at the evening ritual. They carried small statues in processions, and placed others in the sun for rejuvenation in special festivals, such as those marking the beginning of the New Year. Monumental masonry entrance gates or pylons lined processional routes to represent the eastern mountains of Egypt through which the divine early-morning sunlight emanated. Despite their rambling plans and numerous additions, New-Kingdom temples maintained axial circulation spaces for the penetration of solar rays and the movement of priestly processions (Fig. 1.37). The pylon gates were not only symbols of the entrance through which the sun was reborn each day, but also of the gates to the underworld through which the eternal spirit must pass.

Five generations after Hatshepsut, the pharaoh Amenophis IV (1353–1335 BCE) made a major break

Pylon II
Hypostyle hall
Pylon III
Temple of Ptah
Pylon IV
Great Temple of Amun
Festival Temple of Thutmose III
Avenue of ram-headed sphinxes
Pylon I
Temple of Ramesses III
Temple of Khonsu
Sacred lake
Festival Hall of Amenophis II

N

0 _____ 250 m
0 _____ 750 ft

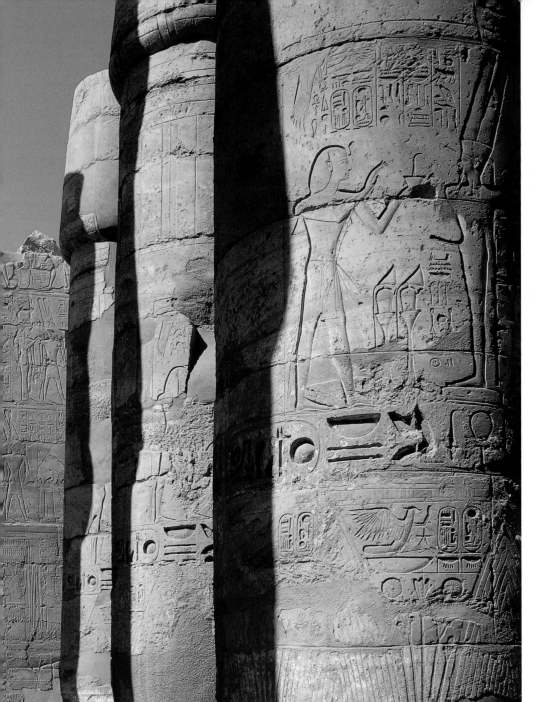

1.36 Papyrus columns, Hypostyle Hall, Great Temple of Amun, Karnak, Egypt, ca. 1390–1224 BCE.

Carved detail on these columns depicts daily ritual and processional scenes, including the pharaoh bringing offerings to the gods. The photograph on page 8 shows the context for these columns.

with Egyptian religious tradition by disavowing the multitudes of deities and instituting a monotheistic religion devoted to the sun disc Aten. Changing his name to Akhenaten, which means "all is well with Aten," Amenophis abandoned the old capital at Thebes about 1350 BCE to establish a new capital 300 miles to the north at Akhetaten (the modern Tell-el-Amarna). From what is known from incomplete excavations of its ruins, Akhetaten was a linear town nearly seven miles long, bounded on the west by the Nile and on the east by mountains, and lacking a consistent overall plan. Transportation was facilitated by the waterway, and a river road linked the various residential sections of the town (Fig. 1.38). Temples had altars set in open courtyards, and there were no segregated areas for the priesthood. Private houses of the wealthy were commodious, walled off from public view, with rooms grouped around open courts looking into garden areas planted with trees. Thick mud-brick

walls moderated the extremes of heat and cold. No wall surrounded the city, protection being provided by free-standing guardhouses.

What we know of other Egyptian city plans is meager indeed. Aside from Akhetaten, only a few construction villages and military encampments survive to provide an indication of Egyptian urban patterns, and these may not be at all typical of the whole. There is consistency in the layout of construction villages, however, to judge from the surviving El-Lahun (built for Middle-Kingdom workers constructing the pyramid of Sesostris II), Deir el-Medina (a New-Kingdom construction near the Valley of the Kings), and the workers' village to the east of Akhetaten (Fig. 1.39). All were built on a grid layout, with a wall to control access to the camp. Individual workers' houses were built to similar plans, with rooms running in series. Overseers and senior officials lived in a separate section, divided from the workmen's houses by a brick wall, and

1.37 First court, Great Temple of Amun, Karnak, Egypt, begun ca. 1550 BCE.

Massive columns and colossal statues of Ramesses II define the axial path to the second pylon gate, built by Sethos I (1306–1290). Beyond is the Hypostyle Hall illustrated on page 8.

these administrators were provided with more commodious houses organized around internal courtyards.

The so-called Amarna period brought a change in artistic conventions. For a brief interval, stiff and highly stylized artistic canons were relaxed in favor of more naturalistic approaches. This can be seen immediately in the portraits of Akhenaten and his family, who are shown in informal poses. Akhenaten himself is depicted with distorted facial features. Innovative as they were, Akhenaten's religious reforms perhaps contributed to the downfall of the Eighteenth Dynasty. There is little evidence that the common people abandoned the old pantheon of gods, and the deposed priesthood of Amun, largely a hereditary group, resented the cult of Aten and its followers. Akhenaten neglected imperial defense needs in the provinces, and repeated appeals from Syria for help in the struggle against the Hittites went unanswered. (These communications, along with correspondence from other kingdoms throughout Mesopotamia, were found as archaeologists excavated Akhetaten.) By the time Akhenaten died in about 1335 BCE, the cult of Amun had been revived and former religious practices reinstated. Thebes again became the capital as Akhetaten was abandoned and its buildings deliberately ruined, with stones from the temple of Aten

1.38 Plan of the central section, Akhetaten (Tell-el-Amarna), Egypt, ca. 1350 BCE.

This was the new capital city of Akhenaten, located away from traditional religious centers in an effort to break from the powerful, established Egyptian priesthood. Rites for the sun disc Aten were celebrated in temples containing large open courtyards, lit directly by the sun's beneficent rays.

Great Temple

Great Palace

King's House

Small Temple

N

0   500 m

0   1500 ft

quarters for workmen   quarters for supervisors and administrators

Deir el-Medina

N

0   100 m
0   300 ft

El-Lahun

1.39 Plans of El-Lahun, ca. 1800 BCE and Deir el-Medina, ca. 1400 BCE

Because modern cities are located on the sites of ancient Egyptian cities, we cannot say much about their design. These abandoned towns, built to house workers on pharaonic building projects, show a tendency toward orthogonal layouts and uniform house plans, but one cannot say whether this characterized larger cities or not.

being used to construct new pylon gates at Karnak. Akhenaten's successors, Smenkhkare (who reigned for two years) and Tutankhaten, embraced the old religion. Tutankhaten even changed his name to Tutankhamun to show his allegiance to the old religion at Thebes.

There would be little to say about the brief and rather uneventful reign of Tutankhamun (1333–1323) were it not that his burial in the Valley of the Kings remained virtually unplundered until its discovery by Lord Carnarvon and Howard Carter in 1922. The astonishing richness of the artifacts crammed into the two chambers of his tomb, in addition to the precious objects included with the mummy encased in a golden mask, adequately demonstrate why grave-robbing flourished in ancient Egypt. If a minor pharaoh such as Tutankhamun merited such a lavish burial, imagine what treasures were entombed with an important ruler. The discovery of Tut's tomb greatly increased knowledge of Egyptian life, for the everyday objects—furniture, a wig box, camp bed, fire-making tools, and so forth—are as informative as the bejeweled objects are valuable.

Tutankhamun was the last pharaoh of the Eighteenth Dynasty. His chief advisor and his military officer seized power in succession after his death and founded the next dynasty, of which Ramesses II (1290–1224 BCE) was the

most outstanding pharaoh. In addition to his military and political accomplishments, including a peace treaty with the Hittites, Ramesses II constructed a number of great monuments during his sixty-six-year reign. His contributions to the temple at Karnak have already been mentioned. At Abu Simbel, he had two temples carved into the rock cliffs adjoining the Nile, thus exploiting ideas from the Giza Sphinx (monumental sculpture carved in living rock), Beni Hasan (rock-cut tombs), and the New-Kingdom temples (pylon gates). The larger temple at Abu Simbel (Fig. 1.40) has four colossal statues of Ramesses II seated, each measuring sixty-five feet in height; these dominate the entrance face and continue the sloping contour of the cliff. Diminutive statues of family members, including his queen Nefertari, stand beside the pharaoh's legs. None of these secondary figures is as tall as Ramesses's knee, to indicate their inferior status. Behind this sculpted façade is the temple proper, excavated into the rock for a distance of 180 feet. The plan is axial, with an entrance hall, colonnaded chamber, and shrine in the center flanked by long, narrow storage rooms to either side. The interior surfaces are richly carved. Columns in the large chamber are composed of standing images of Ramesses as Osiris, wearing the crown of Upper Egypt on the north-side row and the double crown of unified Egypt on the south-side row. The smaller temple is similar, with thirty-three-foot-high standing colossi representing Ramesses and his queen set between buttresses that continue the slope of the rock face. Both temples have been repositioned today, the result of an international effort to save them from inundation in Lake Nassar, which was created behind the Aswan Dam. Their new locations on higher ground vary only slightly from the original orientations.

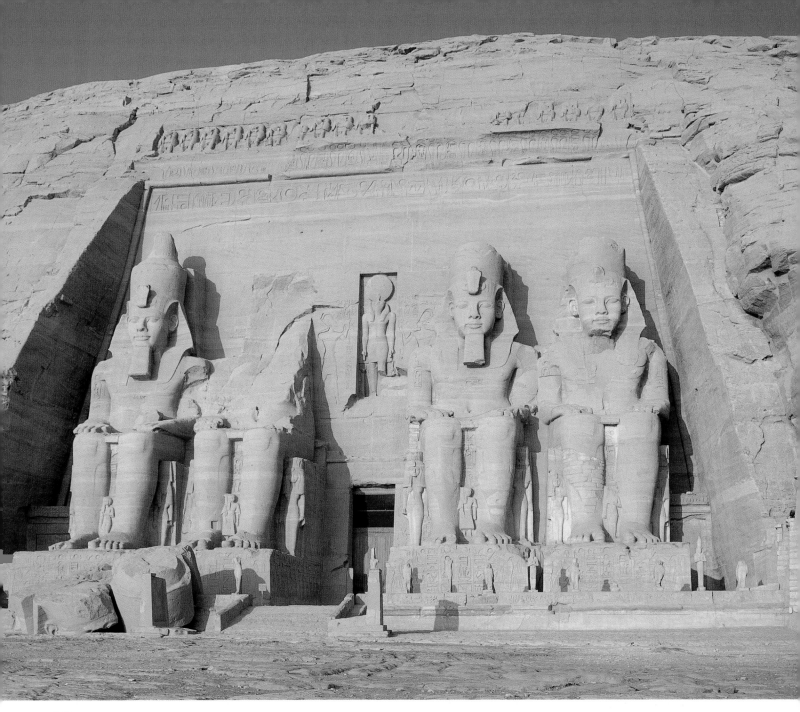

1.40 Great Temple of Ramesses II, Abu Simbel, ca. 1285–1255 BCE.

Ramesses II selected a site near the southern boundary of his domain to build temples honoring himself and his queen, Nefertari. Carved in the rock face, his temple combines the monumentality of the Giza Sphinx, the axial design of rock-cut tombs, and the battered façades of pylon gates into an arresting composition.

Later rulers of the Twentieth Dynasty did not eclipse Ramesses's glory, but they maintained some of the same vigor as leaders. With the advent of the Twenty-First Dynasty (ca. 1070 BCE), however, Egypt began a long slide into decadence and ceased to be a major influence in either art or culture. While at its zenith, however, Egypt produced some of the most astonishing constructions of all time. The sheer volume of stone moved to construct the great pyramid at Giza has not been equaled by any single project of more recent eras, and the gigantic scale of New-Kingdom monuments such as Abu Simbel continues to impress modern visitors. That such an early civilization should have created these monumental and enduring works is eloquent tribute to the skills of Egyptian architects, engineers, and builders.

CHAPTER 2

THE GREEK WORLD

The Aegean Sea, bounded by the peninsula of Greece on the west, the mountains of Macedonia on the north, and the coast of Anatolia on the east, is studded with numerous islands. To the south is the island of Crete. By the beginning of the second millennium BCE (about the time of the Middle Kingdom in Egypt), the seafaring people of this region had learned how to exploit natural resources—timber, stone, metallic ores, clay for pottery—to produce distinctive artifacts. With these, in addition to other agricultural products, they engaged in trade with Egypt and settlements along the eastern Mediterranean, where they constructed small fortified settlements and agricultural villages on islands and along the coast.

An examination of artifacts made in the Aegean suggests strong influence from Mesopotamia as well as contact with Egypt. Early Cretans worshiped nature deities associated with mountains, trees, and animals (most notably snakes), as well as flowers, including lilies and poppies. Since there are no snakes on Crete, the snake cult appears to be an imported practice, probably derived from the Sumerian water god Ea, whose attributes included creativity, wisdom, magic, and slyness. Bull-baiting was a sport of the Sumerians, and bull-jumping seems to have become a ritual game in Crete. Lions were associated with royal symbolism in both Egypt and Mesopotamia, and they also came to be used in fortified royal settlements on the Greek mainland. Egyptian artifacts from the Eighteenth Dynasty have been retrieved from the harbor at Kairatos, Crete, and 1300 pieces of Aegean pottery dating from 1370–1350 BCE have been excavated from the rubbish heaps of Akhetaten.

North entrance, Knossos, ca. 1700–1380 BCE.

This section has been partially restored, complete with the typical Minoan columns with bulbous capitals and downward-tapering shafts.

THE MINOANS

Historians recognize two separate civilizations in the Aegean during the second millennium: that of the Minoans, based on Crete, and that of the Mycenaeans, established at several sites on the mainland of Greece. They share some artistic and cultural traits, including a reliance on trade with other communities in Egypt, Mesopotamia, Asia Minor, and Cyprus. Both produced luxury goods that were traded extensively around the eastern Mediterranean—Minoan envoys bearing characteristic pottery from Crete are included in Egyptian wall paintings from the reign of Queen Hatshepsut—and Mycenaean sites were involved in the Trojan War (ca. 1250 BCE), chronicled by Homer in the *Iliad*. Both civilizations contributed to the cultural patrimony of classical Greece. Most of what we know about this Minoan civilization comes from archaeologists, who are still making new discoveries and reinterpreting older finds as a result of analysis with more sophisticated scientific tools. Not surprisingly, there is more than one theory related to the development and demise of the Minoans.

The civilization is named for Minos, which might be the name of an early king or simply the title (like pharaoh) that denoted a ruler. The later Greeks created legends associated with King Minos and his palace and labyrinth at Knossos, where the fearsome Minotaur that ate youths and maidens lived. Although numerous Minoan sites have been excavated on Crete, Knossos remains the largest and best known. Four thousand years of Neolithic settlements lie under this Minoan settlement, which began in about 1900 BCE as a series of detached structures erected around a large rectangular court. When these were destroyed by a major earthquake in about 1700 BCE, the complex was rebuilt in a unified scheme on multiple levels, with ritual or ceremonial rooms, storage areas, and living accommodation connected by long corridors and staircases built around light wells, open cores that admit sunlight to the lower levels. The courtyard continued as the central element in the composition. Tablets

theater area

North entrance

stairs to lustral basin

West entrance

storage rooms

Throne Room

lustral basin

Hall of the Double Axes

bath

Central Court

Queen's megaron

processional corridor

Upper level plan
(conjectural restoration)

N

0   50 m

0   150 ft

Ground level plan

2.1 Plan of the palace, Knossos, ca. 1700–1380 BCE.

The plan is organized around an open rectangular courtyard, off which major reception rooms open. As only the ground level of this three- or four-story building survived destruction, many aspects of its design are conjectural.

inscribed in Linear A, a script that has still not been deciphered, appear in the archaeological record in about 1600 BCE. In about 1450 BCE, Knossos and all other Minoan palaces on Crete were destroyed, but Knossos alone was rebuilt. Traces of Mycenaean cultural influences, including writing in the script known as Linear B, an early form of Greek, are found in the rebuilt palace, suggesting either collusion or a forced alliance between Mycenaeans and the Cretans at Knossos. The final destruction of the site, this time by fire, came in about 1380 BCE.

Understanding the extensive ruins at Knossos is no easy task (Fig. 2.1). Sir Arthur Evans started excavations at the ceremonial center in 1900 CE. Archaeological investigation continues on the site today, and the associated town has yet to be unearthed. Evans was confident that he had found the palace of the legendary King Minos, but his chronology and efforts at reconstruction are now regarded as controversial and a recent assessment suggests that what Evans found was actually a sacred center. The function of the building may in fact have changed from a temple to a palace in its final years, but frescoes depicting priestesses and celebrants suggest the continuing centrality of religious practice. The charred remains of the final buildings present ambiguous evidence at best. While parts of the lower levels of the building were built in **ashlar** masonry,

most of the upper floors were supported on walls built of rubble contained within squared timbers, wooden columns, and large wooden beams, the combustible portions of which were consumed in the conflagration. Evans relied on impressions of the bases and capitals where these touched stone to reconstruct the characteristic Minoan column, a downward-tapering shaft with a bulbous torus ring and abacus block capital (see page 38). (The columns on-site today are in concrete.) On the basis of what he found, Evans also reconstructed major ceremonial rooms and several light-wells (Figs. 2.2–2.3).

Even after considerable study, however, the function of the whole complex is a matter of scholarly deliberation. Storerooms containing pottery jars for wine, oil, olives, and grain are unmistakable, but the function of other sections of the building, where several stages of construction can be detected, is still conjectural. The appearance and uses of the upper floors we cannot know, so photographs of the site today can only begin to suggest the grandeur that must have characterized the whole. When one realizes that the mainland Greeks of this period were living in far simpler buildings, it is possible that they preserved memories of the site in the legend of King Minos, using the term "labyrinth" to describe the large, rambling, and complicated plan that is the complex at Knossos. (Although the etymology of labyrinth is uncertain, the equivalent Egyptian term was applied to an enormous mortuary temple built during the Middle Kingdom for Amenemhet III [1844–1797 BCE] at Hawara.)

So far as we know, Knossos was unfortified. The palace/temple complex sat on a hill overlooking the

2.2 Restored light well, Knossos, ca. 1700–1380 BCE.

Located on the upper story, this light-well hall is over the Throne Room (see Fig. 2.3). The fresco shown here is a restoration.

2.3 Throne Room, Knossos, ca. 1700–1380 BCE.

Named for the elaborate "throne," this room is provided with bench seating along the adjacent walls. Frescoes show griffins in lush foliage. Since a lustral basin adjoins this room, it is possible the space was used for religious ritual rather than royal audiences.

harbor below. Nearly four acres of buildings surround a central courtyard measuring 174 by eighty-seven feet. In the three-story western wing, which contained ceremonial spaces, there is none of the axiality characteristic of Egyptian architecture. Instead, visitors to the palace during its final years entered through the west *propylaea*, or gateway, then followed a corridor lined with frescoes depicting priestesses and celebrants bearing offerings, before turning left twice to approach the courtyard from the south. On the left (west) wall near the north end of the courtyard was the entrance to the antechamber of a **lustral-basin** (depressed pool) sanctuary called the throne room because of an elaborate alabaster seat found there. On a lower level, along the southern edge of the throne room, was a lustral basin, one of several found in the complex that are thought to have been used in initiation rituals. This basin, which is only about eighteen inches deep, is further concealed by a low wall and a screen of Minoan columns. Cult statues and votive offerings indicate that the site was sacred to a female deity linked to the earth and fertility. Long rows of underground storage rooms occupy the western side of this wing, dug into the slope of the hillside, with tall ceramic containers for olive oil, grain, and wine still in position.

2.4 Reconstructed light-well staircase, Knossos, ca. 1700–1380 BCE.

As major ceremonial rooms were located partially under ground, stairs to reach them were constructed around open shafts to bring light and fresh air to lower levels. The original wooden columns and supporting beams were destroyed in the fire that consumed the palace about 1380 BCE.

Buildings on the eastern side of the courtyard have been interpreted as being residential, although some of the suites may have functioned as textile workshops and others were definitely used as storage areas. Rooms on the east had views out over the valley below. The primary entrance to this section was through a grand staircase approached from the middle side of the central court and illuminated by an open light well. The stair led down to the Hall of the Double Axes, from which a corridor connected to the room Evans dubbed the Queen's **Megaron**, a pleasant space decorated with frescoes of rosettes and flying dolphins. Smaller rooms behind the megaron contained a bathtub and a water closet (toilet) connected to the palace's drain system. Standards of water supply and drainage at the complex were exceptional for the time. Terracotta water pipes brought clean water through a series of settling tanks and siphons to supply baths, and sanitary sewers carried off waste water from basins and water closets, although the tub in the so-called "queen's apartments" had to be emptied by bailing.

At the northwest corner of the complex was the oldest and deepest (six feet) lustral basin, accessed by a staircase and light-well (Fig. 2.4), and beyond this was a series of broad steps, set into a slight rise in the ground and connected to the palace proper by a ceremonial road. This area has been labeled as a theater, although its precise use, as with so much else at Knossos, remains unclear. It seems that the large central courtyard provided the setting for theatrical ritual, including perhaps ceremonial games involving acrobatic feats by young men and women performed on running bulls. Frescoes preserved on some palace walls illustrate these amusements or rituals.

The naturalistic portrayal of the young men and women in these frescoes creates the impression that the Minoans were an energetic and cheerful people who took delight in their own beauty and that of the natural world. In contrast to the stiffness and formality of Egyptian art, frescoes and carvings in Minoan sites seem relaxed and open, emphasizing movement. Women held positions of high status, an unprecedented situation among contemporary civilizations. There is, however, a great deal that is still not clearly understood. The language(s) recorded in Minoan pictographs and on Linear A tablets remain undeciphered; the significance of the double-headed axe widely found in Minoan art is also a puzzle. We do not know whether the appearance of Mycenaean culture in the final phase of Knossos came as a result of invasion or peaceful assimilation. Continued study of Minoan sites may reveal answers to these and other questions.

THE MYCENAEANS

Mycenaean civilization takes its name from Mycenae, the largest but not the only citadel in a trading society that appears to have been led by warrior-kings. Mycenaean settlements located on the mainland of Greece date back to about 1600 BCE. Graves from this period preserve a large number of golden objects as well as weapons of various sorts. Heinrich Schliemann, the nineteenth-century excavator of Mycenae, found golden masks, drinking vessels, and other treasure that convinced him he had found material related to the Trojan War. In fact, his finds predate the era of the Homeric tales by four centuries.

MYCENAE

Mycenae reached its period of greatness after about 1450 BCE, perhaps invigorated by contact with the more sophisticated Minoan culture. In contrast to the seemingly undefended complex at Knossos, the citadel at Mycenae was built with a strong concern for defense. The city is on high ground, protected by mountains on the north and south and flanked by two ravines, allowing surveillance of a wide area down to the coast (Figs. 2.5–2.6a,b). Fortifications erected in the fourteenth century BCE were expanded in about 1300 BCE to enclose the palace compound and an earlier grave circle. These walls are eighteen to twenty-four feet thick and up to forty feet high, constructed of boulders set in position with minimal shaping and no mortar, except for the sections immediately adjacent to the gates, where the stone has been cut into large blocks. The later Greeks thought this the work of giants, the Cyclopes, hence the adjective **cyclopean** to describe their construction.

2.5 Ruins of Mycenae, ca. 1600–1250 BCE.

This fabled city was strategically situated to control major routes in the vicinity. The enclosing wall is composed of roughly shaped boulders. Ruins of the palace are at the high point of the site.

2.6a Plan of Mycenae, ca. 1600–1250 BCE.

This shows areas that have been excavated. Notice how the fortifications' walls extend to provide additional protection at the Lion Gate, as is also the case at the secondary gate on the northeastern side. The palace megaron, one of the largest rooms in the city, is located in the center.

2.6b Plan of Tiryns, ca. 1300 BCE.

The palace section is located on the southern end, where two megarons can be seen, and the northern extension enclosed the lower citadel. The entrance ramp along the eastern side passed through two fortified gates and between high walls that served as fighting platforms.

Entrance to Mycenae was through the Lion Gate, which was added when the citadel was enlarged in about 1300 BCE (Fig. 2.7). It was positioned so that the approaching visitor had to pass along an increasingly narrow passageway parallel to the enclosing wall, allowing defenders inside the settlement ample opportunity to attack hostile forces before they could reach the entrance. The actual gateway is of considerable artistic interest. Single upright stones support a fourteen-ton lintel across the opening, above which is a corbeled arch. The space of the arch is filled by a triangular stone with relief sculpture of two lions with their forefeet on an altar bearing a column of the tree cult. (Mesopotamia had a tradition of venerating trees.) The lions' heads are missing; they were carved separately and attached with dowels, the holes for which are still visible. Even in its damaged state, however, the Lion Gate indicates contact by its creators with the Minoan world, for the column of the tree cult is unmistakably the same as the columns used at Knossos. On the north side, the walls have a second smaller gate of the same age as the Lion Gate but without sculpture. There are also inconspicuous back entrances or postern gates built to provide access to a cistern and to provide outlets in case of need.

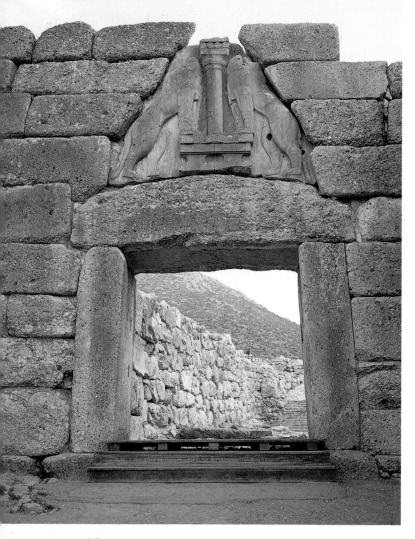

2.7 The Lion Gate, Mycenae, ca. 1300 BCE.

Notice that the carved lion figures flank a column of the type seen at Knossos. The use of guardian beasts associated with royalty links Mycenae with both Hittite and Egyptian traditions.

the largest room, roughly forty feet square. Bases for the four columns that supported the roof are still visible, as is the central hearth. This part of the palace was built in part on fill, supported by a retaining wall, and there is still a splendid view out over the valley from the court in front of the megaron. To the north, a smaller room with a stuccoed bath has been identified as a bathroom which legend associates with the murder of Agamemnon on his triumphal return from Troy. Other rooms of the palace were lost when the area was cleared for a later temple.

The citadel at Mycenae was surrounded by smaller settlements, perhaps comprised of extended family groups who lived in houses associated closely with tombs of their ancestors. Nine of these tombs in circular form (tholoi) have been found in the neighborhood of Mycenae: of these, the largest and best preserved is the **tholos** or beehive tomb commonly called the Treasury of Atreus (ca. 1330 BCE) (Figs. 2.8–2.10). It is a corbeled stone chamber rising forty-four feet in thirty-three horizontal courses from a circular plan forty-eight feet in diameter, with a small chamber to the right of the entrance. All the stonework, except for the stone-walled dromos, or entrance way, is covered by an earthen mound, whose weight adds stability to the dry masonry. The corbeled construction employed here is the same technique used by prehistoric megalith builders in northern Europe and by Egyptian masons as early as the Fourth Dynasty. Originally the entrance doorway was elaborately decorated, and there is evidence that the interior was embellished with bronze

Beyond the Lion Gate are the remains of shaft graves where Schliemann uncovered so much golden treasure. Originally these lay outside the citadel walls, but when the fortress was enlarged the grave circle was carefully incorporated into the fortified area. The administrative and ceremonial spaces that lay beyond exist only as ruins, but from remaining foundations it appears that the palace at the highest elevation of the hill had many features derived from Crete, including a megaron as the major ceremonial space. Homer used this term to describe a large palace hall (hence Evans's use of the term at Knossos for the Queen's Megaron). In architectural usage, the word megaron is generally reserved to describe a simple rectangular space (**domos**) having solid long walls without openings and an entrance in the center of the short side, generally with an attached anteroom (prodomos) preceded by a court (see Fig. 2.11). It is an elementary house form still employed in Mediterranean countries, and it has been used by twentieth-century architects including Le Corbusier in his Citrohan houses (see Fig. 15.56). At Mycenae, the palace megaron is

2.8 Plan and section of the Treasury of Atreus, Mycenae, ca. 1330 BCE.

This corbeled tomb assumes the shape of a beehive. Its construction may be compared to the tomb at Er-Mané and the passage grave at New Grange (see Figs. 1.2–1.4). The function of the side chamber is unknown, but it may have been used for burials.

0   20 m
0   60 ft

2.9 Façade and dromos of the Treasury of Atreus, Mycenae, ca. 1330 BCE.

This shows the stone-walled dromos and the triangular corbeled relieving arch that diverts weight from the massive lintel stone. Ornamentation and paint that originally decorated the exterior have disappeared.

2.10 Interior of the Treasury of Atreus, Mycenae, ca. 1330 BCE.

Although the interior space is relatively large, it is also dark, deriving its only light from the open doorway and triangular transom above. The even courses of shaped stones are visible, as is the portal to the side chamber.

plates. Whatever the tholos contained in the way of burials or goods for the afterlife disappeared long ago.

Some of the houses outside the citadel have been excavated, and their remains provide an indication of what the dwellings of this period were like. Near to the Treasury of Atreus are the foundations of four closely grouped houses, of which the West House provides the easiest plan to interpret, as its main floor (rather than the basement) is preserved (Fig. 2.11). Entrance was into a court, probably open to the sky, off which there is the three-room megaron sequence of porch, vestibule, and domos as the major spaces of the house. Off a corridor extending along the

The "Megaron" of the West House, Mycenae

House I of the Panagia Houses, Mycenae

The Megaron of the Palace, Mycenae

The LH IIIB Megara, Tiryns

House at Priene

0   20 m

0   60 ft

2.11 Plans of megarons at Mycenae and elsewhere.

The West House, located just outside the walls at Mycenae, combines a courtyard, porch, antechamber, and megaron. The palace megarons at Mycenae and Tiryns are considerably larger, with remains of the four column bases that supported the roof around a central hearth. Note the survival of the megaron form in the much later Greek house from Priene (see Fig. 2.35b)

atop a limestone ridge protected by a massive wall of cyclopean masonry that dates to the fourteenth century BCE (see Fig. 2.6b). After a fire destroyed the citadel in ca. 1300 BCE, the whole was rebuilt to its present outline, including enclosure of the lower citadel with a twenty-five-foot-thick wall. An earthquake and fire in the mid-thirteenth century BCE damaged the complex, leading to the construction of the buildings whose remains are visible today. The surviving walls around the upper citadel vary from sixteen to fifty-seven feet in thickness. Like Mycenae, the citadel at Tiryns had several postern gates through which people inside could slip out unobtrusively. Corbeled galleries built into the thickness of the walls on the southeast side are handsome examples of masonry (Fig. 2.12). The approach to Tiryns has a more strongly defensive design than the entrance to Mycenae. An almost single-file passage beside and then between the walls

2.12 Corbeled gallery, Tiryns, ca. 1300 BCE.

These passages, built within the thickness of the walls, provided access to guard chambers or postern exits for emergency use.

west side are a series of five rooms and a terrace that was probably unroofed. Stairs at the end of the corridor led to an upper floor whose layout cannot be determined, as the house was destroyed in antiquity by fire. The roof was probably flat, and both it and the upper story were framed in wood, which accounts for the survival of only the rubble stone foundations. Except for the court area, which was paved with stone, all the floors were of clay. A large drain extends across the court and exits under the foundation of the east wall, while a lesser drain is located in the megaron's domos. The use of the small rooms off the corridor has been determined from pottery and clay tablets found in them: all were storerooms, except for the chamber directly off the court, which had both a hearth and drain and was probably the kitchen. It is surmised that the house belonged to wealthier persons engaged in the manufacture of scented oils, for which Mycenae was famous. While not all Mycenaean houses had megaron layouts, the form is commonly enough encountered for the West House to be considered a typical design.

A megaron layout on a grand scale is found in the palace at Tiryns, where the citadel sits

2.13 Approach to Tiryns, ca. 1300 BCE.

This shows the imposts of one gateway. Although the actual gates are now gone, their positions may be seen in the cyclopean masonry. As one advanced up the ramp, the walls of the citadel rose on the right-hand side, placing right-handed shield-wielding soldiers at a disadvantge.

made would-be attackers vulnerable well before they reached the first of two gates (for which the portals are gone) (Fig. 2.13). Beyond the second gate was a courtyard bounded by porticoed chambers corbeled into the mass of the wall. These face the relatively narrow palace gate that opens into a courtyard and through a colonnaded court to the palace megaron of porch, antechamber, and domos (see Fig. 2.11). As at Mycenae, four column bases surround the substantial central hearth, indicating the location of the roof and its opening to let out smoke. Fragments of wall paintings depicting processions of women and the hunting of boars were found in the excavations. A smaller megaron located to the east has an outer and inner court preceding the domos. Tiryns was again devastated by an earthquake in about 1200 BCE.

Between 1200 and 1100 BCE, Mycenaean settlements declined, perhaps in the face of invasions by nomadic peoples from the east, the Dorians and the Ionians, pushing down into the peninsula of Greece. The invaders used mounted cavalry with iron weapons that may have enabled them to defeat the Mycenaeans who had only bronze armory. Several centuries of cultural obscurity followed, during which the invading tribes settled down, mastered the art of writing, and assimilated certain aspects of Mycenaean history and mythology as their own. Out of the confusion of this "dark age" rose the brilliance of Classical Greece.

GREECE: THE ARCHAIC PERIOD

During the "dark age," population on the Greek peninsula began to exceed the land's limited agricultural possibilities, where only relatively narrow strips along the coast and in the river valleys could be productively farmed. Seeking additional farmland, as well as looking for metal ores and new trading opportunities, the city-states began a program of colonization, establishing new towns around the eastern Mediterranean in Asia Minor, Sicily, southern Italy, and North Africa. These colonial settlements were laid out in orderly fashion, generally in elongated rectangular blocks grouped around the market and temples at the center of the city. There were public facilities for recreation and entertainment, and a protective wall surrounded the whole colony.

In addition to grid-plan towns, the major contribution to architectural history made by Greek architects and builders during the Archaic period (ca. 700–500 BCE) was the temple, which originated as a home for the gods and was based on the design of the houses of the Greeks themselves. From what we know from surviving small clay models, the early temples were simple one-room structures, built to accommodate a statue of the deity. They had a covered portico or porch at the entrance; walls were mud-brick, and the roof was thatch. In the eighth century BCE, the small Temple of Artemis at Ephesus was constructed with a row of wooden columns surrounding the temple chamber, giving it additional distinction. The Temple of Hera at Olympia (ca. 600–590 BCE) continues this same idea at a larger scale (Fig. 2.14a). Here the original wooden columns were later replaced with stone, perhaps to provide better support for roof tiles that were significantly heavier than thatch. The transition to stone construction appears to have been a gradual process, doubtless influenced by Egyptian precedent and technology. Stone columns in Greek architecture are characteristically fluted (incised with concave grooves) in a manner similar to Hatshepsut's mortuary temple at Deir-el-Bahari. The Greeks also developed a highly stylized treatment for columns, capitals, and the supported members, the **entablature**. In the sixteenth century CE these were termed the **orders** of architecture, the term by which we know them today. Vitruvius, the Roman architect whose first-century BCE treatise was based in part on earlier now-lost Greek texts, names three such orders: the Doric, the sturdiest, was

2.14a Plan of the Temple of Hera, Olympia, ca. 600–590 BCE.

The original wooden columns of this early Greek temple were rebuilt in stone, perhaps to provide better support for heavier roof tiles that replaced thatch.

N
0   20 m
0   60 ft

2.14b Plan of the Temple of Hera, Paestum, ca. 550 BCE.

This is one of the earliest surviving examples of the Doric order. It is unusual in having an odd number of columns across the short side, placing a column in the center where one would expect an intercolumnar space.

2.14c Plan of the Temple of Apollo Epicurius, Bassai, ca. 430 BCE.

All three of the Greek orders were used in this temple. Doric formed the external colonnade, Ionic columns (partially attached to the cella wall) lined the sanctuary, and a single Corinthian column was placed on axis. Light shone on the cult statue from an opening in the east wall.

based on the proportions of a man; the Ionic was lighter in character to reflect the proportions of a woman; and the Corinthian, slenderest of all, had a highly decorated capital to suggest the form and proportions of a young maiden. The Doric originated on the mainland of Greece, while the Ionic developed on the islands of the Aegean and the coast of Asia Minor. The Corinthian order only appeared later.

Each order has its own particular combination of elements. The Doric column has no base and has the simplest capital atop the fluted shaft of the column; its entablature consists of a plain architrave and alternating metopes and triglyphs in the frieze, which is crowned with a cornice (Fig. 2.15). The Ionic has a base supporting its fluted column shaft and a capital with **volutes** (scrolls). Its entablature is also composed of an architrave and frieze. There is regional variation in the Ionic: along the coast of Asia Minor, the frieze is usually treated as three stepped bands of masonry, while on the mainland of Greece the frieze often features continuous sculpted relief (Fig. 2.16). A cornice with dentils concludes the order. There were also general conventions regulating the proportions of the parts, the overall height, and the column spacing, which the ancient Greeks adjusted according to particular circumstances. Italian architects of the Renaisssance 2000 years later codified the practice into a set of mathematical ratios based on the column's diameter at the base, but measurements of surviving temples provide no evidence that the Greeks ever reduced temple design to a single formula. The orders of architecture were thus at once

2.15 The Doric order as found on the Parthenon, Athens.

This shows the names of various parts. The Doric's clear articulation of elements catches sunlight in an ever-changing play of shade and shadow across the carved surfaces. This may be one reason it has endured even to the present as a part of Western architecture.

2.16 The Ionic order as found on the Erechtheion, Athens.

This shows the names of various parts. The Ionic's decorative flourishes may reflect influence from oriental sources. Although its entablature is simpler than the Doric's, its capitals and bases are subject to considerable artistic variation.

specific and flexible, not a straitjacket for designers but an expressive medium that could be adapted.

The origins of the architectural orders remain obscure. Vitruvius maintains that the orders were derived from earlier architecture in wood, a material that we know was once used for temples. In Doric temples, for example, triglyphs have been seen as echoing the protective ends of wooden roof beams, and metopes the infill panels between. In its stone incarnation, the wooden end grain of the triglyph was stylized into vertical grooves, and the blank metope panel became a place for sculpture. Recent scholarship questions this derivation, proposing instead that the orders developed from a monumental decorative style using molded terracotta details, with no particular reference to structural features in wood. Even after the walls and columns were built in stone, wooden beams continued to be used for framing the roof, and these have not survived.

Builders of the early Doric temples made use of locally available material, most often limestone. This imposed

structural limitations on the length of span for lintels and the diameter of columns needed to support the heavy tile roof. Ionic temples used marble, a superior stone, and thus had a more slender profile. At Paestum in southern Italy, the Temple of Hera in the former colonial city of Poseidonia is one of the most substantial of surviving Archaic temples (Fig. 2.17). Built in about 550 BCE, it has sturdy Doric columns. The column shafts swell, then diminish, as they rise to the bulbous echinus molding that forms the capital. This change in column diameter is called **entasis**, and it was thought to be comparable to the muscular strength of an arm or leg, expressing visually the physical load sustained by the shaft. Each flute in the column has a precise edge, an **arris**, where the curved sections of adjacent flutes intersect, and these arrises run absolutely straight up the shaft on every column. Above the echinus is a flat square block, the **abacus**, which provides the transition from the cylindrical form of the column to the rectangular and linear architrave above. The logic of the Doric order is that alternate triglyphs are

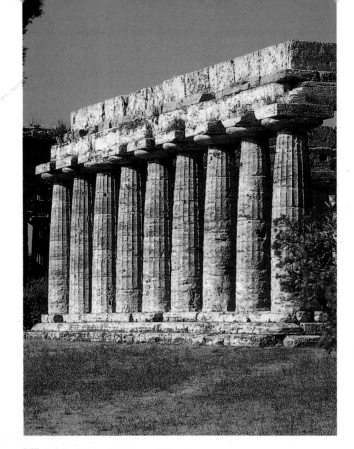

2.17 Temple of Hera at Paestum, ca. 550 BCE.

We see here the end elevation, with nine sturdy columns with entasis, capitals with flattened echinus profiles, and substantial abacus blocks. Notice how shadows cast by fluting on the column shafts enhance the sense of volume.

placed above columns, with metopes in between. This works well except at corners, where the established rhythm would make two half-metopes intersect. To avoid this, the final complete metope before the corner is generally elongated to allow the end triglyphs from both sides to meet at the corner. Columns near the corners may also be placed closer together—look at the rhythm of the frieze to see if this is the case. Joints between limestone blocks are easily seen at Paestum, and the limited spanning capability of the stone is reflected in the close column spacing. On the interior, the central span across the sanctuary required additional support, so a line of columns extends through the middle of the **cella**. This corresponds on the exterior to the nine columns across the short side of the temple, one of few times the Greeks would plan a temple with an odd number of columns on the entrance end. An even number places an intercolumnar space at the entrance axis.

GREECE: THE CLASSICAL PERIOD

During the Archaic period, the Persian Empire flourished in Mesopotamia, and Persian forces under Darius and Xerxes attacked Greek cities, both on the peninsula and around the Mediterranean. Ionian cities of Asia Minor had been under Persian domination from the middle of the sixth century. They revolted and were reconquered, and Darius attempted an invasion of the mainland, where his army was defeated in 490 BCE by the combined legions of Greek city-states at the battle of Marathon. In 480 the Persians attacked again, devastating the region around Athens and sacking the city itself, but the Greek navy scored a decisive victory over the Persian fleet near Salamis. In 479 the Persians were defeated on land and at sea, effectively ending the invasion threat to the peninsula.

A period of relative peace followed, and Athens emerged as the leading city on the mainland. To prevent further incursions by the Persians, it united with Ionian cities to form the Delian League. By 454 the League's treasury had been transferred from Delos to Athens, and a considerable portion of the money was controversially spent on rebuilding the ravaged Athenian Acropolis, which had been a military, political, and religious sanctuary since Mycenaean times (Figs. 2.18–2.20). The four buildings erected there after 479 ushered in the mature phase of Greek architecture known as the Classical period (479–323 BCE).

2.18 The Acropolis, Athens, ca. 479 BCE, from the entrance side.

The Propylaea and the Temple of Athena Nike stand out in the foreground, with the gable end of the Parthenon visible on the right.

Propylaea   Statue of Athena   Old Temple of Athena   Erechtheion

Temple of Athena Nike   Parthenon

N   0   100 m
0   300 ft

2.19 Plan of the Acropolis, Athens, ca. 479 BCE.

The shaded temple plan in the center represents the foundations of an earlier temple to Athena Polias that was destroyed by the Persians. The Erechtheion's porch, with the Caryatid maidens, encroaches on these foundations, in a perpetual reminder of the destruction of the Persian War.

2.20 The Acropolis, Athens, ca. 479 BCE, from below.

The Parthenon sits on the highest point and still rises above the modern city. Part of the Erechtheion is visible at the extreme left, while the Temple of Athena Nike stands clearly on the right side.

THE PARTHENON, ATHENS

Largest and most famous of these temples was the Parthenon (448–432 BCE), a great temple to Athena, patron goddess of the city (Fig. 2.21). An earlier temple, known as the Older Parthenon, had been begun in the general euphoria that followed the victory at Marathon in 490, but was still incomplete when the Persians destroyed it in 480. The new temple, designed by the architects Iktinos and Kallikrates and built of the finest marble from Mount Pentelicus, was erected on the same site, with enlargements, and probably made use of column drums and metopes carved for the older temple. It is a Doric temple, eight columns wide by seventeen deep, but it incorporates Ionic attributes, including slender column proportions, a continuous frieze around the exterior of the cella wall, and actual use of the Ionic order in the western **opisthodomos** (back room) that housed the Delian League treasury, where four Ionic columns support the roof. The use of eight columns across the gable end, unusual in the Doric, has connections to earlier Ionic temples (Fig. 2.22). Entasis, which was rather obviously handled in the Temple of Hera at Paestum, was used here to create a sense of repose. Minute adjustments in the horizontal and vertical lines of the structure enhance the perception of orthogonal geometry: the **stylobate** (the platform from which the columns rise) is actually convex; the columns incline imperceptibly away from the viewer; and the central axis of each column is not vertical but radial from a point over 6800 feet above the ground. The

2.21 The Parthenon, Athens, 448–432 BCE.

This is how the Parthenon appears after one leaves the Propylaea. As is the case with many Greek temples, the building is set so that one looks up to it and sees more than one side at once.

columns are not the same diameter—the end ones are larger—nor are they equidistantly spaced: the corner ones are closer together. In minute ways, the architects made slight variations in the column spacing and other details to avoid strict geometrical perfection and thereby give a sense of life to the composition.

Sculpture adorned both the outside and the inside of the Parthenon. The two end pediments were filled with over-lifesize figures representing, on the east, the birth of Athena witnessed by the gods, and on the west, the contest between Athena and Poseidon for control of Athens. The

metopes contained relief sculptures depicting struggles between Greeks and Amazons, Greeks and Trojans, gods and giants, and Lapiths and centaurs, all commemorating the triumph of Greek civilization over barbarism. A continuous frieze ran around the cella walls inside the colonnade, portraying a sacred procession of Athenians bringing gifts to Athena, possibly as a thanks offering for victory over the Persians or as a representation of the Panathenaic Festival held every four years. The procession shown on the frieze begins at the southwest corner and moves in both directions to meet again in the center of the east side, where Athena and other enthroned gods receive the offerings. The sculptor Phidias served as artistic coordinator for the rebuilding of all monuments on the Acropolis, and he was responsible for the sculptural detail on the Parthenon, including the large cult statue of Athena housed in the cella. The latter was portrayed standing, with a Nike (goddess of victory) in her right hand and a shield resting at her left. The statue had a wooden armature finished with valuable materials. Ivory was used for all exposed

2.22 The Parthenon, Athens, 448–432 BCE, seen from the west.

The Doric used here is elongated to an almost Ionic slenderness. Not all optical refinements are readily discernible, but note the widening of the central intercolumniation and the slightly closer spacing of the end columns.

parts of Athena's body; her drapery, armor, and helmet were represented in gold; and precious stones were used for her eyes and for decorating her robes and armor.

The cella of the Parthenon was one of the largest interiors built in Classical Greece. It was intended to provide a fitting setting for the enormous cult statue, which was the grandest of its time. Scholars differ as to whether the cella was completely roofed or not, as spanning the forty-foot width between the internal colonnades posed constructional challenges. Some speculate that the cella was open to the sky. A relatively dark interior would be an appropriate location for the dramatic image of Athena, for the Parthenon was oriented so that the sun would penetrate the cella interior on the morning of Athena's birthday to shine on the great chryselephantine statue.

Time and civilization have not been kind to the Parthenon. The statue of Athena had been broken up by the second century CE, probably for the value of its materials, and various adaptive reuses of the temple did little to preserve its best features. It became a Christian church, and then a mosque after the Turks occupied Greece. By 1687 it was being used for munitions storage, at which time it was bombarded by the Venetians as they attacked the Turks. A direct hit caused an explosion that ripped out the cella wall and dislodged many sculptures. The victorious Venetians carried some off as trophies. Lord Elgin, the British ambassador to the Ottoman Empire from 1799 to 1803, negotiated for the remaining sculptures, which he had removed from the temple and shipped to England; his son later sold them to the British government. Known as the Elgin Marbles, they are now housed in London's British Museum, but the Greek government is eager to have them returned to a new building that has been constructed for them in Athens. Industrial air pollution from the Greek capital is now the biggest threat to the surviving

bits of the Parthenon. Sulfur dioxides combine with ever-present water vapor to form sulfuric acid, which is dissolving the marble on this and other ancient buildings. A major restoration project on the Acropolis is under way as part of an international conservation effort.

OTHER BUILDINGS ON THE ACROPOLIS

The other buildings on the Athenian Acropolis are disposed in a manner that seems almost random yet is actually carefully planned to respond to particular qualities of the site when experienced on foot. In the case of the Acropolis, the site is a plateau rising abruptly above the plain of the city below. From the earliest times, the route of the Panathenaic Way from the civic and commercial center (the **Agora**) to the **Acropolis** traversed a winding, stepped path up the western side of the escarpment. (As most Greek temples face the east, this means the initial view one has is of the back sides of buildings.) In about 437 BCE construction began on an appropriately scaled entrance gateway, the Propylaea, designed by the architect Mnesikles. In a highly original design, Mnesikles created a dignified symmetrical entranceway on an asymmetrical site, accommodating a fragment of the original Mycenaean fortification wall and a gradient change through the depth of the building. His building marks the transition from the secular world to the sacred precinct of the Acropolis.

The Propylaea is essentially a Doric portico flanked by projecting wings (Figs. 2.23–2.24). The central intercolumniation is wider than the rest, reflecting the processional way that passed through the axial colonnaded space into the sacred precinct of the Acropolis. This required two (rather than the usual one) unsupported triglyphs over the

2.23 Plans of the Propylaea (437 BCE) and Temple of Athena Nike (ca. 425 BCE), Athens.

The Propylaea defined the entrance to the Acropolis, while the small Temple of Athena Nike stood on a forward projection, visible at an angle by those entering the Acropolis. See Fig. 2.24 for a reconstructed view of this ensemble.

megaron

entrance to the Propylaea

N

0   20 m

0   60 ft

Temple of Athena Nike

CELEBRATING ATHENA'S BIRTHDAY

by David Lewis

This account of the Great Panathenaic procession (Fig. 2A) is an excerpt from the fictional journal of an aristocratic Athenian woman. It is a description of the eighth and final day of the Great Panathenaic Festival in 424 BCE to celebrate the birthday of Athena.

2A Horsemen, Panathenaic Festival, Parthenon north frieze, Athens, 424 BCE. British Museum, London.

28 Hekatombaion—the first month and our goddess Athena's birthday. The sea's wind blew warm even before the sun rose on this midsummer's day. Thousands gathered outside the city's walls. We wives and maidens dressed in purple robes and carried kannephoroi, bronze and silver trays filled with cakes, honeycombs and oak branches. Armed infantrymen, the victorious athletes, and the four men bearing the prize amphora were inside the Pompeion, while the young men who escort the 100 sacrificial cows, the equestrians and warriors on chariots, were next to the Dipylon Gate.

At the head of our procession were two maidens proudly bearing the sail-peplos of Athena, its breadth extending the whole width of the Sacred Way and facing the cavalcade, and the champion athlete with the ceremonial torch. The peplos's saffron and sea-purple linen threads glistened in the morning sun and torchlight while its silhouetted figures of Athena, Zeus, and other gods did battle with the giants. [Sail-peploi were commissioned every fourth year for the Great Panathenaic Festival and produced by professional male weavers. For the other three years, young daughers, arrephoroi, and wives of aristocratic citizens would spend months in the workshop, or arrephorion, *on the Acropolis, producing a human-sized robe.]*

As we walked fifteen abreast on the Sacred Way through the cramped Kerameikos, the potters, who lived there, cheered proudly as the prize amphorai filled with sacred oils passed by. These men spent the last year sculpting and painting elaborate scenes on the 1400 trophies. Even from this outer precinct we could discern the Parthenon atop the Acropolis.

Continuing downhill, we entered the Agora at the Eridanos river bridge alongside the Poikile Stoa, with its jugglers and street musicians, and the Royal Stoa. We continued diagonally through the Agora, passing the Orchestra, where athletic events took place this week. As we approached the South Stoa, we began our ascent to the Acropolis, winding around its western rock face.

At the base of the ramp, we turned to face the Acropolis. Resplendently will it embrace our procession. Delicate Athena Nike to the south perched on her own askew promontory temenos [sacred precinct] while the Propylaea meets us head on. We marched up the ramp, for all of the polis to view. We stopped at the Propylaea's *blue step, allowing us to see to the north the Agora below, over our right shoulder the same battle between the gods and giants on the Athena Nike's east pediment, and ahead glimpses of the grand Athena Promachos statue beyond the Propylaea's doors. We sift through the gateway, animals and chariots led by the peplos through the central walkway, while those of us on foot walk to the outside of the Ionic columns and through the smaller doors.*

Stepping over the east threshold and between the monumental Doric columns, we entered the temenos as the sun appeared over the mountains; Athena and Pericles's glorious pentelic temples glimmered. As we marched eastward on the Sacred Way along the north face of the Parthenon, the morning sun illuminated the cella frieze. As we proceeded to the east, so did the brightly colored figures as if telling us how and where to proceed. Like the frieze, our procession broke off into two groups; the men ushering the cows, and maidens bearing the kannephoroi walked to the Great Altar, while the remainder went to the open area to the east of the Parthenon.

As the two maidens, led by the high priestess, carried the peplos into the cella, we heard "IOIOIOIOIO," cries signaling the sacrifice of the first cow.

2.24 Theoretical reconstruction of the entrance to the Acropolis, Athens.

Note the wide intercolumniation in the center of the Propylaea. A large exterior statue of Athena (no longer extant) dominated the view, balancing the Parthenon on the right.

central space, as the architect had to take liberties with the exacting Doric. Three pairs of Ionic columns line the passageway, because the rising ground level and scale of the space dictated the choice of a more slender order. A second Doric portico terminated the Propylaea's central section. Its northern wing was a megaron, perhaps used as a picture gallery or banqueting hall, while on the south

side there was a porch preceding the freestanding Temple of Athena Nike.

The overall layout of the Acropolis was designed to enhance the sense of procession. A visitor would first emerge from the eastern portico of the Propylaea to see a great statue of Athena close by, just left of center, balancing the majestic Parthenon, which rose farther back on the right-hand side. Even though the entrance to Greek temples is placed axially, it was the intention of the architects of the Acropolis that visitors should first view the Parthenon from below, at an angle where the west pediment and long north colonnade presented the essence of the temple's volume at a single glance. One reached the sanctuary entrance by traversing a rising pathway running the length of the Parthenon, passing the exposed foundations of the Temple of Athena Polias (destroyed by the Persians) and turning the corner to ascend the steps into the eastern portico. Only after experiencing the totality of the exterior would the drama of the interior be unfolded. Mnesikles's Propylaea both echoes the volume of the Parthenon and establishes the viewpoint that enhances the major temple on the Acropolis.

There are two other important temples on the Acropolis. The small Temple of Athena Nike (Athena Victorious) perches on rocks that were once the site of an ancient

2.25 The Erechtheion, Athens, ca. 421–407 BCE.

This shows the entry to Athena's shrine (right) and the porch of the Caryatid maidens (left). In the left foreground are the remains of the Temple of Athena Polias, on which the Caryatids gaze in perpetuity.

2.26 The Erechtheion from the northwest, Athens, ca. 421–407 BCE.

The entrance to Poseidon's shrine is through the portico on the left (this is also the Ionic order drawn in Fig. 2.16). In front of the building is an olive tree, located where Athena is said to have presented her gift to Athens.

bastion (projecting fortification) on the edge of the hilltop forward of the Propylaea. Possibly designed as early as 448 BCE by Kallikrates but not constructed until the 420s, it is a simple sanctuary that housed a wooden image of Athena holding her helmet and a pomegranate, a symbol of fertility. Four Ionic columns create a portico before the eastern entrance, and an identical set is placed at the western (rear) side, which is the elevation seen clearly from below the Acropolis. Although it is an Ionic building, it has side walls that incline slightly in a visual refinement common to the Doric.

Across from the northern side of the Parthenon stands the more complex form of the Erechtheion, begun in ca. 421 and completed in 407 BCE to the designs of an unknown architect, on the site of the Mycenaean palace that was also regarded as the location of the contest between Athena and Poseidon (Figs. 2.25–2.26). Myth has it that in a competition to decide who should be named as patron of the city, Poseidon struck his trident on a rock and created a spring, while Athena brought forth an olive tree. The contest was judged in favor of Athena by Kekrops, the first legendary king of Athens, whose tomb is also commemorated here. Under the temple is the Sea of Erechtheus, a salt-water spring that made the sound of the sea and had a rock bearing the mark of Poseidon's trident. The Erechtheion knits together these assorted strands of site-specific history while also deferring to the dominance of the Parthenon. The Ionic was chosen as the most suitable order for a temple built on two different levels to accommodate the uneven site. The eastern portico, distinguished by its slender Ionic columns, led to Athena's sanctuary, where an ancient wooden image of the goddess was housed, while the north porch, ten feet lower, gave access to Poseidon's shrine through an even more elongated Ionic portico. Four Ionic columns, partially engaged in the

wall, extend across the west façade to the south, where the roof of the splendid porch facing the Parthenon is supported by the six Caryatid maidens. Their pose is graceful, with one knee bent slightly and drapery revealing the form beneath. The base of the caryatid porch is the north foundation wall of the destroyed Temple of Athena Polias, and the caryatids look out to the Parthenon across the ruins of the former temple, which were deliberately left exposed as an eternal reminder of the devastation wrought by the Persians. Although female figures had been used as columns (**caryatids**) before, the Roman architect Vitruvius explained their origins as follows:

> Caryae, a state in Peloponnesus, sided with the Persian enemies against Greece [Athens]; later the Greeks, having gloriously won their freedom by victory in the war, made common cause and declared war against the people of Caryae. They took the town, killed the men, abandoned the State to desolation, and carried off their wives into slavery, without permitting them, however, to lay aside the long robes and other marks of their rank as married women, so that they might be obliged not only to march in the triumph but to appear forever after as a type of slavery, burdened with the weight of their shame and so making atonement for their State. Hence, the architects of the time designed for public buildings statues of these women, placed so as to carry a load, in order that the sin and the punishment of the people of Caryae might be known and handed down even to posterity.

We may find this punishment unjustified, given that it was the men of Caryae, not the women, who committed treachery, but it reminds us that even under Athenian democratic rule, women were no better than slaves when it came to legal and political rights.

As an example of the Ionic order, the elaborate detail of the Erechtheion has no equal in later Greek works, and the multiple complexities and scales that have been united here in a single temple are also exceptional in Classical architecture. The exquisite decorative detail may well have influenced the later Corinthian order.

In all four of the Acropolis temples, one sees the architects fusing new constructions with elements from the site's history, be it the Persian Wars or the Mycenaean period. Evidence of Persian destruction was deliberately preserved in the ruins of the Temple of Athena Polias, while historical references to the origins of the city are the very essence of the Erechtheion's design. Mycenaean fortifications were incorporated into one wall of the Propylaea, and the older Parthenon's base and architectural elements were reused for the existing building. The architects also sought to integrate the Doric architecture characteristic of Attica (the region around Athens) with Ionic elements (from Asia Minor) in an attempt to express the unity of the Delian League and Athens's ascendancy among the city-states of Greece.

GREECE: THE HELLENISTIC PERIOD

Athens's moment of architectural glory, epitomized by the buildings on the Acropolis, came to an end in 431–404 BCE with the protracted and ultimately disastrous Peloponnesian War. Rival city-states quarreled with one another, weakening themselves in the process and opening the entire peninsula to opportunistic external powers. The eventual conqueror, Philip of Macedon, came from the north and effectively annexed all of Greece in 338 BCE. The close of the Classical age in Greece is generally associated with the reign of his son, known as Alexander the Great, but the influence of Greek culture continued to spread east owing to Alexander's conquests. From 336 to 323 BCE, his armies swept through much of the civilized world, including Asia Minor, Egypt, Mesopotamia, Persia, and parts of what today are Afghanistan, Pakistan, and northern India. Alexander died at the age of thirty-three, unable to consolidate his vast territories, but his enthusiasm for Greek heritage and his adoption of oriental aspects of the Persian court accelerated the assimilation and adaptation of Greek culture far beyond the Aegean. The term "Hellenistic" is applied to the art and architecture associated with the extended empire of Alexander and his successors, including the Seleucids, who ruled the area stretching from Anatolia to the Indus, and the Ptolomies, who ruled in Egypt.

Hellenistic architecture differs from that of the Classical period by shifting away from staid traditions associated clearly with the region around Athens in favor of showier and freer interpretations as found along the western coast of Asia Minor. As the Doric order was intimately connected with the mainland of Greece, its use diminished in favor of the more ornate Ionic order, which reflected an oriental exuberance typical of the Ionian colonies. The meticulous sculptural ornamentation and coordination of column spacing required by the Doric were not part of either the Ionic or Corinthian orders, which overcame the Doric's limitations by eliminating the troublesome features. Their column flutes are jointed by flat fillets to simplify the carving, and the frieze runs continuously without metopes or triglyphs.

Even in the Classical period, the use of a particular order on the exterior of a building did not preclude the use of others within, as has already been seen in the Parthenon and the Propylaea. The Temple of Apollo Epicurius at Bassai (ca. 450–425 BCE), designed by Iktinos, employs all three orders: the Doric for the external colonnade, the Ionic for the cella side columns (which are connected to the cella wall by extended buttress-shaped piers), and the Corinthian for the single axial column placed at the end of the cella (Fig. 2.27). A statue of Apollo was set adjacent to this column so that it faced to the east through an opening in the cella wall. Among Greek temples, this one is unusual for its orientation; the main entrance faces north, rather than east. The temple at Bassai is the first known use of the Corinthian order, and also marks the first time the Ionic was used for a cella interior. These forward-looking features are counterbalanced by some seemingly old-fashioned ones which must have been included for positive reasons, for the architect was thoroughly familiar with what was being built contemporaneously on the Athenian Acropolis. The temple's elongated plan and narrow cella have been explained as deliberate references to history (the cult of Apollo had long existed on the site, and there had been three predecessor temples

2.27 Temple of Apollo Epicurius, Bassai, ca. 450–425 BCE.

This is one of the few Greek temples on which one can look down. The building is undergoing repairs necessitated by earth tremors.

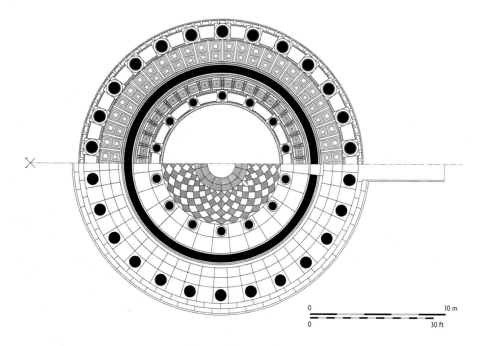

2.28 Floor plan (bottom half) and reflected ceiling plan (upper half), tholos, Epidauros, ca. 360–330 BCE.

Parts of the beautifully detailed ceiling coffers have survived as indications of the high standard of Hellenistic design.

2.29 Elevation of the Choragic Monument of Lysikrates, Athens, ca. 334 BCE.

Engaged Corinthian columns ornament this small structure. Nineteenth-century American architects who worked in the Greek Revival style used this building as a basis for their designs.

here), and the earlier temples may also be the source of the spur walls connected to the Ionic columns. It has been proposed that the single Corinthian column likewise made reference to the distant past, when wooden columns were sacred symbols of the gods. The temple may thus be interpreted as a fusion of historical references with innovative design.

The Corinthian order was employed on a substantial scale in the tholos at the Sanctuary of Asklepios at Epidauros (ca. 360–330 BCE), a circular building approximately seventy-two feet in diameter, known now from its foundations and reassembled fragments preserved on the site (Fig. 2.28). Epidauros was dedicated to the god Asklepios, the son of Apollo, and both gods were venerated here in a large complex dedicated to healing through exercise, diet, and medical care. The tholos is but a small part of a site that included a stadium, gymnasia, a theatre, altars, fountains and baths, temples, and accommodation for patients. Its external colonnade was composed of twenty-six Doric columns, and there were fourteen freestanding Corinthian columns in the inner circular colonnade fitted into a black-and-white rhomboidal flooring pattern. The ceiling had ornate coffers with floral decorations. An unused Corinthian capital found buried at the site shows the delicacy and grace achieved by Polykleitos, architect of the tholos. The corner volutes, derived from Ionic columns, are small, and their scroll form is complemented by the stylized curls of acanthus leaves that enrich the bell of the capital. How exactly this building was used is unknown. It has been suggested that its form at the upper story matches that of a shelter for a tomb (a **baldachin**) and that the circular corridors evident from the foundation remains were evocative of passages through the underworld to the tomb of Asklepios. Much of the healing at Epidauros took place during sleep, either through dreams or perhaps through actual medical procedures performed while patients were unconscious.

In a better state of preservation is the Choragic Monument of Lysikrates (ca. 334 BCE) in Athens (Fig. 2.29). This small cylindrical structure was erected to display the prize awarded to Lysikrates for the entry he sponsored in a dramatic contest honoring the god Dionysos. Here the Corinthian order is used on the exterior of a building, with six columns being built into the cylinder so that they appear as half-columns. (Recall that the Erechtheion likewise had engaged columns on its western elevation. The decorative possibilities of the orders as wall articulation were exploited in Hellenistic and later Roman work.) The frieze they support illustrates the mythological story of Dionysos and the pirates of the Tyrrhenian Sea. There is no accessible interior space. Nineteenth-century American architects adapted the form of the Choragic Monument for quite varied purposes. It inspired the form of the Philadelphia Exchange and the cupola atop the dome of the Tennessee State Capitol in Nashville (see Fig. 14.14), both by William Strickland.

When discussing the buildings of ancient Greece, it is important not only to imagine them complete, but also to remember that the Greeks never saw them as the bare stone structures we see today. Architectural and sculptural detail was generally painted in vibrant colors, perhaps

with gilding, and plain walls may well have had murals. Traces of the original paint remain in protected crevices to confirm written accounts of the buildings' original appearances. If they were restored and repainted in authentic hues today, Greek temples might well appear surprising to our eyes.

During the Hellenistic period, permanent buildings for theatrical performances were constructed in many of the outlying cities. Many of these elegant designs postdate the plays by Euripides, Sophocles, and Aristophanes that were originally presented from carts to audiences grouped on wooden benches in public open areas. Athens constructed the Theater of Dionysos on the south side of the Acropolis hill in the fifth century, using the rising embankment to provide support for a concentric seating focused on the circular orchestra, a flat area for dancing. Behind the orchestra was a backdrop structure, the skene, and the area directly in front, the proskenion, was a raised platform from which actors declaimed their lines. (Note how this terminology continues to be used today: the framing arch over the stage of today's theaters is known as the proscenium, while orchestra seats are those placed directly in front of the stage.) Several doors set in the skene served

2.30 Plan of the theater, Epidauros, 350–2nd century BCE.

Virtually every Greek city had its own theater which could accommodate a good portion of the population: attending dramatic performances was encouraged to promote civic values.

2.31 Theater, Epidauros, 350–2nd century BCE.

This shows the rows of seating. The original skene or backdrop building shown in the plan is no longer extant.

as entrances and exits as needed in the drama, and actors spoke lines from the gods from the roof of the building.

Although the theater in Athens has been modified, surviving auditoria at Delphi, Dodona, Ephesus, Epidauros, Megalopolis, Pergamon, and Priene give a clear image of what Greek theaters originally looked like. The theater at Epidauros is exceptionally well preserved and beautifully sited in the landscape, looking out to distant hills (Figs. 2.30–2.31). Tradition assigns its design to Polykleitos, architect of the tholos, but not all scholars agree with this attribution. The theater was built in two stages, the lower 5000 seats in thirty-four tiers dating from 350 BCE, with the upper twenty-one tiers being added in the second century BCE, extending the total capacity to about 14,000 seats. The ring of seats closest to the orchestra were provided with backs and used by dignitaries, while everyone else sat on continuous benches raised slightly above the row in front of them. An efficient system of radial and cross aisles provided circulation from entrances at multiple levels. Most remarkably, the acoustical design worked so well that words spoken in a normal voice from the orchestra projected intelligibly to all seats. The theater is still used for performances.

GREEK CITY PLANNING

THE ATHENIAN AGORA

We have seen how the spatial experience of buildings on the Acropolis in Athens affected the placement and design of temples on the site, so that what appears on plan to be a haphazard arrangement unfolds before the visitor as a logical sequence in an ordered and balanced universe. The static poise of a colonnaded temple is enhanced by the subtle arts of the site planner, who has used surprise and a changing perspective to reveal the full drama of the architectural forms. A similar spatial approach was taken in the layout of the Athenian Agora, the civic and commercial heart of the city, which developed around the ancient track of the Panathenaic Way entering the city from the northwest and leading to the Acropolis (Fig. 2.32). Development of the public structures in the Agora began in about 600 BCE, and by the end of the Archaic period its boundaries were defined. A group of civic buildings, including temples, a shrine to Zeus, and a senate house (**bouleterion**), had been built on the western side at the base of the Agora Hill (Kolonos Agoraios). The bouleterion was an ambitious project, built on a nearly square plan to accommodate the 500 senators who comprised the elected government of Athens. A columned porch led directly to the senate chamber, with seats in rows along three sides of the rectangular space. The roof was supported on the exterior walls and four intermediate columns. Another government building was the Royal Stoa, erected on the northwest corner beside the Panathenaic Way for the city's chief religious magistrate, who was responsible for official sacrifices, administration of the city's festivals, and adjudication of priestly disputes. The Royal Stoa was a small rectangular building with a colonnade and steps along the long side facing the Agora, the first of a type that would be constructed on a larger scale for various purposes in the Classical and later eras.

After the Persian Wars, when the Acropolis was being reconstructed with its famous temples, new works were undertaken as well in the Agora. On top of the hill to the west, the Hephaisteion, a temple to Hephaistos (god of the forge) and Athena (goddess of the arts), was

Royal Stoa

Painted Stoa

Shrine of Aphrodite

Shrine to the twelve Gods

Arsenal (?)

Shops

Hephaisteion

Bouleterion

Stoa of Attalos

Metroon

Monument to the
Eponymous Heros

Tholos

Middle Stoa

Fountain

South Stoa

Mint

Heliaia

Panathenaic Way
to the Acropolis

N

0   50 m

0   150 ft

2.32 Plan of the Agora, Athens, ca. 150 BCE.

Buildings from the Classical era are indicated by shading. The
diagonal route crossing the central space is the Panathenaic
Way, the processional path that led from the city gate
(south) to the Acropolis and toward the north.

constructed in about 449–444 BCE. This Doric temple,
still remarkably intact, was enriched with relief sculpture
and an elaborate ceiling of stone coffers. Three broad rows
of seats were constructed at the base of the hill to extend
the eastern axis of the temple across the Agora. Within the
Agora, war damage to the Royal Stoa was repaired and the
building slightly enlarged, while new stoas were built. The
Painted Stoa (so named because it displayed paintings of
military triumphs, mythical and real, of the Athenians)
had an external Doric colonnade and Ionic columns
within. It was used for informal meetings (the Stoic
philosophers were fond of meeting there and eventually
took their name from it) as well as jury trials. The Stoa of

Zeus replaced the earlier shrine and was used as an informal meeting place. The first South Stoa, whose small
rooms behind a double colonnade were used for commercial activities and perhaps also for dining, was constructed adjacent to the Heliaia, which was probably the
main law court. A new boulererion was constructed ca.
415–406 BCE directly behind the existing building (which
was renamed the Metroon to honor Rhea, mother of the
gods of Olympus, and used for city archives). Its internal
arrangements are not clear from the excavations, but
archaeologists believe it had a curved U-shaped configuration of seats. Adjacent was a circular building, the tholos,
that was used for meals served to the fifty senators who
happened to be on duty. The open spaces of the Agora
were used both as a racetrack and as a setting for theater
and dancing.

Building in the Athenian Agora continued after the
conquests of Alexander the Great. In the Hellenistic
period, some Classical buildings were modified, and other

2.33 Stoa of Attalos, Athens, 159–132 BCE (reconstructed 1952–56).

This building was contributed to the city by Attalos of Pergamon. It and the Hephaisteion are the only structures from antiquity remaining in the Athenian Agora. The stoa has been extensively restored in modern times to serve as a museum.

entirely new ones were constructed to create a more complete sense of spatial order and closure. The dominant Temple of Hephaistos and its axial approach remained. The old Metroon was replaced by a more elaborate building serving the same functions, with an external colonnade fronting onto the open civic space. The South Stoa was rebuilt on a shifted orientation, with an additional Middle Stoa extending parallel to it on what had originally been open land. Across the Panathenaic Way, which remained unchanged, the Stoa of Attalos (Fig. 2.33) was erected at right angles to the Middle Stoa, and its southern end worked with the eastern terminus of the Middle Stoa to establish a narrow entrance, in contrast to the openness of the Agora beyond. In the colonnaded walkways of the stoas, one had a sense of shelter while at the same time being connected to the larger open space. The stoas were thoroughly urban buildings, providing space for merchants to trade in and inviting citizens to participate in the public life of the city, an important aspect of Greek society. The concept of a colonnaded or arcaded space containing shops and facing major public open spaces will reappear in later urban designs.

HELLENISTIC CITIES

Greek city planning was not always as asymmetrical and evolutionary in form as the Agora in Athens. The Greeks were perfectly capable of producing regular, orthogonal town plans and frequently employed them for colonial cities, as may be seen at Paestum (Poseidonia), which had a street pattern from the mid-seventh century BCE that produced greatly elongated rectangular blocks (Fig. 2.34). While many cities grew organically over time, others were rebuilt, often after suffering war damage, according to the new, more regular town-planning principles. Such was the case in the fifth and fourth centuries BCE, when a number of towns were provided with grid blocks and carefully considered open spaces according to the theories of the fifth-century pupil of Pythagoras, Hippodamus of Miletus, who is often regarded as the father of city planning. This label is misapplied if taken to mean that he "invented" the grid plan, for orthogonal plans existed long before Hippodamus. More properly viewed, his contribution seems to have involved consolidating and articulating the religious, social, and commercial elements of the city center with regular blocks of houses adjusted to fit the particular circumstances of the topography. Hippodamus's birthplace, Miletus, a harbor town on the coast of Asia Minor, was in its day the leading city of Ionia. After its destruction by the Persians in 494 BCE, the city was rebuilt in the period following 479 BCE with a plan of rectangular residential blocks and an orthogonal agora. Hippodamus's design went beyond specifying the location of civic buildings, the layout of streets, and the positioning of open spaces, to encompass design of typical single-family houses for an estimated population of 15,000 to 20,000. Houses were consistently oriented with their major rooms opening to the south, and the megaron form already familiar from Mycenaean times was used again as the basic living unit of the house.

The application of Hippodamus's principles can be seen in the ruined neighboring city of Priene, where extensive archaeological work has revealed details of the major buildings and houses (Figs. 2.35a,b). Reestablished in ca. 353 BCE in conscious emulation of Athens, which was by then in decline, Priene featured a substantial Ionic temple to Athena, financed in part by Alexander the Great. The architect Pytheos is credited with both the town plan and temple design; according to Vitruvius, he also wrote a book on architecture (now lost). A regular grid of streets extended across the hillside site, its orientation aligned with the cardinal directions. The population is estimated to have been about 5000, mostly farmers who worked fields in the fertile valley below the town.

Priene's major public spaces were clustered in the center section of the plan. The agora occupied the largest level site within the town walls, defined on the west and south by a continuous colonnaded stoa, on the east by the Altar and Temple of Zeus, and completed on the north side by a raised sacred portico set parallel to the main east–west street. Just to the west of the agora was the marketplace, flanked by shops and a two-story market hall. Stairs from the west side of the agora led up to the Temple of Athena, raised on a terrace above the market and bounded by another east–west street that also passed the theater, built into the slope of the hill. Other stepped streets led from the agora up to the council house and the prytaneion, or shrine of the city's hearths, and the gymnasium. At the bottom of the town, a long, level plot of land was reserved for a stadium. Walls enclosed considerably more land than was ever occupied by the town, and it appears that the unbuilt sections may have included outlying farm settlements and probably provided protected grazing room for cattle. There was also a high acropolis on the escarpment north of the city on which no buildings were constructed.

Most north–south streets were fitted with stairs to accommodate the uneven terrain. Blocks were subdivided into eight house lots, each about thirty by eighty Greek feet (twenty-nine by seventy-seven modern U.S. feet). The slope of the hillside was sufficient to permit staggered levels for houses within each block, thus increasing exposure to the warming southern sun in winter while overhangs restricted solar access at the height of summer. The

houses share a typical plan: the narrow lot is divided into thirds, with an open court comprising the central section. On the southern end are shops (if the lot faces a street) and storage rooms or workshops connected to the household. At the northern end, facing south, are the living areas in a two-story house. The major living suite is the domos of a megaron, complete with hearth, preceded by an open porch with wooden columns. Off to one side of the porch is the men's room (andron), where the head of the house and a small group of friends could recline on couches, eat, and talk. From the domos, a ladder/stair led to the second floor, where there were bedrooms and a sitting room for women above the andron. A small room on the first level behind the andron may have been a bathroom. Walls and the small number of openings to the street preserved privacy for the occupants, while the open courtyard provided sunlight and encouraged the circulation of air within the house. The simplicity of houses in Priene contrasts with the care lavished on public buildings, reflecting the value the Greeks placed on civic life. Freemen in a democratic society spent most of their waking hours in the public sphere in the company of others, and the noblest occupations were those involving the use of the mind: literature, philosophy, the arts and sciences, and politics. Manual work was disparaged, despite its importance to the well-being of society as a whole, and was usually left to menials and slaves. Women were generally secluded, and men's and women's spaces within the house were kept separate.

During the Hellenistic period, both architecture and city planning became more elaborate and theatrical, as can be seen in the design of Pergamon, another city in Asia

2.34 Plan of Paestum (Poseidonia), 7th century BCE.

This Greek colonial city was laid out with elongated blocks on an orthogonal pattern. Across the center was the public sector, with commercial structures, government buildings, and temples, including the Temple of Hera (identifiable by its row of central columns in the lower right). The site was submerged by the sea during the Middle Ages, but is dry land again today.

0   500 m

0   1500 ft

Minor that between 282 and 133 BCE aspired to imitate the glory that once pertained to Athens. It became the capital of the Attalid Dynasty, whose leaders took the title of king in part to celebrate their military victories over the Galatians (Celtic tribes). Originating as a hilltop fortress, Pergamon grew in terraced steps down from the summit, with level sites for buildings supported on well-engineered retaining walls and linked by monumental stairs. On such a precipitous site, a grid plan was out of the question; the road has switchbacks to minimize the slope. On the acropolis were temples, a distinguished library, the Sanctuary of Athena, and palaces, above a banked theater carved into the hillside that could seat 10,000 people. One of the most celebrated buildings at Pergamon was the Great Altar (ca. 181–159 BCE), dedicated to Zeus and Athena. The high

plinth on which the altar stood became the location for a frieze over 300 feet in length and sculpted with scenes of battles between gods and giants, an obvious allusion to recent battles with the Celts (Fig. 2.36). Intertwined wings, arms, and writhing snake bodies create a dynamic composition: even the hair on the gods' heads and beards falls in animated coils. The highly dramatic frieze contrasts with the colonnaded building above, and it also complements the equally dramatic site, an architectural tour de force that has little of the restraint and sublimated feeling that governed the design of the Athenian Acropolis.

After the conquests of Alexander the Great, the desire for independence and seclusion on the part of city-states on the mainland of Greece stood in the way of any larger alliance for mutual defense, and Greek colonial cities were

2.35a Plan of Priene, ca. 353 BCE.

This city applies the principles of Hippodamus to the layout of a city that straddles the side of a hill. Major public buildings are located in the center. From the top down, these include the theater, the Temple of Athena, the governmental center with council meeting hall, the agora and associated stoa buildings, the market, the Temple of Zeus, and the gymnasium and stadium. Regular blocks of housing flank the center section.

2.35b (inset) Plans of houses, Priene, ca. 350 BCE.

Based on courtyard designs. The megaron is still evident as the principal living space, flanked by an andron (eating and meeting room for men). Rooms for women and children were primarily on the second floor.

Temple of Athena

Sacred portico

Theater

Agora

Temple of Zeus

Stadium

2.36 Great Altar of Zeus, Pergamon, ca. 181–159 BCE.

This has now been reconstructed in the Pergamon Museum in Berlin. This impressive shrine, originally set on a hillside above the city, features a dramatic frieze of large sculpted figures that contrast with the serenity of the colonnade above.

slowly lost to expanding powers in Italy and the Crimea. Meanwhile, on the western side of the Italian peninsula, in Rome, the next great culture was developing. The Greek mainland itself became a Roman possession in 146 BCE, but much of its artistic legacy had long since been transmitted to the rest of the civilized world. Hellenistic art traveled eastward along the trade routes to India and China, where its influence was reflected in both buildings and sculpture. More significantly, Greek artistic and cultural patrimony was transferred to Rome, where it affected many aspects of life, including architecture, as we shall see. Greek architecture also has a much later revival in the United States during the early nineteenth century, when Greece achieved independence from the Ottoman Empire. Americans applied aspects of ancient Greek forms and details to schools, banks, houses, churches, and similar structures to express links with the earliest democracy. In many ways, ancient Greek architecture continues to serve as a symbol for Western civilization.

CHAPTER 3

THE ARCHITECTURE OF ANCIENT INDIA AND SOUTHEAST ASIA

The prehistory of India is largely an account of settlements along the Indus Valley and its associated coastal plain, now part of the modern countries of Pakistan and Afghanistan, where various regional cultures flourished from ca. 3000 BCE. Its mature phase lasted about 1000 years, starting in about 2700 BCE, when Harappa (in the northeast portion of the valley) and Mohenjo-Daro (on the Indus, nearly 400 miles to the southwest) seem to have functioned as the leading cities of an extensive region. Many details about the culture remain sketchy, for there is no agreement among scholars concerning the decipherment of the Harappan script which has over 400 characters; in any case, much of the surviving writing is on personal seals, which hold little promise of revealing much about the civilization. The basis of the economy was agriculture, facilitated by irrigation and periodic flooding of the rivers. There was also commerce, both internal and with settlements in southern Arabia and Mesopotamia, as a result of which some cultural influences were adopted. Literate civilization in the Indus Valley was later in developing and of shorter duration than in Mesopotamia or Egypt, but the region over which it exercised control was larger. Over 1000 Harappan sites have been identified across an area of nearly 500,000 square miles.

Archaeology reveals that Harappan settlements were laid out according to an orderly grid oriented to the cardinal directions. Orthogonal town plans are generally an indication of a high level of central governmental control, and that seems to have been the case in Harappan culture.

Buildings were durable, being constructed of fired bricks of uniform size throughout the region, and houses were provided with underground drains connected to a well-planned sewer system. As the cities were built on plains beside the river, flooding seems to have been a constant menace. Mohenjo-Daro (Figs. 3.1–3.2) was repaired at least nine times after damaging floods. Cities accordingly featured a walled, terraced citadel on high ground, provided with ceremonial buildings, large public storehouses for grain, and mills that could be used in time of peril to shelter and feed the population. Rising forty feet above the plain, Mohenjo-Daro's citadel also had a great stepped bath measuring thirty by forty feet with a depth of eight feet: this is thought to have served some ritual function. However, there are no clearly identified large shrines or temples like those found in Egypt or Mesopotamia. Small figurines suggest a reverence for trees and animals, a mother goddess cult, and a male god that may be the precursor of the later Hindu deity Shiva. Water and fire may have been associated with rituals that are still not understood.

In contrast to both Mesopotamia and Egypt, the Indus settlements seem to have been relatively egalitarian societies. There are neither palaces nor royal tombs, and no great temple complexes to indicate a concentration of power and wealth. Excavated residential areas of Mohenjo-Daro, the best-preserved and most extensive city, estimated to have had a population of 40,000, show tightly packed houses organized around internal courtyards that were open to the sky for light and air. The plans vary, but all houses presented virtually blank façades to the street, as external openings were set high in the perimeter walls. Rooms were small, perhaps because there was a scarcity of wood to serve as beams for second floors and roof framing. While the buildings themselves do not seem elegant in terms of architectural refinement, the clear urban layout, careful provision of a water supply through wells, and drain and sewer system are without parallel at the time and are marks of an efficient, highly organized society.

Kandariya Mahadeva Temple, Khajuraho, 1025–50.

This shows the plinth and entrance terrace in the foreground. From this angle, the orderly progression of roof masses simulates a mountain range.

RESIDENTIAL SECTOR
(shaded areas have been excavated)

CITADEL

Great bath

Granary

3.1 Plan of Mohenjo-Daro, Indus Valley,
ca. 2400–2000 BCE.

The city was located on a plain beside the river, with a
higher citadel section (left) that featured granaries and a
large stepped bath. Shaded areas represent residential
quarters that have been excavated, with one section (top
center) showing outlines of the foundations. As the valley
was subject to flooding, storage of foodstuffs on a high
point was a sensible precaution. Notice the orthogonal
character of the residential quarter.

3.2 View of the remains of Mohenjo-Daro, Indus Valley,
ca. 2400–2000 BCE.

Excavations of Mohenjo-Daro began in the 1920s, when
archaeologists uncovered remains of the citadel and
portions of the lower-lying residential area. Bricks made to a
uniform size are the major construction materials used.

N

0   500 m
0   1500 ft

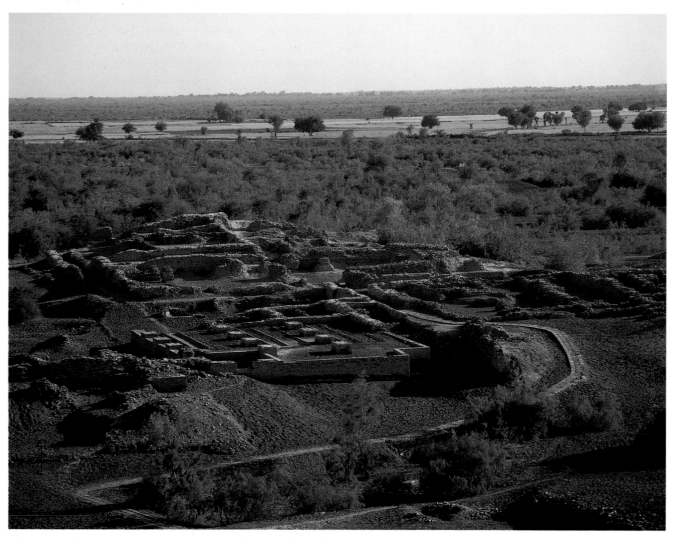

Reasons for the rapid decline of Harappan culture by about 1700 BCE are disputed, but natural factors (changes in river courses, failure of irrigation systems, earthquakes) and incursions by northern ethnic groups appear to have played a part. Harappan cities ceased to be inhabited, and over the next two centuries the countryside was raided by nomads from the north. In about 1500 BCE great invasions by Aryan tribes from eastern Iran began, and the Aryans eventually spread over the Indian subcontinent, displacing indigenous settlements. By 500 BCE their Indo-European language, the original root of many of the languages of Europe as well as Sanskrit in India, had displaced native tongues, a sign of cultural dominance. There was an ethnic factor here too: the invading Aryans were light-skinned in comparison to the darker-skinned native Indian populations. The distinction between conqueror and conquered became the earliest basis for the caste system that still operates in Indian society today.

Out of the confusion attending the invasions arose numerous small principalities. At about the time Alexander the Great was leading his army to the Indus (326 BCE), a young member of the Maurya tribe, Chandragupta, succeeded in bringing much of northern India under his command, eventually controlling most of what today is Pakistan and the eastern sections of Afghanistan as well. The empire continued to expand into southern India under his son and then grandson, Asoka (reigned 272–232 BCE), perhaps the greatest prince of the Maurya line and, as far as architecture is concerned, the first ruler of consequence. Asoka advanced the art of building in stone, bringing masons and stonecutters from Persia to construct monumental freestanding pillars, excavate caves for religious hermitages, and improve Buddhist shrines. His works have survived, and they will be considered below in the discussion of early Buddhist architecture.

A study of the ancient architecture in India and Southeast Asia is to a very large extent an examination of the development of temple architecture, for there are few structures not erected for religious purposes that have survived the passage of time. Temples were the primary buildings erected in durable materials, stone and brick, while houses and even palaces were constructed of less permanent wood, thatch, or stuccoed rubble and are therefore preserved only incidentally as, for example, in the backgrounds of scenes carved on temples. Princes, kings, and occasionally wealthy merchants were the major patrons of masonry temples, and thus architectural developments and religious preferences are closely related to political dynasties. In the period under consideration (up until about 1000 CE), the Indian subcontinent was not a unified country, although a certain level of cultural continuity was afforded by religious ties. A closer examination of Indian architecture would recognize the development of regional styles and the influences of powerful dynasties, but these will be given less emphasis here in the interests of creating a broad overview.

RELIGIONS OF INDIA

Since religious buildings assume such a prominent position in Indian architecture, it is necessary to understand the rudiments of the faiths that inspired their construction. During the sixth century BCE, the Indian subcontinent witnessed the development of three major religions that all shared a general belief in the transmigration of souls. This doctrine, which was as pervasive in India as the belief in life after death was in ancient Egypt, held that living souls passed through an endless cycle of rebirth and suffering. In somewhat differing ways, Hinduism, Buddhism, and Jainism proposed means by which people could transcend the sorrow of temporal existence.

Never the spirit was born; the spirit shall cease to be never;
Never was time it was not; End and Beginning are dreams!
Birthless and deathless and changeless remaineth the spirit
for ever;
Death hath not touched it at all, dead though the house of it
seems!
Who knoweth it exhaustless, self-sustained,
Immortal, indestructible,—shall such say, "I have killed a
man, or caused to kill?"
Nay, but as when one layeth his worn-out robes away,
And, taking new ones, sayeth, "These will I wear to-day!"
So putteth by the spirit lightly its garb of flesh,
And passeth to inherit a residence afresh.

Bhagavad Gita (translated by Sir Edwin Arnold)

The common background for all three religions was a synthesis of traditional beliefs indigenous to the Indian peninsula and sacrificial cults brought by Aryan invaders from the north. The oldest sacred writings, the Vedas, date from 1500 to 900 BCE. They contain hymns and prescribe rituals for worship of a pantheon of gods identified with the natural elements. From an early date, there was also a cosmology that invoked the joining of male and female as a metaphor for the union of the individual with the Universal. Simple shrines gave physical expression to this idea through an upright stone (*linga*) emblematic of the male element surrounded at the base by concentric circles (*yoni*) representing the female principle. Observation of religious rites and sacrifices required to maintain proper relationships between people and the gods was entrusted to a group of priests or Brahmins, who came to hold considerable power within society. Ascetic cults that developed during this period promoted the view that the physical world is but a small part of a much greater cycle of birth, death, and rebirth, and they offered their followers guidance for escaping repeated reincarnations.

Partly in reaction to the dominance of the Brahmin priests and their elaborate rituals, a number of individuals sought simpler means to religious understanding and ethical living. Two lasting religious movements—Jainism, which is still practiced by about two million Indians, and Buddhism, one of the world's major religions, which is now virtually extinct in India but flourishes elsewhere—were founded by identifiable historical figures. Jainism was inspired by the life of Vardhamana, also known as Mahavira (great hero) and Jina (the victor). In 546 BCE Vardhamana found his version of the path to salvation in a complete rejection of the complex formulations of the Brahmins. He taught that escape from the world's unhappiness was attainable only through rigorous asceticism to purify the soul and by maintaining reverence for all living creatures. His followers, mostly merchants and bankers whose livelihoods enabled them to avoid all forms of violence against animals, established Jainism (literally, religion of Jina), in which participants seek to acquire spiritual merit through charity, good works, and, whenever possible, monastic retreats. In architectural terms, Jainist temples never developed a distinctive style, borrowing elements instead from other religious groups.

In contrast, the religion founded by Siddhartha Gautama (ca. 563–ca. 483 BCE) was destined to become a major influence on architecture, not only in India, but also in Sri Lanka, China, Tibet, and southeast Asia. Born into a wealthy family, Gautama left his wife and fortune to travel as a beggar and seek an understanding of the causes of suffering. After six years of ascetic mortification and contemplation, he achieved enlightenment while sitting under the bodhi tree. Gautama's Four Noble Truths proclaimed that the world was worthless, that ignorance must be overcome, that vain craving could be renounced through yoga, and that the true path to salvation lay in the middle way between self-indulgence and self-mortification. These Truths, in conjunction with the Eight-fold Way (right views, resolve, speech, conduct, livelihood, effort, recollection, and meditation), formed the basis of his teachings, which were intended to enable his disciples to overcome worldly suffering caused by human desires and thus to achieve *nirvana* or liberation from the eternal cycle of birth and rebirth. Buddhism, the religion he inspired, took its name from the word Buddha, the Enlightened One, the name given to Gautama after his conversion. As initially expounded, the religion required neither complex worship rituals nor a specific architectural context.

The religion of the Brahmins, which evolved into Hinduism, responded to Jainism and Buddhism by incorporating popular devotional images of gods and spirits into its rituals of worship and making these rituals relate more closely to people's daily lives. Hinduism, which remains the major religion in India today, had no single founder, and it still has no clearly defined religious hierarchy. Essential to its beliefs are acceptance of the Vedas as sacred texts, and maintenance of the caste structure, whereby society is organized immutably into four classes (priests, warriors, merchants/craftsmen, and laborers). Hindus hold that each individual accumulates the consequences of both good and bad actions through a series of lifetimes, and they pursue freedom from the cycle of rebirth through reverence to the gods and the elimination of passions. Of the innumerable Hindu deities, many with multiple and sharply differing aspects, there are three supreme gods: Shiva, Vishnu, and Brahma. Shiva, the great lord whose essential characteristic is procreative energy, but who can also be the great destroyer, has as his consort Devi, the mother goddess, whose alternate form includes Kali the destroyer. Shiva's mount is the bull Nandi. Vishnu is the creator who embodies mercy and goodness, sometimes youthful romance, but who also has powers of destruction. His consort, Lakshmi, is the goddess of wealth, and his mount is the eagle Garuda. Brahma, the creator who is reborn periodically from a lotus growing in the navel of the sleeping Vishnu, has as his consort Sarasvati, patroness of learning and music.

EARLY BUDDHIST SHRINES

The Buddha had not prescribed any particular architectural setting for worship, but his disciples established shrines to give permanent form to the religion. The first shrines were created after the death of the Buddha, when his cremated remains were divided by his followers and placed in ten locations associated with his life and teaching. To mark these places, a simple mound of rubble and earth known as a **stupa** was erected over the relics, in a manner comparable to traditional village memorials or **chaityas**, where the ashes of deceased leaders were placed in a mound, often located on the outskirts of their settlement. It was this traditional form and placement that served as the genesis of later Buddhist architecture. In time, Buddhist monks settled in the vicinity of stupas to form small monasteries (**viharas**) of individual cells organized around open courts. Their rituals included walking around (circumambulating) the stupa while chanting verses from scripture. A processional path, generally followed in a clockwise direction, remains central to Buddhist temple design.

3.3 Diagram illustrating the origin of the stupa.

The traditional practice of placing stones and earth over the graves of distinguished people evolved into the construction of a hemispherical form that incorporated the cosmological associations of a circle (in plan), the world mountain and dome of the heavens, and the vertical world axis.

3.4 Great Stupa, Sanchi, ca. 250 BCE–250 CE.

This shows a torana gate and portion of the enclosing fence. The harmika (fence) and chatra (stylized bodhi tree) on top of the mound symbolize the enclosure surrounding the tree under which the Buddha received enlightenment.

3.5 Plan of the Great Stupa, Sanchi, ca. 250 BCE–250 CE.

This shows the four gates and their bent-axis entry design that creates a swastika, perhaps linked to ancient sun symbols. Openings correspond to the cardinal directions. Stairs on the south side lead to the elevated circumambulation path used by priests.

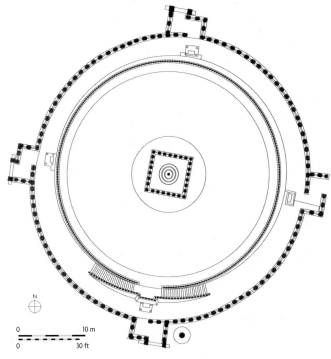

The oldest surviving Buddhist stupas were enlarged with successive coverings or constructed anew during the reign of Asoka, the early Indian emperor who was converted to Buddhism. Through his contacts with Persian architecture and the Hellenistic world, Asoka brought to India builders proficient in the art of stonework, which until this time had not been used in construction. He also caused the roads leading to Buddhist shrines to be marked with tall columns inscribed with Buddhist teachings, known afterward as Asoka columns. These featured ornamental carving clearly modeled on Persian originals (see Fig. 1.21). Whereas the columns in Persian architecture supported a roof, in India they were freestanding elements used as commemorative markers in the landscape.

Under Asoka's patronage, the original simple stupas were enlarged and new shrines were created. All were regularized into hemispherical forms, reflecting the simplicity of the circle in plan, section, and elevation and creating a symbolic link to the cyclical nature of existence (Fig. 3.3). To provide for greater permanence, the stupas were paved over with brick or stone. To indicate their sacred character, they were protected by an enclosing fence that delimited the path for circumambulation. And to mark their special association with the Buddha, they were crowned with a square railing (**harmika**) and a three-tiered umbrella form (**chatra**), stylized stone versions of

the sacred enclosure fence and famous bodhi tree under which the Buddha received enlightenment. The triple parasol was emblematic of royalty, and its supporting stalk symbolized the axis of the world passing through the precise center of the hemispherical form of the stupa, symbol of the heavenly dome.

The monastery at Sanchi, founded by Asoka and enlarged over the next 500 years, illustrates the fundamental elements of Buddhist shrines in India. The Great Stupa, originally constructed as a mound about seventy feet in diameter, grew to become a dome that was almost 120 feet in diameter and fifty-four feet in height (Figs. 3.4–3.5). At its top, the stupa is crowned by a triple umbrella set inside a square fenced enclosure. Its base is for the monks (Fig. 3.8). In contrast to the permanent materials employed for the shines, viharas were constructed of wood, and only their masonry foundations survive to indicate their layouts, which in many respects are an enlargement of the courtyard house already familiar from the early Indus Valley constructions and also used throughout Mediterranean civilizations. Buddhist monks lived in simple cells that were grouped around a square or rectangular open court containing community facilities, including the water supply. Sanchi also featured several enclosed chaitya halls, buildings permitting year-round devotions by enclosing a small stupa at the end of a rectangular hall. The end of the hall embracing the stupa was curved to reflect the shape contained within, and thus created an architectural form that could be erected as a freestanding structure raised on a base, or plinth, as in the

3.6 The fence and torana gate, Sanchi, ca. 250 BCE–250 CE.

The fence is composed of massive stones, treated in a manner analogous to wooden construction, while the gates are richly carved.

3.7 The fence and torana gate, Sanchi, ca. 250 BCE–250 CE.

As seen from the inside, the space for circumambulation is effectively screened from the outside world by the stone rails of the fence.

encircled by a two-tiered ambulatory: the upper level is reserved for priests, leaving the ground level path for pilgrim use. Enclosing the stupa is a massive stone fence (**verdika**) (Fig. 3.6), nine feet in height, with four carved gates at the cardinal points of the compass. The construction of this fence shows how early masons were influenced by wooden construction. Octagonal upright posts and rounded horizontal rails replicate forms already familiar in wood, raised here on a much larger scale. The elaborate entrance gates (**toranas**) (Fig. 3.7), added in about 25 BCE, reflect bamboo prototypes. When built in stone, however, the size increases and it is possible, as here, to embellish the work with carved figures representing Buddhist legends, symbolism that may have been inspired by similar work on Asoka columns. The relative lack of modeling on the figures makes these gates seem more the work of wood carvers than masonry sculptors. All four gates are set in front of the encircling fence, and they are part of a staggered, or bent-axis, approach designed to reduce distractions outside the sacred enclosure from disturbing the meditations of pilgrims circumambulating the stupa.

The shrine at Sanchi is an accumulation of buildings constructed over time, including three stupas and viharas

3.8 Reconstruction view of the temple complex, Sanchi.

In the center is the Great Stupa, and to the right is the so-called Temple 40, an early chaitya hall. The rectangular-plan building at the upper left is a vihara, a residence for monks, of which only the foundations now remain.

3.9 Section and plan through the cave temple, Karli, ca. 100 BCE.

Excavated in a rock cliff, this temple consists of a chaitya hall with an ambulatory around the stupa shrine at the rear. Two freestanding columns (one now gone) flanked the entrance, while stone and teakwood carvings screened the opening to the cave.

so-called Temple 18 at Sanchi, or excavated from solid rock, as in the temples cut into cliffs at Ajanta, Ellora, and Karli.

Construction of these cave-temples coincided with a period when the rulers of India's principalities favored Brahmin practices, and Buddhism was the religion primarily of wealthy merchants. Even though Buddhist shrines were thus financed by substantial donations, the monks increasingly sought remote sites for construction to avoid conflicts with Brahmins. Rock cliffs and gorges provided isolated locations, and the living rock contained durable material for masons to carve without their having to enclose space with stone beams. At the great cave-temple of Karli (Fig. 3.9), which dates from the first century CE, the chaitya hall faithfully replicates the form and details of wooden architecture that provided its prototype, including the semicircular arched ceiling patterned after flexible bamboo structures. Karli's dimensions, however, exceed those of wooden buildings of the period: the hall is forty-five feet wide, a difficult span to achieve in timber, but one that presented no problem to the excavators. Starting from the cliff face, which was smoothed and shaped to resemble the façade of a chaitya hall, workers drove two tunnels 150 feet into the cliff to establish the

BAMIYAN AND THE COLOSSAL BUDDHA

by C. Murray Smart

Traders transported Indian design and iconography east by sea to Southeast Asia and Indonesia and west through the mountain passes to Central Asia by Silk Road caravans. The main text here deals with the most spectacular examples of Indian architecture in Southeast Asia—the great works at Borobodur and Angkor. Equally important, however, is the great Buddhist pilgrimage complex of Bamiyan in what is today Afghanistan; it was here that the colossal image of the Buddha first appeared. Bamiyan was the western terminus of three of the trade routes that connected China, India, the Near East, and the Western world. At Bamiyan, a great monastic complex more than a mile long was carved into a sandstone cliff overlooking a fertile valley between the Hindu Kush to the east and the Koh-i-Baba mountain range to the northwest. The site was visited in the seventh century by the Chinese pilgrim Hsüan-tsang who described it in glowing terms. Another visitor, Genghis Khan, apparently found less to admire: legend has it that he massacred the entire population, turning Bamiyan into the deserted complex of today.

The monastery is terminated at each end by a colossal Buddha statue (Fig. 3A). The figure at the eastern end, designated "Sakyamuni" by Hsüan-tsang, is 120 feet tall; the more spectacular figure at the western end, which Hsüan-tsang simply called "the Buddha," is 171 feet tall. It is the larger figure that is of greater importance, not only because of its size, but also because its iconography and style were replicated in small souvenir statues and exported to the home countries of visiting pilgrims. A comparison of the Bamiyan figures with those of the Tun-Huang caves in China reveals that the Buddhist iconography

of China was influenced directly by the figures at Bamiyan.

The two Buddhas illustrate the cosmopolitan nature of the Buddhist art at Bamiyan. They are quite different in style. In every respect except its size, the smaller figure is a typical Gandharan Buddha figure of the second or third century CE. Its construction is interesting. Only the basic armature of the body was carved; over the rough stone body and head, facial features and voluminous drapery folds were modeled in plaster made of mud and straw. The figure was finished with a coating of lime-plaster which was painted and gilded. At the time of

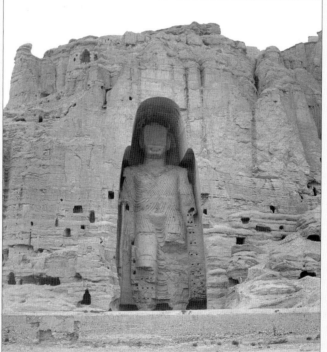

3A Great Buddha, Bamiyan, Afghanistan, late Gandhara school, 7th century. Height 171ft (52m).

Hsüan-tsang's visit, the statue was completely covered with gold leaf and metal ornaments, leading him to the erroneous conclusion that it was made of metal.

As interesting as the statue are the fragments of fresco that remain. Originally, the niche in which the figure stands was completely covered with paintings symbolizing the vault of

heaven. The central image of the fresco above the Buddha's head is a sun god driving a chariot drawn by horses and attended by winged angels. It could be Apollo, or Surya, the Hindu sun god, or perhaps Mithra, the Persian sun god. Two of the four flanking angels have human form and are inspired by Persian and Mediterranean prototypes; the other two are derived from Greek harpies and have birds' feet.

The drapery of the larger Buddha was modeled on ropes attached to wooden dowels driven into the stone armature. The result was an enormous replica of a late Gandharan Buddha type in which the robe was reduced to a series of lines that clung to and revealed the body form beneath. This statue is two centuries or more later in origin than the smaller figure; it probably dates from the fifth century CE. It stands in a trefoil niche that creates a double halo about the body and head; this double halo was much copied in both China and Japan.

These two figures are the first of many colossal images of the Buddha that would appear throughout the Buddhist world. Both Greece and Rome produced colossal figures that served as prototypes. And just as the colossal portrait sculptures of Roman emperors were intended to portray them as divine rulers of the world, the Bamiyan figures portray the Buddha as cosmic man, the source and substance of the universe.

Unfortunately, since this essay was written, the fundamentalist Muslim sect formerly in power in Afghanistan, the Taliban, destroyed both of these two colossal Buddha figures in 2001. Since the overthrow of the Taliban, there has been talk internationally of restoring the statues, but no plans have yet been announced.

length of the temple, then enlarged the excavation to create a barrel-shaped ceiling with arched "ribs." Rock on the chamber floor was cut away and columns carved as workers completed excavating the entire interior space. Rubble extracted from the cliff became material for construction of a platform extending to the cave's entrance, a recessed, arched porch marked by paired freestanding columns supporting lion sculptures. This porch was adorned by relief carvings and (originally) painted scenes from the life of the Buddha. Inside the chaitya hall, the relatively dim light penetrating through high grilles of the windows allows the pilgrim to discern slowly the enormity of the space, measured by the stately rhythm of colonnades and dominated at the far recess by a stupa carved with the image of the Buddha. The architects of the temple at Karli achieved that elusive synthesis of space, light, and detail which characterizes the finest buildings of any era.

THE SPREAD OF BUDDHIST INFLUENCE

Particularly in northern India, where Buddhists came into contact with late Hellenistic Greek and Roman traditions, followers of the Buddha began to revere their founder as a god and savior, and they included increasingly large images of the Enlightened One as an object of worship. The cave temples at Ajanta (ca. 450 CE) organize the chaitya hall in such a way as to focus on images of the Buddha rather than the stupa form seen at Karli. Stupas built in the mountainous country of the north were given cylindrical drum bases to increase the sense of their verticality, and the triple-umbrella top became more prominent. In one of the greatest of these northern stupas, the now-vanished shrine of the Mahastupa at Sha-ji-ki-Dheri (near Peshawar), the stupa was constructed over a brick base with projections at the cardinal points, supporting a 628-foot-high timber tower of thirteen receding stories, which was in turn crowned by twenty-five superimposed copper-gilt umbrellas as a finial. Although this remarkable building was destroyed by lightning in the seventh century, Chinese traders and pilgrim travelers on the Silk Roads across Central Asia used it and similar northern Indian stupas as the basis for the **pagoda**, the typical Buddhist tower associated with both China and Japan (see Fig. 4.3).

Indian influence also spread to Southeast Asia through merchants, who were active in an area around the Bay of Bengal and the eastern Indian Ocean from the fourth and fifth centuries CE. These traders introduced new technology, including the potter's wheel and the use of elephants and horses as draft animals, and they also brought Hinduism and Buddhism with them. In Indonesia, the synthesis of native artistic traditions and Indian religion found magnificent expression in the stupa shrine of Borobudur (ca. 800–50) on the island of Java (Fig. 3.10). Set on a plain ringed by mountains, an enormous pyramidal form was constructed around a natural rise in the terrain to become an artificial hill, covered in stone carved in place and supporting a Great Stupa Shrine that symbolizes the center of the universe. The entire composition is symmetrical and oriented to the cardinal directions. In plan, it is a great square with projecting and inset corners, having a stair in the center of each side. Visitors to the temple walk around the base and then ascend the stair to repeat the circumambulation on each of the four galleries as they climb. On their journey they encounter three rising terraces, circular in plan, containing seventy-two miniature stupa shrines holding images of the Buddha, before they arrive at the central Great Stupa Shrine. The galleries on this pilgrimage route are enriched by more than 500 Buddhas and *bodhisattvas* (individuals who achieved enlightenment but chose to remain in the world as a model for others) set in niches. Over three miles of sculpted friezes along the galleries present events from the life of the Buddha, including his earlier incarnations that form the core of Buddhist legend. On the upper terraces,

3.10 Plan and half-section of the Great Stupa shrine, Borobudur, Java, ca. 800–50.

The lower four tiers are composed of galleries containing carved representations of Buddhist legends, while the upper three terraces are concentric platforms containing seventy-two Buddha figures set in bell-shaped perforated stupas.

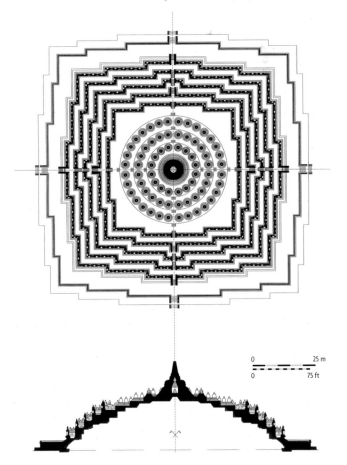

the lively scenes of the galleries are replaced by calm statues of the Buddha, sitting in the lotus position and displaying *mudras*, distinctive hand gestures symbolizing spiritual virtues. Each freestanding statue is protected by a bell-shaped perforated stone stupa that permits glimpses of the figure within. Scholars still argue over the precise function of the temple when it was constructed: was it accessible to all pilgrims, or the province of a select few who had attained higher spiritual understanding? Could ordinary visitors have understood the complex meanings embodied in the architecture and iconographic program? Was it primarily a place where priests were trained? It is not necessary to have firm answers to these questions to appreciate the monument. Borobudur embodies the spirit of its particular place in the landscape, harmoniously blending a peaceful aspect with a form designed to promote meditative reflection by the visitor. As a synthesis of the natural environment, sculpture, and architectural form, it is a powerful and moving monument, fully worthy of the major preservation effort now being undertaken by UNESCO experts.

HINDU TEMPLES
EARLY BUILDINGS

Buddhist and Hindu traditions have a long history of coexistence on the Indian subcontinent, and among followers of various sects there has been a certain commingling of beliefs as well as temple forms. Although Hinduism draws strongly on some of the most ancient

3.11 Diagram illustrating the basis for most Hindu temples.

This shows a womb-chamber (garbhagriha) that radiates energy to the cardinal and ordinal directions; a passage for circumambulation in a clockwise direction; and the sacred mountain defining a central axis that towers over the garbhagriha.

indigenous beliefs, it only developed a particular architectural expression for itself later. Buddhists built the earliest surviving shrines and thereby established the model on which early Hindu architecture was based, but from the fifth century CE onward, Hinduism became the dominant religion in India. Today few Buddhist sects remain there.

As in Buddhist practice, the Hindu temple creates a link between the gods and the worshiper. However, unlike the Buddhists, who focus on the life and teachings of one leader, Hindus venerate a multitude of deities. Their temples are simultaneously dwellings of the god, places for worship, and objects of worship in themselves. Aspects of the cosmos (and thus of the gods) are incorporated into the temple by the use of specific forms, sacred geometry,

3.12 Ladkhan Temple, Aihole, 7th century CE.

Notice that a columned porch precedes the pillared main hall of the temple, translating into stone architectural forms previously built in wood as village assembly halls.

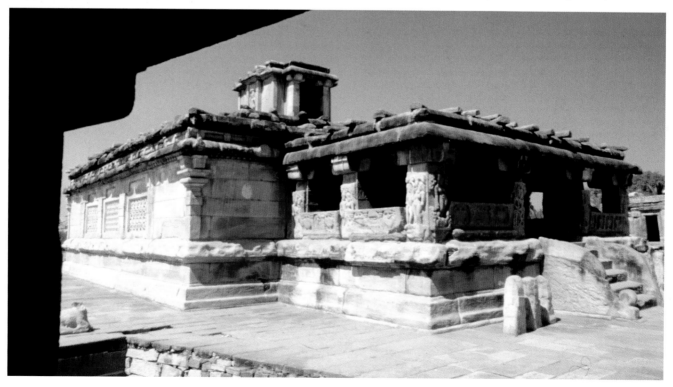

careful orientation, and axial alignments. Most Hindu temple designs include forms that are symbolic of the holy mountain, the sacred cave, and the cosmic axis (Fig. 3.11). Geometry derived from a subdivided square or **mandala** is commonly used, together with a single unit that sets all proportions. Numbers associated with the gods are important in constructing and interpreting the mandala, which provide links to divine proportions, hence harmony with the cosmos. Temple complexes are usually aligned on the cardinal points, representing the four corners of the earth, with the major entrances facing east. Priests perform sacred rites at regular times for the benefit of the entire community, and private devotions may be offered at any time. Since there is no congregational worship, there is no corresponding need for a large enclosed space. Rather, the temple as a three-dimensional form in the landscape becomes a focal point for community life, much as a Christian church might serve social and artistic purposes as well as religious functions.

Some of the earliest surviving Hindu shrines are found in the rock-cut temples of Udaigiri, near Sanchi, and these show clear influence from Buddhist work. Temple 17 at Sanchi, dating from the early fifth-century CE, is modeled on the rock-cut temples at Udaigiri, set on a plinth and featuring a square sanctuary preceded by a pillared porch. This two-chambered temple form is amplified and embellished in virtually all later developments. The sanctuary is typically quite small. Known as the womb-chamber (**garbhagriha**), it contains a sacred image or element as a symbol of the god's presence. If proper rituals are not observed, the god may choose to inhabit another place, so worship involves priestly ceremonies that welcome, entertain, and honor the deity with music, food, dancing, the recital of religious texts, and the singing of hymns. The covered porch provides a transition between the outside world and the sanctuary, and on its pillars and the exterior walls of the temple the visitor can generally find sculpted panels and images that complement the image of the deity within.

Hindu gods have a particular affinity for mountains and caves. As builders became more skillful in working in stone (or occasionally brick), they gave increasingly elaborate formal expression to the vertical mound (mountain) arising over the sanctuary (cave). As an example of this process, consider the Ladkhan Temple (Fig. 3.12), built in the seventh century CE at Aihole, which preserves in its stonework the traces of a wooden village assembly hall that served as its model. The masons resolved questions of overall form and building details as a carpenter would. When translated into stone, however, the light and pliant wooden structure became overscaled and heavy.

LATER TEMPLES

Later Hindu temples rise more dramatically, as builders exploited architectural form as the basis for sculptural

3.13 Vishnu Temple, Bhitargaon, 5th century CE.
Constructed in brick, this is one of the earliest Hindu temples to have a towering mass constructed over the garbhagriha.

embellishment, sweeping masses upward in imitation of entire mountain ranges. At Bhitargaon, the brick Vishnu Temple, dating perhaps to the first half of the fifth century, presents an early example of a more prominent superstructure erected over the sanctuary (Fig. 3.13). Even in its somewhat ruined state, the temple's profile shows an unmistakable allusion to mountain forms. The passage connecting the sanctuary and the porch is unusual for incorporating true-arch construction. Most Indian temples are built using post-and-lintel or corbeling techniques, but this temple demonstrates that builders had knowledge of the arch even though it was seldom employed. The source of the characteristic mountain-peak roof (**shikhara**) of mature Indian temples has been traced to lightweight thatched bamboo structures with curving sides rising from a square base. No matter how elaborate the masonry temple forms became, with their exteriors covered with carved ornament and walls adorned with sculpture, the essence of a square sanctuary housed under the curving shikhara roof, preceded by one or more columnar halls or porches in axial alignment, remains the distinctive design paradigm for the Hindu temple (Fig. 3.14). The enormously thick masonry walls required to sustain the towering roof amplified the womb-like seclusion of the central shrine room, enveloping the chamber within the sacred mountain.

3.14 Temple, Khajuraho, 10th century.

This shows the shikhara roof commonly found over the garbhagriha of many Hindu temples. Its towering form creates a symbolic holy mountain over the sacred cave.

Two temple groups dating from the eighth to thirteenth centuries illustrate the prolific magnificence of northern Hindu architecture. Bhubaneshwar, in the state of Orissa, has over 100 temples constructed across a period of five centuries. The plan of the celebrated Lingaraja Temple (mid-eleventh to mid-twelfth century) is an elaboration of the two-celled form, with three pillared halls on axis preceding the sanctuary. From east to west, these comprise a hall of offerings, a hall of dance, an assembly hall, and finally the sanctuary proper (Fig. 3.15). Pyramidal roofs over the halls resemble foothills, contrasting with the massive central shikhara over the sanctuary, whose form is echoed on a smaller scale by the subsidiary shrines erected inside the walled rectangular temple precinct. Within the worshiper's field of vision, there are sculpted figures carved with a high degree of fine detail as well as sensuous beauty to enrich the wall surfaces. Unlike a number of other historic temples, this massive shrine remains in active use.

At Khajuraho, royal city of the Chandella Dynasty, there were at least twenty-five temples constructed over a

200-year period, with sculptural programs reflecting lavish artistic patronage as well as devotion to mystic Tantric rites. Among the best-preserved is the Lakshmana Temple (ca. 950) (Fig. 3.16), raised on a rectangular platform anchored by four small shrines at the corners. The axial approach from the east brings the visitor up several flights of steps, whose ascent is repeated in the successively rising roof forms over an initial open porch, a second porch, a great pillared hall, and finally the internal sanctuary. The devotee may circumambulate the sanctuary by following an enclosed passage surrounding the shrine room. Light for the ambulatory is provided by openings placed above eye level so that the elaborate interior wall sculpture may be seen without admitting distractions from the external world. Images represented here include many animated scenes of loving couples, generally interpreted as both a

3.15 Plan of the Lingaraja Temple, Bhubaneshwar, ca. 1050–1150.

More elaborate than some, this temple plan has three separate halls preceding the garbhagriha at the end of the processional axis. Each hall is provided with a distinctive roof profile so that the composition builds to the high shikhara.

Sanctuary

Assembly hall (Room of the Faithful)

Pavilion of Offerings

Hall for dancing

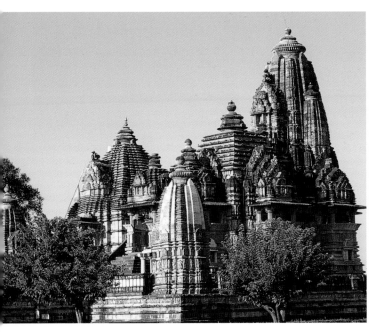

3.16 (above) Lakshmana Temple, Khajuraho, ca. 950.

This shows the platform or plinth on which the temple is raised. Shrines at the corners of the plinth reflect the main shrine at miniature scale.

3.17 (right) Kandariya Mahadeva Temple, Khajuraho, 1025–50

Upper levels of the roof are deeply carved with geometric ornament, which has the effect of making the massive form seem lighter while accentuating its contours. Ornament in the lower bands includes sculpted figures.

literal representation of Tantric practices (which included sexual intercourse) and a symbol of the rapturous union of the human with the divine that was a goal of Hindu theology (page 66 and Figs. 3.17–3.18).

All the Hindu temples considered thus far are products of dynasties who ruled primarily in the north and central sections of India. In the south, a distinctive regional style developed that featured roofs with rounded finials, walls with engaged columns or pilasters for articulation, multi-columned halls, and temple complexes that had sets of concentric walls with massive gateway entrances. As with architecture in northern India, the origin of this style can be traced to the early seventh-century rock-cut temples that generally featured a pillared hall as a prelude to a sanctuary set deep in the interior. In cave architecture, the pillared hall functioned much like a portico or porch, a transition between the outside world and the shrine. (The early temple of Ladkhan at Aihole may well have served as

3.18 Kandariya Mahadeva Temple (detail of shikhara), Khajuraho, 1025–50

In the lower registers, where figures are close enough to be seen by visitors, figural sculpture is extensively used.

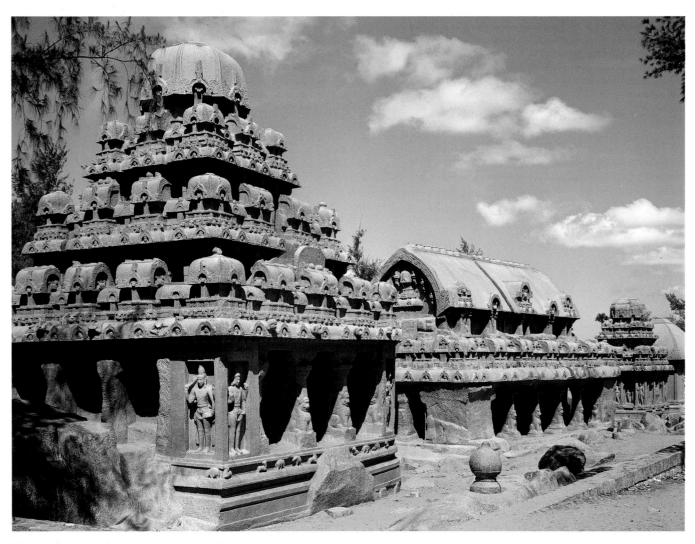

3.19 Dharmaraja Ratha, Bhima Ratha, and Arjuna Ratha, Mahabalipuram, 7th century.

These three monolithic temples, cut from a granite outcropping, replicate in stone an earlier temple architecture in wood. Note the chaitya-like roof on the Bhima Ratha that resembles thatch. A clear geometric conception underlies all three.

a model for the scheme.) The same stone-cutting skills that were used to excavate cave temples were put to more sculptural use in about 650, when a remarkable set of temples was carved out of a granite ridge at Mahabalipuram (Fig. 3.19). The temples, known as **rathas** (wheeled carts or chariots), are similar to large-scale architectural models; each one is different. Some are obviously derived from the barrel-vaulted roofs of chaitya halls, while others are based on simple wooden shrines or elaborations of centralized designs. All are set on a raised base and make use of engaged columns or pilasters for wall articulation. Images of deities, mythological beings, and the royal family (the Pallavas) who commissioned the work are set in recesses defined by the pilasters. Multiple roofs in layers add verticality to the forms. When one realizes how much of the hard granite was cut away to create these diminutive

masterpieces, it is apparent that the art of working stone had reached a high level of sophistication and taste.

What began at small scale was continued at much greater size in the eleventh-century Brihedesvara Temple at Tanjore (Figs. 3.20–3.21). Here the builders succeeded in erecting a tower over the garbhagriha that was three times the height (200 feet) of anything else that had been attempted prior to that time. The base is substantial, an eighty-two-foot square on plan, but there is a processional space around the central shrine included in the lower story, so it is not a solid mass. Half-columns and niches define a two-story elevation rising above the base, while uncounted roof levels recede as they ascend in the towering pyramid roof, which is capped by a monolith weighing over eighty tons that forms a dome-like finial. As one might expect, the temple complex is axially arranged, with a porch and two multi-columned halls preceding the shrine proper. A separate pillared shrine honoring Nandi the sacred bull is placed on axis between the temple and the great entrance gate. The enclosing wall is composed of a continuous double colonnade, and several lesser temples occupy corners of the courtyard.

3.20 Plan of Brihedesvara Temple, Tanjore, 11th century.

Compare this to the plan of the Lakshmana Temple at Khajuraho to see how all elements of the temple have been greatly increased in size. The central axis is defined by a gopura or towering entrance gate on the east side.

3.21 Brihedesvara Temple, Tanjore, 11th century.

The pyramidal shikhara roof over the main shrine rises from a square base, towering over 200 feet to dominate the extensive temple. Its domed top is cut from a single piece of granite in a form that resembles a Buddhist stupa.

Particularly in the southern tip of India, where the influence of Islam never really penetrated, Hindu temple complexes were enlarged over many centuries in response to the growing crowds who came there in increasing numbers to celebrate festivals. Such was the case with the Ranganatha Temple at Shrirangam (dedicated to Vishnu), which began in about 1000 as a modest garbhagriha and

3.22 Gopuras of the Raganatha Temple, Shrirangam,
ca. 1000–1500.

In southern India, Hindu temples were surrounded by multiple sets of
perimeter walls, each provided with a towering gate (gopura). This
photograph shows a series of these gates forming a protective line.

3.23 Satiangam Temple, Kanchipuram, ca. 1300.

Hindu temples in southern India developed greatly
elaborated portals (gopuras) that define the processional
axis and tower over the secular community outside the
temple precinct.

pillared hall set within a walled courtyard (Fig. 3.22). As
the site grew in popularity over the next 500 years, it was
expanded by constructing additional sets of enclosing
walls that maintained the unorthodox north–south axial
alignment but otherwise made little effort at architectural
continuity or formal coherence. The new courtyards contained additional shrines, multi-columned halls, pools for
ritual bathing, and long passages lined with columns, in
addition to stables for temple elephants and housing for
the extensive staff involved in the ritual and operation of
the holy site. By the time of the fourth expansion, the
temple wall engulfed the town itself and enclosed an area
of nearly a quarter of a square mile. In the course of expansion, the rather modest original temple was given a
grander enclosure, but it is still overshadowed by the great
gateways (known as **gopuras**) constructed on the axial
approach to the complex. The outermost wall has three
gopuras, built at the midpoints of the sides so that they
correspond with the cardinal points of the compass. Exterior surfaces of the gates rise in a gentle inward-stepped
curve to ridges that are embellished with boldly modeled
finials, while the layers of the gateway roof become the
occasion for elaborate carved ornament. Shirangam illustrates several enduring traits of Indian architecture: the
preference for repetition, both in exterior articulation and
for rhythmic elements in plan; a tendency to extrapolate
from small-scale models into large compositions; and
the dominance of surface decoration over architectural
form. Shirangam's overall composition of gopuras and

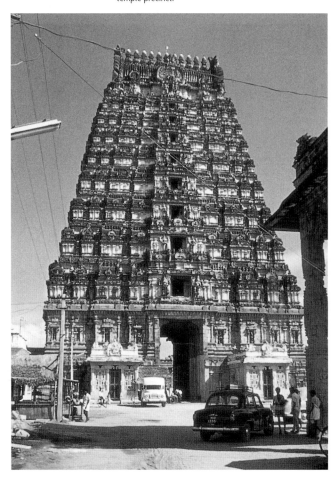

　　　　　CHAPTER 3　THE ARCHITECTURE OF ANCIENT INDIA AND SOUTHEAST ASIA

concentric walls becomes a model for later temples, even those that did not develop by accretion as did the complex here (Fig. 3.23).

Hinduism continues to the present day as the major religion in India, but its preeminence was challenged from the eleventh century onward as Muslim invaders conquered the northern portions of the country, destroying many Hindu sites. Islamic religious architecture differed fundamentally from both the spatial conception and architectural detail of either Buddhist or Hindu constructions, so the new rulers had little appreciation for buildings associated with the older religions. (The Islamic phase of Indian architecture will be considered in Chapter 7.)

ANGKOR WAT

Hinduism spread to other regions in Southeast Asia through the activity of Indian merchants, just as was the case with Buddhism, and the religion remains a force in those regions today. Among the numerous monuments of Hindu art outside the Indian subcontinent, one cannot overlook the vast temple of Angkor Wat in Cambodia, which represents a fusion of Indian religion and native Khmer tradition (Fig. 3.24). The scale of the project makes it one of the largest religious structures ever built, with a rectangular perimeter wall measuring 4275 by 4920 feet. Visitors wishing to make a complete pilgrimage according

Third enclosure galleries

Main shrine

First enclosure galleries

Second enclosure galleries

Cruciform courtyard

Library

Library

Pool

Pool

Pool

Pool

N

0   100 m
0   300 ft

3.24 Plan of Angkor Wat, begun ca. 1120.

The clarity of this design is comparable in its way to Borobudur. Nested sets of galleries focus on the central shrine, the symbolic representation of Mount Mehru, home of the gods.

to Hindu practice would walk about thirteen miles to visit all the galleries within the complex. Begun in ca. 1120 as a temple to Vishnu, one of the Hindu gods, Angkor Wat was finished as the royal shrine of the Khmer Dynasty that ruled Cambodia at that time before later being converted to Buddhist worship.

Earlier Khmer temples consisted of a tower sanctuary within a walled enclosure. The tower of course represented the sacred mountain, while the garbhagriha inside evoked the holy cave at the center of the cosmos. This theme was elaborated in later temples that featured multiple tower sanctuaries on a terrace. Later still, forms resembling step pyramids gave more vivid expression to the concept of the cosmic mountain. Until the construction of Angkor Wat, the most extensive interpretation of these themes in Khmer architecture came in temples that placed the tower sanctuary at the summit of a stepped pyramid, with open galleries for circumambulation extending around all four sides. Angkor takes this as the point of departure for an even more magnificent articulation, adding multiple towers, extended cruciform galleries, corner pavilions, and elaborate entrance gates to the central tower and elevated platform (Fig. 3.25). At the heart of the composition is a 215-foot-tall central tower (Fig. 3.26), built on a pyramid base whose corners are marked by four stepped towers that collectively are meant to symbolize Mount Mehru, the home of the gods. Two additional sets of square concentric galleries surround this core, punctuated by entrance gates in the centers of the four sides to reinforce the cardinal directions. The main axial approach passed through a square courtyard featuring artificial ponds before entering the second gallery and ascending the steep stairs to the innermost platform sanctuary. A moat nearly two-and-a-half miles in length encircles the entire site, symbolizing the oceans out of which the mountain rises.

Angkor Wat is built entirely in stone, and since it does not employ arched construction, only corbeling, there are no large enclosed spaces. Once laid, the stone became the

3.25 Angkor Wat, begun ca. 1120.

This shows how the plan is translated into a three-dimensional architectural form that fuses elements of horizontality and verticality within a relatively simple building technology.

domain of sculptors, who adorned walls and even roofs with ornament and shallow relief carvings. Some of the subjects are drawn from epics familiar from Hindu tradition, but these are blended with references to Khmer cosmology, and the whole serves as a mortuary shrine for Suryavarman II, the king who commissioned the work. In India, Hinduism never involved the concept of a god-king or ancestor worship, but these aspects are part of the Cambodian tradition and inform the design of Angkor Wat. Overall, the form captures the qualities both of horizontal expanse and vertical expression in a single composition. The architecture is symmetrical, balanced, and grand, the culminating expression of religious concepts begun centuries earlier in India.

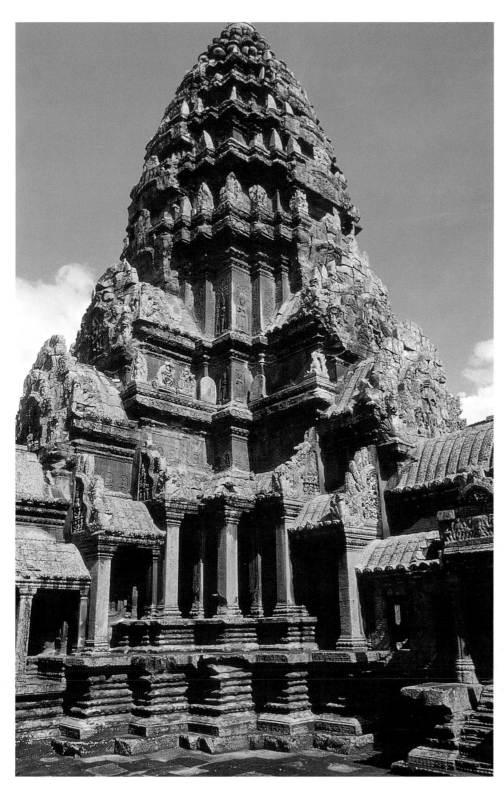

3.26 Central tower, Angkor Wat, begun ca. 1120.

This tower was constructed over a garbhagriha or womb-chamber that is the core of every Hindu temple.

CHAPTER 4

THE TRADITIONAL ARCHITECTURE OF CHINA AND JAPAN

China is a vast country, encompassing today nearly one-third of the world's population. We tend to regard it (correctly) as an ancient culture because, even though historic civilization developed there slightly later than in Mesopotamia or Egypt, China holds the distinction of having maintained the greatest degree of cultural continuity across nearly 4000 years, absorbing only limited outside influences. China's nearly ten million square miles contain varied geographical conditions and over fifty different ethnic groups, but its society has generally been defined by the Han Chinese. Unified government under strong emperors encouraged uniformity in many societal structures, including city design and building practices, and Chinese architectural traditions were remarkably stable over the centuries until the forcible intrusion of Western culture during the Opium Wars of the nineteenth century and the toppling of the last emperor in 1911.

For buildings from the period before about 2000 BCE, there is little information because so many of the sites are still occupied and thus excavations necessary to understand early architecture have not yet been made. Archaeologists have found remains of farming and craft villages in the Yellow River Valley, most notably at Banpo, where small houses of both circular and rectangular plans have been reconstructed based on foundation remains (Fig. 4.1). The rectangular houses were recessed a half-story into the ground and had a pyramid roof (no walls) of lightweight wooden members lashed together at the top. Earth-sheltering helped to stabilize the interior temperature in both summer and winter. Smoke from the central hearth escaped through a gap at the apex of the thatch-covered roof, and the sloping entranceway was protected

by a gable roof. The circular huts had side walls of wattle covered inside and out by a thick layer of clay for insulation, and the same treatment was given to the conical roof, with an opening left at the peak for ventilation, just as was the case with the rectangular houses. The doorway was recessed, and some houses seem to have had internal partitions or screens. Painted pottery remains suggest that skilled ceramists were working in these villages, and there are indications of weaving, although the textiles themselves have long since vanished. The next millennium saw the development of larger houses that still fall within the same architectural vocabulary of timber frame, earthen plastering, and thatch.

From these humble prehistoric origins came the legendary beginning of Chinese history with the Shang Dynasty, which emerged in about 1766 BCE to dominate the Yellow River Valley and extend its control as far south as the Yang-tze. Shang technology included skill in bronze casting and pictograph writing preserved on oracle bones (the shoulder blades of sheep). With the Shang begins the series of dynastic successions—Zhou, Han, Tang, Song, Yuan, Ming, and Qing, to name the major ones—that continue to dominate Chinese history until the early twentieth century.

In China, the primary impetus for building came from government (the imperial court and state investments) rather than from religious organizations or private patrons. The most obvious manifestation of this is the Great Wall, begun by the first Qin emperor in 221 BCE and largely rebuilt and completed during the Ming Dynasty (1368–1644 CE) (Fig. 4.2). Though we speak of it as a single structure, the Great Wall was constructed in segments over time, and there are several branch sections. The whole was intended to keep the nomadic Mongols from the hilly north out of China's agricultural lands; it was not entirely successful in this respect. Nonetheless, the Great Wall is an astonishing piece of construction, 4500 miles long, ranging from the coast through varied terrain to its terminus in the Gobi Desert. Originally it was largely made with rammed earth, but during the Ming Dynasty

---

Phoenix Hall, Uji, 1053.

This hall was built by a wealthy nobleman who had become a devotee of an apocalyptic sect known as the Pure Land Buddhists. The graceful lines of its columns and eaves are reflected in the adjacent lake water.

4.1 Reconstructions of Neolithic houses, Banpo, ca. 2000 BCE.

These reconstructions show early and late designs. As was the case with prehistoric houses in western Europe, these dwellings used readily available materials—wood, thatch, and earth—to provide shelter. A central hearth is also part of many houses at Banpo.

in finding answers to perplexing questions. Aspects of Daoism may be found particularly in the Chinese approach to garden design, where carefully contrived views and experiences are based on the model provided by nature itself. By contrast, the philosophy expounded by Confucius relied on respect for authority as established by the state. Its innately conservative tenets have dominated Chinese social and political structures throughout history. Those in power are to act benevolently on behalf of their subjects, and ordinary people are to show proper deference to the superior wisdom and understanding of their revered leaders. Ancestor worship and respect for one's elders in the family, hallmarks of a well-ordered Confucian family, had exact parallels in the veneration that society in general owed to the reigning emperor, regarded as a virtual deity whose welfare was crucial for the stability of the state. Chinese city planning and traditional house design embodied Confucian principles in their layouts and axial alignments of buildings.

4.2 Great Wall of China, 221 BCE–1368 CE.

This view shows watchtowers and wall sections with battlements. The crenelated wall provides protection on the north side, while on the south side (toward China) the parapet is lower and unfortified.

the height of most of the wall was raised and given its present casing of brick or stone. As it exists today, the Great Wall varies from nineteen to thirty-nine feet in height, with an average width at the top of sixteen feet. The north-facing side is capped by crenelated battlements, with watchtowers connected by a road extending along the top. In the event of attack, beacons could be used to summon reinforcements from garrison camps that were strategically located on the southern side. Only a highly organized, powerful state could command the resources required to construct and maintain an engineering work on this scale. One should not be surprised to find the Chinese achieving similarly consistent building standards in more modest projects.

Indigenous Chinese religious traditions were based on a belief in life after death, ancestor worship, and animism (a reverence for natural features such as trees, rocks, and hills, as well as cosmic elements including the sky, sun, and moon). From early times, indigenous religions had included the concept already mentioned in the chapter on Indian architecture of the complementary duality of female and male, or *yin* and *yang*, which carries over as an artistic principle into architecture and landscape design. Chinese philosophy received its clearest articulation in the fifth century BCE through the lives and writings of two sages, Laotzu and Confucius. Laotzu's philosophy, Daoism, was mystical in approach, seeking harmony of human action and the world through the study of nature. Daoist philosophy is largely anti-rational and anti-authoritarian, as may be seen in the *I Ching*, or *Book of Changes*, an oracle text consulted in conjunction with the casting of coins to determine what part should be read for guidance

CHAPTER 4 THE TRADITIONAL ARCHITECTURE OF CHINA AND JAPAN

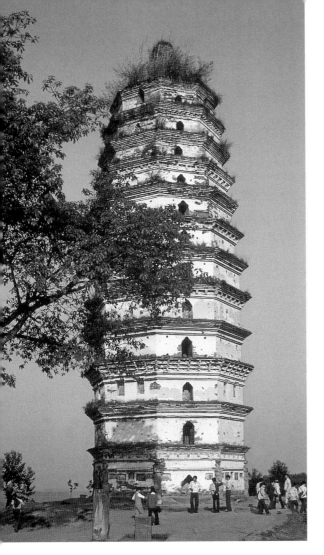

4.3 Pagoda, Dazu, 12th century.

The pagoda's overall design is ultimately based on the chatra or stylized bodhi tree set atop Indian stupas. The parabolic form of the entire pagoda here may owe something to the shikhara roofs of Hindu temples.

vines—as well as dwindled aspects of Hellenistic art, such as acanthus leaf foliage. Modern photographs cannot do justice to the original conception of these cave façades, as their appearance has been damaged by erosion over the centuries.

More widespread than the creation of cave temples was the practice of building Buddhist temple complexes with a hall for venerating images of the Buddha and a separate pagoda, or tower, erected over relics symbolic of the Buddha's presence. The pagoda was inspired by the parasol-like finials atop northern Indian stupas and by multi-storied watchtowers from Chinese military construction. (The word pagoda is derived from the Sanskrit word for stupa, *dagoba*.) As a religious structure, the pagoda became a graceful multi-story building with layered roofs. Early versions can be found as carved pillars inside

4.4 Fogong Temple, Yingxian, 1056.

Notice the axial alignment of elements from the entrance gate to the octagonal pagoda.

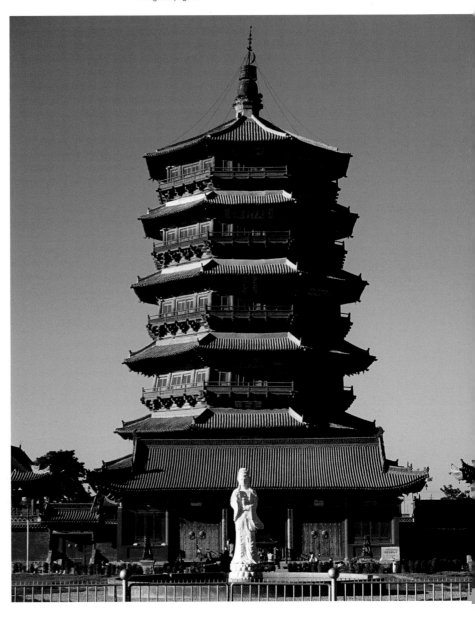

While Confucianism and Daoism are not religions in the Western sense of the term, they are philosophies that have influenced the way many people think. Buddhism would become the most widespread organized religion in China, transmitted to the country during the first or second centuries CE by merchant caravans moving along the Silk Roads across Central Asia, connecting China, Persia, and India. Architectural ideas accompanied Buddhist teachings, resulting in Chinese buildings that have roots in Indian practice. For example, the northern Indian cave temples around Gandhara, furnished with towering images of the Buddha, inspired similar cave temples with gigantic statues built in China as early as the fourth century CE. At Yungang (near Datong), over twenty large caves were cut into the steep sandstone cliffs during the fifth and sixth centuries. In their carved images and detailing, they exhibit artistic influences from India—elephants, lotus plants, scrolling

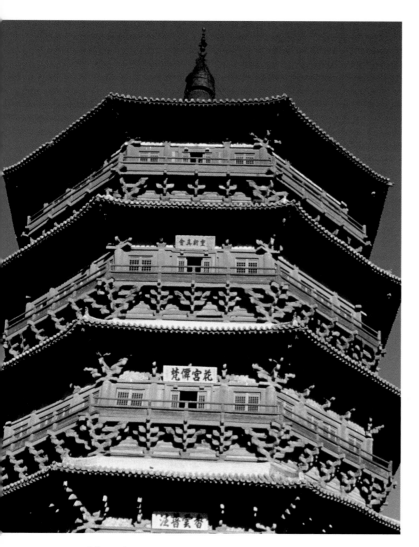

4.5 Pagoda, Fogong Temple, Yingxian, 1056.

Built entirely in wood, this massive pagoda is constructed in alternating layers of wood frame and horizontal log with cantilevers to create five roof and gallery levels.

balconies. On the exterior, these levels are expressed as intricately bracketed overhanging roofs and galleries that contrast with trabeated wall sections. The entire structure tapers slightly to the center, which contributes to stability and also gives the impression of greater height.

CHINESE ARCHITECTURAL PRINCIPLES

Although the earliest surviving Chinese buildings date only from the sixth century CE, there is archaeological and written evidence of older practices. Ceramic objects found in Han-Dynasty burials were cast in the form of houses or watchtowers, so preserving some indication of long-vanished timber structures. Wood was the primary material of early Chinese architecture, and it was used most often in post-and-beam construction. Roof structures were based on a series of beams set in parallel tiers, augmented over time by intricate bracketing for beam–column junctions and cantilevered overhangs. A modular unit called the **jian** (about ten by fifteen feet) was defined as the basic measure in construction (Fig. 4.6). More elaborate buildings contained additional jian, usually in odd numbers so that the distinction of a central bay was preserved, much as the even number of columns on Greek temples emphasized a space between the central pair. Since the structure was separate from the system of enclosure, Chinese buildings have a certain interior freedom in plan, as lightweight, non-load-bearing walls can be located in response to internal needs.

Except for the humblest single-jian houses, Chinese buildings tend to occur in ensembles organized around courtyards. Different functions are generally located in separate structures linked through connecting corridors or set in careful relation to common open spaces, rather than being contained under a common roof. From the exterior, there is little to distinguish buildings with different

cave temples. The pagoda's original purpose, to house relics and sacred writings, was expanded to make the structure itself into a vertical marker in the landscape (Fig. 4.3). Among the earliest freestanding examples is the 130-foot-tall Songyue Pagoda at Dengfeng, built in 523, the oldest surviving brick structure in the country. This is a tapering, twelve-sided, parabolic cylinder, hollow through the center, with fifteen tiers of roofs but without means of access to the top. The parabolic shape may have been inspired by shikhara roofs on Hindu temples, and the rounded finial shows close affinity to Indian stupa designs. The Longhua Pagoda in Shanghai (977) has a brick core and wooden perimeter galleries for viewing the landscape. The ends of the roof tiers cantilever outward and upward in a graceful fashion that was to become characteristic of Chinese roof profiles. At Yingxian, the Fogong Temple (1056) includes the oldest surviving pagoda constructed entirely in wood and one of the tallest wooden constructions in the world (Figs. 4.4–4.5). The 220-foot-tall octagonal building rises five levels in ten structural tiers, alternating upright posts with cantilevered roofs and

4.6 Diagram of a typical Chinese house.

The jian serves as the basic unit for wooden construction. Houses tend to be built with separate pavilions for different functions. This diagram shows the modular basis of the house presented in Fig. 4.16.

4.7b Elevation and section through the main hall, Nanchan Temple, Shaanxi, 782.

This shows details of the roof bracketing system. Note also the slight curvature given to the roof ridge and the wider spacing applied to the central intercolumniation, both of which give grace and liveliness to the structure.

4.7a Section and plan of Nanchan Temple, Shaanxi, 782.

Among the oldest surviving wooden buildings in China, the main hall of this temple is set on axis in the position of greatest importance, preceded by two courtyards and steps to change the level.

functions. Chinese architecture relies on axial arrangement, formal cues, and sequencing to establish dominance, for few buildings (aside from watchtowers and pagodas) are over one story tall. More important buildings are elevated on a podium and distinguished by greater size, central location, elaborate ornamentation and timber bracketing, hipped roofs, and symbolic color schemes (yellow and red), while ordinary buildings are smaller and have simpler framing, gable roofs, and somber (black, brown, and white) coloration. Axiality governs all compositions.

Both Confucian and Daoist principles are evident in Chinese attention to building placement. Orientation to the cardinal directions is common, with principal buildings tending to face south to take maximum advantage of the sun and prevailing winds. Buildings of secondary importance face east or west, shielded wherever possible by generous overhangs or vegetation. The approach axis extends from south to north, and a southern courtyard ensures that the most important rooms have ample exposure to light and air. This rather predictable arrangement

gives physical expression to Confucian ideals of hierarchy while also incorporating Daoist teachings regarding harmonious living with respect to natural forces. *Feng shui*, the Chinese art of adjusting the building to particular features of the individual site and its microclimate, is but a further elaboration of the Daoist principle that human actions should be in accord with the cosmos.

The earliest extant examples of wooden buildings are Buddhist temple halls on Wutai mountain in Shaanxi province. The main hall of Nanchan Temple, dated to 782, is a relatively modest structure of three bays, about thirty-eight by thirty-two feet overall, set in a south-facing courtyard with flanking structures (Figs. 4.7a,b). When the hall's doors are opened, the courtyard provides a space for worshipers to view from outside the statues housed inside the hall. Monks circumambulate around the altar and place offerings on the platform. The hall's central bay has extra width to emphasize its axial placement, and its roof has wide, flaring eaves, crowned by a ridge with curving, hooked ends. Essentially horizontal eave and ridge lines have been transformed into a subtle upward curve by the addition of extra eave rafters and layered bracketing, thereby creating a feeling of delicacy and lightness. Even the end columns are slightly inclined to the center of the hall. The tendency to build curves rather than perfectly straight elements is part of the optical refinement found in

4.8 Foguang Temple, Shaanxi, 857.

Here the landscape has been terraced to create a higher platform for the main hall, which as one might expect is set on axis in the position of greatest importance.

4.9 Main hall, Foguang Temple, Shaanxi, 857.

The broad eaves present an opportunity for the extensive brackets supporting the roof structure to be displayed.

all Chinese building. It might appropriately be compared to the use of entasis and optical corrections on Greek temples. Similar refinements are seen at Foguang Temple, constructed in 857 (Figs. 4.8–4.9). Its hillside site required terracing of the complex, so the main hall is elevated above the approaching courtyards. The front elevation is seven bays wide, with exceptionally deep overhanging eaves that cantilever over thirteen feet from the supporting column face. On the interior, the statues of the Buddha, bodhisattvas, guardian kings, and attendant figures are placed further back in the hall than was the case at Nanchan Temple in order to create more space for ceremonies. The use of a hip roof (in contrast to the gable roofs on subsidiary structures) indicates the importance of this hall.

Jinci, the Hall of the Sacred Mother, is a temple complex at Taiyuan, erected in 1023–32 to honor ancestors

4.18 Pavilion of the Moon Arriving and the Breeze Coming, the garden of the Master of the Fishing Nets, Suzhou, 18th century.

The irregular and picturesque have been carefully cultivated to create contrast, with rocks, water, and plants selected on Daoist principles.

setting that would foster the free exploration of thoughts and feelings in a state of meditation upon nature (Figs. 4.17–4.18). The formality that governed virtually all building design was never applied to landscape design, and the principles of yin and yang are extended to all elements. Yin encompassed not only the feminine, but also such items as the moon, night, earth, water, moisture, darkness, shadows, and plant materials that reflected these properties. Yang, by contrast, stood for items interpreted as having masculine traits: sunshine, fire, heat, brightness, solidity, and landscape materials with these properties. While some gardens, such as the famous ones in Suzhou, cover extensive tracts, even the smallest space could be made into a garden by the placement of unusually shaped rocks, a tree, sand, perhaps a water feature, and a few selected plants. Garden design became an art form rooted in the imitation of the scenic values of natural forms, exploiting properties inherent in the site. In larger gardens, the experience of the visitor was carefully sequenced and controlled through attention to paving textures, viewing points, framing devices (gates) for controlling vistas, and the like. Even though the whole garden was consciously designed, the aim was to have it appear as if it had grown wholly out of nature. Designing the landscape was a far more intellectual exercise than architectural design, so making gardens was considered a suitable pursuit for poets, philosophers, and men who had risen high in the civil service. Such wealthy and cultured individuals were responsible for the masterpiece at Suzhou.

JAPANESE TEMPLE ARCHITECTURE

Japan occupies an archipelago off the coast of Korea and China. It comprises four main islands and a thousand smaller ones scattered over nearly 800 miles. In prehistoric times, it was joined to the mainland by land bridges at various locations. Volcanic eruptions raised a chain of mountains, of which Mount Fuji is the most celebrated, that forms the spine of most of the islands; volcanoes and earthquakes associated with underlying plate tectonics

have been and continue to be sources of disturbances and at times disasters. Although archaeologists have identified four ethnic groups among the earliest settlers in the archipelago, these have long since merged to create a relatively homogeneous population that, like China, enjoyed lengthy governmental autonomy and minimal contact with other civilizations until the mid-nineteenth century. In matters of architecture, there was early influence from China, particularly associated with the importation of Buddhism, and there are also elements in common with Korea, which functioned as an intermediary between China and Japan during the early centuries CE.

Japan's native religion is Shinto (the way of the gods), which reveres natural forces essential to agriculture through rituals and celebrations at shrines. Although the religion was already well established when its oral traditions were first recorded early in the eighth century CE, there is evidence that its myths and practices were used to help forge previously disparate farming and fishing settlements into a united people; with the rise of a powerful central government modeled on that of Tang China, the ruling priest-king styled himself as emperor and claimed direct lineal descent from the sun goddess, Amaterasu. (As part of the settlement of World War II, this claim was renounced by Japan's emperor in 1945.) But, while Shinto was the official state religion, from the sixth century CE onward it was colored by Buddhism, and in practice the two religions grew to overlap considerably in the ensuing centuries.

BUDDHIST TEMPLES

The geographic spread of Japan's islands ensures that there is considerable diversity in their climates, from northern Hokkaido where snow and cold are features of long winters, to humid subtropical conditions on the southern islands. Wood has always been the primary building material, both because it was readily available and easy to work, and also because flexible wooden structures as built in Japan without significant diagonal bracing are more stable than masonry under earthquake conditions. Fire

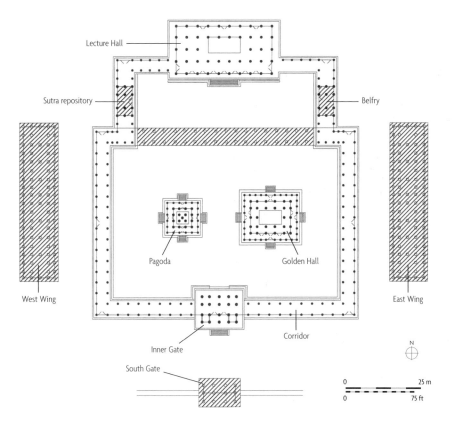

Lecture Hall

Sutra repository

Belfry

West Wing

Pagoda

Golden Hall

East Wing

Corridor

Inner Gate

South Gate

N

0   25 m
0   75 ft

4.19 Plan of Horyuji Temple, near Nara, 670–714.

Note that the composition does not follow strictly symmetrical principles, using instead a dynamic symmetry in which the verticality of the pagoda balances the lower and greater mass of the Kondo. The colonnades defining the perimeter wall were added later, and they incorporate previously freestanding pavilions for bells and sacred texts.

4.20 Horyuji Temple, near Nara, 670–714.

This shows the complex roof structure and eave brackets based on Chinese temple designs.

and natural deterioration have left few buildings extant from earlier than the eighth century, when the major architectural influence was that of China. Post-and-lintel building systems based on elaborately bracketed construction were used in the earliest surviving Buddhist temple, that of Horyuji near Nara (670–714) (Figs. 4.19–4.20). The temple buildings are set within a courtyard defined by a covered perimeter corridor and made accessible through an inner gateway (*Chumon*). Although the axiality one would expect from Chinese influence is there, the symmetry is now dynamic: a five-story pagoda on the left balances the so-called Golden Hall (*Kondo*), which is larger in plan but not as tall as the pagoda. Beyond these is the centrally placed assembly or lecture hall (*Kodo*), used for instructing monks associated with the temple. Small pavilions for housing the sutras, or sacred texts, and a bell, now incorporated into the corridor enclosure, were originally freestanding, as was the kodo, so the monastery as initially constructed had a simple rectangular enclosure wall. As in Chinese practice, the pagoda contained symbolic relics of the Buddha, while the Golden Hall was the repository for religious images. Horyuji's pagoda is constructed around a single wooden column that rises the full interior height of the building (Fig. 4.21), and the pagoda's gracefully flaring eaves are supported by cantilevered cloud-pattern bracket arms. There is no means for ascending to the upper levels, so the pagoda's architectural function is that of a vertical element in the overall composition.

A larger-scale elaboration of this scheme may be seen at the monastery of Todaiji, begun in 760 at Nara as part of a state-encouraged program to construct Buddhist monasteries in every province of the country, with this being the major temple in the capital. The monastery included two symmetrically placed, seven-story pagodas forward of the inner courtyard enclosing the Golden or Great Buddha Hall (*Daibutsuden*) and kodo, all three set on axis. Smaller structures for the monks' living quarters and dining hall flanked the kodo on three sides. The vast Great Buddha Hall housed a monumental gilt bronze statue, fifty-three feet high, of Vairocana, the Buddha of the Ideal World. The hall that survives today is a reconstruction from about 1700 at only two-thirds

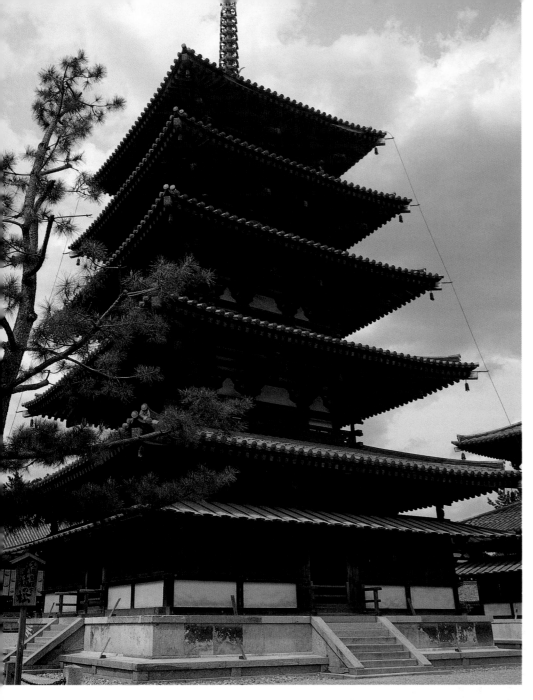

4.21 Pagoda, Horyuji Temple, near Nara, 670–714.

The slight upward curves of the eaves are far more pronounced in actuality than in the line drawing. A single wooden support extends from the base to the finial of the building.

4.22 Great South Gate, Todaiji, Nara, ca. 1200.

The roof structure of this building reflects influences from contemporary work in Song-Dynasty China. Eight layers of cantilevered brackets support the projecting eave of the lower roof, and another seven layers support the upper eave. Bracket ends have a distinctive reverse-curve profile typical of the Great Buddha style.

the size of the original, yet it is still counted among the largest wooden buildings in the world. In overall design and detail, the influence of Chinese temple design is evident. Todaiji was destroyed in 1180 and rebuilt in a manner paralleling that of Song-Dynasty China, which in Japan became known as the Great Buddha style, best exemplified in the Great South Gate completed in 1199 (Fig. 4.22). Here the eave brackets are directly set into the supporting columns that, in turn, are linked to each other by a succession of tie beams extending as tenons through the centers of the posts. Inside, there is no ceiling and thus the entire roof structure is visible, showing how short rafters radiate at the corners to create the cantilevered overhang. Main posts rise to the full height of the structure where, at the peak, a series of so-called rainbow beams with frog-leg struts are stacked to support the ridge.

Pure Land Buddhism arose during the tenth century from an esoteric sect that sought an ideal world (the Pure Land) through devotion to Amida Buddha, the Lord of the

Western Paradise. The movement attracted pious and wealthy nobles, who erected halls on their estates to house an image of Amida, and increasingly these halls sought to capture the magnificence of paradise through elaborate and richly finished architecture. Such was the case with the Phoenix Hall (Hoodo) of the Byodoin, located at Uji (just south of Kyoto), constructed in 1053 by the Fujiwara family as part of the transformation of an existing villa into a family temple (page 86). The plan and massing of the building were inspired by the phoenix, a mythical bird that rises from the ashes of destruction. This was an apt image, for many believed that the year 1052 had marked the beginning of an era of spiritual decline, when hope for escape from the cycle of birth and rebirth was lost. Only Amida was thought to have powers sufficient to save humanity, so this period was a particularly fruitful one for constructing Amida halls.

The Phoenix Hall's plan is symmetrical, consisting of a central hall with open L-shaped wings stretching from either side and a covered corridor attached to the rear like a tail. In elevation, the roof planes and bracketing system create the feeling of upward lift, as if to capture the sensation of flight. The central hall appears to be two stories tall because of its double roof layers, but in fact it is a single high space designed to provide an impressive setting for a gilded wooden statue of Amida, over nine feet tall, seated on a lotus throne in front of a golden mandorla frame and under an elaborately carved wooden canopy (Fig. 4.23). The wooden structure is painted red with golden accents, set off by white infill panels, a color scheme that parallels Chinese practice. The side wings are two story, terminating in gable-roof pavilions and capped by turrets at the corners of the L shape. Viewed across the reflecting pond onto which the hall fronts, the golden image set amid this graceful and delicate architecture conveys the feeling of rising to that perfect paradise to which its patrons aspired.

SHINTO SHRINES

In contrast to the elaborate Chinese-inspired Buddhist temple designs stand the Shinto shrines, typically small in scale and modest in architectural character. The most celebrated is the Ise Shrine at Uji-Yamada, which has been precisely rebuilt at twenty-year intervals since its founding in 690 CE, thus preserving its earliest form with reasonable exactitude, although scholars concede there have been some minor changes over time. Ise actually consists of two shrines set about four miles apart: the Outer Shrine (Geku) dedicated to Toyouke, goddess of agriculture and the earth, and the Inner Shrine (Naiku) dedicated to Amaterasu, goddess of the sun (Figs. 4.24–4.26). As both the sun and the earth were necessary for agricultural prosperity, this union of opposites was in keeping with concepts of harmony and balance. The layout for each shrine is similar: four concentric sets of fences surround the shrine, each entered through a gateway (**torii**), and the buildings are symmetrically disposed around a central axis. At the heart is the main sanctuary, flanked by east and west treasure houses. Subsidiary buildings contain a kitchen and hall of offerings, used by the priests to prepare the daily offering of food for presentation to the deity. White stones cover the courtyard in which the shrine buildings are set, and the tranquillity and emptiness of the site are not disturbed by visitors, who remain outside the fenced enclosure. Immediately adjacent to the shrine is a cleared area, identical in size, which is the site for the next rebuilding.

Many historians see in the Ise shrine buildings the very essence of Japanese architecture. Here, building traditions were preserved and ideas were germinated that would be explored elsewhere in later periods. The architecture probably evolved from vernacular designs for granaries, extraordinary buildings that were raised on posts to protect their contents from damp and vermin. In agricultural cultures, it is not uncommon to find more care lavished on the construction of granaries than houses, for the

4.23 Interior of the Phoenix Hall, Uji, 1053.

This shows the Buddha sitting on a lotus flower in the lake of paradise. The sumptuous materials and intricate detail of carved and gilded figures were used in pious anticipation of a better world to come.

4.24 (left) Inner Ise Shrine, Uji-Yamada, 690 CE–present.

In this view of the fence and treasure-house roofs, archaic forms of wooden construction are employed in all the buildings. Here one can see the chigi, or crossed-gable end rafters, and katsuogi, short horizontal wooden logs set on top of the ridge.

4.25 (middle, left) Elevations and plans of Main Inner Ise Shrine, or Shoden, Uji-Yamada, 690 CE–present.

The simple elegance of the proportions and materials used for these buildings has come to represent the quintessence of Japanese architecture.

4.26 (below) Inner Ise Shrine, Uji-Yamada, 690 CE–present.

The shrine is part of a large complex beside the Isuzu river containing accommodation for pilgrims and priests. The shrine itself is constructed anew every twenty years on adjacent rectangular sites (lower right), where the central post under the main building is retained from the previous rebuilding.

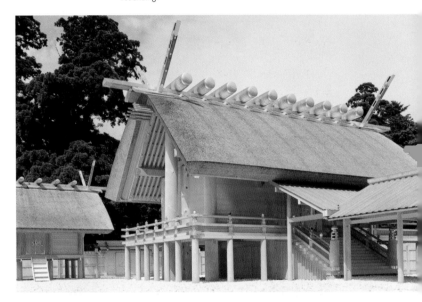

0   10 m

0   30 ft

community's survival depends on stored grain and sufficient seed to plant the fields in the following year. Raised-floor structures were also characteristic of early imperial palaces, another association that was appropriate to a shrine honoring the imperial ancestor. Ise refines this building type to a high art form, creating gabled-roof structures with elegant yet simple detailing.

At the Inner Shrine, the main sanctuary or *shoden* is raised over a vertical post that supports the heart of the shrine: a boat-shaped chest containing a mirror emblematic of the sun goddess and of the imperial family, who claimed descent from her. (This central post is all that remains on the site when the shrine is rebuilt on the adjacent plot of land. Covered and protected by a diminutive roof, it awaits the next cycle of construction, when it will again be the center of the sanctuary.) Only the emperor is allowed to enter the innermost shrine building. The cypress wood of which the shrine is constructed is left unpainted, although the exposed surfaces are finished with a great deal of refinement. Metal ornaments applied to the exterior reflect influence from Tang-Dynasty China. The weight of the roof rests on the shrine's exterior board walls, which over the years will settle and contract so that

the posts and beams touch and thus assume a share of the structural load. Rafter extensions (**chigi**) at the gable ends recall the form of earlier bamboo structures, where rafter ends would cross after being lashed together. Horizontal elements (**katsuogi**) originally set atop the ridge as weights to keep the thatch roof from blowing off in storms became decorative elements whose number signaled the importance of the building. Thus features that originated as practical reflections of construction necessities became highly refined expressions of simplicity, with enormous care being taken over even the smallest detail. This characteristic continues in most traditional Japanese architecture. Through ritual dismantling and re-creation, Ise represents continuity yet remains ever new.

JAPANESE CITIES, HOUSES, AND CASTLES

There is a long tradition of orthogonal city planning in Japan. From about 650 CE onward, planned capital cities that organized buildings were built surrounding the imperial palace. As there was a tradition of building a new palace at the commencement of each emperor's reign in

order to obtain the ritual purity of a fresh location, there was a succession of new foundations, most of which followed patterns similar to that of the Chinese capital of Chang'an. Many of these capitals were set in the Nara basin (between the modern cities of Kyoto and Osaka). Such was the case with Heijo, "Capital of the Peaceful Citadel," established in 710 and occupied until 784. Its plan shared the orientation and orthogonal layout of Chang'an, with the imperial palace at the center of the northern side. A regular grid of streets subdivided the city into square blocks, each named to identify its location relative to the main axis and distance from the palace, much as Cartesian coordinates on a mathematical grid describe precise locations of points in space. Allocation of building lots within the blocks followed court protocols: the higher-ranking officials received larger lots located closer to the imperial compound, some being so large that they encompassed several blocks. Important temples also occupied multiple block sites. The major exception to this regular layout was an eastern extension, known as the outer capital, and a small expansion of three half-blocks along the northwestern boundary. Population estimates place Heijo's maximum population at about 200,000. As soon as the city ceased to be the capital, the land gradually returned to agricultural use.

4.27 Plan of the Heian capital (now Kyoto), ca. 794.

Here one can see influence from Chinese city planning, maintaining similar orientation, grids of blocks, and placement of the palace compound to those found at Chang'an and Beijing.

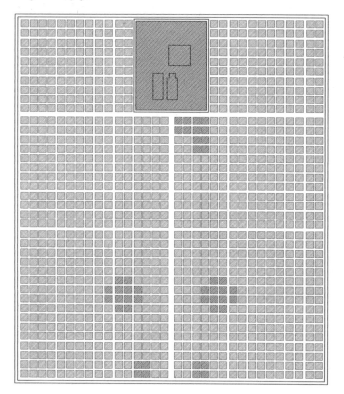

To the north of Heijo, the Heian capital, "Capital of Peace and Tranquillity," was founded in 794 and used until the seat of government was transferred to Tokyo in 1868 (Fig. 4.27). It too had a grid plan, this one perfectly regular with uniformly sized blocks about 400 feet on a side. The grand axial avenue was over 100 feet wide, and it led straight to the imperial palace. Secondary streets were of course narrower, and the lanes subdividing the square blocks into sixteen plots were smaller still. The Heian capital has never ceased to be an urban place. Today it is Kyoto, a city rich in temples and other cultural monuments from the millennium when it was the national capital. Elements of its original plan were lost over the centuries as surrounding development did not maintain the grid layout, and even the Imperial Palace, subject to frequent fires, did not remain in its original location. From the twelfth century onward this palace was increasingly used only for state occasions, with actual living quarters being set in a mansion elsewhere in town. The Imperial Palace surviving today in Kyoto is still used for ceremonies when the country installs a new emperor.

Houses within the capital and other Japanese cities were built of impermanent materials. As a result of frequent fires and natural decay, none has survived to the present. Contemporary scroll paintings capture images of urban life that show streets lined with one-story row houses, often with shops along the street frontage, as commerce was an important adjunct to governmental activity. The construction is simple, with wooden posts resting on foundation stones supporting a plank gabled roof. Floors were of earth, although most houses may have had a raised wooden floor in at least one room. Enclosing walls were of wattle and daub or other lightweight screening, with curtains hanging over entrance doors to provide a sense of privacy. Windows facing the street were set above eye level to admit light but prohibit people looking inside. A small garden might be located behind the house.

Mansions of the wealthy had much in common with Chinese houses. Commonly occupying an entire city block, they were oriented to the south, with an axial main hall (*shinden*) facing a courtyard and flanked by side halls, although conditions particular to each site most often did not permit absolute symmetry of all parts. Perimeter walls ensured privacy from the street, and the buildings might well be complemented by a pond and extensive landscaping.

Traditional building techniques and materials that have long since vanished from urban locations have survived in houses in the countryside. Japan has an unusually rich array of **minka** (wooden folk houses) that collectively illustrate regional diversity as well as the pre-modern living conditions of ordinary people (Figs. 4.28–4.30). In many cases, minka sheltered animals as well as people, with barn or stabling areas connected to the living quarters. In its simplest form, the living space consisted of two areas, an earth-floor section around a central hearth, the

Veranda

Guest room

Anteroom

Vestibule

Sitting room

Veranda

Storeroom

Formal living room

Large living room

Wooden platform

Earthen floor area

Hearth

Storage

0   10 m
⊕N
0   30 ft

4.28 Plan of the Yoshimura House, near Osaka ca. 1620.

Minka were divided into two parts, an earth-floored section (shaded in this drawing) where animals were kept and cooking was done, and the raised-floor living area, covered in modular tatami.

4.29 (right) Interior of a traditional house, Japan, 19th century.

This view shows sliding walls and the raised-floor section covered with tatami. Shelves and storage units hold household equipment, and furniture is minimal by Western standards.

4.30 (below) Traditional house (minka), Japan, probably 19th century.

This minka has a thatched gable roof with a large turret rising above the ridge to provide additional light and air for the interior. Such roofs are characteristic of minka found in the Yamanashi Prefecture, to the west of Tokyo.

chief source of heat and the center of food preparation, and a living section with raised wooden flooring to protect from ground damp. High roofs of thatch, bark, split bamboo, or wooden shingles were desirable to cast off rain and handle snow (in the north), and gable peak vents permitted smoke from the hearth to escape. Minka are generally modular in their structure, and the dimensions of **tatami** (rice-straw woven floor mats roughly three by six feet) determined room proportions and sizes. Elaborations of the basic scheme introduced secondary living/dining areas, guest rooms, and sleeping rooms that could be partitioned by lightweight screens. Although minka seldom have the formal symmetry that characterizes Chinese houses, they have the same flexibility in plan. The typical Japanese house had little furniture. Floor cushions were used for seating, and mattresses for sleeping were rolled out of the way during the day, so rooms could be adapted easily to serve multiple functions. The beauty of these houses lies in their simplicity, careful attention to detail, and the artistry that appears when a feature is made of the natural irregularities of the building materials. It is no wonder that Western architects as diverse as Frank Lloyd Wright and Mies van der Rohe have found

inspiration in the forms and details of traditional Japanese architecture.

Japanese architecture and art often reflect qualities of composure and repose, terms that do not really describe medieval Japanese history. As the imperial family was relatively weak in the thirteenth through seventeenth centuries, feudal warlords competed for control over the country, and the incessant warfare contributed to the construction of a remarkable series of castles, twelve of which survive from the late sixteenth and seventeenth centuries. Based on earlier fortifications that are no longer extant, these castles are unusual in that they were built to accommodate and resist firearms that had been introduced by Portuguese traders in the course of the sixteenth century. The castle at Himeji (1609) is the most spectacular (Figs. 4.31–4.32). Dubbed the Egret's Castle, it shared a number of defensive features with medieval masonry castles in

4.32 Approach to Egret's Castle, Himeji, 1609.

Stone foundations support wooden upper stories of this castle, built on a high point in the landscape. The approach route is protected by battered stone walls and defensive positions with square openings for cannons.

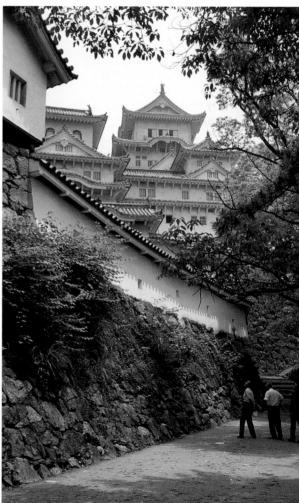

4.31 Plan of Egret's Castle, Himeji, 1609.

This is one of the great surviving medieval wooden castles. Its defenses include a moat and massive stone foundations, but the superstructure is wood covered with thick layers of plaster.

Europe: a strategic location on a promontory, massive foundations for the central donjon, heavily fortified gateways, and walled enclosures protected by moats. What set Japanese castles apart from fortifications elsewhere was their reliance on timber as the primary structural material. Foundations and the lower courses of walls were stone, but the bulk of the superstructure was wood. In all cases, the wooden structure was made more fire-resistant with sand and pebbles before receiving a thick layer of plaster.

The castle at Himeji is composed of three concentric layers of walls and moats, enclosing residential areas in the outer layer, quarters for court retainers in the second ring, and the main donjon and its three subsidiary towers at the center. Within this central section, a maze of passages connects the strongholds to confuse intruders. At intervals, there are overhanging galleries from which rocks or other materials could be dropped on the heads of those below. Walls are supplied with archer's slits and loopholes for firing weapons, and projecting turrets were used for surveillance. The donjon itself is framed into two massive staves that extend from basement to the roof six floors above. An internal courtyard provides light and air to rooms that would otherwise be dismal, for openings to the outside are minimal. The openings become larger in the upper stories, and there is a residential aspect to the fortress interior that is somewhat unexpected in a fortification designed to resist siege. The castle's exterior presents an impressive aspect, with stacked roofs, multiple dormers, and superimposed gables. Like its European counterparts, the Egret's Castle was meant to dominate the surrounding countryside for which it served as the administrative center.

ZEN BUDDHIST ARCHITECTURE: KATSURA

Zen Buddhism, which developed in China and spread to Japan in the twelfth century, gave its name to a style of Japanese architecture that was based on examples from Song-Dynasty China. The essence of Zen is enlightenment through meditation, achieved by discarding conventional modes of thought through methods that can approach the irrational. In medieval Japan, Zen grew in popularity to become the form of Buddhism most practiced by the upper classes, and as such it came to influence all aspects of cultured life, including architecture. The Jizodo of Shofukuji (1404) is the oldest dated Zen temple in Japan, and may be used to illustrate architectural features typical of the style. As with the Great Buddha style, the wooden columns are pierced by horizontal tie beams, but the roof construction differs considerably in that it uses a double or "hidden" structure that presents one pitch and profile on the interior and eave overhang, and a different, steeper one on the exterior. The gentler pitch of the eaves contributes a sense of horizontality to the building. Supports for the external roof were concealed by the ceiling, thereby

giving the appellation "hidden" to the structure. This form of roof construction is distinctively Japanese, having no parallel in China. The layout of Zen monasteries also came to have distinctive characteristics: their bilateral symmetry and predictable placement of structures for different functions reflected in physical form the mental discipline expected of the monks.

For many later Buddhist structures, little distinction was made between sacred and secular architecture. The Katsura Imperial Villa in Kyoto provides a splendid example of a country retreat based on elements from older mansions of the nobility that also embodies concepts from the Zen tradition (Fig. 4.33). Built in stages from about 1616 to 1660 by three generations of the princely Hachijonomiya family, the villa was intended for occasional occupancy as a place for reflection, relaxation, creative works, and contemplation of nature. Katsura's plan is irregular, even sprawling, but all interior spaces are governed by the tatami module (Fig. 4.34). Japanese cedar wood (*hinoki*) is employed for the structural frame, with wooden doors or white paper-covered partitions forming the exterior walls. As at the Ise Shrine, the wood is left unfinished, and it has weathered to a dark chestnut to gray color, depending on exposure to light and weather. The rather somber architecture of the villa itself is complemented by the artistic layout of extensive gardens around a meandering lake. Sliding partitions and doors permit rooms to change dimensions and open up to the natural world in varying ways (Fig. 4.35). Exterior decks become

---

4.33 Katsura Imperial Villa, Kyoto, ca. 1616–1660.

Built as a retreat for contemplation rather than as a permanent residence, this villa presents a series of spaces that can change as partitions are opened or closed, thus blurring the distinction between inside and outside.

Main gate

Gepparo
tea house

Entrance

Moon viewing
platform

Old Shoin

Middle Shoin

New Shoin

N

0   100 m
0   300 ft

0   25 m
0   75 ft

4.34 Plan of Katsura Imperial Villa, Kyoto, ca. 1616–1660.

This shows how the rambling plan is governed throughout by the dimensions of tatami. Terraces and open porches provide opportunities to view the landscape, and link interior spaces with the world outside.

4.35 Interior of the Gepparo tea house, Katsura Imperial Villa, Kyoto, ca. 1616–1660.

Sliding partitions and rice-paper panels have been opened to reveal views to the villa's garden.

4.36 Tea house, Katsura Imperial Villa, Kyoto, ca. 1616–1660.

The tea house is set in a Zen-inspired landscape visually isolated from the villa itself. The tea-house design emphasizes natural materials and controlled views within and without the structure.

extensions of the interior and frame views of the landscape; one serves as a platform for viewing the moon over the lake.

Nestled in the grounds are five tea houses, separate pavilions for practicing the Japanese art of the tea ceremony. Tea as a beverage originated in China, but a succession of Japanese tea masters, including Sen-no-Rikyu (1521–91) transformed informal tea-taking into a spiritual ritual symbolizing detached perfection in the Zen tradition. The ceremony involved with the making and drinking of tea, at once complex and simple, was performed in small structures that are seldom symmetrical or regular but that were constructed expressly to incorporate the qualities of harmony, reverence, purity, and silence that are the very essence of the ritual. Tea houses are usually set, as at Katsura, in isolation from other buildings, and are approached by a path that enables the visitor to view the pavilion only at the last possible moment (Fig. 4.36).

Rustic elements, such as wooden supports with the bark still attached or a wooden element of irregular shape, can be incorporated into the tea house as an extension of the natural world, for the tea ceremony aims at fusing the spiritual and the natural. Terms such as reticent, eloquent, and restrained have been used to describe these buildings. Entrance to the tea house may come through an exceptionally low door, deliberately designed so that one must almost crawl to get in. Shoes are left outside; participants sit on thick tatami and drink from exquisitely shaped vessels obviously crafted by hand. Views are carefully calculated. Windows are at eye level when one is seated, and artfully selected treasures are displayed in an alcove (**tokonoma**) with a raised floor. As the tea master serves the guests, there is time to contemplate the subtle juxtapositions of texture, material, and surface that comprise the room's interior, for the designers have imparted their reverence for materials and spatial harmony, which are intended to promote reflection that will achieve inward simplicity and tranquillity of mind. The refinements of tea-house architecture encapsulate the essence of Japanese traditional design, in which architectural principles seen in the early Shinto shrines are merged with the esthetics and philosophy of Zen Buddhism.

CHAPTER 5

THE ROMAN WORLD

During the first millennium BCE, while Greek civilization originated and flourished on the mainland and around the eastern Mediterranean, an enigmatic people, the Etruscans, were settling and developing their own culture in the area of north-central Italy now known as Tuscany. The origins of the Etruscans are not precisely understood; they are thought to have migrated onto the Italian peninsula from Asia Minor ca. 1200 BCE, after the collapse of Hittite power. From surviving inscriptions, art, artifacts, and architecture, it seems that the Etruscans drew on diverse roots. Greece during its early and Classical eras was a particularly strong influence, but there were other cultural connections as well. The Etruscans' language contained both Indo-European and non-Indo-European elements and was written in a script derived directly from Greek; their religion, which placed great emphasis on providing worldly goods for the afterlife, had much in common with that of Egypt. With that of the Hittites their art shares relief carvings of protective beasts at tomb entrances, and with the art of the Minoans and Mycenaeans naturalistic decorations depicting birds and dolphins. The Etruscan practice of reading omens from the entrails of animals follows that of Babylonia and Assyria, and their use of the arch and vault in monumental gateways indicates links with the architecture of Asia Minor. Even though they assimilated much from their neighbors, the Etruscans were an original people whose accomplishments left distinctive imprints on Roman civilization.

Pont du Gard, Nîmes, 20–16 BCE.

The water channel (aqueduct) is at the uppermost level, where it maintained a constant incline to carry the water through gravity flow into the city of Nîmes. Aqueducts ran along the contours of the land whenever possible, but when a valley had to be crossed, as here, Roman engineers used arches to span the gap. This aqueduct has long been severed, so the Pont du Gard no longer carries water. Projecting stones and inset holes were used for bracing the wooden centering or scaffolds needed to erect the arches, and they were left in the finished work in case repairs were ever required.

ETRUSCAN IMPRINTS

Our understanding of the Etruscans is limited by the dearth of records. Funerary inscriptions comprise the bulk of surviving written documentation, and although these can be deciphered with reasonable accuracy, they tell us little about the language or Etruscan society and how it functioned. Etruscan settlements appear to have been loosely organized into autonomous city-states rather like those in Mesopotamia and Greece, and their economy was based on agriculture and international trade, especially in metals: tin was imported from Britain, silver from Spain, and iron and copper were widely available. Etruscan culture was well established by the eighth century BCE and grew in influence for the next 200 years to encompass the area from the river Po in northern Italy to the region around Pompeii, south of Rome. One of their cities, Marzabotto near Bologna, had a grid plan, with the main streets running perpendicular to one another and intersecting in the center of town (Fig. 5.1). The Romans, who would use similar plans for their military camps (**castra**), labeled the main north–south street the **cardo** and the east–west route the **decumanus**. The orthogonal plan may have owed something to colonial Greek cities, known through trade.

It seems clear that the Etruscans borrowed the orders of architecture and the temple form from Greece, modifying both to suit their own purposes. Greek temples generally had a continuous colonnade surrounding the sanctuary at the center, with entrances on both gabled ends. In contrast, Etruscan temples typically contained a tripartite cella oriented in only one direction, generally to the south (Fig. 5.2). The temple was set on a high podium, covered with a gable roof, and approached through a double row of columns set at the top of a single flight of stairs. The intricate refinement of the Doric and Ionic was forsaken for a greatly simplified original order, the Tuscan, which had the basic characteristics of the Doric but no fluting on the column shafts or sculpture on the frieze. Intercolumnar spacing on Etruscan temples was markedly wider, the roof pitch considerably lower, and the eave overhang greater

5.1 Plan of Marzabotto, ca. 2nd century.

This plan shows a grid of blocks. Excavations of building foundations are shown in some areas. The acropolis is on the northwestern corner of the site, while the river Reno runs along the southern edge.

5.2 Drawing of an Etruscan temple, based on descriptions by Vitruvius.

Compare this to the plans of Greek temples, (see Figs. 2.14a,b,c) Note that the colonnades extend only across the front to create a portico, while the cella has been expanded to several chambers set the full width of the temple. The freestanding building of the Greeks, meant to be viewed on all sides, has been transformed into an axially disposed design suitable for an urban setting.

than on Greek temples, creating a broadly horizontal emphasis. Both the columns and roof structure were built of wood, while the walls were unbaked brick. Terracotta was employed for roofing tiles, pediment ornamentation, and sculpture.

Because of the impermanence of their materials, no Etruscan temples survive, although literary and archaeological sources provide adequate evidence of their form and terracotta elements preserve decorative features. Architectural remains are scarce, and much of what is known about residential designs has been deduced from tomb architecture and funerary urns made in the shape of miniature dwellings. Tomb excavations at Cerveteri provide clues about upper-class housing. The rooms, hollowed out of easily carved volcanic rock (tufa), are entered through a vestibule and grouped around an inner court, which suggests an atrium. In some tombs, the architectural features of doors, roof beams, and moldings have been reproduced, and furnishings, such as chairs, cooking utensils, and other household items, are likewise carved in stone.

At Perugia, which was the Etruscan city of Perusia, there still exists a monumental gateway (the so-called Arch of Augustus) illustrating Etruscan influence, although it dates from after the fall of Perugia to the Romans in 310 BCE (Fig. 5.3). Above the double row of voussoirs forming the gateway arch is a decorative motif consisting of metopes and triglyphs similar to a Doric frieze. Circular shields fill the spaces of the metopes, and the triglyphs are actually short fluted pilasters with volutes at the top. A relieving arch flanked by Ionic pilasters is set atop the band of Doric-inspired ornament. In borrowing from the Greeks, the Etruscans have used elements of the orders with originality, if not with understanding. Later the Romans would forge a coherent and powerful architectural style of their own by employing the arch and vault for structure and using the orders to articulate and enliven the intervening sections of wall.

The Etruscans, together with native Italian peoples, the Latins and the Sabines, inhabited the hills that rose above the marshlands on either side of the river Tiber. Etruscan builders began to drain the marshes by digging the trench that later became the Cloaca Maxima, the major sewer of ancient Rome. According to legend, the city of Rome was founded on these hills in 753 BCE by Romulus, and it was ruled from 616 to 510 BCE by members of the Etruscan royal house, the Tarquins. In about 500 BCE, the Latins overthrew the Tarquins and established the Roman republic. The expulsion of Etruscan rulers from Rome did not signal their complete disappearance from Italy, however; other Etruscan city-states to the north continued to thrive even as Roman authority was growing. From 396 to 88 BCE Roman forces gradually incorporated these northern settlements, but not before many aspects of their culture had merged into Roman life. Etruscan art and architecture influenced Roman work, and Etruscan customs, such as

5.3 "Arch of Augustus," Perugia, after 310 BCE.
The lower portions were constructed by the Etruscans. The Romans later exploited the structural possibilities of the semicircular arch in their buildings.

chariot racing and bloody gladiatorial contests, were also popular in Roman society.

ROMAN ARCHITECTURE

The beginning of Roman civilization was contemporary with that of the Greeks, the Etruscans, and the later Egyptian dynasties. Unlike all of these other cultures, however, Rome continued to grow in importance as the first millennium BCE waned, reaching its apogee in the first and second centuries CE. In time Rome absorbed the Etruscans, Greeks, Egyptians, and many lesser peoples and formed an empire with a remarkably homogeneous architectural style. Roman building practices, like Roman culture, were derived from many sources, especially Etruscan and Greek, but the forms of their architecture were in many respects original.

Above all, the Romans were practical builders. They constructed durable roads and bridges across the length and breadth of their empire, they brought clean water into cities through a series of aqueducts, and they carried away waste water in underground sewers. They also created impressive buildings, making extensive use of the decorative orders (most notably the Corinthian and its more elaborate version, the Composite) on temples and other public structures, and constructed some of the most awe-inspiring interior spaces in the Western world. The Romans used their technical skills in building to provide comfort. They invented underfloor central heating for houses in colder climates, and they built large heated baths for public use in all their cities. They also enjoyed public amusements and spectacles, and their architects developed amphitheaters and stadiums to accommodate crowds for athletic events, gladiatorial contests, and pageants. The Romans built much and they built well, so that a surprising amount of their work survives in whole or in part for modern study.

We are aided in our understanding of Roman construction (and sometimes slightly amused) by a contemporary work, *The Ten Books of Architecture*, composed in the late first century BCE by Marcus Vitruvius Pollio, commonly known as Vitruvius. As literature, his book is not a masterpiece. Like many architects since, Vitruvius was not particularly skilled in the use of words, and the precise meaning of some of his writing is difficult to ascertain. Based in part on Greek originals, his work was doubtless not the only one of its kind, but it is the only intact treatise on architecture we have from antiquity, and as such it has been consulted carefully by architects from the Renaissance to the present seeking to understand the principles of Roman design. Among the topics Vitruvius covers are building design, city planning, military engineering, and the design of machines, which indicates that architects dealt with a much wider array of problems in design and construction then than they do now. His opening comments on the education of the architect are worth reading:

> *The architect should be equipped with knowledge of many branches of study and varied kinds of learning, for it is by his judgment that all work done by the other arts is put to the test. This knowledge is the child of practice and theory. Practice is the continuous and regular exercise of employment where manual work is done with any necessary material according to the design of a drawing. Theory, on the other hand, is the ability to demonstrate and explain the productions of dexterity on the principles of proportion. It follows, therefore, that architects who have aimed at acquiring manual skill without scholarship have never been able to reach a position of authority to correspond with their pains, while those who relied only upon theories and scholarship were obviously hunting the shadow, not the substance. But those who have a thorough knowledge of both, like men armed at all points, have sooner attained their object and carried authority with them.*

BUILDING TECHNIQUES AND MATERIALS

The imposing quality of Roman construction is a result of applying engineering skills to the problems encountered in everyday life. Roman construction exploited structures built in compression: the arch, the vault, and the dome, techniques developed by other civilizations but used in a very limited fashion. In Roman hands, however, these became the basis for hitherto unimagined structures on a scale not possible with post-and-lintel construction.

A true arch consists of wedge-shaped stones (called voussoirs) set in a curved shape, often a semicircle. Building one requires a temporary timber formwork, or centering, to support the voussoirs as they are laid, for the arch will not stand on its own until all the voussoirs, including the central keystone, are set in place. (Contrast this to the technique of corbeling, where each course rests on the preceding one. No centering is required, for the structure is always stable, but the form produced is not a true arch.) If the arch is continued along its longitudinal axis, it produces a structure known as a **vault**; if the arch is rotated on its center, it produces a **dome**. By using arches, vaults, and domes, the Romans could enclose large areas with modestly sized stones cut carefully to shape. The space between supports, necessarily limited when stone lintels are used because stone in tension tends to crack over wide spans, could now be made much larger because vaulted construction carries the structural load primarily in compression, for which stone is well suited. There is a price for this

5.4 "Temple of Diana," Nimes, ca. 80 CE.

This is a fine example of barrel-vaulted masonry construction used to enclose space. Note the use of alternating triangular and segmental arched pediments to articulate the wall.

stability. The weight of the masonry in vaulted construction pushes downward and outward on the walls or columns on which it rests, and this overturning force or thrust must be countered by massive supports. Vaulted construction thus requires walls or piers that are much thicker than those used in post-and-lintel buildings.

The earliest Roman vaults were built for utilitarian structures. Mention has already been made of the Cloaca Maxima, the trench begun by the Etruscans to drain the Roman marshes. By the mid-first century BCE, it was vaulted with stone, and the construction still functions as one of the main sewers of Rome. Discharging wastes into the Tiber, however, made the river water unfit for human consumption, so clean water was brought from rivers or springs in the Sabine Hills beyond Rome, piped in a gravity-fed system of aqueducts to city reservoirs, then distributed to fountains or other uses around the city. As much as possible, the water channel or aqueduct followed the contour of the land, but where it had to cross valleys, it became necessary to elevate the conduit above the land to preserve the constant slope of the supply line. The Romans erected handsome arched structures for this purpose. They completed the Aqua Appia in 312 BCE and constructed three more aqueducts in the second half of the second century BCE to provide water for the growing population of Rome. They added the impressive Aqua Claudia in 38 CE to bring water from Tivoli, some forty-five miles away. The aqueduct's great masonry arches, some more than 100 feet high, extended over the countryside for much of that distance.

Perhaps the most spectacular surviving aqueduct span is the Pont du Gard (20–16 BCE) outside Nîmes in southern France (page 110). Made of unmortared masonry (*opus quadratum*), the aqueduct strides 882 feet over the valley of the river Gard on three tiers of arches, carrying the water channel 160 feet above the level of the river. Its design is remarkably straightforward: the two lowest arch levels are identical rows of semicircular arches, sixty feet in diameter except for the span across the river, which is eighty feet. The uppermost tier has arches set on twenty-foot centers, so that a unifying rhythm ties all three levels together. Projecting stones used for support of the centering and scaffolding add surface texture, and they were retained in case repairs were ever needed. Enclosed above the highest arches is the water channel, about six feet square in section, lined with mortar to prevent leaks. A roadway is carried above the lowest row of arches.

In Nîmes itself, the so-called Temple of Diana (ca. 80 CE) uses barrel vaults to cover interior space (Fig. 5.4). The interior volume was covered by a series of semicircular arches supporting intermediate arched stones to create the barrel vault with transverse bands. A thousand years later Romanesque church builders would revive this roofing system. The temple is interesting too for its blind windows, used as articulation for the interior wall. Since the masonry vault rests equally on all points of the wall,

openings for actual windows were not cut. The blind openings are detailed with alternating segmental and triangular pediments, a treatment that would be revived during the Renaissance. There is speculation that, rather than a temple, this building was used as a library, with the blind openings containing wooden cabinets used for storage of scrolls.

Relatively little of Roman vaulted construction is made in ashlar or cut-stone masonry, however, for the technique was costly and required skilled workmen. The efficient Romans developed a more expedient building method by using a new material, hydraulic cement, derived from volcanic deposits first discovered around Puteoli (Pozzuoli) and named *pozzolana*. Vitruvius noted it as "a kind of natural powder which from natural causes produces astonishing results." What the Romans discovered was that when pozzolana was mixed with lime, rubble, and water, the mixture reacts chemically and hardens to a stone-like consistency, even if under water. The simple lime mortars known to the ancients had some bonding strength, but they were ineffective for the bridge and harbor foundations where Roman builders first exploited the superior strength of pozzolana. (The geologic process that results in natural cements, which are found at other volcanic sites aside from Puteoli, is the basis for the present-day manufacturing method for cement.)

The Romans also found uses for this artificial stone away from the water, and during the third century BCE they gained experience in building with concrete. They placed a liquid mass composed of pozzolana, sand, water, and lime in horizontal courses over rough-laid rubble, which served both as aggregate in the wall and as an enclosure or formwork for the concrete. The mixture solidified into a monolithic material that behaved like solid masonry. Curves and irregular shapes were of course much easier to achieve in concrete than in cut-stone work, but the resulting walls were generally not handsome, so the Romans became adept at nonstructural wall finishes such as stucco, mosaic, and marble veneer.

Because most Roman buildings have lost their finish surfaces, one can see the underlying wall construction today in a way that Roman builders never intended. Early concrete walls were composed of rough stones surrounding a concrete core (*opus incertum*), a technique later refined to squared stones (*opus reticulatum*) which gave a more orderly exterior face. In imperial times (after 37 BCE) the Romans increasingly used bricks as the concrete facing/aggregate (*opus testaceum*), laying their thin triangular shapes to present a smooth exterior and an irregular inner face for maximum bonding surface with the soupy cement mixture. (Stamps impressed on the wet bricks in the factory have enabled archaeologists to date many Roman structures with reasonable precision.) After the second century CE concrete walls with stone rubble striped by horizontal courses of brick bonding every three or four feet (*opus listatum*) became common, the brick courses also serving as a leveling device to keep the work plumb and true. The strength, durability, and economy of concrete construction gave the Romans a versatile material for large-scale building, and by the middle of the first century CE they were using it with rapidly increasing architectural sophistication.

CITY PLANNING

City planning practices in ancient Greece and in Rome had striking parallels. Both Athens and Rome, the cultural centers, grew without preconceived overall plans, while the colonial cities established by each were generally provided with orthogonal plans. Greek foundations might become Roman settlements later, as was the case with Pompeii, one of the best-preserved examples of a Roman provincial town owing to its burial in the eruption of Mount Vesuvius in 79 CE. The fabric of the city, already

shaken by an earthquake in 62 CE, was engulfed by ash, lava, and mud that preserved it until excavations begun in 1748 brought the remains to light.

Pompeii was founded by the Greeks in the sixth century BCE, and it was briefly inhabited by the Etruscans and Samnites before becoming a Roman city. At the time of its destruction, it had a population of about 20,000, including great patrician families, middle-class merchants, retired persons, and slaves. Its irregular grid plan covered about 160 acres within roughly oval town walls (Fig. 5.5). The Roman civic center or *forum* was located in the southwest quarter, near the Marine Gate entrance. The earlier Greek center was two blocks to the east, on an acropolis

5.5a Plan of the forum, Pompeii, founded 6th century BCE.

The various buildings flanking the open space were unified with colonnades. When Vesuvius last erupted in 79 CE, the city was still being rebuilt after suffering earthquake damage in 64 CE.

Arch

Temple of Jupiter, or Capitolium

Latrines

Vegetable market

Temple of Apollo

Basilica

Macellum

Lararium

Temple of Vespasian

Eumachia building

Comitium

City government offices

5.5b Plan of Pompeii, founded 6th century BCE.

This city dates back to a Greek colonial settlement, later occupied by the Etruscans and Samnites. During the Roman period, Pompeii was greatly enlarged to the outlines seen here. The forum is the major civic space in the original settlement, while recreational facilities are located in the southeast corner.

with a Doric temple and a columned portico dating from the second or third century BCE. Streets ran approximately parallel and perpendicular to the forum, their pattern being adjusted to the varying topography.

Public facilities were dispersed around the town. Within the town walls, there were three baths, a large exercise facility (the **palaestra**) with a swimming pool, covered and open-air theaters, and an amphitheater capable of seating the entire population. Nine temples dedicated to various gods—Greek divinities, Roman deities, deceased Roman emperors, patrons of the city, and the oriental mystery cults of Isis and Bacchus—indicate the diversity of religious beliefs in Pompeii. Cemeteries were located outside the town gates.

The Forum in Pompeii was the focus of public life (Fig. 5.6). A two-story colonnade surrounded its rectangular form, 510 by 125 feet, on three sides, the open fourth (north) side being occupied by the Capitolium, the center for state-sponsored religious observances. A triumphal arch marked the north entrance and prevented wheeled vehicles from intruding on the pedestrian domain. Buildings of various designs and uses flanked the forum. On the east side were the macellum, the meat and fish market; the lararium, a temple for the patron gods of the city; the eumachia building, containing guild offices and shops of the cloth workers and dyers; and the comitium, an open area where elections were held. The short southern side contained three halls used for government: offices for judges, public works officials, and the council chamber.

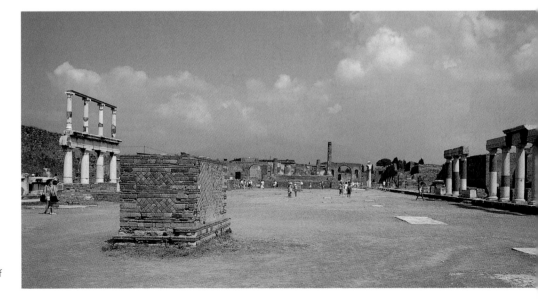

5.6 The forum, Pompeii, founded 6th century BCE.

Remains of the colonnades show the brick used in their construction, which was then covered with a veneer of marble, creating the effect of magnificence at a fraction of the expense associated with using solid marble.

Cardo

Arch

Market of Sertius

Senate House

Capitolium

South baths

Library

East baths

Decumanus

Forum

Basilica

Theater

5.7 Plan of Timgad, founded ca. 100 CE.

This is generally cited as the textbook example of a Roman city because of the great regularity of its plan. It is in fact orthogonal to a degree seldom found in Roman colonial cities.

On the west side, bordered by the road from the Marine Gate, was the large basilica where public assemblies for legal, commercial, and social purposes were held. It functioned much as the stoa in the Athenian Agora did, yet the space here was introverted and enclosed rather than being outwardly oriented, as at Athens. Beyond the basilica were the Temple of Apollo, which dated from the earliest period of Pompeii; the vegetable market, one of the last buildings constructed on the forum; and public lavatories. The use of colonnades linking most of the buildings gave the forum architectural consistency (see Figs. 5.6 and 5.13). Conveying unity within such a diverse grouping of buildings constructed over three or more centuries is no insignificant accomplishment, and it indicates the high quality of Roman design attained in provincial centers.

Some Roman cities began as military garrisons (castra) located in unsettled areas as a means of defense and of bringing civilization to new territories. For these, and for many colonial cities as well, the Romans had a standard plan, perhaps derived from the Etruscans and applied with consistency throughout their empire, from Britain to North Africa, Italy, and the eastern Mediterranean. This basic plan was rectangular or square, with two main roads, the cardo and the decumanus, crossing at right angles in the center of town. A wall surrounded the encampment, and the public spaces—the forum and military headquarters—were usually located at the intersection in the center of town. Residential sectors were laid out in square or rectangular blocks, with land reserved for neighborhood markets and recreational facilities as the town grew. Streets could be numbered sequentially so that a stranger in town could find any given address easily. Large public buildings, such as baths and theaters, served the whole community and were located according to topography.

This standard Roman plan underlies many present-day European cities, including Florence, Bologna, Cirencester, and Trier. Timgad in Algeria is an original example that has not been overbuilt by a modern city, so its major features can be seen even though it is now a ruin (Fig. 5.7). Timgad was founded by Trajan in 100 CE for veterans of the Roman legions and became a thriving regional center until it was destroyed by native tribes in the seventh century. The city walls enclosed a square, with the cardo and decumanus intersecting in the center of town. The forum is to the south, and a large theater was set just south of the forum. (Because of the theater's placement, the cardo did not continue through the forum.) Entrances into the city were framed by triumphal arches, and continuous colonnades lined the major streets to lend dignity and shelter to the sidewalks. Timgad had a population of perhaps 15,000 within a century of its founding, and in the third century CE it began to accumulate suburban developments along the approach roads to the north, west, and south. Large baths were built north and south of the walls, and markets and temples further served the expanding population outside the walls. None of the extramural growth conformed to the grid plan of the city proper.

Trajan is also remembered for the substantial contributions he made to the urban fabric of Rome itself. Civic life in Rome focused on the Forum Romanum at the base of the Capitoline Hill in an area drained by the Cloaca Maxima (Fig. 5.8). Here the functions of commerce, government, law, and religion mingled, and with the growth of the city, the space became increasingly congested. From the middle of the first century BCE onward, the area expanded as new colonnaded forums were constructed adjacent to the existing fabric (Fig. 5.9). Julius Caesar laid

5.8 View of the Forum Romanum, Rome.

This forum was largely transformed during the reign of Augustus (37 BCE–14 CE) to become a splendid civic center for Rome. Visible here (left to right) are three columns from the Temple of Vespasian, the Arch of Septimus Severus (203 CE), columns from the Temple of Saturn, and rows of columns from the Basilica Julia.

5.9 Plan of the imperial fora, Rome, with the great Forum of Trajan, 1st century CE.

Of this vast project, only the markets and Trajan's Column (located between the two library buildings) have survived.

5.10 Axonometric drawing of Trajan's markets, Rome, 100–14 CE.

The markets are built into the hillside in a series of shops that form a semicircle. Further up the hill is the vaulted market hall.

for Latin texts; the column's continuous frieze would have been readable from these neighboring buildings. At the terminus of the axis, in the center of a curving colonnaded courtyard, was a temple dedicated to Trajan and his wife by the later emperor Hadrian.

Needed commercial space adjacent to the forum was carved out of the Quirinale hillside behind the northeast hemicycle. The buildings of Trajan's markets, a good part of which are extant, were set in a multi-story semicircle with adjoining buildings, reflecting the hemicycle of the forum below and becoming an arcaded complement to it (Figs. 5.10–5.11). The markets contained over 150 shops, offices, and a groin-vaulted market hall (Fig. 5.12), all of which could be reached from the forum and from streets on two higher levels. They were built of brick-faced concrete, a contrast to the marble and elaborate ornament of the forum. Durable barrel vaults provided the basic structural module both for the individual shops and for enclosed walkways between them. Trajan's forum and the markets show at once the monumentality of great civic constructions and the ingenious adaptation of geometric forms to a fundamentally utilitarian project.

5.11 Trajan's markets, Rome, 100–14 CE.

This view shows the great semicircle that completed one side of the principal cross-axis of the forum.

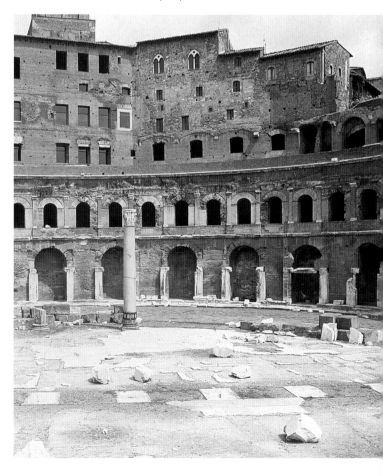

out a forum containing a temple and governmental chambers; Augustus constructed a forum at right angles to the Forum of Caesar to surround the Temple of Mars Ultor; and Vespasian built a forum around a library. The culmination of these constructions was the Forum of Trajan (ca. 100–14 CE), equal in size to all the others put together and built to the designs of Apollodorus of Damascus, who had served with distinction as a military engineer. The site was north of the Forum of Augustus, where a ridge connecting the Capitoline and Quirinale hills was removed to provide a level area and improve access to all the fora from the north. Trajan's forum was symmetrically planned, with a monumental entranceway from the Forum of Augustus leading into the forum proper, a court 330 by 375 feet defined by double colonnades and semicircular elements (**hemicycles**) set on a cross-axis. Dominating the center of the court was a large equestrian statue of Trajan. Opposite the entrance was the Basilica Ulpia, a magnificent judicial building with entrances placed on its long side. Beyond the basilica was Trajan's Column, a marble shaft nearly 100 feet high set on a fifteen-foot-high base and carved with a spiraling narrative relief illustrating Trajan's victories in the Dacian Wars. Spoils from the Dacian campaign (in the region of present-day Romania) were used to finance the forum's construction. Trajan's Column, the sole surviving structure in this part of the forum, was flanked by two library buildings, one for Greek and one

5.12 Covered market hall built by Trajan, Rome, ca. 100 CE.

Constructed in concrete, this is an early example of a groin-vaulted space with clerestory lighting. It shows the care extended by Roman builders to civic structures accommodating such mundane activities as a fruit and vegetable market.

5.13 Triumphal arch, Pompeii, before 79 CE.

Monuments such as these were the pride of the city, reflecting civic virtues and boldly marking entrances to important sites. In this case, the arch also restricted access of wheeled vehicles into the forum.

5.14 The Arch of Constantine, Rome, 315 CE.

This triple-arched form, became an architectural motif for later buildings. Compare the abbey gatehouse at Lorsch (see Fig. 8.4) and the west front of S. Andrea in Mantua (see Fig. 11.17) for examples of later works inspired by this design.

We have noted the presence of triumphal arches in both Pompeii (Fig. 5.13) and Timgad. These freestanding monuments were generally built to commemorate a military victory, and they added grandeur to the public realm by serving as reminders of civic greatness. (The Arc du Triomphe in Paris, erected in the nineteenth century, was constructed in this same tradition, but on a scale greater than that of comparable Roman works.) Of surviving arches, those in Rome are the most elaborate. The Arch of Septimus Severus (203 CE) still stands in the Forum Romanum, while the larger Arch of Constantine (finished 315 CE) stands near the Colosseum (Fig. 5.14). Both are triple-arched structures, the central arch being larger than the side arches, and the attic story (above the arch) is embellished with carved relief panels depicting the particular military victory for which the arch was constructed. Constantine's Arch incorporates panels from earlier monuments. As an architectural motif, the triumphal arch will have a long afterlife, being revived in Carolingian, Romanesque, Renaissance, and later works.

THE ENGINEERING MIGHT OF THE ROMANS

by Dan MacGilvray

It now remains for us to speak of stones, or, in other words, the leading folly of the day . . . as to the mountains, nature has made those for herself, as a kind of bulwark for keeping together the bowels of the earth; as also for the prupose of curbing the violence of the rivers, of breaking the waves of the sea, and so, by opposing to them the very hardest of her materials, putting a check upon those elements which are never at rest. And yet we must hew down these mountains and carry them off . . . for no other reason than to gratify our luxurious inclinations . . .

These very mountains are cut asunder to yield us a thousand different *marbles, promontories are thrown open to the sea, and the face of nature is being everywhere reduced. . . . We now carry away the barriers that were destined for the separation of one nation from another; we construct ships for the transport of our marbles; and amid the waves . . . we convey the summits of the mountains to and fro: a thing, however, that is even less unpardonable than to . . . search amid the regions of the clouds for vessels with which to cool our draughts, and to excavate rocks, towering to the very heavens, in order that we* *may have the satisfaction of drinking from ice!*[1]

5A Altar from Claudian period, 1st century CE. Villa Medici, Rome.

In these two paragraphs from his *Natural History*, Pliny neatly exposes both the arrogance and the capabilities of the Roman civilization. As opposed to the aesthetically sensitive Greeks, the Romans were the mighty engineers of the ancient world, conquering not only all the peoples and nations of the Mediterranean, but subduing the sea itself and even the mountains that surround it.

Not since the Egyptians had architects and constructors had the routine capability of choosing building materials for their projects that came from great distances. Ancient buildings had always reflected the local geology: the sun-dried brick walls and vaults of Babylon were built of mud scooped from the Euphrates flood plain, the gleaming white Parthenon was constructed of marble from nearby Mount Pentelikos. Even the proud Egyptians were limited to materials found within the 600-mile-long watershed of the Nile below the first cataract—limestone for the pyramids came from the Giza plateau or Tura, across the river; sandstone for the temples at Luxor and Karnak was quarried at Silsileh, a few miles conveniently upstream. Only when they required the toughest of all stones, granite, for a 100-foot obelisk or to line the pharaoh's chamber in the Great Pyramid, were the Egyptians called upon to move their stones great distances.

In contrast, Roman architects routinely constructed concrete walls and vaults using pozzolana, a natural cement mined near Naples, and the emperors adorned their temples, palaces, and baths with a polychrome profusion of thin marble veneers and graceful columns: pure white from Carrara overlooking the Lingurian Sea above Pisa, or the island of Proconeseus in the Sea of Marmara; *giallo antico* (antique yellow) from Tunisia; *verde antico* (green) from Greece; onion-skinned *cipolino* from the Aegean isles; purple porphyry, rose and gray granite from Egypt. Romans outdid Egyptians by pulling down the great obelisks from their temple fronts, moving them on specially constructed ships over 1500 miles across the Mediterranean, and re-erecting them in the circuses, villas, and gardens of Rome (Fig. 5A). In the process they seem to have offended not only the Egyptian gods but also Pliny, who comments on Roman "folly" and environmental arrogance.

Just as the ancient Romans indelibly marked the mountains with their quarries, Rome today still displays some of its ancient arrogance (and capabilities) as granite obelisks, marble veneers, and slender columns have been relocated to adorn the temples of the Catholic Church.

---

1 Plinius Secundus, C. (the Elder Pliny), *The Natural History of Pliny, Vol. VI,* translated by John Bostock and H.T. Riley (London: Henry G. Bohn, 1862), p. 305. Pliny is referring to quartz as the material that gives the "satisfaction of drinking from ice."

TEMPLES

Discussion of the Roman fora has indicated the locations of temples, which the Romans built largely on the basis of Greek and Etruscan precedents. Generally speaking, the Romans did not build temples as isolated structures as had the Greeks, but as axially approached buildings in an urban setting, like the temples of the Etruscans. The placement of the Capitolium in the forum at Pompeii and the Temple of Mars Ultor in the Forum of Augustus in Rome was essentially the same, and the temple designs were similar. Both were raised on podiums, so that a flight of steps led up to the colonnaded portico of the cella space.

As the Capitolium and the Temple of Mars Ultor are largely destroyed, smaller Roman temples that have survived more completely provide us with a better image of temple architecture. In Rome the second-century BCE Temple of Fortuna Virilis (Fig. 5.15) superficially resembles an Ionic Greek temple. However, a closer look at the side and rear elevations reveals that the columns are engaged with the cella wall and not freestanding. Expanding the cella to the limits of the surrounding colonnade provides a larger interior space and reinforces the axiality of the whole. This same theme is seen at the Maison Carrée at Nîmes (ca. 10 CE), where the order is Corinthian rather than Ionic and the scale is larger, but the same

5.15 Temple of Fortuna Virilis, Rome, 2nd century BCE.

An early example of a Roman temple, which uses the orders (here, the Ionic) as one might expect from the Greek example, but the building was oriented to an axis in the manner of the Etruscans.

5.16 Maison Carrée, Nimes, ca. 10 CE.

This exceptionally well-preserved Roman temple in the Corinthian order is a larger version of themes already seen in the Temple of Fortuna Virilis.

essential qualities remain (Fig. 5.16). (Thomas Jefferson would later model his scheme for the Virginia State Capitol in Richmond on the Maison Carrée.)

Not all Roman temples were rectangular. The Greeks had built circular tholoi, and the Romans applied the circular ground plan to temples. One of the most striking is the Temple of the Sibyl (ca. 25 BCE) in Tivoli. Set on a promontory, it seems to reflect Greek precedent in both its design and siting. It is, however, distinctly Roman. The approach is axial, via a flight of stairs; the cella wall is constructed of concrete instead of marble blocks; and the ornamental frieze of the Corinthian order has Roman swags and ox skulls. Near the Temple of Fortuna Virilis in Rome is the so-called Temple of Vesta (a temple dedicated to Hercules), a circular-plan temple of the first century BCE that is similar to but slightly larger than the Tivoli example. Later modifica-tions have changed the roof and destroyed the original entablature.

5.17 Pantheon, Rome, ca. 125 CE.

This greatest of Hadrianic architectural projects has become one of the most influential works in Western history, the inspiration for virtually every subsequent domed building. The exterior is imposing, while the interior is overwhelming.

The greatest circular-plan Roman temple is the Pantheon in Rome (118–28 CE), considered by many to be the most influential building in Western architectural history (Fig. 5.17). Its size, the boldness of its design, and the technical accomplishment of its construction combine to make it a memorable work. Dedicated to seven planetary deities, the Pantheon was constructed in the reign of the emperor Hadrian, who is reputed to have been its architect. The entrance is an enormous portico with

5.18 Giovanni Paolo Panini, *The Interior of the Pantheon*, ca. 1740. Oil on canvas, 4ft. 2½in. x 3ft. 3in. (1.28 x .99m.). National Gallery of Art, Washington, DC.

The interior could contain a sphere 142 feet 6 inches in diameter, as the circular plan is surmounted by a hemispherical dome whose height equals the diameter of the circle. Trabeated articulation of the wall belies the actual structure of arches and vaults that sustains the great dome. Concrete is the primary structural material, faced with marble veneers.

emphasizes the depth of both the ceiling coffers and the eight niches below. As one stands in the center of the Pantheon, the building creates the feeling that the space extends beyond the cylindrical drum and that the dome is much higher than its actual dimension.

The conceptual simplicity of the Pantheon's dome-on-drum design should not be mistaken for constructional simplicity (Fig. 5.19). What looks like trabeated construction is in fact a structure based on arches and vaults. Behind the orderly interior columns, veneers, and coffers lies a technical masterpiece, a testament to Roman skill in building with concrete. The immense structural load of the dome is distributed to concrete foundations fifteen feet thick and thirty-four feet wide through drum walls that are up to twenty feet deep. Most of the constructional complexity is not visible on the interior. The first two rings of coffering conceal eight great relieving arches that work with a second set, likewise hidden, to concentrate loads on the wall sections between the niches of the ground story. Even these sections are not solid, but are hollowed by chambers, accessible from the exterior, to equalize contraction of the concrete as it hardened and lessen the dead weight bearing on the foundations, all this without compromising the stability of the whole. Aggregate in the concrete mix is progressively lightened, from heavy basalt in the foundations to sponge-like volcanic rock (tufa) in the oculus ring.

5.19 Axonometric section of the Pantheon, Rome, 118–28 CE.

This view shows part of the plan and the arched construction behind the internal marble veneers. Although none of this is visible on the interior, the exterior wall of the drum does show some of the arches that conform to the actual structure.

twenty Corinthian columns that originally supported bronze roof trusses (since removed). This portico is rather awkwardly joined to the circular cella, a space 142 feet and six inches in diameter and 142 feet high. The bottom half of the cella is a cylinder on which rests a hemispherical dome, with a circular opening or **oculus**, twenty-seven feet in diameter at the top to let in light and air (Fig. 5.18). The contrast of the interior to the exterior is breathtaking, even to modern senses, and it has inspired visitors ever since it was completed. Unlike other pagan temples in Rome, the Pantheon was converted to Christian use and never pillaged for its marble facings, so it remains the Roman building closest to its original state.

The cylindrical cella wall is visually divided into two stories, a ground-level Corinthian order of fluted columns and pilasters supporting an attic story with rectangular openings resembling windows set in a patterned marble wall. The lower story is varied by niches, alternately semicircular and rectangular, set at quarter and eighth points around the circumference. Articulation in the dome is accomplished by five tiers of diminishing square coffers, designed with exaggerated perspective to enhance the sense of depth. The light pouring in from the oculus

5.20 Temple of Venus, Baalbek, Bekka Valley, Lebanon, 3rd century CE.

Although a ruin, this small late Roman temple shows a free geometric interpretation of the circular temple theme. Both the plinth and cornice swing in measured curves.

portico was wider than the cella, and the outermost columns on either side continued in a semicircle around the cella wall. The circular plan of the cella, truncated at the entrance, was crowned by a shallow dome built in stone. Its modest size—twenty-five feet in diameter—does not pose structural problems as extensive as those of the Pantheon, and the outward thrust of the dome is countered by a horizontally arched entablature supported on the external colonnade. Within the width of the cella wall are external niches (**exedrae**) that parallel the curved entablature above and the podium below. Both sets of concave curves respond to the convex shape of the cella interior in a manner suggestive of much later developments in seventeenth-century Italian Baroque work. Although the formal similarity is strong, there is no evidence that Baroque architects knew of the Temple of Venus, so it seems to be a case of similar results being arrived at through independent developments.

PUBLIC BUILDINGS

The Romans developed a number of public buildings for specialized functions: the basilica, a large assembly hall used for law courts; the baths, a many-chambered building containing bathing and recreational facilities; and the theater, which was based on the Greek prototype but made into a freestanding structure and enlarged to become an amphitheater for spectacular entertainment. Each of these building types posed spatial and constructional challenges, and each left its imprint on subsequent architectural developments.

BASILICAS

The basilica on the southwest corner of the forum at Pompeii has already been noted. Dated to ca. 100 BCE, it is the oldest known Roman basilica, though it was probably not the first. While legal activities were its main function, it doubtless also served as a gathering place for social and commercial functions, as did the colonnades of the Greek stoas. In Greek, the word *basilica* literally means king's hall. Rather than surrounding the exterior as in a stoa, the basilica's colonnades define the interior aisles and enclose the central space or nave, as is consistent with the Roman emphasis on internal space. Entrance to the basilica at Pompeii was primarily from the short side adjacent to the governmental offices, but there were lesser entrances on both long sides. Set in a rectangular area in front of the end wall opposite the entrance was the tribunal seat of honor, terminating the longitudinal axis established by the colonnades. The stucco-finished brick columns separating the nave from the aisles on either side probably once supported a wooden gabled roof.

Trajan's Forum in Rome contained the more extensive Basilica Ulpia, which measured 200 by 400 feet excluding

Virtually every domed building constructed since Roman times makes reference to the Pantheon. Sometimes its influence is very obvious, as in Jefferson's design for the Library at the University of Virginia (see Fig. 14.18), and at other times the connection is less apparent, as in Brunelleschi's dome for Florence Cathedral (see Fig. 11.3). Literally hundreds of domed museums, universities, banks, churches, and railroad stations, to mention only some of the building types, may be found that are ultimately connected to this masterpiece from the time of Hadrian.

Another interesting circular-plan Roman temple is the Temple of Venus at Baalbek in the Bekka Valley of Lebanon (Fig. 5.20). Baalbek was a regional religious center before the arrival of the Romans, and under Roman leadership the existing sanctuary was dramatically expanded with some exceptionally large temples dedicated to Jupiter Heliopolitanus and Bacchus. In comparison to these, the Temple of Venus, dated to the third century CE, is small indeed, but its highly original form illustrates well the ornate theatrical qualities of late Roman work. As with the Pantheon, the temple had a pedimented porch preceding the circular cella, but here the

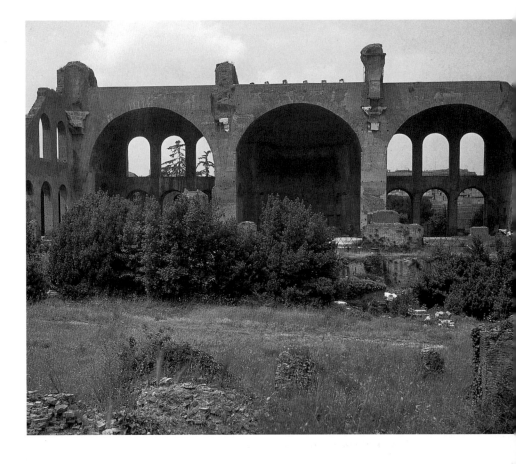

5.21 Plan of the Basilica Nova (Basilica of Constantine), Rome, 307–15 CE.

This large vaulted building had groin vaults across the nave and transverse barrel vaults in the aisles. Illumination was provided by large clerestory windows above the aisles.

5.22 Basilica Nova, Rome, 307–15 CE.

Although the nave vaults have collapsed, the vaulted aisles remain, stripped of their marble finishes, to give an impression of the noble spaces once contained in this building.

the curved end sections (**apses**). Here the entrances were placed on the long façade because the basilica completes one side of the forum. On the interior, double colonnades created two aisles on either side of the nave, and there were triple colonnades across the short sides in front of the semicircular apses there. Architectural restoration drawings show the interior with second-floor galleries over the aisles and clerestory windows illuminating the nave. As at Pompeii, a gabled timber roof covered the building. Luxurious materials, financed by tribute money from Dacia, were employed in the construction: marble on floors and walls, bronze gilding suspended from the roof trusses on the coffered ceiling, and Egyptian granite for the columns. Impressive size, rich finishes, and dramatic lighting combined here to create a setting fit for the dispensation of imperial justice. Of all this magnificence only rude fragments remain, but the basilica form would become the basis for Early Christian church designs.

Not all basilicas were timber-roofed. The Basilica Nova (also known as the Basilica of Maxentius and Constantine) in Rome, dated 307–15 CE, had three great groin vaults over its nave, buttressed by three barrel-vaulted bays comprising each side aisle (Figs. 5.21–5.22). The large size of each aisle bay creates a strong response to the corresponding aisle across the nave, thereby creating a spatial unit at right angles to the axis of the nave. From the straightforward linearity of Pompeii, the basilica form has been manipulated into one of dynamic complexity, with cross-axial interplay between aisles and nave.

PUBLIC BATHS

The interior of the Basilica Nova owed much to the greatest vaulted Roman buildings, the baths. As the name implies, Roman baths (**thermae**) were primarily hygienic facilities, but they also provided for exercise, relaxation, and informal socializing, activities more commonly associated with modern spas or health clubs than with bathrooms. Excavations at Pompeii have revealed three bath complexes within four blocks of the forum. The Romans actually cleaned the body without soap by first anointing with oil and then scraping the skin with spoon-like implements. Bathers induced perspiration in hot steam rooms (rather like Finnish saunas) and then cooled down and relaxed in a sequence of temperate and cool plunges. They might extend their time at the baths by swimming, taking walks, enjoying conversation, or reading in the baths' library.

Such an array of activities required multiple spaces: changing rooms, latrines, rooms for hot, warm, and cold baths; exercise facilities, relaxing areas, and gardens if possible. Adequate water supplies were essential. The Romans used mineral springs when available (Bath in England was one such Roman establishment) and heated the water if

Open-air swimming pool

Frigidarium

Tepidarium

Caldarium

Peristyle

Gymnasium

stadium or theater seats

0   250 m

0   750 ft

5.23 Plan of the Baths of Diocletian, Rome, 298–306 CE.

The large bath building was set within a walled enclosure and provided with landscaped grounds used for exercising, athletic games, or restful walks.

5.24 Remains of the Baths of Diocletian, Rome, 298–306 CE.

The central section of the frigidarium survived and was converted into a church, S. Maria degli Angeli, by Michelangelo. Note the groin vaults and the clerestory windows.

Men's entrance

Furnaces and cistern

Women's entrance

Shop

Shop

Shop

Shop

Stairs to inn on 2nd floor

Shop

Caldarium

Shop

Frigidarium

Shop

Basin for cold baths

Changing

Shop

Tepidarium

Caldarium

Men's entrance

Changing room

Shop

Tepidarium

Shop

Portico

Service court

Shop

Gymnasium
garden

N

Men's entrance

0   20 m

0   60 ft

5.25 Forum Baths, Pompeii, ca. 80 BCE.

This is a small facility with separate but unequal sections for
men and women. A common service area (dark shading) was
used for heating water. Shops occupy most of the street
frontage, since there was no need for an impressive street
presence. See Fig. 5.5b for location within the city.

the supply was not naturally warm. Because bathing was a
healthful diversion for the large urban population, the
later emperors vied with one another to build ever more
elaborate complexes in Rome.

The Baths of Diocletian (298–306 CE) comprised the
largest bath complex in ancient Rome, covering about fifty
acres of land and said to have the capacity for 3000 people
(Fig. 5.23). The entire complex was symmetrically
designed, with the principal sequence of rooms within the
bath building placed on an axis. From the center of the
south façade, these included the groin-vaulted hot baths
(**caldarium**), domed warm baths (**tepidarium**), cruciform
cool baths (**frigidarium**), and open-air swimming pool
(*natatio*). On either side of this central suite of spaces were
oval-plan changing rooms and unroofed rectangular exercise courts surrounded by ancillary service rooms, the use
of which cannot be completely identified. *En suite* rooms
on the south side may have constituted a sequence of dry
steam rooms leading up to the caldarium. Interiors were
finished with sumptuous materials, marble veneers and
mosaics; statues were placed both inside and out; and the
grounds were landscaped with trees and gardens to create
a congenial environment for exercise, conversation, and
relaxation. A large *exedra* in the south exterior wall was
fitted with tiered seats for use as a theatre or stadium. Rectangular rooms to either side may have contained
libraries. Of this vast structure, only parts survive. In 1561,

Michelangelo converted the frigidarium into the Church
of S. Maria degli Angeli (Fig. 5.24), where the interior
reflects the scale and some of the splendor of the Roman
original. One corner rotunda has been transformed into
the Church of S. Bernardo, and a trace of the great southern *exedra* has been preserved in the nineteenth-century
Piazza dell'Esedra near the present railroad station.

The Baths of Diocletian were exceptionally large, even
by the standards of imperial times. Of ancient Rome's over
950 baths listed in a mid-fourth-century inventory, only a
handful were this grand. One can appreciate the more
common baths designs by looking at buildings that
remain in provincial cities, such as the Forum Baths at
Pompeii (Fig. 5.25), Paris (where the Cluny Museum
incorporates part of a third-century CE baths), or Leptis
Magna on the North African coast, where the so-called
Hunting Baths (late second or early third century CE) are
exceptionally well preserved.

THEATERS AND AMPHITHEATERS

Athletic competitions and dramatic performances were
part of the culture of ancient Greece. The Romans, who
inherited these traditions and added to them the gladiatorial combats of the Etruscans, needed theaters and stadiums in which to stage these events. Greek building
practice was to carve the shape of theaters or stadiums out
of hillsides, thus adapting the natural setting for human
use, but the Romans chose to construct their facilities
whether the terrain was favorable or not, so they developed great vaulted structures to create the slope needed for
spectator seating. An early result of this process was the
Theater of Marcellus (completed 13–11 BCE) in Rome
(Figs. 5.26a,b), where a great semicircle of 11,000 seats

5.26a Perspective section through the Theater of Marcellus, Rome, 11–13 BCE.

This view shows the ramps and stairs needed to allow patrons to reach their seats. The lower two stories have survived, reworked as housing, while the upper wooden tier has vanished.

5.26b Plan of the Theater of Marcellus, Rome, 13–11 BCE.

Roman theaters were based on designs already perfected by the Greeks. The difference here is that support for the seats depends not on a convenient hillside but rather on a supporting vaulted structure of cut stone and concrete.

0   50 m
0   150 ft

5.27 The amphitheater, Pompeii, ca. 80 BCE.

This oval-shaped arena was used for the gladiatorial contests of which the Romans were exceedingly fond. Part of its seating is supported on arched construction and part is built into rising ground.

rising in three tiers focused on a rectangular stage building that formed the backdrop for the drama. (This theater had the same capacity as the Greek theater at Epidauros.) Enough of the original construction has survived reuse, first as a medieval fortress and then as a Renaissance palace, to permit reasonable understanding of the structural ingenuity underlying the plan. Stacked radial barrel vaults made of cut stone and concrete extended outward to a massive two-level circumferential ring of barrel vaults containing entrances and internal circulation corridors. A third-story perimeter wall upheld one end of the timber supports for the highest tier of seats. Fragmentary remains of the exterior reflect the arched terminations of the radial barrel vaults. The arches were articulated by engaged half-columns and entablatures of the Doric and Ionic orders on the ground and second levels, respectively.

The design of theaters doubtless inspired that of amphitheaters, which were circular or oval in plan, with raked seating on all sides. The amphitheater at Pompeii, dating from about 80 BCE and the oldest surviving example, was sited so that seats at one end of the oval could be supported on rising ground (Fig. 5.27). Later amphitheaters built in southern France at Arles and Nîmes were constructed almost entirely above ground level.

Greatest of all was the Flavian Amphitheater in Rome, more commonly known as the Colosseum, completed in 80 CE (Figs. 5.28–5.29). Although the building's plan is the familiar oval and its structure is modeled on that of the Theater of Marcellus, the novel element here is size. The exterior of the oval measures 510 by 615 feet, encompassing seats for an estimated 50,000 people in a continuously rising tier with an additional seating band above. Except for this top level of seats, which rested on wooden supports, the entire building was masonry, a combination of cut stone and concrete resting on carefully laid foundations. Under the seating was an intricate network of structural supports, horizontal passageways, ramps, and stairs to accommodate the throngs attending spectacles in the building. The exterior was clad in travertine, usually a cream-colored marble. Stacked half-columns in the Roman Doric, Ionic, and Corinthian orders combined with arches of the supporting barrel vaults to create three stories of the façade. A fourth level of Corinthian pilasters without arches completed the elevation around two upper galleries (reserved for women and slaves). Attached to this wall were brackets for the poles that some historians believe to have been supports for a canvas cover (*velarium*) providing shade for spectators. The area under the arena floor, an oval measuring 175 by 280 feet, was a labyrinth of passageways and chambers for gladiators, beasts, and hoisting machinery to service the spectacles staged above. The Colosseum is inextricably linked with savage and cruel entertainment, including fights to the death by gladiators and the persecution of Roman Christians. During later eras the fine marble work was removed as the building became a source for ready-cut stone. It remains today as a partial ruin, but even in its crumbled condition the Colosseum testifies to Roman construction skill.

5.28 The Colosseum (Flavian Amphitheater), Rome, completed 80 CE.

Grandest of all the Roman arenas, the Colosseum's exterior was clad in travertine. This view shows sections where the veneer has been stripped, revealing the structural arches. Fig. 5.29 shows the original appearance.

5.29 Perspective sections of the Colosseum, Rome, completed 80 CE.

These drawings reveal the Colosseum's internal circulation and structure. On the uppermost wall section were masts to support the velarium that shaded portions of the arena's seats. The top deck had standing room for those who could not afford seats.

RESIDENCES

To study Roman housing, we once again return to Pompeii, for the collection of ordinary dwellings, elaborate town residences, country villas, and farmhouses preserved there provides the most complete record we have of the types of buildings in which people lived. The earliest houses have atrium plans, an indigenous Italian building type in which the principal rooms of the house directly adjoin an open courtyard for access and for light and circulation of air. Such a house presents a blank wall to the street on which it fronts without setback from the sidewalk.

URBAN HOUSING

The House of the Surgeon is the most ancient dwelling found in Pompeii, and an examination of its plan reveals the typical features of atrium houses (Fig. 5.30a). It is an irregular quadrilateral because it exactly fills the plot of land on which it was built. On the street side it has three doors, two of which provide access to shops, one connected to the dwelling and the other forming part of a self-contained shop with living quarters upstairs. The center doorway, dignified by two entrance steps, was the principal entry to the house, and its location defines the axis of symmetry for the house proper. Passing through a vestibule, a visitor would next encounter the atrium, where a roof provided covering and shade except for a relatively small central area that was left open to the sky. Water running off the roof would fall in a basin (**impluvium**) in the center of the atrium. On either side of the atrium were chambers generally used as bedrooms; straight ahead on axis was the main reception room (**tablinum**), flanked by large and small dining rooms. Beyond was a portico that opened onto the rear walled garden. Service spaces, including chambers for servants and the kitchen, were set in the wings beside the dining rooms or tucked away in asymmetrical back rooms. All the internal spaces depended on the atrium or the garden for light, as the exterior walls were without openings. Only the tablinum, the most distinguished room in the house, had direct access to both sources (and thus to the cooling breezes that would pass there); most of the remaining rooms must have been rather dim, even during the day.

The atrium plan had formal dignity and practicality too. The owner could rent the frontage shop with second-floor living quarters to a tradesman or artisan and use the shop connected to the interior of the house as his own place of business. The functioning of either shop was independent of domestic activity, which was in turn isolated from street noise. The scale was ample. The private quarters in the House of the Surgeon covered about 5500 square feet, including the garden. Nevertheless, in the second century BCE wealthier citizens were constructing expanded atrium houses. These newer houses might have

House of the Surgeon

5.30a Plan of the House of the Surgeon, Pompeii, 2nd century BCE.

This is organized around a central open space or atrium that admitted fresh air and light to surrounding rooms. A portico or porch at the rear opened into a small garden. Positioned between these two elements was the tablinium.

5.30b Plan of the House of Pansa, Pompeii, 2nd century.

This house is so extensive that it occupies virtually an entire block by itself and includes a spacious walled garden at the rear. The atrium, peristyle, and rear garden provided this elegant dwelling with multiple public rooms suitable for dining.

House of Pansa

Peristyle garden

Triclinium
(Room of the
Cherubs)

Reception
room

Portico

Garden

Triclinium

Bed | Bed

Office

Waiting
room

Impluvium

Bed

Latrine

Bed

Service atrium

Kitchen

Stable
entrance

Stable

Atrium

Reception
room

Bed | Bed

Entrance

House of the Vetii

0   10 m
0   30 ft

N

5.30c Plan of the House of the Vetii, Pompeii, 2nd century.

The brothers who owned this house had a taste for entertaining. Their house had multiple dining rooms opening off the peristyle.

5.31 Atrium of the House of Venus in the Shell, Pompeii, 2nd century.

The roof has been restored to give an idea of the original space and light quality. Water running off the roof collected in the impluvium at the center of the atrium. The opening to the left gave access to service spaces, while the center doorway entered a bedroom. The rightmost door is the entrance to the house from the vestibule.

more than one atrium, and the garden was greatly enlarged and surrounded by a colonnade to become a peristyle (Figs. 5.31–5.32).

The House of Pansa at Pompeii is an example of the atrium-peristyle house that has been dated to the mid-second century BCE (Fig. 5.30b). It occupies virtually one entire city block (approximately 27,000 square feet, over half an acre) and thus might have had windows on any of its four sides, but it has none, relying instead on an atrium, peristyle court, and a large walled garden for light and air. The entrance establishes an axial disposition of spaces similar to that at the House of the Surgeon. The small rooms around the atrium were used as bedrooms, with the dining rooms set adjacent to the peristyle. Beyond the peristyle, the axis passes through another reception room and portico to the walled garden, which occupied about a third of the site. Such a large house was uncommon in Pompeii. Examples of three smaller houses can be seen along the side street of the House of Pansa, where they were created out of the main house in a later remodeling. Lacking an atrium or internal court, these houses had windows for light and air, but they opened to the street, thus sharing the dust, noise, and smells of the public way.

5.32 Peristyle of the House of Venus in the Shell, Pompeii, 2nd century.

The house takes its name from a fresco found on the peristyle wall (to the left, not visible in this photograph). Fragments of other wall frescoes are evident. The dining room opened onto this garden.

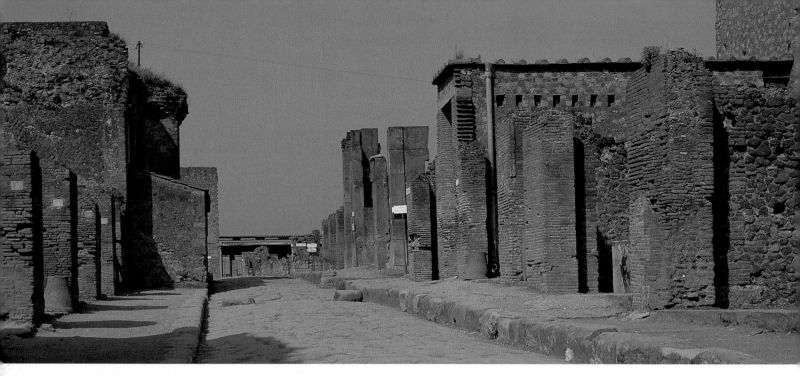

5.33 Street in Pompeii, 2nd century.

Shop fronts predominated along the street, with the entrances to houses being rather modest openings.

The two remaining sides of the House of Pansa contained shops. One can see the masonry mass surrounding the oven of a bakery on the plan.

The House of the Vetii is an example of a house from the last period at Pompeii, although there is evidence that it was built over ruins of an earlier dwelling (Fig. 5.30c). Its owners were two businessmen who evidently enjoyed a relaxed and elegant quality of life. Rather than having a triclinium set between the atrium and peristyle, this house has a grand triclinium on the long axis of the peristyle as well as several smaller chambers that could be used for dining or entertaining if the group attending were smaller. Service areas, including the kitchen and an area for washing, were located around a secondary atrium to the right of the entrance, where there was a tap from the town's aqueduct to provide running water. On the left side of the central atrium were the stables, where stairs in the corridor gave access to a second story (now vanished) on the street façade. The house is notable for the amount of statuary and wall painting it contained, evidence of the prosperity of its owners.

Inward-looking houses such as those at Pompeii present a virtual wall to the street, an effect completely unlike the residential districts of American cities but not so dissimilar to the modern towns in Mediterranean countries. The streets in Pompeii were usually narrow, ranging from under eight to just over twenty-two feet. Major streets had raised walks on either side, and raised stepping stones at intersections enabled pedestrians to cross the street without sinking into the muck that often filled the roadway (Fig. 5.33). These crossing stones also permitted wheeled carts to pass, carefully, and thus controlled traffic speed. The walls in most sections of town were covered with graffiti. Election slogans, public notices, advertisements for commercial establishments and public

entertainments, and obscene remarks have all been found in the excavations of the city. On streets where tradesmen had shops, the walls sometimes contained murals illustrating the particular trade or product available within. Shop fronts opened directly to the street for the display of goods and were secured at night by wooden roller shutters.

Interior finishes in the houses at Pompeii have proven almost as interesting as the architecture. Art historians have identified four styles of wall paintings at Pompeii. One of these, in which imaginary scenes were painted as viewed from high or low vantage points, seems a precursor of the elaborate Baroque creations that were used in the

5.34 Insula (tenement building), Ostia, 2nd century.

Much of the urban population in Rome lived in accommodation similar to this building. Cooking facilities for all units were located on the roof to minimize odors and the danger of fire, and water had to be carried from the public supply.

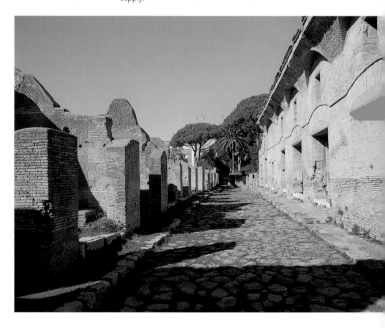

seventeenth century to expand optically the physical boundaries of walls and ceilings.

Stone and brick were the primary materials used in the construction of houses, although a surprising amount of timber was also employed, particularly for roof beams. In less affluent houses, walls were often provided by a wooden structural frame filled with rubble or brick, rather like the half-timbering construction of medieval Europe. Houses were originally one story, but as the city grew and urban land became more valuable, construction inevitably became multi-story, and older houses were converted to apartments. By the time of Pompeii's destruction, in fact, many of the atrium-peristyle houses had been divided into multi-family dwellings, as the wealthier citizens had moved to more spacious residences on estates outside the city.

For city residents, the dominant housing type after the fire that destroyed much of Rome in 64 CE came to be the apartment block or **insula**. An inventory made in the fourth century of buildings in Rome counted 46,000 insulae, while there were fewer than 1800 single-family houses. The best surviving insulae are in the port city of Ostia (Fig. 5.34). These apartment buildings, ranging up to six floors in height, occupied substantial plots of land and were designed around a central courtyard. Shops or commercial ventures were located on the ground-floor street frontages. Unlike the atrium houses, however, the upper-floor walls of insulae had windows opening to the street, so that rooms could draw on both the courtyard and street for light and air. In middle-class districts, the windows had glass panes instead of skin coverings to prevent air filtration.

RURAL VILLAS AND URBAN PALACES

Country residences were called villas, and at Pompeii, a fine example is preserved just outside the city wall. Known as the Villa of the Mysteries (Figs. 5.35–5.36) because of the wall paintings in one room that relate to the mystical cult of Bacchus, it grew gradually over a period of 300 years from a simple house to a complex of sixty rooms. Elements from atrium houses remain in its plan, including the preference for axial symmetry, but the ordering of rooms differs. The entranceway led into the peristyle, followed by the atrium and finally the tablinum, while extensive terraced gardens surrounded the villa on the three non-entrance sides. Based upon the original inward-focused house, the architectural developments at the Villa of the Mysteries seem to suggest a building in which the exterior elevations and their connection with the surrounding countryside were becoming more important.

Truly wealthy individuals, such as the emperor, had elaborate palaces in Rome. The ruins of the Palace of Domitian, built to the design of Rabirius for the emperor Domitian (finished in 92 CE) on the Palatine Hill (Fig. 5.37), hint at the complexity of elements incorporated

5.35 Villa of the Mysteries, Pompeii, ca. 120–80 BCE.

This is an example of a country residence for a family of some wealth. The name derives from splendid wall frescoes depicting initiation rites for one of the mystery cults that flourished during the Roman period.

5.36 Plan of the Villa of the Mysteries, Pompeii, ca. 120–80 BCE.

What is seen here is the result of about 300 years of modification and enlargement. The germ of the plan is still the atrium/peristyle combination seen in urban residences, but the house also opens out to the landscape with numerous porticoes.

Domus Flavia, or official wing | Domus Augustana, or residential wing

Basilica
Audience hall
Lararium
Peristyle

Guest rooms
Vestibule
Guest rooms
Peristyle
Peristyle

Triclinium
Fountains
Library
Library
Peristyle
Walled garden

0   50 m
0   150 ft

5.37 Plan of the Palace of Domitian, Rome, completed 92 CE.

This extensive residence for the emperor has a suite of official reception rooms (left) and a set of more intimately scaled private apartments (right). At the extreme right is an extensive walled garden in the shape of a stadium.

into an imperial residence, in which spaces for public functions and private living had to be combined. (Our word *palace* is derived from this extraordinary building on the Palatine Hill, just as *capitol* stems from the Capitoline Hill, which was the focus of civic activity.) In the Palace of Domitian, the western section contained a suite of official rooms, axially arranged with a grand reception hall, peristyle with a fountain, and a large vaulted dining hall (**triclinium**) with a exedra at the end to mark the emperor's seat. Note that this sequence of rooms follows that of the atrium house, but at a greatly enlarged scale. The more private residence section to the south was also organized on a central axis, connected to the official rooms by a cross-axis terminating in an elongated walled private garden. Its more intimately scaled rooms on two levels present a virtuoso display of architectural ingenuity, incorporating varied volumes, water features, and contrasts in

light and shade. The entire complex was a highly original setting of spatial and material magnificence, reflecting the power and wealth of the empire.

Interest in exploring complex arrangements as seen in Domitian's Palace continues at the imperial villa erected by Hadrian outside Tivoli as a reflection of his extensive travels and personal passion for architecture (Fig. 5.38). Constructed between 117 and 138 CE, Hadrian's Villa is a vast, sprawling accumulation of geometrically controlled building groups sited to follow the landscape and linked to each other by a shifting set of axes and cross-axes. The many shapes incorporated in the buildings, including wondrously convoluted curves, exploit the design freedom afforded by the concrete of which virtually all the buildings were constructed. Hadrian may have intended that his villa should evoke architectural forms from all parts of the world, but there are no Disneyland-like copies of foreign buildings. Rather, it is the sheer variety of interior volumes and exterior vistas, as if the designers were experimenting with imaginative and untried forms, that makes this a treasury of spatial sequences without precedent.

The villa was conceived as a place for both work and relaxation. Hadrian attended to state business in certain areas and enjoyed entertaining, relaxing, and following intellectual pursuits in others. To a greater degree than was the case in other villas of the time, this was a place composed of varied spaces—open courtyards, regularized plantings, long passages, soaring domes, intimate rooms, contained vistas—to be experienced at leisure. The most recent scholarship on the subject has stripped away names traditionally associated with features of the villa in preference for descriptive terms, as the old names were assigned by romantically inclined amateurs and not Hadrian himself. (The old names will be given here in parentheses so that readers may understand them when encountered in other sources.) An enclosed garden built around a rectangular fish pond forms the East–West Terrace (the Poikele), the largest single element in the villa. Here Hadrian could follow the advice of physicians and take gentle walks after eating, seeking shelter under the porticoed north wall from sun or rain. Below the western end of the terrace were tiers of rooms for as many as 700 villa staff and servants, always near at hand but out of sight.

To the east was the Island Enclosure (Maritime Theater), a circular, enclosed, colonnaded area 150 feet in diameter that provided a retreat for meditation or intimate meetings (Figs. 5.39–5.40). A circular water channel isolated the central building from the surrounding walkway. Access to the building was provided by removable wooden bridges, later supplemented by a permanent masonry one. The central structure is also circular, with three suites of rooms: a library or lounge on the east, a salon or dining

area on the south, and a baths complex on the west, communicating with the ring canal through a flight of steps, which suggests that it was also used for swimming. Water is also the central feature of the Scenic Canal (Canopus Canal), a long colonnaded pool that was lined with statuary and focused at its southern end on a grand triclinium (the Serapeum) or banqueting hall that became a grotto.

To the north of the Island Enclosure was the residential area, which included parts of an earlier villa on the site, grouped around a rectangular court. Of greater interest from the standpoint of geometry is the Water Court (Piazza d'Oro or Golden Court), built on the northeast edge of the villa (Fig. 5.41). This consisted of a square courtyard enclosed by both a colonnade and an arcade. The central axis of the composition was defined by an octagonal domed entrance pavilion that sat opposite the famous reverse-curve Nymphaeum or water pavilion. Down the center of the open courtyard was a long rectangular pool of still water, bordered by trees and flowerbeds, a tranquil contrast to the active water in six fountains that played in the Nymphaeum. The rectangular geometry of

---

5.38 Plan of Hadrian's Villa, Tivoli, 117–38 CE.

It is hard to convey in a single drawing the complexity of this sprawling collection of buildings that covers twice as much area as the city of Pompeii. Hadrian's architects exploited the structural possibilities of concrete to build unprecedented forms and compositions around water features.

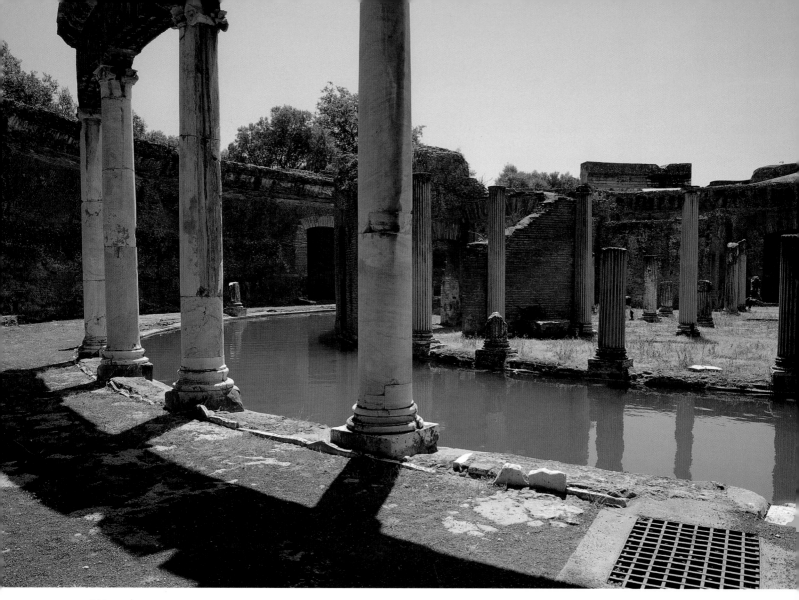

5.39 Island Enclosure (Maritime Theater), Hadrian's Villa, Tivoli, 117–38 CE.

Inside a circular colonnaded walkway, there is a moat surrounding a circular building that contained a library, dining area, and baths. For scale reference, the diameter of this complex is about the same as that of the Pantheon.

5.40 Large Baths, Hadrian's Villa, Tivoli, 117–38 CE.

Hadrian's Villa included both small and large baths with vaults and domes constructed of brick-faced concrete. Even in a ruined state, these buildings give a sense of the varied spaces that made this sprawling villa an inspiration for later architects.

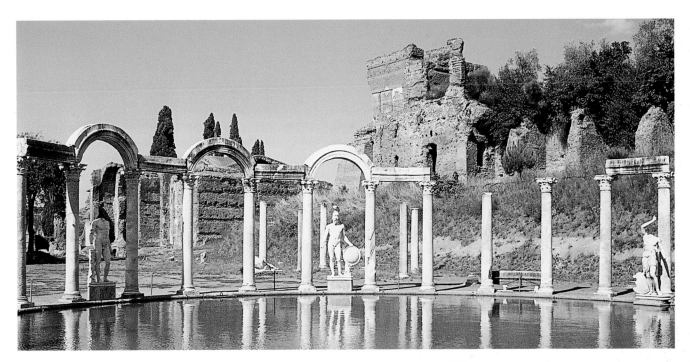

5.41 Columns terminating the Scenic Canal, Hadrian's Villa, Tivoli, 117–38 CE.

Opposite the Grand Triclinium, the Scenic Canal ended with a semicircular curve. Alternating arches and lintels used here could be the genesis for the Palladian motif, or Serliana, that is extensively employed by Renaissance architects (see Fig. 11.50). The Canal itself was probably a swimming pool.

the courtyard also contrasts with the sinuous plan around the fountains, where arcs of circles swing in and out in dynamic interplay. Between the eight piers are pairs of columns supporting a cornice that curved in and out around the center, alternately concave and convex, creating a sensation of space extending beyond the concavities, as did the niches around the Pantheon. There is no agreement on whether this space was roofed or not. As it was probably used as a summer dining room, having no roof would be unusual, but the columns and piers that survive are inadequate to support a masonry vault, and the geometry would make a suitable dome complex indeed. A lightweight timber roof has been hypothesized. Two apartments are placed symmetrically to each side of the Nymphaeum, and the whole ensemble forms a contained inward-focused environment.

As the villa was neglected for centuries after its construction and even today has only partially been excavated, it is difficult to reconstruct a complete image of it as it was in Hadrian's time. A keen imagination is required to envision buildings that exist now only as ruins or foundations marked on the ground. Enough survives, however, to define areas and convey an impression of space. The free use of curves seen here and in other late Roman buildings provided inspiration for architects who visited during the late Renaissance and Baroque periods. Roman architecture as a whole encompasses so many formal variations that it is the single richest architectural legacy for later developments in the West. Designers in the Romanesque, Renaissance, Baroque, Neo-classic, and nineteenth-century Classically derived styles, including the Beaux-Arts, have all found material in Roman architecture from which to generate building forms never imagined by the Romans themselves. Even twentieth-century masters such as Le Corbusier and Post-Modernist designers have drawn inspiration from the varied forms of Roman architecture.

CHAPTER 6

EARLY CHRISTIAN AND BYZANTINE ARCHITECTURE

Christianity, the religion developed by followers of Jesus Christ, began as a reforming sect of Judaism whose members regarded Jesus as the promised messiah. Over three centuries after the death of Christ, the religion developed into an organized church with a hierarchy of bishops and clergy. The earliest expression of its beliefs is found in the Nicene Creed (325 CE with later revisions), still used by the Eastern Orthodox Church, the Roman Catholic Church, and some Protestant denominations:

I believe in one God the Father Almighty, Maker of heaven and earth, and of all things visible and invisible; and in one Lord Jesus Christ, the only-begotten Son of God, begotten of His Father before all worlds; God of God, Light of Light; Very God of Very God; Begotten, not made; Being of one substance with the Father, by whom all things were made; Who for us men, and for our salvation, came down from heaven; And was incarnate by the Holy Ghost of the Virgin Mary, and was made man; And was crucified also for us under Pontius Pilate. He suffered and was buried; And on the third day He rose again according to the Scriptures; And ascended into heaven; And sitteth on the right hand of the Father. And He shall come again with glory to judge both the quick and the dead; Whose kingdom shall have no end. And I believe in the Holy Ghost; The Lord and Giver of Life; Who proceedeth from the Father and the Son; Who with the Father and Son together is worshipped and glorified; Who spake by the prophets. And I believe in one Holy Catholic and Apostolic Church. I acknowledge one Baptism for the remission of sins. And I look for the Resurrection of the dead; And the Life of the world to come.

S. Marco interior, Venice, rebuilt 1063–89.

This late Byzantine church, modeled on Justinian's Church of the Holy Apostles in Constantinople, is finished inside with elaborate mosaic figures on a golden background.

In the context of the late Roman Empire, Christianity was one of a number of religions troublesome to governmental authorities because its followers refused to acknowledge the state-sponsored deities, so the early history of Christianity is one of underground meetings and official persecution. Not until the emperor Constantine proclaimed toleration for all religions of the Roman Empire in the Edict of Milan in 313 did Christians have authority to construct buildings for public worship. Prior to that time services were held in private homes, where common domestic rooms, most often the triclinium (dining room), sufficed for worship. Christians developed congregational worship with a liturgy that focused on the celebration of the Eucharist (also known as communion), symbolic of the Last Supper of Jesus with his disciples and by extension of his sacrifice for humanity. One table was used for the Eucharist and another for offerings, with participants in the service sitting on the remaining furnishings or standing.

As the liturgy became more elaborate and the congregation grew, larger and more extensive sets of rooms were needed. In many cities Christians established community houses with a hall for worship, a baptistery, and rooms for the distribution of alms to the needy. They also organized separate cemeteries to distance their burials from those of other religions. Christians disapproved of cremation, and if suitable land for a graveyard was not available, the community developed underground cemeteries, generally begun in abandoned quarries, which became known as catacombs. Portions of the catacombs in Rome are among the oldest surviving Christian constructions, providing a glimpse of early religious decorative art.

Christian architecture after 313 derived in large measure from Roman precedent, and Early Christian and Byzantine buildings continue certain aspects of classical antiquity. At the same time, stylistic developments in this period contributed to later buildings in the medieval period, thus creating a transition between the classical past and the medieval era in western Europe.

EARLY CHRISTIAN BASILICAS

In giving official sanction to Christianity, Constantine became the sponsor of some of its early church-building efforts, most of which were based on the Roman basilica. Pagan associations rendered Roman temples unsuitable models for Christian worship, but the connotations of assembly hall and court of justice pertaining to basilicas suited the new religion much better. Basilicas could accommodate large crowds, an important consideration for a religion attracting increasing numbers of converts, and their layout created processional space that was part of worship services. With relatively minor modifications, the Roman basilica form was adapted to Christian ritual. The altar was placed in the apse where the magistrate's seat had formerly been, entrances were set in the opposite short wall, and an atrium accommodated gatherings before services and enabled the unbaptized to hear but not participate in the Mass. The longitudinal arrangement of atrium, nave, and apse formed an impressive axis for processions that terminated at the altar.

Constantine gave the Lateran Palace in Rome to the early church to serve as a residence for the bishop, and one of the earliest basilicas was built adjacent to the palace in about 313. Much rebuilt and extended, it stands today as St. John Lateran and is still the cathedral of Rome. (**Cathedral** is the designation given to a church that contains the seat or **cathedra** of a bishop. While cathedrals are often larger or more elaborate than ordinary churches, this is not necessarily the case, nor is every large church a

6.1 S. Apollinare Nuovo, Ravenna, ca. 490.

This early basilica has changed relatively little since its construction, preserving the very plain brick exterior that was common in many Early Christian churches.

6.2 S. Apollinare Nouvo interior, Ravenna, ca. 490.

Grained marble columns define the aisles and nave. Nave walls are finished with mosaics.

cathedral.) The original building had paired aisles on either side of a lofty nave, which was concluded by an apse containing seats for the bishop (the cathedra) and priests. Clerestory windows high in the nave wall illuminated the central space, while smaller windows in the outermost aisle and above the first aisle colonnade provided light for the ancillary spaces. Open wooden trusses spanned the nave and aisles, supported on brick-faced concrete walls and marble columns salvaged from earlier Roman buildings.

A more vivid example of an Early Christian basilica is found at Ravenna in the church of S. Apollinare Nuovo, constructed about 500 as the palace church for Theoderic and given its present name centuries later (Figs. 6.1–6.2). Constructed of brick with single aisles flanking the nave, the church interior focuses on the semicircular apse (not the original). The walls above the nave arcade are finished with mosaics arranged in three horizontal layers. The lowest tier depicts stately processions of female saints (north side) and male martyrs (south side) advancing toward the altar. (This mosaic tier was installed in the ninth century, replacing original work whose subject we do not know.) Between the clerestory windows are single figures that may represent Old Testament prophets and New Testament evangelists and apostles. In the highest sections of the nave wall are scenes representing the Passion story (south side) and the miracles of Christ (north side). This elaborate interior decoration not only communicated Christian teachings to a largely illiterate public, but also symbolized the richness of the kingdom of God to which the soul could aspire. The sober exterior brickwork gives little indication of the shimmering golden mosaic work contained within.

MARTYRIA, BAPTISTERIES, AND MAUSOLEA

Basilicas were not the only religious buildings erected by early Christians. Among the structures raised to serve Christian purposes were **martyria**, buildings erected as memorials to commemorate saints or sites of special importance to the Christian faith. Celebrated martyria might attract large crowds for services and thus need to function as churches, but major importance was always attached to the tomb or shrine around which they were built. Old St. Peter's in Rome (318–22), predecessor of the present Basilica of St. Peter, began as a martyrium marking the tomb of St. Peter and seems to have been used for several centuries as a place of burial for other Christians as well (Figs. 6.3a, 6.4). Its plan is that of a basilica, with double aisles on each side of the nave and a transverse element or transept projecting beyond the side walls and extending across the nave in front of the apse. Placed at the junction of transept and apse was the tomb of St. Peter, surrounded by a railing and marked by a canopy rising on twisted spiral columns that reputedly came from the

Temple of Solomon in Jerusalem. The transept spaces accommodated those coming to venerate the shrine, while the enormous nave (300 by 64 feet) and aisles functioned as a covered cemetery with space for burials and commemorative funeral meals. A spacious atrium preceded the martyrium, and the whole scheme provided the model for a number of churches built later, both in Rome and elsewhere.

A similar program influenced the design of the Church of the Nativity in Bethlehem, constructed under the patronage of Constantine in about 333 over the grotto that tradition identified as the birthplace of Jesus (Fig. 6.3b). As at St. Peter's, this building was a basilica preceded by an atrium, but rather than transepts and an apse, the Church of the Nativity had an octagon at the head of the nave. A passage around the octagon allowed pilgrims to circulate and view the grotto below through an opening in the floor, and there may also have been stairs going down to the actual level of the shrine. The junction of a basilica with an octagon shows Early Christian willingness to explore new forms in the course of seeking appropriate and functional religious buildings.

Baptism is an important Christian rite, and in the Early Christian period special buildings were often erected for this sacrament alone. Most were centrally planned around the baptismal pool, for at the time baptism was by complete immersion, and **baptistery** plans were frequently octagonal to reflect the number eight, which symbolized regeneration or the Resurrection, since Jesus was said to have risen from the dead on the eighth day after his entry into Jerusalem. The Baptistery of the Orthodox in Ravenna (ca. 458) is a domed octagonal volume surrounding the octagonal marble font (Fig. 6.5). The central scene in the ceiling mosaic depicts Christ's baptism in the river Jordan, encircled by the twelve apostles and an outer ring illustrating altars in semicircular niches and empty thrones (Fig. 6.6). As was the case with S. Apollinare Nuovo, the plain brick exterior, articulated primarily by eight arched windows and corbeled arches with pilaster strips, gives no hint of the sumptuous finishes inside.

Mausolea, buildings erected to contain the tombs of important people, were also in the repertory of Early Christian architecture. Following Roman practice, these were often centrally planned, and they served as models for later domed churches. In Rome the mausoleum of Constantine's daughter Constantia was built in around 350 as a circular monument with a cross-section paralleling that of the basilica, having lower aisle spaces flanking the higher nave lit by clerestory windows (Figs. 6.3c, 6.7–6.8). In Constantia's mausoleum, now known as the church of S. Costanza, the basilican cross-section was rotated about the center axis to create a circular building, rather than being extended longitudinally to form a basilica. Originally the resulting dome with encircling ambulatory focused the visitor's attention on the sarcophagus placed in the center. Twelve paired sets of columns

6.3a Plans of Old St. Peter's Rome, 318–22; S. Apollinare in Classe, Ravenna, 532–49; and S. Apollinare Nuovo, Ravenna, ca. 490.

The fundamental elements of basilican church plans are evident here: a longitudinal axis leads from the entrance (through an atrium and/or narthex) through the nave to the terminating apse, where the altar is located. The nave is illuminated by high (clerestory) windows. Aisles flanking the nave provide additional processional space.

Altar
Nave
Aisle
Aisle
Aisle
Aisle
Apse
Transept
Atrium
Old St. Peter's

S. Apollinare in Classe

S. Apollinare Nuovo

N

6.3b Plan of the Church of the Nativity, Bethlehem, ca. 333.

This innovative building combines the form of a double-aisle basilica with an atrium forecourt and an octagonal rotunda over the site of Jesus's birth. The design thus accommodates the functions of worship while providing circulation space required by pilgrims visiting the holy site.

N

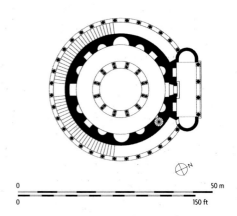

6.3c Plan of S. Costanza, Rome, ca. 350.

This shows the original narthex and stairs descending to the crypt. Paired columns support the drum below the dome.

N

support the drum wall on which the dome rises above twelve clerestory windows. The aisle vaults are finished with mosaic, and the columns are of polished marble.

A smaller monument with even more elaborate decoration is the Mausoleum of Galla Placidia in Ravenna (Fig. 6.9). Built in ca. 425 on a Greek-cross plan (that is, a cross having arms of equal length), it was intended to house the tombs of Galla Placidia and members of her family. Her half-brother Honorius was the western emperor who moved the capital from Milan to Ravenna. After his death, Galla Placidia ruled the western empire in her own right and on behalf of her son. She was a notable patron of church-building

6.4 Perspective section of Old St. Peter's, Rome, ca. 318–22.

This building began as a martyrium, a cemetery based around the grave of the apostle Peter. Notice how the lower aisle roofs permit direct light to enter the nave through high clerestory windows.

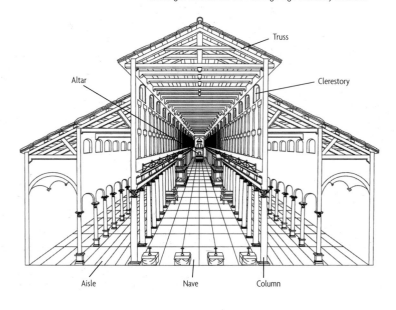

Truss
Altar
Clerestory
Aisle
Nave
Column

6.5 (above) Baptistery of the Orthodox, Ravenna, ca. 458.

This view shows the brickwork embellished primarily by pilaster strips and shallow arches near the eaves. These decorative elements are known as Lombard bands because they originated in Lombardy.

6.6 (right) Baptistery of the Orthodox, ceiling mosaic, Ravenna, ca. 458.

Directly over the baptismal font in the center of the building is an image of Christ's baptism by John the Baptist. The dove of the Holy Spirit hovers overhead, while an old man, a personification of the Jordan, stands in the water on the right side.

6.7 (below) S. Costanza, Rome, ca. 350.

Erected as a mausoleum for the emperor Constantine's daughter, this central-plan building was converted into a church. Note the plain brickwork of the exterior, with two layers of voussoirs placed over the clerestory windows.

6.8 (below, right) S. Costanza interior, Rome, ca. 350.

A section through the building resembles that of a basilica. Rather than being extended longitudinally, the section is rotated about the axis to generate a central plan building.

EUSEBIUS AND CONSTANTINE

by Lynn K. Barker

6A Anon, Eusebius of Caesarea. Engraving.

Around 315, a visiting bishop rose to address the congregation gathered for the rededication of the new cathedral in the Levantine city of Tyre. He turned and both dedicated and addressed his "Festival oration on the building of churches" to his friend, the inspiration behind the cathedral's construction and its bishop, Paulinus. The speaker was Eusebius (Fig. 6A), himself bishop of the nearby coastal see of Caesarea. He was famous both as the "father of Church history" and as Constantine's biographer and panegyrist.

The adage "history is written by the winners" is nowhere more strikingly illustrated than in the generation of Eusebius and his contemporary, Lactantius, whose work *On the Deaths of the Persecutors* recounts the grisly deaths, divinely sanctioned as retribution, of the church's enemies at the turn of the fourth century. In his own *Historia Ecclesiastica*, Eusebius describes with eyewitness authority the sufferings of Palestinian martyrs under Galerius and Maximinius.

When Eusebius came to describe the world that he thought had been transformed by Constantine's practice of toleration of all religions, he thought of no better way to depict the new order than by inserting, at the beginning of Book X of his *Historia Ecclesiastica* a full transcription of his address that day in Tyre.

Soon after peace came building: "The next state was the spectacle prayed and longed for by us all—dedication festivals in the cities and consecrations of the newly built places of worship, convocations of bishops . . . unification . . . harmony . . . There came together bone to bone and joint to joint."

The fine new basilica at Tyre was the inspiration of the bishop, standing second only to Christ. Eusebius the panegyrist styles his friend "a new Bezalel (Exod. 35:30); the "Solomon . . . of a new and far nobler Jerusalem;" "a new Zerubbabel," restoring the Temple to a "glory far greater than the old."

For all its spendor, however, this earthly building pales beside the more sublime truths of the archetypes behind it. The soul is a building, whose fall into sin Eusebius likens to the destruction of church properties at pagan hands. The "divine spiritual edifice in our souls" (what we call the image of God) fell to the battering rams of sin, "til not one stone of virtue was left." The work of Christ was directed to rebuilding the human soul. But while the bishop rebuilds his material church more splendidly than before, the true building project is God's work in history: raising up the edifice of the universal Church, in which God sets the people themselves as "living, securely-laid, and unshakeable stones." Even what Augustine of Hippo would one day call the city of man is a building, composed of most men in the world—"bad builders of bad buildings."

Modern historians have caught Eusebius out in promoting his vision of unity in harmony at the expense of a messier reality called historical truth; Constantine's Church was neither unified nor harmonious. Little wonder, then, that Eusebius' vision of God's edifice would nourish the architects—actual and metaphorical—of a Christian empire for a millennium to come.

in Ravenna, but the mausoleum is the only structure she commissioned that survives. The building also honored St. Vincent, a Spanish saint and martyr whose cult was popular by the early fifth century. Behind the plain brick exterior, enlivened by blind arches and pilasters, is a rich and glowing interior with marble floors and wainscoting, and mosaics on the upper walls and vaults (Fig. 6.10). Barrel vaults enclose the arms of the cross in plan, and the raised crossing is completed by a dome on **pendentives** (spherical triangles used to transform a square bay into a circle for the springing of a dome). Small windows admit light through alabaster glazing to shine softly on the mosaics. The small glass pieces, or *tesserae*, are intentionally set on a slight skew to the plane of the wall so that they do not all catch the light in the same way. This enlivens the surface and makes the inanimate material seem to

6.9 (above) Mausoleum of Galla Placidia, Ravenna, ca. 425.

This building's walls are articulated by blind arches and pilasters, features that were translated into Lombard bands in later buildings. The plain brick exterior gives no hint of the splendid mosaic and marble work found inside.

6.10 (right) Mausoleum of Galla Placidia interior, Ravenna, ca. 425.

While the walls are veneered with marble, the vaults are covered in vibrant mosaics, their colors as fresh as the day they were installed. The lunette over Galla Placidia's sarcophagus shows St. Vincent and the burning gridiron on which he was martyred. Arch profiles are outlined with garlands of fruit and leaves, or geometric patterns.

shimmer. The ceiling vaults, covered with geometric stars derived from textile designs, are set on a deep-blue ground and framed by decorative bands in brilliant colors, while the semicircular panels, or **lunettes**, formed below the barrel vaults at the end walls illustrate scenes featuring the Good Shepherd, the martyrdom of St. Vincent, and the apostles. It is a stunning interior, reflecting a high standard of workmanship and the devotion of its founder.

BYZANTINE BASILICAS AND DOMED BASILICAS

The division between the Early Christian and Byzantine eras is generally made at the reign of Justinian (527–65), who, as emperor based in Constantinople, put an end to factional disputes, reasserted imperial influence in portions of North Africa and Italy that had fallen to heretical rulers, and engaged in a vigorous program of church-building. People living at the time probably did not perceive the change. As historians look back on the period, however, Justinian's reign serves as a convenient marker to differentiate increasingly separate developments in

western and eastern sections of what had been the Roman Empire. Work tied by patronage or tradition to Constantinople is termed Byzantine. One characteristic of much Byzantine architecture is a clear preference for domes on both basilican and centrally planned churches. Like the Romans, the Byzantines saw the dome as symbolic of the heavenly sphere, complementary to the earthly realm of floor and walls below.

Early Christian traditions were not entirely discarded, however. Basilicas were the most common church plan constructed in the sixth century, although none of the examples built in Constantinople survives. We turn instead to the church of S. Apollinare in Classe at Ravenna, constructed under Justinian's patronage from 532 to 549, for an example of a wooden-roofed basilica without transepts (Figs. 6.3a, 6.11–6.12). Its splendid apse mosaics are the glory of the interior, where St. Apollinaris, the first bishop of Ravenna, guards a flock of twelve sheep (representing the disciples by number and the people of Ravenna by extension) grazing in a lush meadow. Overhead is a golden cross with the image of Christ in the center, set in a starry blue sky, and figures of four early bishops of Ravenna are installed between the windows. Rich marble columns form the nave arcade, with portraits of saints set in roundel frames above the arches. In character and design the church is similar to the earlier S. Apollinare Nuovo, but its scale is considerably larger. In the century after its construction, the apse floor was raised to permit access to the crypt tomb of Apollinaris.

6.11 S. Apollinare in Classe, Ravenna, 532–49.

Many Byzantine buildings continued the tradition of sober exteriors and rich interiors already seen in Early Christian times. The volume of the basilica and its narthex porch reads clearly.

6.12 S. Apollinare in Classe interior, Ravenna, 532–49.

Windows glazed in thin sheets of alabaster reduced the intense Italian sun and provided soft light suitable for appreciating mosaic work and marbled columns. Note the absence of seating: congregations stood or knelt during services at this period.

6.13 S. Irene interior, Constantinople, 532–64.

Lower sections of the pendentives supporting the dome are visible. Galleries erected over the aisles braced the structure and were used by women during services. One needs to imagine the mosaics that were intended for this bare interior.

The innovative domes seen in Justinian's churches are notable contributions to architectural history. In Constantinople, two domed basilicas rose simultaneously and survive as models for the type. The smaller, S. Irene (begun in 532 and remodeled in 564), has a rectangular plan divided into nave and aisles with a projecting semicircular apse (Fig. 6.13). (The church seen today is largely a rebuilding after an earthquake in 740.) Two domes cover the nave, and their thrust is countered by massive rectangular piers, pierced by openings, and effectively strengthened by barrel-vaulted galleries over the aisles. The outlines of the aisle vaults articulate the exterior side walls, where tiers of arched windows admit light to the aisles and galleries. More windows are placed at the base of the dome and around the apse. S. Irene thus represents a new interpretation of the basilica, combining the liturgical logic of the longitudinal plan with the centralizing or heavenly qualities of domed construction. This same idea, on a much larger scale, was carried out at a contemporary church in Constantinople, Hagia Sophia, the Church of the Holy Wisdom.

Hagia Sophia (532–37) is one of the great buildings of the world and is without question the masterpiece of Byzantine architecture (Figs. 6.14a, 6.15–6.17). We know the names and backgrounds of its architects, Anthemius of Tralles and Isidorus of Miletus. Both were mathematicians and scientists skilled in mechanics, geometry, and engineering. These talents were all needed to design and supervise the construction of the exceptionally large Hagia Sophia. In plan it is a basilica with a dome above the central space, complemented by two semidomes along the longitudinal axis. Its 107-foot-diameter central dome, supported on pendentives, rises 180 feet above the floor and is flanked by two lower semidomes of the same diameter, a clear span of nearly 250 feet. In the description of the church written by Justinian's court historian, Procopius of Caesarea, the dome was seen to hover over the interior.

Hagia Sophia, Constantinople

6.14a Plans of Hagia Sophia, 532–37, Constantinople, 532; S. Vitale, Ravenna, 538–48; SS. Sergius and Bacchus, 527–36; and S. Marco, Venice, 1063–89.

These Byzantine churches are grouped to allow comparisons of scale.

S. Vitale, Ravenna

SS. Sergius & Bacchus, Constantinople

S. Marco, Venice

0   50 m
0   150 ft

N

*[It] seems not to rest upon solid masonry, but to cover
the space with its golden dome suspended from Heaven.
All these details, fitted together with incredible skill in
mid-air and floating off from each other and resting
only on the parts next to them, produce a single and
most extraordinary harmony in the work, and yet do not
permit the spectator to linger much over the study of any
one of them, but each detail attracts the eye and draws
it on irresistibly to itself.*

Aisles with galleries above range on either side, while a
colonnaded atrium (no longer extant) and groin-vaulted
double narthex precede the church proper.

The structural problems posed by such an audacious
design were many, yet the necessary supports do not
intrude on the internal space, creating the feeling that the
dome floats effortlessly above the billowing interior
volumes. Nothing could be farther from the actual case.
While the brick used does constitute a relatively light construction material and the vaults are amazingly thin to
minimize both thrust and weight, the size of the building
means that the gravity forces are large. The forty windows

6.14b Plan of monastery churches, Hosios Lukas,
ca. 980–1025.

There are two churches shown here, the Theotokos (*above*)
and the Katholikon (*below*). The Theotokos church is a
quincunx design, while the Katholikon has a single large
dome buttressed by galleries.

Narthex   Theotokos church

Screen

Apse

Sacristy

Saint's tomb

Altar

Apse

Narthex

Nave   Katholikon

0   25 m
0   75 ft

N

at the base of the dome are set between buttresses that stabilize the junction of dome and pendentives. From this point the load is transferred to four great stone piers, which are further buttressed by being extended above the gallery vaults to join in great barrel vaults along the sides of the church. The semidomes, which appear to brace the narthex and apse ends, probably contribute little to the structure's integrity, however satisfying they are visually. The masonry mass of the four piers is more obvious on the outside than internally. Anthemius and Isidorus's structural daring overstepped the

6.15 Hagia Sophia, Constantinople, 532–37 and later.

This audacious building contains the greatest dome of its age, only slightly smaller than that of the Pantheon. The exterior shows massive buttresses added later to repair earthquake damage. Minarets were added when the church was converted into a mosque.

6.16 Axonometric section through Hagia Sophia, Constantinople, 532–37 and later.

This view shows the massive arches that support the great dome. The dome is built of brick which accounts for its relative thinness, and pendentives are used to transform the square bay defined by the piers into a circle from which the dome springs.

6.17 Hagia Sophia interior, Constantinople, 532–37 and later.

This view shows the multiple levels of windows that illuminate the interior. Windows set between the dome's ribs create the illusion that the dome floats unsupported over the major space. Hagia Sophia's architects intended to create a building that would rival the Pantheon, and their work has both inspired and challenged later builders who sought to emulate its space and structural daring.

physical limits of their materials, and the first great dome collapsed in 558. It was reconstructed with a steeper pitch and ribbed construction in 563, but the western half of the rebuilt dome fell again in 989. Following repairs, the eastern half collapsed in 1346; the replacement dome is the one on the building today.

Structural problems aside, the effect of the arches, vaults, exedrae, semidomes, and domes is ethereal. Light pours in from windows at many levels, playing over surfaces enriched by polished marbles and mosaic. From a position at the center of the nave, the repetition of curved forms reflects the great dome overhead and creates a pervasive harmony that is constantly varied. From the aisles and galleries, the view into the nave is dramatic, providing a partial perspective of the interconnecting layered spaces surrounding the interior volume. In the church ritual for which Hagia Sophia was built, the major space was reserved for two groups, the ecclesiastics and the retinue of the emperor. The clergy claimed the sanctuary space before the apse, while the imperial court occupied the region at the narthex end. The meeting of patriarch and emperor under the great dome marked a high point of the religious ritual. Ordinary people were relegated to the aisles and galleries, women on one side and men on the other, where they could observe the impressive ceremonial processions and symbolic joining of church and state in this magnificent setting.

CENTRALLY PLANNED BYZANTINE CHURCHES

Roman temples such as the Pantheon and Early Christian baptisteries and mausolea had featured centralized plans. Not surprisingly, these precedents combined well with the Byzantine fondness for dome-building and contributed to the development of the most characteristic Byzantine churches, which had circular or Greek-cross plans. Justinian's churches again provide the dominant models for later centuries.

SS. Sergius and Bacchus (527–36) in Constantinople and S. Vitale (538–48) in Ravenna illustrate two variations on the theme of central plans. SS. Sergius and Bacchus (Figs. 6.14a, 6.18) is essentially a domed octagon surrounded by aisles and galleries encased in a square, whereas S. Vitale's octagonal dome is echoed by octagonal galleries and aisles. The strong centralizing tendencies of both churches are countered somewhat by apsidal projections opposite the narthex side, and the interior space is more fluid than that seen in S. Costanza, where a similar organizational idea is carried out in circular form. In SS. Sergius and Bacchus, the eight piers supporting the dome are interspersed with two columns, set alternately in semicircular and straight alignments, so that the domed area penetrates the surrounding spaces. The sixteen-sided "pumpkin vault" dome reflects the alternating niches

6.18 SS. Sergius and Bacchus interior, Constantinople, 527–36.

This central-plan church features a "pumpkin vault" in its dome, a form that had been used in Roman times and that reappears in the Baroque era.

below in alternate straight and curved sections above its rather low drum.

Although the dome at S. Vitale (Figs. 6.14a, 6.19–6.20) is smaller, the church design is more sophisticated, with a higher drum and greater internal cohesiveness than at SS. Sergius and Bacchus. Clerestory windows illuminate the nave directly, and between the piers of the octagon all the niches are semicircular, carving into aisles and galleries to borrow additional light from windows in the exterior wall. Semidomes over each of the niches complement the dome that rises over the nave. The proportions of the exterior are equally fine. Red-tile roofs in direct volumetric expression of the internal space cap simple arched windows set in brick walls articulated by pilasters. SS. Sergius and Bacchus has lost most of its original interior mosaic, but S. Vitale displays the beautiful products of imperial workshops in both marble and mosaic. Carved capitals complete richly veined marble column shafts, book-matched marbles face the lower wall surfaces, and both geometric and figured mosaics complete arch soffits, upper walls, apse, and floors. Mosaic donor panels set on the sides of the apse portray Justinian and his court across from the empress Theodora and her attendants. The apse semidome shows Christ flanked by angels, with St. Vitalis to Christ's right

6.19 (above) S. Vitale, Ravenna, 538–48.
Another of the exceptional churches built under imperial patronage, S. Vitale is based on an octagonal plan. Its dome is constructed of hollow clay pots to create strength while minimizing weight.

6.20 (below) S. Vitale interior, Ravenna, 538–48.
This view shows the rich array of book-matched marbles and mosaic work.

and Bishop Ecclesius to the left. The bishop holds a model of the church, and Christ passes a crown to St. Vitalis. The splendor of Byzantium glows throughout this handsome church.

For the Justinian prototype of centralized churches on a Greek-cross plan, we must rely on fragmentary evidence provided by the now-vanished Church of the Holy Apostles in Constantinople. Originally erected by Constantine as his own mausoleum and rebuilt by Justinian from 536 to 550, it was demolished in 1469 to provide the site for a mosque. A standing church built on the model of Justinian's Church of the Holy Apostles is S. Marco in Venice, begun in 830 and rebuilt in 1063–89 (page 140 and Figs. 6.21–6.22). Hemispherical domes cover each arm of the Greek-cross plan, and a central one crowns the crossing. All are set on pendentives, with barrel vaults connecting the large pierced piers that sustain the downward thrust of the domes. Windows at the base of some domes illuminate the upper regions of the church and allow light to sparkle across the gold-ground mosaics of the interior. While the basic design concept for S. Marco stems from Byzantium, much there reflects other architectural traditions. For example, the present exterior portal hoods are fifteenth century, and the external dome profiles, raised on a timber framework above the masonry work, reflect the shape of eastern domes. Nevertheless, S. Marco is substantially Byzantine. It became the model for Romanesque churches in the south of France shortly after its completion.

In addition to the domed Greek-cross plan used at S. Marco, Byzantine churches built in the centuries after Justinian also followed two other general plan types, the cross-in-square and a single dome placed on a longitudinal base. The cross-in-square or quincunx plan has nine bays, with the central one domed, and diminutive domes over the corner bays. All other sections are barrel-vaulted. In cross-domed plans, the arms of the Greek cross are reduced and covered with barrel vaults that surround the crossing dome. Aisles and galleries enclose the church on three sides, and three apses complete the fourth side. Many of these churches were on a rather modest scale, so the vaulting did not pose undue constructional complications.

We can see both these plan types at the monastery of Hosios Loukas, located at Phocis northwest of Athens, where two churches were built adjacent to the shrine erected over the tomb of St. Luke, a local hermit who died

6.21 S. Marco, Venice, rebuilt 1063–89.

A Greek-cross plan based on Justinian's Church of the Holy Apostles in Constantinople, S. Marco has five domes, of which the central one is highest. The west front and raised external dome roofs were added later.

6.22 Section through S. Marco, Venice, rebuilt 1063–89.

This view shows the original dome profile and the taller shells erected in the fifteenth century to increase the exterior effect. Note particularly the turrets atop the dome, which resemble the characteristic onion domes of Russia.

in 953 (not to be confused with the evangelist of the same name). The smaller of the churches, designed on a cross-in-square plan with three apses, was dedicated in about 1000 to the Theotokos, the Greek term for the Mother of God (Fig. 6.14b). Built of squared stones surrounded by brick, the Theotokos church has a central dome raised on a drum. Groin vaults rather than domes were built over the corner bays, perhaps because the scale is so small: the central dome is eleven feet in diameter. Although the interior today is devoid of fresco, mosaic, or marble facing, it is probable that it was once richly finished to accord with the carved screen separating the nave from the chancel that is still in place.

The larger Katholikon was constructed in the following twenty years immediately to the south of the Theotokos church, thereby sharing proximity to the saint's shrine and allowing pilgrims to circulate on all sides of the tomb. Its

6.23 Interior of the Katholikon, Monastery of Hosios Lukas, 1020.

This interior repeats at a greatly reduced scale some of the dramatic lighting and rich interior of Hagia Sophia (see Fig. 6.17). Frescoes in the dome replace the original mosaic work that fell during an earthquake in 1593.

plan is in some respects similar to S. Irene in Constantinople, with a large dome set over the nave, braced on three sides by a second level gallery. Squinches transform the square central bay into an octagon that supports a drum and dome thirty feet in diameter (Fig. 6.23). The interior was sumptuously finished, with marble facing on the walls and mosaics on the vaults and dome. The dome mosaics, destroyed in an earthquake in 1593, were replaced by frescoes of the original subjects. On the apse semidome, in a field of gold mosaic, is a majestic Mary holding the infant Christ.

BYZANTINE CHURCHES IN RUSSIA

Many of the features of later Byzantine architecture are reflected in Russian church designs, for their architecture is inextricably identified with the legacy of Byzantium. In the period under consideration here, roughly from 990 to 1725, Russia included what today are the independent states of Belarus, Georgia and Ukraine. Much of the territory west of the Urals is rolling countryside, covered with extensive grasslands, vast forests, lakes, and marshes. Its rivers were the first tracks through the wilderness, and by the ninth century Viking explorers had settled along water routes requiring minimal portages to travel from the Baltic to the Black Sea, where they traded with the Byzantines. Aside from the rivers, the Urals, and the Carpathian mountains, there are few natural boundaries, so the area has long been open to nomadic incursions. Russian history begins with the legendary Rurik, a Viking who was invited to Novgorod in about 856 to bring order to the scattered trading settlements along the trade route to Constantinople. Although Rurik's descendants ruled the country until the sixteenth century, the history of Russia was severely interrupted for the period from 1239 to the fifteenth century, when the region was effectively a surrogate state of the Mongol khans of Central Asia. For a variety of historical reasons, Russia became isolated from western Europe, so the chronologies and stylistic periods defined for France, Italy, England, or Germany do not apply here. Byzantine work influenced church architecture in Russia for centuries after the fall of Constantinople in 1453. Difficulties in maintaining contact with church authorities in Constantinople and growing differences within the Russian church led to the proclamation in 1443 of a Russian Orthodox Church, having its own primate or metropolitan independent of the patriarch in Constantinople.

MASONRY CHURCHES

Christianity and the Byzantine style came to Russia in 988, when Prince Vladimir of Kiev became a convert to Christianity. According to history, before breaking with pagan tradition, Vladimir first entertained emissaries from four major religious faiths and then sent his own ambassadors to observe the ritual of Judaism, Islam, Latin Christianity, and Greek Christianity in actual practice. His agents were highly impressed with Hagia Sophia, as their report shows:

We knew not whether we were in heaven or on earth. For on earth there is no such splendor or such beauty, and we are at a loss how to describe it. We know only that God dwells there among men, and their service is fairer than the ceremonies of other nations. For we cannot forget that beauty.

Vladimir embraced the Christian church of Constantinople. Willingly or otherwise, his subjects soon joined their leader in espousing Christianity. The patriarch in Constantinople sent missionary priests to Kiev, where they translated the Bible into Slavonic and developed the Cyrillic script based on the Greek alphabet. They also established schools and aided in the construction of churches. Many early churches were built in wood, the most common material for structures of all sorts, and these of course have not endured. Foundations of the first masonry church built in Kiev, the Cathedral of the Dormition of the Virgin (also known as the Church of the Virgin of the Tithe) (989–96), indicate that it had a quincunx plan (Fig. 6.24a). On the exterior, the massing was essentially that of a cube with five domes. Russian builders employed the scheme so persistently that it became the paradigm for the Russian Orthodox Church.

Kiev's earliest surviving church is St. Sophia (ca. 1037–50s), built by Vladimir's son, Yaroslavl the Wise. Its

6.24a Reconstructed plan of the Church of the Virgin of the Tithe, Kiev, 989–96.

This plan, known as a quincunx, is extensively used in Byzantine churches in Russia. Both nave and transept arms are barrel-vaulted, with domed square bays over the crossing and in the corners defining the aisles. Quincunx designs have a clear hierarchy of domes, the central one being dominant.

Hagia Sophia, Constantinople

S. Sophia, Kiev

6.24b (left) Plans of Hagia Sophia, Constantinople, 532–37, and S. Sophia, Kiev, ca. 1037–505.

Russian masons were not able to replicate Hagia Sophia, so they used a clustering of domes in their elaboration on the quincunx theme at S. Sophia. Shaded outer galleries are later constructions.

6.24c Plan of St. Basil the Blessed, Moscow, 1555–60.

The plan shows how eight chapels of varying shape and external expression are grouped around a central sanctuary. Covered stairs lead into the building, which was not intended to accommodate a regular congregation.

which in a subsequent campaign was flanked by additional arcading on the north and south elevations. Finally, two large circular staircase-towers were added on the west as part of a narthex, so except for the east end, two additional layers now surrounded the original church. After being heavily damaged in 1240, the church was left as a ruin until seventeenth- and eighteenth-century restorers repaired and rebuilt missing sections. At that time, Baroque roofs were built over the domes and the open galleries were enclosed, so the exterior today bears little relation to the original design, which is best seen in drawings (Fig. 6.25). The interior is better preserved, with great mosaic figures of Christ Pantocrator in the dome and the Virgin in the apse complemented by frescoed walls (Fig. 6.26). In general, the interior is characterized by extremely vertical space in the nave and transepts. Piers necessary to support the domes and vaults divide the interior into

6.25 S. Sophia, Kiev, ca. 1037–55.

This church still stands, much restored and augmented on the exterior, so this view from the 1600s shows its original massing more effectively than a modern photograph.

6.26 S. Sophia interior, Kiev, ca. 1037–55.

This view looks from the gallery level to the apse. Russian domes do not generally span great spaces, being raised on drums with windows for added vertical emphasis and interior lighting. Note the use of pendentives to support the drum of the dome.

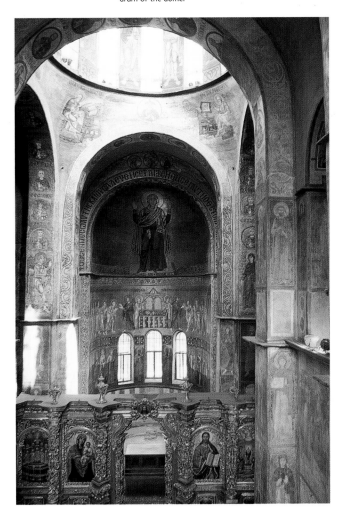

name suggests that its model was none other than Hagia Sophia in Constantinople. A glance at the plan, however, shows that the concept has been considerably modified in translation (Fig. 6.24b). The audacious structure of Hagia Sophia, its soaring dome and luminous interior, was far beyond the abilities of Russian craftsmen, so instead they used multiple domes over parallel bays to evoke the splendor so admired in Constantinople. At its core, St. Sophia is a quincunx plan, with a Greek cross defining the central space, which is vaulted full height to read as the primary volume. As well as the major dome at the crossing, the church has twelve additional domes on high drums, erected as a cluster of four subordinate domes at the intersections of the arms of the cross and eight additional lower domes in the outermost bays, symbolically representing Christ and the twelve apostles. If one ignores the wider bay established for the transept, the plan looks superficially like a nave flanked by pairs of aisles. Both aisles and the nave are terminated by semicircular apses, and second-level galleries over the aisles help to brace the vaults of the transept and nave and the central dome. (Note that the entire design on plan could be erected within the clear span under the great domes of Hagia Sophia.) Soon after its completion, an open gallery surrounding the church on three sides enlarged the church,

6.27 Church of the Transfiguration of the Savior, Novgorod, 1374.

This church was financed by merchants familiar with contemporary architecture in northern Germany. The roofline originally followed the flowing contours of the vaults in a manner similar to the moldings over the grouped windows.

6.28 Axonometric perspective and plan of the Church of the Transfiguration of the Savior, Novgorod, 1374.

These show how the interior space is interrupted by large piers. The axonometric drawing also includes the choir loft, a balcony-like projection over the entrance door, accessed by stairs shown in the plan.

relatively small bays that compartmentalize much of the remainder of the church. Anyone expecting the open spaciousness of Hagia Sophia will be disappointed. Outside the central cross, the second-level galleries diminish the sense of height over the aisles, as does the very limited lighting. Small windows and an overcast climate contribute to the mysterious gloom found inside most Russian churches.

In the context of Russia, St. Sophia is exceptionally grand. Most Russian churches are small and follow a reduced version of the quincunx plan, retaining only a central dome, as may be seen in Novgorod's Church of the Transfiguration of the Savior on Elijah Street, built in 1374 (Figs. 6.27–6.28). Here, there is only a single apse, and the original roofline is suggested by the gentle curves under the eaves. Interior divisions of the plan are reflected on the façade by wall buttresses. Elevations are also enlivened with blind arcading that may reflect influences from Gothic work in Germany. Financing came from wealthy merchants, whose trading contacts exposed them to architectural influences from northern Europe, although the execution here is unmistakably Russian. On the interior, it preserves some of the earliest fresco paintings by the master artist from Constantinople Theophanes the Greek,

whose work would inspire a school of icon painting in Russia. At the rear of the nave, a staircase leads to the choir gallery, which helps to brace the structure. No musical instruments are used in the Byzantine liturgy, so all music is provided by *a cappella* voices. One of the glories of the Russian Orthodox service is its rich tradition of choral song, which emerges from unseen locations above the congregation and reverberates within the hard surfaces of the interior, adding to the mystery and drama of the Mass.

At this point we should consider briefly two features characteristic of Russian churches. The most obvious exterior element is the bulbous or onion dome shape that is built almost universally from the fourteenth century onward. This profile is first seen in Novgorod architecture, but there is no agreement as to its origins. Theories have been proposed that it imitates the form of Indian stupas and ribbed, pointed chaitya hall roofs, which could have been transmitted to Russian builders through intermediary trading contacts. Others have observed that the shape helps shed rain, ice, and snow more effectively than does a hemispherical roof. Ultimately one is left with the impression that whatever the origins, the shape was found esthetically satisfying, thereby explaining its widespread adoption. Russian churches strove for height so as to stand out better in a largely flat landscape. Their domes are raised on tall drums, and the pointed silhouette of the bulbous form emphatically reinforces that sense of verticality.

During the fifteenth century, a screen separating the eastern sanctuary from the nave and aisles partitioned Russian church interiors. This screen, or **iconostasis**, derives from chancel screens such as that surviving at Hosios Loukas's Theotokos church. In Russia, the screen was used to display devotional pictures (**icons**), and over time it came to have multiple tiers of images that made it a virtual wall between the altar and the congregation, thereby adding to the mystery of the ritual. (It should be noted that medieval churches in the Roman Catholic tradition also built screens to separate clergy from laity, and many of these interrupted the view down the church.) The priests during services use three doors in the iconostasis. In the metaphysical interpretation of the Russian Church, the iconostasis does not so much conceal the spiritual world, however much it may hide the architecture, as reveal it and provide a connection to invisible realms.

Icons are painted on wooden panels and affixed to gilded frames in the iconostasis. When their gilded or silvered backgrounds catch the flickering light from candles, the church gleams softly with an other-worldly shimmer, and one seems transported into an ethereal world outside of daily experience.

WOODEN CHURCHES

Masonry architecture records only part of the story of Russian architecture. Until the twentieth century, wood was the dominant building material in Russia. It was readily available, easily worked, and its insulating qualities were superior to masonry for comfort during the long winter. Horizontal log construction, employing notched corner joints similar to those seen in American log cabins, was used for houses, fortifications, and churches. (A major

6.29 Church of the Raising of Lazarus, Muromansky monastery, now at Kizhi, ca. 1391.

Reputedly the oldest wooden church surviving in Russia, it has three different roof pitches and two different forms of wall construction. The diminutive dome on a stalk marks it as a church rather than a simple log house. (Church of the Transfiguration in the background; see Fig. 6.33.)

6.30a Elevation and plan of the Church of the Raising of Lazarus, Kizhi, ca. 1391.

The three sections are an entrance porch, nave, and sanctuary.

6.30b Section and plan of the Church of the Transfiguration, Kizhi, ca. 1391.

While the external effect is spectacular, the interior is not particularly exceptional and the iconostasis cuts abruptly into the nave. The same three-part division in plan seen in the small Lazarus church is repeated here.

difference between Russian, indeed European, log construction and that usually seen in the United States is the sturdiness of the former and the relative impermanence of the latter. European log buildings were meant to last for centuries, whereas most American examples were hastily erected then abandoned as soon as something better could be built.) Foreign visitors remarked repeatedly on the fact that Russian cities seemed to be composed entirely of wooden buildings. Wood of course is subject to both decay and fire, and these destructive forces have greatly reduced the number of old buildings available for study.

Both legend and physical evidence suggest that the oldest surviving Russian wooden building is the small Church of the Raising of Lazarus (ca. 1391) from the Muromansky monastery, now relocated to the open-air museum at Kizhi (Figs. 6.29–6.30a). It is a simple, three-celled structure, composed of a vestibule, nave, and chancel, each covered by its own gable roof and each roof having a slightly different pitch. The oldest sections are the nave and chancel, constructed in horizontal log work, while the vestibule has wooden planks inserted into upright wooden beams. A small shingle-covered dome on a stalk-like drum rises over the nave. Aside from the dome and the slight outward flare to the upper wall sections, there is little about this building that is different from what might be built for a house, but from these humble beginnings, far more elaborate designs would develop. Larger churches with higher gable roofs were built to stand

out more prominently in the countryside, and their floor levels were raised a story off the ground so as to keep the entrance above winter snow levels. Covered access stairs and enclosing galleries were added to provide a protected place for those who may have traveled considerable distances to attend services.

These elements may be seen in the Church of the Nativity of the Virgin (1593), originally in the village of Peredki and now preserved at Novgorod (Fig. 6.31). The

CHAPTER 6 EARLY CHRISTIAN AND BYZANTINE ARCHITECTURE

church has a Greek-cross plan, with an octagonal tower over the crossing that is capped by a tent roof (**shatyor**) to create a strong vertical marker. Logs in diminishing lengths are well suited to support such a roof, and shatyor roofs became common not only for churches but also for fortress towers (Fig. 6.32). The church also has a great external gallery that wraps around three sides of the building, supported on stacked cantilevers (**pomochi**) extending from the wall underneath. One gets a clear idea of the depth of winter snow from the height of this gallery! Russian builders understood the properties of different woods and how to use them effectively. Larch logs that resist rot well are used for the lowest log rounds, while pine is the usual material for the upper sections. Wall logs are cut away on the bottom edge to match the rounded profile of the log below, thus ensuring a tight joint and providing no place for water to collect. Birch bark is used for flashing where roofs intersect walls. Aspen wood was employed for shingles because it weathers to a smooth silvery color. Shingles were split or rived along the grain and then cut to create an interesting pattern and texture when installed. Boards used for the roof have pointed

6.32 Diagram of the construction of a shatyor roof.

Logs of diminishing length are laid in an octagonal plan to create a tent-like shatyor roof. The weatherproof exterior is made of long wooden boards with angled terminations to cast water away from the building.

6.31 Church of the Nativity of the Virgin, Peredki, now at Novgorod, 1593.

This building is clearly more elaborate than the Lazarus church, having a Greek-cross plan and a shatyor roof over the crossing to increase the sense of verticality.

ends to encourage water to drip quickly at the edges. Roof pitches on the towers change near the base to cast run-off clear of the supporting walls. Not everything is so strictly functional, however, for there is also poetry. Folk symbols that date to pre-Christian times are seen in the sun signs on barge boards (decorative trim at the gable ends), and a carved bird may grace the ridge to bring good fortune.

Both practical concerns and symbolic elements are turned to stunning advantage in the masterpiece Church of the Transfiguration (1714) at Kizhi (Fig. 6.33), the only survivor of what were at least three churches with multiple domes constructed under the patronage of Peter the Great. Its plan is based on a Greek cross with the crossing transformed into an octagon (Fig. 6.30b). What at Peredki was treated as a tent roof here becomes the entire external composition, a central tower that steps back in two stages with reverse-curve gables (**bochki**) and domes (Fig. 6.34). The church in fact has twenty-two domes on slender drums, creating a pyramidal composition. Counting from the top, there is a large single dome at the summit, four domes on the middle stage of the octagon, and eight on the lower octagonal story. Two more sets of four domes each are stacked at the bochki gables over the arms of the Greek cross, and the lowest single dome is placed over the sanctuary. This church continues the tradition begun nearly 700 years earlier at St. Sophia in Kiev: an elaborately domed exterior and an interior of smaller compartmentalized spaces not necessarily reflected in the overall massing. At Kizhi, there is a suspended ceiling across the octagonal tower, so the interior does not share the soaring volume suggested by the tower of domes. Furthermore, the internal space division in plan is not what one might expect from the outside. The vestibule wraps around the Greek cross, obscuring the actual shape of the nave, and the iconostasis projects into the center of the octagon, resulting in an irregular shape for the congregation. Kizhi

6.33 Church of the Transfiguration, Kizhi, 1714.

This masterpiece church of 22 domes rises from a Greek-cross plan. Aspen used for shingles on the domes and bochki (reverse-curve gables) weathers to a silver gray that gleams like polished metal. To the left is the companion Church of the Intercession, built for use in winter and provided with a stove.

is dramatic in the expansive northern landscape. On the inside, it is the icons that capture one's attention rather than the volume of the space.

The widespread destruction and economic upheaval that accompanied the invasion by the Mongols or Tartars in 1238–40 brought an end to the dominance of Kiev as a center of Russian government. Russian cities paid annual tribute to the khans of the Golden Horde, leaving little for investment in major buildings at home, so there was a corresponding decline in construction skills. Over the course of the fourteenth and fifteenth centuries, Moscow gradually established itself as the leading Russian city and

became the seat of the metropolitan of the Russian Orthodox Church. Church and state combined efforts to overthrow the domination of the khans. Moscow's central fortress, the Kremlin, was gradually reconstructed in stone from the original wood, and new churches were erected there under patronage of the princes of Moscow, who now styled themselves as tsars (from the Latin *caesar*).

Motifs from wooden architecture found their way into masonry building, particularly the tent roof already seen in the church from Peredki, which came to be used for votive churches (as opposed to churches needing to accommodate a congregation) built in Moscow during the sixteenth century. The most famous of these is Moscow's Cathedral of the Intercession on the Moat, more usually known as St. Basil the Blessed (1555–60) (Fig. 6.35), erected on Red Square just outside the Kremlin walls to commemorate Ivan IV's victory over the Horde at the battle of Kazan in 1552. The architects were Barma and

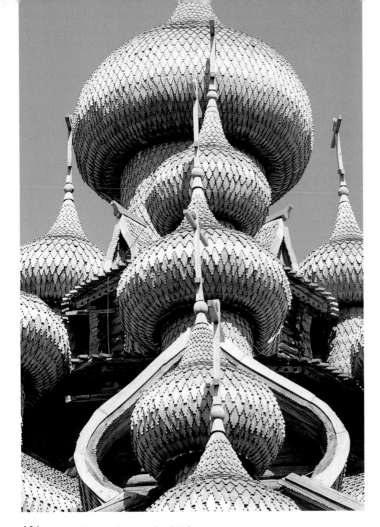

6.34 Church of the Transfiguration detail, Kizhi.

This view shows the elaborate shingle work and framing of bochki. Note the stepped shapes of shingle ends, cut not only for decorative effect but also to promote water run-off and minimize capillary attraction.

compartmentalized. Since the volume under each tower is open to the chapel below, processing through the church is like traveling along a passage connecting a series of discrete chambers, each the size of a domestic room but having an enormously tall ceiling.

St. Basil's is a reasonable place to conclude this consideration of the Byzantine architecture of Russia. Even though its construction coincides chronologically with buildings of the late Renaissance in Italy, St. Basil's is still rooted in traditions begun a millennium earlier in the eastern empire centered in Constantinople. Byzantium's lasting impact would continue in Russia as foreign architects came to build Baroque churches during the seventeenth and eighteenth centuries. Under Peter the Great, who avidly sought to end Russia's cultural isolation and overcome its perceived backward ways, secular Russian architecture came to resemble contemporary European architectural movements more than honoring its own historical past.

6.35 St. Basil the Blessed, Moscow, 1555–60.

Barma and Posnik utilized forms from wooden churches to create an extraordinary design in masonry. The riot of forms and colors on the exterior is more memorable than the interior.

Posnik, who came from Pskov. Their design is fundamentally a central sanctuary surrounded by four large octagonal chapels and four smaller chapels that are square in plan (Fig. 6.24c). Eight of the chapels are dedicated to saints whose days coincided with key dates in the siege of Kazan, and the ninth is dedicated to the Entry into Jerusalem, so in some respects this building is really nine chapels sharing a common foundation. The central sanctuary is covered by a tall shatyor roof, while the eight subsidiary chapels receive individual vertical expression as domed towers. It is a tribute to the architects that this diverse array of elements, including also the covered entrance galleries and stairs, reads not as a random collection of parts but as a complex, intriguing whole, interesting from whatever angle it is approached. A close look at the outside shows decorative elements including layers of semicircular and triangular gables, pilasters, and diamond-shaped motifs, along with the expected onion domes, which are actually seventeenth-century replacements for helmet domes of the original design. These replacement roofs are a riot of glazed tiles in faceted, zigzag, spiraling, and striped designs that contribute additional color to the already elaborate red-brick and white-stone trim of the exterior. Interior space is highly

CHAPTER 7

ISLAMIC ARCHITECTURE

As we have seen, the Early Christians went through an extensive process to develop architectural forms suitable for and expressive of their religion. Followers of the religion founded by the prophet Mohammed experienced a similar evolutionary process, but one that led to different results as they created buildings to serve and symbolize Islam.

Islam originated in Arabia. In 610 the angel Gabriel is said to have appeared to Mohammed in Mecca and expounded the revelation of God, or Allah. These revelations were collected into a holy book, the Qur'an, which expressed in Arabic the message of Islam, a word signifying submission to the will of Allah. Each Muslim accepted five basic truths or duties: to believe in the oneness of God, and that Mohammed was the messenger of God; to pray five times daily; to fast from sunrise to sunset during the month of Ramadan; to give alms to the poor; and to make at least one pilgrimage to Mecca, wealth and health permitting.

Conversion of the tribes to Islam was accompanied by an intense awakening of Arab fervor, and the courage and fighting skill of Arabic tribes, previously exploited by the Sassanian and Byzantine empires, was turned against these masters in a fury of rapid conquests, frequently aided by local contempt for the corruption associated with Byzantine rule. By 661 Islamic armies had swept through what is today Iran, Iraq, Israel, Syria, and Egypt, and they then moved across the North African coast to enter Spain in 711. From Spain they pushed northward into France, where forces led by Charles Martel stopped their European expansion in 732 at the battle of Tours. Islamic settlers remained in central and southern Spain until 1492,

however, and their armies continued to batter the southern borders of the Byzantine Empire until they finally conquered Constantinople in 1453. Through trade, Islamic dynasties made contact with China and India, where their religion would eventually take root. With military conquest came economic, social, and cultural dominance as Islamic customs and the Arabic language replaced surviving Roman practices. Islamic policy toward conquered populations was generally one of accommodation. Islamic rule was often preferred by the natives of occupied lands to that of harsh Byzantine governors, and the multi-cultural society the invaders fostered provided a model of respectful interaction that the modern world might do well to rediscover. The heady mix of learned men from Islamic and Jewish traditions, sometimes joined by Christian theologians, contributed to a highly productive era in the arts and sciences from the ninth through sixteenth centuries.

EARLY SHRINES AND PALACES

For their earliest buildings, the largely nomadic Islamic Arabs assimilated techniques and forms from the civilizations they encountered. Syrian and Christian influences are clear in one of the most prominent early shrines, the Dome of the Rock (687–91) in Jerusalem (Figs. 7.1–7.2). Its location on Mount Moriah was sacred to the Jews, both as the site on which Abraham had offered his son Isaac as a sacrifice to the Lord and as the location of Solomon's Temple. Muslims honored it for Abraham's presence, but also venerated it as the place from which Mohammed ascended in his night journey to paradise. At the center of the Dome of the Rock is a rock, under which is a small cave with a single opening. The shrine is carefully positioned around this rock, the domed central portion enclosing the rock and a concentric aisle permitting circumambulation. The building's form was probably derived from Christian precedent. Constantine's Church of the Holy Sepulcher in Jerusalem had featured a similar

---

Qibla iwan of the Friday Mosque, Isfahan, 12th century.

What began in the ninth century as a columnar hall mosque was transformed over time into a more elaborate plan, culminating with a large four-iwan courtyard. Note the iwan's use of muqarnas vaults.

7.1 Dome of the Rock, Jerusalem, 687–91.

One of the earliest Islamic shrines, this octagonal domed building has a double ambulatory surrounding the rock from which Mohammed ascended on his journey to paradise.

rotunda, and there were many centrally planned domed churches throughout the Byzantine world. Unlike most Byzantine domes, however, the structure here is of wood. (There is evidence that early Christian shrines also had wooden domes, although none has survived to the present day.)

The dome of the Jerusalem sanctuary, sixty-seven feet in diameter, is constructed of a double shell, each shell having thirty-two converging wooden ribs, and the whole rests on a cornice atop a masonry drum. The inner ribs are plastered and adorned with painted and gilded designs (fourteenth-century reconstructions), while the exterior is sheathed with boards and finished with lead and gold leaf. The drum is supported on four piers, with three columns set between each pier. Between this inner ring of columns and piers and the outside wall is an intermediate ring of eight piers alternating with paired sets of columns, all supporting a circle of wooden tie beams overhead. The location of major elements in the plan is governed by a geometric figure contained in the circle circumscribing the octagon formed by the exterior walls. If two rotated squares are inscribed in this circle so that their corners are opposite the center of the octagon faces, the piers of the

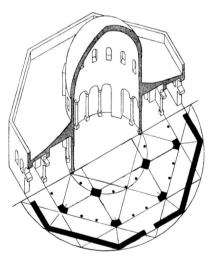

7.2 Axonometric section of the Dome of the Rock, Jerusalem, 687–91.

This section shows the sophisticated geometry involved in its design.

intermediate ring occur at the intersections of the lines forming the squares. Furthermore, the four innermost piers fit into the grid of lines drawn across the plan from the eight intermediate piers. Such a harmonious relationship indicates that the architect had a sophisticated understanding of geometric order.

Rich materials covered both interior and exterior surfaces. Marble facings were used on some interior piers and walls, and elegant mosaics portraying stylized palm and acanthus plants finished other piers and vaulted surfaces. Windows had ornamental stone grilles based on contemporary patterns, and the arches around the rotunda were set with alternating red and white stones, a technique called **polychromy**, which is seen in many later Islamic buildings. An inscription in Arabic at the base of the dome proclaims Islam as the true religion, the successor to Christianity. In building the Dome of the Rock, Islam created a monument to rival the wealth and magnificence of other temples and churches, thereby providing a tangible symbol of the new religion's ascendancy and that of the Umayyad Dynasty that was responsible for its construction.

The general scheme employed at the Dome of the Rock, that of a central shrine around which the faithful could circulate, was used earlier at Mecca in rebuilding the Ka'ba, the goal of Islamic pilgrimage. This cloth-draped cubical shrine contains the Black Stone, believed to have been given to Abraham by the angel Gabriel. The stone was venerated in pre-Muslim times. Mohammed destroyed the idols placed around it, and his successors cleared neighboring buildings in order to provide clear circulation space around the stone. At the Hajj, or annual pilgrimage, the devout process seven times around the Ka'ba, following the sets of concentric rings set in the pavement encircling the shrine.

Early Islamic rulers or caliphs preferred life in the desert to life in cities, and they constructed a number of desert palaces in the Middle East. In about 711–15 (or as late as the middle of the eighth century), such a settlement was built at Qusayr Amra (Figs. 7.3–7.4a), about fifty miles east of Amman, Jordan, by Caliph al-Walid I. The complex is still under archaeological study, but it appears to have included an agricultural community. The surviving buildings are an audience hall and a small baths, both interesting for their vaulted construction. The audience hall is nearly square in plan, twenty-four by twenty-eight feet, with a central alcove on axis from the entrance flanked by side rooms. This division into thirds corresponds to the ceiling vaults of the audience hall, where two longitudinal arches support three transverse barrel vaults. Both arches are slightly pointed; Qusayr Amra is one of the first places where this feature is found in Islamic work. The design is thought to be of Syrian origin

---

7.3 Desert palace, Qusayr Amra, 711–15 or later.

The masonry buildings that survive were used as an audience hall and a small baths. Other foundation remains indicate that this was part of an agricultural settlement.

Chamber

Changing room

Furnace under floor

Throne room

Audience hall

Open court   Caldarium   Tepidarium

0 _____ 20 m
0 _____ 60 ft
N

7.4a Plan of the audience hall and a small baths complex, Qusayr Amra, 711–15 or later.

Three parallel barrel vaults of the nearly square audience hall were supported on two longitudinal arches springing from piers. Small apsidal rooms off the central recess were probably used for sleeping in.

7.4b Plan of the palace, Mshatta, 743–44.

Only a portion of this palace was ever completed. Rooms adjacent to the entrance include ceremonial halls and courts, with mosque. The palace portion (shaded on plan) is organized around a triple-apse basilican hall.

Latrine

Throne room

Court   Court

Bayt, or domestic living unit for wife

Basilican hall

Central court

Bath House   Court

Mosque

Entrance   Mihrab

N

0 _____ 50 m
0 _____ 150 ft

7.5 Carved ornament from Mshatta, 743–44.

Note the fine-scale detail set behind the bolder zigzag diagonals and rosettes. Removed from the palace in the nineteenth century, this fragment is now in Berlin.

since pointed arches are unknown in Roman building. Attached to the audience hall are the three small rooms of the baths: a barrel-vaulted changing room, a groin-vaulted tepidarium, and a domed caldarium warmed by under-floor heating and supplied with piped water in the Roman manner. Interiors were finished with frescoes throughout, and the dome was embellished to represent the vault of heaven, with the northern constellations of stars and the signs of the zodiac. On the exterior, the articulated roofs directly reflect the vaulting patterns, and the massing of the whole complex is reminiscent of Roman work such as the Forum Baths at Pompeii.

Some other desert residences were based on the designs of Roman frontier forts combined with influences from Sassanian audience halls. Such was the case with the Mshatta Palace (Fig. 7.4b), located about twenty miles south of Amman, Jordan, and started in 743–44, although never completed. Stone walls, reinforced by towers set at regular intervals, form the square enclosure, measuring about 475 feet on a side. There is only one entrance, in the center of the south wall, establishing the central axis through an entrance hall, a rectangular secondary court, the large square central court, and a concluding basilica hall terminating in a triple-apse square chamber. Four vaulted apartments, probably for the caliph's four wives, open off side courts and are accessed through the audience hall. Secondary rooms, including a mosque on the south side balanced by a baths, were planned for the section just inside the portal. The flanking side sections seem never to have been built, although tie courses in the stonework indicate that apartments were to have been constructed there. As with the Dome of the Rock, an orderly geometry underlies the plan—proportions of the sections are established by diagonals drawn from opposite corners—while the scheme relies on precedent established in the area since Roman times. The formal plan and central axis recall castra plans, while the entrance to the basilica hall is formed by a triple-arched gateway, with the central span being wider than the side spans in the manner of a Roman triumphal arch. Carved reliefs (removed from the lower portions of the outer wall in the late nineteenth century and now in Berlin) were set in a continuous frieze nearly fifteen feet high (Fig. 7.5). They include a ground of stylized vines in intertwining geometric patterns, accented by rosettes set amid a great zigzag projecting molding, demonstrating the same love of surface ornament found in the Jerusalem building and presaging the intricate ornamental elaboration so characteristic of mature Islamic architecture.

DEVELOPMENT OF THE MOSQUE

The building type most closely associated with Islam is the mosque, the primary place of worship, which evolved from several sources, including the House of the Prophet at Medina (ca. 622), Christian churches, and perhaps the audience halls (**apadanas**) of Persian kings. Beside Mohammed's house was a square enclosure, with small chambers set in the southeast corner for his living quarters (Fig. 7.6). The remainder of the space was a partially open central court. Although constructed originally for domestic purposes, it also served as a gathering place for his followers to hear sermons and prayers, and after

7.6 Reconstruction of the House of the Prophet, Medina, ca. 622.

This building became a prototype for the mosque. Followers of Mohammed assembled in the open courtyard to hear sermons and participate in group prayer, functions that became key in mosque design.

Mohammed's death its form was imitated in simple worship facilities built in other settlements. When territorial expansion brought the forces of Islam into established cities, readily available spaces, particularly Christian churches, were converted to mosques by removing Christian images and orienting the prayer wall, or **qibla**, to face toward Mecca. In areas formerly controlled by Sassanids, the remains of apadanas were renovated to provide space for worship. The size of the mosque was usually proportional to the size of the community. The five daily prayers required of the faithful did not necessarily take place in mosques, but on Friday all the men in the community assembled in the main mosque for communal noontime prayers.

The Great Mosque at Damascus (706–15, with later rebuildings) is the oldest extant mosque and illustrates the process through which the form developed (Fig. 7.7b).

7.7a,b Plans of the Great Mosque, Córdoba, 785; 833–988; and the Great Mosque, Damascus, 706–15.

Both these mosques have columned prayer halls preceded by open courtyards or sahns.

The site is an ancient one on which had stood a Roman temple dedicated to Jupiter and a fourth-century Christian church dedicated to St. John the Baptist. For a time after the Islamic conquest of the city in 635, both Christians and Muslims worshiped on the site, but in 706 the church was pulled down and an impressive mosque, based in part on tripartite aisle-and-nave basilican church plans, was constructed under the caliphate of al-Walid I. The mosque's outline was determined by the shape of the Roman shrine, a walled irregular rectangle 1262 by 1004 feet, entered through a gateway in the center of the shorter, east side. Four towers, once part of a Roman temple enclosure on the site, provide an elevated platform at the corners of the site from which a caller (*muezzin*) could summon the faithful to prayer. The general design of these towers, known as **minarets**, may have been based on earlier fortification towers or lighthouses, but, with their incorporation at Damascus, they became standard features of subsequent Friday mosques. Just as belltowers or raised domes do for churches, minarets serve to identify the mosque in the landscape. Much later, particularly important mosques were sometimes given multiple minarets, but one generally sufficed.

Over half of the inner space is given over to an open arcaded courtyard, the **sahn**, containing a domed fountain pavilion for ritual ablutions and an octagonal pavilion originally used for the public treasury. The covered prayer hall, or **haram**, extends along the entire long south wall. Two parallel rows of columns divide this hall longitudinally into thirds, near the center of which the arcades are interrupted by a broad transverse element similar to a nave, with a wooden dome over its central bay. This element develops in later designs into the **maqsura**, a special processional area reserved for the retinue of the caliph, thereby justifying its dome as a special architectural accent. The entrance to the maqsura from the sahn is through a triple-arched entry that historians believe was based on the design of the now-destroyed Chalki Gate of the palace in Constantinople. (That design also influenced the entrance to Justinian's palace in Ravenna, which is illustrated in the mosaics of S. Apollinare Nuovo.) The south wall being the qibla, there are three niches or **mihrabs** set into it to indicate the direction of Mecca. A raised pulpit or **minbar**, from which Qur'anic readings, sermons, or official proclamations and addresses are given, is located to the right of the central mihrab. Extensive mosaics originally covered the upper walls and arches. Although little remains of them today, their subjects are known: calligraphy and naturalistic vegetation, as in the Dome of the Rock, together with a frieze of villages, townscapes, and running water, thought by some to be the Islamic image of paradise. Islamic ornament relies greatly on geometric abstractions (arabesques) and the stylized use of Arabic calligraphy, as strict interpretation of religious laws forbids the depiction of animate beings—people and animals—in places of worship. (Many religious scholars also objected to writing.) The Great Mosque at Damascus is one of the glories of early Islamic architecture, and some of its features influenced later mosque designs.

REGIONAL VARIATIONS IN MOSQUE DESIGN

As Islam spread, the form of the mosque was adjusted to suit local building traditions and conditions. Scholars have categorized mosque designs into five broad groupings: the columned hall with perhaps several small domes (found in Arabia, Africa, and Spain); a large central space covered either by a large dome braced by semidomes (common in Anatolia) or pyramidal roofs (typical of Indonesia); a rectangular court flanked by large roofed or vault spaces (**iwans**) open to the courtyard in the center of each side (found in Iran and central Asia); the triple-domed mosque with a large open courtyard (developed in India); and mosques composed of a series of pavilions set on axis within a walled garden (typical of China). To provide an introduction to the diversity seen in these different geographical areas, we will consider a few examples from each group in turn.

COLUMNAR HALL DESIGNS

The Great Mosque begun in around 785 in Córdoba, Spain (Fig. 7.7a), follows the pattern established by the Great Mosque of Damascus, having been founded by Abd al'Rahman I, a descendant of the Umayyad line who brought Syrians with him to Spain. In the first construction period, the mosque occupied a nearly square plan, half comprising the sahn and the other half the haram, which contained ten rows of eleven columns to create an eleven-aisled sanctuary. In the haram, superimposed arches connect the columns, the lower arch being horseshoe-shaped and the upper one not quite semicircular. The effect of this work is light and delicate, and although both the tiered arcades of the Damascus mosque and the stacked arches of Roman aqueducts have been suggested as the inspiration for the superimposed arches, their treatment here is entirely original. Both arch levels are polychrome, composed of white stone voussoirs set alternately with red brick ones. The salvaged Roman columns on which they rest are of various designs, some fluted and some plain, with Corinthian capitals. Since the ceiling above the sanctuary was originally flat, the builders facilitated roof drainage by a parallel series of gable roofs with sloping drains in the valleys to discharge water to the sides of the building. Each aisle opened to the sahn, where eleven horseshoe arches framed as many entrances to the sanctuary. The sahn itself was large, 240 by 197 feet, and its entrances were set in the midpoints of the wall enclosing the entire mosque.

7.8 (left) The Great Mosque interior, Córdoba, 833–988.

This view shows the horseshoe-shaped polychrome stacked arches that dominate the interior. Eventually 610 columns defined the prayer hall.

7.9 (right) The Great Mosque vault, Córdoba, 833–988.

Note the use of lobed arches, polychromy, and the interlaced-arch structure of the dome.

7.10 (below) The Great Mosque, Lantern of Hakim II, Córdoba, 833–988.

This lantern also employs interlaced arches in its construction.

Starting in 833, this mosque was enlarged three times. In the first renovation campaign (833–48), the prayer hall was extended southward by the addition of eight new bays that maintained the alignment and rhythm of the original mosque but necessitated reconstruction of the qibla and mihrab. The hall was again expanded to the south in 987–88, when another twelve bays were added along with a new qibla and mihrab. The new mihrab was a richly ornamented niche, given prominence in the interior by a maqsura of lobed and cusped arches (Fig. 7.8), covered by a dome formed by boldly interlacing arches (Figs. 7.9–

7.10), flanked by smaller domes also composed of interlaced arches in the bays to either side. So far as we know, these exceptional domes are an original invention here, and they are the probable inspiration for similar domes built in the Baroque by Guarini (see Fig. 12.27). The final extension of the mosque was constructed in 987–88 along the eastern side, adding another eight aisles running the full length of the existing prayer hall, and enlarging the courtyard as well to create the largest mosque in all Spain. In the sixteenth century, after the Moors were expelled from Spain, the cathedral of Córdoba (Fig. 7.11) was inserted inside the mosque, disrupting the colonnaded expanse of the prayer hall but perhaps inadvertently preserving a good portion of the Islamic fabric through the mosque's conversion to a place of Christian worship.

IWAN DESIGNS

To the east, in Central Asian lands now part of Iran, Uzbekistan, Turkmenistan, and Afghanistan, mosque designs developed initially from multi-columned halls, familiar in the region from Persian audience halls. The earliest mosque about which we have reliable archaeological information is the Friday mosque in Isfahan (Fig. 7.12a), begun in the ninth century and reworked repeatedly until the seventeenth century. The original form seems to have been a rectangular multi-columned hall, with colonnades on all four sides, soon changed into a sahn and haram surrounded by arcades. To this in 1086–87 a domed chamber was introduced at the south end of the existing building, probably to serve as a maqsura. It differed significantly in scale from the domes already seen as part of the maqsuras

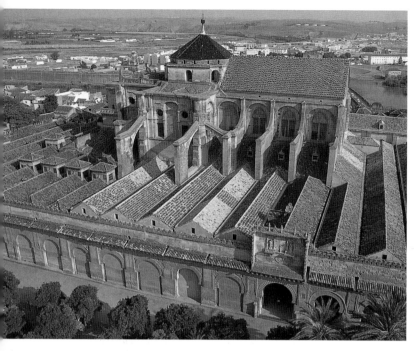

7.11 The Great Mosque from the minaret, Córdoba, 833–988.

Parallel rows of ridge-and-valley roofs cover the prayer hall, and the foreground trees are growing in the sahn. One regrets the intrusion of a later Christian church in this splendid Islamic building.

7.12a Plan of the Friday mosque, Isfahan, 8th–16th centuries.

This mosque is interesting for its early incorporation of substantial domes within a multi-columned prayer hall. In its final form, the mosque evolved into a four-iwan type, having a large central courtyard bisected by cross-axes established by the iwans.

7.12b Plan of Masjid-i-shah, Isfahan, 1611–ca. 1630.

At the top is the public square. Entrance to the mosque is centered in the arcades defining the square, but the axis turns to bring the mosque proper into alignment with Mecca. Theological schools are located beside the mosque.

at Damascus and Córdoba: rather than covering one bay of the columnar hall, the southern dome covered twenty bays. In 1088, a slightly smaller dome was added in an axial line to the north. It is not clear what function it served initially, for it was outside the building at the time of its construction but was soon incorporated into arcades.

At some later date, Isfahan's Friday mosque was modified again to include four iwans set in the center of each side of the courtyard (page 164). Courtyards of this design were known from Parthian palaces built in Persia in the third century CE, but the reason for adapting the idea for use in a mosque is unclear. While two iwans at right angles to the qibla wall could help define the focus on Mecca, having four symmetrically disposed makes less sense. It has been proposed that the four-iwan courtyard became popular for esthetic reasons. A boldly scaled arched

7.13 Masjid-i-Shah, Isfahan, 1611–ca. 1630.

In order to respect the direction of Mecca, the mosque is turned forty-five degrees to the axis of the public square (left side of the photograph) laid out by Shah Abbas.

7.14 Iwan, Masjid-i-Shah, Isfahan, 1611–ca. 1630.

Two-story arcades flank the central arch, which is finished with elaborate tile decoration and a muqarnas vault. In the background is the rear of the entrance iwan on the public square.

7.15 Masjid-i-Shah, entrance to prayer hall, Isfahan, 1611–ca. 1630.

This view shows the elaborate blue-glazed tilework and muqarnas vault.

Entrance to the mosque comes in the center of the southern side of the market, so as to provide a monumental portal to the public area and match the gateway to the bazaar at the opposite end of the square, but the mosque itself is turned forty-five degrees so as to be correctly aligned with Mecca. The skill with which the designers accommodated the change in axis is one of the most admired aspects of the plan. From the entranceway, one can look directly at the iwan constructed in front of the qibla, but the circulation path leads one aside, past the ablution area, before entering the four-iwan courtyard, thereby accomplishing the axial shift with finesse. Apart from the transitional elements at the entrance, symmetry governs the entire design. A still pool at the center of the courtyard reflects the blue-background painted tilework covering the iwans and the great dome of the mosque. Among the decorative elements portrayed in the tiles are peacocks, reflecting the builders' willingness to depict animals in art rather than confining ornament to recursive geometric elements and calligraphy. The domed prayer hall is augmented by rooms on either side, also covered by a succession of smaller domes, that served as a winter mosque, and it is further complemented by two religious schools (**madrasas**) in courts located parallel to the qibla, thus continuing an established tradition of incorporating education with worship. (The study of law and religion are inseparable aspects of Islamic higher education.)

COURTYARD DESIGNS

Islam came to India in successive waves of military invasions in the eleventh through thirteenth centuries, challenging the established religions of Hinduism and Buddhism with its fundamentally different religious perspective. India's cave-like temples with interiors used only by priests and covered inside and out with intricately wrought sculpted figures were totally alien to the Islamic idea of the mosque with accessible open courtyards, spacious prayer halls, and scrupulous avoidance of the human figure in representational art. Hindu and Buddhist temples were replaced with mosques initially based on multi-columned hall designs. Beginning with the ascendancy of the Mughal Dynasty (mid-sixteenth to eighteenth centuries), however, one sees a distinctly Indo-Islamic style come into being, spurred on in large measure by the arrival of foreign craftsmen from Central Asia. Some of these masons were descendants of Indian craftsmen taken captive by the Mongol conqueror Timur the Lame in 1398. Their return in the sixteenth century brought skilled builders familiar with the Islamic architecture of Persia to India, and the resulting works done for the Mughal rulers are some of the most magnificent to be found in the Islamic world.

Akbar, the third Mughal emperor, who ruled 1556–1605, was responsible for constructing an entirely new capital at Fatehpur Sikri (1569–ca. 1580), a site

opening that provided builders with an opportunity to exercise their skills in geometric ornament interrupts the regular rhythm of the colonnades. In the case of Isfahan, this included the application of glazed tiles in shades of blue, turquoise, white, and yellow, and **muqarnas** vaults, the ornamental treatment of curved wall surfaces with corbeled concave elements that has the overall effect of dissolving the material presence of the wall into facets that seem to hover in space. The mosque is also renowned for its intricate brickwork patterns in the domes.

During the reign of Shah Abbas I, the core of Isfahan was greatly expanded as a whole new market area was developed at some distance from the older settlement around the Friday mosque. Included in the new construction was a congregational mosque, the Masjid-i-Shah (1611–ca. 1630), built to designs of Badi' al-Zaman Tuni and Ali Akbar al-Isfahani (Figs. 7.12b, 7.13–7.15).

7.16 Plan of the palace, Fatehpur Sikri, 1569–ca. 1580.

This remarkable palace has building groups and pavilions organized around courtyards that open from one to another without an overall sense of hierarchy. Akbar's personal retreat was the Diwan-i-Khass, a pavilion in the center of a square pool accessed by four bridges.

7.17 Plan of the Friday mosque, Fatehpur Sikri, ca. 1568–71.

The monumental gate is on the southern side of the mosque, preceded by a wide stairway, while the prayer hall is set to the west.

abandoned after his death and preserved now as a national monument in India (Fig. 7.16). The monumental palace buildings are all that remain, but sixteenth-century accounts describe it as a city larger than London at the same period, which explains in part the grand scale employed for its Friday mosque (ca. 1568–78) (Figs. 7.17–7.18). Constructed in red sandstone, the mosque has an immense courtyard, 312 by 387 feet, entered from the south through a monumental gate enlarged in 1596 (Fig. 7.19). From the palace, the entrance was through the eastern side, placing it on axis with the prayer hall on the western side. Behind the western iwan is the major dome of the prayer hall, flanked by two smaller domes, setting a pattern for Indian mosques that would often be repeated.

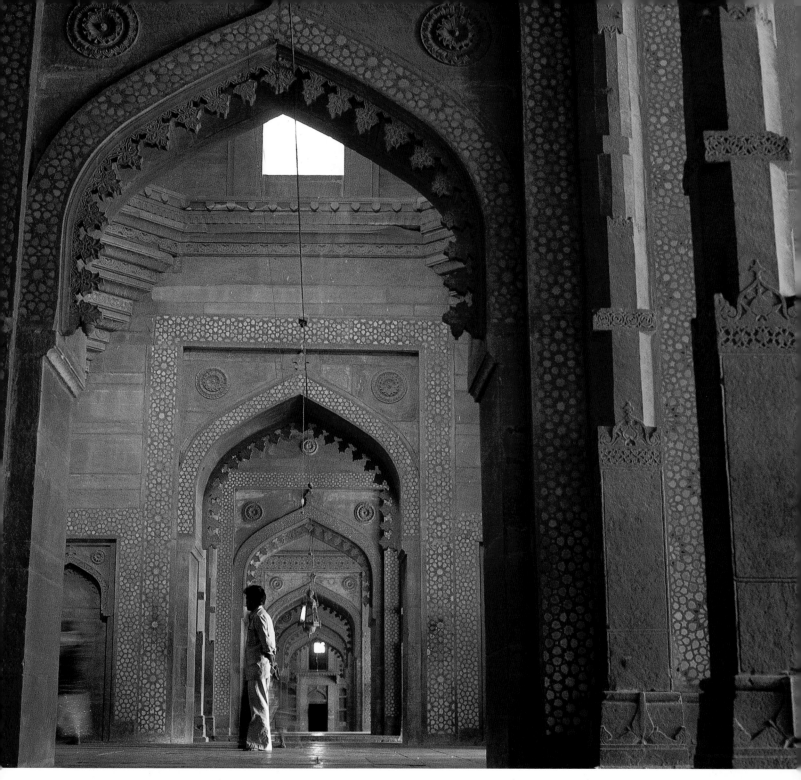

7.18 Friday mosque interior, Fatehpur Sikri, ca. 1568–71.

This view shows the distinctive detail developed by Akbar's architects as they fused Islamic forms (the pointed arch, for example) with elements from Hindu and Buddhist traditions already well established in India.

In its architecture, the building reflects arched and domed forms familiar from examples in Iran, but some of the detail also borrows elements from the Hindu and Buddhist architecture of India, a blend that contributes a distinctive quality to Islamic buildings on the subcontinent. The mosque's courtyard contains the exquisitely detailed marble tomb of Salim Chishti (d. 1572), a holy man who had predicted that the childless Akbar would have three

sons. Fatehpur Sikri was built in celebration of the birth of Akbar's son Jahangir in 1569, and the east–west axis through the Friday mosque aligns with Chishti's hermitage, which was already on the site.

It is common for a mosque to include the tomb of a founder or holy man. Monumental tombs, usually with domes, had been built for Islamic rulers in Central Asia, including Timur the Lame, and with the construction in Delhi of the tomb of Akbar's father, Humayun, this idea came to India (Fig. 7.20). The architects for the tomb, which was built in 1562–71, were Mirak Sayid Ghiyath and Muhammad Sayid, a father-and-son team who had worked previously in Herat and Bukhara. Their innovative design combines the domed tomb, symbolizing a heavenly mansion, with the Persian garden, evocative of paradise, in a majestic memorial. Within a square enclosure, the tomb is centered on a raised podium. The structure is brick, faced with red sandstone trimmed in geometric marble inlay, rising to a central double-shell dome-on-drum that dominates the composition. Surrounding garden areas are subdivided into quadrants by channels of flowing water that border planted areas, where flowers and fruit trees delighted the senses. Arched gateways mark axial entrances in the center of each side of the enclosing wall.

A similar idea is found at the Taj Mahal in Agra (1631–47), where the tomb and its associated garden are

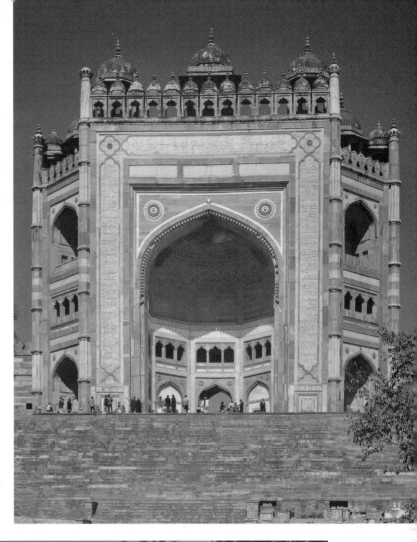

7.19 (right) Friday mosque gateway, Fatehpur Sikri, ca. 1568–71.

As Akbar's city was set on a plateau above the surrounding terrain, a monumental flight of steps is required to gain entrance to the mosque from the southern side. These serve as a plinth for an impressive arched gateway.

7.20 (below) Tomb of Humayun, Delhi, 1562–71.

This building combines Indian and Iranian architectural traditions. Four corner chambers join to support a double-shell dome at the center of the tomb, while the gardens are eight quartered squares subdivided by watercourses.

7.21 Taj Mahal, Agra, 1631–47.

This is one of the world's best-known buildings. The famed serenity of this marble tomb derives in part from its elegant design and its placement in an appropriate landscape with plants and water.

7.22 Plan of the Taj Mahal, 1632–47.

This plan shows how the tomb (*top*) is set in a larger landscape of square courts divided into quarters by watercourses, creating a nested hierarchy of axes and cross-axes that allude to the garden of paradise.

River Jumna

Mosque

Guest house

Tomb

Gardens

Main gate

Servants' quarters

Servants' quarters

N

0   200 m

0   600 ft

complemented by a mosque (Figs. 7.21–7.22). Its builder was Jahangir's son, Shah Jahan, who ruled from 1628 to 1658 and is remembered as a prolific Mughal patron of building. Aided by a well-trained group of architects attached to his court, Shah Jahan promoted a style that included an emphasis on bilateral symmetry, the use of cusped arches, and white marble or stucco facing instead of red sandstone for exterior finishes.

The Taj Mahal is unquestionably one of the world's most celebrated buildings, built as a tomb for Shah Jahan's beloved wife, Mumtaz Mahal. A trio of architects was responsible for the work, Ahmad Lahawri, assisted by 'Abd al-Karim Ma'mur Khan and Makramat Khan, assisted by craftsmen from Persia, Central Asia, and India. The site adjoins a river to the north, and the tomb is placed next to the river, rather than being in the center as was Humayun's. Entrance is from the south, through a gateway set on axis with the tomb. In between is a square garden, with canals dividing the square into quarters to set the central axis and cross-axis, and each quadrant is twice further subdivided into quarters. Flowering trees, cypresses, and blooming plants originally grew in the garden areas as symbols of rebirth and immortality. The tomb itself is symmetrical, crowned with a large bulbous dome raised on a drum and graced by smaller octagonal pavilions with domical

178

roofs set at the corners. Highly polished and inlaid marble is used for the exterior, so the building appears to glisten in the sun. The whole is raised on a square platform, the corners of which are marked by minarets. Flanking the tomb are symmetrically placed red sandstone buildings, to the west a mosque and to the east a guest house, whose color contrasts deliberately with the shimmering white marble. Against a verdant foreground of plant material, accentuated by reflecting water channels, the Taj Mahal seems ethereal, its proportion and detail so finely wrought as to capture the beautiful memory of the woman whose untimely death prompted its construction.

PAVILION DESIGNS

Islam was introduced to China in the mid-seventh century through contacts in port cities. Some of these foreign traders assimilated Chinese culture and remained in the country, retaining their religious practices. Another source of Muslim influence came over land through the armies of Genghis Khan, whose troops included Islamic peoples living on the routes of conquest. These troops settled in garrisons located throughout the country, spreading the religion over a broad area and attracting converts. Over time, traditional Chinese architectural forms were adapted for Islamic worship, so in contrast to the masonry and domed mosques of Central Asia, one finds mosques in China that conform closely to architectural models already developed for wooden buildings. (There are also mosques resembling those of the Islamic heartland, but these were built by predominantly Muslim ethnic minorities.) Three major adjustments to traditional Chinese designs were necessary to fit Islamic practice. First, Chinese halls generally faced south, aligned on a north–south axis. In order to be directed toward Mecca, however, the mosque had to face west, with access from the east, so the axis had to be rotated ninety degrees to normal custom. Minarets came to be linked in some mosques with portal gates and identified with moon-viewing pavilions, an interesting fusion of Islamic and native traditions. Finally, the mihrab recess generally has a small masonry semi-dome built over it, but on the exterior it is covered by a Chinese gable roof rather than being expressed.

The Great Mosque in Xian provides an early example of these modifications in practice. Built in 1392 with later renovations, it consists of a series of wooden pavilions and courtyards arranged along a central axis running from east to west (Fig. 7.23). After passing the entrance gate, there are four portal pavilions defining the entry to the

7.23 Pavilion, Great Mosque, Xian, begun 1392 with later renovations.

This mosque is organized like Buddhist temples in China, with a series of courtyards and pavilions with up-turning eaves, symmetrically arranged around a central axis leading to the prayer hall.

successive courtyards before one reaches the substantial timber-framed prayer hall, raised on a granite platform. In the third courtyard is a triple-roofed octagonal Pavilion for Introspection, which closely resembles a pagoda and was used as a minaret. A courtyard containing fountains for ablutions precedes the prayer hall, and the hall itself is large enough to accommodate a congregation of nearly 2000 people. So thoroughly have Chinese building traditions been adhered to in meeting Islamic requirements that there is very little on the exterior to mark this as the distinctive structure it is in actuality.

DOMED PRAYER HALL DESIGNS

In Anatolia, the spread of Islam came at the expense of the Byzantine Empire, which was gradually reduced in size until the fall of Constantinople in 1453 brought an end to a civilization over 1000 years old. The victors were the Ottoman Turks, led by Sultan Mehmet II, who thus completed the Islamic conquest of the Balkans. Hagia Sophia, the most impressive church in the eastern Mediterranean, was converted into the city's congregational mosque; minarets were eventually added. Ottoman architects, who had already had experience in building domed structures set on cubical masses, received new inspiration from the city's great Byzantine churches which now stood before them as models, and in succeeding centuries they constructed a number of mosques which in structure and architectural detail rank with the best religious buildings that Byzantium produced.

Among these one must count the works of Koca Sinan (ca. 1490–1588), a distinguished engineer and architect who has been compared with his Italian contemporary Michelangelo. Born to a peasant family of non-Muslim background, Sinan was recruited for governmental service as a youth and trained in the corps of Janissaries, elite infantry units of the Ottoman army composed of non-Muslims abducted as children and forced to convert to Islam. After participating in military campaigns in Austria, Greece, and Mesopotamia, he served as court architect in Constantinople for fifty years, during which time he

7.24 Shehzade Mosque, Istanbul, 1545–48.

Sinan's first major mosque, this building is notable for its clearly articulated geometry of squares. One square comprises the courtyard, while the second defines the domed prayer hall. Minarets are incorporated into the corners where the squares join.

7.25 Section and plan of the Shehzade Mosque, Istanbul, 1545–48.

These show how Sinan took Hagia Sophia's theme of the central dome with flanking semidomes and expanded it into a completely centralized design. The square plan of the sahn matches the square enclosed space of the prayer hall.

7.26 Shehzade Mosque interior, Istanbul, 1545–48.

This view shows the piers supporting the great dome and the flanking semidomes.

designed and supervised construction of a large number of projects, including waterworks, bridges, fortifications, and buildings. Sinan's career coincided with the reigns of generous sultans, and he was undoubtedly fortunate to have the vast Ottoman building corps of skilled workmen at his command. Without both liberal patrons to finance them and capable assistants to carry them out, major projects could not have been realized, no matter how brilliantly designed.

Sinan's first major architectural commission in Constantinople was the Shehzade mosque complex (1545–48), commissioned by Sultan Süleyman in memory of his son, who had died as a young man. Constructed on the site of Justinian's Church of the Holy Apostles, the mosque is composed of two joined squares (Figs. 7.24–7.26). One square contains the sahn, which has a central fountain and is surrounded by domed bays behind arcades. The second square is the enclosed prayer hall, where the central dome is complemented by four semidomes set at the sides, with smaller domes and semidomes filling the remaining spaces. The elegantly symmetrical geometry of the plan is matched by the balanced volumes of the interior space and the exterior

massing, punctuated by paired minarets at the corners where the two squares adjoin. Sinan has handled the great piers and necessary buttressing so as to minimize the apparent bulk of the masonry. As a result, window openings are larger and the volumetric massing on the exterior presents a harmonious composition of successive layering of domes and semidomes. Associated with the mosque are the tomb of Shehzade Mehmet, a madrasa, a hospice for the infirm, a school, and a **caravanserai** (accommodation and markets for foreign merchants who sold at wholesale prices), reminders that even in a well-established city, mosques provided space for both civic and sacred functions. It was Ottoman practice to provide separate buildings dedicated to different particular needs.

A similar quality marks Sinan's celebrated mosque (**Külliye**) of Süleyman the Magnificent (1550–57), a vast complex containing a mosque and cemetery at the center, with five madrasas, a primary school, a medical school, a hospice, a community kitchen to feed the poor, a caravanserai, public baths, a hospital, small shops, and even a house for Sinan grouped at its sides (Figs. 7.27–7.28). It was sited on the sloping side of a hill fronting on the Golden Horn (harbor of Constantinople), and Sinan

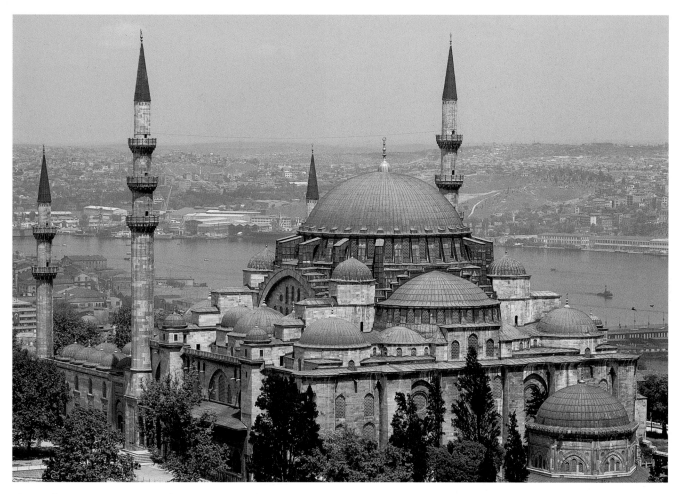

7.27 Mosque of Süleyman the Magnificent, Istanbul, 1550–57.

Constructed as the centerpiece of a larger complex of schools, shops, and community facilities, the mass of this mosque is balanced by the slender vertical accents of its four minarets, only two of which are visible in this photograph.

7.28 Plan of the Mosque of Süleyman the Magnificent, Istanbul, 1550–57.

This plan shows the related structures that are part of the project. Sinan's own house is set at one corner.

Hospital

Hostel

Latrines

Sinan's house

Medical school

Shops

Kitchen for poor

Madrasa

Courtyard

Prayer hall

Madrasa

Madrasa

Mausoleum of Süleyman

Cemetery

Madrasa

0   100 m
0   300 ft

7.29 Selimiye Mosque, Edirne, 1568–75.

Generally held to be Sinan's masterpiece, this mosque is essentially a single dome supported on eight great piers and braced by external buttresses. The minarets are exceptionally tall and provided with internal spiraling staircases of considerable geometric complexity.

7.30a,b Plan and cross-section of the Selimye Mosque complex, Edirne, 1568–75.

Sinan attempted here to equal the dome of Hagia Sophia and exceed its integration of interior space.

located the complex so as to exploit the dramatic possibilities of the terrain, which required that the layout be asymmetrical. Marked by four slender minarets, the mosque dominates the ensemble of buildings. Its plan is familiar: an arcaded sahn, a domed haram, and a walled cemetery set on a linear axis. The prayer hall is a variant of Hagia Sophia, having a central dome flanked by two semidomes, but here the aisles, also domed, are so configured as to contain the entire building within a square. Spatially, the interior functions as a single volume, with aisles and nave available for prayer. (There is no second-level gallery as at Hagia Sophia.) The whole presents a more consistent articulation, both inside and out, than was achieved in the Byzantine building. Buttressing elements, arches, vaults, and domes work together structurally and visually to create a satisfying architectural composition. The octagonal tomb of Süleyman (d. 1566), placed in the center of the cemetery behind the qibla wall, has a plan inspired by the Dome of the Rock, although this is not evident from the exterior treatment.

Sinan's final major work was the Selimiye Mosque in Edirne, built in 1568–75 for Selim II, successor to Süleyman (Figs. 7.29–7.30a,b). The complex contains the usual madrasas and commercial buildings (whose revenues helped to offset the running costs of the mosque and its related educational and charitable facilities), but it is the domed prayer hall that commands particular attention. Sinan boasted that here he had built a dome both wider and taller than Hagia Sophia, which is not quite the case, but his method of conceiving the space transcends that of the Byzantine original. There are no semidomes. The dome is set directly on eight piers, six freestanding and two engaged in the qibla wall. Arches connecting these piers support the dome, which rises above ranks of windows pierced in the exterior wall. Buttressing necessary to brace the dome's thrust is hidden within the walls and

Madrasa

Cemetery

Mosque

Court

Madrasa

Kavaflar Arasta, or cobblers' market

0   50 m

0   150 ft

0   50 m

0   150 ft

seen more clearly on the exterior. As daring as is the dome, one must also marvel at the four slender minarets that mark the corners of the prayer hall. Of exceptional height (232 feet), they are grooved to accentuate their verticality. Inside two of the minarets are separate staircases leading to each of the three balconies, a complex exercise in spiraling geometry and a structural challenge that Sinan boasted proudly that he had met successfully.

HOUSES, PALACES, AND URBAN PATTERNS

Across the broad geographic area that comprises the Islamic world, there is obviously considerable diversity in climate, traditional house forms, and construction materials, making it impossible to propose a single definition for an Islamic house. From the Qur'an and related texts comprising traditions and laws, however, there developed certain principles governing both private and public life that also regulated aspects of house forms and city planning. Islam recognizes the fundamental right of privacy for the family within its own house, hence in many places houses present plain exterior walls to the street. In hot, arid climates, residences tend to be designed around courtyards that preserve privacy and also modify the microclimate advantageously (Figure 7.31). Doorways of houses on opposite sides of the street must be located so that one cannot look from one dwelling into the other when both doors are open, and ground-level windows are set so high that those passing by cannot look in. Windows above the ground floor may be larger, but they may not be placed so as to overlook courtyards or rooftop areas of other houses and thus invade their privacy. These upper-floor windows may project beyond the plane of the wall, and they are frequently provided with elaborately carved screens to restrict the view from the outside. Within the family, women and children are segregated from men and visitors, so the family living area (**haram**) is separated from reception facilities provided for male guests, and from the entrance to the house one cannot see directly into living areas. Privacy and seclusion are often achieved by the use of separate doors and carved screens or grilles,

Roof terrace for sleeping in summer

Screens covering projecting windows overlooking street

Internal screens to protect family privacy

Interior courtyard

Underground chamber serving as summer cooling

7.31 (left) Axonometric section through a traditional house, Baghdad.

This house incorporates many characteristics of Islamic urban dwellings in hot, dry climates. Under the courtyard floor is an earth-sheltered room that provides cooling air during the day. Screened rooftop areas are used for sleeping in hot weather. Grilled windows at upper levels can be opened for air circulation while preserving privacy.

7.32 (below) Plan of the Maidan-i-Shah (public square) and related developments, Isfahan, 1590–1602.

Shah Abbas had an ambitious new city center laid out around a twenty-acre urban square. The Masjid-i-Shah (Shah Mosque) was built at the south end to draw the faithful from the older Friday Mosque.

Friday Mosque

Caravanserai

Covered bazaar connecting to old city

Palaces of Nobles

Entrance to bazaar

Maidan

Lutfallah Mosque

Ali Kapu Gate

Shah Mosque

Chahar Bagh Avenue

Ziyanda River

N

0   500 m

0   1500 ft

Khwaju Bridge

which admit light and air while also allowing those behind to look out without being seen.

Islam has a lengthy urban tradition, and aspects of the Prophet's teachings were applied to the problems inherent in establishing rights when living in larger communities. Pre-modern Islamic society made no distinction between the sacred and secular realms. In many traditional settlements located from North Africa to the Middle East, the essential features of an urban area were a Friday mosque large enough to serve the community and surrounding settlements, a governor who exercised control of the territory, and a bazaar or market with covered stalls for the city and surrounding countryside. The Friday mosque and the bazaar were inseparable. Market stalls were grouped by trade or type of merchandise, with those of highest status (perfume, books) located closest to the mosque entrance, and those associated with noise or noxious odors (coppersmiths, leatherworkers) farthest away. Interspersed with the public areas might be fountains, cafés, caravanserais, public baths, and madrasas. This whole public area was the domain of men, and its plan tended to be irregular, built up over time. The city's neighborhoods or residential quarters began as homogeneous groupings of families affiliated by a common trade or religious and ethnic connections. At one time, many quarters had a gate or door that could be used to close off the area when desired. Within the neighborhood, families shared

a mosque, fountains, public baths, communal ovens, and shops. Knowing about the organization of residential quarters helps explain why the street plans of traditional Islamic cities such as Tunis or Isfahan have few through roads, on which are found the major public places and markets; a limited number of secondary streets; and hundreds of cul-de-sacs, off which most houses open. The street pattern resembles a maze with many dead ends, far more than in the grid layouts more common in Europe.

Isfahan provides perhaps the most handsome example of the application of Islamic principles of city planning, although one must admit from the start that its royal quarter and new section as laid out by Shah Abbas I (1587–1629) are not typical of the growth by accretion associated with traditional Islamic urbanism (Figs. 7.32). In the older part of town, around the Friday mosque, one finds the traditional network of streets and cul-de-sacs. The historic trade route extending toward the river grew into a linear covered bazaar (Fig. 7.33) of small shops that

7.33 View of the bazaar at Isfahan.

The bazaar is composed of a street linking merchants' stalls and small shops, interspersed with baths, workshops, and theological schools. Vaults over the street provide relief from the intense sun, while skylights admit necessary daylight and fresh air.

meandered past entrances to other facilities that lay behind the merchants' stalls: caravanserais, madrasas, mosques, baths, fountains, and craft workshops. Shah Abbas, determined to bring greater glory to his capital city, undertook redevelopment of the public square established just outside the traditional area and defined it as a formal rectangular square, the Maidan-i-Shah, lined with shops and punctuated by major monuments: two mosques, the Ali Kapu gate (the imperial porch, which served as a viewing stand), and the entrance to the Qaysariya, the shah's bazaar. The center of the open space was normally available for small vendors to sell their wares in, but it could also be cleared and used for military or athletic events, the two-story arcades around the edges providing a good base for observation.

The Shah's contributions to this grand urban scheme included construction of a complex of governmental buildings on the western side of the square behind the Ali Kapu gate. Directly opposite the gate was the imposing entrance to the small Sheikh Lutfullah Mosque (1602) that has a bent-axis entry around two sides of the square prayer hall to bring the faithful into the mosque on the axis aligned with Mecca. The Masjid-i-Shah, or Shah's mosque, occupies the short southern end of the square, set opposite the grand entrance to the shah's bazaar on the northern side. This formally conceived space comes as a surprise after the more organic city core, but its layout is not out of character, for it does at large scale what many of the older buildings, including the Friday mosque, had become over a longer period of time; spaces with biaxial symmetry and uniform perimeter articulation, whether in

arcades or colonnades. Shah Abbas's ambition was to link the Maidan-i-Shah with a grand new avenue leading to the river and a new bridge leading to the commercially important Armenian settlement on the other side, but not all of his program came to fruition.

Some of the formal concepts that characterized the planning of Isfahan are also seen in the fortress-palace of the Alhambra, a royal citadel erected above the city of Granada (Fig. 7.34). Built in the thirteenth and fourteenth centuries, the Alhambra was the work of the Nasrid Dynasty, who governed the dwindling Islamic territories of southern Spain until their expulsion in 1492 by Ferdinand and Isabella, the monarchs who also financed Columbus's expedition to the Indies in the same year. Some parts of the Alhambra are now ruined, and the center of its site on a ridge overlooking the city is crowded by the later palace of Charles V. The red-brick exterior wall bristles with towers capped by crenelated battlements. Originally these enclosed an entire palace city, including common dwelling houses, craft workshops, the royal mint, several mosques, public baths, and a military garrison, in addition to seven palace buildings. Archaeological work on the surviving buildings is still ongoing as historians try to understand the construction history of the structures on this hill.

Of the surviving palace chambers, the two most impressive are grouped around open rectangular courts;

7.34 Plan of Alhambra, Granada, 13th–14th centuries.

This plan shows what were originally two separate palaces. In the center is the Court of Myrtle Trees and the associated hall, constructed on the foundations of a military tower. To the right is the Court of Lions.

Comares Tower with Hall of the Ambassadors

Sala del Mexuar (original Throne Room)

Court of Myrtle Trees

Hall of Two Sisters

Court of Lions

Hall of the Abencerrajes

N   0   25 m
     0   75 ft

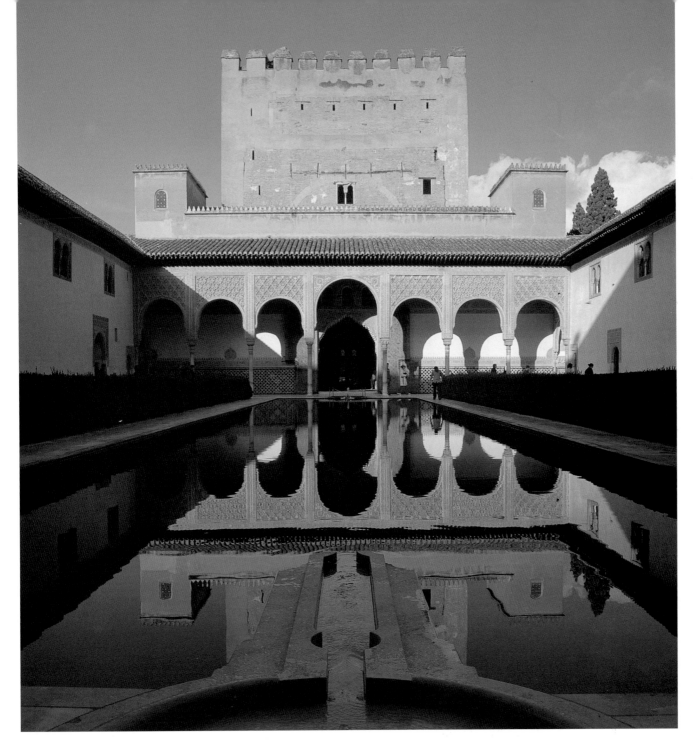

7.35 Court of Myrtle Trees, Alhambra, Granada, 14th century.

This view shows the reflecting pool and the Comares Tower in the background. The delicacy and grace of late Islamic architecture in Spain is evident in the arcade.

one known as the Court of Myrtle Trees, which provided access to the Hall of the Ambassadors; and the other called the Court of Lions, so named for the fountain at its center. The Court of Myrtle Trees has a central rectangular pool fed by gently overflowing fountain basins at opposite ends (Fig. 7.35). Arcaded galleries are set across the short sides, and rows of myrtles parallel to the pool on the long sides are reflected in its smooth surface. At the north end is the Comares Tower, which contained the square-plan Hall of the Ambassadors, thirty-six feet on a side, with a soaring sixty-foot ceiling (Fig. 7.36). This was the throne room of

the sultan, and its domed ceiling, composed of over 8000 wooden sections, captures the effect of thousands of stars in the seven levels of heaven as described by Islamic theology.

The Catholic kings who later occupied the Alhambra palaces cut an opening from the Court of Myrtle Trees to the rectangular Court of Lions, which was originally the heart of a separate palace (Fig. 7.37). Its perimeter is set with arcades resting on slender columns, and its center is divided into four parts by shallow watercourses emanating from the lion fountain at the center. As with the Tomb of Humayun and the Taj Mahal, this layout is thought to symbolize the Qur'anic vision of paradise—a garden below which four rivers flow with water, wine, honey, and milk—and the courtyard was originally planted. Square axial pavilions on the short sides project into the court with clustered columns supporting intricately carved

7.36 Ceiling and upper wall, Hall of the Ambassadors, Alhambra, Granada, 14th century.

Thousands of small wooden pieces are suspended from the roof timbers to transform this ceiling into the seven layers of heaven surrounding a small dome at the center representing the heavenly throne. Pierced grilles filter sunlight.

arcades. There has been considerable scholarly discussion about the dates and origins of the twelve lions, which as figurative representations of animals would seem to have no place in Islamic art. The basin is clearly Islamic, as attested by its fourteenth-century inscription, but it does not match the animals in style. It has been speculated that the lions originated in a Jewish palace formerly on the hilltop, where they may have replicated the animals supporting the great bronze basin that was found in the courtyard of the Temple of Solomon. Opening off the short axis of the court are two chambers, each of which is a jewel of ornamental vaulting. To the south, the Hall of the Abencerrajes is covered with a splendid muqarnas vault in

the shape of an eight-pointed star. The northern room, the Sala do las Dos Hermanas (Hall of the Two Sisters), has an octagonal drum supporting what appears to be a star-shaped muqarnas vault that is actually suspended from wooden trusses above.

In contrast to its simple exteriors, the Alhambra's interiors are enriched by a profusion of decorative detail that covers all surfaces, conveying splendor, ineffable lightness, and the ethereal quality of a dream world. Marbles, colored ceramic tiles, and carved and gilded wood or stucco screens create changing patterns of shadow as light reflects on water and polished surfaces, or flickers through pierced walls and ceilings. Pattern and texture abound in both geometric arabesques and stylized plant forms embellished with flowing Arabic inscriptions; arches are lobed and cusped; windows have elaborate grilles; and ceilings feature stalactites of carved wood or plaster. Behind the ornament, the underlying rubble masonry construction is not of the highest quality—it was the effect of magnificence that was desired rather than its actual substance.

Even without its interior furnishings and original courtyard plantings, however, the Alhambra's sumptuous character can still be appreciated today.

By 1492, when the Moors were expelled from Spain, many aspects of Islamic architecture had long since found their way into buildings in western Europe. During the medieval period, interactions between learned men from Islamic, Hebraic, and Christian traditions had generally been amicable, undermined primarily by intolerance for non-Christian religions on the part of the Catholic Church. Elements that became important features in Western architecture, among them polychromy, the pointed arch, and domes with interlacing ribs, originated in mosque designs, and the gracious elegance of palaces integrating landscape and architecture, such as the Alhambra, were unmatched by comparable buildings in northern Europe.

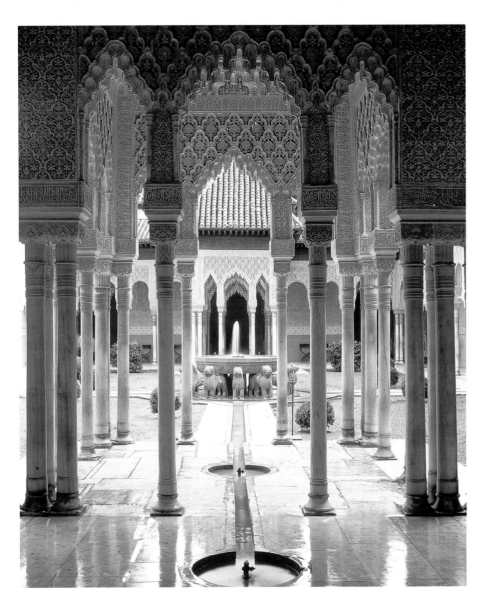

7.37 Court of Lions. Alhambra, Granada, 13th–14th centuries.

This view shows the central fountain and the water channels dividing the court into four quadrants. In the background is the roof of the Hall of the Two Sisters.

CHAPTER 8

EARLY MEDIEVAL AND ROMANESQUE ARCHITECTURE

While Byzantine and Islamic cultures were flourishing in eastern Europe and around the southern rim of the Mediterranean, those portions of western Europe that had been part of the Roman Empire entered a sustained period of decline. From the first centuries of the Christian era, outposts of the empire had been repeatedly besieged by waves of nomadic peoples migrating from Central Asia. These tribes, called barbarians by the civilized Romans, eventually overran the frontiers established by Rome and occupied the city of Rome itself by 476. Many place names across Europe preserve the memory of these nomadic tribes. The Franks settled in what eventually became France. The Burgundians in east-central France and the Lombards in northern Italy gave their names to Burgundy and Lombardy, respectively. The Goths and the Visigoths were memorialized in the architectural style called Gothic, and the behavior of the Vandals, who went everywhere, is remembered in the word "vandalism." Gradually the nomads settled down, became converts to Christianity, and attempted to continue Roman governmental traditions, which they greatly admired although they lacked the necessary administrative expertise. The period in western European history extending from the decline of Roman authority until the beginning of the Renaissance (approximately 400 to 1400) is known as the medieval period or the Middle Ages, because historians saw it as a middle era separating antiquity from modern times.

Roman culture was based on city life and depended on a strong central government. In the chaos that accompanied the barbarian invasions, the basic skills required to maintain governmental authority, such as literacy, virtually disappeared. Urban settlements and the money economy that sustained them were replaced by small agricultural units organized by local strongmen, who lived in fortified dwellings and controlled the surrounding land by force of arms. Peasants tilled the land in exchange for meager sustenance and the physical protection afforded them by the strongman's military might. Over the centuries this arrangement of mutual service and protection developed into the feudal system, embracing all levels of society from peasant to king in an intricate social, political, and economic order.

CAROLINGIAN ARCHITECTURE

Outside the Italian peninsula and the Mediterranean coast, where Early Christian traditions were maintained in a number of masonry basilicas and baptisteries, very little architecture in western Europe has survived from the period 400–800. Caught in the chaos created by barbarian invasions, most of northern Europe experienced several centuries of unsettled life, during which the stability necessary to design and construct durable buildings was lacking. From the many strongmen who were leaders in the developing feudal system emerged one whose strength and military might enabled him to dominate his rivals. Known as Charles the Great, or Charlemagne, he was the grandson of Charles Martel, the Frank who had led assembled forces to victory over the Islamic army at the battle of Tours in 732. During his reign (768–814), Charlemagne unified a large portion of present-day France, the Low Countries, and Germany through a series of successful military campaigns. Charlemagne's influence extended even to Rome where, on Christmas Day in the year 800, Pope Leo III crowned him Holy Roman Emperor. This illiterate descendant of barbarian chieftains had become the spiritual heir of the Roman empire, the temporal equivalent of the pope.

St. Sernin east end, Toulouse, ca. 1077–1119.

Brick trimmed in white stone was used for the exterior, and the rounded volumes of the radiating chapels complement the form of the apse.

THE REVIVAL OF MASONRY CONSTRUCTION

Charlemagne aspired to a renaissance of Roman achievements, including the excellence Rome had exhibited in government, literature, and the arts. He summoned the greatest minds to his court, established schools for the training of governmental administrators, and encouraged architecture by donating lands and money for the construction of churches and monasteries. The resulting buildings, termed **Carolingian** (from *Carolus*, the Latin name for Charles), are in many cases based on the Early Christian buildings Charlemagne visited during his travels in Italy. Such was the case with the palace complex built at Aachen (Fig. 8.1). The overall plan is

8.1 Plan of Charlemagne's palace, Aachen, 792–814.

The sixteen-sided building is the Palatine Chapel, connected by a passageway to a basilican audience hall. Note that the chapel was preceded by a forecourt or atrium. From a loggia at the second level of the chapel, Charlemagne could address an audience assembled there.

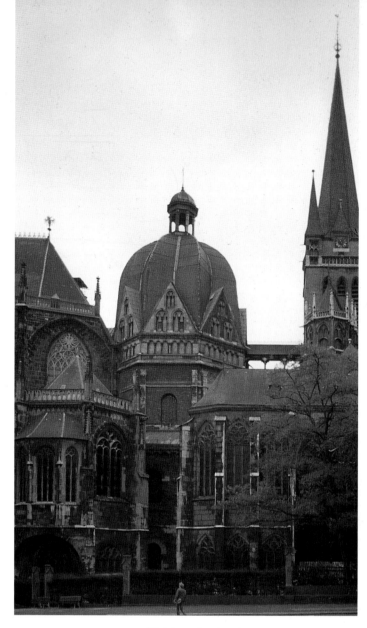

8.2 Palatine Chapel, Aachen, 792–805.

The Carolingian building has been modified by the addition of a Gothic choir and higher roof over the dome. Only the lower wall sections of the central part are authentic from the time of Charlemagne.

modeled on the Lateran Palace in Rome, with the chapel derived from S. Vitale at Ravenna and the audience hall being a Roman basilica. In keeping with Roman tradition, the whole complex was laid out on the module of a square grid. What survives today is the buildings (or foundations) that were constructed in stone, but there were doubtless wooden buildings that contained living accommodation. Much as Charlemagne and his architects admired Roman buildings, they lacked the construction skills necessary to duplicate them, so in comparison to their Roman prototypes Carolingian buildings may seem somewhat unrefined. We should not judge these works too severely, however, for Charlemagne was effectively reviving monumental masonry construction in a region that had not built in this way for about half a millennium.

The Palatine Chapel at Aachen (792–805) was designed by Odo of Metz and probably built by Lombard masons using stone salvaged from nearby Roman structures (Figs. 8.2–8.3). A

8.3 Palatine Chapel interior, Aachen, 792–805.

S. Vitale at Ravenna served as a model for this building, but the chapel also contains original features. The second level was used by Charlemagne and his court to observe services without interfering with those celebrating holy offices. This view includes the choir section added in the Gothic period.

8.4 Abbey gatehouse, Lorsch, ca. 800.

Influences from Roman architecture can be seen in the overall form, derived from the triumphal arch, and the arch-and-column motif used on the ground level.

sixteen-sided aisle with a gallery overhead surrounded its central domed octagon. The construction, including barrel- and groin-vaults and an octagonal cloister vault in the dome, reflects late Roman practice rather than the Byzantine techniques employed at S. Vitale, and its plan simplifies the complex geometry of the Ravenna building. The main entrance is dominated by a **westwerk**, that is, the western façade including the entrance vestibule, rooms at one or more levels above, and one or more towers. The addition of a westwerk to churches is one of the Carolingian contributions to the Western architectural tradition. Early Christian churches featured freestanding belfries, if they had towers at all, but during the Carolingian period towers were often incorporated as integral components of the church.

The interior of the Palatine Chapel has a heavy effect, particularly the eight great piers that support the dome, but the proportions of the arched openings at the ground and gallery levels are well chosen. Polychrome is used in the semicircular arches of the main floor, while sixteen polished marble columns from the Palace of the Exarchs in Ravenna were hauled over the Alps to be reused in the arcade of the gallery. Locally cast bronze grilles in the balustrade and mosaics in the dome contributed to a rich interior. Charlemagne's throne was set on the gallery level on axis with the altar. As the first domed building north of the Alps since the decline of the Roman Empire, the Palatine Chapel is comparable in scale, if not in elegance, to S. Vitale, and it reflects Charlemagne's intense desire to revive classical ideals in architecture.

Of the abbey at Lorsch, which was endowed by Charlemagne, only a small freestanding gatehouse now remains (Fig. 8.4). Its architectural precedents can be found in Roman triumphal arches, such as the Arch of Constantine in Rome (see Fig. 5.14), and also at Old St. Peter's in Rome, where a triple-arched pavilion marked the entrance to the atrium. Arches supported with Corinthian columns articulate the gatehouse at Lorsch, and triangular frames in a decorative pattern derived from late Roman sarcophagi surround the second-floor windows. One could never confuse the gatehouse with an actual Roman building, however, for it features such elements as a steeply pitched roof and decorative red and white tiling, which are distinctly not part of the classical tradition. The roof pitch was dictated by the rain and snow loads of the northern European climate, while the tiled designs seem to have been devised by local masons, perhaps influenced by Islamic polychromy or Roman *opus reticulatum*.

Another small building surviving from Carolingian times is the oratory at Germigny-des-Prés (806–10), which was built for Theodulf, Bishop of Orleans, Abbot of Fleury, and close advisor to Charlemagne (Figs. 8.5–8.7). Conceived as a private chapel for quiet reflection and prayer, the oratory was designed with a Greek-cross plan and a square central tower. (Compare this plan to that of a Russian cross-in-square scheme as shown in Fig. 6.25a.)

8.5 Oratory, Germigny-des-Prés, 806–10.

This small, centrally planned building combines elements from Byzantium (the central plan and an apse mosaic) with horseshoe arches found in Islamic work in Spain and the semicircular arch of Roman work.

8.6 Plan of the oratory, Germigny-des-Prés, 806–10.

The horseshoe arch is evident in the shape of the apse and its flanking chapels.

8.7 Interior of the oratory, Germigny-des-Prés, 806–10.

This view of the crossing and apse shows that horseshoe-shaped arches are used both in elevation and plan.

Horseshoe arches are found in both plan and elevation. Together with the centralized plan, these suggest influence from Mozarabic churches (those in which art and architecture was produced by Christians under Islamic rule) in Muslim-dominated Spain. This assumption is made more plausible by the fact that Theodulf was from Septimania, the area between present-day France and Spain along the Mediterranean coast. Rather surprisingly, the oratory also has a magnificent mosaic depicting the Ark of the Covenant in the eastern apse, the technique and style of which both indicate artistic contributions from Byzantium. In these few surviving Carolingian buildings, one can thus trace elements from Roman, Early Christian, Byzantine, Islamic, and northern European civilizations, combined in what must be seen as the beginnings of an architecture unique to western Europe.

MONASTERIES

Charlemagne's unifying work did not long survive him. In 843, on the death of his son and heir, Louis the Pious, the Carolingian Empire was divided among Charlemagne's

Garden for medicinal plants | Infirmary | Novitiate | Orchard & cemetery | Kitchen garden | Geese

Physicians' house

Kitchen & baths for medical units

Kitchen & bath

Chapel

Chapel

House for bloodletting

Fowlkeeper's lodge

Gardener's house

Sacristy

Chickens

Library

Dormitory

Latrines

Abbott's house

Barn

Reception for visiting monks

Bath

Refectory

Craft workshops

External school

Church

Cloister

Bakery

Mill

Brew house

Distinguished guest house

Wine press

Parlor

Kitchen

Malt kiln

Cooper

Granary

Caretaker's lodge

Kitchen for guest house

Hostel

Bulls

Stable

Bake & brew house for pilgrims

Probably quarters for retinue of distinguished guests

Sheep | Goats | Cows

Barns & stables for animals

Servants | Pigs | Horses

8.8 Plan of St. Gall, ca. 817.

This drawing sets forth the major elements of a Benedictine monastery, establishing a model that would be used for the next 400 or more years as the basis for monastic design.

three grandsons. Governmental power in western Europe gradually reverted to the hands of local or regional lords. The one cohesive social institution that transcended regional groups was the Church, which organized medieval Europe into ecclesiastical dioceses, each administered by a bishop. The seat of episcopal authority was frequently a town that had been a Roman provincial center, and there was much of Roman governmental structure preserved in the organization of the Church.

Complementary to the town-based diocesan units were the largely rural monasteries that grew and flourished widely during the medieval period. Charlemagne had encouraged their establishment as a matter of practical policy for the settlement of conquered territories, in addi-

tion to their spiritual and educational contributions. Few institutions had as extensive an impact on the architecture of the medieval period as monasticism. Indeed, it would be difficult to discuss almost any aspect of medieval history and culture without considering the role played by monks of the various orders. Medieval society was divided broadly into three classes: those who fought (the land-owning lords and knights); those who labored (the peasants); and those who prayed (the priests and monks). The work of each was considered essential to the well-being of all. Prayers of the monks were particularly necessary, it was thought, to provide a never-ending flow of praise to propitiate a God who was justifiably wrathful about humanity's errant ways. Medieval Christians considered their heavenly Lord to be as susceptible to flattery as his earthly counterpart.

The concept of monasticism, the withdrawal from the corruption of everyday life in order to contemplate things spiritual, originated in fourth-century Egypt, where Christian hermits led solitary lives in the desert wilderness. At about the same time, the idea developed that groups of monks might live together communally, and both the hermitic and communal forms of monasticism spread rapidly from Egypt to the edges of the Christian world. Irish monks were active from 432 until 793, when Viking raiders destroyed their settlements. Communal forms of monasticism became the dominant models for the organization of Western monasticism, while hermits continued to be common in the Eastern Church. In most cases, twelve monks and an abbot were sufficient to found a monastery, and the monks often selected remote sites for building. Their major requirement was a reliable water supply. During the Middle Ages, new monastic foundations eventually numbered in the thousands. Monastery schools brought learning to every part of Europe, and monastic building and farming enterprises preserved and advanced the best in architecture, the arts, and agriculture. Medieval civilization throughout western Europe was achieved in no small measure through the work of the monks.

Charlemagne's interest in centralizing and standardizing administration extended to religious institutions. After examining several models of monastic organization, he required that all monasteries within his realm should follow the Rule of St. Benedict, a flexible but rather specific set of regulations formulated by Benedict of Nursia in around 535 for monks living communally under the direction of an abbot. (St. Benedict's precepts relating to the organization and management of a monastery were called a "Rule" because they regulated the lives of those who followed them.) The monastic life of prayer, contemplation, and mental and manual work, marked by poverty, chastity, and obedience, was intended to emulate the example of Christ. In 817 abbots from leading Carolingian monasteries held a conference to resolve differences in interpretation of the Benedictine Rule. Out of its discussions came a document detailing a model layout for a Benedictine abbey. We know of this drawing through a copy sent to the abbot of the monastery of St. Gall, where the plan remained in the abbey's library until rediscovered in the eighteenth century (Fig. 8.8). Known now as the Plan of St. Gall, this manuscript is the oldest surviving architectural drawing from the medieval period, and from it modern scholars Walter Horn and Ernest Born have deduced much about monastic life and building practices in the Carolingian age.

The Plan of St. Gall clearly sets forth the major components of a self-sufficient religious community. The largest building was the church, a double-ended basilica in plan, with a western hemicycle flanked by twin cylindrical towers. Inside the masonry-walled and timber truss-roofed church was the worship space for the monks. Altars were located throughout the nave, transepts, and apse, as medieval religious practice, which placed growing importance on the veneration of relics, required multiple altars to honor individual saints. On the south side of the church was the cloister, 100 feet square, surrounded by a covered, arcaded walk connecting the major buildings on its sides: the chapter house, workroom, and warming room below the dormitory on the east; the refectory (dining hall) on the south; and the cellar or storeroom on the west (Fig. 8.9). A stairway connected the dormitory with the south transept since the monks arose at 2 a.m. for Vigils, returning to sleep until Lauds at daybreak. Six more services—Prime, Terce, None, Vespers, and Compline—completed the daily cycle.

By counting the beds drawn on the plan, Horn and Born have concluded that the monastery was designed for approximately 110 monks. Service buildings were grouped outside the cloister and staffed by an additional 130 to 150 workmen and servants necessary to provide for the monastery's sustenance. A bake and brew house, artisan craft workshops, and a complete working farm, with pens or barns for goats, geese, pigs, horses, and cows, are indicated on the plan to the south and west of the cloister, although their actual arrangement on the land would

8.9 Axonometric section through the cloister, St. Gall, ca. 817.

Following Walter Horn and Ernest Born's deductions, the monks' beds in the dormitory, the tables in the refectory, and the barrels of stored food are shown in the buildings surrounding the cloister, with the south side of the church in the background. The kitchens, warming room, and latrines are also detailed.

doubtless have been adjusted to the location of fields and pasture. They are grouped here to have all the buildings fit on the parchment. To the east of the church, the plan indicates a miniature double cloister to house the novitiate and the infirmary, together with a house for two physicians, a medicinal herb garden, and the cemetery. On the north side of the church was the abbot's house, connected to the transept by a passage. As the administrator and spiritual leader of the monastery, the abbot was responsible for the management of the monastery's life, and as its representative to the outside world he was charged with public relations and with providing hospitality for distinguished guests. Adjacent to the abbot's house were the external school, required by Charlemagne's decree to provide education for young men not intending to become monks, and the guesthouse and stables for high-ranking visitors. The more common sort of traveler would be cared for by the almoner at the cloister gate to the south of the church entrance.

Through its clear ordering of the practical requirements for a monastic community, the Plan of St. Gall encapsulates the high quality of functional planning achieved by Carolingian architects. While no monastery ever built followed the Plan of St. Gall precisely, its general disposition of monastic buildings was employed in Benedictine abbeys throughout the medieval period.

ANGLO-SAXON AND VIKING ARCHITECTURE

ENGLISH CHURCHES

Much of England had once been part of the Roman Empire, and in the waning days of its influence there, Christianity was introduced, coexisting with Roman cults and pagan traditions. Early in the seventh century, the pope sent a Roman monk named Augustine on a mission to revitalize Christianity in the Anglo-Saxon kingdoms. Augustine was hospitably received at Canterbury, where he encouraged the construction of churches, most of which were built in wood. None of Augustine's churches still exists, and only one of the once-numerous wooden Anglo-Saxon structures survives to the present, the nave of the small church of St. Andrew at Greensted (north of London), constructed in about 1000 (Figs. 8.10–8.11). Built of vertical half-logs pegged together, with a three-quarter log employed to turn the corner, the church wall is extraordinary because it does not use the horizontal log construction that was already common in northern and eastern Europe.

Anglo-Saxon parish churches such as that at Greensted were generally small, consisting of a nave and a chancel. In plan these churches were extremely simple versions of the Roman basilica, with the Roman semicircular apse often replaced by a square-ended chancel. Construction of the nave was the responsibility of the local community, while

8.10 St. Andrew's, Greensted, ca. 1000.
The stave-built nave of this Anglo-Saxon church is the only wooden building to survive from that period. It is remarkable for its construction in upright log sections, work that links it with stave constructions in Scandinavia.

the church authorities financed the chancel. (Indeed, because of these different sources of funding, the naves and chancels of later English parish churches are frequently in different styles.) The major entrance, protected by a porch, was usually on the south side rather than the west as in Early Christian churches. Towers to hold bells were built from an early date as freestanding belfries, but these were soon incorporated into the church proper. Small splayed windows with either arched or triangular-headed openings dimly lighted interiors.

8.11 St. Andrew's wall details, Greensted, ca. 1000.
This view shows how the logs are positioned vertically. The brick sill under the base is a nineteenth-century insertion to protect against rot.

The best-known example of Anglo-Saxon masonry building is the tower of All Saints Church at Earl's Barton, Northamptonshire, which dates from about 1000 (Fig. 8.12). Although built of stone, the tower's vertical strip-work and horizontal cornices appear to imitate wooden construction. In fact, the surface articulation is bonded firmly into the rubble stonework of the tower that is concealed underneath a stucco-like finish coat. Corners are strengthened by long-and-short work (bonding stones at corners alternately as vertical and horizontal elements for reinforcement), a technique frequently found in Anglo-Saxon masonry. Notice the thick columns supporting carved lintel blocks framing the belfry opening on the fourth story. The present battlemented parapet above is an incongruous fifteenth-century addition.

NORWEGIAN STAVE CHURCHES

Anglo-Saxon England was repeatedly assailed by raiders from Scandinavia. These pirates, known variously as Danes, Norsemen, or Vikings, both terrorized western Europe and served as intrepid explorers and traders, maintaining contacts with places as remote as Constantinople. (Recall that one of their number, Rurik, was invited in 856 to become the founder of the ruling family in Russia, and that Leif Ericsson led an expedition that reached the North American continent in about 1003.) In Britain, they harried the Anglo-Saxon kingdoms occupying the whole of East Anglia and land as far north as York, which became a Viking city. The Danes extracted annual payments (the danegeld) from territories under their control, while also profiting from organized piracy on the cities of Europe. When shallow-draft, swift Viking ships sailed or rowed up the navigable rivers along which medieval settlements clustered, the burning, looting, and massacre visited on these communities only added to the instability of the time.

The artistic legacy of the Vikings is best seen in smaller objects, including jewelry, ceremonial and household objects, and military regalia, which are adorned with intricate interlaced ornament based on stylized plant and animal forms (hence its name, the Animal Style), an artistic tradition that has links to the fierce Scythians who came from the steppes of central Asia. Interlace ornament finds its way into Romanesque architectural decoration.

Scandinavia itself remained outside the Christian sphere until the middle of the eleventh century, when Anglo-Saxon missionaries who returned with Viking raiders from England succeeded in converting the vigorous pagans of Norway. The missionaries brought knowledge of Anglo-Saxon church architecture with them, so the simple plans of parish churches in Britain, themselves based on Early Christian precedent, became the models for equally small Norwegian churches. The combination of these simple plans with native building traditions created a unique and distinctive architecture, the stave church.

8.12 Church of All Saints west tower, Earl's Barton, ca. 1000.

This Anglo-Saxon masonry tower shows influences from wooden construction in its stone details, most notably in the thin vertical strips that break up the wall surface. The belfry opening approximates classical columns and arches.

The church at Urnes, Norway, the oldest extant stave church, dates from about 1125–40, and its design illustrates the type (Figs. 8.13–8.14a). The staves are upright poles, usually pine trees from which the bark has been removed, that form the basic structure for the building. They are supported on four crossed horizontal sills forming a rectangular chassis. The chassis is raised off the ground by large flat stones at the intersections of the sill planks because excavated foundations would have been subject to heaving as the ground froze and thawed. These corner stones also protect the timber structure by isolating it from ground moisture. Low exterior walls, made of vertical boarding anchored by rounded corner posts, rest on an outer chassis sill supported on the short cantilevered ends of the main chassis, while the upper wall, braced above head height by one or more clamping beams that encircle the staves, follows the vertical line of the stave frame up to the roof rafters. A cupola completes the roof ridge visually, although it has no connection to the interior space. The major structural elements, the staves, are kept dry by shorter exterior boards that are renewed from time to time as required. Urnes and other stave churches are very dark inside, for the original design had no windows, depending instead for light and ventilation on small circular openings (wind-eyes) located high in the walls. Scandinavia and Anglo-Saxon Britain are the major places where one finds wooden buildings constructed of upright staves rather than horizontal logs. It is interesting

8.13 Stave church, Urnes, Norway, ca. 1125–40.

Building volumes reflect plan elements: the tall nave with lower aisles, the choir, and apse extension each have a separate expression. The carved portal from an earlier church is installed on the lower side (north) wall.

to note that the stave church at Greensted was associated with a Viking settlement.

Urnes also possesses a remarkable carved portal, now located on the north wall of the church, which probably belonged to a previous church of about 1015 built on the same site (Fig. 8.15). Bands of boldly undercut figures, cut from single planks of wood, represent four-legged beasts and serpent-like animals intertwined in intricate patterns with a scrolling vine. The similarity of this work to Animal Style ornament is immediately apparent. What is less clear at first glance is why such carving should be found as ornament around a church doorway. Although no documents provide absolute proof, scholars believe that these figures represent a carry-over from the pagan past applied to the fresh purposes of the Christian faith. In Norse mythology, the end of the world was to come when snakes and dragons, representing the forces of evil, were locked in mortal combat. Known as Ragnarok, this struggle was the Norse equivalent of the Christian Last Judgment, which became established as a subject for sculpture on the doorways of churches in other parts of Europe. The best explanation for the snakes and dragons on stave churches seems to be that in Norway, as elsewhere, early missionaries found it convenient to adapt established traditions to the causes of the Christian church.

Stave churches were widely constructed in the sparsely populated and isolated valley communities along the fjords of Norway. As late as the nineteenth century, 322 such buildings could be documented through remains or textual references, but today only thirty-two survive. The

CHAPTER 8   EARLY MEDIEVAL AND ROMANESQUE ARCHITECTURE

8.14a (left) Sections and plan of the stave church, Urnes, Norway, ca. 1125–40.

The basis of this building is a rectangular chassis laid on foundation stones resting on the ground. On this frame rest the ends of upright poles or staves that form the structure of the church. The tower shown in Fig. 8.13 is not included in this section.

8.14b (left, below) Sections and plan of the stave church, Borgund, ca. 1150.

Like Urnes, Borgund church also relies on small openings, or wind-eyes, high in the wall to admit light and air, and to relieve wind pressure against the sides of the structure.

8.15 (below) Carved portal from an earlier church at Urnes, ca. 1015.

This portal is now preserved on the north wall of the present church. The intertwined snakes and dragons represent the end of the world according to the Norse legend of Ragnarok. Christian missionaries substituted this imagery for the Last Judgment as a way of conveying Christian teachings.

church at Borgund, dated to about 1150, probably represents the most authentic mature stave church, and aspects of its form and detail have served as models for the restoration of other stave churches that were not so fortunate in preserving their original character across the

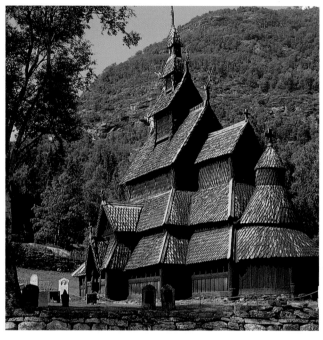

8.16 Stave church, Borgund, ca. 1150

While this church looks considerably more elaborate than Urnes, it is fundamentally the same in structure, having additional roof turrets and an external gallery at the base.

8.17 Diagram showing the construction of a stave church.

The church illustrated here comes from Gol. This is one of a number of stave churches that were restored in the twentieth century according to features seen in the church at Borgund. The internal structure, including diagonal bracing of the staves and configuration of the roof trusses, is shown.

centuries (Figs. 8.14b, 8.16–8.17). Borgund began much as Urnes did, but in the thirteenth century it was embellished with an external gallery and elaborate turret that give it a more complex profile. Crosses and dragons placed on the ends of the roof gables protect the church from the powers of darkness. Pagan forces, though banished by Christianity to remote areas, still remained a potential menace to be countered by prominently displayed symbols.

EARLY ROMANESQUE ARCHITECTURE

The monastery of St. Martin at Canigou (1001–26) survives as an example of the process by which monasticism spread, and its buildings illustrate architectural accomplishments of the early Romanesque period (Figs. 8.18–8.19). Its patron, the Count of Cerdagne, landlord of this mountainous territory in the Pyrenees, endowed the monastery on a rocky outcrop to expiate his sins. Although it never housed more than about thirty monks, its place in the history of architecture is assured because it has survived, with the aid of an entirely sympathetic twentieth-century restoration, as one of the earliest completely vaulted Romanesque churches. In plan the church is a basilica without transepts, having semicircular apses terminating the aisles and nave. The barrel vaults of the nave and aisles rest on ten supports—eight stubby columns and two grouped piers—and the solid exterior walls (Fig. 8.20). The only natural light comes from small windows at the east and west ends, resulting in a very dark interior. From the exterior, the entire monastery forms a harmonious composition. A square-plan tower abuts the side of the church, guarding the entrance to the abbey, while the cloister and its related buildings form an irregular quadrangle on the limited building site rather than the neat square indicated on the Plan of St. Gall. The stone construction is simple, articulated primarily by semicircular arches used over windows and also set as surface relief in horizontal bands. The stepped crenelations atop the tower recall Islamic fortifications found in neighboring Spain.

St. Martin at Canigou exemplifies the early Romanesque style. As the name implies, Romanesque buildings have a certain affinity with Roman architecture, primarily because they tend to employ the semicircular or Roman arch. Beyond this simple generalization (which itself is not always true), it is difficult to characterize Romanesque buildings with great precision. The style flourished from around 1000 to 1250. Romanesque buildings tend to be massive and heavy. The construction problem that Romanesque builders set for themselves, that of efficiently supporting a ceiling made entirely of small stones, posed a real challenge and encouraged varied approaches according to the materials available, the experience of the architect, and the ambitions of the patron. It is perhaps easiest to understand the Romanesque as a great series of experiments to enclose

8.18 St. Martin at Canigou, monastery, 1001–26.

Founded as a pious act by the Count of Cerdagne, this monastery has a mountainous site that is difficult to access even today. The presence of a freely running spring made habitation possible here, and a small monastic community continues to occupy the buildings.

Tower
Barrel vault
Aisle
Nave
Lower church
Cloister

0   10 m
0   30 ft

8.19 Cutaway drawing of the church, St. Martin at Canigou, 1001–26.

The church has two levels, both vaulted. Romanesque architects had to rediscover building techniques used by the Romans, and here one gets a sense of the struggle to construct a durable and fireproof church.

8.20 St. Martin at Canigou interior, 1001–26.

Windows are minimal, for every opening cut in the wall weakened the structure. Since the monks knew the services by heart, dim light levels inside the church were not a major obstacle.

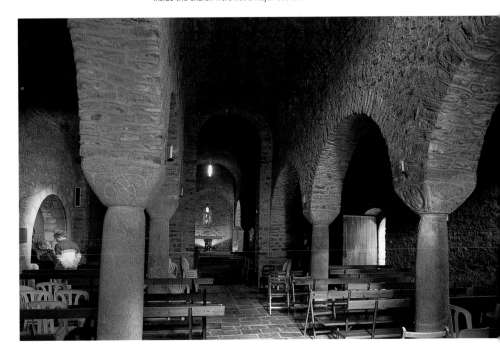

and illuminate interior space, using incombustible masonry construction to reduce the chances of fire and thus protect the valuable relics held in churches.

Most Romanesque buildings rely on the mass of the continuous wall to sustain the weight of the vaulting overhead. Medieval builders could not calculate structure as we can today. (Indeed, the systematic study of materials and structural theory was not sufficiently advanced to be applied to ordinary buildings until about 1850.) Trial and error, based on knowledge of what had worked in previous projects, formed the basis of building practice. Yet within the span of 150 years the structural experiments of hundreds of Romanesque builders led to the refined masonry techniques that made Gothic architecture possible. It was a long

Speyer Cathedral

St. Philibert, Tournus

St. Michael, Hildesheim

8.21 Plans of Speyer Cathedral, 1030–61; St. Philibert, Tournus, ca. 950–1120; and St. Michael, Hildesheim, 1010–33.

Speyer Cathedral was one of the most ambitious Romanesque buildings of its time, with groin vaults on a scale with major Roman baths. St. Philibert is notable for its radiating chapels off an ambulatory and transverse barrel vaults in the nave. St. Michael is an interesting example of a double-ended basilica with wooden roofing.

8.22 St. Philibert interior, Tournus, ca. 950–1120.

This view shows the transverse barrel vault covering each bay of the nave, the clerestory window, and groin vaults in the aisle.

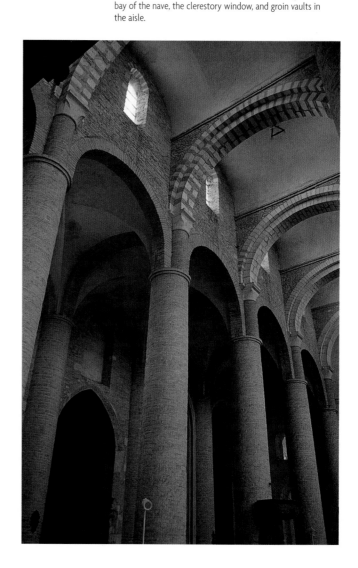

process, however, for the semicircular arch is not a particularly efficient structural element. The Romans had employed it extensively for its esthetic qualities and ease of construction (the arch scaffolding or centering is relatively uncomplicated to build), qualities that doubtless recommended it to Romanesque architects as well, even though the outward, overturning thrust it generated caused problems, which were commonly resolved by building massive supporting walls. Since cutting openings could weaken the supporting wall, Romanesque builders used windows very sparingly to avoid damage to the structure's integrity. The semicircular arch, the barrel vault, and the groin vault (two barrel vaults intersecting at right angles) also imposed geometric constraints. Square or rectangular bays could be handled easily, while irregular or circular sections posed esthetic and structural difficulties.

During the early Romanesque period, large expanses of exterior wall were often articulated, as at St. Martin at Canigou, by decorative devices commonly used by masons in Lombardy, particularly in the region of Como. These so-called Lombard bands consist of vertical pilaster strips and corbeled arches set in shallow bands on the wall surface. Arches on the early Christian buildings of Ravenna, such as the Mausoleum of Galla Placidia, have been suggested as the origin of Lombard bands. Lombard work spread from Italy to the rest of Europe, and it can be seen on the westwerk of St. Philibert at Tournus, a monastic church in central France (roughly contemporary with Canigou) that exhibits both traditional and novel features in its fabric. While Carolingian architects had added towers and a westwerk to the Early Christian basilica of nave, aisles, and apse, the early Romanesque work further

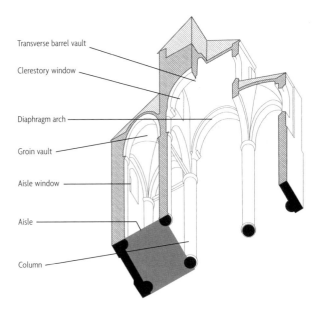

Transverse barrel vault

Clerestory window

Diaphragm arch

Groin vault

Aisle window

Aisle

Column

8.23 Diagram explaining the structure of nave and aisle vaults at St. Philibert at Tournus.

This drawing closely matches the view seen in Fig. 8.22.

elaborated the east end to accommodate additional altars and processions.

Monks had come to Tournus to escape the pillaging of Norse raiders along the Atlantic coast, only to find themselves attacked by the Huns from the east in 937. Given this history, it is not surprising that they wanted a fireproof masonry church to protect precious relics. Work on the present building began in about 950 with construction of the crypt or basement level under the choir. In plan (Fig. 8.21), the east end of the crypt had a central chapel for the relics of St. Philibert, surrounded by a passage recalling the ambulatory of early Christian martyria such as the Church of the Nativity in Bethlehem. The difference at St. Philibert was the inclusion of three rectangular chapels radiating from the ambulatory. Their plan is repeated in the east end of the church above, reflecting the need for circulation around the church and access to additional altars set in each chapel. At the opposite end of the church, the massive westwerk contains a narthex, above which is a chapel dedicated to St. Michael, patron saint of high places. Stubby cylindrical piers at both levels support groin vaults in the narthex and barrel vaults in the chapel.

Similar but elongated piers extend the length of the nave as supports for a unique series of transverse barrel vaults over diaphragm arches defining each bay (Figs. 8.22–8.23). The architects thus resolved several constructional problems. They reduced the clear span required of their barrel vaults to the width of each bay, which was less than the nave width; they countered the thrust of each barrel vault with that of its neighbor, ultimately anchoring the sequence with the mass of the westwerk and crossing tower; and they inserted relatively large clerestory windows in the enclosing walls at the ends of each barrel vault, thus obtaining direct light into the nave. An interrupted ceiling plane on the interior offset these advantages. The unity of the nave and its axial direction toward

the altar were diminished by the vaulting, which may account for the fact that this solution was never repeated over a major space in subsequent churches.

In its choir plan, its ingenious structure, and its unadorned construction, Tournus reflects the struggle between tradition and innovation faced by Romanesque builders. It also illustrates the Romanesque tendency to maintain discrete elements in plan as separately articulated volumes in the three-dimensional reality of the building. From the exterior, most Romanesque church features are readily discernible. The aisle roofs are lower than that of the nave, and the westwerk is a distinct mass, as are the radiating chapels, ambulatory, choir, transepts, and crossing tower. With experience, Romanesque architects achieved remarkable compositions of these plan-generated elements.

ROMANESQUE ARCHITECTURE OF THE HOLY ROMAN EMPIRE

The middle portion of Charlemagne's empire, corresponding roughly to modern Germany and northern Italy, eventually came under the control of the vigorous House of Saxony, whose three successive heads each named Otto gained the title of Holy Roman Emperor in the course of their capable leadership. Their rule, termed Ottonian, extended from 936 to 1002, but its effects lasted nearly a century longer.

Ottonian architecture is in many respects an extension of Carolingian traditions: it is the German expression of Romanesque. An outstanding example is the Ottonian church of St. Michael at Hildesheim (1010–33), which is a double-ended basilica with entrances along the side aisles as in many original Roman basilicas (Fig. 8.21). Its two apses also recall the general church layout indicated on the Plan of St. Gall. On the interior (Fig. 8.24), the eastern apse contains the altar, and the western apse contains a raised platform for seating the emperor and his court. Illumination is provided by clerestories, simple punched openings in the unarticulated nave wall, while the supporting nave arcade has a subtle A-B-B-A rhythm established by piers alternating with two columns. Polychrome arches, boldly carved column capitals suggestive of Italian examples, and an elaborately painted wooden ceiling enrich the interior.

Slightly later than St. Michael at Hildesheim is the spacious imperial cathedral at Speyer, built about 1030 and revised in three successive building campaigns until 1182 (Figs. 8.21, 8.25–8.26). It is a massive and majestic construction, extending over 425 feet from the thick walls of its imposing westwerk to the semicircular apse flanked by a pair of square-plan towers. The nave is wide, long, and tall, framed by semicircular arches surrounding each wall bay. Covered at first by a flat wooden ceiling, the nave received groin vaults set over paired bays and separated by transverse arch bands in the course of building activity

8.24 (above left) St. Michael interior, Hildesheim, 1010–33.

The square module that governs much of the plan is defined by the piers and the bay under the eastern tower, outlined by bold polychrome arches.

8.25 (below left) Speyer Cathedral east end, ca. 1030–61.

Speyer is distinguished by its large scale and multiple towers. The two seen here are set at the junction of choir and transepts, and they are taller than the dome over the crossing. Note the use of Lombard bands.

8.26 (below right) Speyer Cathedral nave, interior looking east, ca. 1030–61.

The groin vaults were erected in 1082–1137, making this one of the highest vaulted churches of its time.

8.27 S. Miniato al Monte west front, Florence, 1062–90 and later.

This façade would not have seemed strange to the Romans, for it continues the use of marble veneers in geometric patterns combined with arch-and-column motifs familiar from the classical past.

8.28 Plans of S. Ambrogio, Milan, 1080–1140; S. Miniato al Monte, Florence, 1062–90; and Pisa Cathedral, 1063.

S. Miniato preserves the plan of simple Early Christian basilicas. S. Ambrogio includes an atrium and two separate belfries, while the cathedral at Pisa has a cruciform plan, with transepts that are treated as smaller basilicas. Pisa's oval crossing dome provided the impetus for Florence to attempt an even more ambitious dome on its cathedral.

S. Ambrogio, Milan

S. Miniato al Monte, Florence

Pisa Cathedral

0   50 m
0   150 ft

from 1082 to 1137. At 107 feet above the floor, these vaults rank as the highest built in the Romanesque period and approach the accomplishments of Roman construction. Interior decoration is restrained, even severe, with the variegated warm yellow-to-pink hues of the stone enlivening the surfaces of walls and piers. Influences from Lombardy are seen in the cubiform capitals of the crypt and the corbel arch tables and pilaster strips of the exterior wall.

In the southern regions of the Holy Roman Empire, the classical heritage of Rome heavily influenced Romanesque architecture. Italian cities developed their own versions of Romanesque architecture, retaining a strong reliance on the classical past with little influence from northern Europe. In general, the Early Christian basilica remained the standard church form, seldom having a westwerk or attached towers as in Ottonian or Carolingian architecture. The church of S. Miniato al Monte in Florence (1062–90 and later) is typical (Figs. 8.27, 8.28). A single pair of aisles flanks the transeptless nave, which is terminated by a simple semicircular apse. Alternate bays of the nave are grouped by diaphragm arches (where a wall is built to create a level, horizontal top), above which wooden trusses support the roof. Its façade is articulated on the ground level by five arches supported by

8.29 (above) Pisa Cathedral west front, 1063; 1089–1272.

Marble arches and columns march around the building, which is further enriched with alternating bands of dark- and light-colored marble.

8.30 (below) Pisa Cathedral and Campanile seen from the east, 1063; 1089–1272.

The campanile is better known as the Leaning Tower of Pisa, a building that has never been vertical because of difficult foundation conditions.

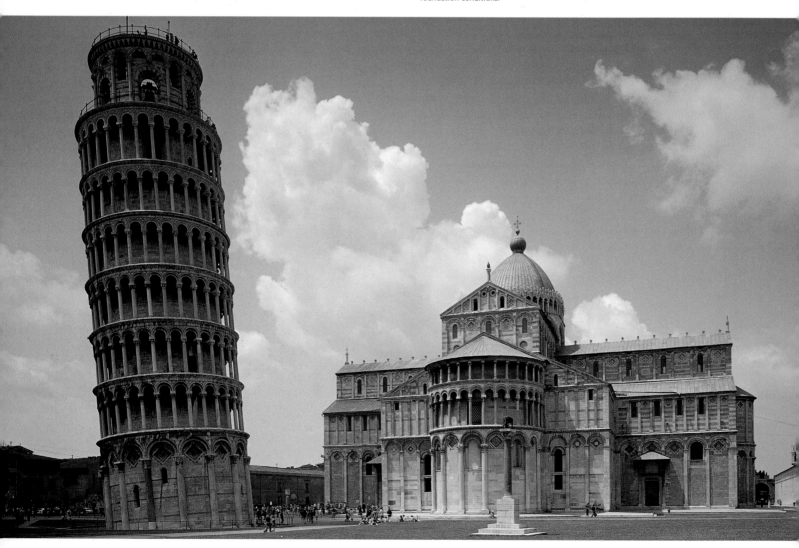

Corinthian half-columns, with Corinthian pilasters and a gable defining the roof of the nave. Geometric patterns set in marble veneers enliven the essentially flat wall plane, and the entire elevation clearly follows the profile of the basilican space behind it.

The freestanding cathedral at Pisa (begun in 1063 and finished 1089–1272) is more elaborate, although still close to Early Christian tradition (Figs. 8.28–8.30). In plan the cruciform basilica has double aisles and galleries flanking the nave, and single aisles and galleries flanking the transepts. At the crossing, an oval dome is raised on squinches and shallow pendentives, recalling the centralized church plans of Byzantium, while wooden trusses roof the remainder of the church. The exterior is sheathed in marble arcades, stacked row on row across the western façade and continuing around the church. The interior is marked by polychromy, in this case alternate courses of dark and light marble set in horizontal bands, and there are Byzantine mosaics in the apse. The cathedral is complemented by two adjacent structures, a circular baptistery and a cylindrical campanile, the famous Leaning Tower of Pisa, now over thirteen feet out of plumb.

In the northern Italian region known as Lombardy, the outstanding Romanesque building is the abbey church of S. Ambrogio in Milan (Figs. 8.28, 8.31–8.32). The dates of this important monument are still a matter of scholarly debate. Research indicates that work on the present structure began in around 1080, and the nave was begun after 1128. The rib vaults of the nave were probably built in about 1140. In plan S. Ambrogio conserves Early Christian practice. An arcaded atrium precedes the church proper, and a semicircular apse and smaller semicircular chapels at the ends of the groin-vaulted aisles terminate the transeptless basilica. Galleries over the aisles help buttress the thrust of the nave vaults, but they preclude the possibility of clerestory lighting.

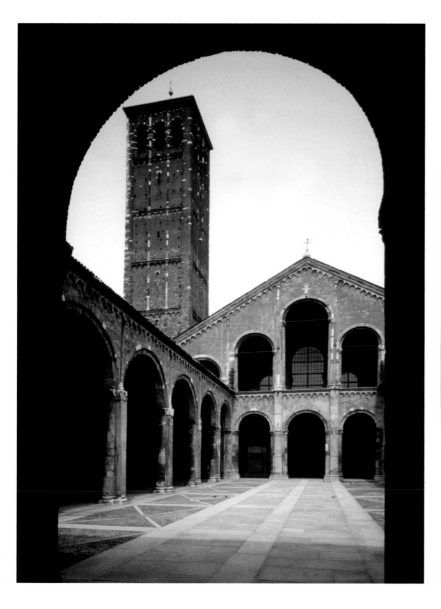

8.31 S. Ambrogio west front, Milan, ca. 1080–1140.

The façade and atrium are ornamented with rows of corbeled arches known as Lombard bands. Lombard work may be seen in Romanesque buildings found in many parts of Europe.

8.32 S. Ambrogio interior, Milan, ca. 1080–1140.

The wide square bays of this church have groin vaults to which brick ribs have been added along the line of the arris. Note the use of corbeled arches continues on the interior

PILGRIMAGE ROADS

In addition to monasticism, the medieval period was marked by another important religious institution: pilgrimage. To atone for sins, seek a cure, or assure salvation, medieval men and women traveled as pilgrims to shrines containing the relics of saints. All churches established since Carolingian times were required to possess relics for each altar, providing local, regional, or international opportunities for pilgrimages. Jerusalem and Rome were the most celebrated centers, but they were also the most expensive and hazardous for northern Europeans to visit.

Around the year 900 a new center for pilgrimage arose to rival the popularity of Rome and Jerusalem, the shrine of the apostle James (Sant' Iago in Spanish), located at Compostela in northwestern Spain. With considerable assistance from the Church, Compostela became the goal for thousands of pilgrims as stories of miracles wrought by St. James encouraged people from all parts of Europe to visit his tomb and pray for his assistance. Gradually an entire network of roads and hospices developed to support the growing tide of pilgrims traveling to Compostela. Monasteries, the traditional centers of hospitality for travelers, found the increasing numbers of visitors disruptive to their prescribed cycle of services. The monks accommodated these pilgrims by modifying the basilican church plan to include an ambulatory, like that found at St. Philibert at Tournus, which worked as an extension of the aisles to provide a continuous passageway around the entire church. At the east end, radiating chapels opened off the ambulatory, and there were sometimes additional chapels located on the east side of the transepts for use by monks who were also ordained clergy. These chapel altars could also be visited by pilgrims without interrupting monastic services being sung in the choir.

Churches built in response to the pilgrimage are common on the major roads to Compostela. Five of the largest are so similar in plan, scale, and architectural detail that they illustrate strikingly the transmission of artistic ideas up and down the roads. The oldest of the five was St. Martin at Tours (now destroyed), where a rebuilding of the apse as early as 918 introduced the scheme of radiating chapels and ambulatory attached to a large nave and spacious transepts. By the middle of the eleventh century, this theme had been picked up by the churches of St. Martial at Limoges (now also demolished), St. Foy at Conques, St. Sernin at Toulouse, and St. James at Compostela, producing a series of buildings with an unmistakable family resemblance (Fig. 8.33).

The church of St. Sernin at Toulouse clearly illustrates the group (page 190 and Fig. 8.34). St. Sernin remains a major monument of the Romanesque even though its west

8.33 Plans of St. Sernin, Toulouse, ca. 1077–1119; St. Foy, Conques, ca. 1050–1130; and St. James, Compostela, ca. 1075–1211

All three of these are churches from the pilgrimage routes to Santiago de Compostela, and they share common traits, including aisles linking to an ambulatory and so providing a continuous path for pilgrims to access relics in the chapels.

St. Sernin, Toulouse

St. Foy, Conques

St. James, Compostela

8.34 St. Sernin interior, Toulouse, 1077–1119.

The church has paired aisles on each side of the nave, perhaps in reference to Old St. Peter's in Rome, and the innermost aisle has a gallery above to help brace the thrust of the nave vault.

8.35 Diagram showing the structure of St. Sernin, Toulouse.

The paired aisles work together with the gallery vaults over the innermost aisle to brace the thrust from the high banded barrel vaults in the nave and choir.

front was never finished and its crossing tower was greatly enlarged in the Gothic period. Begun in about 1077, the choir was consecrated in 1096, and the transepts and nave were probably complete, except for the vaulting, by 1119. In plan the church has paired aisles on each side of the nave, four chapels on the east of the large transept, and five radiating chapels around the apse. At nearly 360 feet it is a long building, with a width of nave and aisles totaling about 100 feet, spaciousness that may have been inspired by Old St. Peter's in Rome. The banded barrel vaults rise about sixty-five feet and are braced by second-floor galleries over the inner pair of aisles (Fig. 8.35). This gives the church a triangular cross-section, but precludes the insertion of clerestory windows to light the nave. Windows at the east end and light from the windows in the crossing tower provide relative brilliance near the altar in contrast to the dim light of the nave. The exterior arrangement of chapels, ambulatory, and choir rising to the great crossing tower is harmoniously composed, and the ensemble is enhanced by its construction materials, red brick trimmed with stone.

The pilgrimage road churches also remain at Conques and Compostela. St. Foy at Conques in a remote region of

central France is the smallest (Figs. 8.36–8.37). In plan it has only a single pair of aisles and galleries flanking the nave, but its structural scheme is identical to that at St. Sernin. Over the crossing is an octagonal lantern built on a **squinch**, a series of corbeled arches that makes the transition from a square bay to an octagon. (Pendentives as seen at Hagia Sophia do the same thing in a different geometric configuration, but the squinch is more commonly

8.36 St. Foy, Conques, ca. 1050–1130.

Set in a remote mountain valley, this is the smallest of the great pilgrimage road churches. Site restrictions limited the length of the building.

more active scene of hell, entered through the mouth of the monster Leviathan. Presiding over various punishments is the devil, identifiable by his spiked hairstyle, and assisted by reptilian minions. Close observation reveals that the Seven Deadly Sins, among other transgressions, are rewarded by appropriate punishments, graphically illustrating the concept that Dante would use centuries

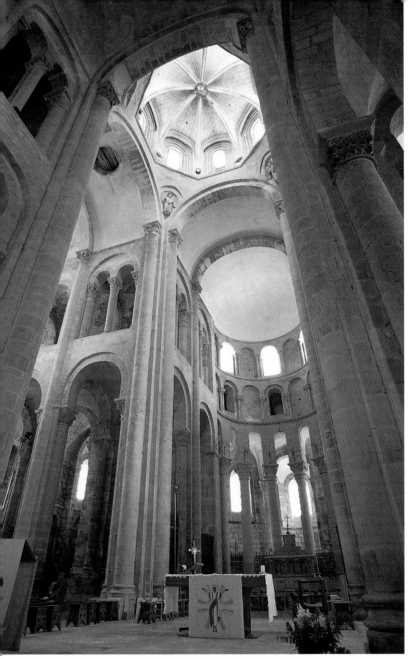

8.37 St. Foy crossing, Conques, ca. 1050–1130.

This view shows the gallery over the aisle and the squinches supporting the crossing lantern. Placement of the altar at the crossing is modern; the medieval altar was set in the choir.

8.38 (above) St. Foy west front, Conques, ca. 1050–1130.

This view shows the large tympanum depicting the Last Judgment set over the doors. Church authorities used sculptures such as this one to communicate Christian teachings to a largely illiterate public.

8.39 (below) St. Foy tympanum, Conques, ca. 1124.

Here we see Christ as the large central figure. Heaven is depicted on the left lintel, while the varied torments of hell occupy the corresponding position on the right. Persons awaiting judgment line up on Christ's right hand.

found in western buildings.) St. Foy preserves on its **tympanum** (the semicircular panel created under the arch of a doorway) a magnificent sculpture (ca. 1140) of the Last Judgment (Figs. 8.38–8.39), including visions of heaven and hell. Christ the judge sits at the center, the largest figure because he is the most important. On his right (your left) is a line of people appearing at Judgment Day, led by Mary, St. Peter (carrying the key), and church personages escorting Charlemagne and his family, who are remembered because they gave money to build earlier churches on the site. Under Christ's feet is the weighing of souls, and on the lintel at the left is the serenity of heaven, where the architecture, fittingly, is Romanesque. On the right lintel is a later in the *Divine Comedy*. Those entering the church could not fail to understand the connection between their actions and their fates in the world hereafter. This tympanum, like most Romanesque sculpture, had a strong didactic purpose in addition to its decorative role.

At Compostela, the church of St. James still functions as a major pilgrim shrine. It was planned with a full complement of nine towers: one at the crossing, pairs at the entrances (west front, south and north transepts), and two more flanking the intersection of nave and transepts (Fig. 8.33). At the east end is an axial chapel with a door to the plaza outside that is opened on jubilee years (those years when St. James's Day, July 25, falls on a Sunday or other years as declared by the church) so that the faithful may enter directly from the east. All three of these churches—St. Sernin, St. Foy, and St. James—reflect the religious devotion that for centuries has motivated pilgrims to travel great distances in search of the holy.

THE ORDER OF CLUNY

In 910, Duke William of Aquitaine, desiring to atone for his less than saintly life and seek divine favor, endowed a monastery on his lands at Cluny, where there was a Gallo-Roman villa or farm. Through an unusual provision in its charter, the new monastery was exempted from the jurisdiction of the local bishop and made directly responsible to the pope. Twelve monks, led by Abbot Berno, came to Cluny seeking a stricter observance of the Benedictine Rule, and the monastery prospered. The exemplary life of its monks attracted more converts and bequests; its position in Burgundy on the route from Paris to Rome and its

virtual independence from local religious authorities allowed it to grow into an influential organization, with 1450 abbeys and priories all over Europe; and the exceptional leadership and longevity of its early abbots brought distinction to the Congregation and Order of Cluny. By 1088, the church and monastic complex (known as Cluny II), built after the original villa has been outgrown, had also become too small, and a new church (known to historians as Cluny III) was begun to accommodate the ever-increasing number of monks.

The church of Cluny III (Figs. 8.40–8.42) had the features of mature Romanesque architecture, for it was appropriate to the monastery's importance that its major church should be the largest and most splendid in Christendom. Based on the basilican plan, the church was enriched by a double set of transepts and further augmented by a series of radiating chapels around the apse and eastern walls of the transepts. The nave, 100 feet high and 496 feet long, was large enough to accommodate impressive processions and was flanked by two aisles on each side, the innermost pair of which continued around the choir as an ambulatory, linking the five radiating chapels of the east end. On the exterior, each of the plan elements was clearly expressed as an individual volume, but all were beautifully integrated into a coherent whole. Towers provided vertical emphasis: a pair at the western entrance, one over each arm of the major transept, the highest tower at the intersection of the major transept and nave, and a shorter tower over the crossing of the minor transept. Viewed from the east, the church appeared as a triangular mass, with roofs ascending from the chapels to the ambulatory, the apse semidome, the minor crossing tower, and finally the major crossing tower. Inside, the effect was even more wonderful,

8.40 Reconstruction view of the monastery of Cluny III, seen from the east, 11th century.

This was the largest church in western Christendom at the time of its construction. To the left, beyond the apse, stretch buildings of the infirmary and the abbot's palace.

8.41 Plan of the monastery of Cluny III, 11th century.

Remains of the atrium and east end of the church of Cluny II survive to the right of the new church. The cloister was enlarged after the great church was completed by demolishing the nave of Cluny II.

8.42 Section through the church of Cluny III, 11th century.

This view shows how the paired aisles worked to brace the nave vaults. Note the use of broken or pointed arches in the profiling of the vaults.

for the sanctuary was filled with light from the many windows in the chapels and clerestories. Images of how this may have appeared come largely from the research of Kenneth John Conant, since the actual church of Cluny III was dismantled for its stone after the French Revolution. Only the south arm of the major transept remains (Fig. 8.43).

Considered from the standpoint of structure, Cluny III shows the great progress made in building art since the completion of St. Martin at Canigou. The paired aisles, which stepped down in height, buttressed the high vaults of the nave. The vault itself was not a continuous barrel vault as at St. Sernin, but a broken barrel vault, banded in each bay for visual articulation and structural reinforcement. Whether by accident or deduction, the monks who served as the architects of Cluny III, the musician Gunzo and the mathematician Hézelon, found that vaults constructed on the profile of a pointed arch exert less outward

thrust than the Roman arch, and they exploited this discovery in the vaulting of the nave and aisles. Even so, a portion of the nave vault collapsed in 1125, but it was repaired before the general dedication of the church on October 25, 1130. Light for the nave was provided directly by rather small clerestory windows located just under the vaulting, since the great loads sustained by the walls severely restricted the possibilities for larger openings. The great vaulted spaces of the church created excellent acoustics for the exceptionally beautiful and elaborate services sung by the monks. The rich splendor of the heavenly kingdom was further reflected in the artistic embellishments, particularly sculpture, lavished on the building. Some of this sculpture survived post-revolutionary destruction, although in considerably damaged condition (Fig. 8.44). To assess the artistic impact of Cluny, therefore, it is necessary to see the better-preserved work at its affiliated foundations, for where the religious influence of

THE MYSTIC MILL FROM VÉZELAY

by Marian Moffett

8A Ste. Madeleine south aisle capital, the "Mystic Mill," Vézelay, France, 1120–38.

Romanesque artists undertook the task of adapting their work to fit architectural frames. Doorways and columns became the domain of sculptors, while wall surfaces were taken over by mural painters. The artists worked not only to ornament architecture but also to make church buildings a visual extension of Christian teachings by using images that could be understood by the largely illiterate population. Within the limitations imposed by functional parts of the building, these artists created memorable scenes that illustrate principles of medieval theology.

One particularly fine example of this is the Mystic Mill capital from the nave of the abbey church at Vézelay (Fig. 8A). Its subject, the grinding of grain to produce flour, depicts a common activity in the Middle Ages, a necessary first step in the production of bread. Grain as harvested from the fields cannot be consumed by people until the hard outer coating (the bran) is broken and the nutritious kernel inside is pulverized, actions accomplished by milling either in hand querns or between the large millstones or a water-powered mill.

For medieval pilgrims, this scene depicts a theological allegory, for this is no ordinary mill, and the figures operating it are not local people. The man pouring the grain on the left is Moses, and the figure bagging the flour is the apostle Paul, while the mill itself represents Christ. Note the cross-shaped brace of the mill's toothed wheel. The two figures, one from the Old Testament and one from the New, are brought together by Christ. The scene thus represents the transformation of promises and prophecies of the Old Testament (the grain) into the teachings and blessings of the New Testament (the flour) through the action of Jesus Christ (the mill). Reconciliation of the Old and New Testaments was a key concern of medieval theologians, and in this one image the artist has captured this abstruse concept through analogy to a process familiar to all. By extension, flour from the mill represents communion bread, the body of Christ. The transformation of grain into flour also implied the conversion of the Jews to Christianity, an event medieval people believed prefigured the Second Coming of Christ.

This scene also embodies a yet deeper meaning that would have been understood by the more learned monks. Just as the bran protects the nutrients of the wheat kernel, the true meaning of scripture is concealed from unbelievers. Through the study of biblical texts and guidance from sacred commentaries, symbolized by the figures of Moses and Paul, those seeking a fuller insight into religious truths could eventually crack the outer shell of appearance and gain spiritual nourishment from the truths revealed only to those who attained the highest levels of religious learning. While not all the capitals at Vézelay are this rich in meaning, they remind us that medieval art existed for more reasons than to delight the eye. Art worked with architecture to advance Christian teachings.

8.43 (left) Cluny III south transept, 11th century.

This is all that remains of the once-grand monastic church.

8.44 (above) Cluny III capital from the choir, 11th century.

This depicts one of the tones of the musical scale shown as a figure playing an instrument similar to a lute. The monks of Cluny were great patrons of the arts, as they believed beautiful surroundings, including lovely music, helped the mind to contemplate spiritual values.

8.45 (left, below) Ste. Madeleine nave, Vézelay, 1120–38.

The nave was constructed while the abbey was part of the Clunaic order. Even though the building does not resemble Cluny architecturally, the tradition of creating a handsomely embellished environment for worship continues here.

8.46 (below) Ste. Madeleine narthex portal, Vézelay, 1120–38.

The portal shows the descent of the Holy Spirit at Pentecost. The apostles look startled, reflecting the surprise at encountering the risen Christ. Faces on many of them were damaged during the turmoil of the French Revolution.

8.47 St. Lazare, Last Judgment, west-front tympanum, Autun, 1120–32.

The subject is the same as that at Conques, although the placement of particular scenes is different. This work was signed by its sculptor, Gislebertus, in the band under the feet of Christ.

8.48 St. Lazare capital (formerly in the choir), Autun, 1120–32.

This work shows the Flight into Egypt, with Mary and Jesus riding a donkey led by Joseph. Note the nimbus or halo behind the heads of Mary and Jesus. Romanesque sculpture often exaggerates the sizes of heads and hands, as these are the most expressive parts of the body.

Cluny traveled, so did its policy of artistic patronage. At Ste. Madeleine, Vézelay, the abbey was enlarged during a period of Cluniac reform, and the church nave preserves its stately Romanesque dignity (Fig. 8.45). (The choir was rebuilt during the Gothic period.) Polychrome semicircular arches divide the nave vault into bays, each of which is groin-vaulted. Splendid sculptural work on column capitals and the narthex portals remains. Nave capitals depict a range of subjects, from Old Testament events to the lives of the saints and allegories illustrating teachings of the Church. The tympanum over the door from the narthex to the nave (dated 1120–32) represents the descent of the Holy Spirit at Pentecost, in which Christ sends the apostles to the corners of the earth to preach, teach, and heal the sick (Fig. 8.46). The sculptor here has bordered the central scene with signs of the zodiac, illustrations of the months of the year shown through agricultural labors, and imaginative depictions of diverse peoples of the world, including Scythians with collapsible, elephant-sized ears, Ethiopians with pig snouts, and pygmies with ladders. As a totality, the tympanum expresses the assertion that Christ and his teachings are present at all times, in all places, to all people.

There is a more austere tympanum at the nearby Cluniac church of St. Lazare at Autun (Fig. 8.47). Here the subject is the Last Judgment, replete with hideous demons and risen souls summoned to the final reckoning. An impassive and enormous figure of Christ occupies the center of the panel, with heaven on his right and the weighing of souls on his left, next to the miseries of hell. (Notice that, as at Conques, the devil's agent in the weighing of souls cheats by placing his hand in the balance pan!) The interior of the church repeats many of the architectural features of Cluny III at a reduced scale, while the beautifully carved capitals of the nave and choir present a range of biblical stories, including a Nativity cycle (Fig. 8.48), as well as fanciful beasts and foliage.

AQUITAINE AND PROVENCE

As one would expect from a period when the means of communication were limited and political control was dispersed, a number of regional variants of the Romanesque developed in present-day France. All share the common heritage of Romanesque influences, but they differ according to the materials, culture, and artistic interests of the individual locales. The major portion of France south of the Loire comprised Aquitaine, an important region that was successively independent, allied with the king of France, and a possession of the king of England. Seat of a flourishing culture, its architecture was perhaps

8.49 Plans of S. Marco, Venice, 1063–89; St. Front, Périgueux, ca. 1120; St. Savin-sur-Gartempe, 1060–1115; and St. Pierre, Angoulême, 1105–28.

St. Front's design seems derived from that of S. Marco in Venice. The cathedral at Angoulême has domes on the scale of those at Périgueux, while the church at St. Savin has a continuous barrel vault in the nave covered with frescoes.

8.50 St. Front interior, Périgueux, ca. 1120.

In the south of France, it is unexpected to find a centrally planned church having domes on pendentives. (Compare this to S. Marco on p. 140.)

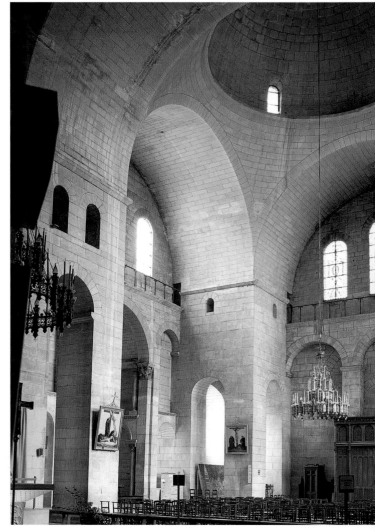

the most open to varied influences from other parts of Europe, especially from eastern Christendom. Aquitaine has a series of some seventy churches with domes, an atypical feature in western medieval architecture. That they reflect Byzantine influence is strongly implied by their use of pendentives, a characteristically eastern device.

The church of St. Front at Périgueux, built largely after 1120, provides an interesting parallel with S. Marco in Venice (Fig. 8.49). S. Marco, itself modeled on the Greek-cross plan of the now-vanished Church of the Holy Apostles in Constantinople, was rebuilt after a fire, with the work being completed about 1089. Nearly thirty years later, the existing church of St. Front at Périgueux was greatly enlarged into a Greek-cross plan remarkably similar to S. Marco. Five domes on pendentives rise from massive pierced piers to cover the arms and crossing of the church. At Périgueux, the work lacks both the typical Byzantine mosaic decoration inside and the exterior profile of later Byzantine domes (Fig. 8.50). Instead the detailing is based on classical architecture, including

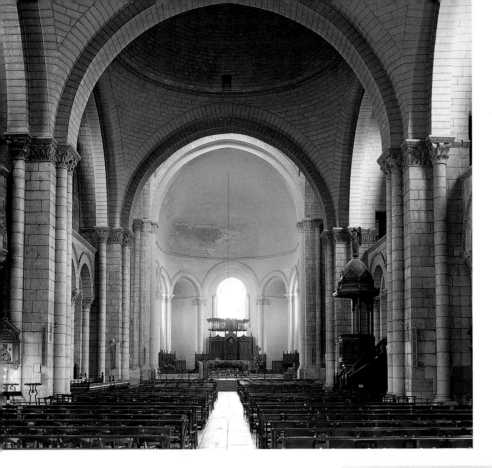

closely spaced classical columns on the lantern turrets above the conical roofs over each dome.

Périgueux is somewhat exceptional even among the unusual churches of Aquitaine. The other domed churches there, such as the cathedral of St. Pierre at Angoulême (1105–28 and later), are aisleless basilicas with domes replacing the customary vaulting in the nave (Figs. 8.49, 8.51). Major structural loads in each bay are concentrated by pendentives to four piers set in the wall, allowing a reasonable area to be opened for windows, thereby providing direct illumination to the nave. The sequence of pointed arches framing each bay provides a stately processional space. On the west front is an inaccurately restored sculpture depicting a vision of the Second Coming of Christ.

Not all Romanesque churches in Aquitaine have domes. There are also fine examples of vaulted structures, including the abbey church of St. Savin-sur-Gartempe, built in stages between 1060 and 1115 (Figs. 8.49, 8.52). It is classified as a hall church because the aisle vaults rise almost as high as those of the nave. Massive cylindrical piers support a continuous barrel vault over the nave, which is braced by groin vaults in the aisles to counteract thrust where it is greatest, just above the springing of the vault arch. As at Angoulême, radiating chapels without an ambulatory form the east end, and a crossing tower provides vertical emphasis. On the interior, the uninterrupted nave vault, the narthex, and the crypt have been adorned with a notable series of frescoes, called the Bible of St.

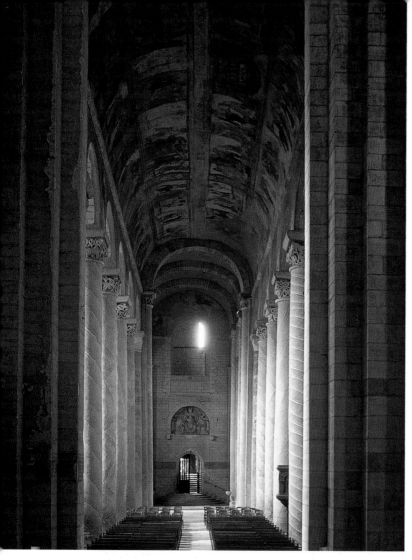

Savin (Fig. 8.53), which form the finest surviving example of Romanesque mural painting.

The region of Provence, centered on the Mediterranean close to Italy, remained most faithful to the classical architecture of ancient Rome. Provence had been a major Roman colony, and well-preserved Roman buildings still exist at Nîmes and other cities. Not surprisingly, therefore, Romanesque architecture there exhibits strong Roman influence in its composition, proportions, and details. The Cluniac priory church of St. Gilles-du-Gard (ca. 1140–70) (Fig. 8.54) has a triple-arched west façade based on the model of a Roman triumphal arch. Accurately proportioned Corinthian columns, some of which were actually recycled from Roman buildings, are incorporated in the work. Aside from the façade, little remains of the original church, which was an important regional center of pilgrimage. The contemporary façade of the former cathedral

---

8.53 St. Savin-sur-Gartempe nave, 1060–1115.

The nave shows the unbroken expanse of barrel-vaulted ceiling surface that was used for displaying a fresco cycle depicting biblical stories.

8.54 St. Gilles-du-Gard west front portals, ca. 1140–70.

The sculpture has a classical feel, and the overall design recalls a triple-arched Roman triumphal arch.

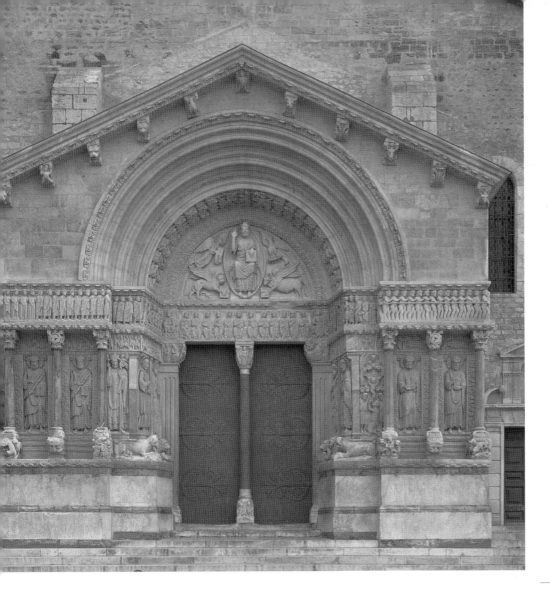

8.55 St. Trophime west front, Arles, ca. 1140–70.

As with St. Gilles, this church façade is based on a triumphal arch and the sculpture recalls Roman models. Provence was relatively close to Italy, and it had a substantial store of authentic Roman works.

of St. Trophîme at Arles also recalls Roman construction in its dignified setting of sculpture in classical surroundings (Fig. 8.55).

CISTERCIAN MONASTERIES

The eleventh century witnessed the establishment of several new monastic groups, including the Order of Cîteaux, known as the Cistercians. Like the Cluniacs, the Cistercians originated in Burgundy, but in terms of artistic and religious development they were in many respects the antithesis of Cluny. The Cistercians were founded in 1098 by a group of twenty-two monks from Molesme who desired to follow a stricter observance of the Benedictine Rule, and their name came from that of their first monastery, at Cîteaux, in a wooded swamp donated by the Viscount of Beaune. The first years were difficult, but the new monastery gained an important convert in 1112, when a young nobleman named Bernard joined the order. His religious zeal and organizational skill shaped the Cistercians into a uniform, highly regulated ascetic community. (Other members of his family also eventually joined the order, and their financial contributions doubtless helped as well.) In 1115 Bernard founded the third

daughter house at Clairvaux, from which he was to continue to act as the guiding spiritual force for all Cistercian houses until his death in 1153.

In time the Cistercians rivaled the Cluniacs in influence. Although their affiliated monasteries totaled only about half the number of Cluniac houses, they spread throughout western Christendom. The Cistercian Order required a great measure of conformity from its dependent monasteries, and this uniformity extended to architecture as well. As was appropriate to the austere life laid out for their monks, Cistercian abbeys were of the simplest possible construction consistent with durable masonry building. In sharp contrast to the Cluniacs, the Cistercians initially did not allow luxurious features like towers, stained-glass windows, or paved floors. They shunned expensive materials and discouraged sculptural ornament. Cistercian monasteries had straightforward, orderly plans based on a square module, devoid of the elaborate articulation of many Cluniac designs. Thus the Cistercians produced an international set of buildings with unmistakable common features.

Cistercian houses were founded at least twenty miles from any existing settlement, preferably at the end of a narrow valley that had a reliable water supply. While the monks did not shun their obligation to extend hospitality

Church

Night stair to dormitory on second floor, over chapter room and workroom

Chapter room

Cloister

Fountain

Workroom, or scriptorium

Guest house

Refectory

Forge

N

0   50 m
0   150 ft

8.56 Plan of the abbey, Fontenay, 1139–47.

This Cistercian plan recalls the Plan of St. Gall, with church, dormitory, and refectory defining three sides of the cloister. The original refectory is missing. On the south side is the forge, a utilitarian building equipped with water-powered machinery that could full cloth, forge iron, or accomplish other heavy tasks. The monastery's vegetable garden was located immediately to the east.

8.57 West front, Abbey Church, Fontenay, 1139–47.

Compared to the embellished buildings of Cluny, this Cistercian church seems rather severe, observing the artistic strictures established by St. Bernard, under whose direction this monastery was founded.

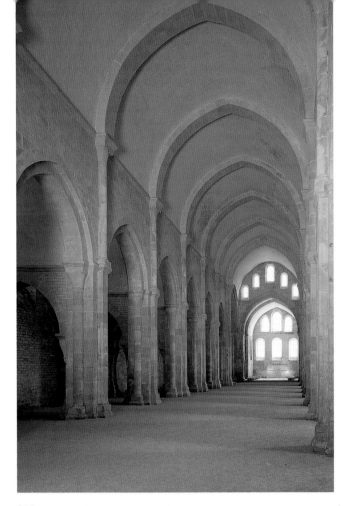

8.58 Fontenay Abbey Church interior looking east, 1139–47.

Note the broken banded barrel vaults and the absence of clerestory windows. The church is not tall, and its architectural detail is austere.

The abbey of Fontenay in Burgundy is today among the best preserved of early Cistercian monasteries. Built from 1139 to 1147, with some portions reconstructed in the thirteenth and sixteenth centuries, it is a clear illustration of Bernard of Clairvaux's architectural ideals. The monastery is closely modeled on the layout of the Plan of St. Gall, having a modular unit established by the square bay of the church aisle (Fig. 8.56). Two of these units determine the width of the nave; four, the area of the crossing; and one for each of the four chapels on the east wall of the transept. The module continues as the standard unit for the cloister walk, and it is repeated in the chapter house, workroom, and forge building. (The non-modular refectory is a sixteenth-century structure.)

The same simplicity distinguishes the three-dimensional reality of the buildings (Fig. 8.57). The nave, modest in height, is covered by a broken banded barrel vault, while the aisles have transverse broken barrel vaults over each bay (Fig. 8.58), reminiscent of the nave vaults at St. Philibert at Tournus. Light for the church comes from windows in the aisles and at the east and west end walls, as there are no clerestories. The church floor is of compacted earth, with only the raised choir section being paved in stone. The harmonious proportions enliven the utter plainness of the construction. The cloister walk, with its semicircular arcading, reflects sunlight softly and creates an appropriately human scale (Fig. 8.59).

8.59 Cloister walk, Fontenay, 1139–47.

The cloister connected major monastic buildings and served as a covered passage for meditation or exercise. In good weather, monks sat on the ledges under arches to read. Modular proportions and restrained architectural detail create a sense of repose.

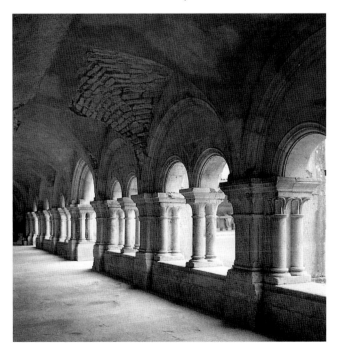

to visitors, they did not locate their buildings so as to encourage pilgrim traffic. Persons able to endow monasteries through gifts of land soon learned that even the most unpromising sites became productive in the hands of the Cistercians, and the example of their superior agricultural management spread to surrounding areas. Whatever long-term spiritual benefits attended the initial donation were generally compounded by very tangible increases in rents and revenues. In the early years the monks provided for all their own needs, supplying their vegetarian diet from garden plots adjacent to the monastery, but soon the care of crops and animals required more time than monks could spare from their religious duties, so lay brothers assumed most of the manual labor, leaving the monks to prayer and the copying of manuscripts. As with many medieval monastic movements, success spoiled the Cistercians. They became wealthy and relaxed the rigors of their religious observances, behaving more like other monastic groups, and when religious institutions came under attack in the post-medieval period, Cistercian abbeys were particularly targeted for their luxury. While their original ideals remained intact, however, they were a powerful religious and architectural presence, contributing much to the spread of learning, progressive agricultural practices, and sound building techniques across western Europe.

The Cistercians built well. Their standardized designs did much to spread sound building practices and the progressive Romanesque style preferred by Bernard across most of Europe. After Bernard's death, many Cistercian houses expanded and built more elaborate structures than those at Fontenay. Choirs in particular were enlarged, as in the plan of Cîteaux, where the original square-ended chapels were replaced with a radial layout, producing a design copied later at many daughter houses. Although minor regional variants are reflected in Cistercian work, monasteries as distant from one another as Fossanova in Italy, Sénanque in Provence, Poblet in Spain, Maulbronn in Germany, and Fountains in England all share the fundamentally straightforward and unadorned character of Cistercian architecture, the first international style of the medieval period.

NORMAN ARCHITECTURE

We have already noted how the Vikings in Norway became converts to Christianity and built stave churches there. Other Vikings became permanent residents outside of Scandinavia: in 911 a group led by Rollo was granted territory in western France in exchange for a cessation of its raids on settlements within the Frankish kingdom. The settlers became known as Normans, their land as Normandy, and their ruler as the duke of Normandy. Within the span of a century they developed into capable builders in stone, and, like Charlemagne, they encouraged the construction of monasteries.

In 1068 work began on the abbey church of St. Etienne at Caen, also known as the Abbaye-aux-Hommes (1068–1120), founded by William, Duke of Normandy, to expiate his consanguineous marriage (Fig. 8.60). Initially the church had a long nave with two western towers. Aisles flanked the wooden-roofed nave, and groin vaults supported the galleries above. Between 1115 and 1120 the wooden roof was removed, and the upper stage of the nave wall was rebuilt to incorporate ribs of sexpartite vaulting constructed across the nave (Fig. 8.61). These vaults, encompassing two bays of the nave for each unit, engage existing major and minor supports in the alternate grouped and single wall shafts so as to continue the line of the vaulting rib down to the floor.

Duke William is remembered in history for more than his endowment of St. Etienne. In 1066 he led an army of Normans across the Channel, defeated the assembled Anglo-Saxon forces at the battle of Hastings, and extended Norman rule to England. Henceforth he was known as William the Conqueror, and his military triumph was to have lasting consequences for English history and architecture. Compared with contemporary Norman work, Britain's Anglo-Saxon buildings were small and poorly built. William reorganized the English church and began a major campaign of building churches and castles. He

8.60 St. Etienne west front, Caen, 1068–1120.
Its façade is austere, with a straightforward ordering of doorways, windows, and wall buttresses. The more florid upper stages of the towers are later additions.

encouraged monasteries, and great cathedrals arose at Canterbury, Durham, Lincoln, Winchester, Gloucester, Norwich, Ely, and other sites.

At Durham, the cathedral of St. Cuthbert (Fig. 8.62) was constructed from 1093 to 1133 under the leadership of Norman bishops as a replacement for an earlier monastic church containing the relics of St. Cuthbert. It remains one of the best-preserved major Norman churches in England, interesting for its impressive massing and early use of rib vaulting throughout the church. Two west-front

8.61 St. Etienne interior, Caen, 1068–1120.

This view shows the sexpartite rib vaults constructed ca. 1120. These are among the earliest such vaults in Normandy, and their introduction there later contributed to the development of Gothic architecture.

8.62 Plan and section of the cathedral of St. Cuthbert, Durham, 1093–1133.

The original semicircular apse was rebuilt in the thirteenth century as a transept with nine altars to house St. Cuthbert's shrine. The builders reduced the height of the gallery over the aisle to leave room for a clerestory window tucked between the folds of the rib vaulting. Compare this section to that of St. Sernin, which uses a similar technique.

8.63 Durham Cathedral vaults, 1093–1133.

Rib vaults were used here in a different geometric configuration from that seen at Caen, still constructed over a semicircular arch profile. Notice how the ribs of the vaults spring from corbels above the triforium.

8.64 Durham Cathedral nave, 1093–1133.

The nave features compound piers alternating with magnificently bold cylindrical columns, each having an incised design.

towers and a square crossing tower announce the cathedral's presence on the hilltop above the river Wear. The original plan was an aisled basilica with transepts, with the choir terminating in a semicircular apse and the aisles concluded by chapels. (The apse was rebuilt to its present transept design in the Gothic period.) Evidence suggests that only the choir was initially planned for vaulting, but eventually vaulting was undertaken throughout the church. In the choir aisle vaults, built in about 1096, the ribs were built integrally with the vault cells. When rib vaults were begun over the nave, in about 1128–33, masons used the ribs as a framework from which to construct vault infill that was significantly thinner than corresponding work in the choir, indicating that they understood rib vaulting's constructional advantages (Fig. 8.63).

Durham's high vaults lack the visual continuity from rib to wall shaft that characterize the interior of St. Etienne at Caen. Although the nave and choir are composed of double bays comprised of compound piers alternating with distinctive cylindrical columns (Fig. 8.64), the vaults are septpartite, and their ribs spring from corbeled heads high on the gallery wall rather than connecting with wall shafts. Transverse arches define the double bays by connecting compound piers across the nave. The heavy quality of construction is increased by the relative absence of figural ornament. Striking geometric designs of chevrons, spirals, and diaper patterns are incised on the cylindrical columns, almost like the abstractions of Viking interlace work, while the arch moldings in the Galilee Chapel attached to the western end of the cathedral in about 1170–75 have zigzag patterning (Fig. 8.65).

What Norman builders explored at Caen and Durham led to structural changes that are associated with the Gothic style. By finding ways to exploit the constructional advantages of rib vaults and the structural efficiency of pointed arches, masons reduced the material (and thus the weight and cost) required to vault a building. The square bays and diagonal groin vaults from Roman times were transformed into rectangular bays having continuity of line from wall shaft to vaulting rib. Uninterrupted walls that were so important to structural stability in early Romanesque vaulted buildings were abandoned in favor of a skeletal system with loads concentrated at particular points, and a new esthetic of spaciousness and light came into being in the style we term Gothic.

8.65 Galilee Chapel, Durham Cathedral, 1093-1133.

This chapel is an example of very late Norman work. This served as Lady Chapel (dedicated to Mary), while also providing space for women, who were prohibited from approaching the tomb of Cuthbert and thus restricted to areas of the cathedral west of the entrance. The roof framing is timber, supported by parallel rows of semicircular arches edged with bar-chevron moldings.

CHAPTER 9

GOTHIC ARCHITECTURE

As we consider the Gothic, the final phase of medieval architecture, we are faced with defining the style. The term Gothic was first applied in the seventeenth century to denote designs not based on precedent from classical antiquity, and the label was applied with derision. By the nineteenth century, pejorative connotations had largely been overcome, but historians have struggled since to clarify what exactly constitutes the Gothic style. The most obvious definition involves key elements employed in many Gothic buildings—the pointed arch and the rib vault—although, as we have seen, these were also found in some Romanesque work. There are, however, elements original to Gothic buildings, including flying buttresses, windows with tracery, and piers composed of colonnettes or shafts bundled around a core, that serve as hallmarks of the style (Fig. 9.1).

Another common definition relies on the way these elements were brought together in the structure of large-scale churches and cathedrals, particularly those built in the region around Paris during the period from 1140 to 1220. Unlike Romanesque buildings, in which a continuous mass of wall is necessary to sustain the load, the Gothic structure is a skeletal system that transfers roof loads down to the ground at discrete points, thereby freeing large expanses of wall to be opened for windows. Secular buildings seldom have this wall section, however, so a purely structural concept is insufficient by itself to define the Gothic. One can define Gothic buildings by their spatial characteristics, which tend to emphasize the vertical, consist of articulated but unified cells of space, and have a sense of openness afforded by the construction system. Lastly the style can be seen as a reflection of the historical era and religious imagery of the period in which it was built, connected both to the growth of urban society and theological analogies to Old Testament tabernacles and temples and concepts of the New Jerusalem. We need to keep all these definitional perspectives in mind as we seek to understand Gothic architecture.

Let us look more closely at the key elements associated with Gothic structure—pointed arches, rib vaults, and flying buttresses. Pointed arches are better approximations of catenary curves that represent the line of compressive force acting in any arch, and thus they exert less outward or overturning thrust. They also present considerable design flexibility, as one can vary to some extent the angle of the arch. Steeper angles generate less thrust. By contrast, the dimensions of a semicircular arch are established by the width of the span. Pointed arches are probably a contribution from Islamic architecture, having been used in Syria and North Africa before their earliest application in northern Europe. They were used in a number of major Romanesque buildings, including the great church of Cluny III and St. Pierre Cathedral at Angoulême. Rib vaults can also be found in late Romanesque architecture, those constructed at St. Etienne at Caen and Durham Cathedral being generally thought to be among the earliest examples. Ribbing a groin vault had the virtue of visually "tidying up" the sometimes awkward arris created at the fold of the groin vault, but builders soon discovered that there were constructional advantages to be gained from laying up the ribs first, then using them as in-situ scaffold for erecting the thinner web sections of the vault. Builders also found they could lighten the webbing, thereby reducing the material weight of groin vaults. As the dead load on the vaulting was created primarily by the weight of the stone, reducing this weight not only economized on materials but also eventually facilitated greater building heights. The third element, the flying buttress, was probably first used at Sens Cathedral in about 1160, but it can be seen in embryonic form in the quadrant vaults over galleries of the pilgrimage road churches. Since Gothic construction concentrates loads at piers rather than

Notre-Dame Cathedral interior, Chartres, 1194–1230.

Chartres has an exceptionally wide nave because of the dimensions of the earlier Romanesque basilica.

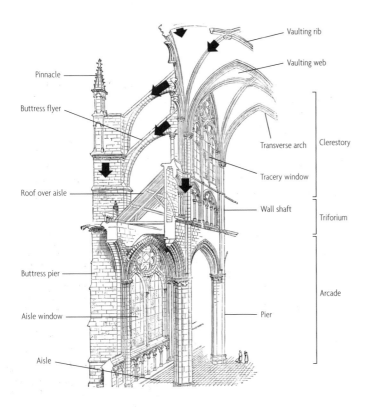

9.1 Section showing the Gothic structure of a major church.

Arrows indicate how dead loads from the vaults are transferred to the columns of the arcade and, through the lower flyer, to the buttress piers outside the building. The upper flyer helps to resist lateral or side loads caused by the wind blowing against the tall building.

distributing it continuously along the wall, the need for reinforcement at specific points is great. Gothic architects soon developed external buttressing, set at right angles to the wall and connected to it at strategic junctions by arches, which appear to "fly" or leap as they reach out to strengthen the upper sections of the skeleton frame. (Gothic can be built without flying buttresses, particularly in smaller structures where wall buttresses suffice to handle the structural loads. In Italy, builders developed alternate structural solutions to obviate the need for flying buttresses, as we shall see.)

Gothic architecture is more than a collection of structural techniques, however, for it embraces an integrated esthetic system. The flexibility of the pointed arch allowed irregular areas to be vaulted while maintaining a common ceiling height. Elements of the church plans that in Romanesque had been expressed as separate volumes (nave, aisle, chapel) could be combined into a unified, ordered composition, thanks to the geometric freedom offered by the combination of rib vaults and pointed arches. Gothic builders learned to integrate vaulting ribs with wall shafts, thus visually anchoring the floating overhead canopy to the ground. With the reinforcement provided by external buttresses, entire wall sections could be devoted to windows, particularly in the clerestory, where increased window height and width contributed to a diaphanous interior effect. Window tracery, the decorative

intersecting stonework in the upper sections of windows, was introduced and became increasingly slender, evolving from plate tracery (punched openings in a solid field) to bar tracery (thin lines of cut stone set in geometric patterns). As the Gothic style developed, one can sense the desire to reduce solid building mass and to enhance the quality of space and light, for both metaphysical and practical reasons, thus stimulating technical and artistic innovations.

EARLY GOTHIC

THE ABBEY CHURCH OF ST. DENIS

The Gothic style originated in northern France, in the region around Paris known as the Ile-de-France. This area had relatively little Romanesque building, so perhaps it was more open to developments from other places. It also was the home of one of the period's most energetic, informed, and innovative patrons of the arts, Abbot Suger, who rose from humble origins to become one of the most powerful church figures of his age. Suger's parents had donated him to the abbey of St. Denis when he was three years old, and he was raised in the monastery school to become a monk. Among his young companions in the school was the future King Louis VII of France. Suger's diplomatic and administrative skills were soon noticed, and he rose rapidly in the church hierarchy. In 1122, at the age of thirty-six, he was elected abbot of St. Denis.

Located about six miles north of Paris, St. Denis was the French royal monastery. It was the burial place of Denis, the first bishop of Paris, who was martyred by the Romans in the third century and later designated the patron saint of France. The kings of France were buried at the abbey, and the royal banner, the Oriflamme, was kept there between military campaigns. For all its prestige, the abbey was overcrowded and somewhat decayed when Suger became abbot. The existing building, consecrated in 775, was a Carolingian basilica that had received an enlarged eastern chapel in 832. Suger wanted to rebuild the church for the greater glory of God and France, but first he had to set the abbey's financial affairs in order and respond to criticism from Bernard of Clairvaux by reforming the religious practices of its monks. While he worked toward these goals, Suger developed images of what he wished the new church to be. He studied biblical descriptions of the Temple of Solomon, a design specified by God; he read writings attributed (incorrectly) to St. Denis, in which there was much discussion of the mystical and metaphysical properties of visual manifestations of spiritual images; and he inquired of travelers from Constantinople for descriptions of Hagia Sophia (see Fig. 6.17), widely regarded as the most splendid church building in Christendom, which Suger was determined to exceed.

By 1137 Suger was ready to build. To enlarge the church he constructed a new west front and narthex

9.2 St. Denis west front, 1137–40.

Generally recognized as the first Gothic building, this church façade has lost its northern tower.

by Suger: "a circular string of chapels, by virtue of which the whole church would shine with the wonderful and uninterrupted light of most sacred windows, pervading the interior beauty."

Planned next for construction was a nave to link the new narthex and choir, but Suger did not live to see the completion of his ambitious dream. Louis VII departed for the Second Crusade in 1147, leaving Suger in charge as

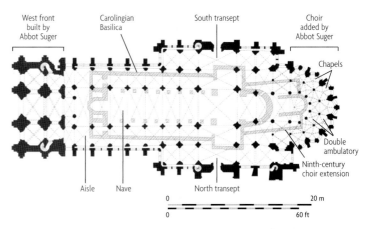

9.3a Plan of St. Denis, 1137–40.

This plan shows in hatched outline the basilica of 775 enlarged in 832. Suger built his new west front well forward of the existing building and had the choir positioned to incorporate foundations of the older building.

9.3b Plans of Notre-Dame, Laon, 1155–ca. 1205, and Notre-Dame, Paris, 1163–ca. 1250.

Notice that Laon has a pronounced cruciform plan, whereas Paris has transepts that scarcely project beyond the line of the buttress piers. The initial design for Paris had no radiating chapels off its double ambulatory, but chapels (shown here) were subsequently inserted between all the buttress piers.

forward of the existing structure, probably to the designs of a Norman architect capable of translating Suger's ideas into reality (Fig. 9.2). This work, consecrated in 1140, incorporated both the twin-towered west façade of Norman churches and the tradition of sculptured portals developed in the south of France. The three doorways had carved tympana and jamb statues, while the articulation of windows, including a circular or rose window, went beyond the linear façade compositions of Normandy. On the interior, rib vaults in the narthex sprang from grouped piers, thus exploiting the potential for continuity of line.

So enthusiastic was the reception of this new work that construction began almost at once on an enlargement of the east end (Fig. 9.3a). Less than four years later (1144) the new choir was dedicated in elaborate ceremonies involving distinguished churchmen and royalty. Suger's preoccupation with colored light is clearly manifested in the seven shallow radiating chapels of the choir, each with two large stained-glass windows (Fig 9.4). The irregular bays of this complex plan are consistently covered by rib vaults rising to a uniform crown height, while slender buttresses, set in the angles between the chapels, reinforce the upper wall. The ensemble creates an airy, luminous, rich interior that glows like jewels, precisely the effect desired

9.4 Abbey Church ambulatory and choir, St. Denis, 1140–44 and later.

The ambulatory (left) dates from Suger's abbacy, while the triforium and clerestory are a century later, constructed anew when the nave of the church was completed. The skeletal nature of Gothic construction facilitated the installation of large windows in the shallow chapels surrounding the apse, creating the wondrous luminosity desired by Suger.

regent of France, with neither time nor money for building. He died shortly after Louis returned from the Holy Land in 1151. The present nave at St. Denis was completed nearly a century later, when the upper stories of Suger's choir were rebuilt to match the height of the new nave vaults.

The wondrous quality of light and space created by the new choir at St. Denis was not lost on the church authorities and lay people who visited the abbey. Within two decades of its dedication, Gothic churches were under construction at several sites in the Ile-de-France, both for monasteries and increasingly for cathedral churches in the growing towns. The style seemed to flourish particularly within the orbit of the king of France's political influence. In regions such as the south of France, where royal control was weak and religious interest in the theology of divine manifestations was not strong, the mature Romanesque style continued to be used for at least a century after the Gothic had been developed.

EARLY GOTHIC CATHEDRALS

Gothic also coincided with an increase in the veneration of the Virgin Mary. As a mother who had suffered great sorrow, she had enormous popular appeal and became an important intercessor figure, standing before Christ the judge and pleading for leniency for erring humanity. Many of the great cathedrals were dedicated to her—she is "Notre Dame" in French, Our Lady in English—and sculpture and stained glass featured her far more often than was the case in Romanesque work. One index of this change is the way in which the Last Judgment was depicted on west-front portals. In Gothic work the scene is more life-like, appealing to the viewer's empathetic identification with theological verities rather than impressing with abstractly conceptual representations of the same spiritual issues.

Two early Gothic cathedrals in northern France are of particular interest. The cathedral of Notre-Dame at Laon was begun in about 1155 to replace an older structure that had become too small for the needs of the prosperous town and the growing cathedral school (Figs. 9.3b, 9.5–9.6). The choir and transepts were finished within twenty years, and the nave, west front, and crossing tower were completed by about 1205. To provide more space for the cathedral's canons, the original semicircular Gothic apse was replaced early in the thirteenth century by the present elongated choir with its rectangular east end. The flying buttresses may not be original to the church,

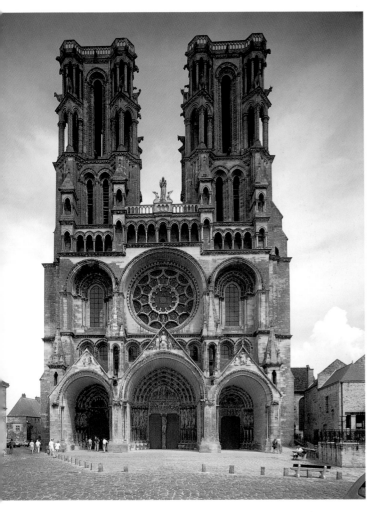

9.5 Notre-Dame Cathedral west front, Laon, 1155–ca. 1205.

This façade has a greater feeling of depth and openness than was seen at St. Denis. Deep hoods protect the entrance portals, and the upper stages of the twin towers change to octagonal plans.

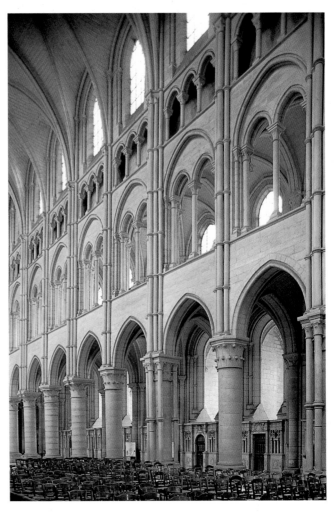

9.6 Notre-Dame Cathedral nave, Laon, 1155–ca. 1205.

The nave has a four-story elevation: aisle arcade, gallery, triforium (corresponding to the section where the roof over the aisle abuts the exterior wall), and clerestory. Bundled wall shafts correspond to ribs of the sexpartite vaults overhead.

because the galleries and their roofs over the aisles stabilize the vaults. Some scholars believe they were added in the thirteenth century to provide additional stability against lateral wind forces.

At Laon one can see how cautious architects and builders were in experimenting with new Gothic techniques. In its pre-1205 state, Laon retained elements from Romanesque works, including the long nave, sexpartite rib vaults, lantern crossing tower, galleries, semicircular apse, and western towers that could be found in Norman churches. The critical difference on the interior is the incorporation of the pointed arch into the profile of the sexpartite rib vaults. Ribs from the vaults and moldings around the clerestory windows continue as clustered wall shafts to the capitals of cylindrical piers in the nave arcade, thus emphasizing verticality. The three-dimensional, sculptural quality of the west front, built in 1190–1205, also departs from Romanesque precedent, for even Caen or the most ambitious of Cluniac churches were never conceived this boldly. Protective porch hoods over the three portals project from the plane of the façade, creating

a sense of depth that is repeated in the arched windows flanking the rose window in the story above. The western towers begin on square plans and are transformed into octagons in the upper stages. Oxen carved from stone peer down from the towers' heights, silent tributes to the patient animals that hauled the construction materials up to the ridge on which the cathedral sits. In the early thirteenth century, Villard de Honnecourt, whose sketchbook has survived to modern times, drew the towers of Laon and noted, "I have traveled in many lands, but in no place have I seen such a tower as the one at Laon." Even with its later modifications, Laon stands as the purest example of the Early Gothic.

In about 1150–55, the bishop of Paris began construction on the new cathedral of Notre-Dame to replace a sixth-century basilica, clearing a site on the Ile de la Cité and laying substantial foundations for the church (Fig. 9.3b). Work began on the choir, progressing to the nave by 1178–1200. The west front was completed between 1200 and 1250. During the course of construction, however, modifications were made to the fabric of the church, so

9.7 Notre-Dame Cathedral south side, Paris, 1163–ca. 1250.

Note the large transept rose window. Thanks to Victor Hugo's *The Hunchback of Notre-Dame* (1831), this building was restored after decades of neglect. It is important both as an early Gothic monument and as a nineteenth-century example of historic preservation.

a double ambulatory, it was the first Gothic building to exceed the height (but not the length) of Cluny III.

The west front, a splendid study in proportions, has a solid, almost military quality, in contrast to the more open character of Laon (Fig. 9.11). At Paris it is the strength of

that what one sees today is an altered version of the original twelfth-century design. Notre-Dame is a tall church, 110 feet from the floor to the crown of its vaults, and the direct light admitted into the nave by the original clerestories proved insufficient for the height of the space. To bring in more light, therefore, the clerestories all around the cathedral were enlarged in about 1225, flying buttresses were added to the choir to stabilize the great hemicycle, and the original nave buttresses were rebuilt (Fig. 9.7). The transepts with their enormous rose windows are another addition. The north transept was built from 1246 to 1257 to the designs of Jean de Chelles, and the south transept was constructed in 1258–61 by Jean de Chelles and Pierre de Montreuil. In the course of the late thirteenth century, chapels were inserted between all the buttresses around the choir and nave. Finally, in the nineteenth century, Viollet-le-Duc restored the cathedral, rebuilding all the flying buttresses, returning the bays at the crossing to their original design, and repairing the sculpture on the exterior (Fig. 9.8).

Despite all these modifications, the Early Gothic qualities of Notre-Dame in Paris are remarkably well preserved on the interior (Figs. 9.9–9.10). Although less pure than Laon, the cathedral remains an important monument of the period. Its original plan was innovative and ambitious on a large scale. A long church, completely surrounded by

9.8 Exterior and interior nave elevations of Notre-Dame Cathedral, Paris, 1150–55–ca. 1250.

This view shows the original form (right side of each drawing) which included a roundel opening in the triforium. When flying buttresses were added in about 1175–80, the clerestory was enlarged.

Exterior

Interior

9.9 Notre-Dame Cathedral nave and choir, Paris, 1163–ca. 1250.

Compare this photograph with the drawings in Fig. 9.8 to see the revised interior elevation built when the clerestory windows were enlarged. Later Gothic cathedrals featured much larger windows.

9.10 Notre-Dame Cathedral nave vaults, Paris, 1163–ca. 1250.

These are sexpartite vaults (six ribs converging in the center) constructed over two bays. Notice how there is continuity of line from the vaulting ribs to the wall shafts, giving the interior a vertical sweep.

the wall that commands attention. Triple portals, each slightly different in size and shape, are surmounted by the horizontal Gallery of Kings, representing twenty-eight kings of the Old Testament. A radiant rose window, flanked by paired lancet windows, forms a halo backdrop for a sculpture of the Virgin and Child with two angels. Below the twin towers is a second arcaded horizontal gallery that lightens the upper wall while completing the basically square configuration of the lower façade. This elevation rewards close study, for the more one looks, the more visually delightful detail one finds. From a distance the basically symmetrical disposition of features within the overall composition is obvious, while the slight irregularities in individual elements become noticeable (and endearing) upon examination. None of the three portals is the

9.11 Notre-Dame Cathedral west front, Paris, ca. 1250.

What seems at first glance to be an obvious symmetrical composition turns out on closer examination to be not entirely so. These small variations and details make this a highly individual building.

same size or shape, and the great towers are unequal in width. The sculptural programs of the three portals extend Christian teachings to those who could not read, just as Romanesque work did. On climbing the stairs to the upper levels, one gets an intimate view of the individually designed crockets projecting from the stones at the corners of the towers and of the fanciful sculpture (generally of the nineteenth century) perched high up on the parapets.

HIGH GOTHIC

The incorporation of flying buttresses at Notre-Dame in Paris integrated the three major structural components of Gothic, and redundant features from the Romanesque could be deleted from subsequent Gothic building. The period of tentative exploration was over, and the mature or High Gothic that followed saw the erection of churches with increasingly refined artistic and structural features.

9.12 Notre-Dame Cathedral west front, Chartres, 1194–1230.

The triple doorways, lancet windows, and tower bases were built ca. 1150 as a new façade for a predecessor church. The horizontal string course just below the rose window marks the seam between Romanesque and Gothic work. The north tower was finished in ca. 1515, creating asymmetrical design.

Labyrinth

Chartres Cathedral

Bourges Cathedral

N

0
0   150 ft

9.13a Plans of Chartres Cathedral, 1194–1230, and Bourges Cathedral, 1195–1250.

These buildings, begun within two years of one another, show different approaches to Gothic design. Chartres continues the tradition of pronounced transepts seen at Laon, while Bourges has a double ambulatory rather like Paris.

9.13b Projected plan of Beauvais Cathedral, ca. 1225–1573.

Built in discontinuous campaigns, the choir, transepts, and one bay of the nave (shown here in black) were all that was completed. After the nave vaults collapsed in 1284, pairs of additional piers were inserted in each of the three choir bays to create sexpartite vaults.

9.14 Notre-Dame Cathedral nave vaults, Chartres, 1194–1230.

Note the use of quadripartite vaults. Chartres preserves large amounts of medieval stained glass, as well as having some modern glass, giving its interior a special richness that is impossible to capture in photographs.

CHARTRES AND BOURGES

The first monument of the High Gothic was the cathedral of Notre-Dame at Chartres, where flying buttresses were planned from the start so that the galleries were unnecessary (Figs. 9.12, 9.13a, page 228 and 9.14). This simplified the interior elevations to three divisions: the nave arcade, the triforium passage, and the clerestory windows. In the process, the clerestory windows increased markedly in size, and vaulting shifted from sexpartite (over two bays) to quadripartite (over one bay).

Chartres Cathedral has an even more complicated chronology than the cathedral of Paris. The site had long been sacred to the Virgin Mary, and the cathedral treasure contained, among other valuable relics, a tunic believed to have been worn by Mary. Chartres became a center of pilgrimage, and from 1020 to 1037 a Romanesque basilica with three deep radiating chapels was constructed to replace an earlier church destroyed by fire. By the twelfth century, this church had itself been enlarged, and a fire in 1134 had damaged the westwerk. Work began that same year to build a new west front and narthex in much the same manner that Abbot Suger was to extend St. Denis. Sculptors from the workshops at St. Denis came to Chartres in

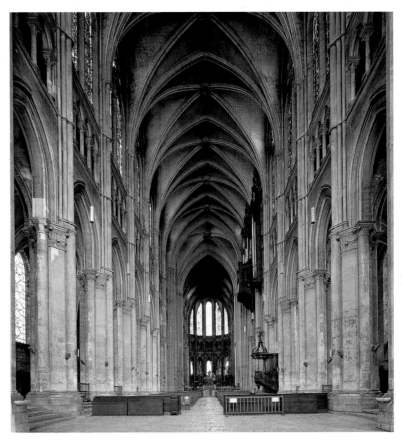

1145–50 to carve the three portals of the new west façade, and the three lancet windows overhead were filled with stained glass depicting themes pioneered at Suger's church: the infancy of Christ, the Passion story, and the Tree of Jesse or the genealogy of Christ.

On the night of June 10, 1194, fire again struck the cathedral and town, destroying the wooden-roofed basilica and eighty per cent of the city. Even though the new west front survived without major damage, the people of Chartres interpreted the fire as a sign of divine displeasure. Sensing the general feeling of hopelessness, the visiting bishop of Pisa called a town meeting, during which the sacred tunic was carried out, unharmed, from the ruins of the crypt. The mood quickly changed from sorrow to jubilation as the townspeople decided that the fire was a sign that Mary desired a larger church. Building funds were raised with remarkable speed and construction commenced. The Gothic cathedral at Chartres was built in the span of twenty-six years, from 1194 to 1220, and the sculpted north and south transept porches were finished between 1224 and 1250. However, the north tower on the west front was completed only in 1513, giving the west front at last a balanced asymmetry of form and style.

In rebuilding the cathedral, the master masons reused the foundations and crypt and incorporated the surviving west front. On the exterior one can still see the seam where the new work was joined to the old, a horizontal string course immediately below the western rose (which itself is slightly off center). The Romanesque apse was transformed into a Gothic choir by the insertion of four shallow chapels between the three existing deep chapels of the crypt, thus creating seven shallow chapels with a double ambulatory on the main level. The builders also added a transept to the original Romanesque basilica plan and, after construction was under way, decided to include three sculpted portals on each transept arm, giving Chartres a total of nine entrances.

The completed cathedral glows inside with a wonderful luminosity, in part because the clerestory window height has increased to equal the height of the arcade, while clerestory width has expanded to consume virtually all of the wall area between the wall shafts. Compare the interior nave elevations of Laon and Chartres (Fig. 9.15) to appreciate how substantially the proportions of window to wall have changed in the shift from Early to High Gothic work. Note also the development at Chartres of plate tracery in the rose windows above the paired lancets of the clerestory. At Chartres, visible structural elements, including the vaulting ribs and wall shafts in particular, are slender and deeply undercut so that they appear to float free of the surfaces to which they are connected. Alternate nave piers have cylindrical and octagonal cores, with wall shafts that are either faceted or cylindrical, respectively. Even the buttresses, particularly the flyers around the choir, have a sense of lightness. Of all Gothic cathedrals, Chartres alone has preserved about two-thirds of its original stained glass. Bold figures of the holy family and the saints dominate the high clerestory windows, while more intricately detailed illustrations of biblical stories and saints' legends predominate in the windows of the aisles and ambulatory. Old Testament subjects are shown in the glass of the north transept, balanced by New Testament themes in the south-transept rose and lancet windows. On the west front, the twelfth-century lancets relating the genealogy and life of Christ were retained from the pre-Gothic church. Suger's ideal of pervasive interior beauty is nowhere more evident than at Chartres.

The west-front doorways, known as the Royal Portals because of the crowned figures in the jamb statues, provide a splendid image of the theology of salvation as it

Laon Cathedral

0   20 m

0   60 ft

Clerestory

Triforium

Gallery

Aisle

Clerestory

Triforium

Arcade

Chartres Cathedral

Flyer

Buttress

Aisles

Crypt

9.15 Elevations and sections of Laon Cathedral nave and Chartres Cathedral nave.

These have been drawn to the same scale. Notice the changes from Early to High Gothic, as well as the greatly increased width and height of the arcade and clerestory at Chartres. Neither drawing includes the wooden roof trusses.

9.16 Jamb figures from the Royal Portals of Chartres Cathedral west front, ca. 1150.

These elongated crowned figures have timeless staring faces and stylized drapery suggesting Byzantine influence. They are probably the work of sculptors from St. Denis, who came to work at Chartres when Suger's west front was completed.

used in the nave and choir. A glance at the interior, however, indicates immediately that Bourges is no copy of Paris, but an original adaptation of High Gothic vocabulary. The paired aisles increase in height to help brace the high vaults of the nave and choir, recalling the triangular cross-section of Cluny III, with the addition here of flying buttresses that follow the slope of the roofs. At Bourges, choir and nave vaults spring from alternating major and minor piers set on a square module plan. The spatial effect is one of breadth and expansiveness, but the layered aisle vaults and roofs preclude clerestory windows as tall as those of Chartres, although here too they fill virtually the entire wall area between wall shafts. On the west front, the

9.17 Jamb figures at Chartres Cathedral south porch, ca. 1250.

The transept sculpture demonstrates the increasing naturalism of later Gothic work. These apostles inhabit bodies that are closer to actual human proportions, and their poses are more animated.

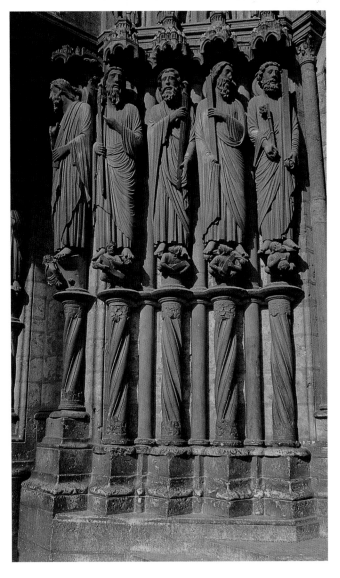

was visualized in 1150 (Fig. 9.16). The influence of Suger's façade at St. Denis can be seen in the stately, elongated jamb figures, while the tympana subjects reflect the teachings of the School of Chartres, a prominent medieval center of learning associated with the cathedral. The portals carved a century later on the north and south transepts provide a measure of increased naturalism that occurred in Gothic sculpture (Fig. 9.17). Some of the subjects shown are repeated from the Royal Portals, but their treatment is far more life-like.

The cathedral of St. Etienne at Bourges (1195–1250) presents a conceptual contrast to Chartres (Figs. 9.13a, 9.18–9.20). Its plan shares features with Notre-Dame in Paris. Double aisles flank the nave and continue in uninterrupted arcs around the choir and sexpartite vaults are

9.18 St. Etienne Cathedral from the east, Bourges, 1195–1250.

This view shows the buttresses that provide bracing for the high vaults.

five major interior volumes are reflected in five portals, completed in about 1285.

Robert Mark, an engineer who has researched the structural behavior of historic buildings, documented the structural logic of Bourges, which achieves a comparable interior height and area to Chartres, yet requires significantly less stone. Despite its cost-effectiveness (for stone was a major expense in building construction), the double-aisle design of Bourges was seldom used thereafter, while the more costly and inherently less stable model of Chartres was adopted for the tallest cathedrals—Reims, Amiens, and Beauvais—of the Gothic era. One suspects that building patrons, in northern France at least, preferred the dramatic luminosity afforded by the tall clerestory windows of the single-aisle design more than structural efficiency, since Gothic was not primarily an expression of technique but an architectural embodiment

9.19 Section through Bourges Cathedral, 1195–1250.

This view shows how the inner and outer aisles function with the buttresses to brace the high vaults of nave and choir.

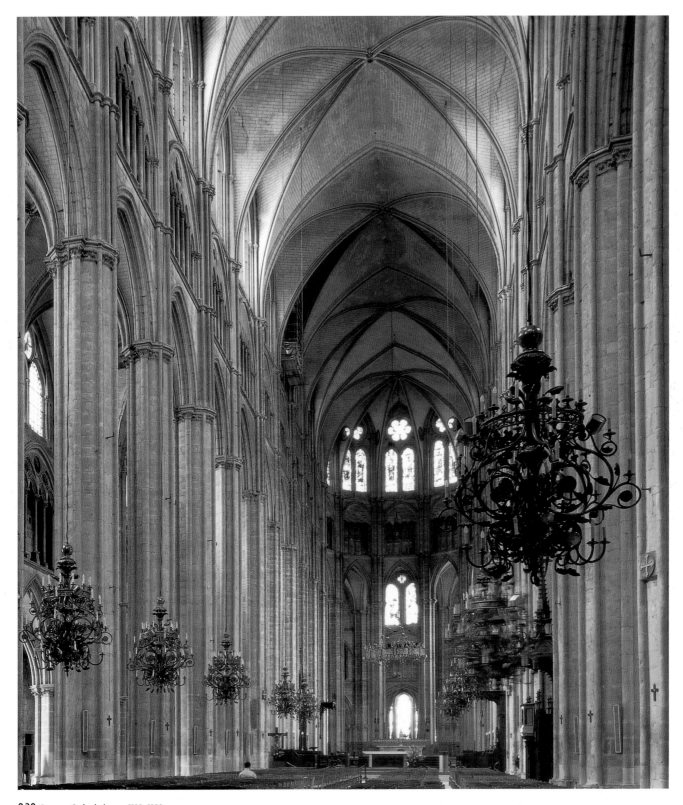

9.20 Bourges Cathedral nave, 1195–1250.

Because of its distinctive cross-section (see Fig. 9.19) Bourges Cathedral has relatively small clerestory windows in the nave and exceptionally tall nave piers. Note also the use of sexpartite vaulting.

of religious and cultural ideals. Cathedrals built on the model of Bourges are found in Spain and Italy, where bright skies prevail. The Cathedral of Milan, a late Gothic building, uses a cross-section similar to Bourges Cathedral to attain a nave vault height equivalent to that of Beauvais.

BEAUVAIS AND STE. CHAPELLE

Builders of the great French cathedrals of the early thirteenth century seemed intent on pushing Gothic technology to achieve soaring interior heights. The nave vaults at Chartres rise 113 feet over a fifty-three-foot-wide nave; at Reims (begun 1211), the vaults are 122 feet high over a forty-five-foot-wide nave; at Amiens (begun 1220), the vaulting is 139 feet high for the same nave width; and at

9.21 (right) Beauvais Cathedral choir, ca. 1225–1573.
This view shows the extreme verticality of the interior space. The glazed triforium contributes to the sensation of a vast airy cage of stone.

9.22 (below) Beauvais Cathedral east end, ca. 1225–1573.
Visible here are the buttress piers between the elongated clerestory windows, glazed triforium, and chapel windows.

9.23 Beauvais Cathedral choir vaults, ca. 1225–1573.

Although originally these were quadripartite, the choir vaults are now sexpartite because additional piers were inserted for strength after the original vaults collapsed in 1284.

Beauvais (begun 1225), the most daring venture of all, the choir vaults rose 158 feet over a choir that is forty-five feet wide before collapsing and being rebuilt in a strengthened form. The cathedral of St. Pierre at Beauvais was never completed, and only the choir and transept stand today to indicate the scale of the intended Gothic building (Figs. 9.13b, 9.21–9.23).

Although structural failure was only part of the problem at Beauvais, it is a recurring element in the history of the cathedral's construction. The design called for a string of seven radiating chapels off the ambulatory, with paired aisles in the choir that continued beyond the aisled transepts as double aisles in the nave. Work on the choir began in 1225, with choir vaulting being completed in about 1260. These vaults collapsed in 1284, probably because wind forces exceeded load capacities on slender intermediate buttress piers, causing them to rotate and fall. The vaults were reconstructed between 1284 and 1322 with six additional piers in the arcade, resulting in sexpartite vaults in the choir bays rather than the original quadripartite design, and thicker piers in the bay next to the crossing. Construction of the transepts was started in about 1500 and completed by 1550. A crossing tower of masonry topped by a wooden spire 497 feet high was added in 1563–69, but, lacking support from bays in the nave which had not been built, the tower proved dangerously unstable and was removed in 1573 after partially collapsing. Damaged transept vaults were rebuilt in 1577–80, and a single bay of the nave was constructed but never vaulted in stone. Early in the seventeenth century, the incomplete west end was shuttered off as the cathedral chapter conceded that the building would never be finished.

Despite this checkered building history, the interior of the cathedral is stunning. The extreme verticality of the arcade is matched by an attenuated glazed triforium, above which rises the fragile cage of the clerestory, where solid wall dissolves into glass, creating the impression that the vault overhead rests on air alone. In the windows, plate tracery used at Chartres has been replaced by bar tracery, thin stone sections carved into geometrical shapes based on circles. Tracery on the enormous transept roses moves into even more elaborate, flame-like shapes. Seen from the east, the exterior is overwhelmingly vertical. At the western end are fragments of Notre-Dame de la Basse-Oeuvre, a small basilica from the tenth century which occupies the site where the nave would have been constructed. Its modest size, juxtaposed against the tallest cathedral in Europe, illustrates how far medieval builders had advanced the arts of masonry construction since the Carolingian era. Beauvais Cathedral continues to be watched closely for structural instability. Its buttress piers have long been linked by iron tie-rods, or beams, and more recently substantial wooden braces have been inserted and electronic sensors installed to monitor structural stresses.

9.25 Sainte-Chapelle, Paris, 1243–48.

Built as a palace chapel by King Louis IX to house relics he had acquired from Constantinople, this small jewel of High Gothic design is a virtual glass-walled structure, with the stone reduced to minimal proportions. The relatively small scale and internal metal tie-rods make flying buttresses unnecessary.

9.26 Section through Sainte-Chapelle, Paris, 1243–48.

This shows the lower chapel (for household servants) and the spacious upper chapel, for use by the royal family.

Construction woes at Beauvais stemmed both from the audacious plan and inadequate funding. By the time the building was under way, popular enthusiasm for large-scale church projects was waning. Enormous sums had been funneled into building cathedrals and monasteries, and the Church no longer commanded sufficient resources (estimated to be about a quarter of the total wealth of all Europe at the time) to sustain extensive building campaigns. Although churches continued to be built or remodeled, the pace of construction seen during the eleventh through thirteenth centuries would never again be matched.

Even as the great French cathedrals were being built, there were also smaller Gothic projects under way. One particularly lovely example is the Sainte-Chapelle

9.24 (opposite) Upper chapel interior, Sainte-Chapelle, Paris, 1243–48.

In great expanses of stained glass, most of it original, these windows illustrate stories from both the Old and New Testaments in sequence from the entrance door.

(1243–48), added by Louis IX to the royal palace in Paris to house relics he had acquired from Constantinople, including the Crown of Thorns and a piece of the True Cross (Figs. 9.24–9.26). The relics cost twice as much as the building. The Sainte-Chapelle has two levels, a ground-floor chapel for use by the household servants and an upper chapel, surrounded by stained-glass windows with bar tracery, for use by the royal family. This upper chapel is a jeweled space in which the walls have been diminished to slender piers set between the great expanses of largely original glass. Wall buttresses are linked together horizontally by iron tie-rods that encircle the building concealed in the masonry, passing across the windows as part of the framework supporting the glass. As a miniature statement of the dematerialization of masonry walls and the wondrous properties of colored light sought by Abbot Suger, the Sainte-Chapelle has no equal.

ENGLISH GOTHIC

Although the Gothic style originated in France, it spread to other parts of Europe, particularly England, Germany, and Italy, and became the predominant style of northern Europe until the fifteenth century. English builders soon formed their own Gothic esthetic, and within a century had created Gothic churches that differed considerably from those built in France.

Nineteenth-century historians who first studied the Gothic buildings of England categorized the work in three overlapping phases, which are still useful for describing the progressive development of English medieval architecture (Fig. 9.27). Early English, built from 1175 to 1265, corresponds roughly to High Gothic work in France. Vaulting is straightforward, usually quadripartite, and windows are lancet-shaped. The Decorated period, built from about

A WOOL CHURCH

by Marian Moffett

Across Europe are legions of parish churches that originated in the medieval period—England alone has about 8000 surviving examples that collectively constitute a national treasure. More than the great abbeys and cathedrals that attract the attention of scholars (and tourists), these modest churches give us an indication of how medieval architecture was experienced by ordinary people of the time.

Parish churches were built in an era when all Christians in a given community worshiped in the same church and regular attendance (not to mention compulsory financial support in the form of tithes) was the norm. When the local economy was strong, well-to-do individuals tended to invest in building churches as a means both of ensuring divine favor and displaying their wealth, which in the late medieval period in England came largely from trade in wool and woollen cloth. St. Agnes's at Cawston in Norfolk (Fig. 9A) is known as a "wool church" because its fifteenth-century nave and western tower were largely financed by Michael de la Pole, Earl of Suffolk, whose fortune derived from the wool trade. (The fourteenth-century chancel from an earlier church was retained.) St. Agnes's size is clearly in excess of what was required by Cawston's medieval population, so we must understand the building as a demonstration of the earl's piety and pride. His family crest is carved above the entrance. Stone imported from France was used for the tower and nave arcade, rather than the cheaper local knapped flint. As is common in English parish churches, the nave and aisles were covered by timber roofs rather than vaulting. Even here, however, the earl's munificence is evident: Cawston's nave has a spectacular hammerbeam roof, adorned with standing angels at the ends of the beams, with three more angels hovering on outstretched wings above each clerestory window.

Not all the medieval work on the interior survives. When Henry VIII broke with the Church in Rome, he set in motion more than a century of religious unrest, during which English churches were stripped of images—altars, sculpture, paintings, and stained glass—that were regarded as being "popish." Traces of a mural over the chancel arch remind us that these walls were originally painted, and remnants of stained glass now set in the south-aisle windows hint at what colored splendor once filled the windows. The wooden screen separating nave and chancel originally supported a gallery on which stood the rood, sculptures of the crucified Christ flanked by Mary and St. John. Its lowest tier still retains sixteen panels painted with figures of the saints, including St. Simon, who most anachronistically is wearing eyeglasses. It's a naïve yet touching detail, like the dragons and wild men carved in unexpected places, reminding us of the fundamental humanity of the artists who created these churches.

9A Interior of the church of St. Agnes at Cawston, Norfolk, 14th–15th century.

Early English   Decorated   Perpendicular

9.27 Examples of English Gothic window tracery.

As many English churches were built over extended periods, variations in window tracery provide one clue to the construction sequence.

1250 until about 1370, uses vaulting elaborated with extra ribs, called **tiercerons** and **liernes**, and window tracery worked into trefoil or quatrefoil cusped shapes, intersecting lines, or flowing curvilinear shapes. The final phase, the Perpendicular, is the most distinctly English. Constructed from about 1330 until 1540, it is distinguished by panel tracery and vaulting in elaborate conical fan shapes. Despite their visual magnificence, **fan vaults** represent no structural advance; in fact, they are best suited to smaller churches where great heights and spans are not required. It is not possible to examine English cathedrals in strict chronological order. Portions of all four medieval periods are represented in the fabric of many English cathedrals. Discussions here will present the buildings as a whole, rather than by chronological periods.

EARLY ENGLISH

Canterbury Cathedral was rebuilt in a Gothic style after the Norman church, begun in 1070, was devastated by fire in 1174 (Figs. 9.29a–9.30). Leading master masons of England and France were summoned to give their advice about rebuilding the ruined site, and William of Sens was selected to direct the work. He convinced the monks to demolish the remaining sections of the choir because the fire's heat had damaged the stone beyond repair, but he confidently retained the fine Norman crypt and aisle walls. Between 1175 and 1184 the choir was rebuilt to a Gothic design based on the cathedral of Sens (Fig. 9.28). During this time, William was severely injured in a fall from the scaffolding, and he returned to France in 1179, leaving his assistant, William the Englishman, to complete the work.

The choir at Canterbury was designed to house England's most popular shrine, that of St. Thomas à Becket, Archbishop of Canterbury and advisor to King Henry II, who in 1170 was murdered in the cathedral by four of Henry's knights. Pilgrims from all over Europe soon flocked to Canterbury to partake of the miracles performed at the tomb of St. Thomas, and the monks, enriched by pilgrims' offerings, needed suitable accommodation both for the steady stream of visitors and their own services. (Recall that the destination of Chaucer's pilgrims was Canterbury.) As was the case in earlier pilgrimage churches, a satisfactory arrangement involved an aisle and ambulatory, which linked the site of Thomas's martyrdom with his shrine in the Trinity Chapel.

Canterbury's somewhat rambling plan can be explained by the reuse of the Norman crypt and the pilgrim traffic to Becket's shrine. The Norman basilica had transepts with two chapels on each east wall and two apsidal chapels set at angles to the main axis rather than radiating from it. Beyond these, William the Englishman built the Trinity Chapel and its single axial chapel, the Corona, which terminates the church on the east. A second, smaller transept was constructed to the west of the choir; and the wider, majestic nave was built early in the

9.28 Sens Cathedral choir, ca. 1135–1180.

Sens was an Early Gothic cathedral that served as the model for Canterbury Cathedral. Compare this image to the choir of Canterbury.

Corona Chapel

Trinity Chapel

St. Anselm's Chapel

St. Andrew's Chapel

Eastern transept

Choir

Crossing tower

Western transept

Nave

Norman church

Gothic church

N

0 ——————— 50 m
0 ——————— 150 ft

9.29a (left) Plans of Canterbury Cathedral, 1175–84.

These plans show the Norman church (*left*) and its Gothic replacement (*right*), which used much of the foundations from the earlier church. Canterbury incorporates the shrine of St. Thomas à Becket, who was murdered here in 1170.

9.29b Plans of Salisbury Cathedral, 1220–58; King's College Chapel, Cambridge, 1446–1515; and Lincoln Cathedral, 1192–1280.

Both Salisbury and Lincoln have plans that reflect Cistercian rectangular chapels and double transepts inspired by Cluny III. The rectangular plan of King's College Chapel was designed for preaching.

Salisbury Cathedral

King's College Chapel, Cambridge

Chapter house

Cloister

West Front

Nave

Greater transept

Angel Choir

Lady Chapel

Lesser transept

Choir

0 ——————— 50 m
0 ——————— 150 ft

Lincoln Cathedral

9.30 Canterbury Cathedral choir, 1175–84.

The choir was built to the designs of William of Sens and William the Englishman. Although many features superficially resemble Sens Cathedral, there are characteristic English elements here, most notably the darker Purbeck marble trim that is used to emphasize horizontal lines.

Perpendicular period, 1377–1405, possibly to the designs of Thomas of Hoo. The crowning element in the cathedral is the 235-foot-high crossing tower named Bell Harry after the bell hung there, which was erected in the mature Perpendicular period (1491–98) to the designs of John Wastell. The fan vaults of the tower are forerunners of those Wastell would erect later at King's College Chapel in Cambridge.

Salisbury Cathedral presents the rare example of an English Gothic cathedral built almost entirely in a homogeneous style, Early English (Figs. 9.29b, 9.31–9.32). It was begun in 1220 on an entirely new site, the cathedral and town having been relocated from Old Sarum to be near more reliable water sources. Construction of the majority of the church progressed with remarkable rapidity and was completed by 1258, leaving only the soaring crossing tower and spire to be built from 1334 to 1380. Salisbury incorporates features from monastic plans, including the double transepts of Cluny III and the square east end of the Cistercians, in a long angular building that is unmistakably English. On the interior, quadripartite vaults rise from three-story nave elevations, yet the continuous vertical line exploited by the French has been replaced by a horizontal emphasis created by a string course under the triforium and another under the clerestory windows. Even the ribs of the vaults do not extend down the wall but spring instead from wall corbels at the base of the clerestory. Surfaces are articulated by shafts and trim in black Purbeck marble, an English stone

9.31 Salisbury Cathedral, 1220–58; tower 1334–80.

A cathedral built almost entirely in Early English Gothic. Note the lancet windows of the west front and clerestory and the horizontal lines that carry across the exterior.

9.32 Salisbury Cathedral nave, 1220–58.
This view shows how horizontality prevails on the interior as well as exterior. Notice how vaulting ribs do not extend as wall ribs down grouped piers, but spring instead from corbels set between the clerestory windows. Horizontal string courses along the triforium direct the eye down the length of the nave.

that is not actually marble but takes a highly polished finish. The exterior receives the same horizontal emphasis as the interior. Flying buttresses do not have a strong vertical character, and the walls are coursed in horizontal bands that extend across the west front. With all this horizontality, the 404-foot tower and spire provide the necessary vertical counterpoint, and their great weight has noticeably deflected the piers at the crossing. The cloisters (completed 1284) are fine examples of early Decorated tracery, and off the east range one finds a lovely octagonal chapter house (begun 1263). Salisbury, like many English cathedrals, was both an abbey and a cathedral. Accommodation was accordingly needed for the brothers to meet daily to hear a chapter from the Rule of St. Benedict read

and elaborated; hence the polygonal chapter house. In Romanesque monasteries, this was generally a square or rectangular room off the cloister, but in English cathedrals it becomes an occasion for elegance in vaulting an octagonal space of considerable size.

DECORATED AND PERPENDICULAR

At Lincoln Cathedral, a more complicated building history has resulted in a splendid combination of English Gothic periods (Figs. 9.29b, 9.33–9.34). The Norman church, damaged by an earthquake in 1185, survives today only in the lower portions of the west front. Rebuilding work, started in 1192, continued harmoniously through 1280.

9.33 (above) Lincoln Cathedral choir vaults, 1192–1280.

Lincoln provides a wonderful sampler of vaulting. The transepts are sexpartite, while the nave features tierceron and lierne vaults of the Decorated period. Most unusual of all are the choir vaults, known as the "crazy" vaults because their centers do not align.

9.34 Lincoln Cathedral, Angel Choir, 1192–1280.

The Angel Choir is the easternmost extension of the church, concluded with an enormous wall of stained glass.

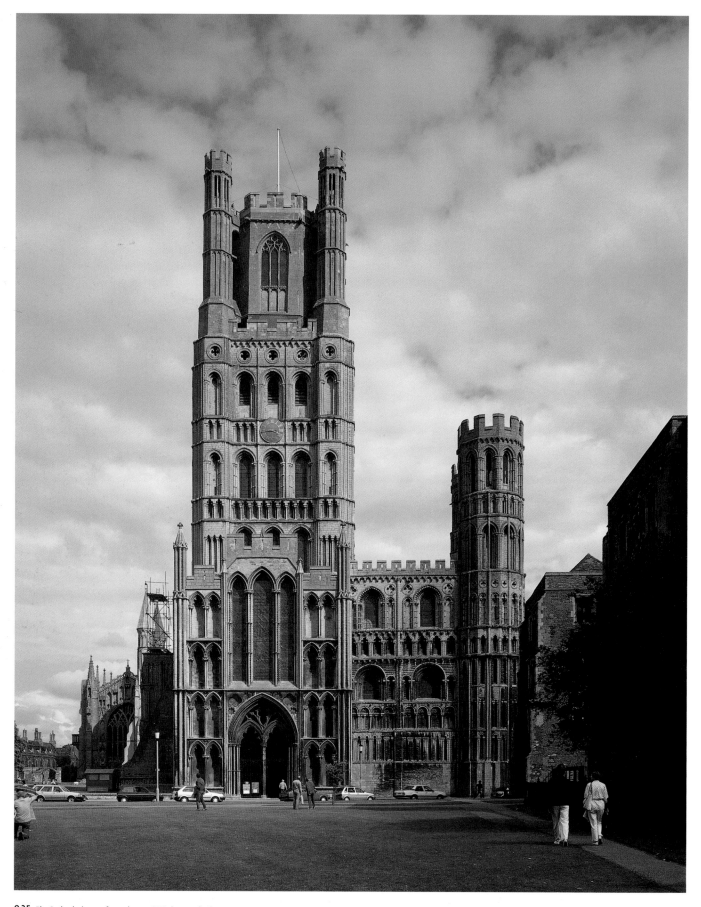

9.35 Ely Cathedral west front, begun 1081; lantern built 1322–36.

Most of the façade dates from the Norman period. The west front was originally symmetrical: a tower to balance the one on the right side no longer exists.

Construction began with the choir and eastern transept, followed by the main western (major) transept, chapter house, nave, and west-front upper portions. The **retrochoir** (meaning "behind the choir" and here known as the Angel Choir) was begun in 1256. Concluded by an enormous eastern window, it was finished in 1280.

Lincoln offers several novel architectural features. Most obvious on the interior are the varied vaulting systems, including the tierceron vaults of the nave which link with an ornamented ridge rib. The "crazy" vaults of the choir are an asymmetrical experiment showing an original and free interpretation of established Gothic conventions. Throughout the cathedral, but above all in the Angel Choir, there is a wealth of elaborate trim in the form of Purbeck marble shafts, stiff-leaf capitals, and the sculpted angels that give the retrochoir its name. The Angel Choir clerestories and east-end window have tracery of the Decorated period. On the west front, a broad screen wall extends from the Norman work to increase the apparent width of the façade, obscuring the bases of the west-front towers, which define the actual width of the church. Finally, the ten-sided chapter house with its bold flying buttresses is a departure from the usual octagonal form.

Ely Cathedral illustrates another aspect of medieval architecture in England, large-scale construction in timber (Figs. 9.35–9.36). Norman work predominates in the nave, which is covered by a timber roof; on the west front, a late Norman project designed with transepts but never finished; and in the transepts east of the nave. The original Norman choir was enlarged (1230–50) by an eastern extension of six additional bays, based on the Early English nave of Lincoln. The collapse of Ely's Norman crossing tower in 1322 provoked the most extraordinary construction. The church foundations were judged insufficient to support a masonry reconstruction, so the tower was replaced by a lantern in wood, the design of which also increased the light and usable space at the crossing. The designer of this masterpiece of medieval engineering was William Hurley, the King's Carpenter. He used eight giant oak posts—sixty-three feet long, forty inches thick, and thirty-two inches wide—for the vertical members of the octagonal tower, which has a diameter of 69 feet. These are supported on hammerbeams tied to the masonry crossing piers. The octagon itself is set at 22.5 degrees to the axis of the nave, providing a spatial contrast at the crossing. Viewed from below, most of the vaulting of the octagon is wood made to look like stone; the actual structural members are visible only if one climbs into the lantern via the access stair.

Ely's exceptional crossing tower is not the only example of English monumental timber construction. A number of late medieval hammerbeam roofs survive, the grandest being Westminster Hall in London (now incorporated into the Houses of Parliament, a nineteenth-century building). The hall itself dates back to the early 1100s, when it was constructed as an aisled hall for royal

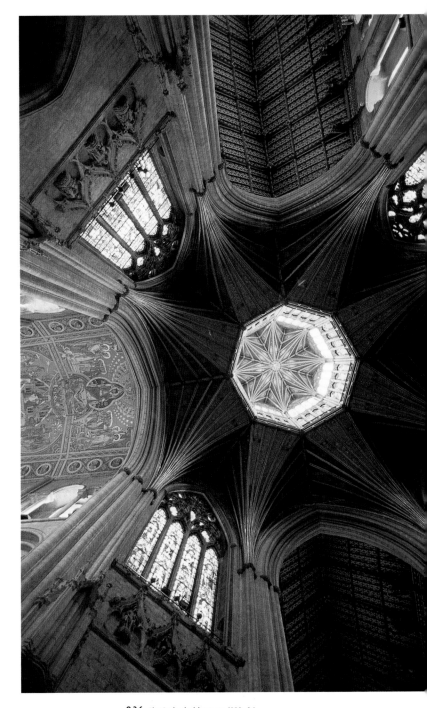

9.36 Ely Cathedral lantern, 1322–36

Notice how the octagon is turned 22.5 degrees to the axis of the nave. Wooden ceilings are treated on the interior as if they were stone vaults. The painted wooden ceiling of the Norman nave extends to the left side.

banquets. By the late Middle Ages, a roof not requiring intermediate supports was desired, so in 1394–1402 the hall was recovered, using hammerbeams that are supported on the older walls (Fig. 9.37). Hammerbeam construction is actually a series of successive short cantilevers that enable builders to roof a span wider than the length of available timbers. The craftsmanship behind the hammerbeam roofs, with their interlocking pegged joints and elegantly carved finials and angels, is a testimonial to the technical skills and artistry of medieval carpenters.

9.37 Hammerbeam truss, Westminster Hall, London, 1394–1402.

This great timber work rests on Norman walls. Notice how the wooden members come to rest on the masonry wall, braced by the arch of the lowest hammerbeam.

9.38 King's College Chapel interior, Cambridge, 1446–1515.

The fan vaults make this glass box a masterpiece of late medieval architecture. As in the Sainte-Chapelle, the walls have been reduced to glass screens set in a stone frame.

As an example of Late Gothic masonry construction in England, the chapel at King's College, Cambridge, deserves attention for its exceptional fan vaults designed by John Wastell (Figs. 9.29b, 9.38). Begun in 1446 with donations by Henry VI and completed by 1515 with contributions from Henry VIII, the chapel was designed for use in an era when the sermon had become an important aspect of worship services, so it was built with a simpler plan and smaller area to reduce reverberation so that speech could be better understood. Medieval monastic chant is enhanced by long reverberation times, but the spoken word is virtually incomprehensible in the same space. Medieval churches still in use for church services employ electronic amplification systems that help cancel out reverberation. King's College Chapel is basically rectangular in plan, with Perpendicular tracery in the large windows and majestic fan vaults overhead. The ornate organ loft atop the choir screen divides the space into two parts, one for townspeople and the other for students. The chapel is contemporary with the High Renaissance in Italy, and the woodwork of the choir screen contains classical detail in what is otherwise a late medieval building.

9.39 St. George Church nave and aisle, Nördlingen, 1427–ca. 1500.

This is a hall church, where the nave and aisle vaults are virtually the same height. Grey stone ribs form intricate geometric patterns on the plastered surface of the vaults.

GERMAN AND ITALIAN GOTHIC
GERMAN HALL CHURCHES

Just as the Romanesque developed regional variants as it responded to local traditions and preferences, so too did the Gothic. German builders initially used French cathedrals as models, occasionally importing master masons, but they were soon creating their own versions of the Gothic style. Particularly characteristic of German Gothic is the hall church, a building where the vaults of both the nave and aisles are essentially the same height. (Recall that St. Savin-sur-Gartempe is a Romanesque hall church.) This is the design used at St. George in Nördlingen (1427–ca. 1500), a church without transepts but which has aisles on either side of the six bays of the nave that continue up the five bays of the choir to a chapel at the eastern polygon (Figs. 9.39–9.40). A massive tower on axis anchors the western front. On the interior, the structure is clearly expressed: gray stone cylindrical columns with attached shaft moldings support a vaulted ceiling where ribs describe intricate patterns. Aisle windows, set between the buttress piers, are treated as punched openings, but they are tall and without colored glass, so they provide ample illumination. Mies van der Rohe, the twentieth-century German-American architect who advocated "skin-and-bones" buildings in glass and steel, found much to admire in German Gothic hall churches.

St. Barbara at Kutná Hora is an extraordinary example of Late Gothic with a complex history and form (Fig. 9.41). The town's economy was fueled by silver mines and the king of Bohemia's royal mint. Construction began in 1388 on the model of a French Gothic cathedral with eight radiating chapels, perhaps designed by Johann Parler, but work stopped in about 1400 and was not resumed until 1481, after the turmoil of the Hussite Wars had subsided. In 1489, Matej Rejsek completed the choir more or less according to the original design. A new master, the royal architect Benedikt Ried, assumed

9.40 St. George Church vaults, Nördlingen, 1427–ca. 1500.

This view shows the pattern created by the ribs.

9.41 St. Barbara Church, Kutná Hora, 1388–1512.

This church has a striking profile and a surprising interior (see Fig. 9.42). The tent-like roof pyramids reduce wind pressure and use less material, a consideration as the economy declined while the building was being completed.

9.42 St. Barbara Church choir, Kutná Hora, 1388–1512.

This view shows the net vaults completed in about 1489. While the choir arcades and clerestory bear a resemblance to French models, the nave was transformed in a later campaign into a hall church design with elegant swirling vaulting ribs.

9.43 St. Barbara Church nave vaults, Kutná Hora, 1388–1512.

The supporting piers rise as unbraced shafts above the inner aisles to vaults that match the height of the nave. Large gallery windows flood the interior with light, illuminating the flower-like ribs that flow gracefully across the vaulting shell.

9.44 (below) St. Barbara Church south side, Kutná Hora, 1388–1512.

This view shows the roof over the outer aisle and the large gallery windows placed between flying buttresses. Two of the three roof pyramids are also visible.

direction of the work in 1512, and in building the nave, he departed from the basilican scheme by building the nave piers as freestanding elements to support the vault of a hall church, with well-lit galleries over the side aisles. Intricate net vaulting in the choir (Fig. 9.42) was joined in the nave by flowing ribs that emerge near the piers to swirl into six-petal forms (Fig. 9.43). Whereas the vaulting ribs at Nördlingen were defined within each bay, the pattern on the thin shell vault here exists almost independently of a bay structure and creates an extraordinary sense of weightlessness. The exterior wall with its flying buttresses gives little hint of the spatial surprises within (Fig. 9.44), although the three tent-like tetrahedrons that comprise the roof are unexpected. Ried probably used these more to reduce wind loads and economize on construction material than for exotic effect, but their profile against the sky is unforgettable. Funding ran out once the nave vaults were complete in about 1557, leaving the west front to be finished in the nineteenth century.

ITALIAN GOTHIC VARIATIONS

Italian designers modified the Gothic style to fit local conditions, and the differences one observes from northern European versions of the style should be understood as adaptations that demonstrate the flexibility of the Gothic to accommodate varying interpretations. Given Italy's bright skies, large windows were not necessary to provide illumination inside buildings. Italian Romanesque builders were proficient in domical vault construction that reduced lateral thrust and thus required less in the way of buttressing. Cultural esthetics predisposed Italians to prefer internal tie-rods instead of visible external buttressing, so flying buttresses appear only rarely. (Tension ties also make sense in earthquake-prone areas.) Many of the religious orders desired churches that maintained a sense

9.45a Plan of S. Maria Novella, Florence, 1279–ca. 1310.

There is a Cistercian-like simplicity to this plan, which was built for the Dominican Order. Its ribbed domical vaults are braced by buttresses concealed under aisle roofs, thereby avoiding the need for flying buttresses.

9.45b Plan of Milan Cathedral, 1387–ca. 1572.

This is the largest Gothic church in Italy, and its structure is based on the cross-section of Bourges Cathedral, where pairs of aisles help to brace the high nave vaults. Master builders from France, Germany, and Italy were consulted concerning its design and construction.

of openness and visibility, qualities that could be achieved using the Gothic.

Gothic architecture first came to Italy with Cistercian monks, who had slipped easily into the style after absorbing the architectural sensibilities of Bernard of Clairvaux. Other monastic orders, particularly the mendicant Dominicans and Franciscans who came to minister to growing urban populations, also tended to build in Gothic. Among the earliest of their buildings was the great Dominican church of S. Maria Novella in Florence (1279–ca. 1310), built to a plan that would seem familiar to a Cistercian (Fig. 9.45a). The nave consists of nearly square bays and a square crossing and chancel. Four square chapels opening off the transept give the church structural clarity. Plain wall surfaces contrast with polychrome stonework outlining arches of the arcade, transverse nave arches, and vaulting ribs in nave and aisles (Fig. 9.46). By

9.46 S. Maria Novella interior, Florence, 1279–ca. 1310.

This view shows the polychrone ribs of the vaults. Notice the small roundels in the clerestory.

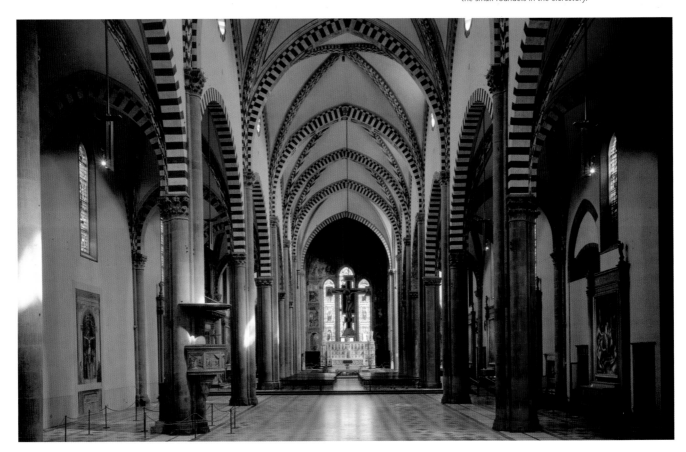

constructing ribbed domical vaults in the nave, the builders minimized lateral thrust to the point where support from the high aisle vaults and buttresses concealed under the aisle roofs was sufficient to brace the structure. A connection to the classical orders is evident in the half-columns engaged in the slender piers of the arcade. Aisle windows are small, and the clerestory consists of modest circular openings punched near the top of each bay. A large triple window in the chancel wall provides the strongest direct light. The internal effect is open and clear, well suited to a church for preaching to a congregation. We will encounter S. Maria Novella again in the Renaissance chapter, when its façade is completed.

At Todi, the Franciscans built S. Fortunato (1292–early 1400s) to a hall church design (Fig. 9.47). Here the highest point (crown) of the vaults is uniform across the church, unlike the billowing ceiling compartments created by domical vaults and transverse arches in S. Maria Novella. Without lower aisles to counter the vaulting thrust, the builders here constructed braces from the exterior wall to the nave piers in order to stabilize the building. As at S. Maria Novella, the nave bays are essentially square. Slender half-column shafts on the piers align with graceful vaulting ribs, giving a sense of considerable spaciousness to the interior. On both sides of the nave, chapels for use of the brothers are set between internally turned abutment walls, set at right angles to the outer wall and functioning as internal buttresses. Tall windows above the chapels provide good light to the interior, complemented by illumination from five windows in the polygonal choir.

In Venice, the nave of the church of SS. Giovanni e Paolo (or S. Zanipolo, in the Venetian dialect) was begun in 1333 by the Dominicans and consecrated in 1430 (Figs. 9.48–9.49). Following the example and proportions of aisle-to-nave height set by S. Maria Novella, it employs domical vaults over square bays in the nave to reduce outward thrust. Minimizing building weight was a real concern here, given that the church's foundations rest on wooden piles sunk into the mud. The church is built of brick, which is lighter than stone, and the vaults are in wood (except for the ribs and transverse arches, which are of stone). Transverse and longitudinal timber ties that are integral to the building link the vaults near the springing. The choir, begun about 1390, has a polygonal apse with three tiers of windows that start near the floor and extend almost to the vaults, admitting a flood of light and emphasizing the vertical. Pairs of chapels open off the transept, and a dome reminiscent of the Byzantine period covers the crossing. The interior of SS. Giovanni e Paolo has both verticality and spaciousness.

Italy's largest and most ambitious Gothic church is Milan Cathedral, begun in 1387 and not finished until 1858, although it was essentially complete by 1572. Its plan features a broad nave with double aisles, an aisled transept, and a polygonal apse with ambulatory (Fig. 9.45b). The

9.47 S. Fortunato interior, Todi, 1292–early 1400s.

This is a hall church, built with domical vaults that have internal stone braces over the aisles. Pairs of chapels are located in each bay along the aisle wall.

aisle bays are square in plan, while the nave bays are rectangular. The structure follows the model of Bourges Cathedral, where the aisles rise in a roughly triangular section to brace the nave vault, and the height of the nave, at 157 feet, is virtually equal to that of Beauvais Cathedral. Remarkably, it was constructed without flying buttresses, the ones on the cathedral today having been added in the nineteenth century.

Less than two years after construction began, decisions of the master builder Simone da Orsenigo were being second-guessed by consultants engaged by the client. Italian master builders, artists, and mathematicians gave opinions regarding theory, design, and technology, and building experts from France and Germany were summoned to give their views as well. Because some of the debate that ensued was transcribed (albeit by persons who did not fully understand what was being discussed) and these written records still exist, documents relating to Milan Cathedral provide an extraordinary insight into the variety of Late Gothic theory and practice, and the contrasting approaches to art and science. Opinions held by these experienced builders and theoreticians reflect differences in regional traditions and esthetics: the Italians favored broad proportions, the French argued for the particular vaulting techniques that they employed, and the Germans advocated soaring verticality. Consultations continued for more than a decade as the work was assigned first to one and then another master. In the end, proportions advocated by the Italian mathematician Gabrielle Stornoloco were used: the cathedral's section, based on an equilateral triangle, establishes the height of the nave at three times the height of outermost aisle and one-and-a-half times the height of the inner aisle (Fig. 9.50). Italian masons, accustomed to building within the load requirements of domical vaults, used them in the aisles and in a

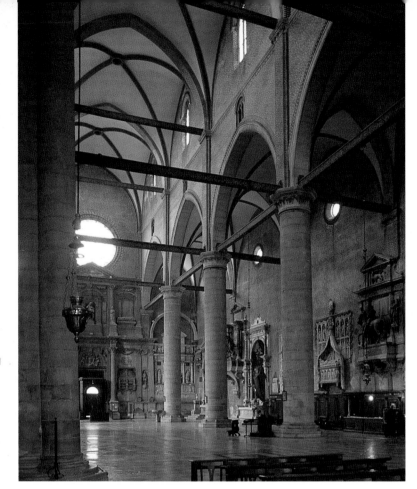

9.48 (right) SS. Giovanni e Paolo interior, Venice, 1333–1430.

This view shows how wooden tie beams were incorporated to brace arches of the nave and aisles. This view is to the west, toward the rose window above the entrance door. Notice the small aisle windows on the north side.

9.49 (below) SS. Giovanni e Paolo, Venice, 1333–1430.

Brick walls and wooden vaults were used here to minimize the building's material weight, as the wooden piles sunk in the mud would not take the dead weight of stone. Notice the dome at the crossing.

9.50 A study of the proportions of Milan Cathedral.

Compare this section to the church at Cluny III and Bourges Cathedral to see similarities in design. Italian builders, who best understood their materials and techniques, erected the building without flying buttresses.

9.51 Milan Cathedral, 1387–1572.

This view shows work that was finished in the nineteenth century. The exterior is in elaborately carved white marble. The west front blends classical and Gothic motifs.

modified form in the nave, reinforcing the vaults with strong iron tie-rods. This approach was foreign to the French and German masters, but it worked.

The resulting building is unlike most other Italian Gothic churches, lacking a sense of spatial openness because of the size and spacing of its piers. The volume is enormous, and as the small clerestory windows are filled with stained glass, even in full Italian sunshine little light enters the nave. Windows in the choir provide brilliance, however, drawing the visitor to the liturgical center of the church. Much of the exterior is post-medieval, but the work was carried out to the very end within the Gothic esthetic (Figs. 9.51–9.52). The exterior of Milan Cathedral is a veritable forest of carved marble and pinnacles from the vantage point of the roof level, which is accessible.

9.52 Milan Cathedral buttresses and pinnacles, 19th century.

Flying buttresses were added in the nineteenth century as the exterior was completed.

MEDIEVAL CONSTRUCTION

Milan Cathedral is exceptional in having preserved documents relating to its design and construction. For most of the great medieval building campaigns, the absence of written or graphic material limits our ability to make definitive statements about the nature of medieval architectural practice or construction procedures. Nevertheless, historians have analyzed the materials that are available—a few sketchbooks, isolated drawings and preserved tracing floors, works accounts, monastic chronicles, and

9.53a The notebook of Villard de Honnecourt, ca. 1225–50.

Villard collected drawings from various places, intending to pass his work on to others. This page shows methods for obtaining the solution to geometric problems, important skills for medieval builders.

9.53b The notebook of Villard de Honnecourt, ca. 1225–50.

This shows a sketch of wrestling men along with the scheme for a Cistercian church and a plan for the choir at Reims Cathedral. While some scholars doubt that Villard was himself an architect or builder, his drawings are the earliest record we have to indicate what medieval builders used as graphic representations of buildings.

9.53c The notebook of Villard de Honnecourt, ca. 1225–50.

This shows plans for two Cistercian church choirs. Some scholars think that Villard was involved in rebuilding the choirs of Cistercian churches to more elaborate designs. Notice that these plans show wall thickness and vaulting ribs.

the evidence provided by the buildings themselves—to piece together an understanding of building in the medieval world.

A building designer in the Middle Ages was usually called a master builder, the title of architect not being used until late in the period. The master builder's training would have included the acquisition of language and mathematical skills in a grammar school run by the local priest or monastery, followed by apprenticeship in one of the building trades (carpentry or masonry) at about age thirteen. The apprentice would be taught all aspects of the craft, including theoretical matters and practical applications. After three to seven years thus spent under the direction of a master craftsman, the apprentice would be certified as a journeyman, a worker qualified to hire himself out for a daily wage. For several years, he would work on different building sites, traveling about and keeping a sketchbook while gaining practical experience. To advance to the level of master he would be required to present a masterpiece—either an actual building or a finely executed model—to the masters of his craft guild, who would evaluate his fitness to direct journeymen and teach apprentices. Only the most capable and experienced master craftsmen would be entrusted with the direction of an entire project and thus acquire the title of master builder.

A collection of drawings made by Villard de Honnecourt, who was active ca. 1225–50, constitutes the earliest surviving documentation from the medieval period (Figs. 9.53a,b,c). His notebook includes a wide range of observations and sketches: geometry problems and their

solutions; timber roof trusses; sculpture and carved ornament; nature sketches; church plans; sketches of details from cathedrals at Laon, Chartres, and Reims; machines and devices; and such esoteric information as how to tame a lion. Other than what is contained in his notebook, little is known of Villard or his works. He claims to have traveled from the Low Countries to Hungary and back, and some historians surmise that he may have been employed by the Cistercians, perhaps in rebuilding chancels in the more elaborate Gothic style employed after the death of Bernard of Chairvaux. Others believe that he was merely a collector of drawings with a particular interest in details. From an inscription on the opening pages of the book, it is obvious that Villard intended his collection to be used by others. He identifies geometry as the basis of drawing, claims to present advice on masonry and carpentry, and asks that readers remember him and pray for his soul. His drawings show the earliest known representations of interior and exterior elevations (for Reims Cathedral) and also contain architectural plans with wall thicknesses specified, unlike the single-line walls marked on the Plan of St. Gall. Whatever his role in the building trade, Villard's drawings show that architectural ideas traveled as workers moved from site to site and also through the exchange of sketches and notations.

Geometry was indeed the theoretical core of medieval architecture. Following Roman practice, the master established basic building dimensions by a module and derived all other measurements from this standard through the manipulation of compass and straightedge. (Medieval people used Roman numerals that were uncongenial for all but the simplest arithmetical calculations.) The "secrets" of the masons were primarily principles of plane and solid geometry and knowledge of how to use triangles, squares, pentagons, and other figures to generate proportional lines, most of which have irrational numbers. Just as beauty in medieval chant was defined by proper relationships in the intervals between musical tones, so beauty in architecture was assured if the proportions of major elements and minor details were in geometric harmony.

Building a church of any size required money to pay skilled craftsmen. Masters and their workshops moved around according to the availability of construction funds, so it is sometimes possible to trace specific crews from project to project. The idea that churches were built either by monks or by volunteer laymen is a misconception. The overall size of the church and its major features would be determined by the master builder in consultation with church officials, and then professional quarrymen, masons, carpenters, sculptors, glaziers, and tilers would be employed to execute the work. Depending on the wealth of the client, a major cathedral could be built in as little as thirty years, as was the case at Chartres, or construction could drag on in discontinuous campaigns stretching over centuries.

MEDIEVAL HOUSES AND CASTLES

Our consideration of Romanesque and Gothic architecture has necessarily concentrated on the design of religious buildings, primarily because the Church commanded the best design talent and greatest financial resources. Medieval buildings remaining for study are from 400 to 1100 years old now, and only the best-constructed architecture can be expected to last that long. In the Middle Ages, churches formed the main group of buildings erected with great care, so inevitably they comprise the bulk of medieval architectural history.

HOUSING

Enough secular structures survive from the Middle Ages to give a general idea of the buildings in which ordinary people lived, and archaeological investigation is providing more information all the time. Rural houses of peasant families were simple, providing minimal shelter for cooking and sleeping. These buildings used local materials, mostly earth, wood, and thatch, and basic construction techniques, as they were probably built by the families that inhabited them. The combined house-barn or longhouse is a type that was widely used throughout the medieval period (Fig. 9.54). It was built on a rectangular plan entered through doorways placed opposite one another on the long sides, thus providing cross-ventilation and dividing the building into two sections. One end centered on an open hearth, around which the family gathered, and sometimes there was a second chamber partitioned off for sleeping or storage. The remaining section housed livestock, whose body heat helped warm the interior. As the building lacked a chimney, smoke

9.54 Reconstruction view of an early medieval longhouse, Bremerhaven, Germany.

Entrances set on opposite sides of the long wall divide the building into two parts, one with a hearth for cooking and warmth, and the other with stalls for animals.

would filter into the high volume overhead, where it could exit through gaps left in the gable ends without igniting the thatch of the roof. Peter Brueghel the Elder depicts just such a house in the background of *The Birdnester*, painted in 1568, which indicates that these rural structures were even then common sights in the countryside.

Land-owning families who were several steps further up the social ladder might inhabit a house (without animals) divided into a hall and solar, a private room on an upper floor. The hall was the major gathering and entertaining space (Fig. 9.55), warmed by a fire or central hearth, and the solar was a more private space reserved for the family. By the late Middle Ages, these basic rooms were usually improved by the addition of a buttery (for storage of drinks and other foods to be kept cool), a pantry (for storage of dry foodstuffs), and a passage screening circulation space to these storage rooms and the kitchen, which was a separate structure. The solar might move to an upper story and have its own stair for greater privacy. Since the nobleman fed his guests and retinue of servants in the hall, meals were important occasions for displaying hospitality and wealth. (It is ironic that the hall in modern houses has dwindled to an entryway or connecting passage, when once it was the major living space.)

Houses built in towns were more compact, often including several floors to conserve available land. The

9.56 Braced heavy timber frames (half-timbering) used in medieval construction.

Notice the slight cantilevers or jetties that extend the floor space on the upper levels. Along narrow medieval streets, these would also reduce available light.

9.55 The hall in a medieval manor house.

This was the main living space, provided with a central hearth for warmth. Meals would be taken here in common with household servants and retainers.

structure would again be wood, the roof would be thatch, and the entire building would accordingly be very combustible. Devastating fires are frequent events in the chronicles of medieval cities. Larger towns eventually regulated building by insisting on masonry construction and tile or slate roofs to reduce the spread of fire. Nevertheless, some wooden dwellings survive in England and on the European Continent to illustrate **half-timber** construction (Fig. 9.56). Buildings so designated have a heavy timber frame, exposed on the exterior, which is completed by non-structural wattle and daub, plaster, brick, or other infill. Whether of masonry or timber, town houses would typically have a shop on the ground floor and the dwelling apartments on the floors above (Fig. 9.57). The kitchen would be on the ground floor separated by a small light court from the rear of the shop to keep its odors and fire hazards away from the main part of the house. Italian cities tended to build houses in brick or stone, with tile roofs, and a number of Italian towns preserve substantial numbers of medieval masonry houses. S. Gimignano is particularly notable for the towers that survive on some houses (Fig. 9.58). While tower houses elsewhere may well have been constructed for defense, the likely function of these was for drying lengths of fabric away from sunlight, a necessary process to fix the yellow dye used here.

9.57 Medieval house, Cluny, 12th century.

This townhouse is typical of many medieval urban residences, combining workshop or commercial space on the ground floor with the owner's living quarters on the floor above.

9.58 Tower houses, S. Gimignano, 13th–14th centuries.

In many northern Italian towns were construction was the norm, medieval families constructed towers on masonry houses out of a sense of competition or perhaps for defense.

CASTLES

Fortified residences or castles were homes of the nobility, although they probably offered little more in the way of creature comforts than the homes of the more modest folk. Castles were constructed for defense, guarding strategic roads or rivers, and they also served as administrative centers for the surrounding territory. The earliest such fortifications were wooden, and only post-holes survive for archaeologists to base their conjectural restorations on. More easily visible are the earthworks that accompanied the early wooden castles, **motte and bailey** (mound and yard) being the most common form for these (Fig. 9.59). For a better command of the surrounding countryside, castles were constructed atop a mound (the motte), based whenever possible on an existing hillock and enlarged by fill from a ditch dug around the base. Between the ditch and the motte was an open area (the bailey) that provided room for the more temporary accommodation of castle retainers—servants, craftsmen, soldiers, horses, and the like. Enclosures of wooden palings, similar to the palisades erected in American frontier forts in the eighteenth

and nineteenth centuries, were built around the bailey, and a watchtower might protect the sole gateway. Hundreds of motte-and-bailey sites are detectable today, their mounds and surrounding ditches still visible in aerial photographs.

The pace of castle construction in England increased markedly after the Norman invasion of 1066. William the Conqueror may have brought pre-cut wooden timbers on his ships to build a castle on the coast at Hastings, for his fortification there was completed in the very short time-span of two weeks. The Bayeaux Tapestry depicts peasants digging the ditch and piling dirt for the motte. (The site of the castle at Hastings has since been claimed by the sea.) When William came to London, however, he desired something more permanent to signify his jurisdiction over the most important city in the country, and he was granted a site on the eastern edge of the Roman wall surrounding the City of London, where he constructed the White Tower (Figs. 9.60–9.61), now better known as the Tower of London (1078–80). It is a three-story masonry keep, basically rectangular in plan, with a semicircular projection reflecting the apse of a chapel constructed within at the

9.59 Plan and section through a motte-and-bailey castle, Castle Acre, Norfolk, 12th century.

The castle buildings are long gone, but the earthworks survive to show the motte or mound and the moat that surrounded the bailey or courtyard associated with the mound.

9.60 The White Tower (Tower of London), London, 1078–80.

Its three floors are vaulted to make them fireproof, and the roof served as a fighting platform. In the rounded section at the second floor is a Norman chapel.

third level. In the years since its construction, turret roofs of the corner towers have changed profile, and layers of enclosing walls and ancillary buildings have been added around William's castle, but the massive strength of the original Norman keep remains.

In succeeding years, partially as a result of the Crusades, European castles evolved from the keep or donjon models to enceinte designs that incorporated multiple towers and an enclosing curtain wall as the primary line of defense. Armies from western Europe were impressed by the fifth-century walls of Constantinople, a double line of fortifications reinforced by two-story towers and further protected by a moat that could be flooded in time of siege. From Islamic castles in present-day Syria, the Crusaders learned to build corbeled stone galleries (**machicolations**) projecting beyond the face of the wall to serve as a fighting platform. Experience gained in attacking, repairing, and defending castles in the Holy Land was brought back to western Europe, where some of the most elegant and soundly fortified works of the late thirteenth century were constructed by the English king Edward I as part of his campaign to subdue Wales. Of his ten castles in the Welsh Marches, Caernarvon (1283–1327) is perhaps the finest (Fig. 9.62). Built to the designs of Master James of St. George, it was both a symbol of English domination and a functioning regional administrative center, provided with a fortified town contiguous with the castle walls to create a secure presence in hostile territory (Fig. 9.63). Taking advantage of existing natural features, the castle is set where the river Seiont enters the Menai Strait, and a moat separates it from the town. In plan, the castle is

9.61 Plan of the Tower of London, 1078–80.

This view shows the ancillary walls and moat constructed since William's day. When first built, the Tower sat just inside the Roman wall around London.

9.62 Caernarvon Castle, Wales, 1283–1327.

An example of an enceinte castle, this is one of the finest medieval castles. The architect, Master James of St. George, was hired by King Edward I to build ten castles to extend English control over the unruly Welsh.

wasp-waisted, with the principal entrance from the town through the heavily fortified King's Gate in the center of the north side. Greatest care was given to the towers of the west or outer ward, where there was a hall (now vanished) set on the southern side and hospitable apartments built into the levels of the Eagle and Queen's towers. This ward was intended to be the residence and seat for the king's deputy in charge of the region.

Caernarvon was lavished with architectural symbolism that made reference to past imperial civilizations and left no one in doubt as to the permanence of Wales's new English master. The site contained ruins of a Norman motte, which were preserved in the eastern bailey (inner ward) as a reminder of earlier English claims to the region. The castle walls, built of masonry set in polychrome bands and reinforced by polygonal towers, recall the walls of Constantinople and thereby link the site to imperial Byzantium, a connection that was strengthened by the finding of what was believed to be the body of Constantine's father, Magnus Maximus, which was ceremoniously reburied in the town's church. The orthogonal layout of the walled city accompanying the castle has similarities to the Roman castrum of Segontium, the ruins of which were nearby, while turrets of the tower most visible from the

9.63 Plan of the castle and town, Caernarvon, 1283–1327.

King Edward I intended that this should become a regional headquarters, so he had a small town laid out on a grid plan and fortified alongside the castle. The former Roman castrum of Segontium is at the lower right.

coastal approach were embellished with boldly carved eagles, the emblem of royalty. Edward's son was born at Caernarvon in 1284, setting the precedent for the heir apparent to be invested as Prince of Wales. For all this majesty, Caernarvon was never completed. As was the case with many other castles, of which there were literally thousands, their defensive benefits were eventually outweighed by the cost of upkeep, and as their strategic value declined, there was little incentive to maintain these relics of a bygone age. Castles ruined either by intention or neglect still crown defensible heights all over Europe.

MEDIEVAL CITIES

There is an obvious connection between medieval castles and cities, for both relied on well-built fortifications to withstand attack, and they are frequently found together. Most medieval cities were provided with a solidly constructed wall with lockable gates that in ordinary times enabled the municipality to collect taxes from merchants entering the city. As the innumerable armed struggles characteristic of the Middle Ages usually had the capture of towns as their objective, the town walls served important defensive purposes as well. Fortunately for cities, medieval warfare was seldom a sustained event with large armies, and weapons before the introduction of gunpowder and metal cannonballs in about 1400 were rather primitive: battering rams, catapults, siege ladders or towers, and bows and arrows. Fire and pestilence could also be used for strategic advantage. A well-built fortification, punctuated by towers, provided defenders with a platform from which to return catapult and arrow fire and to dump stones or boiling liquids on persons trying to sap or scale the wall. The most common form of attack was the siege, in which attackers tried to cut off supplies to the town and thereby force the inhabitants into surrender.

Experience gained over time suggested that the most defensible wall was one protected by projecting towers of cylindrical rather than rectangular shape, equipped with archer slits that would allow defenders to shoot almost parallel to the wall section between towers. Moats or ditches provided useful protection, and a double set of walls made attack that much more difficult. Most of these innovations can be seen at Carcassonne, a strategic site that had been fortified successively by the Gallo-Romans, the Visigoths, and local counts before Louis IX of France gained control of the site in 1248 (Figs. 9.64–9.65). Louis's intention was to make the city an impregnable stronghold as he sought to bring the south of France under royal control. In addition to repairing and strengthening existing work in the old fortified town (the *cité*), he constructed a second ring of towers and walls around Carcassonne. The resulting fortifications were so formidable that the city was never seriously attacked thereafter. Carcassonne's strategic importance waned with the medieval period, but when there was a proposal to pull the crumbling walls down in the nineteenth century, preservationists intervened and restored the battlements and tower roofs to the condition seen today. It is one of relatively few cities to have its medieval defenses intact.

To encourage commerce and trade without overcrowding the *cité*, which had essentially become a military garrison, Louis IX developed a new town in the valley below Carcassonne (Fig. 9.66). Its regular grid plan organized around a central marketplace contrasts sharply with the irregular layout of the hilltop city, which like many medieval towns grew without regulation or advance planning. This lower town is in fact one of about 500 new

9.64 Carcassonne, built 800–1300.

Carcassonne is a medieval French city with fortifications dating back to the seventh century. These early fortifications were extensively repaired and provided with a second set of walls from 1248 to 1290.

9.65 Plan of Carcassonne, built 800–1300.

This plan shows the fortified *cité* (*lower right*) and the grid-plan bastide that was established in 1248 across the river Aude. When the second set of walls was planned for the *cité*, the hilltop became essentially a military camp.

9.66 Carcassonne walls, 1248–1290.

Notice the square holes left near the tops of towers for the construction of timber hourds, projecting galleries that could be quickly erected for defense.

town foundations known as **bastides** that were made in the south of France in the period between 1220 and about 1370. The motive behind establishing new cities was primarily economic: the bitter campaign against the Albigensian heresy had devastated the countryside, and as several parties—the kings of France and England, along with local counts—had claims to the territory, they sought to encourage settlement through the granting of freedoms and economic privileges associated with town residence. Not all bastides were built to the same plan, but many share certain characteristics: an orthogonal street layout, a central market square and hall (often surrounded by arcaded buildings), and uniform lot sizes for houses. The church is usually relegated to a side location. Monpazier, founded by Edward I in 1284, is often cited as the "typical" bastide, but its actual layout is not so regular as the idealized plan would suggest. The plans of Revel, Mirande, and Villefranche-de-Rouergue illustrate some of the variations found in bastide layouts (Fig. 9.67). While the architecture of bastide towns is usually not extraordinary, the clarity conferred by the plan creates a unifying harmony that makes many bastides small gems of urban design (Fig. 9.68).

A similar colonizing intent in central Europe resulted in the founding of hundreds of regularly planned towns under German influence in Poland, Slovakia, and Hungary. Trade was the prime objective, because the founder collected sales taxes from commerce, so the cities encouraged settlement with charters based on the Law of Magdeburg that guaranteed citizens freedoms of the market. One particularly handsome example of a deliberate foundation under Magdeburg

Revel   Mirande   Villefranche-de-Rouergue   Monpazier

N   0   500 m
    0   1500 ft

9.67 Plans of four bastide towns, southern France, 1220–1375.

Note the tendency to provide a square arcaded marketplace at the center of town. In most cases, the church is set away from the square, where commerce was most important.

9.68 Montpazier market square, ca. 1300.

This is one of the bastides of southern France. The architecture here, as in many bastides, is not exceptional, but the clear urban pattern and use of arcades around the square gives these cities particular charm.

9.69 Plan of Kraków, Poland, generated by the Great Charter of 1257.

The orderly town plan (shown in dark hatching) includes a large market square. Building lots were laid out to maximize frontage on important streets and around the square.

customs may be seen in Kraków, the historic capital of Poland, where an old castle and related settlement pre-dated the new foundation created with the granting of a Great Charter in 1257 (Figs. 9.69–9.70). An area immediately north of the built area was laid out around a major market square, 600 feet on a side, with uniform building plots marked on the surrounding square blocks. The only exceptions to the grid were two existing churches, which remained where they were. In time, a substantial cloth hall, large and small weigh houses, market stalls, and the city hall were built in the market square. Fortifications added in the fourteenth century linked the town and castle. Although few medieval houses survive, the original street layout and plot divisions continue to govern the fabric of the historic core.

Italian towns and cities experienced a slightly different situation during the medieval period. There, the commercial activity on which all urban life depends never completely ceased in the period following the decline of Rome, although urban services, most notably the public water supply, tended to fall below standards established under Roman jurisdiction. Medieval Italian communes participated vigorously in the revival of long-distance trade that characterized the later Middle Ages. Larger city-republics

9.70 Kraków market square, showing St. Mary's Church (*left*) and the Cloth Hall.

Textile merchants were very important, and their trading hall had stalls on the ground floor and rooms for the cloth guild upstairs.

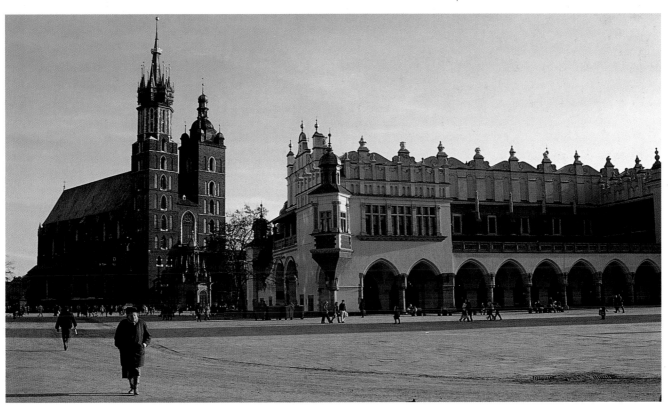

functioned as independent states, controlling smaller communities in the region and squabbling with other city-states for rights to border areas. At Siena, a medieval town formed by combining three separate ridgetop settlements, citizens celebrated the merger by building a new urban center on a marshy field (campo) where the ridges joined (Fig. 9.71–9.72). The town hall or Palazzo Pubblico (1298) dominates the bowl-shaped open area, which is an irregular fan-shaped plaza. Even though it has no

9.72 Plan of the campo, Siena, 1298.

The fan-shaped plaza slopes down to the Palazzo Pubblico, set at the lowest part of the site. While this is often not the best location for a prominent building, the citizens of Siena made sure that all buildings fronting on the Campo were compatible with the town hall.

9.71 Palazzo Pubblico, Siena, 1298.

The slender brick belltower, one of the tallest in all Italy, serves as a vertical marker for the town hall.

regular geometry, the campo was deliberately shaped and governed by municipal regulations that required façades of surrounding structures to harmonize with the town hall. The Palazzo Pubblico is nominally Gothic in style, but elements of the style have been used more for surface articulation than for structure. Crenelations and machicolations atop the building and its slender belltower are likewise ornaments in the modern style rather than serious attempts at fortification.

In Venice, a maritime republic that dominated trade between Europe and the Byzantine Empire, a decorative variant of the Gothic developed in which northern European features were blended with exotic influences from the East. The result is an airy, delicate architecture animated by the shimmering light reflected by the city's canals. The Doge's Palace is perhaps the most famous example of Venetian Gothic (Fig. 9.73). A blocky structure with an open courtyard, it has a solid exterior wall resting on two stories of open arcades. Pink and white diaper patterns enliven and lighten the visual impact of solid wall, so that it does not appear to overload the delicate filigree of the arcades below. The Ca' d'Oro illustrates Venetian Gothic applied to the traditional merchant's house, with its central section of large arcaded windows that open onto

9.73 Doge's Palace, Venice, 1309–1424.

This is a splendid example of the Gothic style adapted in Venice. Mixed with exotic influences from the East, the Gothic in Venetian hands becomes a lacy filigree to adorn buildings.

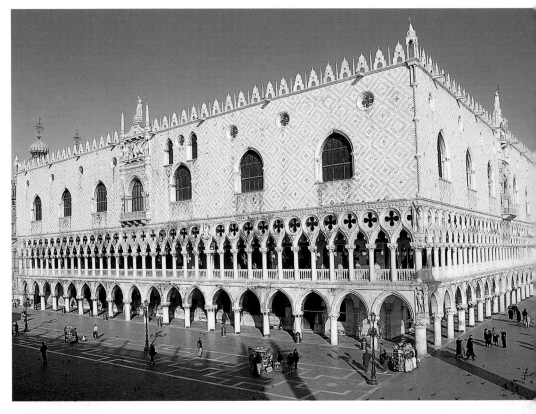

9.74 Ca' D'Oro, Venice, begun 1421.

This is an exceptionally fine merchant's house facing onto the Grand Canal. Its name, House of Gold, came from the gilding that was once applied to exterior detail. Even without the gold, its lace-like arch tracery and marble walls shimmer in the light reflected off the water.

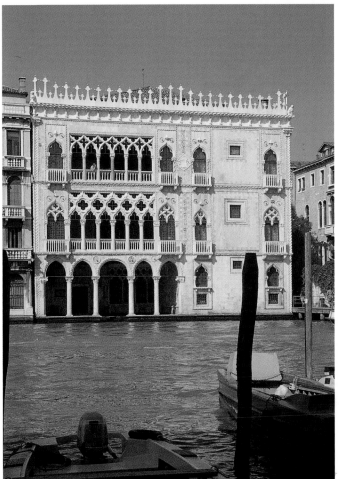

the **grand salon**, the major living space that extends the full depth of the house (Fig. 9.74).

In general, however, the Gothic was strongly identified with northern Europe and never attained great significance in Italy. By the fifteenth century a new artistic movement, based on the ideals of classical antiquity, was developing in the urban centers in the north of the country. In the following centuries this new style, the Renaissance, would spread to the rest of Europe. In isolated communities, however, medieval building traditions continued with little change until the nineteenth century, and medieval house forms are reflected in the earliest American architecture, particularly in New England and Virginia. There is even an American church built in 1682, St. Luke's in Smithfield, Virginia, that is considered part of the Gothic survival. In the nineteenth century, the Gothic Revival originated with reform-minded Victorians as a second flowering of medieval art and architecture.

CHAPTER 10

INDIGENOUS ARCHITECTURE IN THE PRE-COLUMBIAN AMERICAS

As in Europe and Asia, indigenous architecture in North America responded to complex social, economic, political, and environmental forces. However, its salient characteristics were a directness of construction and an honest use of materials. To some extent, such directness and honesty were inevitable, as most native cultures did not build road systems or construct large ships, and, while there was extensive trade between different peoples, it mostly involved smaller objects. This meant, with a few notable exceptions, that construction materials were drawn from local sources. Yet a feeling remains among many that the indigenous cultures of the Americas maintained a connectedness to place, a reverence for nature, and a noble forthrightness in their building that has been all but lost in today's society. Figure 10.1 shows the geographical distribution of the North American tribes.

TRIBES OF THE GREAT PLAINS AND THE GREAT LAKES

Tribes like the Lakota Sioux, hunting bison on horseback and led by their famous chief Sitting Bull in his eagle-feather headdress, have come to represent the Native American in the modern imagination. At their peak, some sixty million bison roamed the Great Plains, and Plains tribes based their cultures on these huge but skittish animals, using their meat for food, their hides for clothing and housing, and their bones for tools. In the seventeenth century, the Spanish introduced horses into New Mexico.

Native Americans quickly recognized their value, and horses soon became available in the Great Plains, where they made it possible for nomadic peoples to accumulate wealth, carrying large quantities of valuable possessions with them in the form of food, housing, clothing, and other amenities. With this rise in the standard of living came a dramatic growth in population. These conditions, in turn, increased warfare between tribes over the best grazing lands.

Because tribes moved about frequently, or at least had separate summer and winter dwellings, their architecture was necessarily temporary, rapidly constructed, mobile, and reusable. The best known of such nomadic structures is the *tipi*, a conical skeleton of poles covered with bison hides (Fig. 10.2). It was preferred by such tribes as the Arapaho, Blackfeet, Cheyenne, Comanche, and Crow, all names made familiar to movie-goers during the heyday of so-called "westerns." Most often depicted in this medium only as savage obstructionists bent on thwarting white settlement, these Plains-dwellers were in fact able designers who developed the tipi as a flexible solution to the contradictory problems of raging winds, numbing cold, internal fires and smoke, and blazing heat. Accordingly, the tipi had its vertical axis tilted and its plan distorted to an egg shape in order to combat prevailing winter winds, while its covering could be opened up for hot-weather ventilation. This covering also provided a mural surface for painted images, which typically depicted sacred symbols and the significant events of inter-tribal warfare. The tipi achieved its great size, requiring a covering of thirty or more bison hides, only after a horse became available to drag it on a travois of two poles joined by a frame.

Other tribes produced temporary buildings in different forms and using different materials. The Kiowa-Apache of the northwestern Plains constructed the *wikiup* as well as the tipi. To build it, they bent saplings into arch-shaped profiles, collectively forming a domical skeleton that they covered with smaller saplings and finally thatch. Tribes of the southern Plains assembled their similar grass houses

Machu Picchu, Peru, ca. 1450.

One could hardly imagine a more dramatic site. However, its exact function—ritual center, military outpost, or something else—remains unclear.

Arctic
Eastern Aleut
Central Aleut
Western Aleut
Trans-Arctic Eskimo

Subarctic
Eastern Aleut
Central Aleut
Western Aleut
Trans-Arctic Eskimo

Plains
Crow
Hidatsa
Mandan
Omaha
Arapaho
Blackfeet
Cheyenne
Kiowa-Apache
Pawnee
Comanche

Northeast / Great Lakes
Chippewa
Kickapoo
Micmac
Naskapi
Penobscot
Iroquois
Winnebago

Southeast
Creek
Natchez
Cherokee

Northwest Coast
Haida
Chinook
Quinault
Tillamook

Plateau
Nez Perce
Kutenai
Umatilla
Yakima

California / Great Basin
Yurok
Hupa
Tolowa
Karok
Pomo
Maidu
Miwok
Wintu

Southwest
Navajo
Papago
Pima

10.1 Distribution of Native American tribes in North America.

10.2 A Great Plains tipi.

A response to both numbing cold and blazing heat, the tipi was also portable. It has become one of the most vivid images in movies depicting the conflict between indigenous American people and European and American settlers.

by bending saplings like ribs over a ring of wooden posts, then covering the saplings with overlapping bundles of thatch.

Various Plains tribes, including the Mandan and Hidatsa, built earth lodges. They began by constructing a post-and-lintel rhombus of logs; next they leaned poles against it in a conical configuration; finally they covered the poles with earth to produce a cone- or dome-like enclosure. The Mandan and Hidatsa founded agricultural towns along rivers in Missouri, making some of them into market centers. Nomadic groups from the north and west brought exotic and precious items like dentalium, a type of mollusk shell, to trade for the local surplus of maize.

TRIBES OF THE NORTHEAST

In the northeast, hunting tribes such as the Penobscot, Micmac, and Naskapi constructed their versions of the tipi and covered them with bark. Various others, including the Great Lakes Chippewa, moved the tipi cone along a horizontal axis to form an extended version that was used as a multi-family dwelling.

Similar to the tipi and wikiup was the wigwam (Fig. 10.3), which was made by bending enough saplings into arch-shaped cross sections to form a vault- or dome-like volume, then covering it with mats or bark. In the northeast, various Algonquin tribes, including the Chippewa, Kickapoo, and Winnebago, favored the wigwam. When the first English settlers arrived to found the Massachusetts Bay Colony, they also lived in wigwams until they could erect larger structures like the ones they were accustomed to in England.

In what is today upstate New York, tribes of the League of the Iroquois erected longhouses, vault-like wigwams extended along their primary axes, sometimes to a length of more than 300 feet. The Iroquois used these large buildings as community halls for holding religious rituals. They practiced agriculture, growing maize, beans, and squash, and trapped animals for their pelts. They established a fur trade with Europeans in the early seventeenth century, competing with and eventually dominating their Algonquin neighbors. By the late eighteenth century, the English and the French were themselves competing for furs, and the Iroquois threw in their lot with the English. Though the Iroquois attempted to remain neutral during the Revolutionary War, they soon found themselves fighting a losing battle with the settlers and retreated to reservations, as would many other Native Americans as the new arrivals spread across the continent.

TRIBES OF THE MISSISSIPPI RIVER BASIN

Tribes of the Ohio River Valley and the southeast were distinguished by their construction of earth mounds. The Adena culture (ca. 800 BCE–400 CE), in what is today Ohio, is admired for its earthwork depictions of animals. Perhaps the best known of these, the so-called Serpent Mound, meanders some 600 feet in an oscillating curve. The Adena people also constructed conical mounds, some more than sixty feet tall, covering log structures used for burials or as depositories for cremated remains. A full explanation of the motivations that so inspired these ancient builders has not yet been developed; some mounds were obviously effigies and some were funerary, others apparently defined ritual spaces, and others still may have been built to provide relief from periodic flooding.

Tribes throughout the Mississippi Basin found abundant wildlife and other natural resources around them and cultivated maize, beans, and squash like their neighbors to the northeast. They also established

THE BIRTHPLACE OF THE CHOCTAWS

By Jack D. Elliott

*The reality of things, it appears, cannot be fully understood
in terms of the world and its time; for the things are cir-
cumfused by an ambience of mystery that can be understood only in terms of the myth.* Eric Voegelin

10A Nanih Waiya mound, rural Mississippi, ca. 100 CE.

The landscape is suffused with symbolism. Even for information-obsessed moderns who fancy themselves to be detached and objective observers, it still has evocative associations. Like most peoples, early Native Americans lived in landscapes replete with mythological symbols. In particular, mounds, relic landscape features built by earlier settlers who were forgotten by their successors, often took on mythical associations.

Nanih Waiya (Choctaw—"bending hill") is an earthen mound that stands in rural central Mississippi (Fig. 10A). Today it is approximately twenty-five feet high and covers about seven-tenths of an acre at its base. Early accounts indicate that the site also once possessed a smaller burial mound and a surrounding earthen breastwork. These features have been destroyed as the result of agricultural practices during the nineteenth and twentieth centuries. Recent research conducted by Ken Carleton, archaeologist for the Choctaw tribe in Mississippi, suggests that the mound

dates to the Middle Woodland period, that is, about 2000 years ago, almost certainly predating by centuries the emergence of the Choctaw tribe.

The mysterious mound came to be regarded by the historic Choctaw tribe as sacred through linkage to their origin myths; it was the "ishki chito," "the great mother." Two basic themes are to be found. According to the more prevalent story, the Great Spirit created the first Choctaws in the interior of the mound, whence they crawled forth wet and moist through a cave or hole into the daylight and lay out in the sun to dry. During the early nineteenth century there was a "large and deep" hole in the top of the mound. The Choctaws' regard for the great mother mound was such that if they were hunting in the vicinity, they would bring a portion of their kill and throw it into the hole, feeding their mother, as they saw it.

The second story was the migration legend, in which the ancestors of the Choctaws moved from the west led by prophets, who envisioned a land with

fertile soil and abundant game, carrying a pole. They traveled eastward, and at the end of each day they camped and planted the end of the pole in the ground so that it stood vertically. In the morning they would find that the pole had tilted, and their journey would resume in the direction in which it had tilted. The journey continued for months until one evening they arrived at Nanih Waiya and planted the pole; the next morning they found it still standing erect. This was interpreted as an oracle indicating that they had arrived at their new home.

We often smile today at the mythologies of the past; the details, for the most part, are not factually true. Yet there is more to our appreciation of these stones than whether they contain strict historical fact or not; the linkage between mythic story and place makes us see places as we might not otherwise see them. They evoke in us a sense of wonder at things that we have all too often lost in a world where the mystery of Being is often ignored.

long-distance trade routes. Excavations in Cahokia, Illinois have unearthed copper objects from the Great Lakes, mica from the southern Appalachians, and seashell ornaments from the Atlantic coast. In around 1000 CE, Cahokia was the largest city north of Mexico, covering five square miles and having a population of some 30,000 inhabitants. Among Cahokia's platform mounds is the so-called Monk's Mound, built entirely of earth, which is half the size of the enormous Temple of the Sun at Teotihuacán near modern-day Mexico City. This pyramidal structure is situated at the head of a great plaza and large posts in the ground nearby probably once facilitated astronomical observations.

Development of the vast Poverty Point site, in what is today northeast Louisiana, is believed to have begun in about 1200 BCE. Some have argued that it was a regional trading center established by the Olmecs of eastern Mexico. Poverty Point consists of concentric semicircular, ridge-like mounds enclosing a plaza 1800 feet across. In order to shape such a landscape, the amount of earth that had to be moved was prodigious. Light wooden houses, long since gone, once stood atop the ridges. Mound-building was still being practiced by the Natchez tribe on nearby sites in the early eighteenth century when the phenomenon was observed and commented on by French explorers.

To the east, Native Americans also constructed mounds, such as those in Moundville, Alabama (Fig. 10.4), which are situated on a high bluff above the Black Warrior river. On a site covering 300 acres, there are twenty mounds, most with their ramps still visible, surrounding a large plaza. Dwellings once ringed the mound complex and were protected by a wooden palisade. Atop the mounds stood timber-frame structures with walls covered in plaster on lath formed of smaller limbs and twigs and with roofs covered in bark.

At Moundville, a museum was opened in the 1930s which allowed visitors to look at skeletal remains in an excavated burial site. While this display seemed reasonable at the time, the modern view is that such exhibitions, made without the permission of associated parties, represent inappropriate intrusions upon the most personal kind of human settings. Consequently the excavation has now been sealed off from public view. Likewise, museums throughout the country have returned for reinterment Native American remains removed unilaterally by archaeologists in years past.

While mound-building has received the most attention, more modest Native American constructions in the southeast are equally interesting. The Creeks of Alabama and Mississippi erected buildings with mud-over-timber-frame walls, which they arranged around square courts, as well as octagonal townhouses and, as communal centers, buildings on round or polygonal plans with conical roofs. They sealed their walls using a whitewash made of ground oyster shells and covered their roofs with a variety of

10.4 Earth mound, Moundville, Alabama, 1200–1500.

This earth mound at Moundville in west-central Alabama was constructed as a base for a temple or residence of an important person. Unlike the pyramids in Mexico, it was never encased in a stone veneer

materials including thatch and bark. Farther south, the lower Creeks built the *chickee*, a raised platform protected by an openwork wood frame supporting a thatched gable or hipped roof.

ARCTIC AND SUBARCTIC TRIBES

The Aleuts of the Aleutian Islands in Alaska favored whale meat for food, but made use of the entire animal, from its intestines to its bladder and tongue. They hunted whales in boats called baidarkas, constructed, appropriately, with whalebone frames. These boats seated as many as forty men, though a typical hunting party usually had only ten or so. They also plied the waters in kayaks in search of smaller game such as sea lions, seals, and porpoises. On land, they used sleds, but still had no dogs as late as 1000 CE. The Aleuts called their semi-subterranean sod-covered house a *barabara*, and entered it through a roof hatch. Underground buildings took advantage of soil mass to create moderate temperatures. In the Arctic, the Canadian Inuit (Eskimos), also lived in subterranean houses, which they built of stone, wood, and almost any other available material. Traditionally, Inuits have hunted sea mammals and caribou, living in villages in winter and then separating and moving inland in the summer. To this day, they continue to construct the well-known *iglu* (Fig. 10.5), a structure made of snow blocks. They cant blocks inward to create a stable domical profile, but rather than laying them

10.5 Inuit iglu.

While the iglu is shaped like a dome, it is actually made of spiraling courses, with the bed of each block sloping inward. The blocks are cut from packed snow, meaning ice crystals rather than solid ice, so that trapped air provides insulation.

10.6 Diagram of a northwestern shed house.

Shed houses could be quite large, with eaves rising to twenty feet and main rooms stretching up to 100 feet across. The production of individual planks by splitting and finishing them with an adze was a technological challenge in a culture that had no power-drive saws.

in courses, spiral them upward. They enter the completed iglu through a small barrel-vaulted porch.

The tipi form was adaptable even for the subarctic region. Here, tribes built the *tupik*, a tipi-like structure that they covered with animal skins. During the summer months, Arctic Inuit constructed a tupik that appears at first glance to have been a type of extended tipi, but was actually a tent made of poles covered with skins that mimicked the form of their winter iglu, even to the inclusion of a tunnel-like entry.

TRIBES OF THE NORTHWEST AND NORTHERN CALIFORNIA

Native American cultural patterns were similar along the Pacific coast from Alaska to Baja California. Diet was diverse, including plentiful fish and sea mammals and a variety of indigenous plants. The Quinault tribe of Washington state is famous for its potlatches, enormous feasts celebrating a child's coming of age, a death and subsequent memorialization, or the annual salmon run.

Along the northwest Pacific coast, the Quinault, as well as the Chinook and Tillamook, built **shed houses** (Fig. 10.6), log frames sheathed in cedar planks and covered with single-sloping or gable roofs. Such constructions were long on a locally abundant building material but short on technology, using inefficient structural cross sections such as circular beams and joists and simple fasteners such as cedar-bark ties. Farther north, tribes such as the

Haida built plank houses and also erected **totem poles**, carving them with images of stylized animals. Some scholars argue that such carving could have been done with bone and shell tools; others see it as a later development dependent on the appearance of metal. The tribes of the northwest also applied similar painted images to the exterior walls of their chiefs' houses.

The Nez Perce, famous for their hospitality to the Lewis and Clark expedition in 1805, wintered in small villages along the Columbia river in carefully chosen, sheltered locations. They lived off salmon, root vegetables, and bulbs, which they preserved by drying them on racks or in earthen ovens. They then stored the processed items in baskets lined with salmon skins, and finally placed them in specially designed storage houses or stone- or bark-lined pits. They also hunted game and, having horses, bison as well. The Nez Perce and Yakima occupied **pit houses** (Fig. 10.7), timber frames set above three to four-foot-deep pits and covered with pine needles, reed or grass mats, and earth. They erected these timber frames in a configuration akin to conventional post-and-lintel and hipped-roof framing.

Northern California is a land of rugged topography and dense forests. The preservable carbohydrate that Native Americans here favored was flour made from acorns and buckeyes, and their preeminent craft was basketry. The Yurok, Karok, Hupa, and Tolowa tribes built gable-roofed frames above pits but covered them with planks from locally available redwoods. In central California, the Maidu and Miwok tribes constructed oval and

10.7 Overhead view and cross-section of a northwestern pit house.

Such domestic environments took advantage of the insulating qualities of surrounding rather than covering earth. While rarely seen in Europe, the entry from above was not uncommon in North America.

octagonal pit houses using radiating poles set atop polygonal frames. Over the poles, they layered sticks, then grass or tule mats, and finally a coating of earth.

TRIBES OF THE SOUTHWEST

In the southwest, members of the Pima and Papago tribes lived in **ki** or **ramada** depending on the season. A ki was a domical structure made by covering sapling frames with brush then mud. A ki consisted of a shallow pit surrounded by walls made from the excavated spoil; both features lessened the effects of winter cold and winds. Both tribes made a warm-weather ramada by planting upright posts in the ground to support a brush-covered roof. Family groups lived in *rancherías*, communities of farmsteads located near water sources.

Unique conditions in the southwest also led to a permanent indigenous architecture. Three cultures contributed: the Mogollan—named for the Mogollan mountains in southwestern New Mexico; the Hohokam—their name taken from a Pima word meaning "those who have vanished"; and the Ancestral Pueblo, long called the

Anasazi, which has often been translated as "Ancient Ones." By 300 BCE. the Mogollan culture of central Arizona and southwestern New Mexico had established villages atop mesas, or steep-walled plateaus. They built pit houses enclosed by timber frames covered with brush and earth and entered down a ramp or ladder. Along the Gila and Salt rivers, the Hohokam people developed sophisticated systems of irrigation and built castle-like structures with adobe walls as much as five feet thick.

The Ancestral Pueblo began their culture in what is today Utah, then gradually migrated into southwestern Colorado, eastern Arizona, and western New Mexico. They developed a distinctive form of black-and-white pottery, as well as and methods for conserving and managing precious water for irrigation. Their building of compact, permanent settlements reached a zenith in 1100–1300 near the Four Corners region at Mesa Verde and Chaco Canyon, and consisted respectively of extensive alcove dwellings beneath protective mesas (Fig. 10.8) and agricultural and trading townships.

Ancestral Pueblo architecture began as pit houses entered from above, with excavated floors covered with timbers and then earth. In around 700 the Ancestral Pueblo modified their construction practices, erecting their houses for use during the summer months at ground level, using sandstone masonry for walls and adobe over small timbers for roofs. They combined these houses in a party-wall fashion, arranged them around irregular plazas, and continued to provide entry into them only from above. In around 1000, they began to transform their remaining pit houses into sunken, circular **kivas**, sacred

10.8 Mesa Verde, southwest Colorado, 1100–1275.

The Mesa Verde site was chosen for habitation for practical reasons rather than for its dramatic landscape: it offered protection from winter winds out of the north and security against potential invaders.

10.9 Pueblo Bonito, Chaco Canyon, New Mexico, 900–1120.

This view gives a sense of the expanse of the site. Its semicircular arrangements of terraces, now in ruin, responded to the path and inclination of the sun. A disadvantage of this kind of tiered arrangement was that it created a high percentage of unlit interior rooms.

and social spaces that celebrated their clan-oriented society. Each kiva contained a **sipapu**, or ceremonial opening, to the world below. Around a kiva, the Ancestral Pueblo distributed several suites of living spaces. As their population increased, they added second and third stories to their already-dense housing complexes, called **pueblos**, probably relegating the largely unlit lower-level rooms to use for food storage. The vast Ancestral Pueblo alcove dwelling or Cliff Palace at Mesa Verde contains some 200 rooms and twenty-three kivas. While Mesa Verde's stone masonry is today much admired for its intricate workmanship, it was originally covered with adobe plaster to protect it from the elements.

The Ancestral Pueblo developed numerous settlements, typically in smaller, compact, naturally sheltered locations like Mesa Verde, which enabled them to combat invaders, mitigate the effects of harsh climate, and orient structures to important celestial events. Atop the mesas at Mesa Verde, they developed terraced gardens like those of the Incas and constructed reservoirs for agricultural- and drinking-water retention.

At Pueblo Bonito in Chaco Canyon, the Ancestral Pueblo built an intricate irrigation system that included dams, ditches, and flood gates. They erected a great five-story, tiered, semicircular megastructure with some 800 rooms and at least thirty-seven kivas facing the arc of the

sun as it traversed the southern sky; only ruins remain today (Fig. 10.9). They built walls from bonded wythes of stone set in thin beds of clay mortar and applied a veneer of coursed ashlar covered with adobe plaster. As at their other sites, they arranged for entry into rooms only from above via ladders. They also developed an extensive system of roads, many of them still apparent in aerial photography. Based upon the exotic artifacts found here, such as seashells and parrot feathers, it seems clear that Pueblo Bonita was the major trading center in the Ancestral Pueblo southwest.

The Ancestral Pueblo culture declined rapidly after 1300 for reasons that are not yet adequately understood. The most likely cause was an extended drought resulting from changing weather patterns. Their descendants, including the Zuni, the Hopi, and the Navajo, still dominate in the region. The Navajo nation, in what is today northeastern Arizona and northwestern New Mexico, represents the largest tribe in the United States, some quarter of a million strong, and occupies some nine million acres of reservation land. Traditionally, the Navajo lived in hogans (Fig. 10.10), which consisted of various configurations of log frames covered with earth. Some of these log frames were conical; some began as post-and-lintel squares against which smaller logs were then leaned; and some had notched log walls and corbeled log roofs. The Navajo are particularly noted for their silver work and their blankets. They also made sand paintings by sprinkling colored sand and maize meal over flat surfaces.

10.10 A southwestern hogan.

To build a hogan, a log frame was covered with earth, producing a living environment compatible with climatic extremes. Wood provided the structural integrity, while the earth covering provided the insulation.

MEXICO, CENTRAL AMERICA, AND SOUTH AMERICA

The following discussion of Pre-Columbian Mexico, Central America, and South America covers eight cultures and fifteen sites, from the Olmecs at La Venta in about 1100 BCE to the Aztecs at Tenochtitlán, and the Inca in Peru up until the time of the Spanish conquest.

THE OLMECS OF THE EASTERN MEXICAN COAST

Men and women migrated east across the Bering Straits more than 10,000 years ago. They settled all along the way, traveling as far south as what are today Peru and Bolivia. The earliest evidence (ca. 1500 BCE) of a sophis-

10.11 Olmec stone head, before 900 BCE.

This artifact, relocated from its original site, displays the distinctive Olmec facial features and ceremonial headdress.

10.12 Diagram of La Venta, Tabasco, Mexico, 1100–400 BCE.

The conical earth mound and stepped pyramid stand at the ends of an axis defined by earthen platforms and walled enclosures. Such a sequential organization of space and mass can be compared to Egyptian pyramid complexes and Mesopotamian ziggurats and their compounds.

ticated culture comes from the Gulf Coast of Mexico in the northern portion of the state of Tabasco and southern portion of the state of Vera Cruz. This was the land of the Olmecs, best known for their jaguar motifs and great bodyless stone heads (Fig. 10.11) with seemingly oriental features. Olmec sculptors carved these heads from six- to eight-foot-tall basalt blocks weighing up to thirty tons that had to be imported from quarries located in the Tuxtla mountains some distance away. They are probably depictions of real rulers, but this is only a supposition as the Olmecs left behind no written records. Olmec art also frequently depicted were-jaguars, a human-jaguar hybrid, as well as the serpents that would appear at most subsequent Mexican sites. The most impressive Olmec ceremonial center is La Venta (Fig. 10.12), where the oldest known earthen pyramid in America, almost 100 feet tall, served as the terminus for an axis defined by an orthogonal arrangement of earthen platforms surrounding a ceremonial plaza lined with basalt columns. The basic elements of this composition would be repeated again and again throughout the region, as would the alignment of buildings with important astronomical events.

TEOTIHUACÁN IN THE VALLEY OF MEXICO

During the Classic period of Pre-Columbian Mexican culture (ca. 200 BCE–1000 CE), a vast, planned urban development was created at Teotihuacán (Fig. 10.13), meaning "place of the gods," in the Valley of Mexico, by a people whose name we do not know. It arose northwest of the Olmec sites subsequent to the Olmec decline, covers some thirteen square miles, and once served a population as large as 200,000 people. In the city's ritual center, designers laid out a great north–south causeway, terminated on the north by the stepped Pyramid of the Moon. Alongside the causeway, they placed a series of earthen terraces with battered walls faced with stone veneer; a great stepped pyramid—the Pyramid of the Sun (Figure 10.14); and walled enclosures, some sunken and some defined by trabeated construction covered with low-relief sculpture.

The horizontal plane dominates here, perhaps inspired by the sprawl of the valley floor. This horizontality is celebrated by means of two distinctive ordering devices. The battered walls of the terraces and pyramids display the **talud** and **tablero** motifs that would be repeated with many variations throughout Mesoamerica. The talud is a sloping plane and the tablero a frieze of random stones framed by plain moldings (Fig. 10.15).

Exquisitely carved columns in the so-called Palace of the Quetzalbutterfly, located on the west side of the plaza and in front of the Temple of the Moon, document the appreciation among Teotihuacán's inhabitants of the hard-edged quality of stone. The plan of the Palace of Ateltelco (Fig. 10.16), located west of the causeway and between the Temple of the Sun and the so-called Citadel,

Pyramid of the Moon

Plaza of the Moon

Causeway, or Avenue of the Dead

Pyramid of the Sun

Great Compound

Citadel

N

0   500 m
0   1500 ft

10.13 Plan of Teotihuacán, Valley of Mexico, ca. 200 BCE–800 CE.

As at La Venta, the principal forms are pyramids and platforms, here stretched out beside a long causeway.

10.14 Pyramid of the Sun, Teotihuacán, begun ca. 100 BCE.

Made of earth with a stone-veneer covering, this giant structure is similar to stepped pyramids in Egypt and Mesopotamia.

10.15 Talud and tablero motifs, Teotihuacán.

The variations on a basic theme offered by the talud and tablero motifs provide unity among diversity at the many Pre-Columbian sites in Mexico and Central America. These motifs appear as pyramid tiers, building walls, and even roofs.

10.16 Plan of the Palace of Ateltelco, Teotihuacán, ca. 300 CE.

This pattern of interlocking orthogonal geometries attests to the sophisticated design ideas of the people of Teotihuacán. Notable are the cross-axial organization, the column screens, and the resulting rich sequence of spaces.

demonstrates—in its complex geometry of interlocking squares, its many level changes, its proportioning systems, and its layering of columns, piers, and walls—a sophisticated understanding of geometric ordering and spatial sequence.

THE ZAPOTECS AND MIXTECS AT MONTE ALBÁN, OAXACA

In Oaxaca, south of the Central Plateau of Mexico, the Zapotecs also rose in prominence after the decline of the Olmecs. They transformed their local culture into a territorial one, with the populace scattered throughout the Oaxaca Valley. At Monte Albán (600 BCE–1000 CE), they organized their great ritual center quite differently from that at Teotihuacán. By leveling the top of a mountain some 1300 feet above sea level, they developed an earthen platform on which they built a series of stepped pyramids as bases for their temples (Fig. 10.17).

The Zapotecs arranged these pyramids around the perimeter of their site, creating a great plaza, 1000 feet long and almost 500 feet wide, and, within this plaza, they placed two additional pyramids, making them built objects inside a larger built environment; such ideas can be compared conceptually to those of Hellenistic Greece in the fourth to second centuries BCE. Equally spatial is the ball court at the southwest corner of the site. This form type appeared throughout Mesoamerica where its misleadingly serene composition of talud-and-tablero-like battered walls and platforms provided a setting for ritual games played with a small resilient ball, games in which the consequence of losing was death (Fig. 10.18).

10.17 (above, left) Monte Albán, Oaxaca, Mexico, 600 BCE–1000 CE.

Unlike Teotihuacán's axial organization, Monte Albán's is spatial. Platforms once capped by temples define a plaza in which the Zapotecs placed two structures, one certainly an observatory that was canted in plan to align it with significant stars or planets.

10.18 (left) Ballcourt, Central America, before 800.

This ball court, like that at Monte Albán, has sloping talud walls resembling modern stadium seating. However, these slopes were a part of the playing field, with onlookers standing on the platforms above. The game was not a sport but a ritual.

10.19 (above, right) Talud–tablero wall, Mitla, Oaxaca, Mexico, ca. 800.

The contrast between the geometric ornament here at Mitla and the organic Maya ornament farther south (see Fig. 10.26) is striking. Perhaps it has to do with the differing contexts in Oaxaca and the Yucatán.

The Zapotecs built their pyramids using talud–tablero motifs but emphasized wide stairs often bracketed by sloping cheekwalls. Their interpretation of the talud–tablero was strongly linear, with corbeled layers configured as if overlapping and turned down at their extremities. Atop their pyramids, the Zapotecs placed temples with notable plan configurations. Each temple was one or two cells deep (like an ancient Greek cella and porch) with frontal columns *in antis* or prostyle. Particularly interesting is the sunken court at the southern end of the site which is comparable in its plan to the Palace of Ateltelco. A square with four smaller, overlapping squares at its corners, it was approached by means of a wide stair, then through a portico with a double file of square columns. Such an exploitation of ranks and files of columns was rare in Pre-Columbian America, but would appear again among the Toltecs in both northern Mexico and Central America. Excavations here have unearthed the tombs of the Zapotec nobility and the largest cache of jewelry found in North America.

The Mixtecs followed the Zapotecs in Oaxaca (ca. 800). Their sacred city of Mitla includes the Palace of the Columns. Here the tablero motif took on a much more intricate character than any seen before. A plain talud serves as the base from which rise tiers of tablero elements framed by corbeled bands. The tablero is formed of inlaid panels of geometric ornamentation in both orthogonal and diagonal patterns (Fig. 10.19).

THE MAYA

East of Oaxaca, in what today is Guatemala and the Mexican state of Yucatán, another great Pre-Columbian culture developed, that of the Maya. At its height, the Maya civilization included some fifty independent states and more cities than anywhere else in the Pre-Columbian Americas. The Maya developed irrigation systems and cultivated a wide variety of crops, particularly maize, which they made into tortilla-like pancakes. Maya society was rigidly stratified, with peasant farmers at the base and the priest class, merchants, and warriors above. At the top was a hereditary king, who was both a civil ruler and a priest.

The Maya were unique in the Americas in developing a system of writing, recording their history and ritual practices on paper. While their libraries were destroyed by the Spanish, many of their hieroglyphic texts survive, carved in stone, modeled in stucco, and painted on pottery or in murals. Their glyphs, long a subject of intense study, have only recently been deciphered. They include signs that represent both individual sounds and whole words. Unfortunately, because the only extant texts are displayed on public architecture, they represent the official government interpretation of events and do not allow for alternative points of view. Still, they offer rich insights into such matters as the Maya concept of time and their world view.

The Maya solar calendar included 365 days broken down into eighteen months of twenty days each, with five residual days. A separate religious calendar had 260 days, and the two calendars coincided every fifty-two years. This interval was viewed as a birth–death–rebirth cycle and was celebrated with lavish rituals. The rebirth was accompanied by the igniting of a ritual flame and by the reconstruction of significant temples and pyramids. The Maya used the zero, which was also independently discovered by the ancient Babylonians, making it possible for them to keep accurate mathematical records and make accurate astronomical predictions.

The Maya saw the world as being made up of three distinct regions, the starry world of the heavens above, the middle world of the earth where fecundity could only be guaranteed by the blood of the kings, and the dark underworld. They viewed the middle world as sacred and the cardinal directions as part of a sacred geography. In ritual acts, the king, reaching a trance-like state and offering his blood atop a pyramid or in a public plaza, was expected to communicate among these tiered worlds.

TIKAL

Perhaps the most impressive Maya city is Tikal, set within the lowland jungles of the department of El Petén in Guatemala. The city was not only a ceremonial site, but also a true urban center with a permanent population of some 45,000 inhabitants. The site plan (Fig. 10.20) is

10.20 Plan of Tikal, Guatemala, 600 BCE–ca. 900 CE.

This site contains thousands of structures and stone monuments, with the most extensively excavated areas located around the North Acropolis at the junction of the three causeways. Archaeologists must uncover such ruins advisedly, as they then become vulnerable to the effects of wind, sun, and rain, and must somehow be protected from the encroaching jungle vegetation.

organized by means of causeways laid out in a rough triangle and linking major building complexes. At the southeast corner of this triangle stands the so-called North Acropolis, a closely packed cluster of pyramids facing a great plaza to the south. This plaza is defined on its eastern and western extremities by large pyramids and bristles with **stelae**, upright slabs with inscriptions. The units of pyramid composition are again the talud and tablero. Talud elements, in the form of sloping embankments, define platforms. Atop these platforms sit stepped pyramids formed of largely unarticulated sloping talud and equally plain vertical tablero motifs relieved only by horizontal returns and recessed panels, both of which cast sharply defined shadows (Fig. 10.21). Tikal's pyramids are its most distinctive built forms with their steep but plain tablero and talud walls and surmounting temples (Fig. 10.22). Atop the talud-like roofs sprout flamboyant, richly carved roof combs, repetitive talud-like elements that rest on the temples' corbel vaults. Steep stairs rise up one side of each pyramid and lead to the temple doorways. The original stucco reliefs have now almost completely vanished. Inside, modest spaces are created by the Maya's use of the corbeled vault, a structural device not seen at Teotihuacán or in Oaxaca. The complete ensemble of pyramids is extraordinary for its verticality, all the more so when the multiple pyramids are viewed as an urban unit; today they rise like great stalagmites from the jungle floor in so dramatic a fashion that George Lucas chose an aerial view of

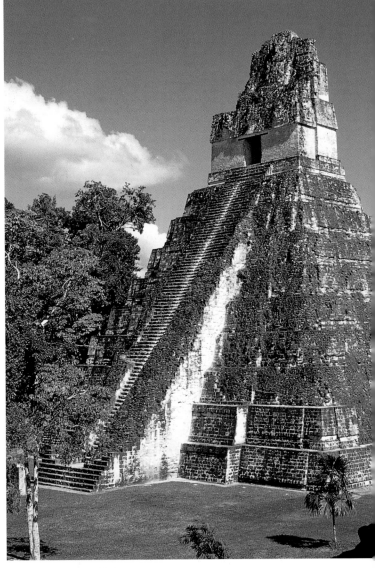

10.22 Pyramid, Tikal, ca. 650.
Most striking about Tikal's pyramids is their verticality. However, they were once part of a densely developed urban fabric rather than being isolated towers amid a dense jungle canopy as they are today.

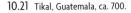

10.21 Tikal, Guatemala, ca. 700.
The portion of the city seen here includes the great plaza in the foreground, with stelae and the pyramid bases of the North Acropolis beyond. The Maya used temples and their bases to shape outdoor spaces intended for ritual spectacle.

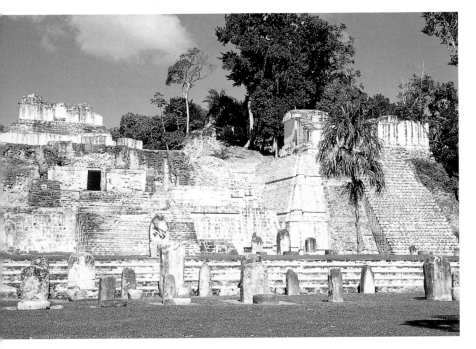

them to represent a moon of the rebel planet in the first *Star Wars* movie. Together with ball courts, a rain-storage reservoir, and the low-rise market structures, also composed using talud and tablero elements, the ritual pyramids at Tikal define a series of linked acropolises, open markets, and plazas.

COPÁN AND PALENQUE

Also located in Central Yucatán are the Maya cities of Copán and Palenque. Copán lies southeast of Tikal and was famous for its periodic gathering of astronomical experts. The ceremonial center is roughly rectangular, with a great plaza to the north and acropolis to the south. Perhaps its most distinctive feature is the many stelae: in this case, vertical, carved monoliths, conceptually not unlike Aluit totem poles (Fig. 10.23). The style of carving has been characterized as "baroque" and "oriental" because of its

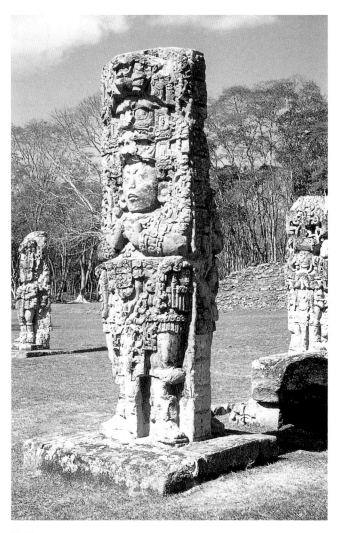

10.23 Stelae, Copán, Honduras, 600–800.

Upright stone objects have appeared in cultures around the world, the most obvious type in the West being the tombstone or grave-marker. The Maya erected them for various purposes, including the commemoration of significant events.

10.24 (above) Temple, Palenque, Usumacinta, Mexico, after 600.

This stepped pyramid is notable for its wide temple with five openings.

10.25 (below) Temple interior, Palenque, Usumacinta, Mexico, after 600.

Inside the temple is an inefficient corbeled vault. The Pre-Columbian cultures never discovered the true arch, or vault.

organic complexity, but was perhaps derived from of the lush jungle environment in which it was created.

At Palenque, similar elements appear but with distinctive adaptations: earthen platforms; stepped pyramids, sometimes with wide stairs; and temples, often with elongated plans. The Temple of the Inscriptions is unusual for having within it a tomb built contemporaneously with the pyramid and reached by a series of subterranean passages that were long ago sealed off. The burial chamber is twenty-three-feet long, twenty-three feet high, and about twelve feet tall. Within it resides a huge sarcophagus carved from a single block of stone and covered with a richly ornamented slab. A skeleton draped with jade jewelry was found inside (Figs. 10.24–10.25). Many façades and some interior walls of Palenque's temples were once covered with stucco, ornately modeled in low relief and painted, and their roofs are crowned by lattice-like roof combs.

UXMAL AND CHICHÉN-ITZÁ

At Uxmal in the Puuc region, the Maya laid out their ceremonial center as objects on raised platforms, several of them taking the form of quadrangles, freely distributed in space. The geometric ornamentation here is reminiscent of Mixtec work, while the contrasting organic ornament reaches its highest level of elaboration in the interlocking masks of the rain god Chac (Fig. 10.26).

Two of Uxmal's most distinctive buildings are the so-called Governor's Palace and Nunnery (Figs. 10.27–10.28). The Governor's Palace is a single, elongated rectangle in plan, some 328 feet long, while the Nunnery consists of four smaller such rectangles defining a quadrangle. The Governor's Palace is divided into three parts by inset bays

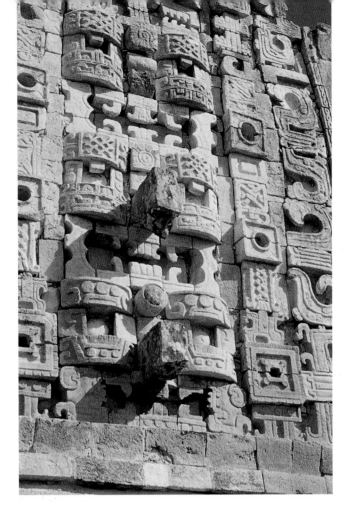

10.26 Nunnery masks, Uxmal, Yucatán, Mexico, ca. 900.

Here, the ornament is both highly geometric and highly organic, the latter reflecting the Puuc style developed in northwest Yucatán. While the individual stones are modular, the images, dominated by the nose piece of the rain god Chac, are boldly sculpted.

10.27 Governor's Palace, Uxmal, ca. 900.

This building has a three-part composition, with a dominant central mass separated from smaller masses to each side by a setback, or recessed strip. This composition is comparable to the schemes developed by celebrated sixteenth-century Italian architect Andrea Palladio for his villas.

with corbeled vaults, making for a five-part composition. On the interior, some twenty rooms of various sizes are covered with corbeled vaults. At their lower levels, both buildings display large areas of mural wall surface and windows with recessed frames. In the frieze above, sculptors at the Governor's Palace combined orthogonal and diagonal geometries with multiple Chac masks. At the Nunnery, stunted columns appear on the north side, supporting a frieze similar to that at the Governor's Palace. Around the perimeter and inside the quadrangle, the frieze is alternately aggressively geometric and organic, with Chac-mask compositions above some openings and projecting dramatically at corners.

Chichén-Itzá, in southern Campeche at the delta of the Usumacinta and Grijalva rivers, is a Maya site that combines native elements of the Putún culture with those of Toltec invaders. The Putún, who were merchant seafarers in control of the ocean trade routes around the Yucatán, were called Itzá in that area. In around 900 they conquered new lands, including Chichén, hence the name of the Chichén-Itzá site. By the eleventh or twelfth century, the city was controlled by the Toltecs.

The most notable buildings here are the so-called Caracol (Fig. 10.29), Castillo, and the Temple of the Warriors. Located to the south of the central section of the city and used as an astronomical observatory, the Caracol, meaning "snail," is unusual in Maya architecture for its circular-plan tower. It is ornamented with Maya masks of

10.28 Nunnery, Uxmal, ca. 900.

The ornamentation of this tablero can be compared to the frieze of the classical Greek or Roman temple. Here, however, the effect is created not by large panels but by many small geometric units that interlock.

10.29 The Caracol, or Observatory, Chichén-Itzá, Yucatán, after 900.

This unusual structure displays not only the Maya-inspired masks for the rain god Chac, but also depictions of the plumed serpent brought south by Toltec invaders.

Chac but also with elements brought here by the Toltecs: images of the plumed serpent and heads of Toltec warriors. Inside the Caracol's central cylinder, a series of openings made possible specific observations of the planets and the stars. The Castillo, or Temple of Kulkulkán, is equally distinctive, a pyramid with stairways leading up each of its four sides. This configuration is explained by its location inside a colonnaded plaza; it is an architectural object placed within an urban space, making Chichén-Itzá comparable in its spatial conception to Monte Albán. The Castillo's form may also have cosmological symbolism, as each stair has ninety-one risers, making a total of 364 in all. If one adds the base on which the pyramid sits, the total becomes 365 or the number of days in the Maya year. Furthermore, a plumed serpent at the base casts a shadow across the stair at an equinox or solstice. Standing east of the Castillo and overlooking the plaza is the Temple of the Warriors, which bears a striking resemblance to the pyramid complex at Tula, both in its planning and execution. Here, finely carved ranks and files of columns flank two sides of the pyramid, as densely placed as the columns in an Egyptian **hypostyle hall**. The carving includes eagles and jaguars devouring human hearts, plumed serpents, and Toltec warriors.

THE TOLTECS IN THE VALLEY OF MEXICO

In around 900, the warlike Toltecs from the north of Mexico settled in the Valley of Mexico, at a time when the culture of Teotihuacán was in decline, and eventually continued south to interact with the Maya. From among the Toltecs sprang the myth of Quetzalcóatl, the plumed serpent, who, they believed, set out on a journey to the east,

promising one day to return. Subsequently, this prophecy would have profound implications for the Aztecs.

The greatest Toltec city was Tula (Fig. 10.30) in the state of Hidalgo. Its ritual center includes the remains of a multi-columned palace and a pyramid supporting huge carved male warrior figures, once inside a temple but now

10.30 Temple-palace, Tula, Mexico, after 900.

In its ruined state, this building at Tula makes clear the Toltecs' dramatic use of the column. As much symbols of militancy as structural elements, the ranks and files capture the warlike nature of the culture that created them.

exposed. The most striking features of the complex are the two- and three-deep files of columns that define one end of the ceremonial plaza and continue around the west and south façades of the palace. Ranks and files of columns are repeated inside the palace, where three great rooms, once roofed except for central openings, stand side by side.

On the north side of the pyramid, portions of talud and tablero motifs remain. On its other three sides, its talud-like stepped layers have only individual projecting stones as shadow-casting ornamentation. In this Toltec interpretation of the decorative form, a plain talud supports a two-tiered tablero, its upper levels stepped back, that serves as a frieze displaying images of coyotes, jaguars, eagles devouring human hearts, and effigies of gods. On both flanks and the rear, a so-called serpent wall once enclosed the pyramid and was crowned by seashell-shaped symbols of Quetzalcóatl.

THE AZTECS AT TENOCHTITLÁN

The sun-worshiping Aztecs arrived in the Valley of Mexico in the thirteenth century and proceeded to assemble a large military and economic empire there. Their rituals included the gruesome practice of cutting human hearts from living victims, using knives made of obsidian, and placing the still-beating hearts on an altar where their blood, the Aztecs believed, served to guarantee the sun's continued motion across the sky. While requiring adjacent tribes to provide captives for these sacrifices, they did not subjugate or exercise civil control over them; still, this practice contributed to the Aztecs' demise when the Spanish arrived, as their neighbors were eager to overthrow them.

Legend held that their capital of Tenochtitlán (Fig. 10.31), the remains of which lie beneath modern-day Mexico City, had been identified to the Aztecs through the sighting of an eagle grasping a snake while perched on a prickly pear or *tenochtli*. By the time of the Spanish conquest in 1519, Tenochtitlán had a population of some 200,000 people, and the Aztec Empire extended from northern Mexico as far as present-day Guatemala and El Salvador.

Tenochtitlán was established on a series of small islands. The Aztecs filled in earth among them to produce a unified setting which, ironically, dazzled their Spanish conquerors. They constructed four long causeways that divided the city into quarters, each with its own neighborhoods, shrines, and administration buildings. In the center, they laid out a great ritual plaza and built the by-now-requisite platforms, pyramids, ball courts, and temples, once again using the talud and tablero as their basic ordering forms. The centerpiece of this architectural ensemble was the macabre skull rack displaying the heads of sacrificial victims.

Unfortunately, the Spanish conquerors destroyed virtually all Aztec architecture, thus leaving us with only

10.31 Plan of Tenochtitlán, location of present-day Mexico City, Mexico, after 900.

Focused on the skull-rack at its center, the orthogonal layout makes use of the same platform and pyramid types seen centuries earlier at nearby Teotihuacán. What set this city apart and what first amazed Spanish explorers was its dramatic location at the center of a lake. The lake has long since disappeared, as have the remains of Tenochtitlán beneath the modern-day city.

archaeological evidence, such as modest pieces of sculpture, as a guide to its former character. Among the remaining carved-stone objects is a statue of the earth goddess Coatlicue. With a head of two coiled snakes, a skirt of writhing serpents, a belt buckle consisting of a human skull, and a necklace of human hearts, Coatlicue's bizarre appearance attests both to the Aztecs' cruelty and their profound skill in carving stone.

The Aztec practice of taking large numbers of captives from nearby tribes for ritual sacrifice made them susceptible to civil uprisings. When the conquistador Hernán Cortés appeared with his small army, the Aztecs believed him to be Quetzalcóatl returned from his journey which, in turn, caused their king, Moctezuma, to become submissive. Together with rebellious local tribes, the Spanish forces quickly conquered the Aztec Empire, bringing an end to Pre-Columbian Mexico.

THE INCAS IN THE ANDES

In Pre-Columbian Peru, the Chimú Empire unified settlements in coastal river valleys in what was otherwise an arid land. In the Moche Valley, the indigenous people erected adobe pyramids, the largest being the Pyramid of the Sun.

In the principal Chimú city of Chan Chan, the inhabitants organized their urban settlement of some 50,000 people by arranging multi-celled, linear, adobe-brick structures around rectangular courtyards. The city had orthogonal streets, two large plazas, pyramids, reservoirs, gardens, and cemeteries. The Chimú Empire fell to the Incas in about 1465–75.

No culture in the Pre-Columbian Americas occupied an environment as dramatic as that of the Incas. A militaristic and intensely socially stratified people, they organized the precipitous terrain of the Andes by terracing the rugged mountainsides and by providing sophisticated irrigation systems for agriculture. The Incas eventually controlled an area stretching some 2500 miles throughout much of modern-day Columbia, Ecuador, Peru, and Bolivia; their greatest era of empire-building was 1438–1532, only a short time before the appearance of Francisco Pizarro and the Spanish conquest. All Inca land was held in common. While they had no written language, they kept numerical records using knotted cords. Their knowledge of medicine and surgery was highly developed, and included the practice of cutting circular openings in human skulls, perhaps to relieve internal pressure. They domesticated the alpaca and llama, and grew a wide variety of crops, from maize to sweet potatoes and tomatoes to peanuts, and even cotton from which they wove cloth. They built extensive road systems and suspension bridges, and formidable stone fortresses. No other contemporary culture in the western hemisphere was so skilled at fashioning and laying Cyclopean stone masonry.

The Incas expanded the Chimú city of Cuzco, located between the Huatanay and Tullumayo rivers. While the construction does not exceed one story in height, the site is impressive for the rigor of its linear stone buildings grouped around quadrangles and for the great fortress of Saqsaywaman, where enormous stone blocks were exquisitely set without the use of mortar (Fig. 10.32).

Perhaps even more impressive is the dramatic development at Machu Picchu (page 274), which is located at a height of 3000 feet in the Andes. The site includes 200 or so houses that could have sheltered only about 1000 persons, in a climate that can only be described as inhospitable other than in the summer months. Consequently, its exact purpose—military outpost, ritual center, or something else—remains uncertain. What can be said conclusively is that the Incas transformed the saddle of land they chose for their settlement into a cohesive ensemble of agricultural terraces, distinctive house types, meeting halls, and carefully defined plazas. The houses are notable for their stone construction, sometimes battered walls, trapezoidal openings, and distinctive plans, many of which are devoid of masonry or have only a pier or piers on one long side. Their light wooden roof framing and covering of thatch have long since disappeared, leaving their isolated, tall gables to form the dramatic Machu Picchu skyline.

10.32 Cyclopean masonry, Cuzco, Peru, ca. 1500.

In Inca stonework, each stone was dressed, then placed adjacent to its neighbors without the use of mortar. Masons then marked the outline of the new stone on those already in place, removed it, and pounded out a new profile to receive it. This process was repeated again and again until a tight fit was achieved.

Pizarro, who had been among Cortés's men at Tenochtitlán, returned to the New World with only 180 troops in search of more riches. Arriving in Peru, he found the Inca Empire recovering from civil war and two brothers, sons of the previous Inca emperor, vying for power. Pizarro captured one brother just after he had ordered the murder of his sibling. The Inca political system was so hierarchical that he was able to take complete control and ransack the culture. It was a sad end to an unfortunate period of Spanish-led cultural destabilization.

If we look back over the contents of this chapter, the similarity of form types preferred by the mound and stepped-pyramid builders of Mexico and Central and South America to the pyramids and ziggurats of Egypt and Mesopotamia becomes obvious. This cross-cultural condition reveals much about mankind's innate design inclinations: that civilizations so far removed could reach such similar, dramatic conclusions reflects a common response to gravity through experimentation with the angle of repose, to recognition of the power of the horizon, and to the belief that the gods resided in high-up places. Likewise, anyone who has spent a night in a tent can feel an affinity for the tribes that built tipis, and for those impressed by the accomplishments at Mesa Verde, a visit to the Taos Pueblo near Santa Fe affords an opportunity to see such housing still in use. Finally, ornament employed by Frank Lloyd Wright on buildings such as Unity Temple (see Fig. 15.14) and by the Art Deco designers of the 1920s and '30s (see Figs. 15.37–15.43) was inspired by the stonework of Pre-Columbian cultures. In a time of globalization, an awareness of such similarities helps us to appreciate Native American traditions as well as those imported from Europe, Africa, Asia, and elsewhere, and the connectedness of them all.

CHAPTER 11

RENAISSANCE ARCHITECTURE

Christopher Columbus arrived in the West Indies in 1492 at a time when European architecture was undergoing a dramatic change from the Gothic of the late Middle Ages to the Renaissance. To understand this change, we must examine the design culture then developing in Italy.

The chapter on the Gothic contained little discussion of buildings in Italy. Here, Romanesque churches were never completely purged of their classical elements. Monumental Gothic religious architecture remained something of an interloper in the one-time center of the Roman Empire, where the vestiges of a grand classical past loomed portentously throughout the Middle Ages.

Still, the fabric of most Italian cities, particularly the everyday residential buildings, was woven in the eleventh through fourteenth centuries. In such inland centers as Florence and Siena, these buildings were rather plain: heavy masonry blocks punctured with arched openings and sometimes provided with shady **loggias** or porches; but from this stock would develop the grand fifteenth-century palazzo type. In seafaring Venice, residential buildings took on a more exotic character as designers enthusiastically embraced Gothic ornament and structural devices such as the pointed arch and manipulated them with a vigor expressive of Venetian connections to Constantinople and the Orient.

Likewise, medieval governmental buildings anchored the civic cores of Italian cities and caused to form around them the open spaces or piazzas that to this day speak the very language of urbanism. It was upon this most solid of medieval foundations that Renaissance architects would base their radical proposals for a new kind of architecture.

While both France and England were unified monarchies by the end of the Middle Ages, Italy remained an assemblage of fractious but vigorous city-states and fiefdoms. Trade flourished as a result of Italy's position between Byzantium and a western Europe undergoing an urban revival. Aggressive merchants exported luxury goods and organized textile industries. Civic life in the principal Italian city-states became dominated by families whose wealth arose not from inherited landholdings but from mercantile profits.

Nowhere was this change more dramatic than in Florence, the city regarded as the birthplace of the Renaissance. Here, the newly wealthy wool merchants and bankers sought prestige and status through their patronage of arts and letters, and artists and architects displayed this support through their development of new forms in painting, sculpture, and architecture.

The spirit of these revolutionary works was derived from the new world view of humanism, which celebrated rationality and mankind's ability to make and act upon empirical observations of the physical world. Humanist scholars and artists recovered classical Greek and Roman texts and aspired to create a modern world rivaling that of the ancients.

Renaissance architects derived whole-number ratios, such as 1:1, 1:2, 2:3, and 3:4, from the musical consonances discovered by Pythagoras, and believed that the innate harmony of these ratios would be impressed upon anyone experiencing spaces determined by them. Humanists were convinced that God's cosmic order could be expressed on earth through such mathematical proportions, which were inevitably related to the mensuration of the human body. In this context, the circular church represented the most perfect form, absolute, immutable, echoing celestial harmony.

Renaissance architects continued the interest in geometry that had so strongly influenced medieval architecture.

Filippo Brunelleschi, Pazzi Chapel, S. Croce, Florence, 1430–33.

Brunelleschi chose as his precedent for this façade the Roman triumphal arch. Here, rather than massive, as in ancient examples, it appears somewhat brittle. The shed roof above and the drum with conical roof and cupola were not part of Brunelleschi's design.

Rather than using the complex, geometric transformations of medieval master masons, Renaissance architects favored simple forms such as the square and circle. They made drawings of the human figure inscribed within the basic outline of the circle and square, thereby demonstrating that human proportions reflected divine ratios. Of these drawings, the most famous is the *Vitruvian Man* (Fig. 11.1) in the notebooks of Leonardo da Vinci, which, like the other drawings, illustrates the precedent established by Vitruvius in the third book of his *De architectura*. Vitruvius wrote:

For if a man be placed flat on his back, with his hands and feet extended, and a pair of compasses centered at his navel, the fingers and toes of his two hands and feet will touch the circumference of a circle described therefrom. And, just as the human body yields a circular outline, so too a square figure may be found from it. For if we measure the distance from the soles of the feet to the top of the head, and then apply that measure to the outstretched arms, the breadth will be found to be the same as the height, as in the case of plane surfaces which are perfectly square.

11.1 Leonardo da Vinci, *Vitruvian Man*, ca. 1485.

Probably no image has been more frequently used than this one to convey the spirit of the Renaissance. Here, Leonardo has drawn the so-called *Vitruvian Man* to illustrate the era's belief that the human body was proportioned according to divine ratios.

FILIPPO BRUNELLESCHI

The son of a notary, Filippo Brunelleschi (1377–1446) was trained as a goldsmith. In 1400 he entered the competition to design a new set of bronze doors for the baptistery of Florence Cathedral. His main competitor, and the man who won, was Lorenzo Ghiberti (1378–1455). Discouraged by his loss, Brunelleschi set off for Rome with his friend, the sculptor Donatello (1386–1466), and his subsequent career as an architect owed much to the extended visit he paid to the Eternal City and the observations he made there.

During his stay in Rome, and perhaps as a means to record more accurately what he saw, Brunelleschi codified the principles of geometrically accurate linear perspective, making possible the exact representation of a three-dimensional object on a two-dimensional surface. Various artists in Italy had struggled with the question of how best to depict spatial relationships in their paintings, but their solutions fell short of the precision achieved by Brunelleschi. In making careful drawings of such repetitive elements as the arches of aqueducts, he realized that parallel horizontal lines converge at a point on the horizon and that elements of like size diminish proportionally into the distance. His development of this new system of spatial representation had a profound effect on art, architecture, and civic design during and after the Renaissance.

Brunelleschi must have assisted his friend, the painter Masaccio (1401–1428), in the application of linear perspective to a fresco painting, *The Trinity* (1427–28) at S. Maria Novella in Florence (Fig. 11.2). It depicts God the Father standing on a large sarcophagus supporting the crucified Christ. Below are Mary and St. John with two kneeling donors. The holy figures are framed by modified Ionic columns supporting an arch that creates a coffered, barrel-vaulted chapel, accurately projected according to the rules of perspective. Masaccio, it would seem, was illustrating Brunelleschi's momentous discovery.

FLORENCE CATHEDRAL

By 1407 Brunelleschi was again living in Florence. In that year the directors of the cathedral works consulted distinguished engineers and architects from France, Spain, England, and Germany for advice on the cathedral's dome. The cathedral was begun in 1292 to the designs of Arnolfo di Cambio and continued by Francesco Talenti. It was always intended to have a dome exceeding the Romanesque cathedral of Pisa in size. Arnolfo and Talenti produced a building with some obvious Gothic characteristics such as pointed arches and ribbed vaults atop piers. Their work proceeded to the level of the octagonal drum, from which a dome reaching nearly 150 feet on the diagonal was to spring, but without anyone having a firm idea about how to achieve such a huge span. The outward

11.2 Masaccio, *The Trinity*, S. Maria Novella, Florence, 1427–28.

Brunelleschi first demonstrated his invention of mechanical perspective by displaying his painted view of the Florence Cathedral baptistery. He obviously showed the artist Masaccio his method, and Masaccio used it to create this illusion of a coffered barrel vault housing the crucified Christ.

thrust of such a dome, built using conventional techniques, without internal tension members, and unbraced by extensive buttresses, would have burst the drum. In addition, the scale of centering required to support the masonry while construction was in progress vastly exceeded anything attempted in the medieval period. This was the situation that Brunelleschi inherited when the works directors eventually turned to him (Fig. 11.3).

Brunelleschi drew upon his knowledge of ancient Roman construction as well as lingering Gothic traditions to produce an innovative synthesis (Fig. 11.4). In order to reduce the outward thrust, he employed a Gothic pointed-arch cross section instead of a semicircular one. In order to reduce the dead load, he created a double shell of radial and concentric ribs, a strategy traceable both to ancient monuments such as the Pantheon and to Florentine medieval work such as the nearby cathedral baptistery. In order to reduce the amount of temporary construction, he devised portable centering that supported concentric courses of masonry until they were completed as stable compression rings, and he used this rising masonry to support scaffolding which in turn supported more centering.

The cleverness of Brunelleschi's system of ribs is worthy of more detailed description. He devised as his principal structural members sandstone ribs rising from each of the eight corners of the octagonal drum. At the springing of the dome, they have a cross section of eleven by seven feet, and they taper upward to an apex ring beneath the cupola. Between each of these corner ribs, Brunelleschi placed a pair of intermediate ribs, making a total of twenty-four vertical ribs. To hold the inner and outer shells apart, he inserted five horizontal rings of sandstone, connected by tin-plated iron clamps: he had observed such imbedded metal fastenings in the ruins of Roman construction. Finally, near the base of the dome, he placed twenty-four chestnut timbers, each one foot square and twenty-three feet long, banded together with straps and bolts into a continuous wooden tension ring that resists the outward thrust of the dome. However, according to modern structural analysis, the action of this ring is negligible.

No less interesting than the dome are the various machines that Brunelleschi designed to facilitate construction. Many practical problems had to be resolved on a job of this magnitude, and Brunelleschi proved adept at inventing the devices necessary to tackle them. A hoist with a worm wheel and endless screw and safety brake was required to lift the large blocks of stone up to the working platform. Brunelleschi designed a hoist

11.3 Filippo Brunelleschi, Florence Cathedral, 1242 and later.

11.3 Filippo Brunelleschi, Florence Cathedral, 1242 and later.

The body of Florence Cathedral was designed by Arnolfo di Cambio and Francesco Talenti, but the dome was only completed by Brunelleschi in the fifteenth century. The campanile, or belltower, was begun by the painter Giotto in the fourteenth century.

11.4 Filippo Brunelleschi, Florence Cathedral section, 1242 and later.

The pointed-arch profile of the Florence Cathedral dome reveals its medieval inspiration. However, internal construction techniques such as a double shell resulted from Brunelleschi's close observation of ancient Roman building methods.

0   25 m
0   75 ft

with an oak gear that wore out quickly, which he replaced with a gear cast in bronze by Ghiberti from a mold made by Donatello. The rope required to raise the stones had a diameter of 2½ inches; 600 feet of it weighed half a ton. Brunelleschi found ropemakers in Pisa who could manufacture the required length, and he devised block-and-tackle pulleys that allowed the lifting of stones weighing up to nineteen tons. Brunelleschi also used efficient management procedures to expedite the work. For example, a canteen provided lunch for crews on the scaffolding so that no time was lost descending from and ascending back to the high platform for midday meals.

Brunelleschi was involved with the cathedral work from at least 1404. The exedras and drum of the dome were not completed until 1418, and he must have contributed to their design. He had demonstrated his proposal and novel construction procedure for the dome itself by having a one-twelfth-scale model constructed in masonry beside the cathedral. It was this that had led to his being awarded the dome commission in 1420, even though he had no completed buildings to his credit at this time. Ghiberti was appointed co-architect, for his proficiency in sculpture was, to Renaissance thinking, proof of competency in all the arts. As construction proceeded, however, it became obvious that Brunelleschi alone was capable of directing the work, and Ghiberti was eventually eased out of his heavy architectural responsibilities. Brunelleschi's success was summed up by Giorgio Vasari, the painter, architect, and biographer of Renaissance artists: "The world having for so long been without artists of lofty soul or inspired talent, heaven ordained that it should receive from the hand of Filippo the greatest, the tallest, and the finest edifice of ancient or modern times."

OTHER FLORENTINE BUILDINGS

Work on the cathedral dome continued throughout Brunelleschi's lifetime; the cupola was completed after his death. Concurrently, he was able to build several smaller projects in which the ideals of Roman architecture could be expressed more directly than in the cathedral dome. In these commissions, which had fewer troublesome technical problems, Brunelleschi was able to express outwardly his empathy for ancient Rome. The earliest, the Ospedale degli Innocenti or Foundling Hospital (Fig. 11.5), is often considered the first building of the Renaissance. Designed in 1419 and built from 1421 to 1444, it continues the link with classical tradition that had been maintained in Florence through such proto-Renaissance buildings as the Romanesque S. Miniato al Monte and the cathedral's baptistery. The Foundling Hospital has a continuous arcade, carried on Corinthian columns across its main façade and around an internal courtyard, that is comparable to the ground-floor arcading in marble veneer that adorns both S. Miniato and the baptistery; these Romanesque elements were ultimately based on Roman architecture. At the hospital, the arcading is three-dimensional, creating a loggia with domed vaults in each bay. Semicircular arches span the width of the loggia, from the freestanding columns with abaci to corbeled brackets on the opposite wall.

A similar columnar arcade is found in the aisles of the Latin-cross church of S. Lorenzo (Figs. 11.6–11.7), begun in 1421. Here, Brunelleschi defined each bay with arches that spring from columns of the nave arcade to pilasters set between side-aisle chapels. This configuration achieves a more balanced effect than the wall corbels at the hospital, yet Brunelleschi found an even more satisfactory resolution in his design for the church of S. Spirito (Fig. 11.8), begun as late as 1445, where he attached half-columns to the wall in place of the pilasters he had used at S. Lorenzo. This may seem an undue emphasis on Brunelleschi's part on admittedly minor architectural details, but such attention to each element and to the relationship of all elements to one another characterizes the proper manipulation of the classical language of architecture.

11.5 Filippo Brunelleschi, Foundling Hospital, Florence, 1419–44.

Brunelleschi placed this arched loggia in front of the cloisters, dormitories, and service spaces of his Foundling Hospital. Eventually the arches were carried around most of the Piazza S. Annunziata, giving it a built regularity expressive of Renaissance design theory.

11.6 Filippo Brunelleschi and Michelangelo Buonarroti, plan of S. Lorenzo, begun 1421.

The church of San Lorenzo is part of a larger monastic complex that includes chapels and the Laurentian Library by Michelangelo. The major spaces are organized around a square cloister that corresponds to the modular regularity of Brunelleschi's church plan.

11.7 Filippo Brunelleschi, S. Lorenzo interior, Florence, begun 1421.

The nave and aisle configuration of S. Lorenzo is no different than that of Romanesque and Gothic churches in Florence. Brunelleschi simply substituted classical elements for medieval ones: Corinthian columns and an arcade as at the Foundling Hospital. His design innovation is the modular regularity in plan, visible here in the floor pattern.

In both S. Lorenzo and S. Spirito, Brunelleschi sought to accommodate the traditional practical requirements of his clients within a unifying system of mathematical proportions. At both churches, the square bay of the aisles defines a module that is repeated throughout. Four modules form a double bay of the nave, and this larger square is repeated four times down the nave and then once for each transept, the crossing, and the choir. Equally carefully proportioned Roman elements such as the semicircular arch, Corinthian columns, and coffering impart a classical monumentality to the interiors of both churches.

Brunelleschi made prominent use of simple numerical ratios in three of his smaller commissions. For the church of S. Lorenzo, he erected the Old Sacristy (1421–28) in a corner of the north transept. The floor, walls, and pendentives are contained in a cube, capped by a hemispherical dome with an oculus. Pilasters, an entablature, and arches of gray *pietra serena*, a local stone much favored for architectural detail, are set against the white plaster of the walls, giving a linear definition to the interior. The thinness of the pilaster strips as they turn the corner and the isolated, undersized brackets "supporting" the entablature have been pointed to as signs of Brunelleschi's "uncertainty" in manipulating the still-new classical language.

Slightly larger than the Old Sacristy is the Pazzi Chapel (1430–33), erected off the major cloister at the monastery

11.8 Filippo Brunelleschi, Plan of S. Spirito, Florence, begun 1445.

Brunelleschi perfected his system of modular planning at S. Spirito. Perhaps he intended for the building's exterior perimeter to have a continuous series of projecting semicircular chapels. If so, these proved objectionable to his patrons as the walls were infilled to be externally flat.

11.9 Filippo Brunelleschi, Plan and elevation reconstruction of the Pazzi Chapel, Florence, 1430–33.

Here is one possible reconstruction of Brunelleschi's dome. If it is accurate, it displays on the exterior the perfect circular form on which the plan was based.

11.10 Filippo Brunelleschi, Pazzi Chapel interior, Florence, 1430–33.

As with the Florence Cathedral dome, Brunelleschi looked here to local traditions for design motifs, in this case the gray *pietra serena* stone used for the framing elements: pilasters, entablatures, and arches. New is the classical language and the geometry based upon squares, half-squares, semicircles, and circles—comparable to the squares and circles bounding Leonardo's *Vitruvian Man*.

of S. Croce. While it is not certain what Brunelleschi intended the façade (page 294 and Fig. 11.9) to be like above the Corinthian columns that support a series of square panels flanking a central arch, the interior is entirely his (Fig. 11.10). The space is a carefully conceived but occasionally awkward essay based on numerical ratios, the classical language, and local building practices. The plan is generated by placing the circle of a dome above a square divided into three bays, and expanded one barrel-vaulted bay to each side and one domed square bay in depth. All these bays are defined by Corinthian pilasters supporting a continuous entablature with arches above, and all delineated in gray *pietra serena* against white plaster.

Renaissance architects considered the central plan to be an ideal type. Brunelleschi's design for S. Maria degli Angeli (1434–37) was the first such structure of the fifteenth century (Fig. 11.11). While it was left unfinished at Brunelleschi's death and subsequently badly reconstructed and altered in the 1930s, engravings probably based upon the original drawings survive to indicate Brunelleschi's intentions. The church's plan and massing were to be Roman, with a domed octagon expanded by eight lozenge-shaped chapels. Piers composed of clustered pilasters provided support for the dome, and the overall spatial effect would have suggested that the chapels were carved from the solid exterior wall. Had the dome been constructed, its monolithic single shell would have been true to Roman prototypes.

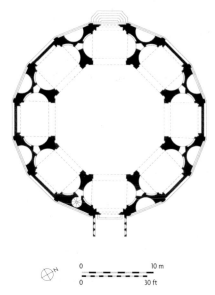

11.11 Filippo Brunelleschi, Plan of S. Maria degli Angeli, Florence, begun ca. 1436.

Brunelleschi had observed the circular temples of antiquity. His proposal for a pure, central plan was the first of the Renaissance, but it was a theme that would be explored by almost every Renaissance designer thereafter.

MICHELOZZO BARTOLOMEO AND THE PALAZZO MEDICI

Michelozzo Bartolomeo (1396–1472), a student of Brunelleschi, worked not only in Florence but also in other northern Italian cities. Although not so celebrated a designer as Brunelleschi, Michelozzo was a capable architect and was awarded several commissions by those archetypal Renaissance patrons, the Medici. Most noteworthy of these was the Palazzo Medici (Fig. 11.12) in Florence, begun in 1444 after an earlier design by Brunelleschi was rejected as being too ostentatious. The client, Cosimo de' Medici, did not want to arouse feelings of envy among other important families in the city. Michelozzo's design reflects his awareness of traditional Florentine domestic buildings and his admiration for the Foundling Hospital arcade and its traditional Florentine courtyard plan. The

11.13 Michelozzo Bartolomeo, Plan of the courtyard of the Medici Palace, Florence, 1444.

The fortified quality of the Medici Palace's exterior walls belies the delicate openness of the arcaded cortile or courtyard. It is as though Michelozzo had taken the external arcade used by his friend Brunelleschi at the Foundling Hospital and made it an internal element reflecting humanist preoccupations.

11.12 Michelozzo Bartolomeo, Medici Palace, Florence, 1444.

The palazzo form of this urban house built by the Medici family can be added to the temple, stoa, and basilica as fundamental form types that have been repeated and reinterpreted down to the present day. The Medici intended its fortified quality to afford them protection in a Florence accustomed to political intrigue.

palazzo's square plan includes such a central courtyard serving as a circulation core for perimeter rooms that open to one another *en suite*, that is, without a continuous corridor (Fig. 11.13). Michelozzo made use of **rustication**, stone blocks with deeply recessed chamfered joints. He arranged the street elevation in three tiers of graduated textures, beginning with rock-faced stone at the street level and concluding with smooth ashlar at the third level below a ten-foot-high crowning cornice with **modillions**, **egg-and-dart moldings**, and a **dentil** course, the first such cornice since ancient Roman times. The cornice projects out eight feet from the building, supported by acanthus-leaf modillions or large brackets, and it combines with the string course between the floor levels to create a strong horizontal emphasis, even though the façade is eighty-three feet high.

The ground floor originally had three open arches along the street, the central one giving access to the courtyard and rooms serving the Medici banking business. From the courtyard a staircase led to the major family rooms on the second floor, or **piano nobile**. Deep shadows in the courtyard make the palazzo's core cool and quiet, and the upper-level galleries provide access to and shade for the individual rooms. Typical Romanesque windows with circular heads are used throughout. While without radical innovations, the Medici Palace reflects Michelozzo's connection to Renaissance circles through its symmetry, inclusion of classical elements, and careful use of mathematical proportions.

LEON BATTISTA ALBERTI

In contrast to the pragmatic and technically skilled Brunelleschi, Leon Battista Alberti (1404–1472) was a classical theorist who saw architecture as a way to address societal order. The Renaissance architect, in Alberti's mind, was to be a universalist, an intellectual, a man of genius, and a consort of those in positions of power and authority. In his autobiography (written in the third-person), he offered this description of himself:

> [He was] assiduous in science, and skilled in dealing
> with arms, horse, and musical instruments; as well as
> the pursuit of letters and the fine arts, he was devoted to
> the knowledge of the most strange and difficult things.
> His genius was so versatile that you might almost judge
> all the fine arts to be his. He played ball, hurled the
> javelin, ran, leapt, wrestled, and above all delighted in
> the steep ascent of mountains. He could leap over the
> shoulders of men and had almost no equal among those
> hurling the lance. . . . He was considered an expert
> among the leading musicians.

Alberti was not being immodest: an accomplished scholar from an exiled Florentine family, he became one of the most influential thinkers of his time. His education at the universities of Padua and Bologna included mathematics, music, Greek, Latin, philosophy, and Roman law.

On completing these studies, Alberti entered the Papal Chancery in Rome as secretary to the chancellor. Living in Rome provided him with many opportunities to meet artists visiting the monuments of antiquity, and his travels gave him the chance to observe the works of artists in many cities throughout northern Italy. Because Alberti searched the writings of Plato, Aristotle, Plutarch, and Pliny the Elder for references to the arts and carefully studied the collections of antique sculpture that were being assembled by patrons of the arts, his writings reveal a mixture of scholarly research and informed observations.

WRITINGS

The manuscript of Alberti's *Della pittura*, or *On Painting*, completed in 1435, documents Brunelleschi's theories of perspective. It was dedicated to the five young artists of Florence whom Alberti most admired and who came closest to creating a personal style that reflected the art of ancient Rome. We now regard these five—Brunelleschi, the sculptor Ghiberti, the painter Masaccio, and the sculptors Donatello and Luca della Robbia (1399–1482)—as among the founders of the Renaissance.

Alberti's interest in architecture was probably first aroused when he came across the already well-known manuscript *De architectura libri decem*, Vitruvius's *The Ten Books on Architecture*. While there may have been many such treatises, it is the only one to have survived. Vitruvius was a mediocre writer at best, and owing to the uncertainty of his language, his text is often ambiguous; nevertheless, as an authentic book from Roman times, the work was greatly respected by Renaissance architects. In response to the obscurities in Vitruvius's text, in order to discuss principles of Roman buildings designed after the time of Vitruvius, and in order to argue that architects should be highly educated humanists, like himself, Alberti began writing his own treatise, modeled on the antique text and, like it, organized into ten books or chapters. He worked on his book, which he titled *De re aedificatoria*, or *On Building*, from the early 1440s until his death, completing a first version by 1452, which was circulated in manuscript form. The text as we know it was published posthumously in Florence in 1485. As the first architectural treatise of the Renaissance, it is important for cataloging the features and proportions of the orders of antiquity and establishing a theory of harmonious proportions to be observed in buildings. Alberti adapted proportional systems expounded by Vitruvius because he believed that they should unify plans, elevations, and sections of a building. For example, church plans could be centralized, using a circle, hexagon, octagon, decagon, dodecagon, or based on a square, such as a square-and-a-half, square-and-a-third, or double square. Whatever the plan selected, the three-dimensional realization was to be

Alberti's palazzo proposal owes more to ancient models than Michelozzo's Medici Palace. Superimposed orders like those used at the Colosseum articulate the three floors, and diamond shapes at the base of the first floor mimic Roman *opus-reticulatum* masonry.

derived from it. Furthermore, to assume their proper symbolic role in the cityscape, churches needed to be centrally located, isolated from other structures so that they could be seen from all sides, and raised above ground level on a plinth or base.

Although Alberti was concerned with the theoretical and esthetic implications of proportional systems, he was equally attentive to the practical aspects of architecture and city planning. Vitruvius had written of public health considerations in the siting of towns, and Alberti extended this approach to include other factors such as the purity of the water supply and the distribution of land uses. He suggested that arrangements should respond to both convenience and hygiene. He recommended that facilities for noxious trades, such as dyeworks and slaughterhouses, be positioned away from residential districts, and he studied the location of recreational facilities and the dimensioning of streets and open spaces with respect to the heights of buildings. He proposed individual house plans with consideration for the needs and ordinary uses of the inhabitants. As kitchens are noisy, he proposed that they should be away from quiet parts of the house and yet near enough to the dining room. Bedrooms should face east toward the rising sun, and the parents' rooms should be near the children's quarters. Old people should have rooms without drafts, and guests should have rooms near the entrance to enable them and their friends to enter and leave without disturbing the whole household. A country house could be more elaborate in design than a town house, where restrained ornamentation could add to the unity of the streetscape. He even described the quality of basic building materials in a manner not too different from the style used in modern specifications. Sand, he said, should be clean and free of impurities, lime should be well slaked, and timber should be straight, well seasoned, and free of knots and checks.

THE PALAZZO RUCELLAI, FLORENCE

Some of this advice is reflected in Alberti's design for the façade of the Palazzo Rucellai in Florence (1446–51) (Fig. 11.14). To organize this façade, he applied superimposed Doric and Corinthian orders to demarcate the individual floors; this was the first use of the classical orders on a Renaissance domestic building. He raised the order of the ground floor on a high plinth scored into diamond shapes in imitation of Roman *opus reticulatum*, where diamond-shaped masonry units were used as formwork for concrete walls. Here, however, the subdivision serves only as a surface texture reflective of antique practices.

CHURCHES IN RIMINI AND MANTUA

Alberti's four other major commissions were ecclesiastical. Sigismondo Malatesta was his client for the modernization of the thirteenth-century church of S. Francesco in Rimini (Fig. 11.15), begun in 1450 but never completed. Malatesta was a consummate Renaissance despot as defined by the Florentine political theorist Machiavelli in his influential treatise *The Prince*. Alberti's wrapping of the existing medieval building with new walls is so thoroughly classical that the building is known to this day as the Tempio (Temple) Malatestiano.

Malatesta wished the structure to serve as a tomb for himself and his wife and for the scholars of his humanist court. For the sepulchers of the scholars, Alberti chose to subdivide the building's flanks using heavy round arches modeled on those of the Tomb of Theodoric (ca. 526) in nearby Ravenna. This composition inspired a series of

11.16 Leon Battista Alberti, S. Maria Novella, Florence, 1456–70.

Alberti's façade composition for this church became a prototype much reinterpreted by other Renaissance designers. Its two-story central bays capped by a pedimented temple-form conceal the gable-roofed nave of a basilican cross section, and the flanking volutes mask the shed roofs over the aisles.

11.15 Leon Battista Alberti, S. Francesco, Rimini, begun 1450.

Alberti never saw this church completed, but he certainly visited the site, modelling his façade on the nearby Arch of Augustus.

subsequent buildings including McKim, Mead, and White's late-nineteenth-century Boston Public Library (see Fig. 14.31). At the front façade of S. Francesco, Alberti superimposed a temple front over a triumphal-arch form, like the ancient Roman Arch of Augustus a few blocks away and proposed to place the tombs of Malatesta and his wife in the arched portals flanking the central entry. Alberti's on-site assistant, Matteo de' Pasti, updated the Gothic interior of the church but never constructed the huge Pantheon-like dome that Alberti envisioned.

The task of adapting classical details to the façade of a church with a basilican cross section was a compositional problem for Renaissance architects. Alberti's work on S. Maria Novella in Florence (ca. 1456–70) produced the first completed design for a church façade in the Renaissance, but in some respects it is an extension of eleventh-century Florentine traditions with its geometric panels of white and green marble (Fig. 11.16). Alberti was obliged to preserve some Gothic aspects of the existing church, particularly the pointed arches of the lower level and the

11.17 Leon Battista Alberti, S. Andrea, Mantua, 1472–94.

Here Alberti built upon his experience in Rimini to produce a confident synthesis of the temple and triumphal-arch forms. The two are effectively interlaced by the entablature of the Serliana that disappears behind the Corinthian columns of the temple front.

11.18 Leon Battista Alberti, Plan and section of S. Andrea, Mantua, 1472–94.

In contrast to Brunelleschi's S. Spirito and S. Lorenzo, S. Andrea has no internal files of nave columns. Rather, it is based upon the ancient Roman basilica. The chapel walls provide the buttressing necessary to resist the lateral thrust of the monumental barrel vault.

central rose window above. Rudolf Wittkower's analysis of Alberti's façade emphasizes the predominance of the square as a unit of composition. As at S. Francesco, Alberti attempted to unify the façade by linking lower aisle roofs to the pedimented higher nave with flanking scrolls, a solution that was much repeated throughout the Renaissance.

Farther north, in Mantua, Alberti worked for the Gonzaga family. Here he gave the church of S. Andrea (1472–94) an entrance portico based, like S. Francesco, on a temple front and triumphal arch, and he intended to extend this treatment to the east and west transepts (Fig. 11.17). The temple portion's order of Corinthian pilasters stands on pedestals; this order reappears on the interior, supporting the great barrel vault of the nave. A shorter Corinthian order supports the arch of the central portal and an entablature that disappears beneath the temple-front pilasters; it also reappears on the interior in the jambs of the barrel-vaulted chapels.

The church's plan (Fig. 11.18) is that of the ancient Roman Basilica of Constantine, with the transverse barrel

PIUS'S RESOLUTIONS

by Charles R. Mack

11A Bernardo Rossellino, Cathedral (left) and Palazzo Piccolomini (right), Piazza Pio II, Pienza, 1459–64.

Although respect for the visible presence of the ancient past was not universal during the Italian Renaissance's first century, there is abundant evidence for a renewed interest in the remains of classical Italy and for a desire to record and preserve its monuments. This preservationist impetus is nicely seen in the actions of Pope Pius II (ruled 1458–64, the humanist Aeneas Silvius Piccolomini). It is true, of course, that Pope Pius did have marble transported from the Colosseum to rebuild the steps leading up to St. Peter's and despoiled the Portico of Octavia for columns to be used in the new Benediction Loggia that he ordered built across the front of the same basilica. But Pius also issued a papal bull (probably the first official document in the history of the historic preservation movement) on April 28, 1462 forbidding the destruction of antiquities in the Roman region. That the document accorded the Pope the privilege of violating his own injunction is interesting and demonstrates two aspects of the Early Renaissance's attitude toward its antique heritage. It prohibited the unrestricted dismantling of Roman ruins by the lower classes, but it allowed the utilization of the surviving remnants of ancient glory in new campaigns of officially sponsored construction. The melding of the remains of pagan antiquity into the fabric of a reconstituted Christian Rome was typical of the age's attitude toward the past.

Curiously, the same Pope Pius, while still a cardinal in 1456, could criticize the title of Flavio Biondo's *Rome Restored* by complaining: "Even if all the forces of Europe were to unite, they could not restore Rome to its early form, for towns also have their end; the fallen ones cannot rise any more than the old can grow young." Perhaps the future pope was just expressing a momentary fatalism inherited from some ancient Etruscan forebear or was simply imitating the cyclical view of history found in the writings of Augustan Age Roman philosophers during the reign of Caesar Augustus (31 BCE–14 CE). In any case, the concept of rebirth was very much on the mind of the confident new pope Pius II only a few years later. It formed a conscious part of his plans for the refurbishing of the Vatican and was very much evident when he set about reforming his very own rustic birthplace of Corsignano, renamed Pienza in his honor (Fig. 11A). Pius must have recollected his earlier comments concerning the futility of attempting a Roman restoration when he visited his hometown in February of 1459. There he found both the companions of his youth and the community itself "bowed down with old age," but, instead of accepting the inevitable, that towns like people "also have their end," he determined upon a truly Renaissance course of action which led to an extensive reconstruction of the town, incorporating much of the classicizing vision he must have held for Papal Rome. Pienza exists today as the very model of the integrating spirit of Pope Pius's generation, a generation that adapted the vocabulary of ancient art and architecture to new, post-medieval circumstances.

vaults of the chapels and their bearing walls resisting the lateral thrust of the longitudinal barrel vault of the nave. It would serve as the pattern for many subsequent churches. The assemblage of classical elements on the interior presents the first Renaissance vision rivaling the monumentality of the interior spaces of such ancient Roman monuments as the basilicas and baths. Unfortunately, Alberti did not live to walk through his creation, as he died early in the construction process. (S. Andrea's choir and transepts cannot be positively attributed to Alberti. Its dome was added by Filippo Juvarra in the eighteenth century.)

S. Sebastiano (begun 1460), which stands not far away, was designed as a Greek-cross plan with a hexastyle pilastered temple front, the second and fifth pilasters having been omitted. Some have argued that Alberti intended to build steps the full width of the portico, as in the temples of antiquity. The central interior space is spanned by a groin vault, not a dome as one might expect; the stubby arms of the Greek cross are barrel-vaulted. In its present incomplete state, the church does not clearly reflect its designer's intentions.

THE IDEAL CITY

Alberti's goal of a centrally planned temple was also represented in Perugino's fresco *Giving of the Keys to St. Peter* (1481–82), Raphael's *The Marriage of the Virgin* (1504), and the *cassone* panels (the sides of a wooden chest) in the Palazzo Ducale in Urbino, painted perhaps by Luciano Laurana. Each of these art works depicts the Albertian ideal of the temple of God in the center of a geometrically planned city. Alberti's design for S. Sebastiano, as well as his theoretical writings, emphasized the ideal-city form, in which a centrally planned church is set in a broad piazza in the middle of the town. The horizontal cornices of the buildings along the approach streets converge as lines of perspective at the focal point, the church. This ideal was less often realized by architects than painters, who were not restrained by the physical dimensions of actual cities and the costs associated with demolition and new construction. Renaissance planning contrasts with medieval practice, where the church commonly formed part of the piazza's edge, if there was a sizeable open space at all. Ideal-city schemes drawn by various Renaissance architects often extended the centralized concept to include radial streets and a polygonal town wall with arrowhead-shaped bastions at the vertices. Such fortifications are also a departure from the towers and turrets of medieval city walls. Changes in military technology, most notably the introduction of metal cannonballs and gunpowder after 1400, rendered high city walls vulnerable, as a well-aimed shot could shatter the masonry. Renaissance town walls were thus low and earth-sheltered, to absorb the impact of projectiles, and complex outerworks of ditches and moats set in the cleared area beyond the wall impeded an attacking army's advance. Cannons pivoted on the bastions could direct their fire over a range of more than 180 degrees, even firing in enfilade, or parallel to the town walls, if necessary.

OTHER RENAISSANCE CITY PLANS

Antonio Averlino, called Il Filarete (ca. 1400–1469), a Florentine architect and sculptor, became interested in centralized Renaissance geometry, writing a *Trattato d'architectura*, or *Treatise on Architecture*, in 1461–64. One copy was dedicated to Piero de' Medici, son of Cosimo and father of Lorenzo, and another to Francesco Sforza, his patron from 1451 to 1465. To flatter Sforza, Filarete projected an imaginary ideal city named Sforzinda. However, Renaissance architects were rarely able to build complete new cities according to their ideal plans. One spot where they did succeed is Palmanova, built late in the sixteenth century on the mainland north of Venice in order to protect that city from an anticipated invasion by the Turks that never came. Because Palmanova was primarily a military outpost, it had the commander's headquarters in its central space rather than the church, which was placed at the side of the piazza.

Fifteenth-century Poland experienced a cultural awakening of its own. The University of Krakow was celebrated throughout Europe, and humanist scholars, artists, and architects brought influence directly from Italy. Lord Chancellor Jan Zamoyski (1542–1605) studied in Italy and wrote a celebrated humanist treatise. He invited the Italian architect Bernardo Morando (1518–1600) to Poland to design the fortress town of Zamość, located northeast of Kraków (Fig. 11.19). Morando planned a civic and residential area with adjacent palace, all surrounded by fortified walls with **salients**. He laid out a grid of streets and blocks, a central, arcaded plaza with a town hall, a heavily rusticated arsenal, and a host of churches—Catholic, Lutheran, Armenian, Ukrainian, and a Jewish synagogue. This wide variety of denominations gives evidence of the religious tolerance and internationalism fostered by Zamoyski in this town intended for trade. In the plaza, Morando's heavy, groin-vaulted, unifying arcade gives way to individualized pilastered façades of shops with housing above. Those buildings designed for Armenian tradesmen are capped by a riot of parapets with curvilinear pediments and urn-like finials cast in plaster. The arcade and pilasters also appear on the town hall (Fig. 11.20), but its most distinctive features are the multi-tiered, onion-domed tower and split staircase that reaches proboscis-like into the civic open space. Strong belt courses give the building a sobriety befitting its governmental function. Morando designed the Catholic church with a groin-vaulted nave and transverse barrel-vaulted chapels, like Alberti's S. Andrea, even to its articulation by two different sizes of pilasters. At the ground level, its walls are subdivided by Doric pilasters with arched openings

11.19 Plan of Zamość, 1579.

Surrounding the central plaza are commercial buildings with housing above, and the town hall on the north side, its stair projecting into the space. Streets around the square conform to a grid. Enclosing it all are fortified walls protected by salients.

Labels on plan: Lutheran Church, Synagogue, Academy, Salt Market, Armenian Church, City Hall, Catholic Church, Franciscan Church, Zamoski Palace, Corn Market, Orthodox Church

N 0 200 m 0 600 ft

between them. The upper reaches of the entrance façade masking the side aisles and clerestory have a sinuous outline typical of central European work in the sixteenth and seventeenth centuries. Morando's influence in the region, particularly in L'viv to the south eventually produced a Gothic–Mannerist fusion with connections to England and the Netherlands.

11.20 Zamość Main square and town hall, 1579.

The town hall, with its tower and cascading staircase, dominates the urban center. To the right of the hall are the elaborate houses of Armenian traders, one of many ethnic groups encouraged to settle in Zamość. Note that buildings around the square have ground-level arcades.

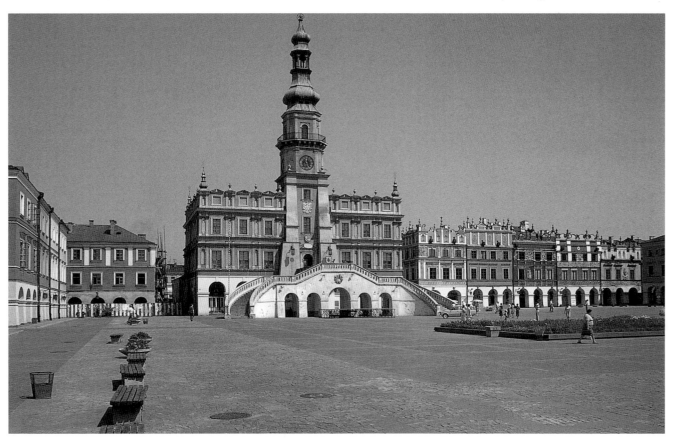

OTHER RENAISSANCE CITY PLANS

THE SPREAD OF THE RENAISSANCE
URBINO

As the Renaissance expanded beyond Florence, it developed different qualities. Not far from Sigismondo Malatesta's Rimini is Urbino, situated in hilly terrain about twenty miles from the east coast of Italy. Here the humanist and condottiere Federigo da Montefeltro held court, governing an area of about 3600 square miles that included 400 villages. Federigo was a loyal commander who served the dukes of Naples and Milan and three popes, and raised an army for Florence in 1448. His military accomplishments were balanced by his patronage of liberal learning. Humanists resided at his court, and dozens of scribes were employed to hand-copy ancient manuscripts.

Francesco di Giorgio was Federigo's engineer, and the Dalmatian-born Luciano Laurana was the architect who began his Palazzo Ducale in Urbino (1465–72) (Figs. 11.21–11.22). The palace surrounds a **cortile** but is slightly more rambling in plan than a typical Florentine merchant's residence; its rooms are light, airy, and carefully proportioned. The walls of Federigo's small study are

11.21 Plan of the Palazzo Ducale, Urbino, 1465–72.

The irregularity of this plan reflects the need to fit it onto a precipitous but dramatic site. Once inside, one finds light, airy rooms that made it an island of Renaissance culture in a sea of medievalism.

11.22 Palazzo Ducale court arcade, Urbino, 1465–72.

The cliff-like façade of the palace conceals this three-story arcade around the courtyard. Its informed manipulation of the classical language includes pilasters above arcaded columns.

11.23 Guiniforte Solari, The Certosa, Pavia, begun 1396, façade built 1473–ca. 1540.

The composition is typically medieval in its stacking up of many small motifs without a concern for overall unity. Its use of brick and terracotta reflects local Milanese practices.

covered with exquisite variegated wood **intarsia** or inlay executed by Baccio Pontelli to designs by Botticelli. Cupboards apparently with doors ajar exhibit their contents. A spinet, a squirrel, and a basket of fruit on the ledge of a colonnaded opening are all rendered in varied types of wood on the two-dimensional surface. Even the distant landscape is shown beyond the simulated open window. Such unified extension of space beyond the actual walls of a room illustrates the complete assimilation of perspectival space in fifteenth-century art and anticipates the trompe-l'oeil effects of sixteenth-century design. In Urbino, what began as a fortress overlooking the Valbona river became a monument to humanist optimism. It celebrates man's ability to observe, to reason, to act effectively in the physical world, and to create civilized society.

MILAN

For almost thirty years before being sacked in 1499 by the forces of Louis XII of France, Milan was a focal point of the Renaissance, attracting both Leonardo da Vinci (1452–1519) and Donato Bramante (1444–1514) in the early 1480s. Renaissance influence had come early to Milan when the local duke, Francesco Sforza, gave Cosimo de' Medici a palace for a branch of the Medici bank, which was vital to Florentine trade links with the north. Michelozzo's alterations to the two-story palace, which became the Banco Mediceo in the 1460s, paid homage to the applied brick-and-terracotta decorative traditions of Milan. The bank's elaborate central entrance, while composed of nominally classical elements, approaches northern Gothic flamboyance. On the piano-nobile level, Gothic cusped and pointed arches are set between classical roundels.

More typical of Milanese architecture than the combination of Gothic and Renaissance features in buildings by Michelozzo and Il Filarete is the Certosa (Fig. 11.23), a Carthusian monastery located just outside Milan in Pavia.

The brick-and-terracotta church was begun in 1396 and finished in 1497. Completion of the marble exterior to the designs of Guiniforte Solari (1429–81) marked the climax of building operations begun in 1473 and not completed until ca. 1540. It incorporates both Gothic and Renaissance elements in profusion. Niches, medallions, arcades, columns, cornices, and buttressing compete within an all-over pattern of surface relief.

MOSCOW

In some cases, Italian architects were called far afield to present the new style. In the early 1470s, Tsar Ivan III (the Great) commissioned a new Cathedral of the Dormition of the Virgin to replace a dilapidated one in the Moscow Kremlin, but the building collapsed while still under construction. When stonemasons summoned from Pskov were unwilling to assume responsibility for continuing the work, the Tsar decided to look abroad for assistance. His emissary to Venice identified Aristotele Fioravanti, an

11.24 Aristotele Fioravanti, Cathedral of the Dormition of the Virgin, Moscow, 1475–79.

This church is the work of an Italian architect. Aristotele Fioravanti, who brought Renaissance ideas of proportion and construction to Russia. His interpretation of the quincunx parti established a new model that was followed in later Russian churches.

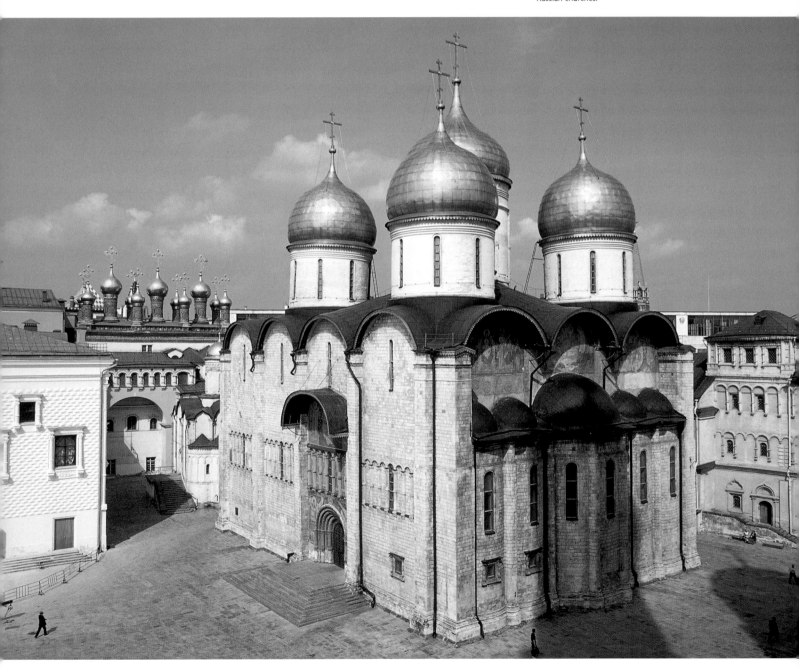

engineer and architect from Bologna, as a suitable professional to design and direct construction on the cathedral. The Tsar's envoy mistakenly thought that Fioravanti had been responsible for the construction of S. Marco (see Figs. 6.21–6.22), whose recently completed exterior dome roofs have profiles similar to Russian churches. Fioravanti came to Moscow in 1475, marking the first time design ideas from the Italian Renaissance entered Russia. Within a week, he had demolished the masonry that had taken three years to build and set to work on new foundations. The cathedral that rose over the next four years adhered in its overall conception to the well-established Russian cross-in-square plan, but modified by Italian construction techniques and Renaissance concerns for geometry and proportion to create a new interpretation of old themes (Fig. 11.24). Rather than stone, the vaulting was done entirely in brick, fired in a new manufacturing facility established by Fioravanti. Stronger brick and improved mortar allowed the vaults to be thinner than usual, thereby lessening the weight on the walls and interior piers, and the bays of the interior were groin-vaulted rather than being given barrel vaults as was traditional. Iron tie-rods were used to relieve tension loads in the arched sections. These structural innovations did away with the need for external galleries to buttress the vaults. Fioravanti also dispensed with the second-level choir gallery, so the interior space is a lofty volume.

In plan, the cathedral is a rectangular solid with proportions of 3:4, realized internally as three square bays in width (the nave and aisles) by fours bays in length. At the east end, each aisle has two apses, and their curved terminations are incorporated into the thickness of the wall so that only the central apse is expressed on the exterior of the building. There are five domes, the central one over the crossing being given dominance by having a larger diameter from the drum level upward and greater height than the four subsidiary domes. The Golden Section, a ratio of approximately 5:8, was used to set proportions of the west façade. As the Cathedral of the Dormition was used for coronations and the investiture of church authorities, its blend of Byzantine and Renaissance features was widely imitated.

LEONARDO DA VINCI

Leonardo prepared sketchbooks illustrating his inventions, observations, experiments, and discoveries in order to demonstrate his potential to prospective clients. Pages from these sketchbooks, which have been widely dispersed over the centuries, include anatomical drawings; studies of geological formations, air currents, and water movements; proposals for architecture and city planning; and a host of drawings, sketches, and studies related to his paintings and sculptures. Other drawings illustrate his inventiveness with such diverse devices as canal locks;

11.25 Leonardo da Vinci, Sketches for centralized churches, ca. 1490.

The central-plan church interested Renaissance designers more than any other architectural problem. Even Leonardo carried out investigations, possibly as a result of his contact with Bramante.

underwater craft; parachutes; helicopters; wing attachments for flying; and tanks, guns, cannons, and other instruments of war. Leonardo's experiments and research brought him close to understanding blood circulation in the human body, to verifying that the earth was more than 5000 years old (as was believed at the time), and to proposals for magnifying glasses to observe the moon, all discoveries that would later be made independently by other men. In his sketchbooks, Leonardo noted various designs for centrally planned churches (Fig. 11.25).

S. Maria della Consolazione at Todi (begun in 1508) (Fig. 11.26) is so similar to some of Leonardo's sketches that its master mason, Cola da Caprarola, must have been influenced by them, perhaps through Bramante's works. The church at Todi is square in plan, with one semicircular and three polygonal apses. Projected into three dimensions, the square generates a cube, while the apses are capped by semidomes. Above the major interior space rises a dome set on a drum and pendentives.

At the Sforza court in Milan Leonardo designed costumes and masques for the marriage and entertainment of Ludovico and his wife Beatrice d'Este; he proposed a two-level city with pedestrian and vehicular separation; and, when the 1485 plague in Milan killed 5000 people, he suggested building ten satellite towns, each of 30,000

11.27 Donato Bramante, Plan and section of S. Maria delle Grazie, Milan, 1492–97.

Here Bramante grafted a central-plan crossing onto an existing medieval nave. The union is awkward. The problem was more satisfactorily solved by Andrea Palladio in the Venetian church of Il Rendentore.

11.26 Cola da Caprarola and Donato Bramante (?), S. Maria della Consolazione, Todi, 1508.

Various architects, including Bramante, have been associated with the design of this church. Compare its design to the central-church plans by Leonardo in Fig. 11.25.

people, to reduce the likelihood of subsequent outbreaks. Between 1487 and 1490, he and Bramante worked on designs for the central crossing of Milan Cathedral; these were never built. The 1499 attack on Milan by French forces brought down the Sforza family, and Leonardo briefly sought employment as a military engineer to the infamous Cesare Borgia. Leonardo later returned to Milan to work for the French military governor, Charles d'Amboise, eventually becoming a painter and engineer for King Louis XII. In 1516 he moved to France under the patronage of Francis I and lived in comfort near d'Amboise until his death in 1519.

DONATO BRAMANTE

In Milan from 1482 to 1499 Leonardo was a close associate of Donato Bramante, and he undoubtedly influenced two of the younger architect's commissions that emphasized the concept of central planning. The first was an addition to the wide Milanese church of S. Maria delle Grazie (Fig. 11.27), a medieval building consisting of a nave, aisles, and chapels. Between 1492 and 1497 Bramante added the centralized crossing, capped by a dome sixty-five feet in diameter and completed on either side by transept apses and a choir with apse. Although in harmony with the spirit of Leonardo's sketches of centrally planned churches and consistent with Renaissance detail on the interior, Bramante's design is behind the times, its highly decorative exterior details falling into the Milanese tradition of brick-and-terracotta appliqué. The church's major interior feature, the hemispherical dome, is not even expressed on the exterior.

A far more original design is Bramante's earlier church, S. Maria presso S. Satiro (1482–92), a rebuilding that included part of the old ninth-century church and campanile of S. Satiro (Fig. 11.28). Bramante's design for the interior included a barrel-vaulted nave and transepts that intersect at a central crossing with a coffered dome on pendentives concluded by an oculus. An existing street restricted the site east of the crossing, preventing Bramante from adding a conventional choir. While the wall behind the altar is almost flush with the east wall of the transepts, Bramante created there a low relief that, when viewed on

Ninth-century chapel

Bramante's new nave

Bramante's octagonal sacristy

Illusionistic choir

N

0 ———————————— 25 m

0 ———————————— 75 ft

11.28 Donato Bramante, Plan and section of S. Maria presso S. Satiro, Milan, 1482–92.

The oddity of this plan, with its stunted nave, resulted from site conditions that prohibited Bramante from building a spacious chancel. His solution was to have painted on the slightly telescoping chancel walls a perspective image of a barrel vault.

11.29 Donato Bramante, S. Maria presso S. Satiro interior, Milan, 1482–92.

Here is the visual effect of Bramante's clever illusionistic manipulation of the shallow chancel wall. The effect works perfectly, of course, only for someone standing along the center line of the nave.

axis, has the convincing appearance of a barrel-vaulted choir (Fig. 11.29). Using the illusionistic potential of linear perspective, he simulated the space he wished to build in actuality, creating in the process what must be the ultimate use of this device in fifteenth-century architecture. Bramante's reworking of the quincunx or nine-part plan of the ninth-century chapel, and his addition of an octagonal sacristy similar to Brunelleschi's sacristy at S. Spirito in Florence, both anticipate his more ambitious central-plan proposals in Rome, culminating with his designs for a new St. Peter's basilica.

THE TEMPIETTO, ROME

Leaving Milan after its sack by the French in 1499, Bramante moved on to Rome where, like Brunelleschi and Alberti before him, he was able to study the ancient monuments first-hand; the effect on his design thinking was profound. In 1502 he was provided with an ideal opportunity to create a cerebral synthesis of humanist worldliness and Christian piety. The clients were conveniently remote: King Ferdinand and Queen Isabella of Spain, most famous for their support of the voyages of Christopher Columbus. The program called for the erection of a monument atop the spot where St. Peter was believed to have been martyred and adjacent to the recently completed church of S. Pietro in Montorio.

11.30 (above) Donato Bramante, Plan of the Tempietto, Rome, begun 1502.

Bramante planned for his interpretation of the circular temple to be placed in this ideal environment. As was so often the case with such grand Renaissance plans, it was never fully realized.

11.31 Donato Bramante, Tempietto, Rome, begun 1502.

Bramante placed the principal door opposite the altar. However, the only absolutely logical way geometrically to enter the circular plan would have been in the center and from below.

Bramante's site plan (Fig. 11.30), though never realized in this form, is critical to an understanding of his complete vision. It called for the creation of a circular cloister, a perfect hermetic architectural environment, and the insertion into it of a circular temple. Bramante designed his building to embody both the Platonic preference for ideal form and Christian reverence for tradition, in this case reverence for the circular martyrium of the early church. His command of form and detail approaches perfection.

Known as the Tempietto (Fig. 11.31) the completed building is a two-story cylinder capped by a hemispherical dome and surrounded by a one-story Doric colonnade with entablature and balustrade. The metope panels of the frieze display symbols connecting the current authority of the pope to the grandeur of antiquity. Only the doorway is awkward in its random positioning within one of the sixteen repetitive column bays, its uniqueness celebrated only by a modest set of steps.

ST. PETER'S, ROME

In 1505 Michelangelo was at work on a tomb for Pope Julius II. Because such a huge monument would not fit readily into the old and crumbling basilica, now almost 1100 years old, the Pope hired Bramante to help him explore his options. They first considered a centrally planned addition for the tomb at the western end of the existing church, similar to Bramante's addition to the church of S. Maria delle Grazie in Milan. Eventually, however, they decided to replace the old building entirely.

This was not the first Renaissance attempt to modify or add to St. Peter's. Pope Nicholas V had instructed Alberti to report on the condition of the building. Not surprisingly Alberti found the walls out of plumb and the aging fabric in such a dilapidated state that he considered repairs inadvisable. Nicholas accepted this recommendation and in 1451 appointed Bernardo Rossellino to design an apse as the first stage of an anticipated new St. Peter's. The deaths of Nicholas in 1455 and of Rossellino in 1464 terminated this project, even though Rossellino's choir was eventually built.

After this tentative beginning, the project to rebuild St. Peter's languished for another fifty years. Eventually Julius II decided that a completely new church was the only suitable accommodation for the tomb he envisioned for himself, and Bramante created an appropriately bold Greek-cross design in 1505 (Fig. 11.32). A medal cast in 1506 depicts Bramante's scheme, which represented a building on the scale of the Baths of Diocletian capped by a dome comparable to that of the Pantheon. This combination was carefully considered by Bramante. A drawing of the church in his notebooks shows it surrounded by gardens and a colonnade; on the reverse of the sheet is his drawing of the baths. Rather than merely continuing patterns of antiquity, Bramante was attempting to outdo Roman builders by proposing a domed structure more

11.32 Donato Bramante, Plan of St. Peter's, Rome, 1505.

The delicacy of the plan, almost like embroidery, foreshadows the problems Michelangelo would face when he replaced Bramante as architect at St. Peter's. The central piers proved to be insufficient to support the projected dome.

ambitious than any ancient edifice. The structural concept of a dome and drum supported on pendentives and semicircular arches actually had more in common with Byzantine work, which had itself developed from Roman models, than with any authentic Roman construction. Bramante's audacious design exceeded his structural understanding, however, for the piers he proposed would undoubtedly have been inadequate for the great loads imposed by the dome.

The cornerstone of this vast project was laid on April 18, 1506, as a labor force of 2500 began the foundations for the crossing piers. Bramante died in 1514, when they were scarcely above ground level. By the time the church was completed nearly 150 years later, almost every major architect of the sixteenth and seventeenth centuries had been engaged here at one time or another. Thus, the rebuilding of St. Peter's embraces work of several periods, from the High Renaissance to the Baroque.

High Renaissance buildings were generally more Roman and three-dimensional in spatial conception than the less massive Early Renaissance ones. Architects such as Bramante had reconciled the theoretical positions of Vitruvius, Alberti, and Leonardo with the realities of Roman construction practices and had developed the confidence to design buildings suitable to the requirements of their own age, while at the same time maintaining the spirit of antiquity. They handled matters of proportion, the manipulation of space, and correct detailing skillfully and subtly, so that in the span of less than a century the explorations of Brunelleschi had matured into the calm, self-assured style of the High Renaissance.

THE BELVEDERE COURTYARD AND THE HOUSE OF RAPHAEL, ROME

Pope Julius II also directed Bramante to organize the land north of the basilica into a great palace. Bramante inherited a modest irregular palace contiguous with Old St. Peter's and, some 900 feet away, a fortress-like **belvedere** used as a summer residence. Intent upon the creation of a complex rivaling the imperial villas of antiquity, he masked the irregularity of the existing structures by adding new façades: the one to the south eventually made into a semicircular theater, and the one to the north organized around a central hemicycle (Fig. 11.33). His strategy for connecting them produced the first great landscaped urban space of the Renaissance and involved the first use of monumental stairs since ancient times. It looked back, as was by now expected, to various inspirations from antiquity, including the villas described by Pliny the Younger. In order to tame the irregular topography, Bramante took inspiration from the Roman Sanctuary of Fortuna Primigenia at Praeneste (now Palestrina) near Rome, specifically its use of stairs and ramps as a means of organizing space within a view based upon a contrived perspective vista (Fig. 11.34). For the flanking east and west walls, he chose as his model the Colosseum, in effect turned inside out, articulating the three stories at the lower, south end of the site with first Doric, then Ionic, then Corinthian pilasters defining bays for arcades and windows, and articulating the one-story section to the north with arcaded openings flanked by Corinthian pilasters. The stairs, ramps, and punctured east and west walls provided vantage points for spectacles staged in the lower court. Many changes have been made to Bramante's scheme in the final built version, most notably Pope Sixtus V's insertion of a library which cuts across the court, eradicating the ramps and stairs and subdividing the space.

Bramante also built a house for himself in Rome (ca. 1512) (Fig. 11.35). It was purchased by the artist Raphael (1483–1520) after he had been summoned to Rome to decorate the papal apartments, and so became known as the House of Raphael; unfortunately, it has long since been demolished. Like many urban dwellings and following the model of the ancient Roman insula, it had shops at the street level, treated by Bramante as the rusticated base for pairs of engaged Doric columns articulating the

---

11.33 Donato Bramante, Belvedere Courtyard, Rome, begun 1505. Engraving.

This great outdoor space adjacent to St. Peter's was intended by Pope Julius II to re-create the grandeur of ancient Rome. One can imagine him and Bramante walking through the ruins on the Palatine planning to recapture the site's former glory.

VERO DISSEGNO DELI STVPENDI EDEFITII GIARDINI BOSCHI FONTANE ET COSE MARAVEGLIOSE DI BELVEDERE IN ROMA

11.34 Donato Bramante, Transverse section through the Belvedere Courtyard, Rome, begun 1505.

This view makes clear Bramante's use of the Roman Hellenistic Sanctuary of Fortuna Primigenia at Praeneste (now Palestrina) as one of his models. It also demonstrates the continuing Renaissance fascination with a single viewpoint—the station point, or position of the observer, in mechanical perspective.

```
0                              50 m
0                              150 ft
```

11.35 Donato Bramante, Elevation of the House of Raphael, Rome, ca. 1512.

This modest building has been as influential a prototype as any created by a Renaissance architect. Its rusticated, arcaded ground floor and columned piano nobile with entablature would reappear at various scales in France and England and eventually in America. Its own model was the ancient Roman insula or apartment house.

piano nobile above. It was a distinct innovation in palace design because it produced a more three-dimensional façade, especially when compared with the flat modeling of the orders on Early Renaissance buildings such as the Rucellai Palace. It became one of the most influential models for façade designs in Western architecture, particularly in England and France in the eighteenth century.

THE LATE RENAISSANCE, MANNERISM

While the architects of the Early and High Renaissance saw the buildings of antiquity as models to be emulated, those of the Late Renaissance, often called Mannerists, sought to achieve a more personal artistic expression through the imaginative and individualistic manipulation of the classical language. Mannerism began in the 1520s and has sometimes been associated with the political destabilization surrounding the Sack of Rome by the army of Charles V, emperor of the Holy Roman Empire. While the High Renaissance designers were disciplined and resolute and attempted to produce integrated, harmonious buildings, Mannerists favored disharmony, discord, imbalance, tension, distortion, and unresolved conflicts. However, the difference in the two periods was not quite so simple.

The term Mannerism was derived from the Italian word *maniera*, which, in the sixteenth century, connoted virtuosity, refinement, and grace, but, by the seventeenth century, had come to mean self-indulgence, self-consciousness, and superficial artifice. Both definitions can reasonably be applied to Mannerist work, depending upon the talent of the practitioner and the attitude of the viewer.

Among the more inventive Mannerists were Raphael, Giorgio Vasari (1511–74), and Giulio Romano (ca. 1499–1546). The genius of Michelangelo Buonarroti (1475–1564), whose career was contemporary with these men and whose designs share some qualities with theirs, transcended any stylistic label. Likewise, Andrea Palladio (1508–80), at work during the same period, was inspired at one point by Giulio Romano but looked back more to the models of Bramante. In the end, Palladio produced a body of work that arguably has been the most written about in all of Western architecture.

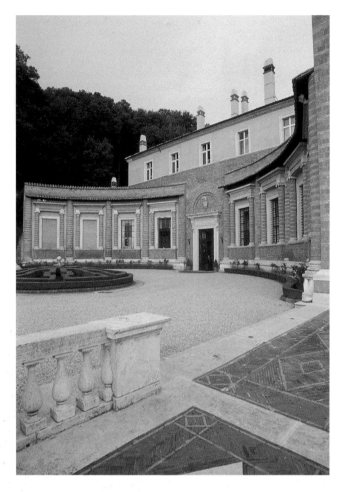

THE VILLA MADAMA, ROME

A good place to begin is the Villa Madama, designed by Raphael for Cardinal Giulio de' Medici, who was later Pope Clement VII; intriguingly it was left half-completed (Figs. 11.36–11.37). The villa was to become a characteristic building type for Renaissance architects. In contrast to the urban dwelling or palace, it was a country retreat, ostensibly inspired by the Roman *villa rustica* or estate farm. The villa's essential architectural attribute was a loggia or open elevated porch, from which visitors could view carefully designed gardens and perhaps enjoy a distant vista. The wealthy owner of a villa would come there to escape the city's summer heat, to rest and relax, and to stroll about and talk with friends. At the Villa Madama, the building was set into the hillside on a south-facing slope of the Monte Mario, beyond the walls of

11.36 Raphael, Villa Madama rotunda, Rome, begun ca. 1516.

As constructed, this villa represents only half of Raphael's plan. If completed, the central feature would have been an open rotunda, modeled perhaps on the Island Enclosure at Hadrian's Villa; but it was left incomplete as a semicircle.

11.37 Raphael, Plan and longitudinal section through the Villa Madama, Rome, begun ca. 1516.

The plan shows constructed and unconstructed portions of the villa. The section along the principal axis shows, left to right, the half-completed rotunda, the short passage to a domed bay of the loggia, the loggia, and the parterre atop its arched terrace. Raphael and Giulio Romano painted the vaulted bays of the loggia with grotesques based on the wall paintings in the recently discovered Palatine wing of Nero's Golden House.

Garden theater

Loggia

Unbuilt portion of the villa

Courtyard

Parterre

Overlook

0   50 m
0   150 ft

Rome, with a view over the city and the Tiber. The hillside, terraced into a number of levels, had formal gardens with fountains spouting and pouring water from level to level. Had its buildings been finished, the villa would have had a circular courtyard with a design based, like the Belvedere Courtyard, on the superimposed orders of the Colosseum, off which loggias, a theater, and an overlook would have radiated. Only half the work was completed, however. Its major space consists of a loggia opening onto a **parterre**, inspired in part by the three partially extant groin-vaulted bays of the Basilica of Constantine, except that the middle space here is covered by a dome on pendentives. Pavements are set in mosaic tiles, and walls and ceilings are covered with frescoed festoons containing mythological, religious, and Medicean symbolism inspired by the excavations then going on at Nero's Golden House. Most of the paintings were completed after Raphael's death by his two major assistants, Giovanni da Udine, who

rediscovered the lost technique of Roman stucco, and Giulio Romano.

The building and its grounds posit new conditions and problems for sixteenth-century designers. Movement through the site offers choices and potential moments of indecision. The various areas—courtyard, garden theater, and parterres—offer abrupt and dramatic contrasts. At the Villa Madama, the classical language reached a new level of sophistication, particularly in the frescoed loggia, but also began the change from the self-assured countenance of the High Renaissance to the anxiety and ambiguity of Mannerism.

THE UFFIZI, FLORENCE

Giorgio Vasari's design for the Uffizi in Florence (Fig. 11.38), begun in 1560, illustrates the Mannerist attitude toward urban design. The building, an office annex for the

11.38 Giorgio Vasari, Uffizi, Florence, begun 1560.

Vasari so composed his Uffizi complex that it framed this view of the medieval Palazzo Vecchio. Such urbanistic interaction of existing and new construction was a significant contribution of Manneristic planning.

Palazzo Vecchio, consists of a long, narrow courtyard flanked on its two long sides by multi-floor wings to which Vasari applied crisply modeled window surrounds and broken **belt courses** that move aggressively forward and back. One end of the courtyard terminates at the Arno river with a series of three openings, the center one wider and arched, and the opposite open end discharges into Piazza della Signoria, with the tower of the Palazzo Vecchio standing off-center. While both ends of the courtyard essentially dissolve into empty space, a view in through the central arched opening captures the perspective diminution of the Uffizi cornices together with the Palazzo Vecchio's tower. Rather than creating a static, hermetic urban ensemble as Bramante had chosen to do with the Tempietto, Vasari created an open-ended interactive one in which he dexterously combined old and new and stressed the dynamics of motion and change over time.

THE PALAZZO DEL TE, MANTUA

Unlike many artists of the High Renaissance working in Rome, Giulio Romano was actually born there, so his understanding of the buildings of antiquity came from his personal, intimate experience of the city rather than from study undertaken for professional reasons. Therefore, it is not surprising that, as one of the creators of Mannerism, Romano chose to represent the ruined condition of ancient monuments as his contribution to sixteenth-century architecture. This can be seen in one of his early paintings, *The Stoning of St. Stephen* (1523), in which Roman ruins in the background provide the setting. Giulio's architectural works feature the willful and amusing misuse of classical elements. In his own house at Mantua (1544), he built a Pantheon Salon, with an

image of Julius Caesar, his namesake, carved over the fireplace.

His most important building is the Palazzo del Te (1525–34), designed for Federigo Gonzaga as a honeymoon villa on an island at the edge of Mantua. The Gonzaga family were horse-breeders, supplying steeds to the courts of Europe, and they were also extensively involved in political intrigue and military alliances. The palace was originally conceived as an enormous stable complex. It consists of a large square courtyard, enclosed on all four sides by a series of rooms arranged en suite, with central entrances on the north and east sides. A loggia on the west side leads into a garden, at the end of which is a semicircular colonnade. The garden is laid out in geometric flowerbeds, and a moat used for staging miniature naval battles was dug adjacent to the villa, which is linked to the garden by a bridge. The loggia is barrel-vaulted and supported on alternate paired and single columns, while the north entrance has rusticated columns, deliberately made to appear unfinished. These columns support lintels with keystones, above which is an octagonally coffered ceiling as in the Basilica of Constantine. In the courtyard, heavy Doric columns support parts of the architrave and entablature with triglyphs dropped down out of place as if part of an ancient Roman ruin (Fig. 11.39). Together with the unframed niches and windows, pediments lacking a bottom cornice, and heavy rustication, these features create extreme contrasts and a sense of ambiguity and tension.

11.39 Giulio Romano, Palazzo del Te courtyard, Mantua, 1525–34.

It is unclear whether the effect was intended to shock or amuse, but Giulio Romano designed some of the stones of the entablature to be displaced downward as if part of a ruin.

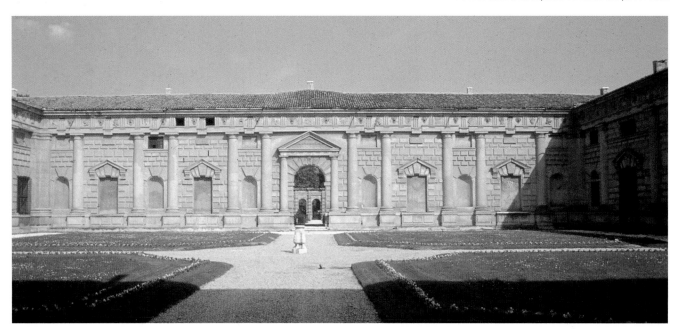

The illusion of imbalance and the perverse use of classicism continue on the interior. The wall and ceiling surfaces of the rooms around the courtyard are filled with frescoes by Giulio Romano and his assistants, with additional enrichment provided by inlaid doors and mantels of oriental jasper, gold, and marble. Cracked brick lintels painted on the wall surfaces above doors create an uncomfortable feeling in visitors passing beneath them. Above the cracked lintels in the Sala dei Giganti is painted a scene of great destruction, with the weight of collapsing columns crushing the limbs and bodies of giant figures, one going cross-eyed as his head becomes trapped between two falling boulders. Walls merge into billowing clouds painted on the ceiling, the center of which carries a representation of a colonnaded drum supporting a hemispherical dome. Horses painted in the Sala dei Cavalli stand on cornices more than half the height of this large chamber, and behind them are landscapes seen through painted window surrounds between the pilasters and architectural detailing.

The Palazzo del Te was never finished, yet it remains a masterpiece of the Late Renaissance, designed by a sophisticated architect as a play on the conventions of revived classicism. Only those who share Romano's understanding of Roman architecture could fully appreciate his accomplishment.

MICHELANGELO

Michelangelo Buonarroti, widely regarded as one of the greatest geniuses of Western art, made important contributions to the fields of sculpture, painting, and architecture during the course of his long and productive life. The second son of a minor governmental official in Florence, he was apprenticed at the age of thirteen to the painter Domenico del Ghirlandaio, despite his father's reluctance to have his son become an artist. His training in sculpture began a year or so later when Michelangelo was invited to join the workshop sponsored by Lorenzo de' Medici as part of the Medici effort to revive the sculptural arts of antiquity. Until the death of Lorenzo in 1492, Michelangelo lived in the Medici Palace as a member of the household, gaining a humanist education from the eminent scholars, writers, and poets who gathered there under Lorenzo's patronage.

S. LORENZO, FLORENCE

Under Pope Leo X, the younger son of Lorenzo de' Medici and successor to Pope Julius II, Michelangelo embarked on the first of three architectural commissions for the monastery of S. Lorenzo, Florence, in 1515. His design for the façade of the basilican church was a screen consisting of two equally developed stories divided by an attic, forming a backdrop for relief panels and sculptures set in niches. Nothing had come of this design by the time Leo died in 1521, and the church exists today without a façade, but Michelangelo's proposals established a second tradition in façade architecture, providing an alternative to Alberti's S. Maria Novella type.

Before the façade design was abandoned, the Medici asked Michelangelo to design a funerary chapel adjacent to the south transept for the burial of Lorenzo de' Medici and four of the lesser Medici. This New Sacristy, or Medici Chapel, was to complement Brunelleschi's Old Sacristy located off the north transept.

Michelangelo paid homage to Brunelleschi by employing a similar form, a hemispherical dome on pendentives, over the cubical main space, and using some of the same materials: white stucco walls trimmed with gray *pietra serena*. The tombs themselves are marble. The number of statues and Michelangelo's placement of them underwent a series of changes; his sketches show that he considered a central mausoleum, but he finally placed two sarcophagi on either side of the chapel. Each supports symbolic but unfinished sculptures of the Times of Day, with seated figures of the dukes Lorenzo and Giuliano placed above in niches set into the wall. The large symbolic figures of Day and Night, on Giuliano's tomb, and Dawn and Dusk, on Lorenzo's, recline precariously on top of the sarcophagi, their very weight seeming to cause them to slide off the curved lids. The ghoulish mask on Night suggests nightmares. These sculptures are in the lowest of three levels within the chapel, where a profusion of architectural elements—heavy blank tabernacles above the doors, tapering blank windows, and even pilasters without capitals—vie with one another. Above are lunettes, punctuated with tapering windows; and surmounting the whole ensemble is a coffered dome with oculus, capped by a cupola.

Pope Leo X's illegitimate cousin, elected to the papacy as Clement VII, wished to house the Medici library for use by scholars within the cloister of S. Lorenzo, the family parish church, perhaps to emphasize that the Medici were no longer mere merchants but members of intellectual and ecclesiastical society. Michelangelo therefore began work on the so-called Laurentian Library in 1524 (Fig. 11.40). It was built above existing monastic quarters on the east range of the cloister, with an entrance from the upper level of the cloisters. Michelangelo wanted to use a skylight over the vestibule, but the Pope believed that this would leak, so clerestory windows were incorporated into the west wall overlooking the cloister instead. Thus the vestibule (Fig. 11.41) is shocking in its verticality, almost half as tall again as it is wide. Blank tapering windows, framed in *pietra serena*, surround the interior of the vestibule; these are separated by paired columns set into the wall. The normally illogical recessing of columns into a wall would seem to be a Mannerist invention, yet the column positions are actually necessitated by the location of the existing walls of the building beneath the library. The walls between columns are like a taut skin stretched

11.40 Michelangelo Buonarroti, Plan and section of the Laurentian Library, Florence, begun 1524.

One should not forget that the sculptural drama of Michelangelo's entry vestibule is only a prelude to the principal space: the reading room for Greek and Latin texts. Here he abandoned his preferred tension and dynamics in favor of a modular serenity befitting the space's function.

between the vertical supports. Michelangelo further emphasized the seeming instability of the whole by having the columns appear to be supported on consoles, so that weight seems to be carried on rather weak elements, and one cannot determine visually whether the columns or walls support the roof. The sense of ambiguity is increased further by the apparently unorthodox forms of the tabernacle windows, and all of the architectural elements have been compressed together, creating a sense of tension and constrained energy.

The tour de force of this restless space is the huge staircase leading up to the reading

11.41 Michelangelo Buonarroti, Laurentian Library vestibule, Florence, begun 1524.

The vestibule stairs appear to cascade downward from the reading room doorway as though its treads and risers were once molten. The impacted columns astride this doorway create in architecture the same kind of tension expressed in the reclining figures at Michelangelo's Medici Chapel.

room. Michelangelo's original sketches for the library show the stair as divided flights placed against the wall. By 1558–59, when the present stair was designed, his proposal had grown into a piece of dynamic sculpture that appears to pour forth from the upper level like lava and compress the limited floor space of the vestibule. As it descends, the stair divides into three flights, the outer ones having no handrails. On the central flight, the convex treads vary in width, making the whole arrangement somewhat disquieting. By contrast the library's reading room is serene, quiet, and restful, entirely appropriate for research and study. In the manner of monastic libraries, it is a long room lit by evenly spaced windows set between pilasters in the side walls. Thus reading desks, arranged perpendicular to the side walls, were amply illuminated by natural light.

THE CAMPIDOGLIO, ROME

In 1534, with both the Medici Chapel and the Laurentian Library still incomplete, Michelangelo left Florence for Rome, where he remained until his death in 1564. Only seven years before, in 1527, Rome had been sacked by Charles V. One of Michelangelo's first architectural commissions there came from the local government authority, which decided to reestablish the grandeur of Rome by developing the Campidoglio, the ancient seat of government on the Capitoline Hill occupied since the twelfth century by a communal palace. Shortly thereafter Pope Paul III had transferred the great equestrian bronze of Marcus Aurelius specifically for use as the centerpiece of the site. Thus Michelangelo was required to provide a setting for the statue and to bring order to an irregular hilltop already encumbered by two crumbling medieval buildings set at an acute angle to one another. Despite these conditions, it was in one sense a Renaissance architect's ideal commission, for it offered the opportunity to build a monumental civic plaza for a major city. Michelangelo produced a brilliant response to this awkward commission. He planned a trapezoidal piazza to regularize the difficult geometry established by the existing buildings, and intended to inset an oval paving pattern that would focus attention on the equestrian statue in the center (Fig. 11.42). Precedent for this general disposition of elements can be found in Rossellino's plan for the cathedral piazza at Pienza (1456–64), although the scale and coherence of Michelangelo's design are much greater.

Axiality and symmetry govern all parts of the Capitoline Hill work. Michelangelo gave the medieval Palace of the Senators (Fig. 11.43), remodeled in ca. 1547 and later, a central campanile, a renovated façade, and a grand divided external staircase. He designed a new façade for the colonnaded Palace of the Conservators, with a giant order of Corinthian pilasters extending over two stories,

11.42 Plan of the Campidoglio, Rome, 1537.

This plan is based upon a nineteenth-century engraving by Paul Le Tarouilly, but with Michelangelo's design (since executed) for the central oval superimposed.

11.43 Michelangelo Buonarroti, Campidoglio, Rome, begun 1537. Engraving by Le Tarouilly.

Le Tarouilly's view is deceptive. The absolute regularity gives no hint of the previous disorder of this formerly rutted hill with its hulks of medieval buildings disposed in an asymmetrical and non-orthogonal configuration. Michelangelo's genius was to unify the unrelated parts.

and projected an identical structure, the Palazzo Nuovo (now the Capitoline Museum), for the opposite side of the piazza. On the narrow side of the trapezoidal plan, Michelangelo extended the central axis with a magnificent ramp-stair to link the hilltop with the city below. Work on the Capitoline Hill was incomplete when Michelangelo died, but his designs were carefully followed in subsequent centuries, down to the installation of the paving pattern in 1928.

THE PALAZZO FARNESE, ROME

In 1546 Pope Paul III employed Michelangelo to continue construction of the Palazzo Farnese (Fig. 11.44), his family residence, begun in 1517 by Antonio da Sangallo the Younger. At the main façade, Michelangelo added the cornice and the central window with coat of arms at the piano-nobile level. In the courtyard, he added the two upper floors, compressing the pilasters, attached columns, and windows in a manner not unlike the entry vestibule at the Laurentian Library. As an expression of the social position and wealth of the newly rich Farnese family, the palace commands the piazza on which it fronts, lending an impassive dignity to the space.

ST. PETER'S, ROME

Pope Paul III had been in office five years before the Vatican had amassed adequate funds to resume the building of St. Peter's, begun in 1506 by Bramante. Plans had been submitted by Raphael, Giuliano da Sangallo, and Baldassare Peruzzi, but the sack of Rome by the army of Charles V in 1527 had emptied the Vatican coffers and prevented much actual construction being carried out. Antonio da Sangallo the Younger spent the amount required to build a small church in making a model to illustrate the ungainly agglomeration of underscaled classical orders he proposed for the north and south transept ambulatories. Even though these admitted only indirect light into the great central space, the southern transept was completed according to his designs in 1546, the year in which he died. Michelangelo's appointment as architect-in-charge provoked Vasari to write that Paul III

11.44 Antonio da Sangallo the Younger and Michelangelo Buonarroti, Palazzo Farnese, Rome, 1517–46.

This joint effort became the model for a variety of urban monuments in the late nineteenth and early twentieth centuries. Unlike the Florentine interpretation of the type, this palazzo has rustication in the **quoins** and at the entry has classically inspired window surrounds.

was indeed fortunate that God had ordained that Michelangelo should live during his pontificate, saying: "How great are thy merits elevated by his art." Michelangelo, who considered himself primarily a sculptor, agreed to the assignment as a pious act for the glorification of God, and he accepted no more than a minimum living wage for his architectural work on St. Peter's. He quickly saw the faults of Sangallo's unimaginative scheme and razed the exterior walls of the transept ambulatories, in part because they encroached on the Vatican Palace and would have necessitated the destruction of several buildings had they been completed around the church. They would also have provided dark internal passageways in which, Michelangelo said, vagrants could hide and attack pilgrims. Michelangelo made a small clay model of the church, from which a wooden model was then constructed; the design restored Bramante's initial conception of a Greek-cross plan, but in a reduced and simplified version (Fig. 11.45), and increased the size of Bramante's under-structured central piers, the foundations of which were already in the ground.

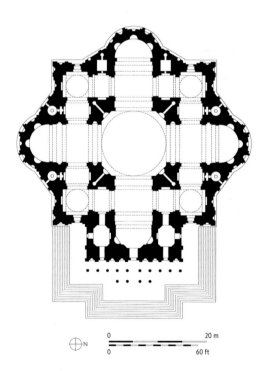

11.45 Michelangelo Buonarroti, Plan of St. Peter's, Rome, begun 1546.

A comparison of this plan to Bramante's reveals that the column screens have disappeared, the central piers have been enlarged, and an entry portico developed. If completed in this form, it would have represented the culmination of centrally planned church explorations during the Renaissance.

Michelangelo corresponded with his nephew in Florence to learn the dimensions of Brunelleschi's cathedral dome there, a design he admired and wished to emulate. "I am going to make its sister bigger, yes, but not more beautiful," he wrote.

Although construction on the dome of St. Peter's was not begun in his lifetime, Michelangelo endowed its design with internal and external unity. Brunelleschi's dome for the Florence Cathedral has a tall Gothic profile; Michelangelo chose instead a hemispherical form. He also increased the number of stone ribs expressed on the outside of the dome from eight to sixteen in order to eliminate the faceted octagonal massing of the Florence Cathedral. Had the dome been constructed as planned by Michelangelo, the outward thrust of the ribs would have been enormous, and it is doubtful whether a masonry drum could have withstood the accumulated forces. Giacomo della Porta, who constructed the dome after Michelangelo's death, employed a slightly taller profile in order to decrease the lateral thrust and used the lantern cupola to force the weight of the dome downward to the drum (Fig. 11.46). He used columns, attached visually to the drum by a broken entablature, to act as buttresses that further force the loads downward to the arches and four great piers of the central crossing. Even so, tension chains were subsequently incorporated into the brickwork of this double-shelled dome, which is only five feet smaller in diameter than the Pantheon dome. The triangulated massing of the whole project rises to a height of 452 feet, enough to have strong visual presence had Michelangelo's façade been built as planned. Eventually, however, St. Peter's was completed early in the seventeenth century with a nave and entrance façade designed by Carlo Maderno (see Fig. 12.5) that diminished the presence of the dome.

PORTA PIA, ROME

In his later designs Michelangelo anticipated the Baroque in several ways, as in his design of the Porta Pia (Fig. 11.47), a city gate built at the end of the Via Pia. Rather than a defensive gateway within a fortified city wall, it was

11.46 Michelangelo Buonarroti, St. Peter's, Rome, begun 1546.

It takes a view such as this one to get a sense of the centrally planned massing intended by Bramante and Michelangelo. The dominant feature here is the great dome, which is no longer the case today as a result of the extension of the nave by Carlo Maderno.

11.47 Michelangelo Buonarroti, Porta Pia, Rome, 1561–65.

This gateway still welcomes people approaching the city from the east. When first constructed, its unorthodox elements, ambiguous structural systems, and discordant textures must have shocked anyone seeing it for the first time.

capitals; the concatenation of architectural details recalls Renaissance stage-set designs for the theater. Begun in 1561, the Porta Pia was almost complete, unlike so many of Michelangelo's other architectural commissions, at the time of his death.

SFORZA CHAPEL, ROME

His most adventurous project spatially is the Sforza Chapel at S. Maria Maggiore in Rome (Fig. 11.48), built for the same family that had employed Leonardo da Vinci in Milan. Like the Laurentian Library, it is both dynamic and ambiguous. The chapel combines central and longitudinal planning and emphasizes not orthogonal but diagonal directionality, defined by four columns attached to rotated

and is a scenic backdrop terminating a vista. Stone architectural elements, many of them unusual, are isolated against a plane of brick: a broken pediment stuffed with an oversized swag and plaque, oddly draped-over roundels, and volute-topped crenelations. Michelangelo emphasized the central passageway demarcating the edge of the city by packing within it an array of redundant structural elements—arch, rusticated arch, and broken pediment above deeply grooved pilasters with **mutules** in their

11.48 Michelangelo Buonarroti, Plan and section of the Sforza Chapel, S. Maria Maggiore, Rome, 1564.

There was no more revolutionary Renaissance building than this one. Its column and vault configuration and resulting spatial dynamics and spatial interpenetrations inspired designers throughout Europe for more than a century afterward. While stone obviously cannot billow, this word does express the feeling that Michelangelo captured. The vault appears to be held down by the columns rather than resting heavily upon them.

piers and supporting a groin vault that can be described as "billowing." The curving wall segments that cradle the lateral altars are the boundaries of an incomplete circle with the vaults above them equally incomplete and sail-like. The principal altar opposite the entrance, as at the Pazzi Chapel, resides in a subsidiary square. The Sforza Chapel offered a source of inspiration for a host of spatial experiments by designers for at least the next 150 years.

ANDREA PALLADIO

Andrea Palladio was born Andrea di Pietro della Gondola in 1508 and was trained as a stonemason. When he was about thirty, he was employed on a building site, where his talents attracted the attention of the humanist Count Giangiorgio Trissino. Trissino became his mentor, renaming him Palladio after a character in his epic poem *Italy Freed from the Goths*, and providing him with a humanist education. Along with several study trips to Rome, this

gave Palladio an education in architecture. In particular, by measuring the buildings of ancient Rome, he collected accurate information on classical proportions, which he later used in designing his own buildings.

Palladio's profound influence on the development of Western architecture can be attributed to both his writings and his buildings. In 1570 he published his *I quattro libri dell'architettura* or *The Four Books of Architecture* (Fig. 11.49), in which he illustrated and discussed his own work as well as that of antiquity. Palladio wrote about the orders of architecture, domestic architecture, public buildings, town planning, and temples, "without which," he said, "no civilization is possible." Although he could measure and illustrate actual Roman temples, theaters, bridges, triumphal arches, and baths, Palladio had to speculate about the design of Roman houses, so he included ideal versions of his own buildings—often at odds with these designs as built—to demonstrate antique ideals. Numerals printed on the plans give the widths and lengths of rooms, and sections and the text sometimes have indications of heights. Making reference to his buildings and their dimensions, he published the Renaissance's most coherent system of proportions. He began with modules based on

11.49 Frontispiece to Isaac Ware's English edition (1738) of Palladio's *I quattro libri dell' architettura*.

While various garbled editions of Palladio's book had appeared in England from the mid-seventeenth century, this was the most reliable and the first one approved of by the Neo-Palladians.

wall thicknesses, then determined all of his rooms' dimensions using ratios derived from the musical consonances, and arranged these rooms according to modulated grids. Here, as in all his architectural designs, he was concerned with practical convenience as an essential component of good design; firmness, commodity, and delight were to him the basic tenets of all architecture. Eventually many architects, beginning with Inigo Jones in England in the seventeenth century, used Palladio's publication as a guidebook and made close observation of his buildings their primary objective during travels through Italy.

BUILDINGS IN VICENZA

Palladio's first public commission was a new skin for the medieval market and council hall, or basilica, at Vicenza; he added a two-story arcade of Doric and Ionic columns (Fig. 11.50). He submitted proposals for the project in 1546 at the request of the civic authorities, who accepted them with modifications in 1549. Construction was based on Roman brick groin-vaulting techniques, but the dominant element of the design is the repeated unit of three openings, the central one arched, supported on pairs of small columns, set off with a larger half-column between each bay. The end bays are smaller to give the appearance of strength to the corners, which have double columns. Although Bramante was the first Renaissance architect to use an arch flanked by square-headed openings, the unit is sometimes known as a Serliana because it was first illustrated in Sebastiano Serlio's publications. In using the Serliana here, Palladio was undoubtedly most directly influenced by the use of the motif at Jacopo Sansovino's Library of S. Marco (1537–53) in nearby Venice (see Fig. 11.61).

Some of Palladio's palazzo designs in Vicenza reflect his Roman experiences. The Palazzo Valmarana, for instance, includes the giant order used by Michelangelo at the Campidoglio. More original is his Palazzo Chiericati (1550–52), which was erected on a very shallow site with a long frontage onto a public open space (Fig. 11.51). Palladio treated the building like a Roman palace, two stories high, fronting onto a forum, with a ground-level Roman Doric colonnade intended to link with other colonnades (never constructed) on buildings around the remaining sides of the square. Like those of many Palladian houses, the palace's façade is divided into three parts, the central section being a pavilion or projecting bay accentuated by clustered columns that create an impression of strength. The second floor is composed in the Ionic order, with loggias flanking the main salon. Thus, by projecting the salon over the public colonnade below, Palladio gained additional space for the largest room in the house. The palace is open and airy. Because of the restricted site, the long axis of its entrance hall and the majority of its rooms run parallel to the street, rather than being perpendicular to it.

11.50 Andrea Palladio, Basilica, Vicenza, 1549.
The roof is a nineteenth-century addition. Palladio's two levels of arches conceal the medieval vaults of the old basilica or town hall.

VILLA DESIGNS IN THE VENETO

Rather than his urban houses, it was Palladio's villa designs that gained him such a wide following among later architects. Unlike most Renaissance villas, his country estates were generally working farms owned by the younger sons of Venetian nobles. Their lands were located on the mainland north of Venice, the Veneto, to which capital generated by maritime commerce had been redirected as Venetian trading opportunities diminished. Although isolated from sophisticated Venetian society, these gentleman farmers maintained an elegant and cultured life in appropriately grand houses. Two of Palladio's early clients were Daniele Barbaro, a scholarly author and editor of a published version of Vitruvius, and his brother Marcantonio. Palladio designed the Villa Barbaro at Maser for them (1557–58) (Fig. 11.52). As with all his villas, the scheme is symmetrical, the central living block balanced by end pavilions connected by flanking arcades. The building is sited on a slight rise, so although it is strongly horizontal, it affords a view out into the landscape. The elegance of the composition

11.51 Andrea Palladio, Palazzo Chiericati, Vicenza, 1550–52.

Palladio intended for the first-floor Doric colonnade to be continued around a forum-like piazza. The openness of the façade is surprising, particularly the cage-like corner spaces on the second floor.

belies the building's practicality. Following ancient Roman practices, Palladio combined the many functions of a large farm into a single structure, including storage for hay and equipment, provision for livestock, and spaces for threshing grain.

Inside the Villa Barbaro, the rooms are gracefully proportioned, well lit, and ingeniously ornamented with perspective frescoes by Paolo Veronese (ca. 1528–1588). Through the skillful application of pigment, walls merge into barrel-vaulted ceilings. In one room, balustraded balconies appear to support spiraled columns, behind which

are painted openings where the mistress of the house can be seen emerging with a page boy, a domestic servant, a lapdog, and a parrot. Shadow projections increase the sense of depth in a series of rooms where actual architraves and pedimented doorways may be confused with those painted on flat wall surfaces. Huntsmen and children appear in open doorways, and sculptures stand in niches flanked by columns, all conjured into existence by the painter's brush. Landscapes lead the eye beyond columns and pilasters in the dining room into imaginary vistas inspired by scenes from antiquity.

With the Villa Barbaro, Palladio made a significant contribution to the development of residential design that continues to influence the architecture of our own time, even though he had no idea that he was being innovative: this was the application of the columns and pediment of a temple front to a house. He had interpreted Vitruvius as saying that Greek temples had evolved from houses, an observation that may refer to the similarity of the megaron and the cella of a temple. Having no knowledge of the megaron, Palladio assumed Vitruvius's remark to mean that Greek houses looked like Greek temples, which he knew to have columns and a pediment. Therefore, in using these elements on the façade of a house, Palladio believed that he was following Greek precedent, when in fact he was breaking new ground.

Palladio designed the Villa Foscari at Malcontenta (1559–60), located on the Brenta Canal outside Venice, on a single axis, with the intention that side courts would mask the end elevations, but the courts were never built (Figs. 11.53–11.54). Dog-leg stairs lead to a portico on axis at the piano-nobile level, and the entrance from the portico opens into a vaulted cruciform space extending the full depth of the building. One of the barrel vaults in the arms of the cross is expressed on the rusticated garden front. There is a consistent proportioning system used throughout the house, all rooms having ratios of 1:1, 2:3, 1:2, or 3:4. In plan the building's measurements of length to width conform to the Golden Section ratio of 8:5, while the height is the same as the width.

By far the most famous residence by Palladio is the Villa Americo-Capra, also known as the Villa Rotonda, located just outside Vicenza (1566–70) (Figs. 11.55–11.56). The client for this villa was a retired churchman, who used the house for elaborate entertainments as well as for agricultural processing. The Villa Rotonda is square in plan, with, as the name implies, a central two-story rotunda. According to Palladio, "there are loggias made on all four fronts" so that "it enjoys from every part most beautiful views, some of which are limited, some extended, and others which terminate with the horizon." Internally the central domed space radiates out to the four porticoes and to the elegantly proportioned rooms in the corners. It is a simple yet powerful scheme, one that would be copied many times.

11.52 Andrea Palladio, Villa Barbaro, Maser, 1557–58.

Palladio's combining of living and agricultural functions into a single, extended structure enabled him to make farm buildings monumental. He was the first Renaissance architect to use the temple front extensively on domestic buildings.

11.53 Andrea Palladio, Plan and elevation of the Villa Foscari, Malcontenta, 1559–60.

Compare this elevation to the adjacent perspective view. The prominent roof disappears through foreshortening, while the portico becomes more dominant.

11.54 Andrea Palladio, Villa Foscari, Malcontenta, 1559–60.

This perspective view reveals Palladio's genius for creating monumentality without relying on great size. He relied instead on large mural wall surfaces and careful proportioning, and avoided scale-diminishing elements.

11.55 Andrea Palladio, Villa Americo-Capra (La Rotonda), Vicenza, 1556–57.

Careful study of the bricks in the stairs has revealed significant changes since the villa's construction. Arched openings at the center of these stairs once allowed carts to carry grain into the ground floor.

11.56 Andrea Palladio, Plan and elevation of the Villa Americo-Capra, (La Rotonda), Vicenza, 1556–57.

These orthographic views show how Palladio illustrated his work with woodcuts in *I quattro libri*. He included the whole-number proportions of his rooms in the plan.

11.57 Andrea Palladio, Plan and elevation of the Villa Trissino, Meledo, begun 1567.

While never completed, this villa design anticipated the sprawling Neo-Palladian compositions of early eighteenth-century England. The quarter-circle connectors between the central block and wings were to become a popular motif in eighteenth-century America.

Palladio started from the same plan in his project for the Villa Trissino at Meledo (Fig. 11.57), an ambitious scheme of which only a tiny end fragment was ever built. To the basic cube of the house, he added quarter-circle colonnades on either side of one porticoed entrance, widening it out to define a rectangular forecourt. Such colonnades would become a popular feature in gigantic Neo-Palladian country houses in England and in the smaller American Georgian houses of the eighteenth century. Comments made by the architect about the villa indicate that the ground floor was to be given over to domestic services, while the dependencies were to shelter farm activities.

CHURCHES IN VENICE

Palladio's most significant church is S. Giorgio Maggiore in Venice (Fig. 11.58), which has a façade design derived from his earlier S. Francesca della Vigne, also in Venice. Both churches offered a new solution to the Renaissance problem of placing a classical façade in front of a basilican cross section. Palladio combined two temple fronts: a tall one, consisting of four Corinthian columns on pedestals that support a pediment at the end of the nave, superimposed over a wide one, with smaller Corinthian pilasters, that matches the sloping aisle roofs. Vitruvius had discussed a double arrangement of gables, and the idea of using double pediments on one façade was further legitimized by the example of the Pantheon, where an attic level with cornice stands between the portico and the rotunda. At S. Giorgio, the Corinthian columns and pilasters on the front carry through to the interior arcading between nave and aisles, providing an Albertian unity in this ecclesiastical building. Palladio looked to the Roman

11.58 Andrea Palladio, S. Giorgio Maggiore, Venice, 1565.

Three scales of orders and three sizes of pediments give this façade clarity and richness. Palladio's overlapping temple forms would be much copied in America.

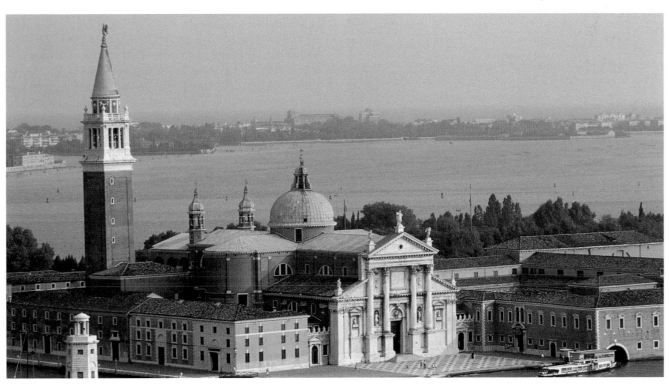

thermae for a precedent in handling the interior. Barrel vaults are illuminated by the semicircular clerestory windows or thermal windows found in such baths as those of Diocletian, and the whole is painted white to reflect light and emphasize the church's volumetric clarity.

THE TEATRO OLIMPICO

One of Palladio's last works was the Teatro Olimpico in Vicenza (1579–80), inspired by Roman theaters with a proscenium like the Theater of Marcellus, but roofed here with a ceiling painted to depict the sky. Steeply banked rows of seats are arranged in a semicircle facing the stage; to this day, the original stage set, designed by Vincenzo Scamozzi (1552–1616), remains as the scenery for all productions in the theater. Scamozzi's set shows an urban piazza, from which three streets extend back into the distance, their apparent length exaggerated by the false perspective of a sloped floor plane and artificially diminishing building heights (Fig. 11.59). When the actors leave the stage, they appear to recede along the

11.59 Andrea Palladio and Vincenzo Scamozzi, Teatro Olimpico interior, Vicenza, 1579–80.

This stage set by Scamozzi was not intended to be permanent. It represents the kind of ideal cityscape imagined by many Renaissance town planners. The buildings' façades are configured so as to create a false perspective. Not only do the cornices and belt courses converge in reality, but so also do the floor and ceiling planes.

street, even though their own height does not diminish according to the perspective of the set.

The continuing influence of Palladio on Western architecture is in no small measure due to the logical planning, careful proportioning, and conceptual clarity that characterize his designs. Indeed, the principles Palladio advocated have been found applicable to a variety of circumstances. Both his writings and buildings demonstrate the achievements of this stonemason turned architect who declared, "Vitruvius is my master, Rome is my mistress, and architecture is my life."

PALLADIO'S VENICE

Palladio's Venice, located in Italy but with commercial connections to Constantinople and farther east, developed its own exotic form of Gothicism, which it overlaid with selected Renaissance ideas. Although Venice ultimately contained a considerable amount of Renaissance architecture, the style developed as a variant relying on local traditions, climate, and disposition. The Palazzo Vendramini-Calergi (1500–10) of Mauro Coducci (ca. 1440–1504) has Corinthian pilasters, columns, and cornices framing large round-headed windows that are also decorated with classical detailing. These windows catch the breezes coming off the lagoon and cool the loggia and central hall that replaced the courtyard found in Florentine palaces. Martino Lombardo employed perspective relief panels, executed by Tullio Lombardo, at the ground level of the Scuola di S. Marco (1487–90). The scenes depict lions, the animal identified with St. Mark, peering out from an implied barrel-vaulted space behind the plane of the façade.

Perhaps most vivid in the mind of anyone who has visited this dowager queen of the Adriatic is the Piazza S. Marco (Fig. 11.60). Located at the point where the Grand Canal empties into the lagoon, it is one of the great civic spaces in Western urban design and offers a cross section of Venetian architectural developments in the fourteenth to sixteenth centuries. The piazza is L-shaped with a wide shaft of space extending from the water between the Doge's Palace and the Library of S. Marco to the campanile, around which it pivots to form a long trapezoid, which, though it evolved over a long period of time, appears as a perfect spatial response to the exotic cathedral of S. Marco that faces it.

The Doge's Palace (see Fig. 9.73) and S. Marco (see Figs. 6.21–6.22) have been discussed earlier. The campanile collapsed in the nineteenth century and was rebuilt. The loggetta at its base and the adjacent library (begun 1537, completed 1583–88) (Fig. 11.61) were the creations of Jacopo Sansovino (1486–1570) and Vincenzo Scamozzi (1552–1616). Sansovino was a friend of the Venetian painter Titian, whose nudes and landscapes have a supple, luxurious, and slightly mysterious character. The library

11.60 Plan of the Piazza S. Marco, Venice, 1487–90.

The space between the Procuratie Vecchie and the Procuratie Nuove, both housing offices for city officials, was gradually hollowed out to produce the piazza's present form. While Venice has many smaller piazzas, this one symbolized the power of one of the West's greatest trading cities in the tenth through eighteenth centuries.

11.61 Jacopo Sansovino, Library of S. Marco, Venice, begun 1537, completed 1583–88.

The library's façade can be read as three layers: the arched openings, the columns and entablatures, and the lavish ornamentation. The resulting scenographic effect appealed to the sensual nature of sixteenth-century Venetians.

11.62 Jacopo Sansovino, La Zecca, Venice, begun 1536.

Heavy rustication conveys a sense of security in the building where Venetians minted their coins. Its massive, highly textured walls are particularly impressive when seen across the Venetian lagoon.

has the appearance of a Titian interpreted in stone. Its bays are defined by attached Doric and Ionic columns with open Palladian motifs between them. The composition is capped by a balustrade and a deep frieze filled with a fecund array of swags, **putti**, and masks. The effect, often described as scenographic, is one of sensuality and vividly contrasts with the brittleness of Renaissance monuments in Florence and the gravity of those in Rome. Adjacent to the library and facing the lagoon is Sansovino's La Zecca, or mint building (begun 1536) (Fig. 11.62). Its complete rustication obviously reflects the influence of Giulio Romano, and its related massiveness is ideally suited to its function as a great vault. The third story is a later addition.

The sculptural quality of these public buildings also carried over into Venetian palazzi. The Palazzo Grimani (begun ca. 1556) (Fig. 11.63) by Michele Sanmichele (1484–1559) has robust attached columns, in this case of the Corinthian order, and a heavy overhanging cornice.

GARDEN DESIGN

The history of landscape architecture is in some respects more difficult to reconstruct accurately than the history of architecture, because without continual maintenance and

11.63 Michele Sanmichele, Palazzo Grimani, Venice, begun ca. 1556.

Venetian palazzi like this one became models for cast-iron façades applied to wood and masonry commercial buildings in nineteenth-century America. The repetitive columns, elaborate windows, and detailed cornices were ideal for mass production.

replanting, the living materials that constitute the designer's work decay more rapidly, and change and vanish more completely than do most buildings. We know that the sacred enclosures and sanctuary precincts of Egypt, Mesopotamia, the Aegean, and Rome were landscaped, although the appearance of these gardens is known now only from reliefs, descriptions, or other representations of them. Better preserved are many Islamic works, such as the Alhambra, where the garden embodied the idea of paradise. The medieval gardens illustrated in manuscripts and described in literature tended to be functional, laid out in orderly beds and contained within a wall or hedge. Many of these were purposeful plantings for culinary or medicinal herbs.

During the Renaissance the garden as an extension of architecture became important once again, with designs that originated as free adaptations of antique landscapes. Roman terraced gardens, for example, influenced both Bramante's design for the Belvedere Courtyard (see Figs. 11.33, 11.34) and Raphael's designs for the Villa Madama (see Figs. 11.36, 11.37). At the Villa Madama, geometric perimeters of miniature box hedges encircled colorful planting beds, and the taller backdrop of trees defined the limits of the garden. During the Renaissance, however, landscape architecture was raised to the level of a major art, providing a stage setting for the enactment of the splendor of the aristocracy and princes of the Church. Pope Julius II, who commissioned the Villa Giulia just outside Rome, made use of its loggias and courts for theatrical performances and leisurely promenading. Late Renaissance gardens were elaborate, using water, sculpture, and foliage in an architectural manner. A number also provided a foretaste of Baroque urban planning.

Renaissance gardens began modestly, as at the Medici Villa (1458–61) in Fiesole, north of Florence (Fig. 11.64). Designed by Michelozzo and intended as a retreat for the Medici family and their humanist associates, it includes two levels of parterres, a lemon garden, and an occasional fountain, whose quietly flowing waters once provided an environment for scholarly contemplation.

Larger and more dramatic is the Villa Lante at Bagnaia near Viterbo (begun 1566) (Fig. 11.65), probably designed by Vignola, which uses perspective as an organizing agent. While the gardens were originally entered from below, the mature vegetation now makes the most dramatic view one from above, where a square upper parterre is extended down the sloping site through a shaft of space or **allée** defined by a **bosco**, a dense planting of trees. The allée is reinforced by twin casinos that act almost like sighting mechanisms for the perspective view; stairs and ramps occupy the space between them. Water features appear at the various levels, beginning with the Fountain of the Deluge at the top. Water then disappears and reappears at intervals down the central axis, sometimes as fountains, sometimes as a cascade, and finally as four placid pools in the center of the parterre on the lowest level.

0   50 m
0   150 ft

11.64 Michelozzo di Bartolommeo, Plan and section of the Medici Villa, Fiesole, 1458–61.

Florentine gardens of the Early Renaissance were quite small compared to the Roman gardens of the next century and the French gardens that appeared around seventeenth-century châteaux. Here the villa's loggia opens out onto a parterre, with another parterre one level below. The back side of the villa looks out over a smaller lemon garden.

The first major Mannerist garden was built at the Villa d'Este in Tivoli (Fig. 11.66) outside Rome, to the designs of Pirro Ligorio (ca. 1510–83). His client, Ippolito II Cardinal d'Este, owned a site that included both a north-facing slope and a large reliable water supply. Anyone visiting the gardens today during the hot summer months is struck by the marvelous microclimate—cool by virtue of shady trees and water everywhere. As designed by Ligorio, however, the gardens were intended as a setting for the Este family's sculpture collection, with plantings mostly in the form of low shrubs and hedges. Furthermore, while visitors enter today through the villa on the garden's high ground, the original entrance was from below. This lower access meant

11.65 Giacomo Barozzi da Vignola, Plan and section of the Villa Lante, Bagnaia, begun 1566.

The Villa Lante's typically Roman organization includes stairs and water features and a parterre at the lowest level. The central axis in the form of an allée is defined by boscos or dense groves of trees.

11.66 Pirro Ligorio, gardens of the Villa d'Este, Tivoli, ca. 1565–72.

Most striking in the fully developed gardens are the myriad water features. In this view a waterfall stands behind fishponds.

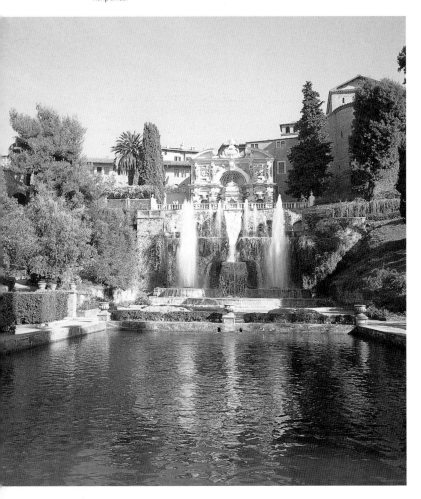

that the entire site could be taken in at a single glance rather than being experienced as a series of episodes along channels of large-scale greenery, as it is today.

Ligorio took as his principal theme the god Hercules, to whom the Este family traced their lineage mythologically. Hercules's strength and the magnitude of his labors were represented metaphorically by the efforts required in modeling the site, constructing aqueducts, and digging tunnels up to 3200 feet long. Ligorio's plan emphasized orthogonal and diagonal cross axes above; large rectangular fishponds and parterres below, with every manner and scale of water feature; architectural environments from an artificial cave to a huge water organ to a model of ancient Rome; and myriad pieces of sculpture, much of which now resides in the Capitoline Museum in Rome and elsewhere.

BOBOLI GARDENS, FLORENCE

Contemporary with the gardens of the Villa d'Este are the Boboli Gardens (Fig. 11.67), another major Mannerist work located in Florence behind the Palazzo Pitti. When the Medici acquired the property in 1549, they enlarged the building by adding substantial front wings enclosing the forecourt and extensive new construction at the back of the original palace. The rear extension was organized around three sides of a rectangular courtyard, the fourth side of which was attached with a semicircular stairway up to the Boboli Gardens beyond. Work on the gardens, to the designs of Niccolò Tribolo, began even before work on the palace. The garden layout was governed by a strong central axis rising up the hillside from the rear courtyard. In sequence it traverses a large horseshoe-shaped theater, rises up a ramp to a pool adorned with a fountain sculpted with an image of Neptune, and finally arrives at the highest terrace, which features a statue of Abundance

11.67 Niccolò Tribolo, Plan and section of the Boboli Gardens, Florence, begun 1549.

In this plan, long, staight pathways separate green spaces. A related use of long, straight streets would dominate city planning in the late sixteenth and seventeenth centuries, beginning with the replanning of Rome by Pope Sixtus V and others.

set in a background of foliage to terminate the vista. Over the next 150 years, others continued this ambitious design down the slope to the northwest, almost parallel to the long façade of the palace, developing this extension around a secondary axis that cuts arbitrarily across the original and primary axis projecting north from the center of the palace. All this work provided an elaborate setting for parties, spectacles, and concerts staged by the Medici.

THE RENAISSANCE IN FRANCE

The extension of artistic developments from Renaissance Italy to France was hastened in part by French military interventions in the peninsula. In 1494 the armies of King Charles VIII invaded Italy in pursuit of his claims to the kingdom of Naples; in 1498 Louis XII attacked Milan, toppling the Sforza family from power (precipitating Bramante's departure for Rome), and Francis I campaigned in Italy until 1525, when his defeat at Pavia brought a halt to French pretensions in the region of Milan. Although these military excursions ultimately resulted in no permanent expansion of French territory, the reverse flow of Italian artistic ideas was to have lasting consequences for architecture in France. By the end of the fifteenth century, France was changing from a feudal society into a strong centralized state headed by the king. Unlike urban-centered Italy, where merchant princes eclipsed the landed nobility and commissioned works from the great Renaissance artists, the court was the dominant force in French society, and the king led the way in supporting design in the Italian style. As Milan was the center of French contacts in Italy, the early Renaissance buildings there, including the Certosa at Pavia, were the best known and most generally admired structures, perhaps because their combination of highly ornamented surfaces and classical details was not far removed from the Late Gothic style with which the French were most familiar. From the last years of the fifteenth century, the French transported Italian art back to their own country, invited Italian artists and architects north to undertake commissions, and sent French artists to Italy to train in Renaissance workshops.

CHÂTEAUX IN THE LOIRE VALLEY

The cultural center of France in the early sixteenth century was not Paris, but the valley of the Loire, where the king and his nobles maintained elaborate châteaux or castles for leisure, entertaining, and attending to the pleasures of the hunt. Within these châteaux are found some of the earliest French architectural manifestations of the Renaissance style. Blois in particular illustrates the transition from the Middle Ages to the Renaissance through the successive stages in its construction. The château was begun in the thirteenth century with the erection of a large medieval hall and associated rooms. Between 1498 and 1504, Louis XII added an east wing, incorporating an entrance gate to what would ultimately be a large courtyard. The construction, in red brick with light-colored stone trim at corners, doorways, and window surrounds, reflects the continuity of medieval traditions. Above the entrance way there is an equestrian statue of Louis set into a large niche with double-cusped pointed arches and other Gothic detailing in stone. Windows align one above the other, culminating in elaborate Gothic dormers in the steeply pitched roof; these dormers read as a series of vertical elements, even though string courses and the cornice establish horizontal lines. Between 1515 and 1524, Francis I embarked on extensive building operations at Blois, adding a north wing to the medieval hall to form the north side of the court, with the opposite side facing

11.68 (above) Château, Francis I wing, Blois, 1515–24.

The medieval-Renaissance style of Francis I resulted from the King's contacts with new architectural developments in Italy while on a military campaign. Though a hybrid, the château was much admired as a source for early twentieth-century residential designs in America.

11.69 (below) Domenico da Cortona, Château, Chambord, 1519–47.

Chambord appears as a Renaissance trunk with medieval branches sprouting above it. The outbreak of steep roofs, dormers, and chimneys reflects an accommodation of the classical language to the northern climate.

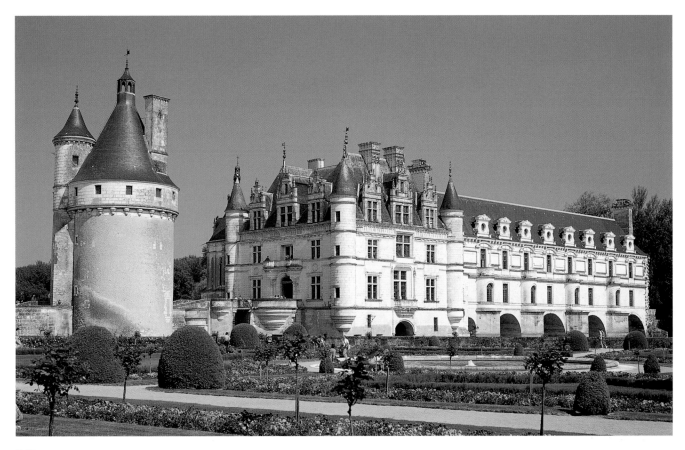

11.70 Philibert de l'Orme, Jean Bullant, and others, Château, Chenonceau, begun 1515.

There is no more picturesque château than this one. To the rear of the main block, the bridge was first added by Philibert de l'Orme. It then became a base for the grand dining hall designed by Jean Bullant.

over the town. Francis demolished an old tower and upon its foundations built the famous open spiraling stair (Fig. 11.68). It features decorative carving of wreaths, porcupines, and salamanders, emblems of the royal family. Windows on the courtyard façade are regularly arranged, although once again their vertical emphasis clashes with horizontal elements. All rooms are en suite, an arrangement the French long preferred. On the town façade, the Francis I wing is like a cliff face, with two loggias and an open third story with freestanding columns, modeled on papal palaces at the Vatican and at Pienza. Its mixture of classical columns and details also includes Gothic motifs.

In contrast to this town-based château, the château of Chambord (1519–47) was built in the countryside in the style of a fortified castle within a bailey or outer wall, thus neatly overlaying Renaissance symmetry and detailing on a fundamentally medieval building type (Fig. 11.69). Its Italian architect, Domenico da Cortona, employed simple cylindrical towers, which were to have been surrounded by open loggias; the latter were never built, however, since shade from intense sunlight was not as necessary in France as in Italy. The keep, or defensible core of the castle, has a suite of rooms in each corner, divided by a cruciform circulation pattern and a double staircase undoubtedly influenced by a sketch of Leonardo's. People ascending

one set of risers in the double-helix staircase can do so without seeing people descending the other. A great lantern above the staircase is one of a whole cluster of cones, chimneys, and dormers on the roof, presenting an almost medieval profile against the sky. Surrounding this abundance of vertical roof features is a terrace from which the ladies of the court could view the progress of the hunt in the wooded countryside beyond the château. The contrast between the ordered clarity of the walls and the wild exuberance of the rooftops reflects the partial assimilation of Renaissance architectural ideas into a firmly established medieval building tradition.

Not all the Loire châteaux were built for the king. Chenonceau (Fig. 11.70) is an example of a château constructed by a wealthy courtier and financier, Thomas Bohier. Begun in 1515, Chenonceau has a regularized plan, with all the major rooms opening off a central corridor, and a straight-run stair that illustrates Renaissance influence in its design, even as its moat, turreted corners, and chapel with rib vaults, pointed arches, and buttresses reflect medieval practices.

SEBASTIANO SERLIO AND PHILIBERT DE L'ORME

A second phase of Renaissance development in France began around 1540 with the arrival of Sebastiano Serlio (1475–1554), an Italian architect who came north at the invitation of the king, and the return of Philibert de l'Orme (ca. 1510–70), a Frenchman who trained in Rome and settled in Paris to practice as an architect and engineer. Both men brought knowledge of High Renaissance work in Rome, especially that of Bramante, and their writings did much to explain Renaissance design principles and modify building practices in France. Little of Serlio's architecture survives, aside from the exteriors of the château of Ancy-le-Franc, a mediocre square-plan building with a central open courtyard. The design, with its corner pavilions, Doric pilasters, and rustication, is almost entirely north Italian in derivation, but the high pitched roof is typically French.

Of greater importance than his buildings were Serlio's writings on architecture, published in several installments from 1537 to 1551 and gathered together in 1584 as *Tutte l'opere d'architettura et prospettiva*, known today as *The Five Books of Architecture*. The first architectural treatises not composed in Latin, these books contained woodcut illustrations, and the text addressed the ordinary builder more than the architectural scholar. Book One explains geometry; Book Two covers the construction of perspective drawings; and Book Three illustrates antique Roman buildings and the High Renaissance works of Bramante and Raphael. Book Four outlines the five orders of architecture (Doric, Ionic Corinthian, Tuscan, and Composite), illustrates arched rusticated door and window surrounds appropriate for each order, and includes notes on construction materials. Book Five features centralized church designs. Three more volumes containing many of Serlio's own designs complete the opus.

Philibert de l'Orme's writings were also practical in nature. His first volume, published in 1561, was *Nouvelles inventions pour bien bastir et petits frais* (*New Inventions for Building Well and Economically*). It considers the construction of vaults and roofs from an engineering standpoint. His major work, *Architecture*, was published in 1567.

While it draws some content from the earlier treatises by Vitruvius and Alberti, it relies extensively on de l'Orme's personal experiences in building to offer architects guidance grounded in both theory and practice.

Of the many projects on which de l'Orme worked, only a few remain. One of the most celebrated is the addition he made to the château at Chenonceau, a bridge over the river Cher composed of five arches of varying span (see Fig. 11.70). The building atop the bridge was added later by Jean Bullant.

THE LOUVRE, THE FRENCH PLACE AND HÔTEL, PARIS

After 1526, when the French capital became fixed in Paris, Francis I decided to update the medieval Louvre Palace, beginning with the removal of the cylindrical keep in the center of the square courtyard. Some years later, he decided to rebuild one wing of the enclosed court, with the possibility of extending the design around all four sides of the palace. Serlio proposed a design incorporating a series of courtyards, but the commission for rebuilding the Louvre wing went instead to the French architect Pierre Lescot (ca. 1500–78). Lescot's design (Fig. 11.71) dates from 1546, and while it is more correct in its use of the classical orders than most French buildings of the same

11.71 Pierre Lescot and Jacques Lemercier, Louvre, Paris, begun 1546.

Very little of the sixteenth-century Louvre is still visible. Here, on the pavilions in the Court of the Old Louvre, the orders are used extensively but in a distinctively French manner of pairs surmounted by pavilion roofs.

period, it could never be confused with Italian work. Lescot's façade emphasizes verticality rather than the horizontal line characteristic of the Italian Renaissance, even though it has cornice lines between floors. The courtyard façade is three stories high including the attic and is composed of Corinthian and Composite half-columns and pilasters, with elongated windows and pavilions at the extremities and in the center. The architecture is complemented by sculpture executed by Jean Goujon, one of the most talented artists of the period. It is possible that Lescot's façade was derived from Serlio's courtyard plan for the Louvre, although it seems that both miscalculated the interior implications of the courtyard's proportions. The great height of the building in relation to the width of the courtyard was such that, had the three additional façades been built to form the intended courtyard, the palace rooms would have received little direct sunlight. As events progressed, however, a later designer, Jacques Lemercier (1585–1654), enlarged the courtyard in 1624 to 400 feet square, more than four times the size proposed by either Serlio or Lescot.

For the last four decades of the sixteenth century, France was tormented by civil strife, the so-called Wars of Religion, which had economic and social causes as well as religious ones. Order was not restored until the arrival in 1594 of King Henry IV, whose policies brought an end to domestic and foreign turmoil. During the relative tranquillity of his reign, France implemented Italian ideas of town planning that were to have an impact on later architecture in both Britain and colonial America. In an effort to unify the aristocracy and rebuild Paris, which was still largely medieval, Henry IV sanctioned the construction of a number of residential squares, bounded by row houses with uniform façades. The Place Royale (now the Place des Vosges) (Figs. 11.72–11.73) was the first of these urban

11.72 View of the Place Royale (Place des Vosges), Paris, 1605–12.

The French *place* is a paved residential square. It focuses inward, in contrast to the subsequent Baroque spaces linked by axial boulevards.

11.73 Place Royale (Place des Vosges), Paris, 1605–12.

Around the Place Royale lie regularized residential façades, all connected by a continuous ground-level arcade. The taller pavilions were constructed by Henry IV, who promoted the project.

squares used exclusively for residential purposes; it was laid out from 1605 to 1612. In addition to lending the enterprise his title, Henry supported the project by constructing two pavilions, one each in the center of both the north and south sides of the square. Thirty-eight plots surrounding the 460-foot-square court were then leased on condition that the row houses to be constructed there conformed to the overall design scheme: each house was to be four bays wide and three stories high, not including the dormered attic story, built of brick with stone trim and roofed with slate. The royal pavilions featured more elaborate details and higher rooflines than adjacent structures, although they shared the continuous ground-level arcade that linked the buildings, a feature derived from Renaissance squares in Italy, such as the Piazza S. Annunziata in Florence onto which Brunelleschi's Foundling Hospital fronts. Originally the central open space of the Place Royale was unplanted and its sand surface used for festivals and tournaments. An equestrian statue of the King later served as the focal monument in the center. The houses proved to be too small for the aristocrats whom Henry wished to attract to Paris, however, so the first residents of the Place Royale were minor nobility and wealthy Parisian merchants instead.

Henry also encouraged a reclamation scheme at the west end of the Ile de la Cité in Paris, where, in 1578, Henry III had begun construction of the Pont Neuf (New Bridge) to link the business center of the city on the north bank to the university on the south. In conformance with medieval practice, houses were to line the bridge, and triumphal arches were to be set at each end. Henry IV ruled out both of these encumbrances to prevent unnecessary blockage of traffic. Instead, a trapezoidal point of land at the end of the island was developed in 1606 for another residential square, the Place Dauphine. This was entered from the center of the bridge, and the entrance axis was further distinguished by an equestrian statue of Henry, commissioned from Giovanni da Bologna by the King's wife, Marie de' Medici, in 1604 and erected in 1614 after Henry's assassination. As at the Place Royale, the houses lining the square had uniform façades; merchants lived upstairs and their shops extended along the ground level, making the Place Dauphine a commercial area.

Marie de' Medici became regent after the murder of her husband, and in 1615 she commissioned the Luxembourg Palace from Salomon de Brosse (1571–1626). The building is symmetrically arranged along a central axis; the three-story main block, or **corps-de-logis**, is a linear building with four corner pavilions, each containing an interconnected suite of rooms, or **appartements**.

The similarity of these arrangements to those in the château of Chambord is significant as appartements became the basic unit for domestic architecture in French town residences, or **hôtels**. The French hôtel generally contained several appartements connected to common reception rooms and salons. Extending perpendicular to

the Luxembourg Palace's corps-de-logis are two long, single-story galleries that terminate with a screen wall and central entrance pavilion enclosing a court. The ensemble has clear massing, with each element in the composition articulated distinctly, yet the whole building is united by overall use of lightly rusticated masonry and steeply pitched roofs.

THE RENAISSANCE IN ENGLAND

As was the case in France, Gothic architecture continued to be the predominant building style in England long after the Renaissance had originated and matured in Italy. Perpendicular Gothic, a particularly English variant, enjoyed favor well into the sixteenth century. The earliest expression of the Renaissance in Britain is found in sculpture and the decorative arts. In about 1511, King Henry VIII brought Pietro Torrigiani (1472–1528) and other artists directly from Italy to work on a number of royal commissions, the most important of which was a tomb for Henry's parents, Henry VII and his queen, in the Late Gothic chapel at Westminster Abbey. Cardinal Wolsey employed Italian sculptors, including Giovanni da Maiano, to make ten glazed terracotta roundels containing busts of Roman emperors. These roundels, which followed antique models and were thoroughly Renaissance in spirit, were ultimately incorporated into the gateways of the Cardinal's medieval castellated palace at Hampton Court, begun in 1515. After Wolsey's fall from royal favor, Henry VIII confiscated the palace and enlarged Hampton Court to more than twice its original size. He added courts, galleries, a chapel, and a hall, but the building remained more medieval than Renaissance, including the hall with its splendid **hammerbeam** truss roof of 1531–36.

Another essentially Gothic building of the same era is King's College Chapel, Cambridge (see Fig. 9.38), begun in 1446 and completed in 1515. Inside, however, the wooden choir screen is a piece of early Renaissance design. It was erected in 1533–35, as a gift from Henry VIII, to separate collegians from townspeople and to support the organ. The artist is unknown, but his work represents the first truly Renaissance design in Britain, exhibiting a wide range of classical details with only a few pendants suggesting Gothic influence.

Henry broke with the Church of Rome in 1534, and numerous Italian artists of the Roman Catholic faith left Britain soon thereafter. Thus, the full flowering of the Renaissance in Britain was delayed until the beginning of the seventeenth century. This does not mean that Italian ideals ceased to influence Britain, but that the direct inspiration from Italian artists resident in Britain stopped, while a more indirect influence continued to come from Italy via the Low Countries and France. The treatises of Scamozzi, Vignola, and Serlio were translated into English from the Dutch, not directly from the Italian, and numerous Dutch

11.74 Robert Smythson, Wollaton Hall, Nottinghamshire, 1580–88.

While Robert Smythson was well aware of the work of the Italian Renaissance, including that of Andrea Palladio, his design decisions reflect a concern for the local context, most obviously in the provision of many windows, a response to the often overcast English climate.

architectural books were exported to England. These illustrated strapwork, low-relief designs based on studded leather straps, that was arranged in geometrical and sometimes interlaced patterns. The strapwork decoration published by Flemish and Dutch architects, such as Hans Vredman de Vries, found its way into the works of the English architect Robert Smythson (1536–1614).

ELIZABETHAN COUNTRY HOUSES

Renaissance influence from Italy continued to come into Britain via Flanders during the reign of Queen Elizabeth I. Her own architectural commissions were insignificant, but her courtiers and governmental officials built on a lavish scale for the Queen and her traveling entourage. Wollaton Hall (1580–88) is an example of a great house built during the Elizabethan era (Figs. 11.74–11.75). Designed by Robert Smythson for the sheriff of Nottingham, the house draws on numerous sources. The building's

11.75 Robert Smythson, Plan of Wollaton Hall, Nottinghamshire, 1580–88.

This plan demonstrates its origins among the English castles of the Middle Ages. In the center is the great hall, and at the corners are the square-plan rooms that were once fortified towers.

11.76 Robert Smythson, Great hall, Wollaton Hall, Nottinghamshire, 1580–88.

Renaissance influence is apparent in the Doric frieze of the wood paneling. The hall is dominated by medieval hammerbeam trusses that support the roof.

symmetrical square plan with corner pavilions is taken from Serlio; in the center of the scheme, the great hall with ancillary accommodation is medieval; and the long gallery for the lodging of courtiers comes from France. Although Wollaton Hall is built of masonry, the huge expanse of windows is comparable to the fenestration found in timber construction. Renaissance pilasters and cornices punctuate the elevations, while the parapets are inspired by de Vries, and the upper clerestory levels of the great hall (Fig. 11.76) protrude above the roofline like a medieval keep with pepper-pot corner turrets.

Another great Elizabethan mansion, in all probability designed by Smythson, is Hardwick Hall in Derbyshire (1590–97) (Fig. 11.77). It shares many of Wollaton's characteristics in plan and elevation, but of greater importance here is the symmetrical arrangement of the main hall and its contiguous exterior colonnades, which reflect contemporary Italian design. Moreover, its plan appears as a Wollaton ripped open, less concerned with defense and more interested in light and warmth from the sun. Like all these

11.77 Robert Smythson, Hardwick Hall, Derbyshire, 1590–97.

"Hardwick Hall more window than wall" went the popular refrain of the time. Above the many windows, the filigree-like gables reflect the importation of Dutch influence based upon so-called strapwork—leather ornament derived from Italian Renaissance ornament in plaster.

grand and pretentious late sixteenth-century residences, Hardwick helped advertise the wealth and social standing of its owner, the extremely wealthy Elizabeth of Shrewsbury, known as Bess of Hardwick. Her initials, E.S., are displayed in the house's decorative crowning balustrade.

Kirby Hall in Northamptonshire (1570–75), sometimes attributed to John Thorpe (ca. 1563–1655), has ranges of rooms around a central symmetrical courtyard. The designer used classical orders freely, but at a variety of scales and in improbable positions, as where roofs butt into gables. The axis of the courtyard is defined by a two-story triumphal arch capped by an elaborate gable, perhaps inspired by the earlier central pavilion of Lescot's courtyard façade of the Louvre in Paris. This same motif dominates the design for William Cecil at Burghley House (1577–87), also situated in Northamptonshire.

INIGO JONES

It is amazing how heterogeneous this second phase of the English Renaissance appears when compared to what was initiated under Henry VIII or what was to come during the reign of Elizabeth's successor, James VI of Scotland, who became James I of England. Inigo Jones (1573–1652), an architect of profound significance in English architecture, emerged during the reign of James I. Jones was born seven years before the death of Palladio, and his first building, the Queen's House at Greenwich, introduced Palladian ideals to England. With the appearance of Jones, English classical-revival architecture immediately mirrored that of late sixteenth-century Italy.

Unlike earlier English architects, Jones acquired his knowledge of Italian architecture first-hand. He was in Italy as early as 1601. Two years later he traveled to Denmark, and he made a second trip to Italy during 1613–14 in the entourage of the earl of Arundel. In his baggage Jones carried a copy of Palladio's *Four Books of Architecture*, which he annotated generously. He met Scamozzi and visited Vicenza, where Palladio's works profoundly influenced him. Upon returning to England, he designed stage sets for the court in which he was able to experiment with Renaissance forms.

His first building commission, the Queen's House (Fig. 11.78), begun in 1616 but still being extended in 1661, was situated astride the road from Deptford to Woolwich, which divided the building in two. A bridge spanned the road at the second-floor level and acted as a **porte-cochère**, or covered drive-through for vehicles, leading to the entrance in the center of the building (Fig. 11.79). From the rather modest doorway, one is led directly into a room with the proportions of a cube. Access to the second floor is gained by a circular stair without a **newel**, or central post, a daring structural accomplishment in its day. A balcony across the cube room connects second-floor rooms, including the queen's bedroom, with the bridge. The garden façade of the house is based on Palladio's Palazzo Chiericati (see Fig. 11.51) at Vicenza; but, whereas

11.78 Inigo Jones, Queen's House from the front, Greenwich, begun 1616.

The change in appearance from Hardwick Hall to the Queen's House is stunning. Its design reflects Inigo Jones's close study of Palladio's work while traveling in Italy.

11.79 Inigo Jones, Plan of the Queen's House, Greenwich, 1616.

The Queen's House plan reflects the same Renaissance rigor as the façades. Its two wings are connected by a bridge that once spanned a road passing through the site.

the Palladian building has a two-story colonnade interrupted in the center of the second floor with a ballroom, the garden front of the Queen's House is a fenestrated wall with a central recessed loggia, well protected from the cool winds of Greenwich. Solid and void have been reversed in the exteriors of the two buildings.

Jones's most famous structure, the Banqueting House (1619–22) at Whitehall in London (Fig. 11.80), was built to replace an earlier building that had burned down. Its design, part of a much larger vision for an enormous Whitehall Palace complex, is an anglicized version of a Vitruvian basilica as interpreted by Palladio. The main interior space consists of a double-cube room with continuous balcony. In Jones's first project, he expressed this volumetric arrangement on the exterior as a two-story composition with a pedimented central pavilion at the principal façade. Jones eventually modified this elevation, articulating it into thirds according to the example of Palladio and omitting the pediment. He placed half-columns on the central

11.80 Inigo Jones, Banqueting House, Whitehall, London, 1619–22.

Notable here is the English emphasis on the surface texture of the stone façade. It was a fixation of English designers at least as far back as the construction of Durham Cathedral, where many of the piers were carved with chevron patterns that defied their circular geometry.

pavilion to provide a contrast in depth with the flat pilasters on either side. He arranged the windows to have alternate segmental and triangular pediments along the piano nobile, distinguishing it from the rusticated masonry of the base, where he employed flat lintels. He masked the roofline with a balustrade.

When Jones proposed a new design for the whole of Whitehall Palace in 1638, the Banqueting House was to be incorporated into half of one side of the central court. The enormous palace, based on Palladio's and Scamozzi's interpretations of a large Roman domus, here expanded to a gargantuan scale, would have replaced an area of rambling medieval structures. Although Jones's palace design was never built, the Banqueting House stood tall and monumental in its surroundings of earlier, domestically scaled medieval buildings, and its basic features were adapted in subsequent centuries for the ranks of over-scaled governmental buildings that form its present-day context.

On a site approximately halfway between the Banqueting House and the City of London to the east, the fourth Earl of Bedford employed Jones in 1630 to design a speculative development, called Covent Garden, in the grounds of Bedford House. Jones collaborated with Isaac de Caux in this work, the first of several English residential squares based on the designs for the French king Henry IV's Place Royale in Paris. As in its French predecessor, the

11.82 Inigo Jones, St. Paul's, Covent Garden, London, 1631–35.

Referring to its use of the rustic Tuscan order, Jones called his church the "handsomest barn in England." It was rebuilt after a fire in 1795.

11.81 Inigo Jones, View of Covent Garden, London, 1658.

With residential units built up into large blocks, this scheme focused on a church (labeled "chapell"), making it the first such composition in Renaissance England. The purpose of the project was to turn the Earl of Bedford's agricultural land into a cash-producing real-estate development.

houses facing Covent Garden had continuous ground-level arcades, masking entrances to the individual houses but providing a covered passageway around two sides of the square (Fig. 11.81). Five streets entered the square, which had Bedford House to its south and, to the west, the first completely new London church erected since the Reformation. Although rebuilt after a fire in 1795, the church of St. Paul (1631–35) (Fig. 11.82) still resembles Jones's original design, a simple box with a Tuscan-order portico, false door and altar at the east end, and the actual entrance at the west. The open space of the square soon became the site of a flourishing market, a use that continues to this day in permanent cast-iron halls constructed during the nineteenth century.

St. Paul's Cathedral in London was in poor repair at the beginning of the seventeenth century, and Jones was commissioned to restore it. He added a Corinthian portico to the west front, incorporating large scrolls to mask the aisle roofs, but the whole church was badly damaged in the fire of 1666, and both church and portico were demolished to make way for the later design of Christopher Wren. Wren's works belong to the seventeenth century and will be considered with those of other Baroque designers in Chapter 12.

CHAPTER 12

BAROQUE ARCHITECTURE

Just as the bankers and merchants of Florence supported Early Renaissance artists and architects, so the Catholic Church was the primary patron of art and architecture around Rome in both the seventeenth and eighteenth centuries, and the works it commissioned gave rise to a new style, the Baroque.

By the end of the Renaissance, the Church had great temporal power, but its moral foundations had deteriorated. The office of cardinal was sold openly; high and low church officials maintained mistresses and sought sinecures for their sons, who were euphemistically called "nephews"; and donations from the pious were spent on projects wholly lacking in spiritual purpose. The popes lived grandly, treating the Church's treasury as personal funds. To finance both sacred and secular projects, the Church instituted questionable fundraising practices, such as the sale of pardons and indulgences to save the payer or a relative from a stipulated number of days in Purgatory.

THE REFORMATION AND COUNTER-REFORMATION

As might be expected, the corruption of the Church brought about calls for religious reform, some as early as the thirteenth century. The most dramatic and influential reaction came from the monk Martin Luther of the monastery at Wittenberg, Germany. In 1517 he nailed his ninety-five theses or propositions to the door of All Saints' Church, in the opening salvo of what would become known as the Protestant Reformation. Until this time the Church had always overcome challenges from deviants within its ranks, usually by declaring them heretics and destroying them by force. This time, however, the discontent was too widespread for inquisitional methods to work, although they were tried.

The Church's more reasoned response was the Catholic Counter-Reformation, a program that involved both reform within the Church and a sustained campaign to win people back to the beliefs of Catholicism. The Council of Trent convened in 1545 and decreed that art was an essential tool for spreading the prestige and teachings of the Church. All the arts were deployed in this public-relations effort, and the artistic style that developed to restate traditional Catholic teachings became known as the Baroque. The results were openly propagandistic, overtly emotional, and long on sensory appeal. Based on an elaboration of classical forms, already made highly individualistic by artists and architects in the early sixteenth century, the Baroque was a didactic, theatrical, dynamic, and dramatic style. Later critics have faulted its exaggerated gestures, excessive ornamentation, and unconcealed emotionalism. In context, however, Baroque work should be seen as aiming to involve people directly with religious ideals. Baroque architecture is characterized by spatial complexity and drama created by light from undisclosed sources. Its effects were achieved through the dynamic play of concave against convex curves; a preference for axial and centralized spaces that found particular expression in the ellipse or oval, at once axial and centralized; and the imaginative integration of painting, sculpture, and architecture to create illusions and dissolve physical boundaries.

IL GESÙ, ROME

Among the new institutions of the reformed Catholic Church was the militant Order of the Society of Jesus, established by Ignatius Loyola in 1534 and commonly known as the Jesuits. Serving as missionaries and educators, particularly in remote areas, the Jesuits reached China

Johann Balthasar Neumann, Würzburg Residenz stair hall, 1720.

Tiepolo's painted ceiling looks down on this stair, which seems to float inside a great room of its own. The level of ornament and drama befits men in uniform and women in court dresses.

12.1 Giacomo Vignola and Giacomo della Porta, Il Gesù, Rome, 1568–76.

Innumerable church designs were based on this one, the mother church of the Jesuit order. The three-dimensionality and accumulation of detail in the central bay suggest a new kind of façade composition.

by 1550 and accompanied Spanish conquistadors to the Americas. Their headquarters were in Rome, however, and it is fitting that one of the earliest Baroque architectural designs, Il Gesù (Figs. 12.1–12.2), was their principal church, begun in 1568 to plans by Giacomo Vignola and completed in 1576 by Giacomo della Porta, who designed the façade as built and the dome.

The Gesù resembles Alberti's S. Andrea at Mantua in plan, having transverse-barrel-vaulted chapels (in place of

12.2 Giacomo Vignola and Giacomo della Porta, Plan and section of the Gesù, Rome, 1568–76.

The stunted nave announces that this is a preaching church of the Counter-Reformation. The use of piers and lateral chapels provided an alternative to the column-and-side-aisle plan inherited by Brunelleschi from the Middle Ages.

12.3 Carlo Maderno, S. Susanna, Rome, 1596–1603.

Compare this façade to Alberti's S. Maria Novella and della Porta's Gesù in order to understand evolving plasticity under the influence of Baroque ideals—the modeling of three-dimensional forms and the creating of dramatic shadows.

aisles with columns) flanking a longitudinal-barrel-vaulted nave. However, Vignola's motives for using such a plan were quite different from Alberti's. Alberti had sought to re-create ancient Roman grandeur and monumentality. By suppressing the transepts and shortening the nave, Vignola produced clear sightlines and acoustics that allowed for preaching to be heard clearly. The Gesù design was also forward-looking in its strong axial emphasis and in the three-dimensionality of elements on its west front. The composition of this façade is traceable to Alberti's S. Maria Novella in Florence, with classical orders replacing the traditional Florentine subdivision based on geometric shapes. At the Gesù, pairs of pilasters step out from forward-projecting planes until, on either side of the entrance, engaged columns support a triangular pediment, which in turn is framed by a segmental pediment supported by flanking pilasters. The original interior design was absolutely plain; the interior seen in the church today reflects a later decorative campaign that began in the late seventeenth century. Looking up at the nave ceiling, one is never sure where the architecture stops and the sculpture begins, or where the sculpture terminates and the fresco of

the *Adoration of the Name of Jesus*, which was painted between 1675 and 1679 by Giovanni Battista Gaulli, begins. Clouds, draperies, and human bodies float in space, and one is swept up by this vision of heaven.

The façade of the Gesù became the model for many Jesuit churches built in Rome and elsewhere. As Jesuit missionaries traveled and constructed new churches, their designs retained features from the mother church in Rome, where all Jesuits received their training. Within Rome itself, one early Baroque church that expands on the theme of the Gesù is Carlo Maderno's S. Susanna (1596–1603), where the façade design progresses from pilaster to half-column to paired engaged columns (Fig. 12.3).

POPE SIXTUS V AND THE REPLANNING OF ROME

Within a decade of the completion of the Gesù, early Baroque influences could be seen in the modifications made to the urban pattern of Rome. Pope Sixtus V

(1585–90) began radical changes, and his design program both guided the city's development for the next hundred years or more and influenced urban design throughout Europe and eventually in America.

Sixtus V was not the first pope to be concerned about the neglected physical appearance of Rome. His work can be seen as a vigorous elaboration and extension of initiatives begun in the 1450s by Nicholas V (1448–55), the first Renaissance pope to gain full control over the city following the long period of unrest when the popes resided instead in Avignon, France. Nicholas had undertaken fundamental repairs to ancient structures, such as the city walls, bridges, aqueducts, and roads on which Romans still relied, and he also had certain monuments modified to meet current needs, such as the conversion of Hadrian's Mausoleum into the Castel Sant'Angelo, a fortress for the papal court. Pope Sixtus IV (1471–84) had restored old churches and commissioned the building of others, and had attempted to improve circulation within the chaotic and densely populated medieval quarter by straightening the streets that led to the Ponte Sant'Angelo, the bridge over the Tiber that connected the bulk of Rome with St. Peter's. Julius II (1503–13) continued Sixtus IV's projects, as discussed in the last chapter in connection with Julius's patronage of Bramante and Michelangelo. In addition to those notable works around the Vatican and St. Peter's,

Julius directed his energies toward civic improvements, including the creation of three straight streets radiating like spokes from the Porta del Popolo, the northern city gate, and the cutting of two roughly parallel straight avenues on either side of the Tiber downstream from the Ponte Sant'Angelo. One of Julius's successors, Paul III (1534–50), commissioned Michelangelo's redesign of the Capitoline Hill. Pius IV (1559–65) laid out a straight avenue, the Strada Pia (1561–62), for which Michelangelo designed the Porta Pia (see Fig. 11.47) as the terminating portal.

These interventions in Rome were accelerated and intensified during the five years and four months of the reign of Sixtus V. Public works were undertaken, including the building of twenty-seven new fountains and the provision of a reliable water supply through the repair of ancient aqueducts and the construction of a new one, and law and order were restored to the city. The wool and silk industries were revived, further increasing employment opportunities. Had Sixtus lived another year, the

12.4 Sixtus V's plan for Rome, 1585–90.

With S. Maria Maggiore at the center, Pope Sixtus V developed axial connections to the city's seven principal churches. With this plan, the Renaissance concept of static, self-contained spaces gave way to the Baroque concept of dynamic axial connections between important urban points.

Piazza del Popolo

Strada del Babuino

Strada del Corso

Strada Leonina (Ripetta)

Strada Pia

St. Peter's

Porta Pia

Strada Felice

N

Colosseum might have been refurbished into a wool-spinning establishment!

The people who most benefitted from the changes wrought by Sixtus were pilgrims coming to see the major Christian shrines. Recognizing that these religious visitors were important to the city's economy, Sixtus planned to link Rome's seven Early Christian basilicas with direct processional routes, punctuated by vertical elements and fountains to mark major points along the way (Fig. 12.4). This was a much larger realization of ideas first developed in sixteenth-century gardens, such as the Boboli Gardens in Florence. Given the irregular topography of the city, it would be no easy task to superimpose a paper plan of straight roads on the terrain. The reworking of the city proposed by Sixtus was so convincing, however, that nearly all architects, planners, and civic authorities who have continued the work in the following centuries have done so in accordance with his scheme.

Sixtus began with the construction of a new street, the Strada Felice, which extended from S. Maria Maggiore to S. Croce in Gerusalemme in one direction and in the other direction to SS. Trinità dei Monti on the Esquiline Hill. The initial intention was to continue this street on to the Porta del Popolo, the major entry point for visitors arriving from the north, but the intervening hills prevented this idea being realized. As a related project, the Piazza del Popolo was later redesigned to provide an appropriate entranceway for visitors. After passing through the gate, visitors entered a space that focused on a central obelisk. Radiating from this center were three straight streets added by earlier popes, which provided direct access to major districts of the city. From the Piazza del Popolo, the left radial street was the Strada del Babuino, which led to a fountain at the base of the Esquiline Hill on which sits the church of the Trinitá dei Monti. Sixtus dedicated the church in 1585, and a stair linking the church and the fountain below was built over a century later.

ST. PETER'S

The most important Christian monument in Rome was the Basilica of St. Peter, located across the Tiber from the older parts of the city. During Sixtus's reign, work was resumed on the construction of the dome after twenty-five years of relative inaction following the death of Michelangelo. Sixtus also turned his attention to the route linking St. Peter's to the rest of Rome. Pilgrims crossed the Tiber on the Ponte Sant'Angelo, at the end of which was the massive Castel Sant'Angelo. The route to St. Peter's continued to the west, but the direct link projected by Sixtus did not become a reality until the 1930s, when the Fascist dictator Benito Mussolini pushed through the Via della Concilazione to provide a majestic axial approach to the great church. From a distance one can clearly see the dome of St. Peter's rising above the nave and wide façade, although Michelangelo's dome, designed for a naveless church, gradually recedes from view as one comes closer to the building.

In the center of what is now the Piazza of St. Peter's is Sixtus's contribution to the shaping of the space in the front of the basilica, the eighty-three-foot-tall Vatican Obelisk, which was installed there in 1586. Technical direction for this monumental feat of engineering was provided by Domenico Fontana, who later wrote a book describing and illustrating the entire process. The Vatican Obelisk was the largest intact specimen of the dozen Egyptian obelisks moved to Rome during the empire. How the ancient Romans maneuvered these into place is unknown, but the presence of several broken ones indicates that their methods were not always successful. Fontana's task was to lower the 681,221-pound obelisk from its position in the former Circus of Nero and move it about 260 yards to its new location in the Piazza of St. Peter's, all without damaging the monolith or its carvings. His solution to the problem involved encasing the obelisk in a protective timber framework, transferring it to a horizontal position by means of ropes and pulleys, which were controlled by the coordinated action of men and horses working thirty-eight windlasses, and then moving it over rollers to the new site. An elevation drop of approximately thirty feet between the old and new sites facilitated the horizontal transport. Once in the piazza, the obelisk was moved down an inclined plane and reerected using the same hoists and capstans employed to lower it. The whole operation was carefully planned and supervised by Fontana, who was empowered by the Pope to appropriate men, materials, and horses as necessary for the completion of the work. As the obelisk was raised in front of St. Peter's on 29 April 1586, the entire College of Cardinals along with the citizenry of Rome turned out to watch the spectacle. Barricades kept the curious at a safe distance, and absolute silence was enforced during the critical lifting stages so that the workmen could hear and respond correctly to Fontana's signals, given by a trumpet and a bell.

Following his successful removal of the Vatican Obelisk, Fontana was commissioned to relocate three smaller obelisks in Rome. Those standing today in the Piazza del Popolo, at S. Giovanni in Laterano, and at the apse of S. Maria Maggiore were all positioned by Fontana. The pyramidal points of these great shafts are prominent landmarks indicating the important surrounding monuments in the city. Sixtus V's work in Rome doubtless had a major influence on Pierre L'Enfant's late eighteenth-century plan for Washington, D.C., Baron Eugène Georges Haussmann's cutting-through of boulevards in Paris in the mid-nineteenth, and even on the twentieth-century city planner Edmund Bacon, who was responsible for major redevelopment work in Philadelphia in the 1950s and '60s. Bacon's use of axial avenues to link major areas of the city and not obelisks but high-rise buildings to mark different areas shows the continuing impact of city planning in Baroque Rome.

GIANLORENZO BERNINI
THE COMPLETION OF ST. PETER'S

After the death of Sixtus V, work continued on St. Peter's; this project, so long in preparation by a series of architects whose abilities, styles, and philosophies varied considerably, was at last brought to completion during the Baroque period. The dome was finished in 1612 under the direction of Giacomo della Porta and Domenico Fontana, and the nave addition, not envisioned by Michelangelo, was made by Carlo Maderno, who also designed the main façade (Figs. 12.5–12.7). The nave shifts orientation imperceptibly to align with the Vatican Obelisk, which Fontana had accidentally set off-center; Maderno considered it easier to turn the nave than to move the Egyptian needle. The largest church in Christendom was finally consecrated in 1626.

12.5 Façade of St. Peter's, Rome, 1546–64, 1606–12.

Maderno's façade stretches the full width of the church. The small cupolas were the work of Vignola. The dome was planned by Michelangelo and executed by Giacomo della Porta.

12.6 Michelangelo Buonarroti and Carlo Maderno, Plan of the completed St. Peter's, Rome, 1546–64, 1606–12.

The extension of the nave after Michelangelo's death documents the clergy's determination to replace the architect-preferred central plan with a Latin-cross conducive to the processional and large crowds.

12.7 Longitudinal section through St. Peter's, 1546–64, 1606–12.

Viewing this section, one would hardly suspect that Bramante and Michelangelo intended this church to be the greatest of the Renaissance central plans. However, the architects did succeed in re-creating the scale and grandeur of ancient Rome.

12.8 Gianlorenzo Bernini, Baldacchino, St. Peter's, Rome, 1624–33.

The size of the Baldacchino, at nearly ninety feet, taller than the obelisk in front of the church, gives some sense of the scale of this great basilica. The twisted columns had connections to Solomon's Temple and to Old St. Peter's.

Urban VIII's favorite artist was Gianlorenzo Bernini (1598–1680), a man who might easily be compared with Michelangelo. Both were recognized as prodigies at an early age; both had long and productive lives; and both were immensely inventive sculptors who also did important work in architecture and city planning. Bernini was the son of a sculptor, and his artistic education had been directed in part by Urban VIII, a noted patron of the arts even before he was elected to papal office. The vigorous building programs of the Catholic Church in the seventeenth century were responsible for the development of the Baroque style, and for over fifty years Baroque work in Rome was dominated by Bernini.

Nowhere is his presence felt more strongly than at St. Peter's, where he served as official architect from 1629 until his death. Much of the present interior's character is the result of Bernini's genius. Either directly or through workshops under his supervision, Bernini was responsible for the flooring in the nave and narthex, for the decoration of the nave piers, and for the design of four sculptural groupings for altars and tombs. His designs for the crossing and main apse of the church, however, are the most substantial contributions he made to the interior. To reduce the scale of the vast space under Michelangelo's dome, Bernini designed the bronze Baldacchino (1624–33), a symbolic protective canopy over the high altar above the tomb of St. Peter (Fig. 12.8). To match the scale of the rotunda, the Baldacchino is nearly ninety feet high; its twisted columns are not a Baroque invention, but a greatly enlarged version of marble columns from the Constantinian basilica, some of which are preserved as part of the reliquaries at the second-floor level of the crossing piers. It was believed that the original twisted columns were brought by Constantine from the Temple of Solomon in Jerusalem, so their continued use here links St. Peter's with the Holy Land. Material for the Baldacchino was obtained by melting down the Roman bronze supports of the Pantheon's portico, a reuse of historic material sanctioned by the Pope over popular opposition; there was even enough metal left over to cast eighty cannons for defense of the city. In the enormous space of the basilica, the Baldacchino distinctly marks the spiritual center of the church, which would otherwise appear insignificant. So large is the interior that the Baldacchino's height, equivalent to a nine-story building, is not overpowering from a distance.

In the angles of the crossing piers Bernini's design placed four dramatic statues of saints associated with the Passion of Christ, all more than twice lifesize. Of these, Bernini himself carved the statue of St.

Longinus (1629–1638), the Roman centurion who pierced Christ's side at the Crucifixion; Longinus is shown at the moment he realizes Christ's divinity. Beyond the Baldacchino, and framed on axis by its columns, is Bernini's culminating work in the basilica, the Cathedra Petri, or Chair of Peter (1657–66), an elaborate reliquary in bronze constructed around the reputed wooden seat of the first apostle. Lightly supported by four figures representing Doctors of the Church, those men who established the doctrine of the faith, the chair floats above the visitor's head against a glorious backdrop where golden rays emanate from a brightly illuminated stained-glass center on which rises the dove of the Holy Spirit. The church of St. Peter's, unlike some Early Christian buildings, is not aligned with its apse to the east but rather to the west, so the rays of the afternoon sun pass through the window and merge with the golden radiance of the sculpture surrounding the chair. By incorporating a window behind the work to provide brilliance for the ensemble, Bernini's design admirably illustrates the theatricality of the Baroque.

In addition to these major features, Bernini designed the Scala Regia (1663–66), leading from the main audience hall in the Vatican to the north colonnade of the piazza and the north end of the church's narthex, as a replacement for the old irregular stair (Fig. 12.9). Bernini's solution turns to full advantage the difficult context into which the work had to be set; he designed a staircase tapering in width and height from bottom to top, thus accentuating the effect of perspective from the bottom of the stairs. A landing halfway up creates a pause in the ascent; lit by an undisclosed source, it becomes a dramatic element in the design. As the Scala Regia is almost perpendicular to the narthex, Bernini made an equestrian statue of Constantine for the side wall at the bottom of the stairs to terminate the axial vista at the end of the narthex. The emperor is depicted at the moment of his conversion on the battlefield; a huge drapery blown by the wind provides a dynamic directional backdrop for the statue.

As the greatest church in Western Christendom, St. Peter's required an appropriate approach and exterior setting, and Bernini was also commissioned to undertake this work. In 1637 he proposed that two belltowers be constructed at the ends of the narthex in order to counter the horizontal emphasis of Maderno's façade. Only the southernmost tower had been partially built when soil subsidence and subsequent cracking of the structure necessitated removal of the campanile in 1645, almost ending Bernini's architectural appointment in disgrace. In 1657, however, Bernini designed the Piazza of St. Peter's, one of the most famous urban spaces in the world (Fig. 12.10). Composed of two parts, the piazza has an oval section, the *piazza obliqua*, which focuses on the Vatican Obelisk, followed by a trapezoidal section, the *piazza retta*, directly in front of the church entrance. Both sections work together to provide a symbolic embrace for Christians

12.9 Gianlorenzo Bernini, Scala Regia, Vatican, Rome, 1663–66.

Here Bernini used forced perspective in plan perspective to accentuate depth; the width of the stair diminishes as it rises. His design can be connected to projects from Bramante's false choir at S. Maria presso S. Satiro to Vasari's Uffizi complex.

12.10 Gianlorenzo Bernini, Plan of St. Peter's complex and part of the Vatican, Rome, 1748.

In this site plan the southern extremity of Bramante's Belvedere Courtyard is visible to the right. The final plan for the church still carries the imprint of its central-plan origins. The quarter east of the piazza is shown densely populated, as it was before Mussolini cleared it to provide open space all the way to the Tiber.

who come to visit the tomb of St. Peter. The *piazza retta* attempts in two ways to ameliorate the proportions of the façade by increasing the apparent height of the church. Its trapezoidal shape, which is perceived as a rectangle, "squeezes" the façade to emphasize verticality, and the flanking colonnade diminishes in height as it extends toward the church, thereby providing a smaller unit to which the engaged Corinthian columns of the façade are compared. Although the converging sides of the *piazza retta* may suggest influence from Michelangelo's Piazza del Campidoglio, the form was probably generated by the oblique placement of the Vatican Palace relative to the narthex of the church.

The *piazza obliqua* is more characteristically Baroque, with curving arms that do not form a true oval but are actually two semicircles connected to a square. Two symmetrically placed fountains and the obelisk establish a cross axis to the approach to St. Peter's, thus introducing an element of tension into the design. The piazza's sides are formed by freestanding Tuscan-order colonnades, thirty-nine feet high and four columns deep, arranged in radial lines to provide a constantly shifting pattern of light and shadow as one moves around the edge. The colonnades generate a sense of enclosure without confinement; the space is defined without being cut off from the fabric of the city. Over 250,000 people can gather in the Piazza of St. Peter's to be blessed from the Benediction Loggia above the central entrance to the church or from a window in the papal apartments, at the right of the piazza. Through its dignified and all-encompassing design, the Piazza of St. Peter's extends the Church's welcome beyond the boundaries of the basilica itself.

S. ANDREA AL QUIRINALE, ROME

Bernini also designed the small oval-plan church of S. Andrea al Quirinale (1658–70) as a quiet retreat for Jesuit novices (Figs. 12.11–12.12). The shape of the interior space is clearly expressed by the convex body of the church. To each side, countercurves turn into concave enveloping arms that connect the building to the street. Entry is made between giant-order Corinthian pilasters supporting a pediment; within this frame a thermal window allows light into the interior and, as though folded down from it, a convex curving portico is supported by Ionic columns. Around the exterior walls at the upper level, volute-like buttresses stabilize the dome.

The entrance and altar lie opposite one another across the short axis of the oval plan. To maintain emphasis on the altar and establish the short axis as the dominant one, Bernini placed pilasters, not chapels, on the cross axis, forcing the visitor's attention back to the origin point of the dramatic action. The architectural space around and above provides the setting for what would today be called a multi-media experience, as Bernini combined painting, sculpture, stucco work, and light effects to dramatize the

12.11 Gianlorenzo Bernini, S. Andrea al Quirinale, Rome, 1658–70.

A reflection of Counter-Reformation policies, S. Andrea has flanking walls that reach out as if to embrace passers-by. Its huge frontispiece is an essay in semicircular geometries: thermal window, portico roof, and entry stairs.

12.12 Gianlorenzo Bernini, Plan of S. Andrea al Quirinale, Rome, 1658–70.

Bernini chose to place the altar along the short axis of the oval. He also chose to terminate the cross axis with pilasters rather than chapels. Both were unorthodox choices in the mid-seventeenth century.

martyrdom and apotheosis of S. Andrea. First, a painted image of the future saint hangs above the altar, lit by a hidden, secondary dome with lantern. Around the painting, sculpted angels and putti levitate among gilded light rays. Above, a sculpted figure of S. Andrea rises through the broken pediment that defines the altar, accompanied around the base of the dome by more sculpted putti and fishermen representing the profession from which the saint was drawn. The coffered dome includes ten ribs, diminishing in width as they rise to visually support the base of the lantern. Here, an audience of still more putti awaits S. Andrea's admittance into heaven, represented by the glow from the principal lantern. All in all, it is a tour de force of Counter-Reformation theatricality.

FRANCESCO BORROMINI

While the completion of the interiors of the basilica and construction of the Piazza of St. Peter's were to occupy a substantial portion of Bernini's time, these were not by any means the only projects undertaken by this enormously gifted and energetic artist. Nor did he accomplish the work on St. Peter's singlehandedly. He had assistants, some of whom became prominent designers in their own right. This was the case with Francesco Borromini (1599–1667), who began his career as a stonecutter in his uncle Carlo Maderno's shop and rose quickly to become a master mason and Bernini's collaborator on the St. Peter's <u>Baldacchino</u>. After a time these two men of strong personalities clashed; before 1630 Borromini had emerged as Bernini's rival. Of his many commissions around Rome, two are of particular interest as demonstrations of Borromini's strikingly original approach to design.

An elaborate canopy erected over an altar.

S. CARLO ALLE QUATTRO FONTANE, ROME

Projects for the monastery and church of S. Carlo alle Quattro Fontane (also called S. Carlino or Little S. Carlo) involved Borromini on and off from 1634 until his death. He began with renovations to the monks' living quarters, including a new refectory and cloister (1634–38), a courtyard in which bulging panels above pairs of columns replaced the customary corners.

In 1638 he designed the diminutive but highly innovative church (Fig. 12.13) at the corner of the Strada Felice and the Via Pia (today known as the Via Quattro Fontane), one of Sixtus V's grand routes linking districts of the city. He embellished the intersection with <u>four fountains</u> set diagonally across each corner, hence the descriptive words "Quattro Fontane" appended to the name of the church. The church plan consists of an undulating oval, its long axis leading to the main altar (Fig. 12.14). The curving side walls swell outward on the short axis to form shallow side chapels in a counterpoint evoking the spirit of a stretched Greek-cross plan. Borromini's own drawings show that he

12.13 Francesco Borromini, S. Carlo alle Quattro Fontane, Rome, begun 1634.

The theme of the façade is set by the figure of S. Carlo above the doorway, his eyes uplifted and his hands positioned as if to pray. This vertical motion extends to the attenuated, superimposed columns and even the oval plaque at the scalloped pediment.

12.14 Francesco Borromini, Plan of S. Carlo alle Quattro Fontane, Rome, begun 1634.

The intensity of Borromini's organizational skills can be read in the dual ordering of the church and the cloister. In each, the theme is sets of paired columns. In the cloister, six sets are freestanding; in the church eight sets are pressed into the undulating surrounding wall.

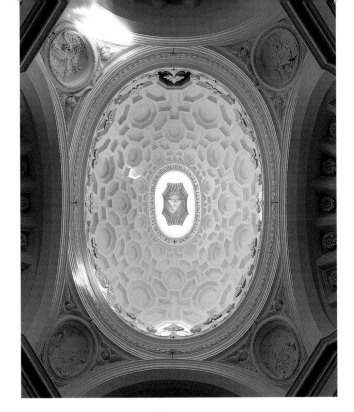

12.15 Francesco Borromini, S. Carlo alle Quattro Fontane, Rome, begun 1634.

At the inside surface of the dome, Borromini introduced a pattern of octagons, hexagons, and trinitarian crosses. These diminish in size as they move upward, creating an exaggerated perspective.

consists of a chapel inserted behind the curved end of an existing two-story courtyard at the Archiginnasio, a college popularly known as La Sapienza and now part of the University of Rome. Giacomo della Porta had designed the façade inside the curve, which necessarily became the visual base for Borromini's dome when viewed from the entry to the courtyard. Borromini proposed alterations to della Porta's façade, but none of them was carried out.

12.16 Francesco Borromini, S. Ivo della Sapienza, Rome, begun 1642.

The first two levels of the courtyard were planned by Pirro Ligorio and Giacomo della Porta. Borromini accepted the extant structure as the base for his unorthodox drum with its exotic cupola crowned by a spiral.

conceived his complex plan by interlocking a series of geometric figures from circles to equilateral triangles, and he based his proportions in section on more equilateral triangles. This reliance on geometry rather than Renaissance arithmetical ratios reflects Borromini's immersion in the more strongly Gothic design and construction practices around Milan where his father had been a builder. Columns at S. Carlo's lower level appear to have been pressed into the surrounding walls. Pendentives above the entablature reduce the undulating plan to an oval drum supporting an oval dome, elaborately coffered with octagons, hexagons, and Trinitarian crosses, diminishing to an oval oculus (Fig. 12.15).

The principal façade, constructed in 1665–67, mirrors the internal play of concave and convex, swinging in and out over its three-bay width with its two stories separated by an intermediate curving entablature. A figure of St. Charles Borromeo with praying hands and eyes uplifted sets the façade's vertical theme, and angels, their wings contorted to form a pediment, shelter the saint and anticipate the almost bizarre character of the interior. This verticality is terminated by a crowning balustrade broken by a large oval medallion. With consummate skill Borromini incorporated one fountain and its mitered corner into the façade design, so that all parts project the dynamism of the Baroque.

S. IVO DELLA SAPIENZA

At S. Ivo della Sapienza (Fig. 12.16) Borromini created an archetypal masterpiece of the Baroque. The building

Pope Leo X donated the site, but the chapel was not begun until 1642 under the patronage of Urban VIII. Urban's coat of arms incorporates bees symbolic of his own family, the Barberini, and Urban was affectionately known as the "King of Bees." Therefore, it is not surprising that Borromini, who had waited ten years for the commission, flattered his patron by incorporating the shape of a flying bee into the form of the plan, which is geometrized as a hexagon (Fig. 12.17a) by the intersection of two equilateral triangles that also create a six-pointed star. The internal entablature between the lower level of the church

12.17a (left) Francesco Borromini, Plan of S. Ivo della Sapienza, Rome, 1642–50.

Borromini made use of two interlocking equilateral triangles as a conceptual structure for his complex plan. The reflected ceiling plan reveals the facets of his "pumpkin" vault, similar in spirit to those apparently used by the emperor Hadrian at his villa in Tivoli near Rome.

12.17b (below, left) Francesco Borromini, Transverse section through S. Ivo della Sapienza, Rome, 1642–50.

This section reveals Borromini's unconventional layering. Atop the pilasters sits the faceted entablature. Springing from this entablature are the ribs, folded against one another and diminishing in width as they rise.

12.18 (below, right) Francesco Borromini, S. Ivo della Sapienza dome, Rome, 1642–50.

With obvious similarity to Gothic ribbed vaults, the dome contains symbols of the Barberini family, the building's patrons.

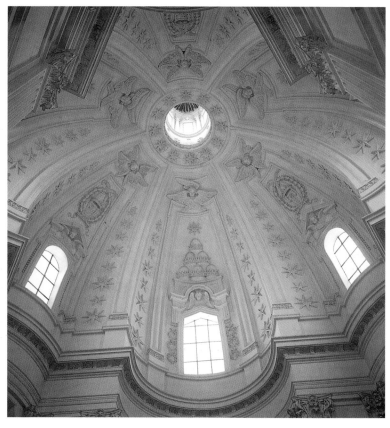

and the dome does not separate the two areas in a conventional fashion. Rather, the concave-convex rhythms of the plan rise in planes through the bent and folded entablature into the ribs of the six-lobed dome (Figs. 12.17b, 12.18). Externally, the bulging walls and stepped cap of Borromini's dome support an exotic lantern tower that spirals upward in a form that admits multiple associations: that of the papal tiara, which contains bands of a triple crown, merged into a continuous spiral, symbolizing the pope's authority in priestly, royal, and imperial affairs; that of a conch shell, one species of which was generally known as the *corona papale* because of its resemblance to the papal tiara; and that of Divine Wisdom, which complemented the symbolism of an upwardly rising spiral. In fact, the iconography of the whole chapel expresses the idea that "all wisdom is from the Lord God" and that "fear of the Lord is the beginning of wisdom" (Ecclesiasticus 1:1).

URBAN OPEN SPACES IN BAROQUE ROME

With a few notable exceptions, urban design is a shared undertaking, occurring across several generations. The bold strokes of Sixtus V's plan for Rome created opportunities for later architects to complete his grand scheme with designs for churches, fountains, and piazzas to enrich civic life. For example, Fontana's placement of the Vatican Obelisk preceded and was therefore not part of Bernini's overall design for the piazza, but its position in front of St. Peter's identified the area as one of major importance within the city and contributed to Bernini's specific spatial conception of it as realized in 1657. The collaboration of talented designers in Rome on various urban projects has endowed the city with many handsome public squares; three particularly fine Baroque ones will be discussed here.

THE PIAZZA NAVONA

Bernini and Borromini jointly created the urban design of Piazza Navona, an unusually proportioned space (177 by 906 feet) that was once the Stadium of Domitian (Fig. 12.19). In the medieval period houses were built on the ruins of the grandstands, while the open center was used for informal games and a market. Pope Innocent X's palace faced the square, and on his election in 1644 he undertook the refurbishing of the piazza and its church, S. Agnese in Agone (Fig. 12.20). The church commission was first given to Girolamo and Carlo Rainaldi, but their designs displeased Innocent, and in 1653, with the foundations already in place, Borromini assumed control of the building process. He retained their Greek-cross plan but pulled back the flight of steps protruding into the narrow square and provided a new concave façade, above which rose a high drum, elongated dome, and slender cupola. After 1657 and the death of Innocent X, Carlo

12.19 Gianlorenzo Bernini and Francesco Borromini, Piazza Navona, Rome, begun 1644.

Piazza Navona's outline results from its origins as an ancient Roman circus or racetrack. Around it are the narrow irregular streets of Rome's medieval core. S. Agnese in Agone is #608; S. Maria della Pace is #599; and S. Ivo della Sapienza is #800.

Rainaldi returned to complete the work, adding the twin towers positioned on either side of the curved façade. In its massing S. Agnese represents the silhouette that St. Peter's might have had without the nave addition.

Bernini, temporarily out of favor for political reasons and because of the failure of the towers at St. Peter's, was not considered as a possible architect for S. Agnese, yet his proposal for the central fountain in Piazza Navona so pleased Innocent that the Pope set aside personal animosities and awarded Bernini the fountain commission. The Fountain of the Four Rivers (1648–51), located in the center of the piazza but off the main axis of S. Agnese so as not to compete with it, has symbolic figures set amid splashing water and representing the major rivers of the continents to which Catholicism had spread. The Ganges figure holds an oar because of that river's great navigable length; the Danube looks toward emblems of Innocent X; the Nile's face is obscured because its origin was then unknown; and the Rio della Plata figure is a highly imaginative figuration of a native South American, bald, bearded, and surrounded by coins to reflect the wealth of the New World. The figures support a central obelisk, crowned with a representation of the dove of the

12.20 Carlo Rainaldi and Francesco Borromini, S. Agnese, Rome, begun 1644.

Borromini chose to place the dome close to the façade so it could be seen between flanking towers. It is the same scheme intended by Bernini at St. Peter's before his towers became unstable.

influential Pamphili family symbolizing the triumph of Christianity over paganism, and, by extension, Catholicism over Protestantism. Thus, in Baroque hands, even so secular an item as a public fountain became an allegory for the Roman Catholic Church. At either end of the piazza are additional fountains; all three provide visual delight while refreshing the air with cooling moisture.

Just behind Piazza Navona is one of Rome's smallest squares, in front of the church of S. Maria della Pace, which is the work of Pietro da Cortona (1596–1669). The main church building dates to the fifteenth century; Cortona gave it a new convex façade in 1656–58 (Fig. 12.21), its plasticity restrained by flanking Corinthian pilasters supporting a pediment. That pediment frames yet

12.21 Pietro da Cortona, S. Maria della Pace, Rome, 1656–58.

Cortona's façade appears to have been bent and expanded from within. The flanking walls are analogous to stage wings and connect the church to existing buildings.

PIAZZA NAVONA—A SPACE FOR SPECTACLE

by Julia M. Smyth-Pinney

12A Giovanni Paolo Pannini, *Piazza Navona Flooded*, 1756. Oil on canvas, 37 ½ × 54 in (95.5 × 137 cm). Landesgalerie, Hanover.

The year is 1756, and this is Piazza Navona, in the heart of Rome (Fig. 12A) Already, the Baroque age is ending and the wonderful monuments of the piazza, created for the glorification of the Pamphili family's pope, Innocent X, are 100 years old. Yet the setting designed by the greatest Roman Baroque architects at the height of their powers, reflected in the waters of the flooded square, re-creates the spirit of Innocent's High Baroque papacy.

Innocent's renovated family palace is on the left-hand of the piazza; from the balconies he and his retinue could participate in the dramatic pageantry occurring in the "royal front yard." Among the Pope's guests would have been visitors from many countries, diplomats representing the absolutist monarchs of expanding European nations, still competing for the Catholic Pope's favor despite his declining power.

Life in Piazza Navona thus offered itself as a permanent theatrical event, managed by increasingly stringent rules of etiquette, supported by New World wealth, and dominated by open enjoyment of artifice and unusual entertainments. Whether it was a festive secular event planned to honor a visiting dignitary, or a sacred cere-

monial occasion, sights and sounds, smells and tastes were organized to delight the senses and to sway hearts and minds. This silent and static painting captures the emotional excitement of the parade, and strives to suggest the shouts and splashes, the rich perfumes wafting along with the carriages, all continuously moving, animated by the bright sunlight striking silk and gilt and silver lamé, light refracting from the active surfaces of spouting, rippling water.

At nightfall, from the interiors of the palaces and churches, more solemn processions lit by tapers and torches flowed out into a Piazza Navona illuminated by bonfires and colored waxed paper lanterns. For ceremonies celebrating the election of innocent to the papacy, the sober surface of the Renaissance church on the right was the background for an enormous wooden, plaster, and canvas construction—Noah's ark on its mount—which later erupted with dazzling firework displays that delighted an audience of rich courtiers, pilgrims and paupers, shopkeepers and soldiers.

Events such as these proceeded with occasional hiatuses for the

harsher realities of the years around 1650: debt-ridden papal finances, serious famines, plague outbreaks, and the terrible battles, both physical and intellectual, among Protestants and Catholics, Christian forces and "non-believers." Statues could sometimes still spout wine, not water. Does all this recall the excesses of ancient Rome? Certainly one of the aims of Baroque rulers was to impress their rivals and subjects, and the underlying classicism evident in the Baroque age arises from explicitly revivalist dreams of an idyllic classical "Golden Age." It is not surprising, then, that Rome was the site of the style's initiation.

Yet fierce inner devotion often animated individual Baroque lives, activating the outward drama of the exuberant public events. Innocent himself, for example, was pious and moderate in his personal habits, and the great sculptor and architect Bernini regularly practiced St. Ignatius Loyola's prescribed spiritual exercises. Combining private piety and public devotion, secular power united itself with religious organizations to demand excesses of scale and emotional effect. Innocent and his architects created the lasting grandeur of Rome's Piazza Navona, and the space has served the city's inhabitants and visitors magnificently ever since.

another pediment with a curved top cornice and a dropped lower one. Cortona improved access to the church by demolishing parts of surrounding buildings to create the tiny piazza. A semicircular portico with paired Tuscan columns protrudes into the square, and the portico's curve is answered by countercurving wing walls. The concave–convex interplay is subtle but effective in this diminutive Baroque stage setting.

THE PIAZZA DEL POPOLO

The next Baroque square to be considered is the Piazza del Popolo. Fontana's placement of an obelisk at the point where its three radial streets converge gave the space a monumental focus. In the mid-seventeenth century, Roman planners wanted to regularize this important gateway to Rome by placing identical domed churches on the trapezoidal sites created by the three streets. This posed a geometric dilemma, however, for the sites were of unequal width. Carlo Rainaldi, assisted by Bernini, solved the problem by giving one church, S. Maria dei Miracoli (1675–79), a circular plan, and the other, S. Maria in

12.22 Carlo Rainaldi and Gianlorenzo Bernini, S. Maria dei Miracoli and S. Maria in Montesanto, 1662–79.

As at St. Peter's, Pope Sixtus V had anticipated the development of a great piazza here by placing an Egyptian obelisk in the formless terrain first seen by pilgrims arriving in the Eternal City from the north. The so-called twin churches were designed by Carlo Rainaldi.

Montesanto (1662–75), an oval plan to accommodate its narrower site. Viewed from the obelisk, the churches look identical because of their domes and porticoed façades, and their profiles enhance the dignity of the piazza (Fig. 12.22). In 1816–20, the architect Giuseppe Valadier carved out an oval volume for the piazza in imitation of Bernini's plan for the Piazza of St. Peter's and added a set of viewing terraces to the east leading up to the Borghese Gardens (Fig. 12.23). The terraces offer viewers the opportunity to appreciate the oval plan from above.

Halfway down the Via del Babuino from the Piazza del Popolo is the point where the route to S. Maria Maggiore envisioned by Sixtus V sidesteps to connect with the Via Sistina at the top of the Pincio Hill. Topographic difficulties here required the route to make a steep ascent, which was imaginatively resolved by the Spanish Steps (1723–26), built by Francesco de Sanctis following designs made a decade earlier by Alessandro Specchi (Fig. 12.24). The project was underwritten by a wealthy Frenchman and constructed on land owned by the French church of the Trinità dei Monte; the steps were so named because the Spanish Embassy was nearby. From the fountain at its base, gentle curves and countercurves form a dramatic cascading stair that narrows and then divides before reaching an intermediate platform, beyond which the stairs again unite, only to split once more into opposing curves that ultimately ascend to the platform in front of the Trinità dei Monti, at the end of the Strada Felice. It is a popular and effective stage setting, inviting promenaders to be

12.23 Giuseppe Valadier, Piazza del Popolo from the Pincio Hill, Rome, 1816–20.

While the former trapezoidal piazza can still be identified, it has been subsumed in Valadier's new oval, its long axis directed up the slope of the Pincio Hill. The steep hillside is made accessible by ramps and has been terraced into platforms serving as overlooks.

12.24 Francesco de Sanctis and Alessandro Specchi, Spanish Steps, Rome, 1723–26.

If architecture can be "frozen music," as suggested in the Introduction to this text, then the Spanish Steps are an excellent example of the phenomenon. The principal elements are the steps with their landings, the obelisk, and the church of the Trinità dei Monte, built at separate times but deftly pulled together by Francesco de Sanctis and Alessandro Specchi in the eighteenth century.

URBAN OPEN SPACES IN BAROQUE ROME

both actors and audience, and the design brings enjoyment to the mundane task of climbing or descending by encouraging the pedestrian to linger and look.

THE SPREAD OF BAROQUE ARCHITECTURE TO NORTHERN ITALY

GUARINO GUARINI

Borromini's work, especially his design for S. Ivo della Sapienza, became the starting point for the work of Guarino Guarini (1624–83), an architect whose buildings in Turin represent the northern extension of Baroque Rome. Guarini was a member of the Theatine monastic order, and he served an eight-year novitiate in Rome from 1639–47. His early work in Modena for the Theatines does not survive; political difficulties led to his expulsion from the city in 1655, and he was to spend the following decade in various places, including France and possibly Spain. On his return to Turin in 1666, he worked on two central-plan churches.

The Cappella della SS. Sindone, or Chapel of the Holy Shroud (Figs. 12.25a,b), was added to the east end of the cathedral of Turin to house the important relic of the Holy Shroud. Guarini received the commission in 1667, after another architect had begun construction on a circular plan, which Guarini was obliged to retain. By inscribing an equilateral triangle in the circle and redesigning the access stairs and landing vestibules, Guarini brought mystery and dynamism to the unimaginative original scheme. The domed chapel pulsates with the counter-curves introduced by the vestibules and an axial niche, and three pendentives touch tangentially the circle of the dome above, which is not really a dome at all but an ascending hexagonal network of arches diminishing to an interlaced-arch oculus topped by a spiraling lantern. Light filters into the upper zone through small windows set within the arch network and pours in from six large windows at the base of the dome.

For his own order Guarini designed S. Lorenzo (1668–80), based on an octagon defined by convex Serliana surfaces bulging into the main space, all set within a square and completed by an elliptical choir (Figs. 12.26a,b). The geometric complexity here is astonishing. Squares, octagons, a Greek cross, ovals, and circles are involved. Again the dome is not a solid vault but an openwork structure with eight interlacing arches. The church is illuminated by oval, pentagonal, and circular openings set between the ribs and by scattered chambers that capture and modulate the light. Over the choir is a lower, six-pointed ribbed-star vault, which, like the main vault, is reminiscent of Islamic ribbed domes at the Great Mosque of Córdoba (see Figs. 7.9–7.10); possibly the mosque was known to Guarini from his travels. S. Lorenzo's dome, drum, and cupola mirror the play of concave and convex forms seen on the interior (Fig. 12.27). Further examples

12.25a Guarino Guarini, Plan and partial reflected ceiling plan of the Sindone Chapel, Turin, begun 1667.

Guarini inherited the plan, but the reflected ceiling plan reveals his innovations: a telescoping, layered vault of rotated polygons.

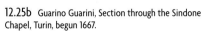

12.25b Guarino Guarini, Section through the Sindone Chapel, Turin, begun 1667.

The drawing reveals the extraordinary organic quality of Guarini's dome construction. It is a dramatic change from the hemispherical domes of Brunelleschi.

12.26a Guarino Guarini, Section through S. Lorenzo, Turin, 1668–80.

Guarini used a cantilevered vault at the first level and interlocking parabolic ribs at the dome. Most interesting perhaps are the many light modulators that form the transition from exterior to interior space.

12.26b Guarino Guarini, Plan of S. Lorenzo, Turin, 1668–80.

This plan, with reflected ceiling plan, reveals the complex patterns of Guarini's vaults. The four pairs of rotunda columns provide a richness through the layering of architectural elements. However, their small diameters indicate that they are false structure, with the loads above being carried by the cantilever.

12.27 Guarino Guarini, Intrados of the Dome, S. Lorenzo, Turin, 1668–80.

The ribbed vaults of the Great Mosque at Córdoba, which Guarini may have seen during his travels, are often mentioned as his inspiration. The lantern appears to float above the ribs.

of ribbed domes on unbuilt projects appear in Guarini's *Architettura civile*, published posthumously in 1737.

BERNARDO VITTONE

Guarini's most notable successor was Bernardo Vittone (1704–70), who edited Guarini's treatise for publication. Vittone's early works share Guarini's exuberance, while those of his later years display more conservatively classical tendencies. In the sanctuary of Santa Maria della Visitazione at Valinotto (1738–39), superimposed equilateral triangles inscribed in the dome recall Guarini's S. Lorenzo, and the plan harks back to Borromini's S. Ivo. On both the interior and exterior, the chapel is a fusion of the circle and the triangle, with ovals worked in as chapels. Throughout, there is a consistent effort to deny the solidity of the wall and to dissolve the physical boundaries of the contained space. Arches support freestanding pendentive-like ribs that function as screens behind which light enters from unseen windows. On the ceiling, legions of painted angels circle around the central lantern, where another painting depicts the Holy Trinity.

The chapel at Valinotto may be contrasted with one of Vittone's late works, the parish church at Grignasco (1750–83), where both interior and exterior are organized using classical elements: columns, piers, entablatures, and pediments (Fig. 12.28). The plan is based on a hexagon extended by means of a square apse terminating in a semi-circle. While the Baroque love of curvilinear geometries is not extinguished completely—the exterior walls gyrate as concave planes, and the clerestory windows assume irregular fan shapes—the more flamboyant elements of the Late Baroque have been considerably subdued.

FILIPPO JUVARRA

Palaces were also built as the Baroque spread into northern Italy and northeast into central Europe. The independent princes who governed this territory aspired to splendid residences, and Baroque architects brought drama and exuberance to their commissions. In Turin the extended front added to the Palazzo Madama in 1718–21 by Filippo Juvarra (1678–1736) for Vittorio Amadeo II of the House of Savoy includes a major feature derived from a functional necessity, the stair. In Renaissance palazzi, stairs were generally sandwiched between rooms leading off the central courtyards; at the Palazzo Madama, the grand staircase occupies the entire width and length of the extension. It begins at the central entrance, leads up to half-landings at the far extremities, reverses to the center, and turns ninety degrees into a bridge element entering the palace. The exterior composition reflects seventeenth-century influences from France with which the House of Savoy had strong connections.

Juvarra later designed the royal hunting lodge at Stupinigi (1729–33) outside Turin. Its symmetrical plan is organized around a large hexagonal entrance court and focuses on a central domed rotunda, off which short wings project diagonally. Rectangular service courts flank the entrance to the hexagon, and secondary wings extend off its vertices and terminate in pavilions. It is an unorthodox scheme, complemented by formal landscaping tailored into geometric plantings. Interiors echo the dynamism characteristic of Late Baroque churches. Spaces interpenetrate, cornices oscillate as though free from the enclosing walls, and stucco ornamentation adorns walls and ceilings. Perspective and the artful application of painted shades and shadows combine to bring drama to the great rotunda hall (Fig. 12.29), where a surprising amount of detail, including fluting on pilasters, scrolls on brackets, and upper-niche statuary, is created with paint, not surface relief.

12.28 Bernardo Vittone, Parish church of Santa Maria dell'Assunta, Grignasco, 1750–83.

For the shell of his church, Vittone telescoped successive masses upward, producing complex, layered space on the interior. The stairs, with their diagonal geometry, provide a dynamic base for the composition.

12.29 Filippo Juvarra, Royal hunting lodge interior, Stupinigi, 1729–33.

The trompe l'oeil, or trick-the-eye, painting in the central rotunda is a descendant of Brunelleschi's invention of perspective some 300 years earlier.

THE BAROQUE IN CENTRAL EUROPE

While Vittone and Juvarra were active in and around Turin, the artistic ideals of Baroque Italy were being spread to the north and east through Switzerland, Austria, southern Germany, and Bohemia. There Italian influences merged with local tastes and surviving craft-guild traditions to create a version of the Baroque distinctive to central Europe. As in Italy, the driving force was the Catholic Counter-Reformation, yet the style received support not only from Church officials, but also from princes and monarchs, who hoped to project a progressive image, and from the common people, for whom it reflected deeply held religious beliefs. In many respects Baroque churches in central Europe continued medieval themes, and architecture, sculpture, and painting advanced a single idea: the evocation of a heavenly realm. Number symbolism is prominent, as are the images of saints serving as intercessors between earth and heaven.

Twin-towered west fronts are commonly found capped by bulbous domes rather than Gothic spires. The impression of lofty volume that is conveyed in the Gothic by soaring vaults is created in the central European Baroque by much lower plaster vaults on which paint and stucco have been expertly applied to create the illusion of an open sky filled with heavenly hosts. These Baroque churches are bright and airy; the windows are glazed with clear glass, and daylight is directed onto white interior surfaces embellished with gold and pastel hues.

The Baroque monuments of Italy were important sources for central Europe. The Gesù in Rome was particularly influential because its design led to the development of the *Wandpfeiler* or wall pillar that characterizes many central European Baroque churches. At the Gesù the barrel-vaulted lateral chapels are separated from one another by cross walls faced at the nave with pilasters. North of the Alps, these cross walls became wall pillars, which Baroque architects exploited for both structural stability and the shaping of internal space. Although the churches may retain side aisles, some even with galleries overhead, the wall pillars were used as space-shaping elements to establish the concept of centrality within what were generally longitudinal plans. Thus, the interaction of axial and centralized plans, already seen in the oval designs of Borromini and Bernini, was continued in the Baroque of central Europe.

The life and work of Johann Bernhard Fischer von Erlach (1656–1723) exemplify one of the ways in which Italian ideas were transferred to central Europe. Fischer von Erlach came from an Austrian family of masons, and he was sent to Rome for training in the studio of Carlo Fontana. During the sixteen years he spent in Rome he became familiar with both ancient and contemporary works there, and these influences, combined with knowledge from travels across Europe, were later reflected in his own designs and in the illustrated *Entwurf einer historichen Architektur* (*Historic Architecture*), a precocious history of architecture which he published in 1721. Fischer von Erlach's architectural fortunes were tied to those of the Hapsburgs. He joined the imperial court at Vienna as architectural tutor to Joseph I in 1689, was raised to the nobility in 1696, and served as chief inspector of court buildings from 1705 until his death. During his lifetime,

Austria experienced a surge of nationalistic pride after decisively repelling the Turkish attack on Vienna in 1683. Seeking to create an impressive international city that would rival Rome or Versailles, Viennese princes built Baroque palaces and raised new churches.

Fischer von Erlach's major contribution to Vienna was the Karlskirche (1716–25), a building that reflects his view that every work should be unique (Fig. 12.30). By borrowing from a wide range of historical sources, he created a highly original design that referred to many major buildings of the past. The church was dedicated to St. Charles Borromeo, the emperor's patron saint, and was built in fulfillment of a vow Charles VI made in 1713 during an outbreak of the plague. Its broad façade is dominated by a dome on a drum rising above a pedimented portico, flanked by columns in a manner recalling the front of S. Agnese in Agone, where the central dome is flanked by twin campaniles. Elements from historical buildings

12.30 Johann Bernhard Fischer von Erlach, Karlskirche, Vienna, 1716–25.

Fischer von Erlach possessed an early knowledge of classical architectural history, which he put to use here. The triumphal columns symbolically connect the Hapsburg Empire to Roman antiquity and the dome alludes to papal Rome.

12.31a Johann Bernhard Fischer von Erlach, Section through the Karlskirche, Vienna, 1716–25.

Compared to the plan and elevation, the section is tame. Cut along the central axis, however, it gives no hint of the cowboy-storefront quality of the façade.

12.31b Johann Bernhard Fischer von Erlach, Plan of the Karlskirche, Vienna, 1716–25.

It is hard to imagine a more unusual plan than this one. The attitude of its designer, who borrowed from numerous sources, anticipates the tide of eclecticism that would reach a high point in the late nineteenth century.

incorporated here include the columned portico from Roman temples such as the Pantheon; Trajan's Column from imperial Rome, repeated on both sides of the rotunda and adorned with scenes from the life of St. Charles Borromeo rather than reliefs of the Dacian Wars; the drum and dome from papal Rome; and an overall composition suggesting the dome and minarets of Hagia Sophia in Constantinople. The interior is impressive for its elongated oval nave (Figs. 12.31a,b), the ceiling of which is embellished with illusionistic frescoes depicting St. Charles Borromeo appealing to the Virgin Mary as intercessor for relief from the plague. Fischer von Erlach had seen the ceiling frescoes being installed at the Gesù during his residence in Rome, so he used painting, rather than coffering or ribs as Bernini or Borromini would have done, to complete the dome's interior.

The rather severe and classical approach of Fischer von Erlach contrasts with the work of his contemporary, the Tyrolese architect Jacob Prandtauer (1660–1726), who was trained in Munich as a mason and practiced as an architect-sculptor. The works of Borromini and Guarini are reflected in his designs, but he was also influenced by Fischer von Erlach. A member of a religious brotherhood, Prandtauer was closely involved with his designs while they were under construction, and he is known primarily for monastic projects, including rebuilding the great abbey of Melk (1702–14), set dramatically atop a rocky ridge rising 200 feet above the Danube. The monastery's

buildings are arranged in an elongated U shape, with the church placed inside the U, its compressed cloister interrupting one long range of rooms. From the river below and the small courtyard that precedes the west front, the twin towers of the main façade dominate, while the drum and dome over the crossing are best seen from the major courtyard at the east end of the church. This is a wall-pillar church with galleries above the oval chapels instead of aisles; a longitudinal emphasis was unavoidable because of site restrictions, and Prandtauer emphasized verticality through fluted pilasters and a dome on pendentives that soars above the clouds and the swirling drapery of the figures in the ceiling frescoes (Fig. 12.32). The undulating cornice of the nave supports recessed arches around clerestory windows, causing the whole ceiling to appear as a floating world. The painted illusion of heavenly figures spilling out from the vaults above provides a dramatic link between earthly matters and the spiritual world.

In Switzerland, Bavaria, and Bohemia, Baroque design was generally the province of families of architects, sculptors, and painters, in which fathers, sons, uncles, and nephews collaborated on building projects. For example, five Dientzenhofer brothers—Georg, Christoph, Leonhard, Johann, and Wolfgang—were active in Bohemia and southern Germany just before and after 1700, where they combined the free-swinging curves found in the works of Borromini and Guarini with Slavic and Gothic motifs; Christoph's son, Kilian Ignaz, also became an established designer. These families of master builders should not be thought of as rustics: a number of them were trained in major centers such as Turin, Vienna, and Prague, and they knew both the built and the unbuilt designs of leading Italian architects, even though they practiced architecture as guild members. Christoph Dientzenhofer (1655–1722)

12.32 (right) Jacob Prandtauer, Abbey church interior, Melk, 1702–14.

The oscillating walls and pillars create a dynamism in sharp contrast to the serene, modular interiors of a Renaissance building such as Brunelleschi's S. Lorenzo, Florence (see Fig. 11.7).

12.33 (below) Christoph Dientzenhofer, St. Nicholas on the Lesser Side interior, Prague, 1703–11.

One of six architect brothers, Christoph Dientzenhofer designed this church using wall pillars. Setting these pillars on the diagonal, he was able to support syncopated, three-dimensionally curving transverse arches that meet tangentially at the centers of the bays, producing dual spatial readings.

designed the church of St. Nicholas on the Lesser Side in Prague (1703–11) (Fig. 12.33) to have a longitudinal plan with deep wall pillars set between chapels below and galleries above. The wall pillars near the nave are splayed to support doubly curving arches. This configuration creates what has been called syncopation: a double reading of the spatial units as either a traditional bay system or a series of overlapping ovals.

DIE WIES, BAVARIA

An alternative strategy of spatial dematerialization was employed by Dominikus Zimmerman (1685–1766) at the church of Die Wies, or The Fields (1746–54) (Fig. 12.34), located in a meadow beneath the Bavarian Alps. Fusing hall church and oval schemes and creating an outer bearing-wall layer and an inner trabeated layer of coupled columns, Zimmerman supported a nearly flat wood-and-plaster vault on which his brother, Johann Baptist Zimmerman (1680–1758), could create an expansive illusionistic fresco of Christ at the Last Judgment. Applied to a background of white plaster dematerialized by brilliant light from large, surrounding windows, paintings, areas of pastel and gold colors, organic stucco ornament, and cut-outs in the vault supports produce an apparently weightless visual unity from this abundance of elements and effects.

The collaboration of two other brothers can be seen in the abbey church of Einsiedeln (1719–35), where the

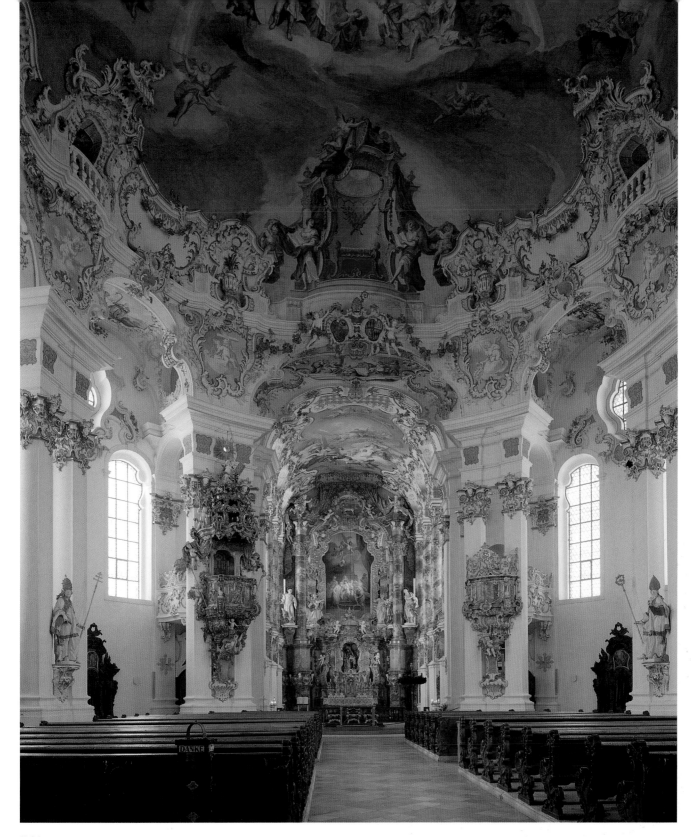

12.34 Dominikus Zimmerman, Die Wies interior, near Munich, 1746–54.

The fairly plain exterior walls and steep draping roof of this small church give little indication of the dramatic, illusory effects waiting on the interior. Die Wies attracted pilgrims who came to see an image of the Scourged Christ said to weep real tears.

design was begun by a lay brother of the monastery, Caspar Moosbrugger (1656–1723), and was finished after his death by his brother Johann Moosbrugger and others.

Einsiedeln is still a major center of religious activity in Switzerland, and the monastery has an appropriately grand façade fronting a sloping plaza at the end of the town. In the center of the composition is the church, its great bowed front with twin towers projecting from the straight line of the flanking monastic buildings. This curved element directly reflects the major element of the interior, the shrine constructed on the site of the cell of St. Meinrad, who is venerated here. A great octagon completed by a dome surrounds the shrine, which thus occupies the first and largest bay of the nave. Wall pillars pierced by aisles and galleries help define this space and form the transition to the smaller, circular domed bays of the nave.

The Asam brothers, painter Cosmas Damian (1686–1739) and sculptor Egid Quirin (1692–1750), were responsible for the wonderfully coordinated fresco and stucco work that graces the interior of the abbey church of Einsiedeln (1719–35). The narrower choir, built to the designs of Egid Quirin, is completed by an enormous altar and embellished with floating stucco figures that complement the ceiling frescoes above. The Asams tended to create pictorial rather than architectural space. With paint and stucco they transformed what appear to be rather commonplace plans and sections into an extraordinary confection of light, color, and illusionistic space. The nave ceilings combine paint and plaster to create a joyous expression of the Nativity, with angels perched on high cornices and putti floating down to earth bearing the good news.

The influence of Einsiedeln's plan can be seen at the abbey church in St. Gallen (1755–68), where a rotunda space has been inserted into a longitudinal basilica, thus accommodating the needs of pilgrims in the nave while

12.35 Johann Michael Beer, Abbey church, St. Gallen, 1755–68.

This façade composition is recognizably Germanic: twin towers flanking a bulging central columned wall capped by a tiara-like parapet.

12.36 Johann Balthasar Neumann, Würzburg Residenz, begun 1720.

This is the garden front of the palace. The second floor contains the royal reception room, reached by one of the great stairs of the period.

reserving the choir for monastic use. St. Gallen is the monastery for which the Carolingian Plan of St. Gall (see Fig. 8.8) was drawn. Although there is evidence that a church following the Carolingian scheme was built, later rebuildings in the Gothic style obscured the older foundations. The present Baroque church, however, retains the double-ended apse of the original basilica. Its design is credited to Peter Thumb (1681–1766), with the towered east façade being the work of Johann Michael Beer (Fig. 12.35). St. Gallen is a wall-pillar church with a central rotunda expressed on the exterior as a bow between flanking towers. There are no transepts, and the west front remains unfinished. Save for the east façade, the exterior of St. Gallen is rather plain, with tall windows evenly spaced. Even the interior fresco and stucco work by Christian Weinzinger is less dynamic and exuberant than the work at Einsiedeln. St. Gallen is the last great Baroque church built in central Europe and one of the last in all of Europe. The style, nourished by Italian inventiveness and responding to the emotional piety of prince and peasant, was losing its vitality in an era that was becoming more interested in rationalism and classical restraint.

Not all central European Baroque buildings were churches. As in Italy and France, the nobility wanted to display their importance by building great palaces, and the theatricality of the Baroque was well suited to providing an appropriate setting. Of these princely abodes, the

grandest was the Würzburg Residenz (Fig. 12.36), begun in 1720 for the prince-bishops of the Schönborn family. Its architect was Johann Balthasar Neumann (1687–1753), generally regarded as the greatest master of the German Baroque. Neumann was trained in mathematics, engineering, and architecture. He served the Schönborns as an artilleryman, civil engineer, and military engineer, before being encouraged to devote his designing talents and engineering dexterity to the creation of architectural spaces. The enormous Residenz was symmetrically disposed around a deep entrance court, with four interior courts providing light and air to the side wings. Neumann's plans for the palace were scrutinized by leading architects in Paris and Vienna before construction began and as the work proceeded; such oversight and changes in the prince-bishops resulted in a twenty-three-year construction period, with an additional five years required to complete the interior decorations. Neumann's masterpiece within this complex was the sequence of major reception rooms, beginning with the low vestibule, made large enough for a coach to turn around in the

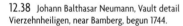

12.37 Johann Balthasar Neumann, Plan of Vierzehnheiligen, near Bamberg, begun 1744.

This drawing shows the vaults above reflected onto the floor plan. Together, they illustrate how Neumann interlocked highly ornamental oval and circular bays within a cruciform plan, with spherical triangles at the intersections.

12.38 Johann Balthasar Neumann, Vault detail Vierzehnheiligen, near Bamberg, begun 1744.

A spherical triangle is created by tracing a triangle onto a spherical surface. Here, craftsmen overlaid these curving surfaces with organic plaster ornamentation.

column-free space, and extending through the majestic Stair Hall to the White and Imperial halls on the second floor.

It is the lofty Stair Hall that most clearly exhibits the architect's technical skill (page 352). At nearly 100 by 60 feet, the hall is the largest single room in the palace, and it is roofed by a clear-span stone vault. The centrally placed stair rises in a single flight to a landing, where it reverses direction and divides before extending to the upper floor—a so-called imperial stair. A balcony placed around the staircase allows onlookers a view of the processional space. The ceiling is enriched by the world's largest fresco, executed by Giovanni Battista Tiepolo and celebrating the sun god Apollo and the prince-bishops as patrons of the arts. Representations of the seasons, the zodiac, Europe, Asia, Africa, and America are assembled at the perimeter, the figures gazing into the clouds opening up in the

heavens or staring down at those ascending the stair. Among the individuals depicted on the parapet are Tiepolo, the stucco artist Antonio Bossi, and Neumann himself, seated with his dog among items of artillery and taking a well-earned rest. Statues on the balustrades and stucco cartouches, swags, and putti above the door and window surrounds harmonize with the allegorical host overhead. Further delights of stucco and fresco await in the subtle shades of the White Hall, which serves as a foil for the Imperial Hall, the most important room in the palace. Its elongated-octagon plan rises to a high oval, vaulted ceiling filled with Tiepolo's allegorical frescoes, alluding to historical scenes of the Holy Roman Empire and peopled with contemporary members of the Würzburg court.

Neumann was also a designer of churches, the most celebrated of which was the pilgrimage church of Vierzehnheiligen (begun 1744), outside Bamberg. Vierzehnheiligen commemorates the hilltop on which a shepherd boy in 1445 had an apparition of the Fourteen *Nothelfer* (a sort of heavenly witness, or guardian angel) for whom the church was named. A previous chapel on the site had become inadequate, and jurisdictional conflicts between the prince-bishop of Bamberg and the Cistercian abbot whose monastery was financing the work led to confusion over Neumann's appointment as architect. Construction was finally begun in 1744, but the foundations were laid too far to the east by the supervising architect, who also made design changes of which Neumann did not approve. Neumann redesigned the church, producing a scheme that is remarkable for the way its basically basilican ground plan is transformed into a composition of Baroque circles and ovals (Fig. 12.37). The freestanding altar of the fourteen saints occupies a central position in the nave, while the transepts become circles and the apse is defined as an oval. Neumann manipulated the interior space by arranging the aisle piers freely, both to support the oval vaults overhead and to form screens obscuring direct vision of windows in the side wall, thus combining the drama of light from unseen sources with swirling, curving forms (Fig. 12.38). He used delicate pastel colors, accented with gold, on marble piers and ceiling frescoes to emphasize the airy volumes of the interior. The warm sandstone exterior is grand but restrained, and the twin towers of the entrance front respond to the axis established by the Baroque abbey of Banz on a hill across the valley.

This discussion of major Baroque monuments should not obscure the fact that the Baroque became an almost vernacular style for churches in the countryside of southern Germany, Switzerland, Austria, Czechoslovakia, and Poland, much as medieval styles characterize the French and English landscape. Existing churches were remodeled and new ones were built in the Baroque style; their distinctive reverse-curve domed towers still dot the rural districts. The Baroque even had an impact in Russia, where St. Petersburg was laid out early in the eighteenth century by French and Italian architects.

THE BAROQUE IN FRANCE

The ideas of the Italian Baroque were transferred, although not without modifications, to France. By the mid-seventeenth century, as Louis XIV was coming into his majority, Renaissance-inspired classicism was sufficiently well established in France to mute the most elaborate excesses of the Roman Baroque. French official patronage of the period was more than ever centered on the royal court, and the propaganda of the Catholic Counter-Reformation was not an important issue. The official court style glorified the monarch, and the primary function of the state-run artistic establishment was to provide splendid settings, furnishings, and objects for the display of royal power. In pursuit of this objective, French architects built impressively elaborate works on a scale seldom seen, and the manners, costumes, and style of the French court became the model for other European capitals.

THE LOUVRE, PARIS

Several building projects exemplify this process. In Paris the rebuilding of the Louvre, begun over a century earlier with the interior court wing by Lescot, was still not complete. First Lemercier and then Louis Le Vau (1612–70) worked on the interior elevations of the square court. During the 1660s a number of architects, including four Italians, were invited to submit designs for the east façade. Bernini, the leading European architect, sent a design proposing a central oval pavilion terminated by end pavilions, the whole composed of giant engaged columns and colonnades better suited to the bright sun of Italy than to the overcast skies of northern Europe. After hearing French objections to the scheme, Bernini sent a second proposal, this time with a concave plan, but Louis XIV and his ministers were still not satisfied. At the insistence of the King, Bernini came to Paris for six months in 1665 to consult directly on the Louvre design, in spite of opposition from French architects who hoped to receive the commission themselves. While in Paris, Bernini prepared a third proposal, not just for the east wing but for the entire palace. In this plan, the original square court was completely shielded by open loggias with blocky staircases protruding at the corners. The exterior façades were no longer curved but articulated by giant engaged columns on the central pavilion and pilasters on the end pavilions; the ground floor was treated as a rusticated base for the giant orders above.

Perhaps because Bernini failed to reflect French taste in his designs, Louis decided not to adopt any of these schemes. Instead he gave the commission to a trio consisting of the architect Le Vau, the painter Charles Lebrun (1619–90), and a doctor of medicine, Claude Perrault (1613–88). While the exact contributions of each remain unclear, these three men were responsible for the present-day east façade (1667–70), composed of a colonnade of paired Corinthian columns with central and end pavilions, all set atop a rusticated ground story (Fig. 12.39). This use of paired columns links the work to Baroque precedent, although the design is far more restrained than contemporary architecture in Italy. In contrast to earlier French Renaissance works, the roof of the east façade is hidden by a balustraded parapet, reinforcing the horizontal emphasis of the whole elevation.

The austerity of the east façade, with its central pediment, end pavilions, and paired columns carrying a continuous architrave, is often associated with Perrault's ideas about architecture. He edited a well-received French edition of Vitruvius in 1673, in which he illustrated the grave monumentality of the trabeated Roman work of the republic. In 1683, he produced a controversial treatise on the orders in which he argued that their proportions were

12.39 Louis Le Vau, Charles Lebrun, and Claude Perrault, East façade of the Louvre, Paris, 1667–70.

The paired columns symbolize the monarchy. The façade composition is distinctly French: end pavilions, central pedimented unit, and connecting stoa-like wings.

not absolute but were best determined by a discerning eye. This attitude of relativism had profound implications for the development of subsequent architectural theory, including twentieth-century Modernism.

FRANÇOIS MANSART

François Mansart is as well known for his difficult disposition as for his design genius. Trained by his master-carpenter father, Mansart was "arrogant, touchy, and unpopular," and perhaps corrupt. His inclination to work and rework projects almost endlessly caused him to lose control over many of them before completion. While owing much to the continuing importation of both High Renaissance and Mannerist forms from Italy, he produced work that was chauvinistic in its emphasis on openwork structure, a continuation of French Gothic traditions, and on **stereotomy**—the art of precise stone masonry. Regarding the latter, his buildings exhibit a precision of detail and conviction of composition that gives them a "severe richness" achieved by few others.

Mansart's St. Marie de la Visitation in Paris (1632), built for a group of nuns who served the sick and needy outside their convent, demonstrates his interpretation of the central-church scheme, a radical innovation in France at the time. He took his plan (Fig. 12.40) through a number of iterations before settling on a rotunda ringed by column screens and apsidal and kidney-shaped chapels cut into the thick, surrounding wall, with one chapel leading to a nuns' choir. His section studies reveal a fascination with telescoping vertical spaces generated by a series of truncated low-slung domes, which were to become his trademark. The entrance façade (Fig. 12.41), with its huge **Serliana** capped by a convex pavilion roof, recalls the work of Salomon de Brosse.

Mansart began the Parisian church of Val-de-Grâce in 1644; it was completed by Lemercier after 1646. Built with funds granted by Anne of Austria after she conceived Louis XIV, it gave Mansart an opportunity to explore the longitudinal church plan in a scheme not unlike the Gesù in Rome. Several projects preceded the design as built. One early scheme included a great baldachin like that at St. Peter's, a truncated double dome at the crossing, and a distinctive combination of intersecting barrel vaults, semi-domes, and domes in the short nave (Fig. 12.42). As built (Fig. 12.43), the structure became much simpler, with a hemispherical dome at the crossing capped by a second, larger dome scaled to be seen above the façade, and a barrel-vaulted nave.

At Maisons-sur-Seine near Paris, Mansart built a château (1642–51) that has few equals in its confident composition and severe masonry treatment. His grand site plan, some of which has been lost, included an elaborate entry sequence with monumental gateways and tree-lined boulevards leading to a forecourt defined by stables and an intended **orangery**. Next comes a moat, an entry court, then the body of the house, the corps-de-logis, surrounded by garden parterres. Mansart arranged the building to have a U-shaped plan (Fig. 12.44) with end pavilions capped by

12.40 François Mansart, Plan of St. Marie de la Visitation, Paris, 1632.

Mansart's central-rotunda plan was unique at the time in France. The column screens were motivated by the need to shield the nuns' choir from the adjacent monastery.

12.42 François Mansart, Early section drawing for the church of Val-de-Grâce, Paris, 1644–46.

Low-slung vaults in the stunted nave and steep, telescoping domes at the crossing connect Mansart's work to spatial investigations in the work of Guarini and Vittone.

12.43 François Mansart, Plan of the church of Val-de-Grâce, Paris, 1644–46.

Mansart simplified his early schemes for this church in order to make it economically viable. The hatched-in portions were added by Jacques Lemercier, who replaced Mansart during construction.

12.41 François Mansart, St. Marie de la Visitation, Paris, 1632.

Here Mansart combined an entry pavilion, based upon the gateway pavilions of earlier French châteaux, with a tall rotunda. While relatively small, the entry pavilion is impressive, illustrating the French preference and aptitude for monumentality.

12.44 François Mansart, Plan of the château, Maisons-sur-Seine, near Paris, 1642–51.

Of particular interest here is the central entry. Its cruciform plan is defined by massive walls inside which stand four pairs of columns. The plan also illustrates the French preference for dominant end pavilions.

12.45 François Mansart, Château, Maisons-sur-Seine, near Paris, 1642–51.

Mansart's façade appears as a thin, taut skin stretched over a sharp-edged skeleton. It reveals the French reverence for stereotomy: the combined results of projective-geometry knowledge and skill in stone carving.

truncated pyramidal roofs and a larger central pavilion with a three-story centerpiece of attached columns and a pediment. The masonry façades (Fig. 12.45), articulated using crisp pilasters, have the appearance of a skin stretched tightly over a structural skeleton beneath. The same sober, assured classicism can be seen on the interior, where the main vestibule appears as a thick-walled masonry box inside which Mansart inserted a set of eight columns, producing an apparently trabeated building inside an arcuated one. Space in the adjacent stair tower extends upward through low, truncated domes like those at St. Marie de la Visitation and his additions to the château at Blois (begun ca. 1635).

THE CHÂTEAUX OF VAUX-LE-VICOMTE AND VERSAILLES

The designers of other French country estates also enthusiastically adopted aspects of the Baroque style. Sixteenth-century châteaux had set a standard of elaborate design that continued into the next century, with increasingly splendid effects culminating in the lavish palace and garden designs of Vaux-le-Vicomte and Versailles. On August 17, 1661, Nicolas Fouquet, the Attorney General and Superintendent of Finances for Louis XIV, invited the King and Queen and 6000 other guests to festivities at his recently completed estate, Vaux-le-Vicomte (1657–61) (Fig. 12.46). The château, designed by Le Vau, stood in 170 acres of land and had a majestic view over the grounds, landscaped by André Le Nôtre (1613–1700) to include formal gardens, fountains, and sculptures extending to the background forest. The château is a freestanding block with pavilions at each corner containing appartements for Fouquet on one end and the king on the other. The axial entrance approach leads across a moat, to a paved terrace, and through triple-arched entrance doors into the vestibule. In the center is a projecting oval salon, entered on its short axis through triple arches corresponding to the triple-arched openings on the opposite wall, through which the gardens beyond can be seen. The painter Charles Lebrun organized the stucco work, gilding, painting, and tapestries of the interior to provide a magnificent setting for living.

Within three weeks of the opening of his château, Fouquet was charged with mismanagement of royal funds and embezzlement, his property was confiscated, and he was thrown into prison, where he died in 1680. Louis bought all of Fouquet's interior furnishings for a token sum and trundled them off to his own château at Versailles. He also commanded the designers of Vaux-le-Vicomte—the architect Le Vau, the decorator Lebrun, and the landscape architect Le Nôtre—to begin work for him.

In 1624 Louix XIII had built a hunting lodge on swampy land at Versailles, some twenty miles southwest of Paris. When the future Louis XIV was a child, he spent

12.46 Louis Le Vau, Charles Lebrun, and André Le Nôtre, Garden façade of the château, Vaux-le-Vicomte, 1657–61.

Prominently displayed in the center of the composition is the projecting wall of the oval salon. Its triple opening on the ground floor, a motif that Le Vau used elsewhere, looks out on extensive parterres laid out by Le Nôtre.

relatively happy times in the twenty-room château there, and on becoming monarch he decided to make modifications. In 1661 Le Vau added two service wings, and in 1669 Louis decided to enlarge the whole complex by building around the original château, keeping the entrance court but adding new work on the garden façade. Louis XIV was sentimental about the original lodge and allowed none of it to be removed during the enlargement of the palace buildings, so Le Vau instead added wings and partially enclosed the central block in a symmetrical design.

From the first, Louis intended Versailles to be the permanent residence of the royal court, dismissing medieval Paris as an unfit setting for the Sun King. A site less suitable for major construction than Versailles would have been difficult to find. The marshy ground was fine for game, but it was incapable of supporting elaborate plant life, and there was no adequate water supply readily available to run fountains. Under the direction of Le Nôtre, the army drained 37,000 acres of land and diverted an entire river thirty miles to supply water for the fountains, which eventually numbered 1400. Vast gardens were laid out, with axial vistas, terraces, sculpture, formal flowerbeds, fountains, water basins, and paths integrated into a grand plan that focused on the King's bedroom in the center of the palace (Figs. 12.47–12.48).

In 1678, when the entire court took up residence at Versailles, the palace was again enlarged, this time under the direction of François Mansart's nephew, Jules-Hardouin Mansart (1646–1708), who continued to work there until his death thirty years later. At one point, in 1685, 36,000 men and 6000 horses were involved in construction of the buildings and grounds. A town of about 20,000 people grew up adjacent to the palace to house the aristocracy, their soldiers and servants, and other minor courtiers. Like the gardens, the town was organized around radiating boulevards extending from the center of the palace—a device first seen in Rome, with the three streets extending south from the Piazza del Popolo. Mansart extended the palace symmetrically on both the north and south ends, continuing the elevations established by Le Vau but destroying in the process the subtle effects of advancing and receding planes that characterized Le Vau's work; Mansart's wings have linear façades that continue without interruption. Mansart also added the Galerie des Glaces, or Hall of Mirrors, and two adjacent salons of War and Peace to the central block. Le Vau's Staircase of the Ambassadors (begun 1671) divided to lead to both salons, so that any ambassador would know of Louis's intentions before these were actually announced to him in the appropriate setting. A large circular panel in the Salon of War depicted Louis as Mars triumphant over his enemies. The King's own suite of rooms included salons where paintings depicted monarchs of antiquity with the

12.47 André Le Nôtre, Plan of the palace and gardens, Versailles, begun 1661.

The vast axial plan at Versailles is a fulfilment of the proposal put forward in the sixteenth century by Sixtus V in his replanning of Rome. The young Pierre L'Enfant lived at the palace and remembered his experience when he laid out the axes-over-grid plan for Washington, D.C.

12.48 Pierre Patel, Bird's-eye View of Versailles from the east, 1668.

This view shows the old hunting lodge at the center, with the addition of Le Vau's wings, and the surrounding gardens by Le Nôtre. The vast extensions of the wings by J.H. Mansart were yet to come.

attributes of the gods representing the seven planets: Mercury and wisdom; Venus and love; Mars and war. His throne room was the Salon of Apollo. The only vertical feature at Versailles is the chapel added by Mansart in 1698–1710, a building of Gothic proportions and spatial conception expressed using the classical language. Its gallery was linked to the King's apartments, while the court was relegated to the lower level.

All of the interior decoration at Versailles was carried out under the direction of Lebrun, and the triumvirate of Le Nôtre, Le Vau, and Lebrun, which had so successfully coordinated the scenic backdrop for fêtes at Vaux-le-Vicomte, achieved a far more grandiose effect at Versailles. Lebrun's decorations, furniture, tapestries, reliefs, and paintings were as elaborate as anything to be found in Baroque palaces of the period. However, while Versailles has much of the grandeur, it has little of the dynamism of seventeenth-century architecture in Italy.

JULES-HARDOUIN MANSART

Jules-Hardouin Mansart also designed structures in Paris. He added the church of St.-Louis-des-Invalides (Fig. 12.49) to the hospital for disabled soldiers. Although the interior of Les Invalides, as it is known, was still incomplete at Mansart's death in 1708, it was essentially finished by 1691. Its plan is based on Bramante's design for St. Peter's, and the drum and dome are derived from Michelangelo's design for the same church, though Mansart gave his interpretation a strong vertical accent. The dome of Les Invalides is buttressed by pairs of Ionic columns protruding from the fenestrated surface of the drum. The dignity of the exterior is achieved by a system of three dome shells (Fig. 12.50). The innermost, truncated masonry dome relates to the scale of the interior space; the intermediate masonry dome caps the truncated

12.49 Jules-Hardouin Mansart, St.-Louis-des-Invalides, Paris, 1670–1708.

J.-H. Mansart made use of drawings inherited from his uncle, François in preparing his design of this church. His central plan can also be compared to Bramante's scheme for St. Peter's.

12.50 Jules-Hardouin Mansart, Section through St.-Louis-des-Invalides, Paris, 1670–1708.

Mansart's triple-shell dome not only creates two scales, interior and exterior, but also pursues his uncle François Mansart's experiments with spatial layers resulting from dome truncations.

one and supports the external timber-framed dome, which is covered with lead sheets and is scaled to the building's exterior silhouette, mass, and composition.

CHRISTOPHER WREN AND THE BAROQUE IN ENGLAND

Mansart's design for Les Invalides was to have a direct impact on the most outstanding architect of the English Baroque, Christopher Wren (1632–1723). Wren came to national prominence as a result of the Great Fire, which began on September 2, 1666 and destroyed 373 of the 448 acres comprising the walled area of the City of London, including 13,200 houses, forty-four city companies, eighty-seven churches, the Royal Exchange, the Custom House, and St. Paul's Cathedral. Numerous prominent men made plans for rebuilding the burnt area. Wren produced a plan dated September 11; the diarist Sir John Evelyn, September 13; and Robert Hooke, Curator of Experiments at the Royal Society, September 19. Wren proposed a grid superimposed with axial routes connecting commercial, religious, and governmental centers within the city. Precedent for this plan organization can be found in the Baroque designs for Rome and Versailles. None of the plans submitted for the rebuilding of London was used in the actual work. Merchants wanted to reestablish their homes and businesses as rapidly as possible, in the same location within the city, without having to wait for radical planning changes to be approved and implemented.

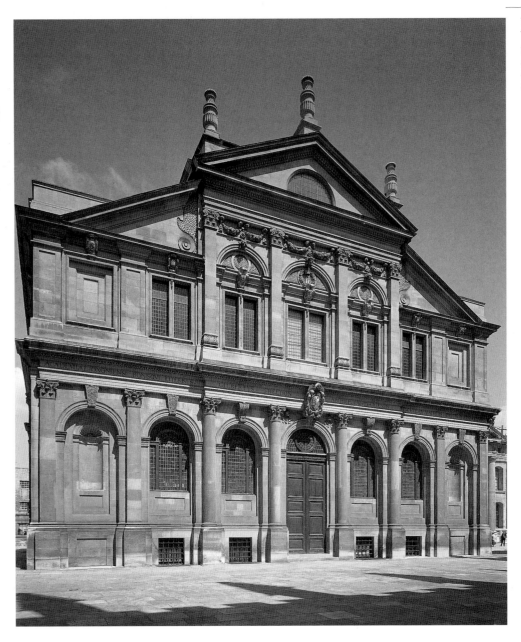

12.51 Christopher Wren, Sheldonian Theater, Oxford, 1662–63.

Wren was just beginning his architectural career when he produced this theater design. It is Palladian in its use of overlapping temple fronts.

Christopher Wren has been acclaimed as Britain's greatest architect. Trained as a mathematician, he was also well connected in the church, his father having been Dean of Windsor. In 1661 Wren became Professor of Astronomy at Oxford University. While there, he designed the Sheldonian Theater (1662–63) for an alumnus, Archbishop Sheldon, basing it on the semicircular plan of the Theater of Marcellus in Rome (see Fig. 5.26b). Huge wooden roof trusses above the theater space support a canvas ceiling, which Wren had painted to resemble the open sky, complete with simulated ropes to hold the shading device taut. The entrance front is a pedimented pavilion with a raking cornice carried down to the perimeter walls (Fig. 12.51). Arcades, half-columns, pilasters, oval dormers, and a cupola complete the design. It was based on a plate in Serlio's *Five Books of Architecture*, as was the pilastered and pedimented design of the street façade of Wren's Pembroke College Chapel, Cambridge (1663–65), created for his uncle, Matthew Wren, Bishop of Ely. The chapel's ceiling is elaborate, and its woodwork was richly carved by the master woodcarver Grinling Gibbons.

Wren visited Paris from July 1665 through March 1666, probably to escape the plague that was sweeping Britain at the time. There he met Bernini and wrote, "I would have given my skin for . . . a few minutes' view" of Bernini's design for the Louvre.

THE CITY CHURCHES

After the fire of 1666 Wren became one of the six commissioners who prepared the Act for Rebuilding the City of London (1667), specifying, among other things, the use of brick walls and slate roofs to reduce the spread of any future fires. Fifty-one (just over half) of the burnt parish churches of the city were rebuilt to designs done by Wren from 1670 to 1686, although much of the detail was probably left to the master carpenter or mason in charge of each individual church since Wren was preoccupied with his major lifework, the rebuilding of St. Paul's Cathedral. The towers and spires of his churches, perhaps influenced by what he had seen in Gothic France, created a distinctive silhouette on the skyline, rising above the lower brick buildings and contrasting with the domed profile being developed in the design of St. Paul's. Wren's parish church designs vary considerably as he had to accommodate many different site conditions; he sometimes provided a reinterpretation of the earlier church destroyed in the Great Fire, so not all the designs are classically derived. Several of the steeples are particularly memorable. The spire of St. Mary-le-Bow rises on a circular plan above a square-plan tower, while St. Bride's, Fleet Street has four diminishing octagons of arched openings in its upper stories. In contrast, the steeple of St. Dunstan-in-the-East was built in a simplified Gothic form that reflected the previous church.

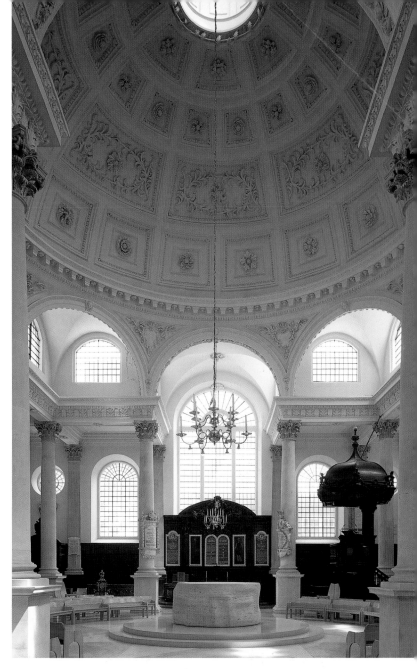

12.52 Christopher Wren, St. Stephen Walbrook interior, London, 1672–87.

Striking in this view is the slenderness and wide spacing of the columns that support the entablature and, in turn, the dome. These proportions are possible because the vaults are not stone, but wood and plaster.

The church of St. Stephen Walbrook (1672–87) served as an experimental model for his dome design for St. Paul's Cathedral. Except for its dome and rather medieval tower capped by a Renaissance crown, the exterior of St. Stephen Walbrook is insignificant, but the interior is an extraordinary centrally planned space developed on a modulated grid, with a stubby nave and a coffered Pantheon-like dome (Figs. 12.52–12.53). The dome rests on eight arches supported by an octagonal arrangement of Corinthian columns on high pedestals. Since the dome was a wooden construction, the supports could be slender and refined; for this reason it did not present any of the structural problems involved in the triple-shelled masonry dome of St. Paul's.

12.53 Christopher Wren, Plan of St. Stephen Walbrook, London, 1672–87.

Wren organized St. Stephen Walbrook by means of a modulated grid—an orthogonal grid with the bay spacing varied. He removed four columns to produce the rotunda defined by an octagon of dome-supporting arches.

ST. PAUL'S

Wren's design for St. Paul's Cathedral went through a number of changes. The so-called "Great Model" (Fig. 12.54), dating from 1673, consisted of a major dome on eight piers ringed with secondary domes forming a continuous ambulatory similar to Bramante's 1506 design for St. Peter's; but this design was too strongly linked with Roman Catholicism to be acceptable by the cathedral's

dean and chapter. A Latin-cross plan, similar to the destroyed Gothic building, was requested, and that was what Wren provided in the "Warrant Design" of 1675. Even its silhouette was Gothic, consisting as it did of a minuscule drum and dome capped by a six-tiered cupola. Construction began on the basis of this design, which Wren modified slowly over the thirty-year building period. The structure completed in 1709 was refined and academic, incorporating elements from a wide variety of sources (Figs. 12.55–12.56). In plan the cathedral is a basilica, a form that Wren admired in the basilica at Fano as published by Vitruvius. Most of Wren's nave-and-aisle churches were based on the Roman basilica. At St. Paul's, the basilican structure is comprised of saucer domes in the nave and aisles, with buttresses above the aisle roofs (Fig. 12.57). To hide these buttresses and impart a classical character to the exterior, Wren raised the aisle walls to create screens articulated in a manner similar to those in

12.55 Christopher Wren, St. Paul's, London, 1675–1709.

Wren's façade composition looks back to such models as Borromini's S. Agnese in Piazza Navona. His triple-shell dome includes the unique feature of a conical intermediate shell that supports both the lantern and the timber superstructure of the outer shell.

12.54 Christopher Wren, "Great Model" plan for St. Paul's Cathedral, London, 1673.

Wren's so-called "Great Model" was unacceptable in England because it had strong Catholic overtones, derived from the churches of the Italian Baroque style in Rome.

12.56 Christopher Wren, Plan and section of St. Paul's, London, 1675–1709.

Remnants of the "Great Model" can be found in the many domed units covering both nave and aisles. It is Wren's interpretation of an ancient Roman basilica.

12.57 Christopher Wren, St. Paul's interior, London, 1675–1709.

In this view from the principal (west) entry, the saucer-domed bays of the nave lead to the octagonal rotunda. Above it rises the triple-shell dome, comparable to the one J.-H. Mansart designed for Les Invalides (see Fig. 12.50).

Inigo Jones's Banqueting House (see Fig. 11.80), while the north and south transept porticos were a restatement of Cortona's façade of S. Maria della Pace (see Fig. 12.21) in Rome. The west front is based on Perrault's façade for the Louvre (see Fig. 12.39), with towers like S. Agnese in Agone in Piazza Navona in Rome (see Fig. 12.20). Wren greatly changed the dome, not begun until 1697, from that proposed in the "Warrant Design" of 1675, synthesizing Michelangelo's buttressing system for St. Peter's in Rome with Bramante's original design for the drum. Such a large dome required substantial supporting piers, necessitating the infill of the sides of the four diagonal arches of the central crossing to create segmental rather than hemispherical arches. The external massing of the dome had to be tall and dignified to dominate the London skyline, but this would have created an excessively vertical internal space. Thus Wren resorted to the triple-domed strategy employed by J.-H. Mansart at his church of St.-Louis-des-Invalides (see Fig. 12.50). The innermost dome is of masonry. Above this, a brick cone supports both the cupola and the wooden superstructure of the lead-covered exterior dome. Despite Wren's background as a mathematician, there is no evidence that he used his academic knowledge to make calculations predicting structural behavior.

The richness of St. Paul's relies equally on the architecture and the internal decoration, which includes work by Grinling Gibbons (1648–1721) and master ironmonger Jean Tijou. Gibbons was born in Rotterdam and discovered there by John Evelyn. He carved numerous Wren interiors, including Trinity College Library in Cambridge and St. James's Piccadilly in London, but he excelled himself in the choir stalls and organ case of St. Paul's. Tijou, a French Huguenot, was patronized by the monarchs William and Mary. He worked mainly at Hampton Court and St. Paul's, where rosettes and embossed leaves distinguish his elaborate creations in wrought iron.

HOUSING IN THE MANNER OF WREN

Wren was much too busy with royal commissions to design private houses. Often presented as a residential building in the manner of Wren is Coleshill, Berkshire (ca. 1650) by Roger Pratt (1620–84) (Fig. 12.58). The two-room-deep or double-pile plan included a transverse service corridor. Such a house can claim ancestry to many Georgian mansions that would appear in eighteenth-century America, although the later buildings would have longitudinal central halls. Uppark, Sussex (1695) (Fig. 12.59) by William Talman (1650–1719) has a façade anticipating many later American works. This house is cube-like, with a central, projecting pedimented bay and an elaborate frontispiece but no use of the orders. Similar houses can be seen in such places as the cathedral close in Salisbury; the related American examples are often more

12.58 Roger Pratt, Coleshill, Berkshire, ca. 1650.

While Wren designed no houses as modest as this one, Coleshill seems to exhibit his form preferences. Its water table, beltcourse, entry frontispiece, heavy cornice, dormers, and rooftop balustrade all became standard features of the English and American Georgian styles. The house was destroyed by fire in the 1950s.

12.59 William Talman, Uppark, Sussex, 1695.

Ironically, Georgian houses in America were more successful than their English models such as this one. In America, designs were often based upon drawings in English and American books, which represented refinements of the built originals.

refined and possessed of finer proportions because they were drawn from publications in which English experience had been codified.

NICHOLAS HAWKSMOOR, SIR JOHN VANBRUGH, AND JAMES GIBBS

While working on St. Paul's, Wren employed a domestic clerk who eventually became his assistant. This man was

Nicholas Hawksmoor (1661–1736), who added to St. Paul's the west-front towers that emphasize massing, in contrast to the linear façades and accurate detailing of Wren's design. Hawksmoor also collaborated with an equally famous contemporary, Sir John Vanbrugh (1664–1726), a gentleman-soldier and colorful character who at one time was imprisoned by the French on suspicion of spying. On his return to England he became a successful comic playwright. In 1699 the Earl of Carlisle chose him over William Talman to design a palace in Yorkshire called Castle Howard (Fig. 12.60). Work on this elaborate and extensive complex began in 1701, with the assistance of Hawksmoor, who contributed architectural know-how to Vanbrugh's theatrical daring. The design is symmetrical, centered around a domed great hall from which the principal apartments extend laterally. Flanking

12.60 Sir John Vanbrugh, Plan of Castle Howard, Yorkshire, begun 1701.

While Palladian in conception, Castle Howard is vast; it has a width of almost 600 feet.

12.61 Sir John Vanbrugh and Nicholas Hawksmoor, Blenheim Palace, Woodstock, Oxfordshire, 1705–24. Engraving.

This sprawling residence was financed by the British crown as a means of rewarding the Duke of Marlborough for his military exploits at the battle of Blenheim.

curved colonnades maintain strict axiality while connecting the main block with subsidiary courts for kitchens and stables.

The most celebrated house of the Vanbrugh–Hawksmoor partnership is Blenheim Palace (Fig. 12.61), built by a grateful England for the Duke and Duchess of Marlborough in commemoration of the Duke's success at the battle of Blenheim in 1704. A large and pompous building following the themes established at Castle Howard, Blenheim is representative of this period of grandiose design and is one of the most monumental pieces of domestic architecture of any period in Britain. The exterior is dominated by giant Corinthian columns and massive corner pavilions. Entrance is made through the north portico which leads on axis from the great court into the hall and salon. Symmetrically disposed on either side of this central group are smaller rooms arranged around two internal courts; on the west front is a long gallery. Colonnades link the main block to the kitchen and stable courts, which balance each other on either side of the great court. Sarah, Duchess of Marlborough, objected to its impracticality as a home, because kitchen and dining room were a quarter-mile apart. The poet Alexander Pope observed, "'Tis very fine, But where d'ye sleep, or where d'ye dine?"

While Vanbrugh designed some ten grand country houses, Hawksmoor's major architectural works were the six churches he built in London; two were paid for under the Act for Building Fifty New Churches of 1711, for which he was appointed commissioner. Most of his basilican planning is derived from Wren, but the exuberance is all Hawksmoor's. At Christ Church, Spitalfields, London (1723–29), Hawksmoor's interest in the late Roman

12.62 Nicholas Hawksmoor, Christ Church, Spitalfields, London, 1723–29.

For this façade, Hawksmoor fully exploited the well-worn Serliana or Palladian motif. A giant version appears as the entry porch, a smaller one as the base of the tower, and a third, still smaller one as the frame for the clock.

12.63 James Gibbs, plan, section, and elevation of St. Martin-in-the-Fields, London, 1721–26.

Gibbs successfully united the temple front, Wren-like tower, and basilican nave to produce a prototype for churches in England and America. He tried out several variants before settling on this tower composition, which begins as a square in plan, moves through sets of octagons, and terminates with a faceted spire.

temples at Baalbek is reflected in his overscaled and unusually detailed scheme. The nave is illuminated by clerestories above elliptical barrel vaults running parallel to the nave. Below these vaults, the nave arcade is composed of cylindrical columns with complete entablatures surmounting each one. The nave is not vaulted but is covered with a flat coffered ceiling, and the whole of the interior is bold. On the exterior, the porch is composed of a large Serliana, above which the tower rises, buttressed at front and back by screen walls containing windows arranged in another Serliana composition (Fig. 12.62). The styles of Vanbrugh and Hawksmoor are very personal and individualistic, forming a rich extension of the more academic work of Wren and thus presenting a distinctive part of the English tradition.

The church of St. Martin-in-the-Fields, London (1721–26) by James Gibbs (1682–1754) is an essay on the Corinthian order, employing giant columns and pilasters both inside and out (Figs. 12.63). A Wren-derived tower and steeple lie on the main axis; the entrance to the church is through their base and is protected by a dominating Corinthian portico. This church set a precedent for countless religious buildings, most notably in the American colonies both before and after the Revolution, mainly as a result of Gibbs's *A Book of Architecture*, published in 1729, which illustrates his numerous designs. For instance, Joseph Brown's Baptist church at Providence, Rhode Island (1774–75), is based on St. Martin, as are St. Michael's in Charleston, South Carolina (begun 1752, possibly by Peter Harrison), and churches in Vermont and Connecticut by Lavius Fillmore.

Gibbs is an architect whose works establish a bridge between the most elaborate examples of the English Baroque and more restrained designs based on the serenity of Andrea Palladio. The designs in his publication illustrate both inspirations. By the middle of the eighteenth century, the return to purer interpretations of classical antiquity emerged as Neo-Classicism, an important movement to which Gibbs gave an impetus.

CHAPTER 13

THE EIGHTEENTH CENTURY

Englightenment

Eighteenth-century architectural developments were complex, encompassing divergent elements and themes, some old and some new. Especially in central Europe, Late Baroque work lingered, particularly in major commissions for the nobility or the Catholic Church. Vierzehnheiligen and the Würzburg Residenz in Germany as well as Blenheim Palace in England and the later stages of French construction at Versailles all date from the eighteenth century.

In some quarters, architects produced confections such as Françoise Cuvillés's Amalienburg Pavilion at Nymphenburg Castle near Munich (1734–39). Within this diminutive garden pavilion, which includes kennels almost as elaborate as the principal salon, Johann Baptist Zimmerman's stucco ornamentation breaks out in a riot of color and texture to accompany the **boiserie** or gilded woodwork. This late flowering of the Baroque during the first half of the eighteenth century is known as the Rococo. The name combines the words **Rocaille**, describing the organic shapes of water-worn rocks, plants, and shells, and **coquille**, meaning "seashell." In France, the Rococo was primarily a style for interiors, typified by the work of J.A. Meissonier (1695–1750), and Neo-Classical architects there eventually reacted against its excesses.

In the work of others there were already harbingers of things to come. While created during the Rococo period, Germain Boffrand's (1667–1754) manner looks back to the conservative classicism of Le Vau, and so anticipates the Neo-Classicism that would dominate French architecture in the second half of the eighteenth century. Boffrand designed the Hôtel Amelot (1712) around an elliptical court with loggias. Its varied room shapes, modest room sizes, and attention to service functions make it a model of convenience and comfort in striking contrast to the megalomania that was Versailles.

Radical new ideas were put forward in other domains. The eighteenth century witnessed the birth of the Enlightenment, the movement in which scientists and mathematicians laid the foundations for modern achievements in their fields; philosophers proposed rational forms of government that were put into practice after the American and French revolutions; archaeologists and explorers probed past and distant civilizations for an understanding of other cultures; and first traditional mechanics, then modern engineers invented devices and machines that were to transform industry, commerce, and transportation. Enlightenment historians also began the first accurate chronology of world events, and with it came an understanding of the architectural accomplishments of the various Western civilizations. Foremost among these were ancient Greece and Rome, and artists and architects traveled south in droves to swarm over the classical ruins, studying and measuring; many published their findings. The result would be Neo-Classicism. Even broader changes were brought about by the beginning of the Industrial Revolution, for convenience dated here to about 1750. It is difficult to find any aspect of modern society that remains untouched—positively or negatively—by this sea change in the way Western society attempted to control the world. As for architecture, new materials, new technologies, and new systems of construction would radically alter traditional building forms and would make completely new building types possible. Finally, the forces of Neo-Classicism and the Industrial Revolution led to an equally forceful countercurrent: Romanticism. For many, Neo-Classicism was too precise, too predictable, and too emotionless. For others, the Industrial Revolution brought not progress, but ugliness, brutality, and numbing sameness. Romanticism offered visual and perhaps emotional relief from these developing phenomena in the form of Picturesque esthetic theory and its application.

Horace Walpole, Strawberry Hill Long Gallery, Twickenham, begun 1748.

Antiquarian Horace Walpole was fascinated by the English Gothic. Rather than being academically correct, this interior is a highly personal architectural statement that expresses the emotion of Romanticism.

THE ENGLISH NEO-PALLADIANS

Even as construction was being completed on the grandiose Blenheim Palace, some English architects were turning away from the style of Wren, Vanbrugh, and Hawksmoor in favor of the simpler approach that they found in the works of Palladio. The leaders of this Neo-Palladian movement included Colen Campbell (1676–1729), a Scottish architect and editor of the influential book *Vitruvius Britannicus*, which appeared in three volumes from 1715 to 1725; Richard Boyle, third Earl of Burlington (1694–1753), a wealthy nobleman who practiced as an architect in addition to fulfilling government duties; and William Kent (1685–1748), an Englishman who originally trained in Rome as a painter and branched out into architecture and landscape design under the patronage of Lord Burlington. All three men were Whigs and staunch supporters of the House of Hanover, which had replaced the Stuart line on the English throne. Both the first volumes of *Vitruvius Britannicus* (1715) and Giacomo Leoni's English translation of Palladio's *I quattro libri dell'architettura* (1716) were dedicated to King George I. Central to the movement they spawned was a great respect for Vitruvius, enthusiasm for the buildings of Palladio, and admiration for the works of Inigo Jones.

Colen Campbell may well have been responsible for converting Lord Burlington to the cause of Palladio. His illustrations of classical English buildings in *Vitruvius Britannicus*, including country houses influenced by Inigo Jones as well as his own designs, brought him to the attention of Lord Burlington, who commissioned him to undertake renovations to Burlington House in London (since further modified and enlarged into the Royal Academy). At Mereworth Castle (1723) in Kent, Campbell designed a near-replica of the Villa Rotonda (as Palladio illustrated it) at a slightly larger scale (Figs. 13.1). He attached four Ionic porticos to a simple cube and crowned it with a pyramidal roof and dome. Mereworth contains

13.1 Colen Campbell, Elevation and section of Mereworth Castle, Kent, 1723.

Colen Campbell was among the circle of Neo-Palladians assembled around Lord Burlington. This is Campbell's English interpretation of the Villa Rotonda.

13.2 Lord Burlington (Richard Boyle), Chiswick House, London, 1725–29.

Lord Burlington was certainly thinking about the Villa Rotonda when he added this pavilion for entertaining to his estate. However, there are features not used by Palladio: the dominant twin stairs, the thermal window placed in the drum, and the Pantheon-like dome.

13.3 Lord Burlington (Richard Boyle), Plan of Chiswick House, London, 1725–29.

The plan is even more unlike Palladio's work than the elevation. It is a nine-part grid of squares, rectangles, circles, and polygons.

several practical and ingenious devices, such as the incorporation of fireplace flues in ribs of the dome, with the cupola used as the chimney exit.

Like many aristocrats of the period, Lord Burlington went on the Grand Tour of Europe, traveling from 1714 to 1715; in 1719 he returned to Italy specifically to study the buildings of Palladio. There he met William Kent, whose work so impressed him that they began a lifetime of friendly collaboration. With Kent's assistance in landscape design and interior detailing, Lord Burlington designed his own variation of the Villa Rotonda at Chiswick House (1725–29) on the outskirts of London (Figs. 13.2–13.3). Chiswick is a smaller version of the Palladian original, enlivened by a certain amount of creative borrowing from

13.4 William Kent, Holkham Hall, Norfolk, 1734.

This sprawling complex continues the vast scale of country houses established by Vanbrugh and Hawksmoor during the period of the Stuart Restoration in the late seventeenth century. Each of its dependencies is the size of a large eighteenth-century Georgian house in America.

various sources. It has one portico instead of four, and its octagonal drum and dome perhaps owe more to Scamozzi than to Palladio. Obelisks placed at the edge of the roof contain the chimney flues in an antique disguise, derived perhaps from similar features on villas in the neighborhood of Vicenza, while the garden elevation is distinguished by three windows of original design, composed of Serliana inside recessed arches. The interior spaces follow Palladian proportions and incorporate elements from designs by Inigo Jones in their details. Lord Burlington used Chiswick to house his architectural library and to provide space for entertainments; he actually lived in an adjacent building that was attached to the new villa only at one corner.

In addition to his work with Lord Burlington at Chiswick, Kent edited a two-volume collection published in 1727 as *Designs of Inigo Jones*. After about 1730 Kent began to practice architecture on his own, designing Holkham Hall in Norfolk in 1734 (Fig. 13.4). It is a grand country seat in the tradition of Vanbrugh and thus much larger than the villas of Palladio. Pavilions, pediments, Serliana, and a certain simplicity in the composition of multiple elements recapture the spirit of the sixteenth-century master in what could be termed a cluster of five Italian residences, consisting of a central reception block and four wings containing the kitchen, a chapel, a music gallery, and private rooms with associated accommodation spaces.

THE RETURN TO ANTIQUITY

The Neo-Palladians in England were among the first, but far from the last, to undertake a thorough study and revival of architecture from the classical past. By the middle of the eighteenth century the artistic elite of Europe had developed a renewed interest in the buildings of antiquity. This had happened before. Carolingian architects had looked to Roman, Early Christian, and Byzantine buildings for inspiration, and the architects of the Italian Renaissance had made extensive studies of the ruins of Rome and the writings of Vitruvius. This eighteenth-century interest in antiquity, however, differed from previous "returns to Rome" in both its focus and its breadth of impact. Artists and architects of the Neo-Classical period sought an accurate understanding of ancient buildings and art works from the past, and historians placed these creative achievements in a proper context through their comprehensive studies of ancient civilizations. Popular curiosity about remote places and exotic cultures encouraged travel by dilettanti or gentleman amateurs as well as artists and architects.

During the eighteenth century, publications of measured drawings from ancient sites greatly expanded the available information relating to architectural history. Remains of the Greek colonial town of Paestum were closely examined, and the Roman cities of Herculaneum and Pompeii were discovered in the course of road construction in the kingdom of Naples. Excavations, begun at Herculaneum in 1735 and at Pompeii in 1748, eventually freed a wealth of buildings from the volcanic ash and mud that had buried both sites during an eruption of Mount Vesuvius in 79 CE. For the first time scholars and architects had abundant detailed evidence of imperial Roman architecture, decoration, and daily life. Thomas Major published *The Ruins of Paestum* in 1768, contributing measured examples of archaic Greek temples to the growing knowledge of Greek architecture; in 1762, James Stuart and Nicholas Revett began publishing *Antiquities of Athens*, a series of four volumes completed by others in

PIRANESI'S VIEW OF ROME

by Michael Fazio

Walking through Michelangelo's Campidoglio (see Figs. 11.42–11.43) and continuing south beyond the crest of the Capitoline Hill, an eighteenth-century visitor to Rome would have found this panoramic view over the ancient Roman Forum Romanum (Fig. 13A) with the triumphal arch of the emperor Septimius Severus in the foreground and the Colosseum (see Fig. 5.28) in the background. Since Giovanni Battista Piranesi engraved this view, the scene has of course changed considerably as archaeologists and modernity have done their work. The valley between the Palatine and Esquiline hills has been cleaned up (of vegetation) and earth that had half-buried the monuments has been excavated. Fallen stones have been reassembled and inferior constructions removed.

In Piranesi's day, the panorama was incomplete, even mysterious, and the artist reveled in it. Raised in densely built-up Venice, surrounded by its tradition of dramatic urban-scene painting by artists such as Canaletto, and trained as an artist-engraver, Piranesi had come to Rome in 1740, where he supported himself by producing views of the city to be sold as souvenirs. Operating from his showroom on the Via Sistina atop the Spanish Steps (see fig. 12.24), he became very successful, even a sought-after celebrity. But Piranesi was much more than a local entrepreneur. Fascinated by the grandeur that had once been ancient Rome, he participated in the radical questioning of the past that grew out of the Enlightenment.

In this view of the Forum Romanum, Piranesi ponders the effects of time and invites the viewer to imagine the scene centuries earlier when the Roman Empire was at its zenith. His moody, atmospheric depiction is enhanced by the eruption of erratic vegetation and an array of actor-like figures, all dwarfed by the ruins around them. This engraving and others like it appealed not only to the casual tourist but also to the

13A Giovanni Battista Piranesi, *The Forum, or Campo Vaccino*, from *Vedute di Roma* (1745).

waves of *pensionnaires*, architectural students who came south from France and England to drink from the fountainhead of classicism.

Pensionnaires such as Marie-Joseph Peyre and Charles de Wailly, designers of the Comédie-Française in Paris (see Fig. 13.19), met Piranesi at the French Academy in Rome. The Englishman William Chambers knew him, and the great rusticated arches of Chambers' Somerset House in London (see Fig. 13.9) demonstrate Piranesi's lasting influence. Robert Adam, who became an inseparable companion of Piranesi in Rome, drew upon the engraver's often fanciful depictions of

ornamental motifs in developing a style of interior decoration in England that became fashionable enough to assume his name, the "Adamesque."

Piranesi's influence did not end with his reproductions of existing views or imaginative illustrations of the past. As his career evolved, he became more and more interested in architectural reconstructions and speculative archaeology. Experimenting with provocative evidence from the past, he sought to give architects a glimpse of architecture's inherent possibilities. Gradually his work became more and more eclectic, more and more fantastic, distasteful to some but ever more inspiring to others.

Piranesi's work illuminates the two major and competing currents in eighteenth-century art and architecture: Neo-Classicism and Romanticism. Firstly, the basis for his art lay with the remains of classical Roman antiquity. He packaged its images in a form that was desirable and portable. He also communicated with young designers studying in Rome. Piranesi's accurate rendition of the Roman monuments provided a ready source of information for these emerging Neo-Classicists. In addition, his personal, perhaps idiosyncratic interpretation of what he saw matched the sensibilities of Romanticism and its manifestation in the buildings and landscapes of the Picturesque. Consequently, it is hard to imagine European Neo-Classicism or Romanticism without considering the work and ideas of Giambattista Piranesi.

13.5 Giovanni Battista Piranesi, from *Carceri*, 1745. Engraving.

Piranesi's views of Rome inspired many architectural students. His depiction of moldering, half-buried monuments appealed to eighteenth-century Romantic sensibilities. The view of *carceri* (prisons) are his most imaginative spatial investigations, depicting as they do the interiors of fantastic, probably unbuildable, but profoundly evocative constructions.

volume *Descriptions de l'Egypte* (1809–22), by Baron Dominique Vivant Denon, encouraged popular enthusiasm for things Egyptian. Public interest in non-Western civilizations had already been sparked by trading contacts and by Jesuit translations of the writings of Confucius and the *Qur'an*; soon architectural knowledge was extended still further by Thomas Daniell's *The Antiquities of India* (1800). Historical information documented through drawings of ancient buildings provided designers with a greater repertoire of artistic styles than ever before; and eighteenth-century publications made possible the freedom in design that subsequently led to nineteenth-century eclecticism.

The leading exponent of Neo-Classicism in Italy and an unabashed promoter of ancient Roman architecture was Giovanni Battista Piranesi (1720–1778), a man known not so much for his architectural designs as for his 3000 or so engravings of architectural subjects. Piranesi even made a large-scale map of ancient Rome, including both actual buildings and imaginary projects composed of complex geometric shapes. From the mid-1750s until the end of his life, he issued a series of engravings called *Vedute di Roma*, or *Views of Rome*. These views of ancient ruins rising enigmatically and provocatively from the accumulated detritus and Renaissance and Baroque buildings designed by the masters of those ages sparked the imaginations of artists and architects throughout Europe. Perhaps even more provocative were Piranesi's *Carceri*, or *Prisons*, a series of fourteen plates made in 1745, and reissued in around 1760, depicting vast spaces teeming with unidentified toilers whose labors are illuminated by obscure light sources (Fig. 13.5). The scale is gigantic, of the magnitude of the great Roman baths, while the spatial organization is even more complex. Arches, vaults, and staircases rise in the gloom and are revealed by shafts of light that perhaps mimic the spotlighting of partly excavated rooms in Pompeii and Herculaneum, where archaeologists tunneled into them from above. Because they were inexpensive, produced in large quantities, and easily transported, Piranesi's engravings were widely distributed across Europe in his own time, and they continue to impress architects and artists today.

1816. Roman settlements around the Mediterranean were also investigated. Robert Wood's *Ruins of Palmyra* (1753) and *Ruins of Baalbec* (1757) documented these important sites in the Middle East. The Frenchman Charles-Louis Clérisseau, later an adviser to Thomas Jefferson, published *Antiquities of Nîmes* in 1778.

This interest in antiquity was not confined to the classical civilizations of Greece and Rome. Napoleon's military expedition to Egypt in 1798 included a large group of archaeologists and engineers whose published reports, notably the *Voyage dans la basse et la haute Egypte pendant les campagnes du Général Bonaparte* (1807) and the twenty-

ROBERT ADAM AND WILLIAM CHAMBERS

An Englishman who traveled to Rome and became friends with Piranesi was the Scottish-born Robert Adam (1728–92). At the age of twenty-six he met and accompanied Charles-Louis Clérisseau to Nîmes. Together they traveled to Split, in the former Yugoslavia, where they made measured drawings, which Adam published in 1764 as *Ruins of the Palace of the Emperor Diocletian at Spalato, in Dalmatia*. Adam was initially as interested in Vitruvius as the Palladians, but during a trip to Italy, which lasted from 1754 to 1758, he became aware that, while the greatest

13.6a Robert Adam, Plans of the Williams-Wynn House, London, 1772.

On a long, narrow site, Adam disposed a variety of spatial types, including basilicas, rectangles, and polygons, without a trace of awkwardness. Not unrelated to developments in French hôtels, such residential designs provided a context for Adam's interior-ornamentation inventions.

13.6b Robert Adam, Williams-Wynn House interior ornament, London, 1772.

This drawing illustrates Adam's delicate, net-like ornament inspired by his investigations of ancient Rome and Renaissance wall paintings.

archaeological interest followed Vitruvius in focusing on the religious architecture of antiquity, little thought was being given to the houses. Adam devoted his attention to what little was known about ancient residential design and interior detailing, in part because he realized that his architectural practice, like that of his father and brothers, would rely on clients who required homes, not temples or churches, based on the classical styles.

Architecturally successful but financially disastrous was his Adelphi scheme (1768–72) fronting on the river Thames in London. It was partially demolished in the 1930s, but a few pieces remain. The Adelphi consisted of brick town houses with stone and terracotta trim facing four streets, two parallel and two perpendicular to the river. Mimicking a typical palatial façade, the eleven houses facing the river had central and end pavilions and tall façade proportions, but not the bold pilasters or columns of an earlier age. Instead Adam introduced decorative panels filled with Greek **acroteria**. The interior decoration was similar, with Greek vine motifs on wall panels complementing the thin, flat geometric designs of the ceilings.

Adam's Williams-Wynn House at 20 St. James's Square in London (1772) demonstrates his dexterous planning and extraordinary system of interior design. On a narrow

site he ingeniously arranged a variety of room shapes in a fashion akin to the French designers of Parisian hôtels (Fig. 13.6a). He employed a distinctive graphic method for representing interior elevations, arranging them orthographically around a room's plan as if they were walls folded down. Thus he could study five related interior surfaces simultaneously. The unified results are evident in the Williams-Wynn House where Adam spread a thin "net" of stucco ornament (Fig. 13.6b), inspired by Raphael's and Giulio Romano's inventive grotesques based on the sixteenth-century excavations at Nero's Golden House, and introduced colors taken from the excavations at Herculaneum and Pompeii. Adam claimed, and probably rightly, that his elegant, attenuated decorations brought about a revolution in English architectural taste.

Adam's work on country houses often consisted of remodeling or adding to late Elizabethan and Jacobean structures. An exception is his Luton Hoo, built in 1767–69 but damaged by fires and rebuilt twice in the nineteenth century. While Adam conceived the exterior (Fig. 13.7) to be rather plain, dominated on its west

West façade

East façade

13.7 Robert Adam, Elevations of Luton Hoo, Bedfordshire, 1767–69.

While most of Adam's country-house designs were remodelings, this one was an exception. The east façade is dominated by a Pantheon-like dome with pedimented portico, while the west façade's central motif is an attenuated circular temple.

13.8 William Chambers, Plan of Somerset House, London, 1776–86.

Unlike most Englishmen, William Chambers went to Paris for his architectural education. The scale and rigor of his plan reflects the French tradition of J.F. Blondel and the Ecole des Beaux-Arts.

elevation by a full-width colonnade and a central temple front preceding a Pantheon-like dome and on the east by an attenuated hexastyle portico, his interior planning is ingenious. Primary circulation occurs along cross axes, with the longitudinal axis passing through an elongated oval expanded by niches, a rotunda with a ring of interior columns, and a rectangle with apse and lateral tripartite columns screens—an overall arrangement reminiscent of Roman baths. To either side, Adam arranged rectangular and double-apsidal rooms until he reached the end pavilions, where he returned to the rotunda and column-screen motifs. The spatial experience for someone moving along the axes or through the enfilade arrangement of banks of rooms must have been extraordinary before the many subsequent modifications.

The other major figure in English architecture of the last half of the eighteenth century was Sir William Chambers (1723–1796). His work says much about the strengths and weaknesses of English designers of the period. Chambers spent four years in Rome as an extension of his studies with J.F. Blondel in Paris. He produced an influential *Treatise on Civil Architecture* (1759) and even published *Designs of Chinese Buildings* (1757) as a result of his travels in China while a young merchant seaman. Chambers's great work is Somerset House on the north bank of the Thames in London, done while he served jointly with Robert Adam as architect to the King. Here Chambers was called upon to centralize the English government offices. After proposing a number of complex schemes, he settled on a rigorous C-shaped plan (Fig. 13.8), some 500 feet square, with a freestanding entry block along the Strand, the road running parallel to the river. It is comparable in formal conception to the many green residential squares developed throughout London. One can only imagine the cleverness and diplomacy required of Chambers in satisfying the myriad political fiefdoms, each determined to have the most prominent and desirable locations within the complex. Along the Thames the façade rises from a great rusticated, Piranesian arcade to linked pavilions reflecting Chambers's French training but marred by an undersized dome that reflects the English difficulty with monumentality (Fig. 13.9). Sculpted figures and groups arrayed throughout the complex celebrate England's maritime prowess.

13.9 William Chambers, Somerset House river-front façade, London, 1776–86.

Along the Thames, Chambers created a façade organized in the French manner, with pavilions punctuating highly textured expanses of masonry walls. At the highly rusticated base, he inserted huge arches with prominent voussoirs, like something from Piranesi's etchings of grand remains in ancient Rome or Ledoux's gatehouses.

ETIENNE-LOUIS BOULLÉE AND CLAUDE-NICOLAS LEDOUX

In France the Neo-Classical movement developed somewhat differently than in England. French Enlightenment architects were interested in the primary geometric solids of the cube, sphere, and pyramid as the logical basis for architectural expression, an approach that paralleled the work of contemporary French philosophers, who were exploring rationality as a basis for human affairs. While there is some similarity in this approach to the early Renaissance interest in the circle, square, and triangle, the Neo-Classical designers of France went beyond previous geometric investigations to propose entire buildings dominated by simple solid geometries.

The most inventive French Neo-Classicists were Etienne-Louis Boullée (1728–1799) and Claude-Nicolas Ledoux (1736–1806), both of whom designed many hypothetical projects as well as real ones. Boullée's imaginary projects give prominence to spheres, cylinders, hemispherical domes, pyramids, and cones, most often at a gigantic scale. His design for a cenotaph for Sir Isaac Newton, the discoverer of the laws of classical mechanics, is a hollow sphere 500 feet in diameter, the top half of which represents the dome of heaven, perforated with holes to give the impression of stars and the moon when viewed from the interior (Fig. 13.10). Suspended inside the sphere is a giant lamp representing the sun. Boullée explained his concept of the design in a tribute to Newton contained in his *Treatise on Architecture*: "Sublime mind! Vast and profound genius! Divine Being! Newton! Accept the homage of my weak talents. . . . I conceive the idea of surrounding thee with thy discovery, and thus, somehow, surrounding thee with thyself." Another project by Boullée, this one for a national library (Fig. 13.11), houses books inside an enormous semicylinder lit by an equally enormous skylight cut into a coffered barrel vault. The vault is supported by stoa-like files of columns, and the columns are in turn supported by terraces of bookstacks working their way down to the main floor so that the books can be lowered from level to level by attendants, obviating the need for hazardous step ladders.

13.10 Etienne-Louis Boullée, Cenotaph for Sir Isaac Newton, 1784.

The most striking feature of Boullée's design is certainly its intended vast scale. The selection of Newton as the figure to be honored expresses Enlightenment admiration for reason through a celebration of the inventor of the clock-like universe.

13.11 Etienne-Louis Boullée, Library of the King, 1788.

Here Boullée's walls are books. They support vast columns and, in turn, a huge, coffered barrel vault. The end wall is an oversized Serliana, its arched opening dwarfing bits of entablature and supporting columns.

Ledoux's designs for Chaux (1775–79) reveal his vision for an ideal town to include a saltworks (Fig. 13.12). Significantly, while completely Neo-Classical in their architectural language, they explore the phenomenon of eighteenth-century industrialization. In plan the community is organized in a great oval of workers' houses, with the buildings for salt-making placed across the lesser diameter. Outside the oval are gardens, recreational facilities, and various communal buildings. Through its integration of planned open space with residential and industrial development, the design for Chaux anticipated the Garden City movement of the late nineteenth century, which was similarly concerned with providing a healthy environment for city-dwellers. In architectural terms the linkage of man and nature at Chaux is expressed in basic geometries. The cemetery building is a sphere, symbolizing the eternal cosmos, and the wheelwright's house is identified by large circles incorporated into its façade. Ledoux's design for the Inspector's House at the Source of the River Loüe (Fig. 13.13) is shaped like a hollow cylinder set horizontally on a podium, with the stream flowing through the lower half of the cylinder and the rooms of the building arranged in buttress-like rectangular blocks along its tunnel sides. None of these highly symbolic projects was constructed, although portions of the plan of Chaux were built between the towns of Arc and Senans. Ledoux's executed designs make use of simplified versions of the classical orders realized in heavily rusticated masonry. The authority of the director of the saltworks is stated emphatically by the heavy banded columns of his house. Under the portico of the main entry gatehouse,

13.12 Claude-Nicolas Ledoux, Plan of Chaux, 1775–79.
Engraving.

In the center of the plan is the Director's House, with
buildings for salt production flanking it and workers' housing
in the surrounding oval.

13.13 Claude-Nicolas Ledoux, Inspector's House at the
Source of the River Loüe, published 1804.

This surprising structure illustrates Ledoux's conception of an
architecture parlante, or a speaking architecture. Here the
river-keeper lives, appropriately, in a house through which
water constantly flows.

with its baseless Tuscan columns, a heavily rusticated apse
beneath huge rusticated voussoirs becomes a grotto, and
the windows of this building take the form of urns spilled
over on their sides to disgourge petrified water. The sever-
ity of the composition reflects the state's jealous monop-
oly of salt production.

Ledoux's Hôtel de Thelluson in Paris (1778–83) is a
remarkable exercise in the manipulation of three-dimensional space, both externally and internally. His composition for a newly developing residential section of Paris
begins with a massive triumphal-arch gateway sunken into
the ground as if it were a half-buried monument in
ancient Rome (Fig. 13.14a). Entry is made through this
arch, then along a two-part elevated carriageway over landscaped gardens, then through the corps-de-logis; a service
court stands to the rear (Fig. 13.14b). A full appreciation
of Ledoux's achievement can only be had by examining a
longitudinal building section cut along the central axis,
where his skill in modulating the ceiling plane and creating various lighting conditions is apparent (Fig. 13.14c).
On the second or piano-nobile floor, one moves along the
principal axis through the curving colonnade—treated like
part of an embedded temple—into a grand oval salon lit
from high windows by means of a truncated dome, then
into an octagonal antechamber lit by a roof **lantern**, then
into a square antechamber with enfilade connections
along the rear wall.

Ledoux also built a series of tollgates for the city of
Paris, most of which have now been demolished. While
they were despised by the Parisian people as symbols of

13.14a Claude-Nicolas Ledoux, Hôtel de Thelluson, Paris, 1778–83. Engraving.

In the foreground, Ledoux placed a gateway like an ancient Roman, half-buried triumphal arch. A walkway at the second level then leads back to the corps-de-logis or main block of the house, with its central motif appearing as an embedded, trabeated temple.

13.14b Claude-Nicolas Ledoux, Plan of the Hôtel de Thelluson, Paris, 1778–83. Engraving.

Built in a developing Parisian suburb, this hôtel was placed on an open site. Consequently, Ledoux had room to combine house, courts, gardens, and systems of pedestrian and vehicular circulation.

13.14c Claude-Nicolas Ledoux, Longitudinal section through the Hôtel de Thelluson, Paris, 1778–83. Engraving.

Perhaps this section gives the most informative view of Ledoux's hôtel. It reveals the bi-level organization, the situation of the building components in the landscape, and the extreme manipulation of the ceiling plane in the corps-de-logis.

tyrannical taxation and criticized at the time of their construction by other architects as inappropriate interpretations of the classical language, they have come to be seen as remarkably successful variations on a common theme: the urban gateway inserted at intervals in a circumferential city wall. Ledoux first argued for a set of triumphal arches based upon those of ancient Rome or the Propylaea leading into the ancient Athenian Acropolis. However, because his tollgates had to include rooms on one or more floors, Ledoux was forced to conceive of new types, drawing upon both ancient and Renaissance precedents. His forms include gable-roofed temples, circular temples akin to

Bramante's Tempietto, several variations on Palladio's Villa Rotonda, pavilions with banded columns like the Director's House at Chaux, and even some compositions that appear, like images from Piranesi, to be half-buried. The still-extant Barrière de la Villette (1784–89) is composed of a cylinder, without a dome but ringed with Serlianas, rising out of a low square block. The massing and the masonry, including baseless, square Tuscan columns, are so handled as to convey a sense of ponderousness befitting the structure's tollgate function. Taken as a group, these gates can be compared to Wren's city churches as evidence of one of architectural history's most fertile minds.

FRENCH ARCHITECTS AND THE AGGRANDIZEMENT OF THE STATE

During the eighteenth century, most French architects still worked for the government, as did Ledoux. Consequently, their buildings were most often intended to serve public functions and to aggrandize the state. In 1771–77, the architect, theorist, and teacher J.F. Blondel set forth his ideas about architecture in his *Cours d'architecture* (*Lectures on Architecture*), really the lecture notes from his own teaching. His writing explains in detail the essential elements of good architecture and the hierarchy of buildings, from common residences to those associated with the king. Blondel discussed *l'art de la distribution*, which involved arranging the plan, and *l'art de la décoration*, which involved composing a façade. Both were governed by *ordonnance, convenance,* and *bienséance. Ordonnance* referred to the correct relationship of parts to one another and to the whole. *Convenance* and *bienséance* concerned appropriateness and the correct form of a building relative to its purpose and social rank. Another influential writer of the period was the Abbé Marc-Antoine Laugier. In his *Essai sur l'architecture* (*Essay on Architecture*), he argued that all proper architecture was traceable to a single prototype in prehistory: the primitive hut. This pure building type, Laugier believed, was entirely rational, composed of columns, lintels, or entablatures, and a sloping roof or pediment. Laugier's theories resonated in the Enlightenment architectural mind.

The architect Jacques-Gabriel Soufflot set out to build a structure according to Laugier's dictates that would exemplify the rich tradition of French architecture since the Middle Ages: the church of Ste.-Geneviève, first dedicated to the patron saint of Paris, since secularized, and now called the Panthéon (1757–90). Soufflot traveled to Rome and farther south to the dramatic ruins at Paestum in the company of the Marquis de Marigny, and it was the Marquis who secured for him the Panthéon commission. The Panthéon's central plan, deftly lengthened at the choir and portico, follows in the tradition of Bramante and Michelangelo at St. Peter's and of Wren's "Great Model" for St. Paul's. However, Soufflot based his design on Laugier-inspired freestanding columns and lintels rather than the traditional piers with pilasters and arches, and he experimented with concealed flying buttresses to stabilize the dome (Figs. 13.15–13.16). Openwork structure had been preferred by such highly regarded French architects as François Mansart and his nephew J.-H. Mansart, who were inspired by the spaciousness of local Gothic cathedrals. Like François Mansart at the central pavilion of his château at Maisons-sur-Seine, Soufflot placed a columnar building inside a bearing-wall building. However, his skeletal system eventually proved to be too open, and the piers of the crossing had to be modified. In addition, some of his windows have since been infilled to make the building serve as a tomb for French notables, and the original

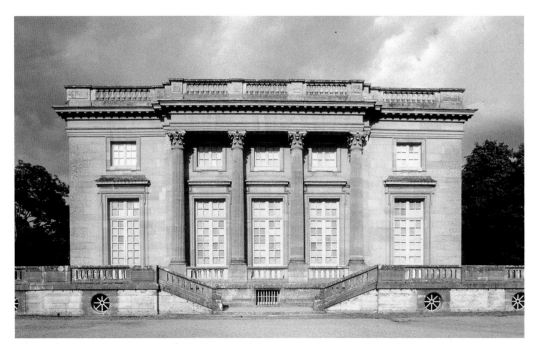

13.17 Ange-Jacques Gabriel, Petit Trianon, Versailles, 1761–64.

Gabriel's cool classicism represents the end of seventeenth-century French Renaissance developments begun by such men as François Mansart. This rigorous design attitude was never completely lost, even during the period of Rococo extravagances.

sculptural program has been destroyed. Consequently, the Panthéon does not express the radical views of Laugier to the degree that Soufflot intended.

Ange-Jacques Gabriel (1698–1782) designed the Petit Trianon (1761–64) in the grounds at Versailles as a convenient and comfortable alternative residence to the sprawling palace. It exhibits a cool, chaste classicism and illustrates the cleverness of French domestic planning in the eighteenth century. The tripartite south, or entry, façade has a rusticated basement, Corinthian pilasters, and a prominent balustrade; it is comparable to some English Palladian villas but is at once more grand and more restrained (Fig. 13.17). To the north, the basement level disappears and the piano nobile opens out only a few steps above the gardens. On the west, freestanding Corinthian columns look out over garden parterres. The east façade offers yet another unique arrangement, having neither columns nor pilasters. These multiple-façade compositions, all symmetrical, in no way compromise the interior planning, where only the larger garden-front rooms are symmetrically placed (Fig. 13.18). Gabriel slid walls about, distributing them around a central service and vertical-circulation core while maintaining spatial order through enfilade connections among the various clusters of rooms. The restrained interior decoration, dominated by rectilinear panelling and mirrors, matches the character of the exterior and looks back to the Versailles interiors created for Louis XIV.

By the mid-eighteenth century, many French students were spending long periods in Rome examining ancient buildings and using them for inspiration. Their academic exercises often reveal a megalomania and almost obsessive fascination with antiquity that, applied to the realities of site, client, and budget, yielded imposing monumental buildings back in France. Such monumentality was essential in Paris, where the range and scale of public buildings were increasing: these larger buildings often covered their sites completely. Compositions were required that successfully included large expanses of unadorned wall surface, that provided adequate light and ventilation, and that were prominently displayed in the cityscape.

This attitude was given an opportunity for expression in the commission for a royal theater, at a time when the

13.18 Ange-Jacques Gabriel, Plan of the Petit Trianon, Versailles, 1761–64.

Each façade of this building is symmetrical. However, only one set of rooms, that on the west front, is symmetrically distributed. Otherwise the partitions are cleverly arranged to achieve internal convenience without sacrificing outward formality.

13.19 Marie-Joseph Peyre and Charles de Wailly, Elevation of the Comédie-Française, Paris, 1770.

Large theaters were a new phenomenon in eighteenth-century Paris. They were more than venues for entertainment, being also settings for social spectacle and something akin to temples of French drama.

theater as a building type was a particular fascination of French culture. Marie-Joseph Peyre and Charles de Wailly, who had also spent time studying in Rome, designed the Comédie-Française with a Piranesian vision of the ancient city firmly in mind. Influenced perhaps by the ancient Roman insula, the theater has shops on the ground floor at its flanks. The main façade of relentlessly rusticated masonry features a temple front without pediment, the first such form used for a theater (Fig. 13.19). The order is Tuscan, a connection, the architects said, to Apollo, protector of the arts. Peyre and de Wailly presented theatre-goers with a social spectacle. From the street, the audience entered into a square vestibule with monumental stairs to either side; de Wailly left a moody drawing of one of the stairs amidst a forest of columns that competes favorably with Piranesi's dramatic perspective scenes. The stairs led up to a domed vestibule and, in turn, to the theater boxes. The circular arrangement of the theater seating, while controversial at the time, was thought by the architects to be the most intimate arrangement.

Jacques-Denis Antoine (1733–1801) designed the Hôtel des Monnaies, or royal mint (1768–75). His challenge was to house what amounted to a foundry within appropriately dignified quarters. On a triangular site, he cleverly arranged the minting shops and their many support spaces around a main court (Fig. 13.20). At the side wall along the Rue Guénégaud, he employed heavy rustication, as did Sansovino at his Venetian mint (see Fig. 11.62), to indicate the security that he had provided for the activities inside. For the main façade facing the river Seine and the city, he chose to cap a central pavilion with a deep attic story but no pediment and to stretch the wings laterally. In so doing, he produced a strongly horizontal, subdued, and elegant composition appropriate for a building that symbolized the strength of the nation's finances (Fig. 13.21). Spaces on the interior, such as the salon for the School of Mines, are ornamented with a

sumptuous inventiveness traceable to the architect's Roman experiences and his admiration for the work of Ange-Jacques Gabriel.

In 1770–75, Jacques Gondoin (1737–1818) built the Ecole de Médecine et de Chirurgie, or School of Medicine

13.20 Jacques-Denis Antoine, Plan of the Hôtel des Monnaies, Paris, 1768–75.

The public front of this mint faces the Seine, with the principal court behind the center of the façade. Still farther to the rear is the great hall of the foundry. To the left of the foundry and around smaller courts are the minting shops.

Minting shops

Main foundry

Service entrance

Court

Rue Guénégaud

Principal court

Court

Court

Quai Conti

Principal entrance

N

13.21 Jacques-Denis Antoine, Hôtel des Monnaies, Paris, 1768–75.

This building has an unusual French façade composition. Its central columns carry no pediment; the wings have no orders; and there are no end pavilions.

13.22 Jacques Gondoin, Ecole de Chirurgie, Paris, 1769–74.

The idea of professional surgeons and a school for them was a new one in eighteenth-century France. At this entry façade, which combines a stoa and a central triumphal-arch-like motif, a sculpted panel shows the goddess of learning, Minerva, the king, and the genius of architecture.

13.23 Jacques Gondoin, Plan of the Ecole de Chirurgie, Paris, 1769–74.

In this plan, the entrance façade is at the bottom. Behind it, the court leads to a temple front, then the semicircular anatomical theatre.

and Surgery. It is characteristic of French Neo-Classicism in its use of decoration to express and even influence societal values. The entrance façade is decidedly un-French, having no end pavilions or central focus, with access provided through a triumphal arch-like opening behind a colonnade capped by a deep frieze and balustrade (Fig. 13.22). A sculptural panel shows the king and Minerva, both surrounded by the sick, ordering the construction of the building; the genius of architecture presenting the plan; and the figures of Surgery, Vigilance, and Providence guiding the actions of the king. Together, these images announce the ongoing elevation of French surgeons to the position of medical professionals, a change sanctioned by the French monarchy. Once through the entry, a visitor passes into a court, with a public hall to the left and chemistry laboratory and hospital ward to the right. Opposite the entry, a temple front announces the semicircular anatomical theater behind, its plan based upon the theaters of antiquity and its coffered semidome with oculus comparable to the Pantheon in Rome (Fig. 13.23). Benjamin Henry Latrobe chose this theater as his model for the old House of Representatives chamber in the U.S. Capitol.

FRENCH ARCHITECTURAL EDUCATION AND THE ECOLE DES BEAUX-ARTS

The famous French architectural school the Ecole des Beaux-Arts has sometimes been presented as a bastion of Neo-Classicism. Actually its teaching was astylar, placing emphasis instead on the architectural-design thought process. Jean-Baptiste Colbert, minister to Louis XIV, founded the Académie Royale d'Architecture in 1671. Its purpose was to direct the arts toward the glorification of the king and, in turn, the state. The academy brought practicing architects together to discuss architectural problems and theories, and it presented public lectures. From 1720 onward, the academy offered regular design competitions for students, but it fell to J.F. Blondel to form the first actual architectural school in 1743. His success encouraged the academy to do the same, and by 1762 Blondel had become one of its professors. By the 1750s students were spending extended periods in Rome as *pensionnaires*. While in the Eternal City, they made careful drawings of ancient buildings and made new designs of their own. Architectural teaching was reorganized during the French Revolution and again under Napoleon Bonaparte. By 1819, the Section d'Architecture of the Ecole des Beaux-Arts was well established, with its own faculty and with quarters in a building adapted for its use by Félix Duban (1797–1870). The name "Ecole des Beaux-Arts" became synonymous with architectural education in France, to some extent in England, and eventually in America, and the Ecole continued to operate in this location until 1968.

While details of the educational system changed over time, the general philosophy did not. Would-be students had to pass a challenging qualifying examination that included diverse subjects from drawing to history. Once accepted, a student or *élève* attended a variety of lectures and was examined on those involving technical knowledge. In addition, he had to enter design competitions, or *concours d'émulation*, in the form of either the *esquisse*, a sketch problem, or the *project rendu*, a fully rendered project; they were held in alternate months. Students worked in an *atelier*, or studio, under the supervision of a *patron*, a practicing architect or a member of the Ecole faculty. When a project was issued, the student was given a *précis*, or program describing the essential elements of the project to be designed. He then entered *en loge*, that is, into a cubicle, and worked for twelve hours to produce a proposal. He would then return to his *atelier* to develop his schematic idea, assisted by comments from his *patron*, until the time of the final submission. At the appointed time, projects were picked up throughout Paris by a cart or *charrette*; students sometimes jumped on board to apply finishing touches, hence the term "charrette" used today by architectural students to describe a period of intense work at the end of a project. Comparing the initial sketch to the final solution, a jury would first determine whether the two represented the same idea, in order to ensure the originality of the scheme; then they would award points relative to the project's merits. It was through the accumulation of these points that a student could graduate from the Ecole. The highest award given was the *prix*, which eventually became the "Grand Prix de Rome" which paid the way for a winner to live and study in Rome.

THE CHALLENGE OF THE INDUSTRIAL REVOLUTION

In the minds of many, a great weakness of the Ecole des Beaux-Arts was its apparent lack of concern for developing technologies. Industrial technology advanced in the eighteenth century as inventors and technicians sought more efficient means for accomplishing the various tasks that were necessary to society: the spinning of yarn, the weaving and finishing of cloth, the mining of metallic ores, and so on. Machine work replaced the handwork of men and women, and engines powered by steam supplanted the motive power of men and horses. The changes these new inventions brought to society were many and far-reaching, including an increase in population, the rise of a new urban working class, the substantial growth of factory towns, some redistribution of wealth, and generally improved living conditions.

Among the developments were new and improved methods for making building materials, while scientific advances increased understanding of the how and why of structural design. Structural calculations were first applied to a new design in the building of the Panthéon in Paris; by the middle of the next century, it was possible to predict the behavior of most structural materials under specified loading conditions, freeing engineers and architects from complete reliance on an empirical understanding of what had worked in the past. Another invention, that of descriptive geometry, enabled designers to depict in drawings the shapes of complex three-dimensional objects, so that they could completely describe a building graphically, which relieved them of the necessity of daily attendance at the job site to direct the progress of the work. A related system for representing land contours made more accurate site work possible, too.

One result of these developments was the increasing separation between architecture and engineering. Since the Middle Ages the architect—described by Vitruvius as a man skilled in the design of everything from cities to buildings, mechanical devices, astronomical instruments, and machines of war—had been gradually released from responsibility for mechanical contraptions and items for defense, which passed instead to the newly recognized fields of mechanical and military engineering. Now a growing body of scientific data on materials provided the basis for civil engineering, which was taught at schools organized apart from architectural academies. Civil engineers were charged with the increasing body of utilitarian construction—roads, bridges, mines, factories, warehouses, lighthouses, and canals—while architects were employed on buildings where esthetics and symbolism outweighed pragmatism. Thus it was the engineer who first experimented with the building materials made possible by industrial technology, and it was in utilitarian structures that they were first used.

Of all the construction materials improved or developed during the Industrial Revolution, none was more important than iron. People had been smelting iron from ore since the prehistoric Iron Age, but the quantity of metal produced was small and its quality was highly variable. Therefore, the use of this material in buildings was limited to occasional ornamental work, fasteners, and hardware. Improved means of producing iron were sought by refiners, including Abraham Darby, whose furnace at Coalbrookdale, Shropshire, in England, began production in 1696. In an attempt to advance his work, Darby imported Dutch ironworkers in 1704 and soon succeeded in smelting cast iron for commercial use. Cast iron has a relatively high (3.5 per cent) carbon content and is brittle, though very strong in compression. By 1713 Darby had pioneered a method for producing cast iron by using coal instead of expensive charcoal in his furnace. The structural properties of his cast iron made it a suitable material for columns, where its 80,000–120,000 pounds per square inch (psi) compressive strength could be exploited. When used as a beam, cast iron is comparatively weak, having a tensile strength of only 15,000–30,000 pounds per square inch. If refined iron with a low carbon content (0.4 per cent) is hammered into shape instead of cast, it is known as wrought iron, a material with 70,000–80,000 psi compressive strength and up to 60,000 psi tensile strength. Its superior tensile properties made wrought iron much better than cast iron for beams.

Builders soon found applications for these two types of iron. Darby's furnaces produced wrought-iron railroad ties as early as 1750 and supplied cast iron for the world's first all-metal bridge at Coalbrookdale in 1779 (Fig. 13.24). Abraham Darby III, grandson of the pioneering industrialist, collaborated with the architect Thomas Pritchard to design a bridge of five parallel semicircular arches to span 100 feet over the river Severn, a watercourse prone to devastating flooding that could wash out intermediate piers. The bridge cost £6000, a large sum but only about one-third the price of an equivalent masonry span. Its design was conservative but it nonetheless represents the first essay in metal construction for bridges.

The incombustible properties of iron, together with its strength, were exploited in the construction of "fireproof" multi-story textile mills. As early as 1793 the Englishman William Strutt designed and built a six-story calico mill at

13.24 Abraham Darby III and Thomas Pritchard, Coalbrookdale Bridge, 1779.

While this bridge has supporting members made of iron, the new material is really treated like stone. It is configured as arches, placing the iron completely in compression and ignoring its great strength in tension.

13.25 William Strutt, Plan of and section through West Mill, Belper, 1793–95.

With masonry exterior walls and a grid of interior columns, this mill has an open, flexible plan. A challenge for architects during the late-nineteenth century would be expressing this internal skeleton on the exterior while covering it with fireproof materials.

Derby with cast-iron columns; his West Mill at Belper, constructed the following year, is similar (Fig. 13.25). The dust-laden air of textile mills, combined with coagulated oil and lint on the floors under the machinery and illumination from open flames, created ideal conditions for mill fires in which equipment, raw materials, and workers' lives were lost. To protect the structure, improve sanitation and ventilation, and reduce the opportunities for fire, Strutt and others designed mills with external walls of masonry, cast-iron internal columns, and protected wood beams. An early version of "fireproof" construction had the large wooden floor beams socketed into cast-iron shoes attached to the cast-iron columns. Segmental brick arches spanned from beam to beam, supporting level floors made of sand, screed, and clay tiles, with wrought-iron rods to tie the structure together. Undersides of the wooden members were coated with plaster; with sand on top and plaster below, the wood was protected from fire. Later improvements to this system substituted wrought-iron rails (forerunners of rolled **I-sections**) for the wooden beams: a surviving example of such a structure is the former Benyon, Benyon, and Bage Flax Mill at Shrewsbury in England (1796). Eventually the segmental brick arches at Belper were discarded in favor of other materials, but even with these changes, the metal-frame structure of today remains essentially the same as that built by Strutt in 1793–95.

Bridge designs, rather than building designs, generally exploited the structural properties of cast and wrought iron most directly, and it is there that the new materials were first used eloquently. For example, Darby and Pritchard's work on Coalbrookdale Bridge was soon surpassed by Thomas Telford (1757–1834), who built an iron bridge three miles upstream at Buildwas in 1795–98. Telford's segmental-arch bridge spanned 130 feet, with a rise of twenty-seven feet; he used less than half the iron required to construct the Coalbrookdale Bridge while achieving a longer span. Engineers in the nineteenth century continued to reduce material-to-load ratios and to experiment with systems, such as tensile structures, that were impossible in masonry or timber. These developments will be discussed in the next chapter.

ROMANTICISM AND THE PICTURESQUE

Industrialization and rapidly developing new technologies hardly pleased everyone. Many saw them as a bane and looked for philosophical positions that would render them unnecessary. Even as Neo-Classical architects and antiquarians were using reason and intellect to reassess the past through archaeological work and scholarly inquiry, a parallel and often overlapping orientation in art and architecture was developing. Its beginnings can be seen in the English landscape movement that accompanied the Neo-Palladians during the first half of the eighteenth century. Developed further and driven by imagination and emotion, it became Romanticism. In some respects Romanticism was a reaction against the order and regularity inherent in Neo-Classicism; in others it was an expression of deeply held religious and moral convictions. Romantics delighted in the asymmetrical and the irregular for their highly picturesque qualities. Contradictory as this may seem at first to the ideals of Neo-Classicism, Romanticism was actually a complementary movement, and a number of established Neo-Classicists designed Romantic works as well. For example, Piranesi's engravings, which were manifestations of Neo-Classicism, fired the Romantic mind. His scenes of fallen vaults and moldering, half-buried monuments populated by enigmatic, tattered beggars expressed the Romantic longing for a perfect place and a perfect time that would remain always remote and unreachable. Ruins in general became a Romantic obsession, as their ruggedness, wildness, and fragmentation illustrated the powerlessness of men and women in the face of irresistible natural forces and the melancholy relentless erosion of their works over time.

The esthetic doctrine of Romanticism was the Picturesque. Edmund Burke wrote about this doctrine in his *A Philosophical Inquiry into the Origins of Our Ideas on the Sublime and the Beautiful* (1756). Here he differentiated between picturesque conditions that were beautiful—possessed of such qualities as delicacy and smoothness—and those that were sublime—possessed of such alternative qualities as power, vastness, and obscurity.

It is clear that Boullée's interest in enormous structures aligns him with the sublime. Looking forward into the nineteenth century, it is equally clear that Romanticism could find fertile ground in an era that would become dominated by new sources of energy and huge machines, as the fruits, both sweet and bitter, of rapid social and technological change altered forever the scale and speed of daily life.

THE ROMANTIC LANDSCAPE

William Kent's Neo-Palladian landscape creations, including the grounds of Holkham Hall (see Figure 13.4), are probably more important than his architectural contributions. He is regarded as one of the founders of the English landscape-garden tradition, in which the landscape architect exaggerated and "improved" on natural qualities. Instead of the rigid geometric plantings favored by the French, English garden designers cultivated a certain irregular wildness. They exploited the natural contours of the land, formed trees into apparently natural patterns, and

developed seemingly fortuitous, but actually carefully contrived, views of carefully sited buildings. Likewise, equally carefully planned views from the windows of buildings extended beyond nearby clumps of trees into the more distant landscape, where cows grazed as in a landscape painting. A ditch with a fence or hedge at its bottom prevented the cows from encroaching upon the lawns in the immediate vicinity of the house; discovery of this concealed barrier was a surprise, causing one to laugh or exclaim, "Aha!"—thus providing the name **ha-ha** for this landscape device. To the Neo-Palladians, who saw "natural" qualities in the architecture of Palladio and Inigo Jones, there was nothing contradictory in having a symmetrical classical house set in a landscape with naturalistic elements that reflected a painter's vision of the Roman countryside.

Lancelot Brown (1716–83) was the leading promoter of this picturesque attitude toward landscape architecture. When asked his opinion of any piece of ground, he would say that it had "capabilities," and thus he became known as Capability Brown. He practiced as an architect in the Palladian tradition, but in that field he was a minor figure compared to Kent, for whom he worked as a gardener at Stowe from 1740. However, he knew much more than Kent about horticulture, expressed his ideas with clarity, and followed up his plans with informed supervision if

13.26 Lancelot Brown, Blenheim Palace grounds, 1758.

The English Romantic landscape garden drew some of its inspiration from the garden traditions of China. The English sought to imitate the irregularity of nature rather than artificially ordering natural elements in geometric patterns as in the Italian and French garden traditions.

13.27 Richard Mique, Hamlet, Versailles, 1778.

Raised in a family of architect-contractors, Richard Mique studied with J.F. Blondel. Once at Versailles, he succeeded Ange-Jacques Gabriel as the king's principal architect. Along with the hamlet he designed a temple of love, a theater, and a grotto with a waterfall.

the client requested it. Among his most celebrated works are the relandscaped gardens and park at Blenheim Palace (Fig. 13.26), laid out after 1764 and still extant. This plan included the creation of a serpentine lake and an encircling drive, the planting of tree clusters that still make a pleasing dappled pattern in the landscape, and intermittent views of the building. Brown's impact on the English landscape can hardly be overstated. Working throughout the length and breadth of the nation, he transformed large areas of unkempt countryside into the kind of lush parkland for which England has become renowned.

PICTURESQUE BUILDINGS

Some designers in France created picturesque architecture as a way of retreating to what were perceived to be simpler, more rustic times. At Versailles, the epitome of formality and pomp, Marie-Antoinette commissioned Richard Mique (1728–1794) to design a *hameau* or hamlet (Fig. 13.27), based on the folk architecture of her native Austria. Here, she and her ladies-in-waiting could escape from the splendors of the court and, in peasant costume, spend an afternoon playing at being simple milkmaids. Mique used a variety of materials, textures, and colors in the hamlet buildings, which were sited intermittently around an artificial lake. The hamlet anticipates nineteenth-century architects' employment of vernacular architecture to evoke national character.

Picturesque architecture in England began with follies, the playful use of medieval-inspired structures or ruins of structures as focal points in the layout of gardens. At Hagley Park, Worcestershire, Sanderson Miller built a sham ruin in the Gothic style in 1747, and other landscape designers soon copied the idea. Horace Walpole had his house at Strawberry Hill near London put up in a medieval manner by a committee of architects and literary friends. Work began in 1748, and the structure soon

emerged as an eclectic assortment of Gothic details. The Holbein Room has a chimneypiece adapted from the tomb of Archbishop Wareham at Westminster Abbey; the Long Gallery (page 396) features **pendant vaulting** based on that in the Henry VII Chapel at Westminster Abbey; and the Round Room has ceiling plasterwork inspired by the rose window of old St. Paul's Cathedral. The Rococo chandeliers and purple wallpapers used throughout contribute to a sense of playfulness in this passionate, picturesque amusement. This early phase of Romanticism in England is often termed "Gothick" (the spelling is deliberately medievalized) to reflect the rather lighthearted character of the work.

While the interior treatments at Strawberry Hill are interesting for their naïve antiquarian enthusiasm, the exterior is equally interesting for its attitude toward Picturesque massing. To understand this, it is necessary first to consider the plan, which has virtually no traditional formal order. Certainly there is a clear functional division between Walpole's rooms and those for his servants and other such practical concessions to the activities of daily life. However, to appreciate the house's design fully, one must view it externally and in three dimensions. Here, it becomes clear that Walpole, amateur though he was, intended for Strawberry Hill to present a rich silhouette against the sky, intended that its character should change as one moved around the perimeter, and intended for the ensemble to appear as though it had been built not all at one time, but had grown up randomly over time as had its medieval inspirations. This was a new way of thinking about building composition and one that would be fully exploited in the nineteenth century. Likewise, nineteenth-century scholars would make an intense study of Gothic buildings, establish a chronology of Gothic stylistic development, and master the recomposition of accurately reproduced Gothic elements. And the return of the Gothic would be only one among many such revivals in an era of rampant borrowing from the past, or eclecticism.

CHAPTER 14

NINETEENTH-CENTURY DEVELOPMENTS

Architecture in the nineteenth century was perhaps more varied than ever before. The freedoms introduced by Neo-Classicism and Romanticism encouraged revivals of historical styles, such as Gothic, Greek, Islamic, Egyptian, Byzantine, and Early Christian, along with inventive new creations, such as the Chinoiserie, Japonais, Moorish, and Hindoo styles. As illustrations of this phenomenon, consider some English and American buildings designed after 1800. Colonial officials returning from India with their fortunes to retire in England built pleasure palaces such as Sezincote (Fig. 14.1) in Gloucestershire, its skin designed in the Indian manner in 1805 by Samuel Pepys Cockerell (1754–1827) for his brother Charles. In the same spirit, between 1818 and 1821, John Nash (1752–1835) built the Royal Pavilion at Brighton for the Prince Regent.

In many cases, styles were chosen because of their associations. For instance, the Egyptian style was proposed for buildings related to medicine, which was considered to have originated in the Nile Valley, and to death, since the great monuments of Egypt were erected for the pharaohs and their journey in the afterlife, or wherever suggestions of massiveness or eternity were desired, as in factories, prisons (Fig. 14.2), suspension bridges, and libraries. In the United States, Benjamin Henry Latrobe (1764–1820) proposed an Egyptian-style Library of Congress within the U.S. Capitol, and Henry Austin built Egyptian cemetery gates at New Haven in 1837. Thomas S. Steward selected the Egyptian style for the Medical College of Virginia in Richmond (1854), as also did William Strickland (1788–1854) for the First Presbyterian Church in Nashville

14.1 Samuel Pepys Cockerell, Sezincote, Gloucestershire, 1805.

This Moorish Gothic Revival structure is perhaps more exotic than most nineteenth-century English country houses, but it does not overstate the era's eclectic attitude. Made possible by the new consciousness of architecture's history, eclecticism made it fashionable to copy, borrow, and mix elements and styles from the past with few reservations.

14.2 John Haviland, City Prison (The Tombs), New York City, 1838.

Eclecticism in America combined Greek, Roman, Gothic, and Italian Renaissance motifs, among others. Here, John Haviland chose Egyptian Revival columns supporting a coved entablature. At the time, the Egyptian style was associated with security because of the many celebrated tombs—hence the prison's epithetical name.

Gustave Eiffel, Eiffel Tower, Paris, 1889.

The Eiffel Tower was seen as a blight on the Parisian skyline when it was built; it was maintained initially in part because of its use as a radio tower. Today it has become a symbol of Paris itself.

(1848). The church has a later but equally remarkable Egyptian interior, including a hypostyle hall painted in perspective on a wall.

Progress in materials science enabled architects and engineers to tackle construction problems in fundamentally new ways, contributing further to the diversity observable in nineteenth-century work. Buildings in Britain and the United States now termed "Victorian" often have little in common with one another, save that they were built during the exceptionally long reign (1837–1901) of Queen Victoria. Amid the stylistic revivals and engineering accomplishments came trends in design that were to have a major impact on twentieth-century architecture. This chapter addresses these developments.

NEO-CLASSICISM

KARL FRIEDRICH SCHINKEL

Nineteenth-century Neo-Classicism in the area equivalent to modern-day Germany is most closely identified with the work of Karl Friedrich Schinkel (1781–1841), who shared some of the formal concerns of Boullée and Ledoux but relied much more on the elements of Greek architecture. Akin to Alberti, Schinkel saw architecture as a means to foster civic consciousness and saw **polis**-driven Greek classicism as its ideal symbolic language. He joined the Prussian public works office at the conclusion of the Napoleonic Wars, at a time when Prussia was seeking to raise its stature to that of a major European state with Berlin as its capital.

The Neue Wache (1817–18), or Royal Guard House (Fig. 14.3), located on the Unter der Linden, Berlin's most important ceremonial street, celebrated the emerging power of Prussia under King Friedrich Wilhelm III. Schinkel's final proposal placed a Doric portico between heavy pylons, both detailed with such austerity that the building achieves monumentality despite its modest size. Here, Schinkel succeeded in uniting the architectural forms of fortification and civic splendor.

14.3 Karl Friedrich Schinkel, Neue Wache, Berlin, 1817–18.

Here Schinkel projected a classical temple front forward from a pylon-like block. While modest in size, it is made monumental by Schinkel's skilful handling of proportions.

14.4 Karl Friedrich Schinkel, Schauspielhaus, Berlin, 1818–21.

For this theater, Schinkel chose a wall treatment of superimposed pilaster strips that anticipates the grid-like façades of twentieth-century skyscrapers. He illustrated it and his other work in his book *Sammlung Architektonischer Entwurfe* (*Collection of Architectural Designs*).

In the summer of 1817, the Prussian national theater in Berlin, designed by Carl Gotthard Langhans in 1800–02, burnt to the ground. By early 1818, Schinkel had produced a new design for the Schauspielhaus (Fig. 14.4) to sit atop the old foundations between existing French and German churches. Schinkel treated the space captured by them and by his new structure as a great vestibule and placed the monumental entry stair on the outside, unlike the practice in Neo-Classical France where the stair became part of the initial, dazzling interior space. Schinkel's stair leads to a building at once monumental, taut, and planar. The entire structure is raised on a high base and is dominated by an Ionic portico with receding planes to either side articulated by plain pilasters and precise, shallow moldings that appear to have been stretched tightly over an internal skeleton. The plan is equally clever and precise, effortlessly uniting multiple room sizes within a symmetrical distribution.

Easily Schinkel's most famous structure is Berlin's Altesmuseum, or Old Museum (Fig. 14.5) (1823–28), the first public art museum in Europe. He sited it opposite the existing palace and arsenal to the south, creating a great civic court with a wall of trees along its east side. The museum's façade is a giant Ionic colonnade raised on a high base and stretching the full width of the building. Its orthogonal simplicity both creates a sense of urban dignity and prepares the visitor for the clever rigor of the plan behind (Fig. 14.6). Here, Schinkel placed a central rotunda flanked by open courts that are surrounded by flexible gallery spaces. Read as an interlocking set of classical prototypes, the museum is like the Pantheon caught between two temples both fronted by a stoa. From the second-floor stair landing, a viewer can look back through the double file of columns for a panoramic view of Schinkel's Berlin.

Schinkel was equally deft in manipulating the picturesque vocabulary of Romanticism. At the Charlottenhof near Potsdam (1829–31), he placed individually symmetrical, classically inspired buildings (Fig. 14.7a) in an informal but carefully conceived landscape setting that includes water features and level changes (Fig. 14.7b), certainly inspired by Schinkel's travels through the Italian countryside as a student.

14.5 Karl Friedrich Schinkel, Altesmuseum, Berlin, 1823–28.

Schinkel carefully planned the setting for his museum along the banks of the River Spree. He also designed a loggia on the second level at the central entry to act as a viewing platform to the urban landscape beyond.

Second Floor

First Floor

Basement

14.6 Karl Friedrich Schinkel, Plans of the Altesmuseum, Berlin, 1823–28.

At the first- and second-floor levels, Schinkel combined a stoa along the front façade with a central rotunda, or pantheon of art, beyond, flanked by twin temples having courtyards in place of cellas and prostyle columns formed by part of the stoa colonnade.

14.7a Karl Friedrich Schinkel, Plan of Charlottenhof, Potsdam, 1829–31. Engraving.

Schinkel was also skilled in planning such asymmetrical compositions as this one. He manipulated architecture, landscape, and water features to achieve calculated vistas and panoramas.

FAÇADE GEGEN DIE TERRASSE.

FAÇADE NACH DEN PFLANZENHÄUSERN.

14.7b Karl Friedrich Schinkel, Charlottenhof, Potsdam, 1829–31. Engraving.

Shown here from the *Sammlung* are two views of the temple-fronted villa that Schinkel made by remodeling a small eighteenth-century farmhouse into a formal ancient Roman *villa rustica*, or elaborate farmhouse.

SIR JOHN SOANE

The leading exponent of Neo-Classicism in England at this time was Sir John Soane (1753–1837), an idiosyncratic architect whose work also has Romantic qualities. His building complex for the Bank of England (1788 and later; now destroyed except for its perimeter walls) used daylight in imaginative ways, since bank security required absolutely blank exterior walls (Fig. 14.8). Soane met the challenge with courtyards, clerestories, and skylights that, when coupled with the pure forms of the rotundas and vaulted spaces of the interior, seem inspired by Piranesi engravings, and indeed Soane may have met Piranesi when traveling in Italy. Decoration was incised into the stone rather than sculpted out of it; detailing is generally linear, simple, and minimal. Soane's own London house (now a museum) at 13 Lincoln's Inn Fields contains a diverse array of spaces and levels, lit by clerestories and top lights, articulated by layered wall planes, and reflected by both flat and convex mirrors (Fig. 14.9). Such a unique design does not fit easily into any one stylistic category, although one can detect traces of Neo-Classicism in the

14.8 John Soane, Bank of England rotunda, London, begun 1788. Drawing by J.M. Gandy.

Gandy was an architect in his own right, but is more celebrated for his many moody renderings of Soane's buildings, some shown complete, some shown during the process of construction, some even shown as ruins. In this drawing, Gandy illustrates Soane's preference for top-lighting, made necessary in the Bank of England by its many densely packed spaces with little if any exposure along the perimeter walls.

14.9 John Soane, The Colonnade, 13 Lincoln's Inn Fields (Sir John Soane's Museum), London, 1812–37. Drawing by J.M. Gandy.

Soane made the rear portion of his own house into a museum. Here he collected paintings by Hogarth, etchings by Piranesi, and shards from classical and medieval sites visited by him or his friends.

14.10 John Soane, Breakfast Room, 13 Lincoln's Inn Fields, London 1812–37.

The vault in this small room is the type preferred by Soane: low-slung arches springing directly from elegant columns or piers supporting a billowing, ribbed dome. His ornament was most often incised, or cut into the surface, in order to emphasize spatial volumes.

form of the shallow saucer-domed breakfast room (Fig. 14.10), where daylighting is brilliantly handled by means of a central lantern and lateral light monitors.

BENJAMIN HENRY LATROBE AND THOMAS JEFFERSON

Soane's contemporary in the United States was Benjamin Henry Latrobe (1766–1820), who was born in England, educated there and in Europe, and practiced as an architect and engineer in and around London, before emigrating to America to become the country's first professional architect. In 1803 Thomas Jefferson commissioned Latrobe to work on the U.S. Capitol, which had been begun by Dr. William Thornton and continued, sometimes haphazardly, by Stephen Hallet and George Hadfield. Latrobe completed both the north and south wings, introducing into the work his own designs for American orders: tobacco-leaf capitals in the rotunda of the Senate chamber and corncob capitals in the north basement vestibule. He also used capitals based on those of the archaic Greek temples at Paestum in the Supreme Court chamber.

In Philadelphia Latrobe designed the Bank of Pennsylvania (1799), combining there Greek Ionic porticoes front and back and a central dome with oculus that covered the monumental banking space. Late in his life, Latrobe was commissioned to design the Roman Catholic cathedral in Baltimore (Figs. 14.11–14.12). For this project he supplied two alternative schemes for the same plan, one based on Gothic precedent and one on Roman. The latter version was selected by the client, resulting in a building of remarkable simplicity, with a dome sixty-five feet in diameter at the crossing.

14.11 Benjamin Henry Latrobe, Roman Catholic cathedral, Baltimore, 1805–18.

Latrobe presented both Gothic and Neo-Classical designs of this church to his client. The classical proposal was selected but did not include the towers seen here; they were added by the architect's son, John H.B. Latrobe.

14.12 Benjamin Henry Latrobe, Roman Catholic cathedral interior, Baltimore, 1805–18.

This view of two piers of Latrobe's crossing shows the simple geometrics, plain surfaces, and minimal ornament of a designer sometimes called a rational classicist. As such, Latrobe was a true child of the Enlightenment.

14.13 William Strickland, Second Bank of the United States, Philadelphia, Pennsylvania, 1819–24.

Strickland's bank stands in the middle of downtown Philadelphia, only a block from Independence Hall. Trabeated on the outside, it is vaulted on the inside, including the impressive former banking room, now a display space.

14.14 William Strickland, Tennessee State Capitol, Nashville, Tennessee, 1845–59.

Late in his career, Strickland left Philadelphia to travel in Europe during a period of economic stagnation. When he returned, he found his client base deteriorated and so accepted an offer to go to Nashville and design the capitol.

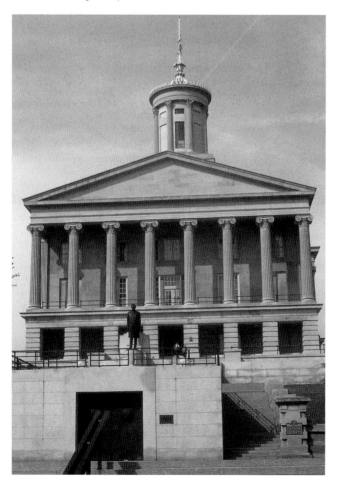

Latrobe's interest in Grecian architecture was to flourish after his death as the national Greek Revival Style. His pupil, William Strickland, worked as an engineer on the construction of canals, railroads, and harbors for most of his professional life. His most notable architectural works include the Second Bank of the United States, built in Philadelphia between 1819 and 1824 to a design that Latrobe claimed had been surreptitiously borrowed from him (Fig. 14.13). The building is Grecian in inspiration, as is Strickland's later Philadelphia Exchange (1834), which is based on the circular Choragic Monument of Lysikrates (see Fig. 2.29). That Greek monument appears again on Strickland's last building, the Tennessee State Capitol in Nashville (1845–59), reinterpreted as a cupola on the roof (Fig. 14.14). The building's interior volumes are surprisingly ungainly in light of the carefully proportioned monumentality of the exterior.

The only other American Neo-Classical architect who was as versatile and talented as Latrobe was the Roman Revivalist Thomas Jefferson (1743–1826), who also penned the Declaration of Independence and served as the country's third president. The son of a land surveyor and a graduate of William and Mary College, Jefferson trained to be a lawyer, yet he made contributions in many fields. He was a statesman, philosopher, scientist, educator, economist, inventor, and gentleman architect—in short, a personification of the Renaissance ideal of an educated man. While serving as minister to France in 1785, Jefferson was asked to propose a design for the State Capitol of Virginia (Fig. 14.15). The model he prepared in response was based on the Maison Carrée in Nîmes (see Fig. 5.16), a building he knew then only through the architectural treatise of Colen Campbell. Jefferson converted the relatively small Roman temple into a two-story legislative building, with a circular domed assembly room that is not expressed on the exterior. He changed the Corinthian order of the Maison Carrée to the Ionic for Richmond because he feared American stonecarvers would lack the skill to handle the more complex Corinthian capitals.

Jefferson began his own home, Monticello (Figs. 14.16–14.17), in 1770 and used it almost as an architectural laboratory, continuing to evolve it until his death more than fifty years later. At first he envisioned a Palladian villa with two-story portico, but the final realization documents Jefferson's experience abroad as a minister to France and his admiration for the new Parisian hôtels. More than any single influence, however, Monticello reveals his extraordinary powers of synthesis. In its final form, the house's central block is two-stories tall above the basement, but through clever placement of fenestration appears to be a single story. The house is crowned by an octagonal dome, not apparent on the interior except as an isolated attic room, and is connected to the landscape by two walkways atop basement spaces that extend to enclose the rear lawn. Here Jefferson placed the service functions—kitchens, storage, the icehouse, stables, and so

14.15 Thomas Jefferson, Virginia State Capitol, Richmond, Virginia, 1785–89.

Jefferson based this temple design on the ancient Roman Maison Carrée in Nimes, which he had seen and much admired while minister to France. Initially designed to stand on open ground, it is now surrounded by additions and high-rise government and office buildings. The flanking wings are not Jefferson's.

on—below the grade of the lawn, so that they remained close at hand yet out of sight. The walkways, which capture rainwater and channel it to a cistern, terminate at the Honeymoon Cottage (above the "Brewins room"), where Jefferson and his wife first lived, and Jefferson's law office (above "Fodder storage"). The house's interior details testify to the sometimes idiosyncratic inventiveness of its owner. A clock in the entrance hall operates on a mechanism driven by cannonball weights that disappear through a hole in the floorboards. Wind direction can be determined indoors from a weather vane set on a tripod atop the east portico. Double doors to the public rooms open together even if only one is pushed because of a mechanism under the floor. Jefferson's bed separates his study and sleeping quarters, and its narrowing of space between the two rooms gives greater velocity to summer breezes.

14.16 Thomas Jefferson, Plan of Monticello, Charlottesville, Virginia, 1770.

This plan shows the ground floor of the central block and the basement level of the wings.

14.17 Thomas Jefferson, Monticello, Charlottesville, Virginia, 1770.

For his own house Jefferson turned the familiar Palladian five-part organization backward in order to focus the complex on spectacular mountain views. This view from the front shows that Jefferson disguised the two-story elevation to appear as only one story.

14.18 Thomas Jefferson, University of Virginia lawn, Charlottesville, Virginia, 1817–26.

Still the most admired example of campus planning in America, the University of Virginia was called an "academical village" by Jefferson. Seen here at the far left is Pavilion IV, then VI, VIII, and X, all connected by the colonnade.

14.19 (left) Thomas Jefferson, Pavilion VII, University of Virginia, Charlottesville, Virginia, 1817–26.

This pavilion design was suggested to Jefferson by William Thornton, winner of the competition for the design of the U.S. Capitol. It is the only pavilion façade given an arcade of arches on piers.

14.20 (below) Thomas Jefferson, Plan of the University of Virginia campus, Charlottesville, Virginia, 1817–26.

Extending from the library at the top of the scheme are the two files of five pavilions each connected by the walkways fronting dormitory rooms or what Jefferson called "ranges." Behind the pavilions are gardens and behind them more ranges as well as dining halls.

In his later years Jefferson turned his architectural talents to the design of the campus of the University of Virginia at Charlottesville (1817–26), an institution that he had done much to establish and for which he served as rector after its opening in 1825 (Fig. 14.18). His early plan for the campus consisted of a U-shaped distribution of student rooms, linked by colonnades and punctuated by larger pavilions serving as lecture halls and faculty residences. Jefferson planned for the design of each pavilion to serve a didactic purpose, informing students about the best of architecture from antiquity. He called this extraordinary complex an "academical village," and he solicited comments on the site plan and pavilion designs through correspondence with William Thornton and Latrobe. Thornton contributed a suggested design for pavilion VII (Fig. 14.19); Latrobe contributed at least two. Latrobe also recommended that the site plan should have a dominant focal element, an idea that Jefferson had originally rejected because of his opposition to centrality in government. The compositional improvement inherent in such a focus became obvious, however, and Jefferson designed a library based on the Pantheon (at half-scale) to serve as the head of the scheme (Fig. 14.20).

THE GOTHIC REVIVAL

A.W.N. PUGIN

Romanticism acquired a more serious tone with the widespread emergence of the ecclesiastical Gothic Revival. In England the leading Gothic Revivalist was Augustus Welby Northmore Pugin (1812–1852), a convert to Catholicism who regarded the Gothic as an embodiment of proper moral and religious values from the past that he felt were all but absent in his own time. Unlike the "Gothick" designers, Pugin was well versed in the realities of medieval buildings, having worked with his father as a draftsman in preparing a four-volume study of Gothic ornament. It was another book by Pugin that brought him into the public eye, however. In 1836 he published (second edition, 1841) *Contrasts; or, A Parallel Between the Noble Edifices of the Fourteenth and Fifteenth Centuries, and Similar Buildings of the Present Day; Shewing the Present-Day Decay of Taste*, a brief volume whose long title sums up the author's message. Pugin compared his view of medieval and modern conditions by means of drawings (Fig. 14.21). The "Catholic Town in 1440" had fifteen church spires and a guildhall tower marking its skyline, while "The Same Town in 1840" had factory smokestacks as the dominant element in an industrial townscape; Protestant chapels of a vaguely classical form had replaced Catholic churches, and many spires had had their tops lopped off.

Pugin's comparison of public charity past and present was even more damning. The medieval "residence of the poor" was shown as a monastery where the almoner received the needy with kindness; fed them a hearty diet of beef, mutton, ale, cider, milk, porridge, bread, and cheese; robed them in clean garments; preached a sermon to enforce discipline; and provided them with a decent Christian burial. By contrast, the "modern poor house" was a prison-like walled building with a temple-front portico. The poor here were kept shackled in cells; fed a diet of small amounts of oatmeal, potatoes, gruel, and bread; cruelly beaten to enforce discipline; and loaded in a box labeled "for dissection" after death. Pugin was of course overstating the virtues of medieval institutions while detailing all the evils of his own time, but to him the medieval town was a total visual and religious environment, while the industrial town, with its vested interests and greedy capitalists, was a detestable degradation of human existence.

In 1841 Pugin published *The True Principles of Pointed or Christian Architecture*, in which he enumerated his ideals: "First, that there should be no features about a building which are not necessary for convenience, construction, and propriety, and second, that all ornament should consist of the enrichment of the essential construction of the building." He regarded the Gothic as the "only correct expression of the faith, wants, and climate" of England and advocated its use for all buildings, including modern secular ones such as railroad stations.

While writing treatises and giving lectures, Pugin was also busy as a designer. He collaborated with Sir Charles Barry on the competition-winning design for rebuilding the Houses of Parliament, which had been destroyed by fire in 1834. The overall conception of the building was Barry's (Fig. 14.22), while the profusion of lively and historically correct detail, inside and out, was Pugin's contribution. On his own Pugin was responsible for the design of at least two dozen churches, chapels, and cathedrals. For himself he designed a house (1843–44) and chapel (1845–51) at Ramsgate, Kent (Fig. 14.23). The design of the chapel, dedicated to St. Augustine, was based on the fourteenth-century parish churches of Kent, and its construction of knapped flint with narrow inset bands of freestone incorporated materials common to the area. The interior of the chapel was finished in ashlar masonry carved under Pugin's supervision. After its completion Pugin donated St. Augustine's to the local Catholic diocese. His nearby house, constructed of coarse brick dressed with stone, had a crenelated tower, gables,

14.21 A.W.N. Pugin, Ancient and modern towns compared, from *Contrasts*, second edition, 1841.

In the lower view, the benign medieval town appears in urban harmony, announcing its values through the silhouettes of its church towers. In the upper view, the malignant nineteenth-century city is a deplorable cacophony of prison, factories, and almost-obscured churches.

14.22 Charles Barry and A.W.N. Pugin, Plan of the Houses of Parliament, London, 1836–68.

The long façade faces the Thames. Behind it, the dominant spaces are the House of Commons and the House of Lords. At the rear of the site is Westminster Hall, saved from the fire of 1834.

14.23 A.W.N. Pugin, St. Augustine, Ramsgate, 1846–51. Engraving.

Pugin's house, called The Grange, stands adjacent to a church he financed himself. As patron, he was able to make every design decision to his own satisfaction.

dormers, and bay windows; but its innovative feature was Pugin's transformation of the medieval great hall into both a horizontal and a vertical circulation space, a feature that would continue in domestic architecture through the end of the century and even appear in the designs of H.H. Richardson and Frank Lloyd Wright. Pugin's work firmly established the Gothic style as a suitable one for modern buildings, especially churches. He died at the age of forty having completed a relatively small number of buildings, but his influence extended to other architects who would be far more prolific, such as Richard Norman Shaw in England and Richard Upjohn in the United States.

THE ECCLESIOLOGICAL MOVEMENT IN ENGLAND AND AMERICA

During the 1830s, the intellectual force of the Oxford Tractarian Movement and the Cambridge Camden Society led to reforms in Anglican church architecture. The resulting Ecclesiological Movement sought a return to forms of medieval ritual that had been swept away on the tide of the Reformation. Architects, clerics, and antiquarians exhaustively examined Gothic buildings and sought to identify features of churches and furnishings that contributed to liturgical and symbolic functions of the worship service and to develop rules governing church design. Pugin was viewed with suspicion by the Ecclesiologists because of his conversion to Roman Catholicism, but his buildings conformed to their views.

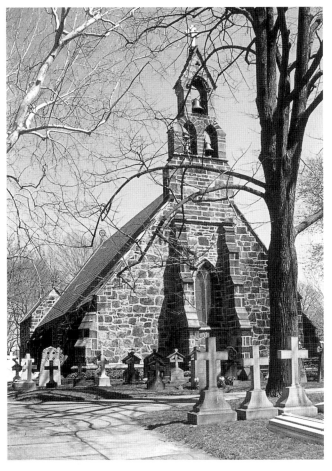

14.24 St. James-the-Less, Philadelphia, Pennsylvania, 1846–48.

St. James-the-Less was modeled specifically on the English church of St. Michael Longstanton. Drawings for it were sent to the United States by the Cambridge Camden Society.

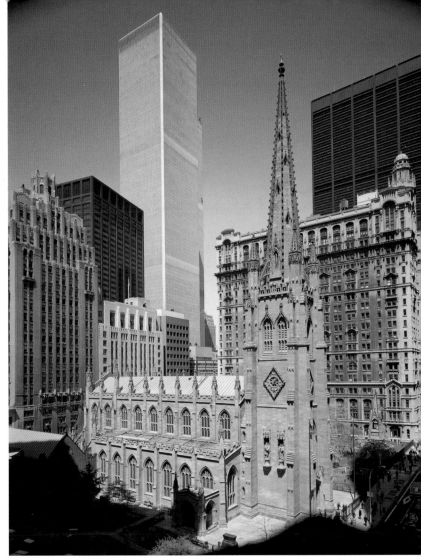

14.25 Richard Upjohn, Trinity Church, New York City, 1839–46.

Trinity Church has been dwarfed by skyscrapers, which once included the now-destroyed World Trade Center. In 1846 the church was a prominent landmark.

The full force of the Ecclesiological Movement in the United States was felt at the Episcopal church of St. James-the-Less in Philadelphia (1846–1848) (Fig. 14.24). Drawings for the church were sent directly by the Cambridge Camden Society, which had based the design on the thirteenth-century church of St. Michael Longstanton in Cambridgeshire. St. James-the-Less was constructed entirely of natural materials, not superficial applications such as plaster, and its small **bellcote** became a typical feature of modest Episcopal churches in the U.S.

Richard Upjohn (1802–78) was the first American architect to follow Pugin's principles, although Upjohn was Episcopalian rather than Catholic and built only Episcopal churches as a result of his sincere belief that it was the only acceptable denomination. His first major commission was for Trinity Church in New York City (1839–46), which was designed for a growing and wealthy congregation. Upjohn used Decorated Gothic for the church, which features an extended chancel, raised altar, and ceiling vaults constructed of wood and plaster rather than stone (Fig. 14.25).

EUGÈNE-EMMANUEL VIOLLET-LE-DUC

The leading proponent of the Gothic Revival in France was Eugène-Emmanuel Viollet-le-Duc (1814–1879), an architect who shared Pugin's enthusiasm for medieval works. However, the moral and religious views that so strongly colored Pugin's writings were not shared by Viollet-le-Duc, who was more interested in the rational basis of medieval structure. He saw the system of rib vault, pointed arch, and flying buttress as analogous to nineteenth-century iron framing, and he aspired to a modern architecture based on engineering accomplishments that would have the integrity of form and detail found in medieval works (Fig. 14.26). His theoretical writings—especially the two volumes of *Entretiens sur l'architecture* (*Discourses on Architecture*), published between 1863 and 1872—stress the importance of rationality in design.

Much of Viollet-le-Duc's time was spent opposing the French architectural establishment's denial of all medieval styles. The only government-sponsored school for architects, the Ecole des Beaux-Arts, was dominated by

14.26 Eugène-Emmanuel Viollet-le-Duc, Iron-frame assembly hall from the *Entretiens*, 1863–72. Drawing.

Viollet-le-Duc was more successful as a theorist than as a practitioner. Interpreting Gothic structure as a highly rational response to the problem of load and support, he proposed the substitution of iron members as a logical use of the products of the Industrial Revolution.

architects working in classical styles, and efforts by Viollet-le-Duc and others to have its courses include the study of Romanesque and Gothic buildings met with little success. However, the extended controversy identified Viollet-le-Duc as an architect knowledgeable about medieval architecture, and from 1840 onward he was involved in scores of restoration projects for the major historical monuments of France, including Notre-Dame Cathedral and the Sainte-Chapelle in Paris; the abbey church of St. Denis; St. Sernin at Toulouse; Ste. Madeleine at Vézelay; the ramparts of Carcassonne; and the cathedrals of Reims, Amiens, and Beauvais. Out of this rich experience in dealing first-hand with medieval projects came the ten-volume *Dictionnaire raisonné de l'architecture française du XIe au XVIe siècle* (*Encyclopedia of French Architecture from the Eleventh to the Sixteenth Centuries*) (1858–65), which remains an important scholarly resource for medievalists. Twentieth-century architectural preservationists shudder at Viollet-le-Duc's philosophy of restoration—"to restore a building is not only to preserve it, to repair it, or to rebuild, but to bring it back to a state of completion such as may never have existed at any given moment"—which is quite the opposite of current attitudes toward this sort of work. Nevertheless, one must acknowledge that many of the buildings restored by Viollet-le-Duc might not have survived into the twentieth century without his intervention. For better or worse, his work marks the beginning of scholarly attempts at historic preservation. While the architectural projects he designed as original undertakings are not particularly distinguished, his theories had a major impact on the development of nineteenth-century rationalism and twentieth-century Modernism.

THE ECOLE DES BEAUX-ARTS

The French school of architecture, the Ecole des Beaux-Arts, remained highly influential in France throughout the nineteenth century, principally producing public work, and had a profound effect on American architecture in both the public and private sectors in the second half of the nineteenth century. Ecole students learned to read closely a *précis*, or program, understand the hierarchical relationships of the various spaces, and distribute these spaces symmetrically along first major, then minor, axes, with an emphasis on the *marche* or movement through the spaces along these axes and in three dimensions. It was this system for ordering space that represented the best of the Ecole's methodology, not the eclectic skin that it encouraged to be applied afterward, almost as an afterthought. However, the extraordinary skills of delineation fostered at the Ecole have sometimes made its designers seem more concerned with superficial appearance than with matters of structure and construction. This complaint played a major role in the supplanting of Ecole principles by those of European Modernism in the early twentieth century.

The elaborate system of Ecole instruction was unmatched in the rest of Europe and in the United States, where apprenticeship in the office of a practicing architect was the norm for architectural education during most of the nineteenth century. Some technical universities in Germany offered architectural studies as part of engineering programs, but it was American landgrant colleges that were to lead the world in placing architecture in the university curriculum. M.I.T. established a School of Architecture in 1861, and fifteen other universities had followed suit before the end of the century. Their curricula were all based on that of the Ecole des Beaux-Arts. Architectural graduates of American universities seeking additional polish would attend the Ecole in Paris, although they were not eligible for the Grand Prix competition, and American universities sought to hire Frenchmen from the Ecole to direct their studies in architectural design. As a result of this cultural exchange, and the economic prosperity and westward expansion that occurred in the United States after the Civil War, the country has far more Beaux-Arts-influenced architecture than France.

RICHARD MORRIS HUNT AND THE WORLD'S COLUMBIAN EXPOSITION

The first American to attend the Ecole des Beaux-Arts was Richard Morris Hunt (1827–1895), who entered the school in 1846. He had lived in Paris since 1832, when his family had moved there after the death of his father. Returning to New York, Hunt established a practice that prospered greatly until his own death. Newly rich industrial magnates wanted houses that imitated the ancestral mansions of European nobility, and of all American architects Hunt was best able to provide the designs desired. His work for the Vanderbilt family—a town house on Fifth Avenue; a "cottage" called The Breakers at Newport, Rhode Island (Fig. 14.27); and Biltmore, their chateauesque country mansion at Asheville, North Carolina (Fig. 14.28)—are well known, but he also designed the base for the Statue of Liberty (1880) and the central portion of the Fifth Avenue façade of the Metropolitan Museum of Art in New York (1895).

Perhaps Hunt's greatest impact on American architecture came through his involvement with the 1893 World's

14.27 Richard Morris Hunt, The Breakers, Newport, Rhode Island, 1892–95.

Richard Morris Hunt was the first American to attend the Ecole des Beaux-Arts in Paris. The knowledge he gained there of academic planning and monumental design made him the architect of choice among the late nineteenth-century American elite.

14.28 Richard Morris Hunt, Biltmore, Asheville, North Carolina, 1890–95.

Among Hunt's residential commissions, none was more grand than Biltmore. He based its form on the Loire river châteaux built during the early French Renaissance.

14.29 Richard Morris Hunt, Administration Building, World's Columbian Exposition, Chicago, Illinois, 1893.

Hunt's Administration Building stands at the head of the Court of Honor and its lagoon. The "White City" captivated the American public. Using widespread exterior electric lighting for the first time, it started a movement that produced proposals for new civic cores in cities nationwide.

Columbian Exposition in Chicago. Landscape architect Frederick Law Olmsted developed the site plan and a committee of the country's most important architects was formed under the leadership of Daniel H. Burnham to design the temporary buildings for the fair. Hunt used his influence as the profession's leading practitioner to direct the entire plan along Beaux-Arts lines. The principal buildings, assigned to different architectural firms, were disposed around a large Court of Honor, with the domed Administration Building (Fig. 14.29) by Hunt at its head and an open peristyle by Charles B. Atwood terminating the vista out to Lake Michigan. To ensure unity around the Court of Honor, it was agreed that all designs would be based on the precedent of the Italian Renaissance; would use a common material, stucco (plaster), painted white; and would maintain a uniform sixty-foot-high cornice line. The effect was stunning. Visitors named it the "White City" and went away greatly impressed by the dramatic spectacle. The 1893 fair did much to advance the ornate and monumental Beaux-Arts style as the appropriate one for important American buildings and civic designs. Train stations, art museums, city halls, post offices, and churches were built across the country in emulation of the White City.

In their enthusiasm for Beaux-Arts architecture, fair visitors completely overlooked the truly innovative buildings in Chicago, the tall metal-framed buildings downtown. Louis Sullivan, an architect who participated in the design of the fair, later remarked that it set the cause of American architecture back by fifty years. His observation is a biased one, however, made late in his life when his career had gone into decline. The construction of great Beaux-Arts buildings was only finally terminated by the economic hardships of the Great Depression, but in truth the fair did no damage to the architects, including Sullivan, who formed the American avant-garde of the late nineteenth century.

McKIM, MEAD, AND WHITE

Among American practitioners following Ecole principles, none was more successful than the firm of McKim, Mead, and White. One author has metaphorically described the careful Mead as the keel, the esthete McKim as the hull, and the flamboyant White as the sail of an imaginary ship in this, the first great architectural partnership in America.

William Rutherford Mead was born into a family of painters and sculptors and began his professional life working in New York for German-trained architect and critic Russell Sturgis, whose Victorian Gothic buildings reflected the influence of architectural critic John Ruskin. Subsequent to travel and study in Europe, he returned to America and met Charles Follen McKim, then working in the office of H.H. Richardson. Always interested in construction, Mead provided the technical and business acumen needed in a large, complex architectural firm.

McKim's parents were Quaker abolitionists; their spirit of idealism remained with him throughout his life. Growing up in a hotbed of mid-century avant-garde culture, Llewellyn Park near New York City, McKim had contact with such luminaries as William Cullen Bryant, Horace Greeley, Henry David Thoreau, and landscape architect Frederick Law Olmsted. McKim attended Harvard's Lawrence Scientific School, worked briefly for family friend Russell Sturgis, then set out for Paris and the Ecole des Beaux-Arts. In 1870 he returned to work for Richardson, where he met Mead. In mid-1872 Mead and McKim set up a practice of their own.

Stanford White's father was an art and music critic for literary magazines. Among his contacts were the architect Calvert Vaux, the painter John LaFarge, and Frederick Law Olmsted. Through Olmsted, White became a precocious apprentice to H.H. Richardson without the benefit of any formal architectural training. In 1878 White left to travel in Europe, and in 1879 returned to enter into partnership with Mead and McKim. He became legendary for his prodigious output of work and indeed for his appetites in general. The firm would eventually have more than 100 employees and produce almost 1000 commissions.

McKim, Mead, and White designed the Villard Houses (Fig. 14.30) in New York City in 1882–85. Consisting of six separate houses arranged around a central courtyard, the building takes on the appearance of a single Roman palazzo. The Villard Houses are large, grand, chaste, and refined, and presented a face of civic decorum in a city then taking its place among world capitals, providing their owner, shipping tycoon Henry Villard, with instant credibility among his nouveau-riche associates.

14.30 McKim, Mead, and White, Villard Houses, New York City, 1882–85.

The firm of McKim, Mead, and White established the model for the large-scale American architectural practice. They based this residential structure on Roman palazzi such as the Palazzo Farnese.

14.31 McKim, Mead, and White, Boston Public Library, Boston, Massachusetts, 1887–95.

Charles McKim looked back to Henri Labrouste's Bibliothèque Ste.-Geneviève for his façade composition. He made numerous studies, including full-scale mock-ups of the cornice, before settling on his final design.

14.32a McKim, Mead, and White, Plan of Pennsylvania Station, New York City, 1902–11

Of all of McKim, Mead, and White's planning accomplishments, none is more impressive than this train station. Here they looked to the Roman baths for inspiration in managing the huge crowds that passed through these vast spaces each day.

Charles McKim was largely responsible for the Boston Public Library (Fig. 14.31) (1887–95), which faces H.H. Richardson's Trinity Church across Copley Square. Then housing the largest public collection of books in the United States, it symbolized Boston's cultural heritage. Its form has layers of precedent, the most recent being Henri Labrouste's Bibliothèque Ste.-Geneviève in Paris (see Fig. 14.38), itself based upon the lateral walls of Alberti's San Francesco in Rimini (see Fig. 11.16), a church that drew inspiration from both the nearby Arch of Augustus and the Tomb of Theodoric in Ravenna. McKim organized the library around a central court, placing the public

14.32b McKim, Mead, and White, Section and elevation of Pennsylvania Station, New York City, 1902–11.

Like the plan, McKim, Mead, and White's elevation and section were inspired by the Roman baths. The dominant features were the great thermal windows that lit the groin-vaulted waiting area. The destruction of this terminal must be considered a tragedy for American architecture.

reading room and elaborate entry sequence to the front of the site. The structure is faced with Milford granite but includes advanced technology such as thin-shell vaults. Sculpted panels above the entry were designed by Augustus St. Gaudens and the bronze entry doors by Daniel Chester French.

Back in New York City, the firm produced the vast Pennsylvania Station (1902–11) (Figs. 14.32a,b) which covered some eight acres on three levels but was tragically demolished in the 1960s. Based upon the model of Roman baths, the station provided a grand portal to the city as it brought in passengers some forty-five feet below the ground level and covered them with monumental vaulted spaces lit by great thermal windows; it brilliantly manipulated the hordes of people passing through each day.

PROGRESS IN IRON FABRICATION
IRON BRIDGES

Eighteenth-century industrial production of cast and wrought iron so increased its availability that iron replaced wood in the frame of any building where heavy loads or the danger of fire were of concern. Cast iron was favored for columns, while the superior tensile qualities of wrought iron made it the recommended material for beams. In the nineteenth century, iron began to be used instead of wood in the fabrication of **truss** bridges built for roads and railroads that crossed rivers or valleys. A

rigid framework composed of shorter members, the truss can be used to span great distances. The Romans certainly used wooden trusses for bridge construction, but during the medieval period the triangulation of elements for rigidity was largely forgotten, and most medieval builders used the king post or queen post truss, which required the bottom chord to be a single member as long as the span. Palladio clearly illustrates trusses in his *Four Books on Architecture,* but he seems never to have used them. The seventeenth- and eighteenth-century revivals of Palladio did not include interest in his truss designs, leaving the truss to be reinvented by builders in the nineteenth century.

Faced with many streams to cross and surrounded by an abundance of timber, American builders soon came to appreciate the principle of the truss for bridge construction. Theodore Burr patented his arch truss in 1817, and Ithiel Town grew rich off his 1820 patent for a lattice truss. Other truss patents soon followed, Long (1830), Howe (1840), Pratt (1844), Whipple (1847), Warren (1848), and Fink (1854) being among the most important. The first iron-truss bridge in the United States, the Frankfort Bridge on the Erie Canal, was built in 1840, and the first

14.33 Robert Stephenson, Britannia Bridge, Menai Straits, Wales, 1845–50. Lithograph by G. Hawkins.

Stone piers support a hollow rectangular beam of riveted wrought-iron plates in order to span more than 1500 feet between three pylons and the shore abutments. Here we see the bridge under construction.

steel-truss bridge was constructed in 1878–79 over the Missouri river for the Chicago and Alton Railroad. The railroads used metal-truss bridges extensively after the Civil War because they offered greater stability than suspension bridges under the moving load of a heavy train.

Bridge builders met the challenge posed by navigable bodies of water by designing long-span structures with high clearances. Robert Stephenson (1803–59) designed the Britannia Bridge (1845–50) across the Menai Straits in Wales as two parallel box tubes, each a hollow rectangular beam of riveted wrought-iron plates spanning 1511 feet between three pylons and the shore abutments (Fig. 14.33). The bridge was constructed by erecting the stone piers, floating the completed tubular sections, each 463 feet long, on pontoons, and hoisting the tubes up with giant hydraulic jacks. Once all sections were in place, railroad tracks were laid inside the tubes, and one open-sea ferry-crossing on the route to Ireland was eliminated.

Stephenson was prepared to reinforce the Britannia Bridge with suspension cables (hence the higher tops of the pylons), but this proved unnecessary. The principle of suspension-bridge construction had been known for centuries; vines, hides, or ropes had long been twisted together and strung across chasms in China, India, and Peru. Modern suspension bridges, using chains of iron links or eyebars, started to be built shortly after 1800, with early work being done by James Findley in Philadelphia, who obtained a patent on his system in 1801. English engineers, including Thomas Telford, learned of Findley's work through illustrations in Thomas Pope's *Treatise on*

Bridge Architecture (1811) and soon applied his findings to their own projects. Telford's bridge over the Menai Straits (1819–26) was supported by sixteen eyebar chains of wrought iron, anchored to cast-iron frames embedded in rock abutments and suspended from masonry towers 153 feet high (Fig. 14.34). At 579 feet, this was the longest suspension span in the world at the time of its completion. The American designer Charles Ellet was the first to see the advantages of using flexible wire cable in place of chains for suspension structures, although the greatest nineteenth-century engineers for cable suspension bridges would be John Augustus Roebling and his son, Washington Augustus Roebling, designers and builders of the Brooklyn Bridge (1869–83).

DEVELOPMENTS IN STEEL

In seeking to expand the market for iron and improve the desirable qualities of the material, nineteenth-century ironmongers experimented with new methods for manufacturing steel, which is an alloy of low-carbon iron and trace amounts of other metals. Small quantities of steel had been manufactured in India as early as 1500 BCE, and Celtic peoples in Austria, Spain, and Britain had made and worked the material at sites where iron ore containing manganese occurred in natural deposits. Blacksmiths, knifesmiths, and swordmakers could work the extracted iron and make steel, which was greatly respected for its ability to hold a superior cutting edge. Industrialization of this process required reducing the carbon content of the molten iron and using less charcoal in the furnace because that fuel was becoming scarce and expensive.

An American ironmonger, William Kelly (1811–1888), was the first to develop a converter that burnt off excess carbon with a blast of air. He constructed seven of them at his works in Eddyville, Kentucky. When he was ready to apply for a patent on his pneumatic process in 1856, however, he found that the Englishman Henry Bessemer (1813–1898) had just been granted one for the same idea. Although Kelly's prior claim to the process was subsequently demonstrated, he received neither the recognition nor the financial rewards that should have been his. Bessemer became known as the inventor of the converter that made reliable quantities of steel efficiently and affordably. From 1875 onward, steel began to replace both cast and wrought iron in construction because its compressive and tensile strengths exceeded those of iron and it was cheaper to produce.

Steel was first used for railroad ties and in engineering works. The first steel bridge built in the United States was the Eads Bridge (1869–74) over the Mississippi at St. Louis. Its designer, Captain James B. Eads (1820–1887), had been a riverboat captain and salvage operator on the Mississippi, and despite his complete lack of engineering training (he was assisted by capable engineers and mathematicians who provided the technical abilities he lacked)

14.34 Thomas Telford, Menai Bridge, Wales, 1819–26.

Suspension bridges achieve beauty through the absolute logic of their use of materials. The great masonry pylons are in compression, while the steel cables that support the roadbed are in tension.

THE COMING OF THE RAILROAD

by Mark Reinberger

14A W.P. Frith, *The Railway Station*, 1866.
Engraving.

No single development had a greater impact on life in the nineteenth century than the railroad. After the first line opened from Stockton to Darlington in England in 1825, the railroad spread with astonishing rapidity. By the 1840s the railroad reached all parts of England. In the 1830s lines were begun in France, Germany, Ireland, Russia, and Italy. The first American line was the Baltimore and Ohio, which began operations in 1830. Ten years later the country had 3000 miles of track, and by the outbreak of the Civil War, 30,000 miles had been laid. In 1869, the first American transcontinental line linked the east and west coasts.

More than any other invention, the railroad linked all regions of countries together, creating unified nations and leading to more integrated economies and the century's stronger sense of nationalism. Regional differences in consumption, fashion, and architecture lessened in the wake of the railroads, which made possible rapid, long-distance mail delivery, the rapid spread of news, and the easier distrib-

ution of products including building materials.

The growth of the railroads spurred, and in turn was dependent upon, nineteenth-century industrialization. A large-scale railroad network was unthinkable without such elements of a modern industrial economy as a large and mobile labor force, the creation of steel for rails capable of withstanding heavy loads, the standardization of tools and machinery, finer tolerances in manufacturing, new structural capabilities for bridges and tunneling, and a prodigious amount of mining for coal. All of these industries, in turn, provided jobs for millions of workers.

Railroads also made possible the modern extended city, and allowed more than just the upper and upper-middle classes (who could afford a carriage) to live in suburbs. Subways and streetcars also made possible denser concentrations of business in city centers, necessitating the development of the tall office building late in the century. In America, railroads also helped open up remote areas to

mining and settlement and were responsible for much town-funding. They also tied together colonialized countries abroad, allowing international powers such as Britain to extract resources more economically and exercise closer control over places such as India.

The accompanying engraving (Fig. 14A), painstakingly composed by W.P. Frith, depicts Paddington Station in London in 1866. The artist's acknowledged goal was the portrayal of modern urban life with its crowds, its mixture of social classes, and its greater bustle. He aimed to create a kind of literary tableau in the spirit of Dickens, then England's most popular author. He also lovingly portrayed the iron-and-glass architecture of a new building type—the railway station—and the details of the train. The many tender family scenes in the image remind us that the train allowed for greater communication between friends and family, and diminished the isolation of rural areas. In both cities and country, the railroad station to some degree replaced the town square as the center of social intercourse.

14.35 J.A. and W.A. Roebling, Brooklyn Bridge, New York City, 1869–83.

No suspension bridge has been more celebrated than this one connecting Manhattan to Brooklyn across the East river. Its steel cables were not raised intact but were woven by a spider-like machine that passed repeatedly from bank to bank.

he was able to gain the confidence of local businessmen who backed the construction of the bridge. Eads understood the behavior of the Mississippi and insisted that the bridge foundations extend to bedrock, which lay under fourteen feet of water and eighty-one feet of sand. The bridge required four stone piers to support three segmental-arched steel spans of 502, 520, and 502 feet; the arches were fabricated of eighteen-inch-diameter cast-steel tubes, interconnected by triangulated bracing to form an integrated unit. Construction was accomplished by sinking pneumatic **caissons** for pier foundations and then cantilevering the arch sections out from each pier until the arch could be closed; using centering to support the arch in construction would have interfered with navigation on the river.

Steel was also employed for the major suspension bridge of the nineteenth century, the Brooklyn Bridge, connecting Manhattan and Brooklyn over the East river with a 1600-foot clear span (Fig.14.35). The bridge was designed by John Augustus Roebling (1806–1869) and constructed under the supervision of his son, Washington Augustus Roebling (1837–1926). They sank two gigantic caisson foundations for the bridge towers, and spun galvanized steel wire for the two main cables that supported the roadway. Each cable contains over 5000 strands of wire, compacted and wrapped with a continuous spiral of softer steel. Diagonal stays radiating from the towers provide wind bracing and are probably strong enough to carry the bridge's loads by themselves should the main cables break, while a stiffened deck checks any tendency the bridge might have to develop destructive vibrations resulting from wind loads.

ARCHITECTURAL APPLICATIONS OF IRON AND STEEL CONSTRUCTION

Iron and steel were not admired for their architectural qualities in the nineteenth century: prevailing Neo-Classical and Romantic attitudes looked to past ages when buildings had always been of load-bearing masonry construction. Everything that architects and their clients admired and felt comfortable with could be constructed by using traditional materials and methods. Thus architects were slow to exploit the possibilities of iron and steel, which were first used in industrial utilitarian buildings, such as textile mills, warehouses, and greenhouses.

Iron was most elegantly employed in landscape gardening. Victorian England, prosperous from the wealth of its empire, had a fascination with the tropical plants that were brought back from India, Africa, and the Far East. Keeping these specimens alive in the cool, overcast climate of Britain required structures that could reproduce the humid heat of their native countries, so builders and gardeners set about erecting greenhouses large enough to contain palm or banana trees. Unfettered by ancient precedent, the builders turned to lightweight iron framing systems with glass infill panes. The Palm House at Kew Gardens, London (1845–47) by Decimus Burton and Richard Turner (Fig. 14.36) is an example of this kind of work, as is the Conservatory at Chatsworth House (1836–40) by Burton and Joseph Paxton. The strength of the building at Chatsworth derived from its glass-and-iron skin, which was arranged in alternating ridge-and-furrow-like folds.

JOSEPH PAXTON

Joseph Paxton (1801–1865) was a landscape gardener by training, acquiring through experience his skill at building with glass and iron for greenhouses. He revolutionized architecture with the unsolicited design he submitted for a building in Hyde Park, London, to house the first modern world's fair in 1851. The building committee for the London exhibition had received 245 designs of all sorts, none of which was entirely suitable, so it had decided to produce its own, a great domed structure with a brick drum and adjacent walls. Even this traditional structure could probably not have been built rapidly enough and within the £300,000 budget. These circumstances made Paxton's tardy submission in July of 1850 all the more attractive (Fig. 14.37a). His design proposed an 1851-foot-long structure of glass and iron at an estimated price of £150,000; and through negotiations with the manufacturers who would supply the materials, Paxton could guarantee completion on time. His scheme was accepted. In constructing the building, the contractors Fox and Henderson made one of the first large-scale demonstrations of prefabrication. The repeated iron-and-glass sections required a limited number of individual components,

14.36 Decimus Burton and Richard Turner, Palm House, Kew Gardens, London, 1845–47.

Greenhouses provided an impetus for the design of lightweight, quickly constructed, transparent structures. Between the iron arches, the glass frames were folded in alternate ridges and furrows, which provided rigidity.

14.37a Joseph Paxton, Crystal Palace, London, 1851. Lithograph.

Joseph Paxton designed a building with prefabricated parts that could be mass-produced and erected rapidly. It stood in stark contrast to traditional, massive stone constructions.

14.37b Joseph Paxton, Crystal Palace interior, London. Lithograph.

Such a structure as this one was not considered to be "architecture" by theorist and critic John Ruskin because it lacked permanence. However, its lightweight, skeletal, transparent construction pointed toward the future.

which meant that supplying factories could easily mass-produce the tremendous quantity of material required for the eighteen-acre building: 3800 tons of cast iron, 700 tons of wrought iron, twenty-four miles of rainwater guttering, 900,000 square feet of glass, and 600,000 cubic feet of wood (Fig. 14.37b). Materials arrived at the site preassembled into subsections, and final assembly proceeded at an unprecedented rate. Once the exhibition opened, the building was visited by about one-quarter of the population of England and was universally acclaimed for its vast, airy interior space. Journalists dubbed it the Crystal Palace, a name it has retained. The construction success and public praise for the Crystal Palace had much to do with the increasing acceptance of a larger amount of glass and iron in buildings designed by architects. After the exhibition ended, the building was dismantled and reerected in a park at Sydenham, outside London, where it remained until it was destroyed by fire in 1936.

HENRI LABROUSTE

Designers in France soon took up the techniques of glass-and-iron construction as well. Henri Labrouste (1801–1875) made a fine architectural use of cast iron in the Bibliothèque Ste.-Geneviève (1842–50) in Paris. On the exterior (Fig. 14.38) the building presents a correct Neo-Classical façade recalling Italian Renaissance palace and church designs; but on the interior at the second-floor level one finds for that time an unprecedentedly great reading room (Fig. 14.39) which extends the length and width of the building, covered by light semicircular cast-iron arches. Sixteen slender cast-iron columns, with proportions previously found only in Pompeiian wall paintings, divide the long space into two barrel-vaulted halves. The ceiling vaults, consisting of interlaced wires covered with plaster, rest on the delicately scrolled cast-iron arches.

In 1854 Labrouste was named architect of the Bibliothèque Nationale (the French National Library), an institution with a rapidly growing collection of books and inadequate quarters in which to house them. Labrouste worked on the buildings for the library for the next twenty-one years, designing around existing structures to create a central reading room (Fig. 14.40) and a separate bookstack, the first to be provided in a library (Fig. 14.41). As in the Bibliothèque Ste.-Geneviève, Labrouste used masonry for the Neo-Classical exterior walls and iron for the interior. The most spectacular use of iron is in the

14.38 Henri Labrouste, Bibliothèque Ste.-Geneviève, Paris, 1842–50.

Labrouste's design would later inspire Charles McKim in his façade composition for the Boston Public Library. The panels between the piers of the arcade contain the names of celebrated members of the French intelligentsia.

14.39 Henri Labrouste, Bibliothèque Ste.-Geneviève reading room, Paris, 1842–50.

Labrouste spanned his great reading room with two sets of cast-iron arches supported down the center line by slender cast-iron columns set atop masonry piers.

reading room, where nine domes, each nearly thirty-five feet in diameter, rest on a grid of sixteen slender iron columns. Illumination for the space comes from clerestories and oculus windows in each dome. Equally important, but less celebrated, is the iron framing of the bookstacks. Here there are six floors of shelving and aisle space, top-lit by skylights and light-wells. The grillwork of the floors and the columns supporting the shelf units form a structural framework independent of the enclosing masonry walls.

GUSTAVE EIFFEL

The most famous French designer using iron in the second half of the nineteenth century was Gustave Eiffel (1832–1923). This engineer gained fame for his graceful bridge designs, such as the Garabit Viaduct over the river Truyère (1880–84) in southern France (Fig. 14.42), and then used his experience with iron construction to build the world's tallest tower, the 1010-foot-high Eiffel Tower, erected for the Paris International Exposition of 1889 (page 418). Not until the completion of the Chrysler Building in New York was Eiffel's tower exceeded in height, and it remains the largest iron construction in the world, for steel was rapidly becoming the preferred material for metal framing. Eiffel's tower design was derided by the artistic elite of France before

14.40 Henri Labrouste, Bibliothèque Nationale central reading room, Paris, 1858–68.

Labrouste's reading room for this library lies in the center of the plan. While the attenuated proportions of the cast-iron columns were new, the domical vaults were based on traditional masonry forms.

14.41 Henri Labrouste, Plan of the Bibliothèque Nationale, Paris, 1858.

Entry is made at the lower left into the large court. The principal axis is the transverse one, through the court, the reading room, and into the stacks.

14.42 (above) Gustave Eiffel, Garabit Viaduct over the river Thuyère, Garabit, France, 1880–84.

Eiffel made the steel-frame bridge into an art form. Striking even today in its grace and lightness, this structure was considered absolutely shocking in the late nineteenth century.

14.43 (right) Gustave Eiffel, Auguste Bartholdi, and Richard Morris Hunt, Statue of Liberty, New York City, 1883–86.

Richard Morris Hunt designed the base in the manner he learned at the Ecole des Beaux-Arts. Gustave Eiffel designed the statue's iron frame, which is seen here without its skin. The sculptor Bartholdi created the figure of Liberty in thin sheets of copper that were painstakingly hammered into shape over wooden forms, then attached to the frame.

14.44 Jules Saulnier, Menier Chocolate Factory, Noisiel-sur-Marne, France, 1871–72.

This was the first all-iron-frame French building. Saulnier gave artistic expression to the diagonal bracing and, structurally, made the building's skin into a lattice truss.

and during construction, but Parisians of all classes were thrilled by the magnificent views from its top, and they soon adjusted to its gigantic silhouette being cast against the skyline. The opening of the tower in 1889 also provided the first large-scale demonstration of the passenger safety elevator, a model designed by the American Elisha Graves Otis.

In New York harbor stands another of Eiffel's engineering projects, the internal skeleton for the 151-foot-tall Statue of Liberty (1883–86) (Fig. 14.43). Miss Liberty's copper skin is supported by iron straps attached to a steel framework that Eiffel designed to withstand the considerable wind loads of the harbor. At the time of its construction, the Statue of Liberty had the most advanced diagonally braced frame to be found in any structure in the United States. Its incorporation of steel members for the major load-bearing posts marked only the second time steel had been used for non-bridge construction there. The first all-iron-frame French building, the Menier Chocolate Factory at Noisiel-sur-Marne (1871–72) by Jules Saulnier, gave artistic expression to the diagonals of its bracing (Fig. 14.44). The iron used efficiently made the building's exterior skin into a lattice truss, and the architect embellished the diamond shapes on the façade with diagonal brick-work and decorative crosses at the intersections.

THE FIRST SKYSCRAPERS

American builders were to become the primary innovators in metal-frame construction for buildings. From about 1865 onward, architects in New York and

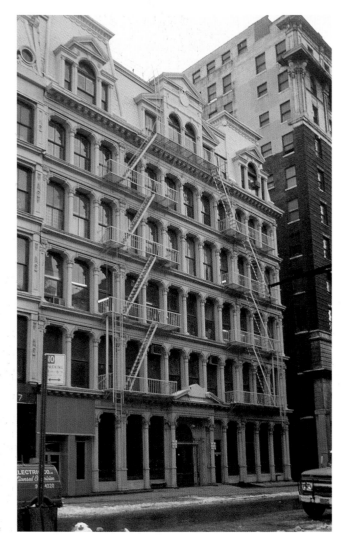

14.45 Cast-iron façade, Richmond, Virginia, ca. 1870.

Such cast-iron store fronts were attached to buildings with perimeter bearing walls of brick and with internal, heavy-timber columns and beams. The cast-iron forms were often based on palazzo façades from Renaissance Venice.

painted to resemble stone or other materials. The simplicity of construction appealed to many businessmen, who built increasing numbers of cast-iron structures from 1849 onward. Whole districts of them, such as SoHo in New York City, sprouted when extensive fires destroyed the previous timber-framed buildings.

In most instances cast-iron buildings lacked the wind bracing essential to high-rise construction, so they cannot be considered the first skyscrapers. However, James Bogardus introduced the European iron I-section, now universally employed as wide-flange sections for steel framing, and his concept of an all-iron building must have encouraged others to think more seriously about the alternatives to masonry bearing-wall construction. In the process of rebuilding the business district of Chicago, largely destroyed by fire in 1871, a number of inventive men perfected fireproofed metal-frame construction for high-rise buildings and thus created the skyscraper. William Le Baron Jenney (1832–1907), the designer of the Home Insurance Building (1884–85), is generally credited with

14.46 William Le Baron Jenney, Home Insurance Building, Chicago, Illinois, 1883–85.

William Le Baron Jenney was only one of the many architects searching for effective ways to fireproof steel-frame construction for late nineteenth-century tall buildings. His Home Insurance Building was among the first successful solutions.

THE CHICAGO BUILDING OF THE HOME INSURANCE CO.

OF NEW YORK

then Chicago developed an original building type, the skyscraper, on a scale and level of sophistication unmatched by European designers. Tall buildings were a response to rising urban real-estate values and the desire of businesses to remain close to established centers of commerce. A whole range of technical improvements—including mass-produced structural components, the safety elevator, and fireproofing techniques—made them feasible, and their structural systems were most logically executed in steel frame, laterally braced to withstand wind loads.

Pre-Civil War building technology included the first structural use of iron for buildings in the cast-iron fronts and building frames that were mass-produced by men such as James Bogardus (1800–1874) and Daniel Badger (1806–1884) in New York and shipped as far as steamships traveled (Fig. 14.45). Cast iron was favored for its strength, fire-resistance, and plastic qualities. The classical detail desired for commercial structures could be economically cast from molds and repeated for as many bays and stories as desired, and the finished façade could be

14.47 Daniel H. Burnham and John Welborn Root, Monadnock Building, Chicago, Illinois, 1890–91.

The front portion of this building—back to the projecting cornice—is original. Built using traditional masonry bearing walls, rather than the new steel frame, it is highly expressive in its use of materials. The need for economy precluded external ornament. As handsome as it is, the Monadnock Building signaled the end of the bearing-wall skyscraper because its thick walls were not economical.

14.48 Daniel H. Burnham and John Welborn Root, Reliance Building, Chicago, Illinois, 1894–95.

The Reliance Building's external skin of terracotta and glass clips onto an internal steel skeleton. This construction method anticipated the curtain walls of the 1950s and '60s.

the early development of the skyscraper, although the Home Life Insurance Building is not entirely metal-framed as the first floor contains sections of masonry bearing wall (Fig. 14.46). Above the ground floor the masonry exterior was supported on shelf-angle supports attached to the frame, and steel rather than iron was employed for the structure above the sixth-floor level. The second Rand McNally Building (1889–90) by Daniel H. Burnham (1846–1912) and John Welborn Root (1850–1891) had all the elements of the modern skyscraper, including a completely 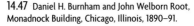 steel frame designed by the structural engineering firm of Wade and Purdy, even though its external appearance looked backward rather than forward. Even where masonry bearing walls were retained, as in Burnham and Root's Monadnock Building (1890–91), an internal iron frame provided lateral bracing through riveted girder-column connections (Fig. 14.47).

Architects who produced the high-rise buildings of Chicago dating from 1875 to 1925 are collectively termed the Chicago School, indicating their common design attitudes and construction technologies. Innovative as the structures of these buildings are, they do not necessarily express their metal frames on the outside; most are clad in masonry, which gives the impression that this is the structural material. Their façades are derived from classical precedents, which, however, offered very few buildings in which the vertical elements dominated the horizontal, and nothing that even approximated their scale of multi-floor construction. Designers solved the problem in a variety of ways. The decorative terracotta cladding on the Reliance Building (1894–95) repeats the same exterior elevation from the third floor to the attic story, expressing in the process the slenderness of its metal-frame columns and the depth of the beams supporting the floors (Fig. 14.48). Other Chicago School buildings were composed by grouping floors in three or four horizontal layers, which could then conform to the proportioning of columns and entablatures and the whole idea of streetscape established by Renaissance architects.

SKELETAL CONSTRUCTION IN CONCRETE AND WOOD

The ancient Romans had, of course, built using concrete. But this material had fallen into disuse for some 1400 years before Joseph Aspdin developed Portland cement in 1824. As early as 1774, the English engineer John Smeaton had experimented with a mixture of quicklime and clay that hardened under water for his famous Edystone Lighthouse. By the late nineteenth century, designers in America and Europe were using concrete reinforced with steel, most notably Ernest Ransome (1844–1917) and François Hennebique (1842–1921). Ransome, whose father had patented a "concrete stone," made innovations in both reinforcing steel and formwork that enabled him to produce a true concrete frame by 1900. Hennebique developed a system that he licensed to others, resulting in the construction of some 40,000 reinforced concrete structures by 1921. By 1894, Anatole de Baudot, a student of Henri Labrouste, had constructed the Parisian church of St.-Jean de Montmartre with a **ferroconcrete** skeleton, which expresses the theories of Viollet-le-Duc with whom Baudot was associated.

Another innovative system of skeletal construction developed in the nineteenth century, this time in wood, was the **balloon frame** (Fig. 14.49). Traditional wood-frame construction had involved heavy timbers shaped by hand and assembled using mortise-and-tenon joints held together by wooden pegs. While it inspired a high level of craftsmanship, it was an inefficient method of construction and one which had only a minimum of lateral bracing in the form of diagonal members. In the nineteenth century, the appearance of dimensioned lumber, that is lumber produced in standard sizes in water- or steam-driven sawmills, and the development of machines to mass-produce nails, made possible a radical change. The balloon frame consists of a sill plate from which rise long studs, placed at fairly close intervals, that are received by a top plate. These wooden members are nailed in place and braced laterally with diagonal studs. It only remained for plywood to appear in the twentieth century, which provided a lateral-bracing diaphragm as a result of diagonal nailing. Balloon framing eventually evolved into platform framing, where the first floor rises to a platform and the skeletal construction is repeated, eliminating the need for two-story-tall studs.

THE ARTS AND CRAFTS MOVEMENT

The rapid pace of industrialization in nineteenth-century England created a new social order based on investment in mechanized and trading enterprises. Factory-made goods from soap to steel were widely distributed and generally raised the material standard of living. Yet the picture was not entirely a rosy one. For instance, factory towns, surrounded by long rows of dreary housing for workers, grew up in the Midlands, where water power and coal were readily available. We have already seen how the unrestrained capitalist system affected individuals such as A.W.N. Pugin, who was dismayed by the decline of the moral and spiritual values that he associated with the Middle Ages. Others were becoming concerned about the decline of artistic standards in manufactured goods because trained designers were not involved in creating such wares for industrial production.

JOHN RUSKIN

These two issues—social values and the artistic quality of manufactured products—were at the heart of the Arts and Crafts Movement, which flourished from about 1850 to 1900 in Britain and later (1876–1916) in the United States. Originating in Victorian England, its ideas spread to Europe and finally found a "modern" resolution in postwar Weimar Germany. John Ruskin (1819–1900), a prolific critic of art and society, may be regarded as the originator of Arts and Crafts ideals. In Ruskin's view, the Industrial Revolution was a grievous error exerting a corrupting influence on society. Ruskin avoided technological progress whenever possible, insisting, for example, on coach transport rather than traveling on the railways and vigorously advocating a return to the handicrafts, where the work produced reflected the shape of the tool and the

14.49 Balloon-frame construction, 19th century.

The origin of the term "balloon" for wood framing remains unverified. This new method of building using mass-produced materials transformed building in wood from a craft practiced by highly skilled labor to an industry.

passage of the worker's hand. Like Pugin before him, Ruskin associated high moral values with certain historical styles in which he believed truth and beauty in building were to be found. Ruskin had only contempt for those who hoped to teach industrial design to students. He wrote:

> The tap-root of all this mischief is in the endeavor to produce some ability in the student to make money by designing for manufacture. No student who makes this his primary object will be able to design at all; and the very words "School of Design" involve the profoundest of art fallacies. Drawing may be taught by tutors, but design only by Heaven; and to every scholar who thinks to sell his inspiration, Heaven refuses his help.

In his *The Stones of Venice* (1851–53), Ruskin wrote skillfully and passionately about an architecture that he felt best reflected the devotion of craftsmen to building. In *The Seven Lamps of Architecture* (1849), he laid out the principles of great architecture. In this seven-part scheme, the Lamp of Sacrifice is dedicated to the craft of building and asks "Was it done with enjoyment. . .?" The Lamp of Truth expresses the moral quality necessary for exemplary building. The Lamp of Power explores the esthetic force of the sublime, and the Lamp of Beauty extols nature as the source of architectural order, while the Lamp of Memory argues for an architecture of permanence. Finally, the Lamp of Obedience urges that no new styles should be created, but that the Pisan Romanesque and the Gothic of northwestern Italy should serve as the only proper models.

WILLIAM MORRIS

Ruskin's speeches and writings had a tremendous influence on a younger generation of sensitive men, who put many of Ruskin's ideals into practice. The leader of this activist group in England was William Morris (1834–1896), an Oxford divinity student who abandoned theology and studied both architecture and painting after encountering Ruskin's teachings. After his marriage Morris could find no house that met his standards of design, so he commissioned his friend Philip Webb (1831–1915) to design what became known as the Red House at Bexleyheath (1859–60), a redbrick structure that harkened back to the medieval domestic vernacular (Figs. 14.50–14.51). Its straightforward approach to structure and its undisguised use of materials surprised contemporary visitors, as did its elaborate use of decorative detail on the interior. Partly as a result of collaborating with his artist friends in the work on Red House, Morris founded the firm of Morris, Marshall, Faulkner and Company in 1862, establishing workshops where artist-craftsmen created wallpaper, textiles, stained glass, utensils, furniture, and carpets using handicraft techniques. Morris's firm reflected his philosophy of dignity and joy through honest craftsmanship. It was intended to be an alternative to the factory system, where mass-produced elements were assembled by

14.50 (above) Philip Webb, Plan of Red House, Bexleyheath, Kent, 1859–60.

The plan seems even less exceptional than the exterior appearance. However, its direct response to light and ventilation and to everyday needs anticipates the functionalism of twentieth-century Modernists.

14.51 Philip Webb, Red House, Bexleyheath, Kent, 1859–60.

This house near London appears to be no more than a comfortable composition using forms familiar in the mid-nineteenth-century English countryside. What sets it apart is Webb's attempt to produce a design true to its materials and means of construction and expressive of the site and local culture.

workers who had become little more than cogs in a machine and had no interest in, control over, or love for the goods produced. Morris believed that the provision of well-designed, handcrafted products in the homes of ordinary working-class people would raise them above the level of disinterested bread-winning employment. His concern for the welfare of the working class extended to his enthusiastic and active espousal of Socialism, and architectural historian Nikolaus Pevsner has argued that Morris's social consciousness represents one of the origin points for the development of European Modernism, with its casting of the architect as a molder of society. Unfortunately the output of Morris's workshops was insufficient to meet the needs of a broad market, and the price of his well-made objects tended to be higher than comparable factory-made goods, so his vision of supplying quality furnishings to ordinary people was never realized. The establishment of his firm, however, marks the first attempt to address the inferior quality of manufactured goods and the dehumanizing aspects of industrial production, a problem that would remain for others to solve. For instance, the writings of John Ruskin and the firm of William Morris and his partners inspired Elbert Hubbard to create his Roycrofters Workshops in East Aurora, New York; Hubbard's work was much admired by the young Frank Lloyd Wright.

RICHARD NORMAN SHAW, C.F.A. VOYSEY, AND HERMAN MUTHESIUS

While in no way a social revolutionary, Richard Norman Shaw (1831–1912) made significant contributions to the development of Arts and Crafts architecture in England.

Pugin's Gothic Revivalism impressed him as a youth. After traveling in Europe, he worked for Gothicist George Edmund Street, whom he considered his mentor. Shaw's early buildings are rationally conceived, as are Street's, but picturesque. Leyswood (1870) (Fig. 14.52) in Sussex has been much published in the form of Shaw's dramatic bird's-eye-view perspective. Its façades of "Old English" character, based upon Shaw's sketchbook studies of medieval buildings in Sussex, are carefully wrapped around a central court and produce a rich silhouette of clustered chimney stacks, multiple steeply sloping gable roofs, and a straightforward use of natural building materials. Much more ornamental, but equally rigorous and attuned to English precedents, is his New Zealand Chambers (1871–73) (Fig. 14.53), which looks back to the red brick and stone trim of the Queen Anne buildings of the early eighteenth century. Shaw designed it to be extremely efficient, including some eighty small offices and a suite for the owners, and composed the façade using tall **oriel windows** and lush wood, plaster, and stone ornament. Shaw's work influenced the development of the Queen Anne and Shingle styles in the United States.

Of the English architects influenced by the Arts and Crafts movement, the most notable was Charles Francis Annesley Voysey (1857–1941), whose early commissions included wallpaper designs that owe much to Morris. He seldom used wallpaper or ornament in the houses he designed, however, preferring instead the purity of white plaster walls or unfinished oak paneling. Because of this omission, he was considered by others (he did not accept the label) as a pioneer Modernist. Voysey's houses, such as The Orchard in Chorleywood (1899) or Greyfriars near Guildford, Surrey (1896), are informal and

14.52 Richard Norman Shaw, Leyswood, Sussex, 1870. Drawing.

Richard Norman Shaw trimmed away the excesses of the Victorian Gothic to produce a rural vernacular known as "Old English." Picturesque Leyswood looks as if it grew over time in response to functional needs and the exigencies of its site.

14.53 Richard Norman Shaw, New Zealand Chambers, London, 1871–73.

14.53 Richard Norman Shaw, New Zealand Chambers, London, 1871–73.

Shaw looked back to both the seventeenth and eighteenth centuries in creating his "Queen Anne" style for urban buildings. Characteristics include red brick, white window sash, and carefully controlled ornament.

reminiscent of the medieval vernacular. They feature wide, overhanging eaves; steeply pitched roofs; broad and bold chimneys; leaded casement windows; and either white-washed masonry or stone walls. Their interiors feature natural-finish materials, such as slate flooring and untreated oak paneling; Arts and Crafts furniture, some of it designed by Voysey himself; and the evidence of hand-crafting in both ornamental and functional fittings, including carpets, pottery, clocks, candlesticks, hinges, and latches. Voysey created a bold but simple scheme in his design for Broadleys (1898), a vacation house on Lake Windermere for A. Currer Briggs (Figs. 14.54–14.55). Three bowfront windows extend through the two stories of the house, interrupting the roofline, to provide views over the lake to the west. The house is constructed of local stone, laid two feet thick in the walls, and is capped by a slate roof with a series of iron brackets supporting the overhanging eaves. The overall composition is asymmetrical yet dignified. With this design and other residential commissions from 1890 to 1905, Voysey helped set the style for much suburban housing built in England and the United States before 1930.

The spirit of Arts and Crafts design was carried to Germany by Herman Muthesius, a representative of the Board of Trade attached to the German embassy in London from 1896 to 1903. Germany was experiencing the same absence of good design in industrial products that had been noted earlier in Britain, and Muthesius was assigned the task of reporting on the state of English architecture and design, by then very highly regarded on the continent. The result was a three-volume report, *Das Englische Haus* (*The English House*), which documented all aspects of late Arts and Crafts work, from architecture to plumbing fixtures. On his return to Germany in 1903, Muthesius was appointed head of the Board of Trade, where he was responsible for selecting notable designers to teach in schools of arts and crafts. The impetus for the formation of the German design school called the Bauhaus can be traced to the work of the men he chose, including Peter Behrens, Hans Poelzig, and Bruno Paul,

14.54 C.F.A. Voysey, Broadleys, Lake Windermere, Cumbria, 1898.

Early chroniclers of the Modern Movement saw C.F.A. Voysey as one of its pioneers. However, he eschewed such an attribution, considering his work to be instead in the tradition of yeoman buildings in the southern English countryside.

14.55 C.F.A. Voysey, Plan of Broadleys, Lake Windermere, Cumbria, 1898.

Broadleys was planned to take advantage of views out over the lake. The great bay windows front each of the principal rooms, while bedrooms and service spaces stretch out to the rear.

although a more complete discussion of that development must wait for the next chapter.

ART NOUVEAU

A new and highly decorative style arose during the era known as "La Belle Epoque" (about 1880 to 1905). Nurtured by a variety of sources, including Late Baroque and Rococo, the Gothic Revival, the Arts and Crafts movement, the Celtic Revival, and the arts of China and Japan, it was a widely practiced style that was given different names in different countries. It was known as Art Nouveau in France, England, and the Low Countries, "Stile Liberty" or "Stile Floreale" in Italy, and "Jugendstil" in Germany. Whatever its name, it abandoned the multiple, backward-looking late Victorian styles and attempted to produce something excitingly new. The linear, sinuous lines found in Late Baroque and Rococo work were developed into free-flowing compositions based loosely on plant and animal forms. In fact, a parallel can be drawn with Celtic art or the Animal Style of the early Middle Ages, although Art Nouveau curves have a freedom to change width and direction that exceeds medieval practice.

14.56 Arthur Mackmurdo, Title page of *Wren's City Churches*, 1883.

The Art Nouveau style is characterized by the long, sinuous curve seen here. Mackmurdo was sympathetic to the writings and work of William Morris, John Ruskin, and Richard Norman Shaw.

One finds the earliest examples of florid ornament in England, although the fullest expression of the style was to come elsewhere. As early as 1876–77, James MacNeill Whistler (1834–1903), an American painter with strong English ties, created the Peacock Room for Frederick Leyland's London mansion, a design marked both by Japanese delicacy and by exotic peacocks—which represented the designer and his client feuding over the fee! (The Peacock Room is now installed at the Freer Gallery in Washington, D.C.) Arthur Mackmurdo's (1851–1942) swirling linear design for the title-page of *Wren's City Churches* (1883) is commonly cited as the first Art Nouveau piece (Fig. 14.56), but its influence was limited. Wallpapers and carpets designed by William Morris at about the same time share this linearity, as do the illustrations and decorative flourishes included in the Kelmscott Press editions of books published by Morris after 1890. Other illustrators, especially Aubrey Beardsley, made woodcuts that exhibit the lively, curving Art Nouveau line.

If one looks beneath the florid surface of Art Nouveau work, however, there are more substantive forces at work. On the one hand, Art Nouveau architecture manifested through its slender iron construction the kind of direct, expressive, skeletal structure advocated by the rationalist Viollet-le-Duc. On the other, there are moments in Art Nouveau interiors when space itself seems to flow and openness dominates, anticipating the more radical spatial experiments of such early twentieth-century architects as Adolf Loos.

VICTOR HORTA AND HECTOR GUIMARD

Art Nouveau architects turned structural necessity into a language of organically derived curves. The earliest architectural innovator was Victor Horta, a Belgian architect and the designer of the Tassel House in Brussels, built in 1892–93 (Fig. 14.57). Horta incorporated swirling tendril designs not only in surface patterning on floors, walls, and ceilings, but also in structural elements such as the staircase, balustrades, and balcony railings. Historian Sigfried Giedion celebrated this "flexible" groundplan with its

14.57 Victor Horta, Tassel House, Brussels, 1892–93.

At the end of the century, designers throughout Europe were looking for new ideas. In urban houses such as this one, Horta explored the tensile and ductile potential of iron.

14.58 Victor Horta, Hotel Van Eetvelde interior, Brussels, 1897.

On his interiors, Horta used iron for columns, ceilings, windows, and handrails. Here he made the stairwell a lighted core in the constrained urban environment.

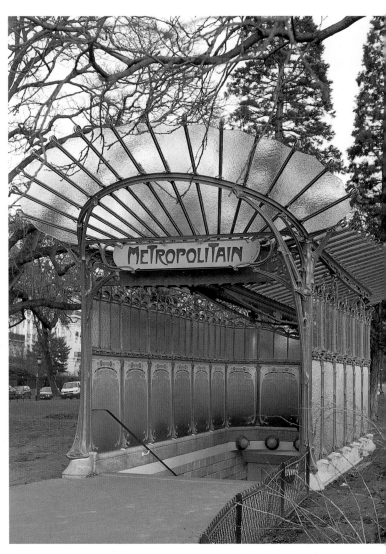

14.59 Hector Guimard, Métro entrance, Paris, 1899–1904.

Guimard's Métro stations still cover the entries into several of Paris's subway stations. In this example, plant-like iron members support a fan-like canopy.

levels and half-levels and interior light-wells, seeing it as the forerunner of the subsequent spatial investigations by Modernists such as Adolf Loos and Ludwig Mies van der Rohe. The interior of Horta's Hotel Van Eetvelde (1897) in Brussels exhibits these same qualities (Fig. 14.58). His later Maison du Peuple (1896–99) exploited its structural relationship to plant forms, particularly in the upper-floor auditorium, where undulating iron ceiling trusses merged with upright supports in the manner of branches leaving a tree. Even the balcony was sculpted into a curvilinear form, its delicate supports terminating as protective railings. While the expressive linearity of iron construction was masterfully handled in this, the first iron-and-glass façade building in Belgium, the plan was quite traditional, with a central axis and cross axis on the ground floor.

Hector Guimard (1867–1942) was the French architect most celebrated for his Art Nouveau designs. The most famous of his works were made fom 1899 to 1904 for the entrances to the Métro, the Paris subway system (Fig. 14.59). These are canopies over staircases that descend from the sidewalk, and Guimard provided several designs that employ wrought-iron swirls and curves, some of which support glass roofs. The unity of these little projects is remarkable, for all the elements are deftly integrated in the plant-like forms. Light standards (upright supports) are terminated by bud-shaped electric bulbs, while patterns derived from vegetable leaves are used as infill on the railings. Guimard's other architectural projects reflect his ability to blend the decorative with the functional, as can be seen at the Castel Béranger (1894–98), an apartment building in Paris, where latent medievalism is nicely balanced by free-flowing asymmetrical decoration in iron and ceramic to form a unified whole.

ANTONIO GAUDÍ

In Spain, Art Nouveau reached its most idiosyncratic expression in the work of Antonio Gaudí (1852–1926), a Catalan influenced by the writings of Ruskin who began as a Gothic Revivalist. Because of his interest in medieval styles, he was asked in 1884 to take charge of construction of the Sagrada Familia (the Expiatory Temple of the Holy Family) in Barcelona, begun two years earlier by another Gothic Revivalist and still incomplete to this day. In the course of work on the Sagrada Familia and on the Colònia

14.60 Antonio Gaudí, Church of the Sagrada Familia, Barcelona, begun 1882.

Partly inspired by the Catalan Gothic, showing traces of Cubism, and commonly associated with Art Nouveau, the Sagrada Familia fits into no single stylistic category. Like many before him, Gaudí drew upon nature and exploited local methods of workmanship.

14.61 Antonio Gaudí, Casa Milá, Barcelona, 1905–07.

This apartment block is so massive and so apparently natural in its use of stone that it is referred to locally as the "stone quarry." The iron railings were made from salvaged material, and at one spot, the roof sculpture creates a framed view of the Sagrada Familia.

14.62 Antonio Gaudí, Parc Güell entrance, Barcelona, 1900–14.

Gatehouses stand to either side of this view. The columns at the head of the stairs support a plaza with undulating seating covered in ceramic shards. The site was intended to be a housing subdivision (parcel of land for multiple houses), but it was never developed to provide more than a residence for Gaudí himself.

Güell Chapel, where he hung sandbags on fabric to determine ideal vault cross sections, Gaudí moved away from the Gothic Revival style to an intensely personal one that he used for apartment buildings, houses, and landscape designs as well as ecclesiastical works. While his three-dimensional curvilinear forms, floral decoration, and plastic, flowing plans link it more closely with Art Nouveau than any other stylistic movement, Gaudí's work ultimately resists categorization. The Sagrada Familia, for example, retains Gothic structural overtones, yet has such a heavy, towering, sculptural presence, enriched with lovingly crafted details, that it is clearly not Gothic. The Façade of the Nativity is an array of grotto-eroded elements flowing together, with four great spires towering above (Fig. 14.60).

Gaudí's design for Casa Milá (1905–07), a large apartment house in Barcelona (Fig. 14.61), has an undulating plasticity in its façade and a curvilinear plan that is made possible by its expressive exterior load-bearing wall. There are no bearing walls inside, giving the designer the freedom to sculpt individual, non-orthogonal spaces, no two alike. His designs for the Parc Güell (1900–14), a real-estate development situated on a hillside west of Barcelona, allowed an extensive merging of naturalistic forms into walkways, stairways, and seating (Fig. 14.62). Vaulting leans at oblique angles in a grotto walkway (Fig.

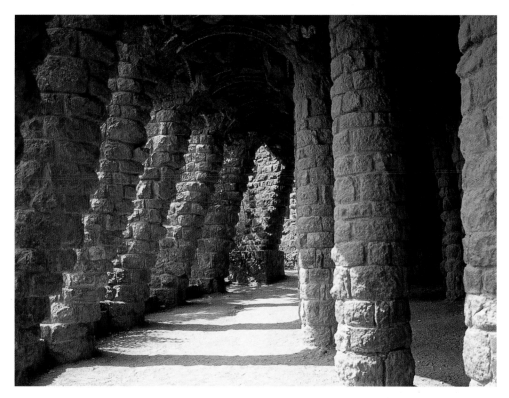

14.63 Antonio Gaudí, Parc Güell viaduct colonnade, Barcelona, 1900–14.

Using ropes, weights, and canvas, Gaudí experimented empirically with the transfer of forces in vaulted construction. One of the results was sloping columns that responded to force vectors, in this case produced by the centrifugal force of cars making turns on the viaduct above.

14.64 Charles Rennie Mackintosh, Glasgow School of Art, Glasgow, 1897–1909.

This is the main façade. The huge windows gather northern light for the painting and design studios. The central entry includes motifs drawn from Glasgow's medieval vernacular.

14.63); stairs flow downward like lava; and benches, conforming to the irregular curves of the seated human form, wind sinusoidally along the upper-level plaza edge. Ceramic-tile finishes and details contribute durable surfaces and an appropriate touch of whimsy. The informal, amorphous, and rambling park is a skillfully inventive total design.

CHARLES RENNIE MACKINTOSH

Gaudí's highly individualistic interpretations of Art Nouveau have a Scottish parallel in the work of Charles Rennie Mackintosh (1868–1928), a gifted designer whose architectural career was brief. Mackintosh and a small circle of friends worked primarily in Glasgow, developing a unique style that is related to Art Nouveau in its use of curves derived from natural forms. Other influences are detectable in Mackintosh's work as well, including the massive forms of Scottish baronial architecture and the delicate interlacing decoration of Celtic art. His architecture tends to have bold massing deftly composed, with light and airy interiors accented by subtle attenuated curves or linear patterns that are usually symmetrical. Like Art Nouveau architects, Mackintosh was greatly concerned with furniture, light fixtures, and details such as window hardware.

The Glasgow School of Art (1897–1909) was Mackintosh's first and largest commission (Fig. 14.64). Located on the north side of a sloping site, the building presents three elevations to the perimeter streets. The main entrance façade on Renfrew Street is a tight monolithic mass dominated by two rows of large, north-facing studio windows and a heavily sculpted central-entry composition, while the later west façade along Scott Street rises austerely as the hill drops, in the manner of medieval

14.65 Charles Rennie Mackintosh, Library interior, Glasgow School of Art, Glasgow, 1897–1909.

The supporting columns are heavy timbers with a dark finish typical of late nineteenth- and early twentieth-century interiors. Mackintosh designed the reading tables and light fixtures as well.

14.66 Charles Rennie Mackintosh, Rear elevation of the Glasgow School of Art, Glasgow, 1897–1909.

While the north elevation provides the proper public face, this rear elevation is no less powerful a composition. Its reliance on the simple application of windows as figures on the plain field of the masonry walls is comparable to Mackintosh's concern for figure–ground relationships in his watercolor drawings from nature.

0   20 m
0   60 ft

fortifications. This elevation, expressing the library, is a bold design broken by the three twenty-five-foot-high windows along the upper section of wall. The library interior is the most celebrated space (Fig. 14.65). Mackintosh designed its furniture and light fixtures to harmonize with the dominant pattern of horizontals and verticals in the windows and mezzanine balcony. A more fluid linearity is found in other rooms, and the southern rear attic level has simple arched openings that are reminiscent of Romanesque work. To the rear or south and facing the railroad yard, the façade (Fig. 14.66) is seemingly perfunctory, with windows punched wherever interior spaces required them. However, Mackintosh so manipulated these simple openings in an otherwise plain, cliff-like wall as to produce a composition of power, variety, and conviction that has few equals.

Other Mackintosh commissions include Windyhill (1900–01), located outside Glasgow at Kilmacolm; Hill House (1902–04) at Helensburgh; and the Scotland Street School (1904–06) in Glasgow. Hill House (Fig. 14.67), designed for a Glasgow publisher, stands like a castle on rising ground, reflecting the influence of the Scottish vernacular in its turrets, expressive chimneys, and dominant roof. The monolithic character of the exterior is achieved by **pebble-dash** stucco. Its plan (Fig. 14.68) is logically compartmentalized into functional areas: the library and cloakroom near the entrance, for the easy conducting of business, followed by the reception rooms and a servants' wing at the end. Upstairs are the bedrooms, with the nursery and servants' bedrooms over the service wing. All interiors are handcrafted in the Arts and Crafts tradition, with custom-designed carpets, light fixtures, stencil decorations, and furniture (Fig. 14.69). Dark woodwork contrasts with pastel colors on floor and wall surfaces. A barrel-vaulted ceiling in the bedroom becomes a canopy over the bed.

Art Nouveau designers in various parts of Europe were aware of one another's work through international publications. Mackintosh's entry in the 1901 German competition to design the

14.67 Charles Rennie Mackintosh, Hill House, Helensburgh, 1902–04.

The picturesque silhouette and massing of Hill House are very expressive of nineteenth-century sensibilities. The stark, unornamented wall surfaces, however, have received much attention from those tracing the origins of twentieth-century Modernism.

14.68 Charles Rennie Mackintosh, First-floor (*below*) and second-floor (*above*) plans of Hill House, Helensburgh, 1902–04.

These plans could not be more straightforward in their functional organization, but the building's perimeter was obviously determined with three-dimensional expression in mind. Notable are the circular stairs that notch into a reentrant (internal, or inside) corner and the stairs that project outward in the form of semicircular landings.

"House of an Art Lover" brought him second prize, and his project drawings became known through inclusion in a publication edited in Darmstadt. Darmstadt had become a center of the Jugendstil in 1899, when Ernst Ludwig, Grand Duke of Hesse, established an artists' colony in the suburb of Mathildenhöhe, attracting artists from Munich and Vienna. While the colony's life as an art center was brief, the houses built in the Mathildenhöhe district remain today a preserve of

14.69 Charles Rennie Mackintosh, Hill House interior, Helensburgh, 1902–04.

On the interior, Mackintosh designed Hill House to have both regimented orthogonals and Art Nouveau curves.

Jugendstil architecture. Major buildings in the Jugendstil included a house for Ernst Ludwig designed by Joseph Maria Olbrich (1867–1908), who came from the Viennese Secessionists, and an elaborate and expensive residence (1899) built for his family by the young German painter Peter Behrens—Behrens quickly outgrew the Jugendstil and went on to figure prominently in the development of modern architecture in Germany. On the whole, the Jugendstil is a late manifestation of Art Nouveau, and its architectural manifestations tend to be linear but less free than comparable work in Belgium or France.

THE VIENNESE SECESSION

Art Nouveau architects in Austria were members of the Viennese Secession, an association primarily of artists formed in 1898. The oldest member of the group, although not one of its founders, was Otto Wagner (1841–1918), a Neo-Classical architect who was promoted to the post of professor of architecture at the Vienna Academy of Fine Arts in 1894. Upon his appointment to academic life, Wagner seems to have undergone a philosophical shift away from archaeologically correct architecture to a more rational, modern expression suited to current-day requirements. The Viennese Secession movement was formed by some of his most outstanding students, and Wagner soon joined them in espousing Art Nouveau ornament.

Wagner's most notable designs in this mode were thirty-six stations for the Vienna subway system, the Stadt-bahn (1894–1901). While not as exuberant as Guimard's work for the Paris Métro, Wagner's designs do employ the characteristic stylized ornament in cast and wrought iron. After 1900, Wagner's enthusiasm for Art Nouveau waned, and he abandoned the style completely for his master-piece, the Postal Savings Bank (1904–06 and 1910–12) in Vienna (Figs. 14.70–14.71). Within an irregularly shaped block, Wagner placed a grand staircase leading up to a wide vestibule, then into the central banking room, which he surrounded with offices. He faced the front façade with white Sterzing marble in shingle-like panels. He attached these panels to the superstructure by means of bolts covered with aluminum caps that create a distinctive grid.

14.70 Otto Wagner, Postal Savings Bank, Vienna, 1904–12.

The pattern of Wagner's façade is created by a marble veneer attached by means of aluminum-headed bolts. Aluminum also appears at the columns and the roof supports of the entry canopy.

14.71 Otto Wagner, Postal Savings Bank interior, Vienna, 1904–12.

Wagner intended for the vault of the banking room to be suspended from masts and cable above it. Against the rear and right-side walls are cylindrical aluminium air-supply standards.

Using more aluminum, a radical choice at the time, he created an elegant entry canopy supported by thin aluminum columns with cantilevered arms. Passing through this canopy to the banking room, one enters a space filled with light brought in through a glass-vaulted roof that Wagner originally intended to support with cables hung from aluminum masts. Some of the light passes through glass-brick floor panels to illuminate the rooms below. Within the banking room, two files of columns create a basilican plan, with the tellers' counters in the "aisles" and with cylindrical aluminum air-supply standards around the perimeter. As at the façade, connectors are everywhere made prominent, from the bases of the aluminum-cladded columns to the newel posts of the handrails.

Wagner's talented pupil, Josef Maria Olbrich, became the leading architect of the Viennese Secession, influenced in part by the work of Mackintosh. Like Mackintosh, Olbrich found an essentially orthogonal basis for his architectural forms, embellishing them with the con-trolled vegetation of Art Nouveau. His first major commission was from the Secessionists themselves, a small building for meetings and exhibitions of art. The Secession Hall (1898–99) is a Neo-Classically inspired mass, crowned by a pierced openwork metal dome (Fig. 14.72). Along the exterior walls between high windows Olbrich set low-relief ornament based on plants and flowers. Compared to French or Belgian work, Olbrich's designs seem rather heavy and symmetrical, but publication of this building brought widespread acclaim to its architect, and the Grand Duke of Hesse, Ernst Ludwig, invited Olbrich to join his artists' colony at Darmstadt.

From 1899 until his death from leukemia in 1908, Olbrich worked at Darmstadt, erecting numerous houses, studio buildings, entrance gates, and a Wedding Tower or Hochzeitsturm (1907–08) to commemorate the Duke's marriage (Fig. 14.73). The tower is a symbolic structure, rising above the colony with an arched and paneled gable that recalls the shape of organ pipes. It is built of brick and trimmed with contrasting stone around doors and windows. These windows are all the more unusual for wrapping around the corner of the tower, seeming to defy the mass required there for strength at the junction of the walls. This feature was to reappear on Modernist buildings in the 1920s and 1930s.

14.72 Josef Maria Olbrich, Secession Building, Vienna, 1898–99.

Olbrich covered his dome with a laurel motif symbolic of Apollo, god of poetry, music, and learning. The building served as a meeting and exhibition space for the Secession.

14.73 Josef Maria Olbrich, Wedding Tower, Darmstadt, 1907–08.

The tower was added last to this complex as a commemoration of the wedding of the Grand Duke of Hesse, sponsor of the colony.

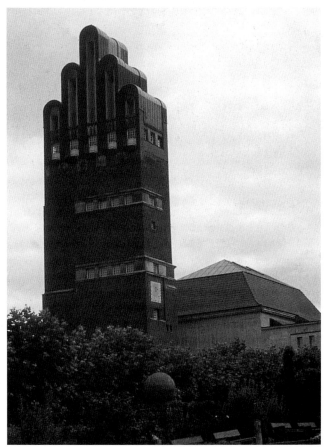

THE SEARCH FOR AN AMERICAN STYLE

A recurring theme in American architectural history is the search for a proper "American" style of building. Jefferson advocated the use of Roman architecture because it symbolized the greatness of the Roman republic, which he saw as a worthy model for the new republic of the United States. Proponents of the Greek Revival cited similar desirable symbolic linkages with the democratic government of ancient Athens, while Gothic Revivalists drew parallels between the Christian values of medieval times and those of the present day. Two American architects of the nineteenth century contributed to the search for a truly American expression in architecture, not by reviving past styles, but by evolving a fresh approach to the materials and building problems presented by life in the United States. Their accomplishments have had a lasting effect on the course of American design.

HENRY HOBSON RICHARDSON

Henry Hobson Richardson (1838–1886) was the first American after Richard Morris Hunt to attend the Ecole des Beaux-Arts in Paris. Born to a wealthy Louisiana family, Richardson completed the course at the Lawrence Scientific School of Harvard University before enrolling at the Ecole in 1860. The onset of the Civil War cut off his financial support from home, forcing him out of school and into the Paris office of Théodore Labrouste (brother of Henri), where he worked until 1865, when he returned to New York. After a few years, he moved his office to Boston and gained national acclaim for his competition-winning design for Trinity Church (1872–77) in Copley Square, Boston.

Trinity Church (Fig. 14.74) was to become the most celebrated building of its age; a national poll of architects in 1885 identified it as the best building in the United States. What was it that designers (and the general public) admired so much about this church? In many respects the design is a pastiche, very much in the tradition of nineteenth-century eclecticism. The plan (Fig. 14.75) is based on a stubby Latin-cross basilica, and the polychrome stonework and general massing come from French

14.74 Henry Hobson Richardson, Trinity Church, Boston, Massachusetts, 1872–77.

It was Stanford White, then working in H.H. Richardson's office, who designed the church's tower, basing it on the Romanesque Salamanca Cathedral. With its three arched openings, the base is quite similar to the Romanesque church of St. Gilles-du-Gard in Provence.

14.75 Henry Hobson Richardson, Plan of Trinity Church, Boston, Massachusetts, 1872–77.

Richardson's plan is remarkably simple. Its vaults are ornamented with murals by John Lafarge. Connected to the chancel end of the church is the parish house, laid up in the same polychromatic stone.

Romanesque churches of the Auvergne; the triple-arched portal is derived from St. Gilles-du-Gard in Provence; and the great crossing tower reflects the tower of the Old Cathedral in Salamanca, Spain. Despite these borrowings, an abundance of original thinking gives Trinity Church its distinctive character. Richardson conceived of the building as a polychrome church, both inside and out, and his design shows a true flair for scale and texture. Ashlar stonework in warm gray contrasts with the red-brown sandstone trim, and slate roofs on the parish house set off the red clay tiles prominent on the tower roof. Murals painted by John LaFarge and his pupil Augustus Saint-Gaudens enrich the plaster walls inside, and William Morris and Edward Burne-Jones made the stained-glass windows, an artistic collaboration that was entirely in accordance with Arts and Crafts ideals. The success of Trinity Church assured the prosperity of Richardson's career, while atoning for the less satisfactory design of his earlier Brattle Square Church (1870), which proved on completion to have faulty acoustics in the nave.

The design of Trinity Church also established what was to become Richardson's characteristic architectural style: an intelligent and personal interpretation of the Romanesque. This was far from a slavish imitation,

Parish house

Church

however, so his work is designated "Richardsonian" to indicate that this was not merely a revival. His adoption of the Romanesque was in fact the starting point in his search for an appropriate American building tradition, for, while he had seen and been impressed by medieval buildings in Europe, he had not been instructed in any medieval modes at the Ecole des Beaux-Arts. Richardson was a romantic who was inspired by the abundant stone of New England, and he worked to evolve a style worthy of its rugged massiveness and load-bearing capacities (technical advances in glass and metal construction had little impact on his work). A chronicle of his major commissions illustrates the progressive development of his thinking about the expression of masonry. In 1878 he designed Sever Hall for his alma mater, Harvard University. It is a classroom building, executed in brick to harmonize with existing structures in the Harvard Yard, but the expression that

Richardson gave to the material, built into a low arch at the entrance and modeled into bowfronts that resemble turrets, conveys a feeling of solidity, quite a contrast to the rather delicate Georgian buildings that are its neighbors. Two years later Richardson designed Austin Hall to house the law school, an almost symmetrical stone structure that was a free and romantic reinterpretation of Romanesque forms.

14.76 Henry Hobson Richardson, Marshall Field Wholesale Store, Chicago, Illinois, 1885–87.

There has been no more satisfying composition in American architecture than this one. Notice the unity of each window bay, which begins with a rectangular opening lighting the basement and terminates with four vertical rectangles over two round-headed windows. Unfortunately the building has long since been destroyed.

14.77 Henry Hobson Richardson, Glessner House, Chicago, Illinois, 1885.

This was Richardson's other commission in Chicago. The most impressive feature of the front (south) façade is the huge semicircular arch made of rock-faced voussoirs.

14.78 Henry Hobson Richardson, Plan of Glessner House, Chicago, Illinois, 1885.

The outside walls of this U-shaped plan are laid up in rock-faced stone, while the walls of the inner court are brick. The scale change is striking, but appropriate. Notice the projecting stairs and bays in the court.

In 1885 Richardson designed two projects in Chicago, the Glessner House for a wealthy industrialist and the Marshall Field Wholesale Store (Fig. 14.76). The store, since demolished, was a revelation to architects in the city, providing a dignified and simple treatment for a six-story block. Richardson eschewed ornamentation and historical trappings, leaving the unadorned rusticated masonry and the great arched openings to convey power and monumentality. It has been proposed that Richardson's model for the great broad arches of the central stage of the store may have been the Roman aqueduct at Segovia, Spain, a construction included in Richardson's collection of photographs. Whatever his inspiration, Richardson succeeded in creating a design as bold and monumental as the Roman engravings of Piranesi. Behind the articulated stone bearing walls of the store was an internal and unexpressed structural skeleton of iron. The Glessner House

(Figs. 14.77–14.78) is similarly restrained and austere on the exterior, opening on an interior courtyard sheltered from street noise and dirt by the building's U-shaped plan. While the courtyard walls are laid up in brick, the street-front façades are constructed in varied courses of rock-faced stone interspersed with orthogonal windows, grills, and a massive semicircular arch. Another late work, the gate lodge (1880–81) for the Ames estate in North Easton, Massachusetts, shows the almost radical directions Richardson was pursuing in his last years (Fig. 14.79). Boulders are set into the masonry walls of the lodge and extend into the interior. A massive red-tile roof caps the structure, eyebrow dormers breaking through its taut surface. Had Richardson lived beyond his forty-eight years, he would doubtless have been an even more powerful force in determining the shape of twentieth-century American architecture. As it is, his masonry works spawned a great number of Romanesque churches, town halls, libraries, and railroad stations, in addition to influencing the directions taken by Chicago School architects in designing tall buildings.

In his residential commissions Richardson also did much to create what became known as the "Shingle Style." Built with wooden frames, these houses were covered with wooden shingles on the wall and roof planes, providing a sense of both volume and simplicity. His design for the Watts Sherman House (1874) in Newport, Rhode Island, has rusticated stone on the ground-floor walls and shingles on the upper-floor walls and roof, stretched like a membrane over the dormers and bay windows that articulate the façade (Fig. 14.80). Great overhanging eaves on the steeply pitched roof and substantial chimneys present an irregular, picturesque profile against to the sky. A later design for the Stoughton House (Fig. 14.81) in Cambridge, Massachusetts (1882–83) shows how far Richardson had gone toward simplifying the rather complex

14.79 Henry Hobson Richardson, Gate lodge, Ames estate, North Easton, Massachusetts, 1880–81.

Richardson here repeated the huge semicircular arch of the Glessner House (see Fig. 14.77) as the carriage portal. The walls are made of uncoursed, Cyclopean boulders.

14.80 Henry Hobson Richardson, Watts Sherman House, Newport, Rhode Island, 1874.

Richardson also worked in wood, in this case assisted by Stanford White. Close observation of the textures created by the mock-heavy timber and the shingles of the roofs and gables reveals the similarity in feeling to Richardson's compositions in stone. The treatment of the wood members is also comparable to the Queen Anne style of Richard Norman Shaw in England.

14.81 Henry Hobson Richardson, Stoughton House, Cambridge, Massachusetts, 1882–83.

Here Richardson drew upon the New England Colonial vernacular to produce a building completely clad in shingles. Particularly effective is the curving shingle-covered wall of the projecting stair.

forms of the Sherman House. Here, the shingle skin covers a bold composition of geometric solids arranged in an L-shaped plan. Although the design owes something to the forms of early Colonial houses in New England, it transcends any one period or style, being as devoid of applied ornament as the slightly later Marshall Field Wholesale Store. The interior of the Stoughton House features a two-story living hall, an element originated in Pugin's design for his own house at Ramsgate.

LOUIS HENRI SULLIVAN

Richardson's scheme for the Marshall Field Wholesale Store was particularly influential on the work of Louis Henri Sullivan (1856–1924), a Chicago architect who has already been mentioned as a participant in the design of the World's Columbian Exposition of 1893, where he was responsible for the design of the Transportation Building. At the time that the Marshall Field Wholesale Store was being completed, Sullivan, then in practice with Dankmar Adler (1844–1900), was designing the Chicago

Auditorium Building (1886–90) (Fig. 14.82). After seeing Richardson's masterpiece, he simplified his design, giving greater emphasis to the arches above entrance doors and arches used for wall articulation.

Sullivan was as original an architect as Richardson. While traces of Neo-Classicism and Romanticism appear in his work, he engaged directly the rapidly emerging building technologies of Chicago and expressed them architecturally. Born in Boston, the young Sullivan spent much of his childhood on his grandfather's farm north of the city, where he became acquainted with the natural plant forms that would later be incorporated in his architectural ornament. Determined to become an architect, Sullivan spent a year in the newly created architectural program at M.I.T. and then worked briefly in the offices of Frank Furness in Philadelphia and William Le Baron Jenney in Chicago. He went to Paris in 1874 to study at the Ecole des Beaux-Arts, where he found the teaching uninspiring. After a year there, he traveled in Italy before returning to Chicago and joining the office of Dankmar Adler and Company in 1879. Adler's engineering and managerial expertise complemented Sullivan's artistic inclinations, and in 1881 the firm name changed to Adler and Sullivan.

Adler's understanding of acoustics gained the firm the commission to design the Chicago Auditorium Building, one of the most complex multi-use buildings constructed

14.82 Dankmar Adler and Louis Sullivan, Auditorium Building, Chicago, Illinois, 1886–90.

Obviously Sullivan was influenced by Richardson's Marshall Fields Wholesale Store. The cantilevered block above the triple arches is the hotel lobby.

14.83 Dankmar Adler and Louis Sullivan, Plan of and longitudinal section through the Auditorium Building, Chicago, Illinois, 1886–90.

The so-called Auditorium Building is actually a hotel and an office building that surrounded an auditorium. It was certainly the cleverest plan composition that Sullivan (together with Adler) ever produced.

in the country up until that time. Its name derives from the huge 4237-seat concert hall located at its center, but the building also contained a ten-story hotel and a seventeen-story office tower, with additional offices at the rear (Fig. 14.83). Erecting such a structure on the muddy subsoil of Chicago challenged the engineering talents of Adler, who also made sure that the sightlines and acoustics were excellent for every seat in the auditorium. Sullivan's task was to give architectural harmony to the diverse elements of the building, and in the process he was influenced, as has already been noted, by the Marshall Field Wholesale Store.

Romantic that he was, Sullivan turned to classical precedent for inspiration when he tackled the problem of artistic expression appropriate to a tall building. In 1890 a commission from a St. Louis brewer, Ellis Wainwright, gave Adler and Sullivan their first opportunity to design a skyscraper, and Sullivan's treatment of the exterior became the exemplar for much of later high-rise construction (Fig. 14.84). Rather than a layering of horizontal elements drawn from one or more historical periods, the Wainwright Building has a base, a middle section, and a top. Sullivan, in his essay "The Tall Building Artistically Considered" (1896), explained his reasons for this organization. He expressed the ground floor (where easy access could be made from the street into banks, shops, or the like) and mezzanine or second floor (still easily reached on foot) as a unit; he placed stacked offices on the third through top floors, where repetitive windows illuminated floor areas that could be subdivided to suit the requirements of various tenants; and he located the mechanical systems, from tanks and pumps to elevator machinery, behind a deep cornice. Sullivan liked nothing better than to discover a general principle, what he characterized as "a rule so broad as to admit no exceptions." His most famous dictum was "form follows function," which was not actually original to him. Sullivan's buildings, however, are generally poor examples of this principle in operation. The Wainwright Building,

for example, has a steel frame with riveted columns behind its red granite, brick, and terracotta exterior cladding. The form of the exterior only partially reflects the structural function of the steelwork, for every second vertical pier is a dummy, covering no steel but necessary for flexible internal planning arrangements and for the visual effect Sullivan desired, and the elaborate, flowing frieze adorns nothing more important than the mechanical floor.

It is better to think of Sullivan's work not in terms of any one maxim such as "form follows function," then, but in terms of the original contributions he made to design. In addition to finding an unashamedly vertical expression for tall buildings, Sullivan evolved a characteristic ornamental style derived from natural plant forms. In fact, this aspect of his work can be considered part of Art Nouveau, although he seems neither to have been directly influenced by, nor to have had a direct influence on, contemporary developments in Europe. Ornament for Sullivan was an integral part of the building's design, and his swirling circular patterns were generally designed for ease of production from a master mold or cast in terracotta,

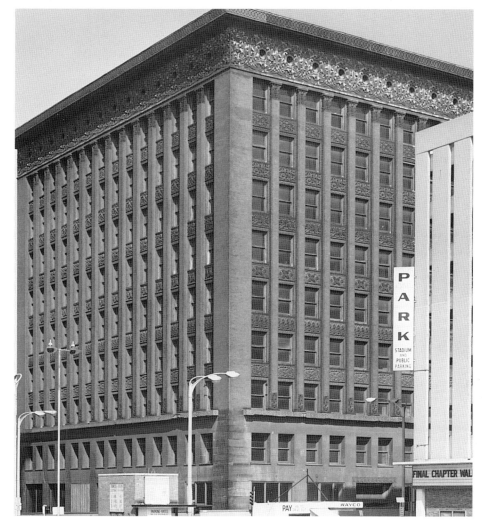

14.84 Dankmar Adler and Louis Sullivan, Wainwright Building, St. Louis, Missouri, 1890.

In his essay "The Tall Building Artistically Considered," Sullivan called for two walk-in, walk-up stories, repetitive office floors, and a cap containing mechanical equipment. Here are his theories at work, with terracotta ornament in the spandrel panels and at the deep cornice. The steel frame is obscured because of fireproofing requirements, but its presence is expressed on the exterior.

14.85 Dankmar Adler and Louis Sullivan, Guaranty Building, Buffalo, New York, 1894.

This office structure exhibits the same tall-building composition as the Wainwright Building. Even more dramatically displayed here is Sullivan's cast ornament that illustrates his principle of organic growth.

iron, or plaster. The Wainwright Building has ornate terracotta spandrels under each window and repetitive patterns on the frieze and roof fascia. He used essentially the same formula in the design of the Guaranty Building (1894) in Buffalo, New York (Fig. 14.85).

With allowance for changing architectural fashions, Sullivan's conception of the skyscraper's composition remains valid today. In place of the brick and terracotta infill panels that Sullivan used, subsequent high-rise construction makes extensive use of glass curtain walls, where the lightweight frames holding the glass are brought forward of the structural columns, a technique first used by W.J. Polk in the Halladie Building (1918) in San Francisco (Fig. 14.86). Under New York's zoning code of 1916, skyscraper façades were required to be tiered back from the street in relation to their height, producing the characteristic stepped profile of landmarks like the Chrysler Building (see Fig. 15.35) and the Empire State Building (see Fig. 15.40). Inspired by the Seagram Building (1958) (see Fig. 15.74) in New York, with an elegant public open space at its base, more recent codes have permitted unbroken vertical façades if a portion of the site is given over to a pedestrian plaza. Unfortunately, this has often resulted in lifeless plazas at other midtown towers. The proper massing, density, and location of high-rise buildings remains a very controversial subject for architects, urban planners, and the general public.

Sullivan used more florid and three-dimensional ornament for the main entrance of the Schlesinger and Mayer Store, now the Carson Pirie Scott Department Store (1899–1904), in Chicago, a building that represents the maturity of Sullivan's design ideas for tall buildings (Fig. 14.87). Here, the large windows are set in wide bays, articulated by white terracotta cladding on the steel columns and spandrel panels. The overall effect of the building is more horizontal than vertical. Display windows on the ground floor are terminated by cast-iron ornamental panels that can be readily viewed from the street level. The ornament becomes far more exuberant around the heads of the doorways, thereby giving emphasis to the entrance, which is further defined by its location at a slightly projecting radiused (i.e. 90° of curvature) corner. Upper-level windows have slender ornamental frames. Thus, the building provides visual rewards from several vantage points. From a distance, its austere white frame reads as a cleanly subdivided rectangular grid resting on a dark base; from a medium distance, the articulated entrance can be easily distinguished; and from a close view, one can appreciate

14.86 W.J. Polk, Halladie Building, San Francisco, California, 1918.

Others besides Chicago School architects were making progress with structural expression in commercial-building walls during the early twentieth century. W.J. Polk anticipated curtain-wall construction with this glass grid projected beyond interior columns.

14.87 Louis Sullivan, Carson Pirie Scott Department Store, Chicago, Illinois, 1899–1904.

At the Wainwright and Guaranty buildings, Sullivan chose to emphasize the vertical. Here he balanced horizontals and verticals and inserted "Chicago windows," windows that have large fixed panes between operable sash.

the abundant detail around windows and doorways. With the Carson Pirie Scott Department Store, Sullivan achieved an integration of uninterrupted line and decorative detail that has seldom been equaled.

Having reached its apogee, Sullivan's architectural practice declined precipitously. The Carson Pirie Scott Department Store was to be his last major commission. He and Adler dissolved their partnership in 1895, and

14.88 Louis Sullivan, National Farmers' Bank, Owatonna, Minnesota, 1907–08.

Sullivan's bank is like a giant lock-box. Upon entering, one is immediately confronted by the thick door of the vault. The effect produced is, appropriately, one of security.

14.89 Louis Sullivan, Foliated ornament design, 1924.

This plate from Sullivan's *A System of Architectural Ornament* (1924) illustrates the organic nature of his system for generating form. Ironically, he argued that ornament was a luxury and that it would be best for his generation first to develop an architecture that was "well formed and comely in the nude."

neither prospered separately. Within a year Adler proposed rejoining forces, but Sullivan turned him down. Sullivan's misanthropy and growing alcoholism estranged him from his family, his wife, his professional colleagues, and most prospective clients. Between 1907 and 1924 he had only thirteen minor commissions, the most impressive of which was the National Farmers' Bank (1907–08) in Owatonna, Minnesota (Fig. 14.88). A simple rectangular box with one enormous semicircular arch on each street front, the bank could be taken for a Neo-Classical composition if one disregarded the large inset ornament in terracotta, cast iron, and glass mosaic. The bank's form expresses security and dignity, desirable attributes for a financial institution, and it led to commissions for several other banks in scattered small Midwestern towns. During this period Sullivan turned to writing, producing the articles that were later collected and published as *Kindergarten Chats and Other Writings* (1934), his autobiography, and plates for *A System of Architectural Ornament* (Fig. 14.89). The pessimistic observations contained in these works reflect his bitterness toward the world, which had by

then virtually forgotten him. The important contributions he made to architecture and the influence he had on the young Frank Lloyd Wright, however, have assured Sullivan's place in architectural history.

CHAPTER 15

THE TWENTIETH CENTURY AND MODERNISM

The development of "modern" architecture has been complicated, an inescapable condition in the twentieth century. Evaluating this complexity has been made more difficult by the polemical nature of much writing by those advocating or disparaging the Modern Movement or European Modernism. While a superficial look at Modernist buildings may suggest that this work is reductivist or stripped of all but its essential parts and, some would say, left with little or no meaning, such is not the case. The founders of Modernism intended that their buildings should be didactic; they intended for them to instruct. But benefitting from this instruction often requires an awareness not only of what can be seen, but also of what cannot, that is, of what has been eliminated from the architecture that preceded Modernism and to which the Modernists were reacting.

THE IDEA OF A MODERN ARCHITECTURE

In the wake of the horrors of World War I, many young architects shared a general disillusionment, indeed a sense that European culture had failed and would have to be replaced by a transformed society; they believed that architecture could and should become an instrument of this transformation. They also believed in the power of rational thought, and ultimately in its handmaidens, economy and functionality, and they believed that their rational designs could best be produced through mechanization,

yielding efficient, somehow machine-made buildings. As a corollary, and following nineteenth-century social and architectural critics like John Ruskin, they revered the direct expression of building materials and their processes of assembly.

Adding to the difficulty in understanding individual buildings from the formative period of Modernism has been the general absorption of Modernist buildings into the broader architectural scene and their construction outside the geographical and social context in which they originated. Frequently Modernist utopianism has given way to mass culture, economy to parsimony, and honesty to banality. Most ironically, this modern architecture, with its often Socialist roots, was appropriated by corporate America, most dramatically for the glass-and-steel towers that became companies' headquarters and projected their capitalist images. In order to begin making our way through these potentially confusing circumstances and to begin exploring Modernism's principal themes, let us identify the authors who have written about it and cast a critical eye on what they have had to say.

THE WAR OF WORDS

In 1927, Gustav Platz published *Die Baukunst der neuesten Zeit* or *The Architecture of the New Age*. This German word *Zeit* is an important one, as the notion of *Zeitgeist*, or the Spirit of the Age, had been assembled from it by nineteenth-century German art historians. *Zeitgeist* combines the notions of newness, inherited from Art Nouveau, and style that somehow encapsulate the aspirations and accomplishments of an era as did, some have argued, the Gothic in France or the High Renaissance in Italy. The publication of Platz's book was sandwiched between Le Corbusier's *Vers une architecture* (1923), usually translated as *Towards a New Architecture*, and Frank Lloyd Wright's *Modern Archtecture* (1931) and Walter Gropius's *The New Architecture and the Bauhaus* (1935). In each of these publications, the author sought to promote his own design philosophy; this had been done before,

Ely Jacques Kahn, Number Two Park Avenue, New York City, 1927.

Ely Jacques Kahn was probably the most prominent practitioner of Art Deco in New York City. While ignored in all accounts of the development of twentieth-century Modernism, he had an extraordinarily productive career that stretched over fifty years.

but, encouraged by the escalating power of the media, it would be done with a vengance in the twentieth century. In fact, by the 1970s, many architects would start publishing monographs about their work before they had built anything of significance, a trend that continues today.

In 1932, architectural historian Henry-Russell Hitchcock and his protégé Philip Johnson, in support of the recently held exhibition at the Museum of Modern Art (MOMA) in New York City that they had organized with Alfred Barr, produced a thin volume entitled *The International Style: Architecture Since 1922*. Here, they announced that European Modernism was a new style and dubbed it international since it had already been transplanted from Europe to America (and would be exported elsewhere). Historians immediately went to work searching for the origins of the newly announced phenomenon, showing the same zeal and promoting the same confusion that had accompanied Baker and Speke's nineteenth-century search for the source of the Nile. None was more persuasive at the beginning than Nikolaus Pevsner. In his *Pioneers of the Modern Movement: From William Morris to Walter Gropius* (1936), Pevsner identified William Morris, as the title suggests, and his circle of Arts and Crafts designers in England, with Herman Muthesius as a connection to Germany, as the forerunners of the *Neue Sachlichkeit* or, as it is often translated, the "New Objectivity," and he saw the various late nineteenth-century art movements as having established a new set of ideals. He discussed developments in iron, steel, and concrete, spent considerable time on Art Nouveau, and concluded with an examination of work in Vienna, including that of Adolf Loos, and of Peter Behrens and his Werkbund associates in Germany. While Pevsner mentioned Futurism, he completely ignored Constructivism, De Stijl, and Expressionism.

Sigfried Giedion took a not dissimilar view in *Space, Time, and Architecture* (1941), a book so persuasive that many Modernist schools of architecture adopted it as a textbook in architectural history classes in the 1940s, '50s, and '60s. Delivered originally as a series of lectures, the text has serious disjunctures, but Giedion wrote with such authority and conviction that these lacunae serve only to intensify, if sometimes confuse, the narrative. His principal themes are truth and honesty, the force of technology, and the so-called space-time conception in art and architecture, all presented in a *Zeitgeistian* context. It is at once a spectacular and insidious book as a result of Giedion's professed method of selecting pertinent materials. In explaining this method, he spoke of constituent and transitory facts, the former being "tendencies which, when they are suppressed, inevitably reappear" and the latter as trends which "lack the stuff of permanence and fail to attach themselves to a tradition." Giedion's critics have seen this differentiation simply as a facile way for him to include those historical events that supported his arguments while ignoring those that did not.

The Pevsner–Giedion Modernist vision held sway almost completely until 1960, when Reyner Banham, in *Theory and Design in the First Machine Age*, argued that the two scholars had got it wrong. He quickly dispensed with the German and Austrian developments in the first section of his book; he spent the entire second section on Futurism, and the entire third section on the De Stijl movement and Expressionism in Holland and Germany, then concluded in part four with Le Corbusier, Gropius, and Mies van der Rohe. Six years later, Dennis Sharp published *Modern Architecture and Expressionism* (1966), an entire book devoted to buildings that Pevsner and Giedion had seen as inconsequential only thirty years before. The year 1966 also saw the publication of Robert Venturi's iconoclastic *Complexity and Contradiction in Architecture*, a publication that both thrilled and shocked students of the time and announced the end of Modernist dominance in education and practice; more will be said about it in the next chapter.

What does this series of publishing events tell us? For young students, perhaps, it presents something destabilizing and even frightening: historical truth does not seem to be a constant; and, indeed, it is not. Things change, human perspectives change, ideals change, and so our view of history, and therefore history itself, changes. Students should not be discouraged, however; in fact quite the opposite is true. History is not dead; it is like a living organism.

Early Modernists were militant; they sought to annihilate by any means available their revivalist enemies, including the entire Ecole des Beaux-Arts. They assumed ultimate power in the role of designers and design teachers for better than thirty years; some of them still linger on. In some cases they behaved badly, arrogantly, even ignorantly, and their architecture sometimes showed it, but many of the so-called Post-Modernists (another term to be dealt with in the next chapter) who replaced them or wrote about those who replaced them in the 1960s and afterward would have us believe that these Modernists were reprobates. How can this be? Can so many, so committed for so long, have been completely wrong? The answer is this: it is just not that simple!

Modern architecture was conceived during a time of tremendous upheaval in Western culture, including a world war and a revolution in Russia and developments in art and science that transformed our fundamental views about both time and space. Designers in the first decade and a half of the twentieth century sought to come to terms with these new ways of seeing, analyzing, and understanding, with tremendous advances in technology, and with the perceived necessity to create a modern art. Subsequent to World War I, the dominant issue became a desperate need for housing. As Modernists competed with traditionalists, the most extreme among them moved toward the New Objectivity, arguing that modern work was more efficient and cost-effective, which in some cases it was. However, their efforts to make modern architecture appear, if not in fact be, machine-producible and to render it functional and expressive of that functionality, led, in the eyes of many, to a reductivistic architecture, one short on character, symbolism, and even "livability." Still, whatever the final assessment, one can only admire the zeal and conviction with which Modernists took to the task at hand.

ADOLF LOOS

Early in his career, Adolf Loos (1870–1933) was affiliated with the Vienna Secession, but he soon became estranged from it. After completing his architectural education, he worked and traveled in the United States in 1893–96, where he saw the buildings of the Chicago School and encountered the writings of Louis Sullivan, such as his essay "Ornament in Architecture" (1892). Sullivan had written: "I shall say that it would be greatly for our esthetic good if we should refrain entirely from the use of ornament for a period of years, in order that our thought might concentrate acutely upon the production of buildings well formed and comely in the nude." Apparently the young Loos took the statement to heart for, when he returned to Europe to settle in Vienna, he soon began to speak against the inclusion of ornament on buildings. This was a difficult position to maintain within the Viennese Secession, for Art Nouveau has nothing if not a highly refined sense of ornament. Some historians have theorized that Loos's turning against the prevailing Viennese school was a

response to losing the commission to decorate and furnish the Secession council chamber. In any case, he set out on an exploration that would lead him to posit a new method of spatial composition: the *Raumplan*.

ORNAMENT AND CRIME

Loos's theoretical writings were extremely influential. The most famous was published in 1908 under the title *Ornament and Crime*. Here he took Sullivan's suggestion to abandon ornament in architecture a step further, proposing that the tendency to decorate surfaces was a sign of primitive culture or infancy. In advanced societies or in adults, he said, the urge to ornamental design was a sign of dependency or criminality. He wrote polemically:

Children are amoral, and so, by our standards, are Papuans. If a Papuan slaughters an enemy and eats him, that doesn't make him a criminal. But if a modern man kills someone and eats him, he must be either a criminal or degenerate. The Papuans tattoo themselves, decorate their boats, their oars, everything they can get their hands on. But a modern man who tattoos himself is either a criminal or a degenerate. Why, there are prisons where eighty per cent of the convicts are tattooed, and tattooed men who are not in prison are either latent criminals or degenerate aristocrats. When a tattooed man dies at liberty, it simply means that he hasn't had time to commit his crime. . . . I have therefore evolved the following maxim, and pronounce it to the world: the evolution of culture marches with the elimination of ornament from useful objects.

15.1a Adolf Loos, Rear elevation of the Steiner House, Vienna, 1910.

Orthogonal massing, punched-out windows, a pipe-rail balustrade, and an absolute lack of ornament announce the nature of Loos's radical architectural proposals. At the front elevation, he made concessions to the surrounding residential context that he would not make again.

15.1b Adolf Loos, Longitudinal section through the Steiner House, Vienna, 1910.

Neither Loos's plan nor section yet suggests the investigations of spatial interpenetrations that will appear in his mature houses.

0   10 m

0   30 ft

15.2 Adolf, Loos, Moller House, Vienna, 1930.

Gone is the symmetry of the Steiner House. Even more dramatically used are the simple window frames and the linear railings. The space on the inside has become the dominant element of the composition.

This was a radical message indeed, and after its original publication in the German art periodical *Der Sturm* (*The Storm*), it was translated into French and published in *Les Cahiers d'aujourd'hui* (*The Notebooks of Today*) in 1913. Loos became the darling of avant-garde artists in Paris, and he moved there in the early 1920s. By extolling the virtues of architecture without ornament, he addressed an issue that had been of general concern to designers in various places around the turn of the century. His writings led to

admiration of the simple vernacular forms of undecorated peasant architecture and the rather plain, functional constructions of engineers, both types of buildings previously considered to have no particular esthetic merit. Furthermore, Loos's admonition to build without ornament suggested a way to build in a style appropriate to a mechanized age.

THE RAUMPLAN AND LOOS'S BUILDINGS

Loos's architectural designs are largely absent of ornament, befitting his theories. Moreover, unlike many revolutionaries, who only identify what to eliminate, Loos had proposals for what should be added too. A sequence of his house designs may illustrate his contributions. His Steiner House of 1910 (Fig. 15.1a) in Vienna is an unadorned white cubical mass with plain modest window openings and a streetfront façade that pays at least lip service to the more traditional surrounding residences. Its plan is straightforward and largely symmetrical, and its section (Fig. 15.1b) shows layered floor slabs of equal height. Its interior offers a slightly richer set of experiences, with considerable use of wood for wainscots, door and window casings, and ceiling grids; but this interior is not unlike the work of many others during this period. His Moller House of 1930 shows several dramatic advances. The exterior mass (Fig. 15.2) is still without conventional ornament, but each element—doors, windows, handrails, parapets, cantilevered slabs—becomes a distinctive and carefully disposed part within an asymmetrical but balanced whole. The plan (Fig. 15.3a) is also asymmetrical, with some

15.3a Adolf Loos, Second-floor (*below*) and third-floor (*above*) plans of the Moller House, Vienna, 1930.

Above the ground floor Loos inserted few full-height walls. However, his plans never had the horizontal spatial interactions of Frank Lloyd Wright's residential designs of the turn of the century.

15.3b Adolf Loos, Longitudinal section through the Moller House, Vienna, 1930.

In this section, Loos has begun to manipulate the floor heights and to cantilever floor plates. Rather than being stacked, the floors are spatial units displaced horizontally across one another.

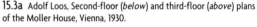

0   10 m

0   30 ft

rooms interconnected spatially by large door openings or low-walled apertures. The section (Fig. 15.3b) is more dramatic than that of the Steiner House in its spatial explorations, as the floor levels vary in height and some become mezzanines. On the interior, the materials are plain but rich by virtue of their natural character, conspicuously grained wood in particular. Of the Müller House (1930) the same can be said of its exterior massing and plans, but the section is even more adventurous, with multiple ceiling heights and an overt use of stairs to unify space vertically. Likewise, the interior materials are richer, particularly the use of marble without moldings such that its grain alone is left to provide scale and detail. Finally, in his earlier but more experimental (and unbuilt) villa on the Lido in Venice (1923), Loos demonstrated the full potential of his style of spatial composition, his *Raumplan*. The section (Fig. 15.4) is the most revealing drawing—multiple ceiling heights, mezzanine levels, and bold openings among spaces. Here Loos accomplished spatially what Giedion could only claim for Victor Horta and prepared the way for Le Corbusier's Modernist spatial compositions based upon his five points and Mies van der Rohe's meticulous compositions using stainless steel, onyx, marble, glass, and water.

Loos also carried out commercial commissions. His Goldman and Salatsch Store on the Michaelerplatz (1910) in Vienna is less shocking than the houses. There is some relief from severe planes in the cornice line, the suggestions of a Doric colonnade along the ground floor, and the window boxes, which were demanded by the Archduke Ferdinand, whose palace faced Loos's building (Fig. 15.5). In fact, the building seems to owe something to Sullivan's compositional rules for tall buildings, and there is also a

15.5 Adolf Loos, Goldman and Salatsch Store, Vienna, 1910.

Loos's seemingly sterile elevation was compared to the gridded storm-drain grates that were then to be found in abundance around Vienna. One of his strategies for maintaining scale without applied ornament was the use of rich materials such as veined-marble veneers both inside and out.

15.4 Adolf Loos, Section through the Lido villa, Venice, 1923.

Ceiling heights vary, and the two adjacent shafts of space have been displaced vertically producing multiple floor levels.

debt to the formal simplicity of Schinkel. In 1923 Loos submitted a late design for the Chicago Tribune Building competition that may be interpreted as either a joke or a serious comment on American architecture, particularly Stanford White's overscaled designs based on the Doric column. Loos's scheme was one enormous Doric column on a multi-story base, with windows arranged in vertical rows corresponding to the fluting. In boldness it matched his writings on ornament.

Three twentieth-century architects are sometimes termed the masters of modern architecture; the first two certainly fit the profile of the heroic figure battling often Philistine forces in the name of their art. They are Frank Lloyd Wright, Le Corbusier, and Ludwig Mies van der Rohe. Walter Gropius is often added to the group, although his most significant contributions were made in the field of architectural education. None of these architects developed their ideas in a vacuum; all were influenced by earlier architects, the use of new construction materials, and other artistic movements. For example, it would be difficult to conceive of Wright without the influence of Richardson, Sullivan, and the Arts and Crafts movement. In turn, Wright had a profound influence on architects in Europe, mainly because of the 1910 publication of his early works by Ernst Wasmuth in Berlin. Through the Wasmuth portfolio, Wright's work influenced the Dutch De Stijl movement, which had an effect on Gropius and the Bauhaus. Both Mies and Le Corbusier admitted their indebtedness to Wright, and in some respects they emulated his designs. In addition to his borrowings from Wright, Mies looks back to Schinkel through the eyes of his master, Peter Behrens, while Le Corbusier is tied into developments in concrete construction by August Perret and the ideas of city planning espoused by Tony Garnier.

FRANK LLOYD WRIGHT

Brief though it was, Louis Sullivan's architectural career profoundly influenced Frank Lloyd Wright (1867–1959). Wright was born in Wisconsin, the son of a domineering Welsh mother and an itinerant preacher-musician father, and he grew up in a variety of locations until his mother moved back near her family in Wisconsin when Wright was eleven. There he worked on his uncle's farm and attended school sporadically, all the while involving himself in drawing, crafts, painting, and printing. Wright's mother had decided before his birth that her son would become an architect, so she encouraged his interest in artistic and spatial investigations. After his parents

divorced in 1885, Wright dropped out of high school and worked as an office boy for a professor of civil engineering at the University of Wisconsin. He later entered the university's evening school as a special student, taking one semester of descriptive geometry and failing to complete a class in French. At the age of nineteen, he went to Chicago and found employment in the architectural office of Joseph Lyman Silsbee, a friend of his uncle's. Wright's ambition, however, was to work for Adler and Sullivan, and he practiced drawing Sullivanesque ornament so that he could make a favorable impression at the job interview.

In 1888 he landed a job there, demonstrating his graphic skill to Sullivan's satisfaction and gaining a five-year contract as draftsman. With an advance on his salary Wright started construction of his own house (1889) in the Chicago suburb of Oak Park. The house began as a modest two-story building, with a Serliana in the shingle-covered gable end turned to the street. Over the years, the house was greatly enlarged and reworked to provide space for Wright's six children and his mother. In the office of Adler and Sullivan, Wright was sometimes given a free hand with residential commissions, such as that for the James Charnley House (1891), a two-story structure on a narrow city lot in Chicago (Figs. 15.6–15.7). Wright's symmetrical design has a central doorway with carved Sullivanesque ornament below a second-level loggia with Doric columns.

DEVELOPING THE PRAIRIE HOUSE

Wright began designing other houses outside of office time, a practice Sullivan denounced as a violation of Wright's contract with the firm. As a result, Wright was fired and established his own practice, which he based in

15.6 Dankmar Adler and Louis Sullivan, Charnley House, Chicago, Illinois, 1891.

For this composition Frank Lloyd Wright, then working in the Adler and Sullivan office, obviously drew upon the Auditorium Building (see Figs. 14.82–83). The projection of the lobby there became a loggia off the central stair hall in the Charnley House.

15.7 Dankmar Adler and Louis Sullivan, Plans of the Charnley House, Chicago, Illinois, 1891.

These carefully balanced plans only hint at Wright's subsequent interior-space designs. The cross axes on both floors intersect at the two-story space of the stair opening.

a studio built onto his Oak Park house. It was the newly developing Chicago suburbs for the rising middle class, like Oak Park, that Wright would use as his first architectural laboratory. While his clients wanted value for money, they were frequently willing to allow Wright to experiment. His early years of independent practice were characterized by explorations of many styles of domestic architecture—Colonial, Tudor, Georgian, Shingle Style, and Queen Anne—although Wright later edited his body of work to include only those designs that obviously

contributed to the development of his Prairie Style. Among these was his first independent commission, a house for William H. Winslow (1893) in River Forest, Illinois (Figs. 15.8–15.9). Like the Charnley House, the Winslow House is symmetrical with Sullivanesque ornament. In common with the later Prairie houses, the Winslow House is organized around a central fireplace and dominated by horizontal lines. The hipped roof overhangs the second floor at the level of the window heads, and the apparent height of the ground floor extends to the second-floor windowsills, effectively reducing the perceived volume of the upper level and creating the impression that the building hugs the ground. Wright even broadened the chimney mass to emphasize the horizontal aspect rather than the vertical.

With the design of the Ward Willits House (1901) in Highland Park, Illinois, Wright abandoned the compact composition of the Winslow House for a cruciform plan (a commonly used plan in many houses of the period 1900–10) of four arms extending out into the landscape from the central chimney mass (Fig. 15.10). Again the horizontal line dominates the exterior, accentuated by the overhanging eaves of the roofline and the extension of the transverse axis of the house to form a porte-cochère (a covered drive-through for vehicles) at one end and a covered porch at the other. The exterior stucco is banded by continuous horizontal strips of dark wood marking the first-floor level and the windowsill line. By lowering the eaves to the level of the window heads and diminishing the chimney's height, Wright again minimized the vertical component of this two-story house.

Wright developed the Prairie house out of his search for an appropriate regional expression for American homes, especially in the Midwest. Taking his cue from the

15.8 Frank Lloyd Wright, Winslow House, River Forest, Illinois, 1893.

This is another case where Wright looked to Sullivan for inspiration. The ornamental frontispiece echoed such compositions as Sullivan's Getty Tomb.

gently rolling land of the prairie, he designed houses that sat close to the ground and seemed to be tied organically to the landscape. The prevailing eclectic Victorian styles, which he had tried and discarded, Wright now dismissed as "pimples" on the land. He also responded to the prevailing materials of construction, including brick and wood cut in standard sizes by sawmills, by trying to devise uses for them that were sympathetic to them and their modes of fabrication.

Environmental factors also affected his designs. The broad overhanging eaves shielded the windows from the hot Chicago sun while permitting the lower winter rays to enter and warm the interior. The central fireplace mass gave warmth to the heart of the home, both functionally and symbolically. All major rooms were oriented to provide cross-ventilation. Some of the most remarkable aspects of the Prairie houses are evident on the interiors, where living spaces flow smoothly from one area to another, creating an integrated spatial experience that was to have a profound influence on early Modernist architects in Europe. Wright's Prairie houses are said to "break the box" because neither the external form nor the internal

15.9 (above) Frank Lloyd Wright, Plan of the Winslow House, River Forest, Illinois, 1893.

Wright often spoke of "breaking the box." That process had begun here, where the front rooms are self-contained and axially connected, while the side and rear rooms project as a porte-cochère and as semicircular and semipolygonal bays, and the terraces are defined by platforms and projecting walls.

15.10 (below) Frank Lloyd Wright, Plans and perspective of the Ward Willits House, Highland Park, Illinois, 1901. Drawing.

Ten years after the Charnley House, Wright had devised a new kind of residence. In it, the center is solidly anchored by a great hearth, and the rooms project out aggressively into space, covered by long, low, hovering roofs. His distinctive perspective-drawing technique was influenced by an interest in Japanese prints.

spaces are contained in tight rectangular units. Even the windows wrap around corners as if to deny the traditional structural corner post. Wright extended the spatial freedom of the two-story living hall used by Richardson and Pugin to the entire interior and gave corresponding freedom to the exterior as it embraced the landscape.

Wright incorporated all these features on even the most difficult of sites, such as the narrow suburban lot of Elizabeth Gale, an Oak Park neighbor for whom he designed a house in 1909. Hemmed in by Victorian hulks on either side, the Gale House had little opportunity to spread out to the landscape, so Wright provided the visual link between interior and exterior through a series of balconies cantilevered off the major living spaces. He would return to this idea later when faced with the far more dramatic hillside site of the Kaufmann House (1935–36) called Fallingwater. The last and by far the most celebrated of the early Prairie houses was built for Frederick Robie on two small corner lots in south Chicago in 1909 (Figs. 15.11–15.12). Robie was a self-made man, a manufacturer who had an interest in engineering, and he and Wright got along exceedingly well. Robie requested a house where he could have privacy from the street and separation from the noise of his small children at play. Wright's response was a three-story design, with the garage, playroom, and service functions on the ground floor, the living and dining areas on the second floor, and bedrooms on the third. A low wall in front of the house shields the ground floor from passers-by, and the elevated windows of the second floor, protected by a balcony, give the privacy Robie desired. A horizontal element was created by the long lines of the walls and balconies, but especially by the great roof of the second floor, which cantilevers daringly at either end of the house. Welded steel beams made this structural bravura possible, and their employment in the Robie House marked the first use of welded steel in residential construction. Bricks for the house, as for other Prairie houses, were custom-made in St. Louis. Shaped like long, thin Roman bricks, they were laid with wide horizontal mortar joints that were sharply raked to cast a horizontal shadow.

In plan the house is organized around the chimney mass. The entrance is off the short side-street frontage into the rear of the house, and the staircase that leads to the second floor is integrated into the masonry of the chimney. The living room and dining room are in effect one continuous space, interrupted only partly by the fireplace, so that the great linear space, illuminated by long bands of windows on either side of the living space, is airy and unified. Wright designed all the interior fittings to complement the space—the light fixtures, furniture,

15.11 Frank Lloyd Wright, Robie House, Chicago, Illinois, 1909.

This is the most celebrated house from the first phase of Wright's career. It is a "Prairie house" that acknowledges the horizontality of the Midwestern landscape.

15.12 Frank Lloyd Wright, Plans of Robie House, Chicago, Illinois, 1909.

The client owned a small lot on a busy street and had young children. Wright responded with a very compact plan. The front section for the family is very open, while the rear service section consists of more conventional, self-contained rooms.

carpets, and even clothes for Mrs. Robie to wear when entertaining. All this was very much in the Arts and Crafts tradition, except for the fact that the designs, especially for the furniture, were based on primary geometric forms and crisp, uncompromising right angles. This made the chairs and tables fit the space well, but all too often Wright's furniture did not fit the non-orthogonal curves of the human body.

EARLY PUBLIC BUILDINGS

Wright's early years as an architect were not entirely devoted to residential commissions. Two notable designs, the Larkin Building in Buffalo, New York, and Unity Temple in Oak Park, illustrate his approach to public buildings. The Larkin Building (1904) (Figs. 15.13a,b) contained offices for a company that sold packaged soap with coupons printed on the labels. Consumers could save

these coupons and redeem them for small gifts, a practice ubiquitous today among merchants of breakfast cereals but novel at the turn of the century. The Larkin Building was populated by rows of young women carrying out clerical tasks and even more rows of filing cabinets holding paperwork. For them Wright designed a frankly vertical six-story building with a full-height skylit atrium at the center (Fig. 15.13c). He placed banks of filing cabinets in partitions or against the exterior wall with windows above them; light from the atrium balanced the illumination on each floor. Massed plantings at either end of the atrium introduced the natural environment into the work space, and uplifting moralizing inscriptions, such as "Honest labor needs no master. Simple justice needs no slaves," were cast in the spandrels and placed around the exterior fountains to inspire the workforce. The custom-designed metal furniture used throughout included chairs connected to the desks, so that, after office hours, the back

15.13a,b (left) Frank Lloyd Wright, Plan and perspective view of the Larkin Building, Buffalo, New York, 1904.

Unfortunately, the Larkin Building has long since been destroyed. Its innovations were many, including air-conditioning and built-in filing cabinets, which are visible in Fig. 15.13c.

15.13c (right) Frank Lloyd Wright, Interior atrium of the Larkin Building, Buffalo, New York, 1904.

A comparison of this interior perspective with the exterior perspective shows the continuity between interior and exterior forms. Notice as well the Wright-designed furniture and light fixtures in this top-lit space surrounded by galleries.

15.14 Frank Lloyd Wright, Unity Temple, Oak Park, Illinois, 1906.

It is remarkable to consider that this landmark work is almost 100 years old. Built for a congregation of modest means, its early use of poured-in-place concrete was an economy-driven innovation.

15.15 Frank Lloyd Wright, Plan of Unity Temple, Oak Park, Illinois, 1906.

To the left is the sanctuary; to the right is the Sunday-school wing. Entry occurs between the two. Notice the way that Wright breaks away the corners from each volume.

would fold down on the seat and the entire chair would swing out of the way of the cleaning crew's mops. The exterior of the building was rather austere, rising as an uninterrupted vertical brick mass to the height of a thin string course carefully placed to mark the parapet wall around the rooftop recreation space. The stairs, located in all four corners, rose as towers distinct from the building mass, leaving the walls in between to be articulated by repetitive bands of windows. As an office building design, the Larkin Building was forward-looking. Entirely ventilation-controlled, with filtered air intake and extract ducts in the stair towers, it was planned for modular furnishings and flexibility, while provisions made for employee recreation anticipated the corporate health clubs of the present day. It became one of Wright's most widely published designs, especially in Europe, where it was emulated by various designers, making it all the more unfortunate that the City of Buffalo demolished the building in 1949 to create a parking lot.

A happier fate has been visited upon Unity Temple (Figs. 15.14–15.15), built in 1906 for the Unitarian-Universalist congregation of Oak Park. The site was on the corner of two particularly busy thoroughfares, so Wright turned the building inward to reduce the impact of street noise. The two major elements of the church, the worship space, called an auditorium in Wright's drawings, and the unity house containing classrooms and a kitchen, are connected by a common vestibule, neatly solving at once the problems of entrance and separation of the noise of Sunday-school classes from adult worship. The worship space is an articulated cube with two levels of balconies on three walls facing the pulpit on the fourth. It is a rich and glowing interior. Light from leaded-glass windows high in the wall balances that from the deeply coffered, amber-colored skylights over the major congregational seating in the center of the main floor. Insofar as possible, the interior trim consists of orthogonal geometries composed of thin strips of wood. The lights, also designed by Wright, are either spheres or cubes of glass suspended from wooden frames.

Equally remarkable is the exterior, which is constructed entirely in poured concrete. Unity Temple was Wright's first essay in concrete, and it was also one of the first attempts anywhere to design straightforwardly with that material, instead of covering it or disguising the surface to resemble stone. Wright designed discrete geometric ornament in the formwork of the piers between the high windows, and gave the same treatment to the smaller and lower unity house. The church stands today, carefully restored, and still serving its original functions.

THE FLIGHT FROM AMERICA

By 1909 Wright was well established as an architect, and his reputation had spread abroad. Public and professional acceptance did not bring happiness, however, and he felt increasingly hemmed in by family responsibilities and office routine. When an offer came from Ernst Wasmuth, a prestigious Berlin publisher, to prepare a portfolio of his work for publication, Wright jumped at the chance to escape. Abandoning his wife and six children, he took with him instead the wife of a client and neighbor, Mamah Borthwick Cheney, who left her husband and three children, and together they traveled to Europe in September of 1909. For the next twenty-five years, Wright's turbulent personal life seriously interfered with his professional work, and he built very little. The publication in 1910 and 1911 of the Wasmuth portfolios, *Ausgeführte Bauten und Entwürfe* (*Executed Buildings and Projects*), had an enormous impact on European architects, but the press in the United States was principally interested in the scandal in Wright's private affairs.

In this difficult period the only major commission Wright received was for the Imperial Hotel in Tokyo (1916–22) (Fig. 15.16), remembered now chiefly for its ingenious foundations and cantilevered structural system. The very muddy subsoil conditions of the hotel site prompted Wright to float the foundations instead of digging further for bedrock. The whole of Japan is prone to earthquake hazard, so Wright sought to balance the building in sections on central concrete pile clusters with a cantilevered concrete slab on top, much as a waiter balances a tray on raised fingertips. The hotel was designed around courtyards with a pool of water in front of the entrance, both for beauty and for firefighting in case of earthquakes. Its form was complex and its decoration

15.16 Frank Lloyd Wright, Plan of the Imperial Hotel, Tokyo, 1916–22.

Wright's tartan pattern of organization is as apparent at this large scale as in his smaller, fully developed residences. However, this building's symmetry and dominant central space give it a kinship to Ecole des Beaux-Arts designs.

lavish, demonstrating little of the spare qualities Wright so admired in Japanese woodblock prints. Indeed, most of the decorative motifs and their manner of application owe more to the Aztec, Toltec, and Mayan cultures of Mexico and Central America than to anything oriental. Decorative caprice aside, the structural system worked as intended in the severe earthquake of 1923, one of the few triumphs Wright could record in that unfortunate year. Over subsequent years, differential settlement, aided by a lowering of the water table under the area, caused large cracks in the building, and the demand for more spacious, air-conditioned hotel accommodations made Wright's structure increasingly obsolete. It was demolished in the late 1960s to make room for a high-rise.

The architectural career of Frank Lloyd Wright was not over, however, for he would enter another phase of great productivity in the mid-1930s. Those works will be discussed later in this chapter along with other projects of the same period.

PETER BEHRENS AND THE DEUTSCHER WERKBUND

Previous discussion of the English Arts and Crafts movement included reference to the German Herman Muthesius, who was sent to England in 1896 to report on all aspects of English architecture, design, and manufacture, with the intention that his research should prove useful in raising the design standards of German products. Muthesius's subsequent appointment of eminent designers to leadership positions at German arts and crafts schools was one result of the reform process begun after his return to Germany. In 1907 another significant step came when Muthesius, together with sympathetic manufacturers and designers, formed the Deutscher Werkbund. (This German title does not translate easily. Perhaps "German products association" would be an appropriate English equivalent.) The Werkbund encouraged fine design in industrially manufactured goods. The motive was primarily economic: Muthesius and others were very much concerned that German products would not be competitive in domestic or international markets unless they could equal the standards set by other countries, especially England. Just what artistic direction the Werkbund would take was the subject of considerable debate in the early years, but the word

15.18 Peter Behrens, AEG Turbine Factory, Berlin, 1909.

Many have commented on the barn-like aspect of this structure's massing and roof profile, suggesting vernacular inspirations. However, the more relevant features for twentieth-century Modernism are the exposed steel supports and the huge, screen-like end-wall glazing set between massive corner piers.

"quality" was used with great frequency. The Werkbund increasingly urged the merits of abstract forms for manufactured products and standardized parts for production ease, and demanded that esthetic quality should be evaluated separately from manufacturing quality. All these ideas were to be of great importance to postwar designers.

Another important event of 1907 was the hiring of Peter Behrens (1868–1940), a member of the Werkbund, by the Allgemeine Elektricitäts-Gesellschaft (AEG), or General Electric Company. Behrens was responsible for all aspects of design for the firm—including its letterhead, electric-light fixtures, and production facilities—a brief embracing the modern fields of graphic design, product design, and architecture (Fig. 15.17). The man entrusted with this work was originally trained as a painter, but he was also influenced by the arts and crafts teachings of William Morris.

The buildings Behrens designed for AEG have a quality of stripped classicism. While they are forceful, bold statements, representing the first architectural attempts to deal with industrial facilities, they are also symbols of the new industrial order arising in Germany. The most famous is the Turbine Factory in Berlin (1909), where the polygonal profile of the roof truss over the large manufacturing assembly hall is reflected on the exterior (Fig. 15.18). Behrens avoided applied ornament entirely and gave the structural materials direct expression. The steel frame is exposed along the side walls, where large windows span between the supports, while concrete panels, slightly battered and articulated in large rectangular coursings,

15.17 Peter Behrens, Poster design for AEG, 1908.

As artistic consultant to AEG, Behrens sought to create a graphic image for a large corporate client. He produced letterheads and advertising graphics as well as trade images such as this one.

dominate the end elevations. The large front window projects slightly from the concrete mass as if to emphasize its non-loading-bearing status. A lower two-story factory block to the left of the turbine hall has banks of vertical windows framed by a concrete surround closely following classical proportions, but treated here without classical detail.

Perhaps because of his AEG work, Behrens's office soon became known as one of the most progressive in Europe, and a number of the young designers who came to work for him became postwar leaders of the architectural profession. Walter Gropius met his first collaborator, Adolf Meyer, when they worked for Behrens; both Mies van der Rohe and the young Le Corbusier were also employed by Behrens before the outbreak of World War I.

FUTURISM AND CONSTRUCTIVISM

Two fairly short-lived movements that had an influence on the development of European Modernism were Futurism in Italy and Constructivism in Russia. The ideas of Futurism were laid down primarily by Filippo Marinetti (1876–1944), who published a foundation manifesto in 1909—the same year that Frank Lloyd Wright was abandoning the United States for Europe. Marinetti was passionate in his belief that Italian culture, including Italian architecture, was in a stupor of decrepitude. He called for a radical transformation of the Italian landscape—his plans included paving the canals of Venice! He praised speed, danger, audacity, and even war as a cleanser of society, and he announced the end of traditional space and time. Around this fiery rhetoric coalesced both artists and sculptors, but they had no appropriate graphic means for expressing themselves. By 1912, they had visited Paris and met with Braque and Picasso. The Cubism they saw there suggested ways in which they could represent episodic experiences, energy, and motion in paintings and sculpture, which they did in works such as Umberto

Boccioni's *Bottle Evolving in Space*. The most celebrated Futurist architect was Antonio Sant'Elia (1888–1916) and with his death Futurist architecture lost its momentum. Sant'Elia is best known for his "Città Nuova" ("New City") exhibition of 1914 and its accompanying publication, *Messagio*, which became the manifesto for Futurist architecture. Using a dramatic perspective technique, he proposed designs for airship hangers, apartment blocks, transportation centers, hydroelectric plants, and power stations (Figs. 15.19–15.20). All were characterized by bold massing without ornamentation, verticality and battered or stepped-back walls, multiple levels of horizontal circulation, external elevators, and exposed power-production facilities.

In revolutionary Russia, Constructivists were in an equally heady mood, but they were doomed to succumb to stultified Stalinist classicism. In a vast land where many in the countryside still lived in environments little changed since the Middle Ages, Constructivists envisioned a Soviet republic with an architecture driven forward by the forces of industrialization, but many of their ideas exceeded the technical capabilities of a backward country in total flux. They sought to exploit modern building materials such as steel, concrete, and large expanses of glass. Like the Futurists, they proposed the dramatic use of external transportation systems, and they added monumental external graphics, prefiguring today's huge digital displays.

Vladimir Tatlin (1885–1953) designed the *Monument to the Third International* (Communist Congress) in 1919 (Fig. 15.21). This tower was to be a fantastic, dynamic double spiral some 1300 feet tall, with revolving cone and cylinders that would have housed governmental and propaganda offices. It was unbuildable, but the vision caught the attention of the world. In 1924, the Vesnin brothers, Viktor (1882–1950) and Alexandr (1883–1959), produced the Pravda Newspaper Building (Fig. 15.22), complete with a loudspeaker system, to house the primary instrument of Soviet propaganda, the *Pravda* newspaper.

15.19 Antonio Sant'Elia, Project for a Milan power station, 1913.

Antonio Sant'Elia died young as a result of trauma suffered in World War I. His extraordinary perspective drawings made him the best-known exponent of Futurism.

15.20 Antonio Sant'Elia, La Città Nuova detail, 1914.

Sant'Elia explored the possibilities of a dynamic city dominated by multiple means of transportation. Particularly dramatic here are the tall elevator towers connected to building flanks by leaping bridges.

15.21 (left) Vladimir Tatlin, Model of the *Monument to the Third International*, 1919.

This tower project, with its dramatic proposal for the use of new materials and construction methods, strongly influenced young Russian designers. Gone are solid walls in favor of a technologically efficient, open frame.

15.22 (right) Viktor and Alexandr Vesnin, Pravda Newspaper Building, Moscow, 1924. Drawing.

Features such as exterior elevators and huge changeable graphics did not become common on modern buildings until the second half of the twentieth century. Equally portentous are the diagonal braces that were to give rigidity to the slender structural frame.

15.23 Konstantin Melnikov, Soviet Pavilion, Exposition des Arts Décoratifs, Paris, 1925.

Melnikov achieved dynamic form through the use of a rotated grid. It was this same Paris exhibition that saw the display of Friedrich Kiesler's Cité dans l'Espace (see Fig. 15.45).

15.24 Konstantin Melnikov, Rusakov Workers' Club, Moscow, 1927–28.

Melnikov's club not only demonstrates the kind of dramatic use of structure typical of the Constructivists; it also housed the kind of collective activity made necessary by the Russian Revolution. However, within a few years, the progressive Constructivist mentality was replaced by the crushing control of Stalin.

To its exposed, skeletal frame of steel, including X-bracing, they attached external elevators and a clock with digital readouts, and atop it all they placed a searchlight as a metaphor for the Communist experiment. Konstantin Melnikov (1890–1974) designed the Soviet Pavilion (Fig. 15.23) for the 1925 Exposition des Arts Décoratifs. Its diagonal grid and cantilevered structure emphasized dynamism, and its interconnected spaces expressed the still-open agenda of Soviet Communism. Melnikov's Rusakov Workers' Club in Moscow (1927–28) (Fig. 15.24) shows the same fascination with dramatic structure, in this case through bold cantilever seating constructed of reinforced concrete.

DUTCH AND GERMAN EXPRESSIONISM

Between 1900 and 1914, painters of the German Brücke (Bridge) and Blaue Reiter (Blue Rider) groups revolted against academic naturalism and sought to express emotions, thoughts, and feelings directly in their paintings. Subsequent to World War I, Expressionist artists and architects reacted passionately to the grinding horrors of trench warfare, as society attempted to come to terms with the guilt, angst, and estrangement of the postwar period. Expressionism in architecture has sometimes been characterized as anti-rationalistic, a twentieth-century continuation of nineteenth-century Romantic sensibilities, and has sometimes been defined by default as everything that did not conform to International Style standards, but its two principal guises—Dutch Expressionism (or Wendigen) and German Expressionism—are better understood by what they were and were for, than by what they were not or what they were against.

The members of Wendigen lived and worked in Amsterdam. Their designs owed much to the work of H.P. Berlage (1856–1934) and stressed the handicraft process of building, the revelation of structure, and the resulting high level of construction-process-related, sometimes fantastic detail. Berlage is best known for his Amsterdam Stock Exchange (1897–1903) (Fig. 15.25), a brick and stone bearing-wall structure of medieval inspiration, but one with a skylit iron-truss roof over the stock-exchange floor (Fig. 15.26). While the Stock Exchange was conceived quite rationally by Berlage, following the precepts of Gottfried Semper—about whom Berlage had learned while a student in Zurich—and P.J.H. Cuipers—a designer in the brick tradition of Amsterdam with connections to the thinking of Viollet-le-Duc, its Ruskinian expression of building materials, particularly through the colors and textures of its carefully composed wall surfaces, provided a starting point for Wendigen explorations.

In 1901 Berlage was commissioned by the City of Amsterdam to lay out residential neighborhoods in the area called Amsterdam South. His proposals for two-story walk-ups of brick, with the street as the primary organizing element, provided the environment for buildings by such designers as Piet Kramer (1881–1961) and Michael de Klerk (1884–1923). Kramer, an outgoing personality with an interest in the occult as well as Communist sympathies, designed his units for the De Dageraad housing association in 1918–23 (Fig. 15.27). He used brick to make taut planar and bulging curvilinear walls, inserted grid-like windows with avian overtones, and applied roof tiles and copings to produce aggressive, prickly silhouettes. De Klerk was perhaps the most talented and original of the Dutch Expressionists. His project for the Eigen Haard housing association (1921) (Fig. 15.28) is more plastic than Kramer's work, its silhouette more irregular, and its detailing more highly textured. De Klerk's abilities went well beyond the treatment of surfaces, however, as his housing on the Henrietta Ronnerplein (1921) demonstrates. Here, he manipulated battered walls, linking chimneys, and composite windows to produce a three-dimensional architecture that is among the most original and provocative of the early twentieth century.

German Expressionism was more diverse than the Dutch, concerned with both form and utopianism. Central to much German Expressionist thinking was the writing of Paul Scheerbart and his vision for a glass or crystalline architecture that would somehow ameliorate the

15.27 Piet Kramer, De Dageraad housing project, Amsterdam, 1918–23.

The Dutch Expressionist movement, called Wendigen, included such highly imaginative works as this one by Piet Kramer. Inspired by the brick masonry investigations of Berlage, its members sought to be expressive through the natural use of materials in the handicraft tradition.

repressive opacity of modern culture. In part a reaction against the directions being pursued by the state-run Deutsche Werkbund, the counter-proposals of German Expressionism appeared dramatically at the 1914 Werkbund exhibition in Cologne where Henri Van de Velde's Werkbund Theater explored the theme of *Kunstwollen*, or the will to form, in contrast to the mechanistic type-form precepts of mainstream Werkbund thinking, and Bruno Taut's Glass Pavilion (Fig. 15.29) gave physical reality to Scheerbart's proclamations. This variety of approaches illustrates the internal stresses at work within the Werkbund: rationality attuned to industrial mass-production versus self-expression made possible by the handicrafts, and, as a corollary to the latter, utopian collectivism and individual romanticism. Taut's Glass Pavilion was quite formal in its organization: a circular concrete base with central, axial stair; a circular rotunda; and a dome. However, Taut so thoroughly exploited the possibilities of glass that the building became a kind of walk-in prism (Fig. 15.30). Glass walls, glass treads and risers, glass panels in the dome, all filtered and reflected light and color to produce a space intended at once to display glass as a product of industrial production and to nourish the human spirit.

Perhaps the most idiosyncratic of all built German Expressionist work was the Goetheanum designed by an amateur, Rudolf Steiner (1861–1925). A philosopher, scholar, and student of the occult, Steiner founded the Anthroposophical Society in 1912 and set out to build a "free high school for spiritual science" called the Goetheanum, so connecting his thinking to the writings of

15.28 Michael de Klerk, Eigen Haard housing project, Amsterdam, 1913–21.

The exotic quality of projects such as this one should not obscure their designers' concerns for making them good places to live. These two-story walk-ups include common areas and landscaped courts.

15.29 (above) Bruno Taut, Glass Pavilion, Cologne, 1914.

This pavilion was on display at an exhibition organized by the German Werkbund, an organization dedicated to the improvement of German manufactured products. Taut sought to dramatize the potential uses of glass as a building material.

15.30 (below) Bruno Taut, Glass Pavilion interior, Cologne, 1914.

Taut's obsession with glass began with his so-called "glass chain" writings in which, following the lead of philosopher Paul Scheerbart, he celebrated a vision of culture made less repressive through the use of the transparent material.

Goethe. There were, in fact, two Goetheanums, both in Dornach, the first built of wood in 1913 and destroyed by fire at the end of 1922, and the second of concrete, which opened in 1928 (Fig. 15.31). Goetheanum I can be compared to Van de Velde's Werkbund Theater; it was dominated by curvilinear shapes, many that seemed melted and deformed. Underlying this deformity, however, was a symmetrical plan composed of interlocking circles, and the roofs were not unlike many traditional German profiles intended to shed snow. Goetheanum II, which is also systematic in plan, is at once more sculptural and faceted, with the most fantastic part of the complex being the boilerhouse with its vegetal chimney stack.

The Einstein Tower in Potsdam (1920–21) (Fig. 15.32) and the design for a hat factory in Luckenwalde (1921–23)

by Erich Mendelsohn (1887–1953) offer yet another Expressionistic approach to architecture. The dynamic qualities of the Einstein Tower, built of brick covered with stucco, demonstrate Mendelsohn's interest in streamlined forms, with little connection to the Italian Futurists, but certainly a kinship to Van de Velde's Werkbund Theater and with the Secessionist productions of Joseph Maria Olbrich. The bold graphic technique of Mendelsohn's sketches for it (Fig. 15.33) and related works displays the powerful and often poetic hand of someone forcefully influenced by the act of drawing itself. The appropriateness of dynamism to the activities of a scientist exploring space and time is obvious. Mendelsohn also exploited metaphorical qualities in his hat factory design; here he produced, upon a foundation of rational decisions, a scheme appropriate both to the realities of industrial manufacturing and the spirit of German economic aspirations. The administration building has a De Stijl quality, with its asymmetrical composition of orthogonal shapes, but in the production facilities Mendelsohn exploited structural and mechanical systems to produce logical but highly provocative forms. The rigid frame supporting the workshop inspired a rhythmic composition of triangles on the exterior, and the ventilating hoods of the dye vats are both purposeful and evocative.

Another much-published German Expressionist monument is Hans Poelzig's (1869–1936) water tower at Posen (1911) (Fig. 15.34). Here Poelzig, a stalwart member of the Werkbund, orchestrated a collision of seemingly heterogeneous functions and an almost hallucinogenic industrial esthetic. The skin of the tower is faceted and highly textured, with disparate masonry and glazing patterns. On the inside, set in a skeletal structure comparable to that seen in Fritz Lang's Expressionist film *Metropolis* and beneath the water reservoir, Poelzig designed an exhibit hall that he planned to be converted into a market hall. The tower is a remarkable amalgamation of purpose and fantasy.

ART DECO

Some have found a kinship between Art Deco and Expressionistic work. Art Deco is a slippery term describing a diverse design idiom that encompassed everything from graphics to ceramics, furniture, and architecture. Art Deco decorative arts, then known as *l'art moderne*, thrived in France from 1910 or so, and Art Deco architecture continued to be popular in America, especially for skyscrapers and theaters, through the 1930s. As a style, it has only been recognized since the 1960s and so did not even make it into Reyner Banham's *Theory and Design in the First Machine Age* (1960); thus evaluation of the work remains incomplete.

Art Deco designers consistently preferred sumptuous materials and produced objects of supple elegance. Like Art Nouveau and various other Modernist investigations, Art Deco was a movement in search of newness for a new century. However, its inspirations were eclectic in the extreme. From Cubism it drew overlapping and faceted shapes, from Russian Constructivism the language of mechanization, and from Futurism a fascination with motion. Add to these sources motifs drawn from ancient Egypt, Africa, the Orient, and elsewhere such as stylized flowers, coiled tendrils, faceted geometries including chevron patterns, and stylized, idealized, heroic human figures. In France, l'art moderne produced lavish ornamentality, so much so that at the 1925 Exposition des Arts Décoratifs in Paris, it succumbed to the tide of European Modernism and its reductivist, mass-production esthetic championed by designers such as Adolf Loos and Le Corbusier.

Ironically, there were abundant French examples of Art Deco architecture at the 1925 exposition, but they were razed at the end of the event. In England, Art Deco designers sought modernity through the expression of function and economy, so the style was considered appropriate for such buildings as power stations, airports, and movie theaters. In the United States, architects of the 1920s were searching for a decorative vocabulary applicable to skyscrapers, which had previously been modeled on everything from campaniles to ziggurats. At a time when European Modernism had not yet taken the field in America, Art Deco ornament was seen as modern, stylish, and appropriate for machine production, making it a viable substitute for the historicism of Gothic-inspired towers such as the Woolworth Building (1913) by Cass Gilbert (1859–1934) in New York City, and reproducible in terracotta, brass, and aluminum. Art Deco offered, if not a machine-age esthetic, a means to celebrate both art and technology.

The most famous Art Deco skyscraper is the Chrysler Building, also in New York (1928) (Fig. 15.35), designed by William Van Alen (1883–1954). Its crown-like dome of stainless steel, with tiered arches filled with sunbursts and capped with a spire, remains a classic for skyline-makers. Its other notable ornamental features include eagle gargoyles and the famous radiator-cap acroteria and adjacent frieze of abstracted car wheels.

New York's most prolific Art Deco designer was Ely Jacques Kahn (1884–1972), whose career spanned some fifty years. Representative of his output is the building at

15.35 William Van Alen, Chrysler Building, New York City, 1928.

There is still no more distinctive silhouette on the New York skyline than the stainless-steel crown of the Chrysler Building. Long ignored by Modernists, this aspect of tall-building design reemerged as almost a fetish in the 1970s and '80s.

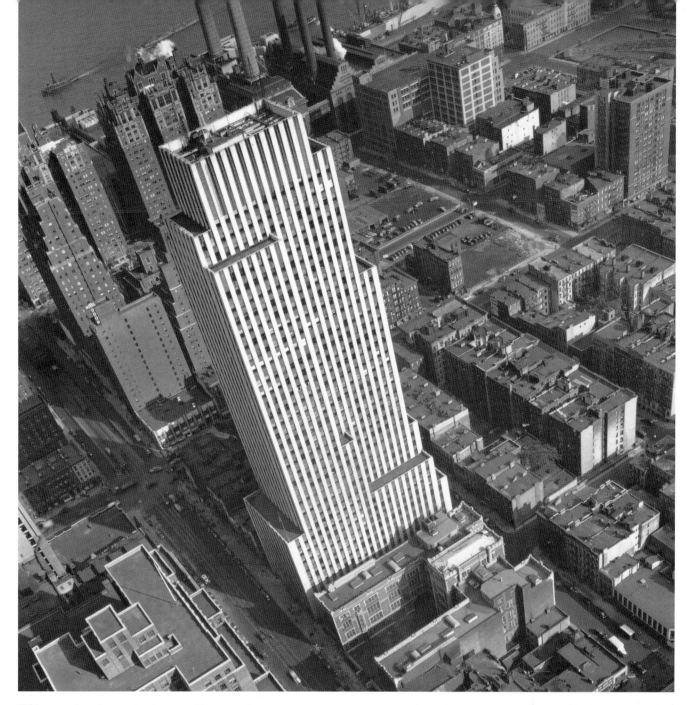

15.36 Raymond Hood, New York Daily News Building, New York City, 1929–30.

Contemporary with the Chrysler and Empire State buildings, the New York Daily News Building approaches International Style minimalism but displays incised decorative panels of Art Deco inspiration.

15.37 Raymond Hood, New York Daily News Building incised ornament, New York City, 1929–30.

The Art Deco Style made its appearance at the base of the tower. The sources for Art Deco ornament were many, from Pre-Columbian imagery to forms responding to the period's penchant for speed.

Number Two Park Avenue (1927) (page 474), with its wealth of faceted and geometric detail both inside and out. In 1929–30, Raymond Hood (1881–1934) designed the New York Daily News Building (Fig. 15.36) in New York, which in some ways approaches the minimalism of the International Style but also displays incised decorative panels of Art Deco inspiration (Fig. 15.37) and includes a

15.38 Reinhard and Hofmeister, Corbett, Hood, Fouiloux, and others, Rockefeller Center, New York City, begun 1929.

While the individual buildings are distinctive, it is the urban ensemble they create and the space they define that has caused the Rockefeller Center to be so celebrated. For many, it is the very heart of Manhattan. At the center of the complex, the tallest tower, with its distinctive setbacks, is the RCA Building.

15.39 Wallace K. Harrison, Radio City Music Hall foyer, New York City, 1933.

Within Rockefeller Center, no single interior space is better known than this one. Its plush furniture, opulent materials and dramatic lighting capture the spirit of New York City in the 1920s and '30s.

subtle color palette of greens and terracottas—colors outside the range of European Modernist dicta. Hood and Fouilhoux, along with other firms, designed the complex of buildings comprising the Rockefeller Center (begun 1929) (Fig. 15.38) and located within it a significant body of public art, including Art Deco sculpture by a variety of artists and the famous Diego Rivera fresco that was destroyed soon after completion because of its sympathetic treatment of communism. An artwork in itself is Radio City Music Hall (Fig. 15.39), with its plush furniture and lush materials and lighting. The tallest structure of the period was, of course, the Empire State Building (1931) (Fig. 15.40) by Richmond Shreve (1877–1946), William Lamb (1883–1952), and Arthur Harmon (1878–1958). Its Art Deco ornament includes a vast number of sandblasted aluminum spandrel panels with zigzag ornamentation.

In Los Angeles, Art Deco buildings took two forms: the so-called "Zig-Zag Moderne" and the "Streamline Moderne." The Wiltern (1931) and Pantages (1929) theaters have façades of stepped-back vertical pylons interspersed with ornamental spandrel panels (Fig. 15.41). Their interiors are a riot of sunburst and faceted geometric motifs, including prism-like mirrors and prismatic fan vaults. The Coca-Cola Bottling Plant (1936) (Fig. 15.42) by Robert Derrah (1895–1946), actually a remodeling, illustrates the streamline mode. It includes nautical motifs such as porthole windows, hatch-like doorways, and offices reached by way of a "promenade deck."

A particularly rich body of Art Deco work can be found at Miami Beach, Florida, where the international idiom was fused with a local color palette and adapted to the subtropical climate (Fig. 15.43). These modestly scaled buildings are painted in vivid pinks, greens, peaches, and lavenders that would be garish inland but are delightful here, and are often outfitted with strongly horizontal sunscreens and balconies and punctuated with dramatically vertical entry

15.40 Richmond Shreve, William Lamb, and Arthur Harmon, Empire State Building, New York City, 1931.

This building would be famous even if the only popular image of it were King Kong batting at airplanes from its summit.

15.41 B. Marcus Priteca, Pantages Theater, Hollywood, California, 1929.

Theaters offered an opportunity for flights of fancy. The Art Deco office building was tame compared to outrageous Mayan-, Byzantine-, and Egyptian-inspired environments that were created in buildings where illusion was the principal commodity.

15.42 (above) Robert Derrah, Coca-Cola Bottling Plant, Los Angeles, California, 1936.

A variation on the already diverse Art Deco was the "Streamline Moderne" style. This production facility, with its sleek curves and porthole windows, was actually a remodeling of an existing building.

15.43 Anton Skislewicz, The Breakwater, Miami Beach, Florida, 1939.

The most popular massing compositions for Art Deco buildings in Miami combine several horizontal floors with a tall, central feature, here a hotel sign and stair tower.

bays and stair towers. Decoration includes stock Art Deco motifs such as sunbursts, but extends to local flora and fauna, including the ubiquitous Miami palms and flamingos.

DE STIJL

The De Stijl movement in Holland had two phases, both of them guided by the painter, designer, typographer, critic, writer, and rabble-rouser Theo Van Doesburg (1883–1931). The origins of the movement can be traced to the work of the painter Piet Mondrian (1872–1944) and the architect H.P. Berlage (discussed earlier in this chapter in the context of Dutch Expressionism). Both men sought a modern expression in their work, Berlage through a moralistic search for truth in building and Mondrian through a reductivism that, he believed, would reveal and subject to criticism the essence of early twentieth-century culture. As Dutch Expressionists tended to be extremely figurative and attuned to handicraft means of building production, so De Stijl designers sought in equal and opposite measure to be ultra-rational, abstract, and mechanistic.

An art student in Amsterdam from age twenty, Mondrian moved to Paris in 1911 and was immediately influenced by Cubism. Back in Holland during World War I, he met Theo Van Doesburg, and they founded the journal *De Stijl* (*The Style*) in 1917. Here, Mondrian set out his doctrine of Neo-Plasticism, influenced by the writings of esoteric mathematician-philosoper M.H.J. Schoenmaekers, who believed that the world functioned with absolute regularity and that this regularity could be expressed through "plastic" mathematics. Mondrian returned to Paris and, following his published philosophy, began a gradual process of abstraction that led him to produce frameless panels laid out in grids, with squares and rectangles painted in only the three primary colors.

Berlage was certainly not an abstractionist, but his writings espoused what he considered to be elementary truths: the primacy of space, the wall as the creator of form, and the need for systematic proportions. It was also Berlage who brought Frank Lloyd Wright to the attention of Dutch designers following the publication of his work by Ernst Wasmuth in 1910–11.

In 1921 Van Doesburg began the first phase of De Stijl, which included as participants Mondrian, several other Dutch painters, and the architects Rob van t'Hoff (1887–1979) and J.J.P. Oud (1890–1963). The group advocated the creation of forms that were universal, spatially unbounded, and attuned to modern technology. Van t'Hoff, who had been to Oak Park, produced a house in Huis ter Heide (1916) that is a convincing adaptation of Wright's work, with its strong horizontals, including clusters of windows, and cantilevered roof and floor slabs. Oud, though never fully committed to De Stijl principles,

15.44 J.J.P. Oud, Hook of Holland housing project, Rotterdam, 1924.

The contrast between Oud's housing and that of the Dutch Wendigen designers is almost shocking. Oud had made contact with members of the Dutch De Stijl movement and at the Hook of Holland housing displayed the latter's reductivist desire to de-emphasize applied ornament.

produced a significant body of related work before he returned to a more staid traditionalism later in his career; the early buildings eventually earned him stature as a first-generation European Modernist. His Hook of Holland housing project (1924) (Fig. 15.44), while not very experimental spatially, is highly reductivist, with its long, seemingly extruded white stucco walls on a base of red and yellow brick, large expanses of glass with plain metal window frames, and details painted in primary colors—a remarkable contrast to the work of Kramer and de Klerk of about the same period.

In 1921–22, the roster of De Stijl participants changed significantly, becoming much more international in profile. Mondrian departed, but Van Doesburg remained as the catalyst. New on the scene were the Russian Constructivist El Lissitzky (1890–1941), Friedrich Kiesler (1890–1965) from the Berlin G Group (which included the young Mies van der Rohe), the planner Cor Van Eesteren (born 1897), and the Dutch architect and furniture-maker Gerrit Rietveld (1888–1964). De Stijl work remained abstract and mechanistic, but became more Constructivist and radical in its exploitation of space in three dimensions. A case in point is Kiesler's Cité dans l'Espace (Fig. 15.45), exhibited at the 1925 Exposition des Arts Décoratifs in Paris. Relieved of the responsibility of serving as a conventional building, this was a three-dimensional grid of linear elements suspended in and

15.45 Friedrich Kiesler, Cité dans l'Espace, Exposition des Arts Décoratifs, Paris, 1925.

While only an exhibit piece and not a building, Kiesler's composition succeeds in translating Mondrian's two-dimensional ideas into three dimensions. Kiesler was a member of De Stijl in its later stages, when it had reached out to German and Russian designers.

15.46 Gerrit Rietveld, Red-Blue Chair, 1917–18.

This chair is still produced. Its apparent construction from discrete elements explains Rietveld's description of his work as "Elementarism."

organizing infinite space. Likewise, in 1923 Van Eesteren and Van Doesburg collaborated on studies for a house in which they used axonometric drawings and a model by Rietveld to show planar spatial compositions in neutral space affected only minimally by any form of context, including gravity. In his furniture designs, Rietveld developed his own idiom, called Elementarism, in which he so assembled individual elements that each maintained its individual integrity, and the completed assembly made clear the entire process of construction. His much celebrated Red-Blue Chair (1917–18) (Fig. 15.46) is still in production today. Rietveld's Schroeder House in Utrecht (1924) (Fig. 15.47) is most often cited as the quintessential De Stijl building, but it is limited by the realities of habitation. From the exterior, it looks like one of Van Eesteren and Van Doesburg's house compositions: planes in various orthogonal orientations intersecting and interconnected by linear steel sections. The interior (Fig. 15.48) is somewhat disappointing—very open, dominated by linear, Elementarist components and primary colors, but hardly an investigation of infinite space as defined by Mondrian.

15.47 Gerrit Rietveld, Schroeder House, Utrecht, 1924.

It is not hard to imagine the shock felt by neighbors in their traditional brick houses when this unfamiliar composition appeared on their street. It had been some twenty years since Adolf Loos first stripped a house of its applied ornamentation.

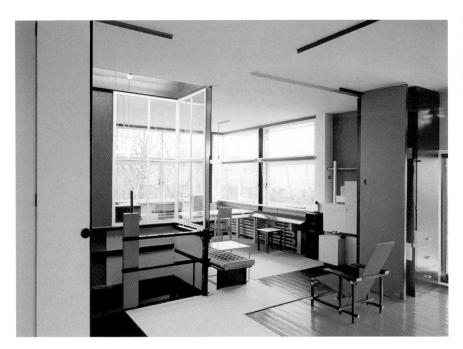

15.48 Gerrit Rietveld, Schroeder House interior, Utrecht, 1924.

Such an interior shows that it was not easy to translate Mondrian's paintings or Van Doesburg's planar compositions into liveable spaces. There is, however, a rigor and, not apparent here, a palette of primary colors like those preferred by Mondrian.

EXPLOITING THE POTENTIAL OF CONCRETE

The development of the open plan depended ultimately on the availability of materials that could be used for post-and-beam structural systems with **moment connections** between columns and beams or slabs. Just as the development of metal-frame construction was one of the major engineering contributions of the nineteenth century, the development of reinforced concrete has been an important aspect of twentieth-century engineering. Although the idea of reinforcing concrete with metal rods originated in the late nineteenth century, the technique was not extensively exploited for building construction until the twentieth century.

Robert Maillart (1872–1940), a Swiss engineer, explored the possibilities of the material. He developed a construction system of mushroom or flared columns supporting flat slabs, thus eliminating the need for beams, and used it most notably in a warehouse in Zurich, Switzerland (1910). An American engineer, Claude A.P. Turner, independently developed the same idea and applied it in the construction of the Johnson-Borey Building in Minneapolis (1905–06); he obtained a patent on the system in 1908. Maillart is perhaps more famous for his reinforced concrete bridges, which combined load-bearing arches and the horizontal surface of the roadway in a unified design. His Tavanasa Bridge of 1905 (destroyed by a landslide in 1927) was the first to use this integration of parts, and he developed the theme further in later works, most notably the Salginatobel Bridge of 1930 (Fig. 15.49) near Schiers in eastern Switzerland. The bridge carries a small mountain road across a narrow valley, spanning 293 feet between steep sides. Maillart

designed it as a three-hinged concrete arch, so the structure can rotate in response to small movements in the abutments. Also impressive is his design for the Schwandbach Bridge (1933), where a curved roadbed with arched supports is built in concrete slabs to create a graceful structure that appears to leap effortlessly across an alpine

15.49 Robert Maillart, Salginatobel Bridge, near Schiers, 1930.

Engineering projects interested many early Modernists because they showed that function, materials, and construction methods alone could sometimes produce exceptional forms. Such is the case with Robert Maillart's ferroconcrete bridges; this one appears to leap across the valley.

merging into base foundations. Maillart also used naturalistic forms in his expressive lines, for the full plastic potential of concrete is not realized in the limiting shapes of traditional square or circular columns, beams, and slabs. Even where the conventions of flat floors had to be maintained, Maillart often found ways to articulate the structural load-bearing functions, as in his customs warehouse at Chiasso, Italy, where the columns branch out to ribs, which in turn support trusses similar in structure to leaves.

In France Auguste Perret (1874–1954) built numerous apartment houses, commercial buildings, and churches, such as Notre Dame, Le Raincy (1922–23) (Fig. 15.50), in reinforced concrete. His earliest notable work was the Paris apartment house at 25 bis Rue Franklin (1902), in which the concrete frame allows an irregular disposition of rooms to reflect the fact that the walls are not load-bearing (Fig. 15.51). This same freedom is reflected in the

15.50 Auguste Perret, Notre Dame interior, Le Raincy, 1922–23.

Auguste Perret was a pioneer in the architectural use of ferroconcrete. Here thin columns support a low-slung longitudinal vault and short transverse ones, all surrounded by a lattice-like enclosing skin.

15.51 Auguste Perret, 25 bis Rue Franklin, Paris, 1902.

Perret's clever design replaced the conventional Parisian interior light-well with a U-shaped plan that increased the percentage of daylight-lit walls. He cast ornament into the building's concrete skin.

ravine. The curved roadbed allows uninterrupted traffic flow, and the design took into account the torsion loads created by moving vehicles on the curving slab.

After designing the reinforcing bars to counter the stress of various loads, Maillart allowed the concrete to follow the shape of the internal steelwork. Thus, the form of the concrete responded to the internal structural forces, resulting in long, diminishing horizontal slabs, with vertical slabs that taper in height and broaden out again before

15.52 Pier Luigi Nervi, Palazzetto dello Sport, Rome, 1960.
Like Maillart, Nervi allowed the logical and efficient use of his building materials to produce memorable forms. In Nervi's *ferro-cemento* process, lightweight precast units were sprayed into their shapes without the need for complex wooden formwork.

disposition of the windows, which are closer together than would be possible in a structure with load-bearing walls. In response to neighbors' complaints about the "rudeness" of the material, the exterior concrete was scored to resemble stone. The young Le Corbusier worked for Perret and gained from him his interest in and knowledge of reinforced concrete, a material he would use extensively throughout his career.

Another Frenchman, Eugène Freyssinet (1879–1962), explored in his work the techniques of pre-stressed and post-tensioned concrete construction. Pre-stressed concrete involves stretching the reinforcing bars before pouring the concrete, so that when the concrete has set and the jacks maintaining the tension are released, the beam or girder has greater compressive and tensile strength. Post-tensioning has much the same effect, except that the reinforcing here is stretched after the concrete has been poured, and the steel cables (which pass through hollow cores in the concrete) are then restrained. Freyssinet is most famous for his two airship hangars at Orly near Paris (1916), which were constructed on a parabolic section with a folded surface and provided a clear height of over 200 feet. Freyssinet also constructed numerous bridges.

Pier Luigi Nervi (1891–1975) and Felix Candela (born 1910) have been the most innovative architect-engineers of our own day working in reinforced concrete. Nervi built an impressive array of concrete structures, beginning with the Municipal Stadium in Florence (1929–32), which has a dramatic cantilevered shell roof over the grandstand. Following the approach of Maillart, Nervi allowed his concrete shapes to reflect internal stresses, so that the edge of the grandstand tapers to respond to the reduction in loading. In 1935 Nervi won a competition to build aircraft hangars for the Italian air force. The program required a clear interior space measuring 330 by 135 feet and an opening 165 feet wide on the long side. Models were built to test Nervi's almost intuitive structure, which could not then be calculated accurately. It involved a thin-layer ribbed vault, analogous to the thin gill structure on the underside of a mushroom, with concrete struts supporting hollow tiles on the roof. (Later hangars employed a similar system with all the elements of precast concrete.) Buttresses extend from the corners to counter the thrust of the roof vault, and box beams span the entrances from one buttress to the next.

After World War II, Nervi experimented with what he termed *ferro-cemento*, a method of construction that involved spraying cement mortar on a form made of fine mesh steel (like chicken wire). Only slightly more than an inch of cement thickness was required to produce a strong structure. Nervi built himself a yacht hull this way and demonstrated its application to buildings in a warehouse for Rome (1945). In his later works, he used *ferro-cemento* for large-span factories, sports facilities, and exhibition halls, where lightweight precast units were sprayed into shape without any need for complicated wooden formwork. The lacy roof of the Palazzetto dello Sport (1960), erected for the Rome Olympics, was created this way (Fig. 15.52).

In contrast, the work of the Mexican engineer Felix Candela (born 1910) has concentrated on the structural possibilities of the hyperbolic paraboloid, a surface of double curvature for which it is difficult to calculate precise structural behavior. Candela has experimented with the form in a series of designs for churches, warehouses, factories, and commercial buildings, basing his buildings on a standard single hyperbolic paraboloid supported at opposite corners or on a grouping of four of these into a monolithic umbrella supported on a central post.

TONY GARNIER AND THE INDUSTRIAL CITY

Tony Garnier, a designer in reinforced concrete, is most famous today for his industrial city scheme. Garnier (1869–1948) was an excellent student at the Ecole des Beaux-Arts. In 1897 he came in second in the Grand Prix

de Rome competition, and in 1899 he won the prize with a design for "A State Bank" that is still recognized as a model of Beaux-Arts planning and composition (Fig. 15.53). During his four-year residence at the French Academy in Rome, Garnier began to turn away from the classical ideal espoused by the Ecole, much to the distress of academic officials, who refused to accept the drawings, required annually of all scholars in Rome, that he began to submit. In 1900 Garnier wrote: "Since all architecture rests on false principles, the architecture of antiquity was an error. TRUTH ALONE IS BEAUTIFUL. In architecture, truth is the product of the calculations made to satisfy known needs with known means." For a graduate of the Ecole des Beaux-Arts, this was nothing short of heresy. To satisfy academy requirements in Rome, Garnier embarked on academic reconstruction studies of the ancient city of Tusculum, southeast of Rome, and, for his own interest, he made plans for an ideal town that he called "La Cité Industrielle."

He chose an imaginary site for the town (Fig. 15.54a). The industrial quarter would be in a valley beside a river, laid out in orthogonal streets and provided with rail and waterway connections. A convenient ridge above would hold the residential and commercial districts, again deployed in an orderly grid, with a monumental civic open space surrounding the important governmental and cultural buildings in the city center. Greenery would be interspersed with houses in the residential sectors, for a building there would be permitted to cover only 50 per cent of the lot. The single-family houses would be small and detached, with Roman atria and unornamented walls, flat roofs with garden terraces, and simple features (Fig. 15.54b). Construction would, of course, be in concrete, and Garnier emphasized hygienic aspects with such features as concave moldings between floors and walls to eliminate the corners where dirt could accumulate. Sunlight and fresh air would penetrate all interior spaces. In theory, the strict zoning of industry (Fig. 15.54c) to the lowlands would keep its noises and odors away from the civic center, although having only a single winding road connecting the industrial sector to the city proper would have insured traffic congestion.

Garnier's work was substantially complete in 1904, but he did not publish his Cité Industrielle designs until 1917, by which time he had supplemented them with designs of actual projects he had constructed as city architect for Lyon. The great importance of his theoretical project lay in the fact that an architect had actually bothered to consider

15.53 Tony Garnier, Grand Prix de Rome competition plan for "A State Bank," 1899.

Tony Garnier's plan follows the Ecole des Beaux-Arts precepts of hierarchy and multi-axial organization. The central feature at the crossing of the principal longitudinal and transverse axes is the tellers' cages.

Hospitals   City Center   Train station   Industrial area

15.54a Tony Garnier, Plan of La Cité Industrielle, 1904–19.

North of the river with its hydroelectric plant are the two sections of the town separated by the rail line. The section to the right is industrial, while the section to the left is residential and commercial and includes a civic center with major buildings and open spaces.

15.54b (below and right) Tony Garnier, Plan and view of residences in La Cité Industrielle, 1904–19.

Garnier designed every building in the town. All were to be built in concrete with a minimum of ornamentation. Each detached house has an atrium and roof garden.

15.54c (below) Tony Garnier, View of the industrial sector of La Cité Industrielle, 1904–19.

Garnier envisioned an industrial city that would be so benign as to need no jails or law courts. While this may have been naïve, his early embracing of industry as a design determinant was not.

the design of an industrial town at all, for the subject was not a common one among designers of his day. Stressing healthful surroundings, the Cité Industrielle connects back to Ledoux's ideal industrial town of Chaux and forward to much housing subdivision construction in the twentieth century. In its use of concrete for residential buildings, Garnier's designs anticipate the work of Le Corbusier, who would also employ flat roofs with garden terraces.

LE CORBUSIER

Charles Edouard Jeanneret-Gris, better known as Le Corbusier, is remembered for his architectural mastery of form and light. Le Corbusier (1887–1965) was born in the Swiss watchmaking town of La Chaux-de-Fonds, and he received his formal art instruction in the local arts and crafts school, which trained its students to do fancy engraving for watch cases. Recognizing his artistic talents, his teachers encouraged him to consider more ambitious goals than a job in the watch industry. His architectural education came from experience garnered in the offices of Auguste Perret (1908–09) and Peter Behrens (1910), sandwiched between sketching travels throughout the Mediterranean, including the Greek islands. He returned to La Chaux-de-Fonds in 1912, taught in the art school, and designed a few houses.

THE DOM-INO AND CITROHAN HOUSES

From Perret he acquired a firm understanding of reinforced concrete, and from Behrens he learned about designing for industry. He combined these two strains in his first noteworthy project, the Dom-ino House (1914), made in response to the outbreak of World War I. Anticipating that destruction caused by the fighting would increase the demand for rebuilding when hostilities ended, Le Corbusier proposed a mass-produced housing scheme that reduced components to a minimum: floor slabs, regularly spaced piers for vertical support, and stairs to connect the floors (Fig. 15.55). Inherent in the design was the possibility of factory fabrication of these parts near the construction site and rapid erection of the frame by crane. The subdivision of the interior and precise

15.55 Le Corbusier, Dom-ino House, 1914. Drawing.

With this system, Le Corbusier separated structure from enclosure. The results were the free plan, with its flexible distribution of walls, and the free façade, which could take on any desired configuration.

weatherproof enclosure (the walls) of the exterior would be left to the discretion of the builders so that local preferences could be observed.

In 1916 he moved to Paris. It was at this time that he adopted the pseudonym of Le Corbusier, a name taken from his mother's family, for his architectural projects. (He continued to paint under his given name.) With the war still raging, there was not much work for an unknown young Swiss architect, and Le Corbusier occupied his time with painting, writing, and drawing projects. In 1920 he and the poet Paul Dermée began a small journal, *L'Esprit nouveau* (*The New Spirit*), which covered all the visual arts, music, and the esthetics of modern life in its three years of publication. A collection of Le Corbusier's essays on architecture that first appeared in the pages of *L'Esprit nouveau* was reprinted as a book, *Vers une architecture* (translated as *Toward a New Architecture*) in 1923. In it Le Corbusier's tendency for poetic overstatement is indulged in the best traditions of Romanticism, and the book is still illuminating to read for the flavor it gives of the arts in Paris during the early 1920s. "Architecture is the masterly, correct, and magnificent play of masses brought together in light," he

15.56 Le Corbusier, Citrohan House, 1922. Drawing.

This house's name was a play on words taken from the Citroën automobile and connecting it to Le Corbusier's conception of a "machine for living." The largely blank lateral bearing walls show that it was really envisioned as one unit within a multi-unit block.

proclaimed, as he endorsed the design of buildings based on the esthetics of the machine. In anticipation of eventual mass-production on a modular basis, he also advocated the use of dimensions derived from both a Golden Section-based system of proportions and the size of an average man, for all elements in a building.

Among the projects illustrated in *Vers une architecture* was the Citrohan House (1922), Le Corbusier's attempt to design a modest dwelling that would be as affordable as the Citroën automobiles then being manufactured in France (Fig. 15.56). The house is built of reinforced concrete, raised off the ground by piers or **pilotis**, with a garage and service-storage rooms on the lowest level. The second floor, in the tradition of the piano nobile, has the living and dining rooms, maid's room, and kitchen; the third floor has the master bedroom overlooking the two-story living room; and children's rooms and a roof garden fill the fourth level. Many of Le Corbusier's later houses would incorporate a two-story living room with overlooking balcony. Fenestration consists of simple punched openings filled with industrial windows that divide the exterior into horizontal bands extending continuously with little regard for the location of interior partitions.

THE VILLA STEIN AND THE VILLA SAVOYE

Later in the decade, Le Corbusier was given the opportunity to build a number of modest and not-so-modest houses, putting his design theories into practice. At Garches he designed the Villa Stein (1927) (Fig. 15.57). As with the Citrohan House, the main living floor is at the piano-nobile level, and the roof becomes an elegant terrace. The regularly spaced structural piers permit freely curving interior partitions, while continuous bands of horizontal windows extend across both the north and south façades. (The end elevations are largely blank, for Le Corbusier was considering this as a prototype for rather narrow suburban lots, where the neighboring houses would create party walls.) The major building proportions were based on Palladio and determined by the Golden Section, the "regulating traces" being included in the published elevation drawings.

More expressive was the Villa Savoye (1929–31) at Poissy, outside Paris (Figs. 15.58–15.60), designed as a weekend house for an art-loving family. The curving ground-floor wall is determined by the turning radius of the motor car that would convey the family here from Paris. The driveway extends under the house, between the pilotis, and continues past the main entrance to a three-car garage and the maid's quarters. From the ground-level entrance hall the visitor has the choice of climbing the sculptural stair or ascending the ramp (which links all three levels) to the second floor. Here, from the main living floor, one obtained an unobstructed view over the clearing in which the house sits to the forested hills enclosing the site. The large living room is separated by an enormous sliding glass door from the exterior patio and the ramp that continues to the upper level terrace with its sculptural windscreen walls. The appearance of regularity is carefully maintained on the exterior. All four elevations are essentially identical, consisting of a ribbon of windows and openings running the width of the façade at the second-floor level, supported by regularly spaced pilotis. In fact, the house is a good deal more complex than this simple exterior skin implies, for a close study of the plan reveals that the structural system is *not* a regular grid, as both Le Corbusier's theoretical writings and the façade would lead one to believe. Regular spacing would have made it next to impossible to park cars in the garage, and it would have inconvenienced interior spaces on the second floor as well. Nevertheless, Le Corbusier scrupulously avoided having interior partitions coincide with columns.

Le Corbusier's choice of interior finishes and fittings reflects his enthusiasm for industrial products and his admiration for the functional aspects of oceanliners. The entrance hall alone has unglazed ceramic tile flooring; simple pipe rails, painted black; a pedestal washbasin,

15.57 Le Corbusier, Plans of the Villa Stein, Garches, 1927.

Here are the results of the dom-ino system in a suburban villa. The walls do not necessarily align with the column bays, and the perimeter wall can be penetrated at any point. The ground floor is at the far right.

Coupe en travers

15.58 (above) Le Corbusier, Plans of and section through the Villa Savoye, Poissy, 1929–31.

The three free-plan floor layouts (ground floor at the right) have almost no correspondence to one another. Continuity is provided by the columnar structural system and by the ramp—an extension of the accomplishments of Adolf Loos.

15.59 (right) Le Corbusier, Villa Savoye, Poissy, 1929–31.

This view reveals the thin enclosing planes made possible by Le Corbusier's dom-ino system of columns and floor slabs.

15.60 (below) Le Corbusier, Villa Savoye interior, Poissy, 1929–31.

The dining area (right) and the living area (left) form a single, long, narrow space lit by continuous strip windows.

freestanding in the hallway; and industrial light fixtures, directed upward to provide reflected light. Skylights, painted intense blue, provide softly colored light reflecting off the white wall surfaces on the second floor, where the master bath has a particularly famous lounging recliner and tub in ceramic tiling. The artful incorporation of varied spatial experiences and light within a simple geometric container testifies to the mastery of form Le Corbusier had achieved by 1930.

THE CITÉ UNIVERSITAIRE AND LE CORBUSIER'S "FIVE POINTS"

At the Cité Universitaire of Paris, Le Corbusier was commissioned to design a dormitory for Swiss students, the Swiss Pavilion (1930). Here the four-story rectangular block of dormitory rooms is raised on the inevitable pilotis to provide a covered entrance for the lower block of common rooms, articulated separately in a sculptural free curve. Rather than using a uniform white finish for all surfaces, Le Corbusier allowed each material to express its own character. The concrete was unpainted and left with the board markings of the formwork, and natural stone was laid in random rubble on the exterior and interior end wall of the common room. Similarly, the varied functions of the two sides of the dormitory block received different expressions: small punched openings illuminated the corridor on each floor, and a window-wall of glass provided unrestricted views from each dormitory room.

Inherent in the Swiss dormitory were concepts of high-rise living that can be found in Le Corbusier's city-planning schemes dating back to 1922. His city of the future involved the construction of widely spaced towers, each allowing the apartment-dwellers within to receive sunlight and fresh air, away from the dirt and noise of the typical urban street. Le Corbusier seems never to have appreciated the social function of the street, where crowds and varied sights, sounds, and smells contribute to the essence of urban life. A romantic individualist, Le Corbusier preferred solitude and natural surroundings, so he provided his buildings with rooftop gardens and raised them off the ground on pilotis, leaving the terrain unobstructed for recreational facilities or parks. By 1926 he had articulated his "Five Points Toward a New Architecture:"

1. The supports (*pilotis*) are precisely calculated, spaced regularly, and used to elevate the first floor off the damp ground.
2. The flat roof or roof garden is used for domestic purposes such as gardening, play, and relaxation—thereby recovering all the built-upon ground for outdoor activities.
3. The interior walls, independent of the support system, can be arranged in a free plan.
4. The horizontal windows, made possible by the support system, assure even illumination from wall to wall and admit eight times as much light as a vertically placed window of equal area.
5. The façade, also independent of the structural supports, can be freely designed.

Some of these points are not logical. Concerning point 4, for example, the amount of light coming through a given area of glass is the same regardless of window orientation, but other conditions in the room, such as color and reflective surfaces, do have a great deal to do with the spatial effect of light in a room. It is also unlikely that the rooftop recreations advocated in point 2 would be equivalent to what was possible on the ground. All the points taken together, however, defined a new esthetic for building design, which Le Corbusier followed in most projects until the mid-1950s. His later works will be treated with contemporary developments later in this chapter.

WALTER GROPIUS

Prior to World War I, thoughtful architects and designers in the United States, England, Austria, Italy, France, and Scotland were struggling with the problem of finding an esthetic expression appropriate to the industrial world. The war brought a temporary halt to these investigations, but shortly after the termination of hostilities, an approach to the vexing problem of industrial production and artistic expression was proposed by the founding of the Bauhaus, a new school of design in Weimar, Germany. Its students, faculty, methods of teaching, and designs were to define the Modern Movement that spread worldwide.

BUILDING DESIGNS

Walter Gropius, the founder of the Bauhaus, was unusual among the masters of the Modern Movement in being the product of a thoroughly academic architectural education at the universities of Berlin and Munich. The son of an architect, Gropius (1883–1969) obtained valuable practical experience from 1907 to 1910 in the office of Peter Behrens and then set up an independent practice with Adolf Meyer (1881–1929). Their first major project, the Fagus Shoe-Last Factory at Alfeld-an-der-Leine (1911), is still considered a landmark in the history of modern architecture because it used elements that later characterized the International Style: glass curtain walls between expressed steel supports, corners left free of solid masonry, and simple rectangular massing with a flat roof (Fig. 15.61). Having received the commission after a previous designer had already begun construction on the complex, Gropius gave most attention to one wing of the factory, where he was able to express his ideals most clearly.

Like Behrens, Gropius was a member of the Werkbund. For its exhibition in Cologne in 1914, Gropius and Meyer

15.61 Walter Gropius and Adolf Meyer, Fagus Shoe-Last Factory, Alfeld-an-der-Leine, 1911.

Gropius and Meyer did not intend to create a new style with their rigorously functional esthetic. However, the strips of steel-frame windows and related spandrels and flat roofs created a type used in the United States not only for factories but also for schools and even gas stations.

designed a model factory to demonstrate the possible architectural expression of a hypothetical manufacturing plant with an attached office block. In consultation with local industry, Gropius devised the building's program to answer the needs of a medium-sized business. The rear of the office block was a glass curtain wall, which extended dramatically around the sides and around the circular stair towers on the front corners, while the front façade was windowless and clad with limestone made to look like brick. Symmetry governed the entire ensemble; the central entrance was placed on axis; and the stair cylinders were overshadowed by tower elements containing roof-level dancefloors connected by a covered restaurant. Separating the office block from the manufacturing plant was a large open courtyard, which led axially to the industrial area, a large basilican hall, itself divided into thirds by the supports for its double-pitched skylit roof. It was far more daring and complex than anything that had yet been constructed for German industry. Significantly, Gropius derived several of his design ideas from the European publication of Frank Lloyd Wright's work. The courtyard side of the office block, for example, relies on the elevation of the Mason City Hotel (1909) in Iowa, and the rooftop recreational facilities of the Larkin Building inspired similar provisions in the Cologne factory. On the strength of this design, the Grand Duke of Sachsen-Weimar-Eisenach asked Gropius to assume direction of the ducal arts and crafts school.

THE BAUHAUS IN WEIMAR AND DESSAU

The outbreak of World War I delayed implementation of the Grand Duke's invitation as Gropius served from 1914 to 1918 in the German army on the western front. At the conclusion of the war the German nobility lost their domains, but the Grand Duke's offer was renewed by the new civic authorities, and in 1919 Gropius combined the former Grossherzoglich Sachsen Weimarische Hochschule für Angewandte Kunst (Ducal School of the Applied Arts) and the Grossherzoglich Kunstakademie (Ducal Art Academy) in Weimar into the Staatliches (State, or Public) Bauhaus Weimar. (Bauhaus can be literally translated as "House of Building.")

In joining the former ducal arts and crafts school with the fine-arts academy, Gropius created a new institution dedicated to training students in all aspects of design. In the early years most of the faculty were painters from Berlin and Vienna whom Gropius had known before the war. Dominant at the beginning was the Viennese painter Johannes Itten, who taught the *vorkurs*, or introductory course. Itten's radical, anti-authoritarian philosophy, austere lifestyle, and eccentric mode of dress spread to the students and eventually created friction with the community. The model used for organizing the curriculum was the medieval guild: students were called apprentices and graduated with journeyman's certificates. Gropius was firmly convinced that fine art came through mastery of craft, and he arranged the teaching program so that students were given manual instruction in one of the many craft workshops (wood, metal, weaving, pottery, mural painting) and were led in theoretical studies in principles of form by separate instructors, most often painters. As Gropius wrote in an essay in 1923:

> By depriving handicrafts and industry of the informing services of the artist, the academies drained them of their vitality, and brought about the artist's complete isolation from the community. Art is not one of those things that may be imparted. Whether a design be the outcome of knack or creative impulse depends on individual propensity. But if what we call art cannot be taught or learnt, a thorough knowledge of its principles and of sureness of hand can be. Both are as necessary for the artist of genius as for the ordinary artisan.

Gropius, himself a product of the European academic system of architectural education, saw the curriculum of the Bauhaus as a sharp break with Beaux-Arts training, and he had harsh words for the older methods:

> The besetting vice of the academy schools was that they were obsessed by that rare "biological" sport, the commanding genius; and forgot that their business was to teach drawing and painting to hundreds and hundreds of minor talents, barely one in a thousand of whom could be expected to have the makings of a real architect or painter. In the vast majority of cases, this

A RUSSIAN PAINTER AT THE BAUHAUS

by Jay C. Henry

15A Wassily Kandinsky, *Accent in Pink*, 1926. Musée National d'Art Moderne, Centre Georges Pompidou, Paris.

Abstraction has been a fundamental principle of twentieth-century art, and with the exception of Pablo Picasso, Wassily Kandinsky stands as the most influential abstract artist of the century. Picasso, however, never totally eschewed representation. *Les Demoiselles d'Avignon* (1907) and *Guernica* (1937) remain images with narrative themes. Conversely Kandinsky, by the time he was teaching at the Bauhaus (1922–33), had evolved to the point of total abstraction. *Accent in Pink* (Fig. 15.A) represents nothing but itself—it is pure form and color. And one can appreciate why a painter who viewed art as pure form without extrinsic content would be a valued teacher at a school like the Bauhaus where design was taught as an abstract discipline. It is this rapprochement between an international abstract art and an international modern architecture that makes the Bauhaus and its extraordinary faculty so vitally relevant to the history of twentieth-century design.

Wassily Kandinsky was born in Russia in 1866, making him a contemporary of Frank Lloyd Wright (born 1869) and other figures of the first Modernist generation. His early interest in Russian folk art establishes a common context with national Romantic movements elsewhere in Europe. In 1896 he moved to Munich to study art, where he fell under the influence of the arts and crafts wing of the German Jugendstil. This exposure to William Morris's ideas—for instance, that craftsmanship and design were just as much fine arts as painting, sculpture, and architecture—may have conditioned Kandinsky's ultimate role as teacher in the century's most important design school. Unlike Behrens or Van de Velde, who matured in the same Jugendstil environment, Kandinsky remained fundamentally a painter, and in 1913 he joined the Blaue Reiter group of German Expressionists and published his essay "On the Spiritual in Art" ("Über die Geistliche in der Kunst"), one of the most influential twentieth-century treatises on art. It argued, among other things, that form and color convey emotional and spiritual values beyond mere representation of images.

As an enemy alien, Kandinsky was forced to return to Russia in 1914 and eventually took up a teaching position in one of the new Soviet art schools of the early 1920s, establishing connections with Constructivists. In 1922 he returned to Germany on a visit and accepted Walter Gropius's invitation to teach at the Bauhaus, where he remained until the school's dissolution in 1933. Fleeing the Nazis, he died in exile in Paris in 1944.

By the time Kandinsky joined the Bauhaus faculty in 1922, Expressionism was a waning influence in German art and architecture. His age and conservative temperament made him something of a father-figure and a stabilizing influence following the departure of the eccentric Expressionist Johannes Itten. Kandinsky joined Paul Klee and László Moholy-Nagy, among other new faculty, and, after 1925, the junior masters Marcel Breuer, Josef Albers, and Herbert Bayer, in the move to Dessau in 1926, where his sixtieth birthday was celebrated with a commemorative exhibition. One of Breuer's seminal pieces of Bauhaus metal-tube furniture, the Wassily chair, was named for him.

15.62 Walter Gropius, Bauhaus, Dessau, 1926.

The plan of this building is a pinwheel, reaching out into space like a Mondrian painting. The workshop wing seen here is a concrete column-and-slab frame enclosed by a glass curtain wall. Considered decadent and expressive of Communist values, the building was shut down by the Nazis in 1932.

hopelessly one-sided instruction condemned its pupils to the lifelong practice of a purely sterile art. Had these hapless drones been given a proper practical training, they could have become useful members of society.

"The ultimate aim of all visual art is the complete building!" Thus began the 1919 prospectus advertising the Bauhaus to students. Through involvement in its workshops, students would become skilled in a craft, learn drawing and painting, and receive instruction in science and theory. It was envisioned that workshop projects would attract outside support, in the form of commissions or production licenses, and that the Bauhaus might soon become self-supporting. Collaboration was stressed from the beginning.

In 1921 Gropius received a commission from Adolf Sommerfeld to design a house, and he saw this as an opportunity to give practical (and paid) experience to some of his apprentices in the woodworking shop. Gropius (with Adolf Meyer) designed the structure, while the Bauhaus apprentices were given a rather free hand to design and furnish the interior. The result was unusual, to say the least. Postwar Germany, saddled with enormous reparation payments to the Allies, had chronic shortages of just about everything. So, to assemble building materials, Sommerfeld, a contractor, purchased a dismantled navy ship for the teakwood it contained, and this wood was used for almost every element. In elevation the house has an affinity with Wright's Winslow House, with due allowance for the peculiarities of its teakwood construction. The interior has been described as "a riot of styles and contemporary clichés," owing to Gropius's encouragement of individual approaches among his students.

As the Bauhaus matured, the thrust of its program, which began with the idea of handicraft as a means to art, shifted to handicraft as a means of making prototypes for industrial production. This adjustment had been made by 1923, in response to three main influences: outside pressure created by growing scandal about flamboyant faculty members and the bohemian lifestyles of the students; the Dutchman Theo van Doesburg's presence and haranguing of these students; and Gropius's own interests in mass production. Moreover, the anticipated support from trade groups or industrial concerns had not materialized, which left the Bauhaus in bad financial straits. If designs could be sold to manufacturers, the income would help alleviate the financial situation. More importantly, in placing emphasis on design for industrial production the Bauhaus had found an appropriate resolution of the relationship of art to the machine. Rather than seeing the two as adversaries, as had Ruskin and the Arts and Crafts movement, the Bauhaus saw the integration of art with mechanized production as the great challenge for the twentieth-century designer, and it organized its teaching to address this issue.

Despite these changes, the position of the school in Weimar became increasingly difficult. Gropius removed the most eccentric members of faculty and requested that the students wear ordinary clothes, but the radio and newspaper attacks on the Bauhaus continued. At Easter in 1925 the progressive mayor of Dessau offered assistance, and the Bauhaus moved to temporary quarters there. By December 1926 the school was established in a new home designed by Gropius in buildings that rank among the finest expressions of the emerging Modern Movement (Fig. 15.62). The reinforced-concrete-frame structures consist of four major elements, arranged freely on the flat site so that there is no "front" in the customary sense. The workshop wing, four stories tall, is the largest mass, containing behind its glass curtain wall the studio spaces for preliminary instruction and workshops for printing, carpentry, dyeing, sculpture, weaving, and wall painting, in addition to exhibition and lecture spaces. A road (added by Gropius) runs through the site beside the workshop building, requiring an enclosed bridge to connect it to the separately administered trade school. In the bridge were administrative offices for the Bauhaus and Gropius's private architectural office. Parallel to the road and extending behind the workshop wing is the low dining hall and auditorium building, equipped with a stage between the two spaces and provided with movable walls for maximum flexibility. Beyond this is a five-story student dormitory with twenty-eight rooms and related facilities.

What made this building complex so remarkable? Several factors can be identified. The asymmetrical, sprawling composition represented a break with the typical monumental disposition employed for educational facilities. Separate articulation was given to each element of the program, resulting in an abstract, sculptural treatment for the whole, and the introduction of a road and bridge reinforced the sense of free-moving space. Bauhaus workshops designed and executed all the interiors, with the metal workshop responsible for lighting fixtures and the tubular steel furniture (designed by Marcel Breuer), the printing workshop for the graphics, and so on. Thus, the building was a total work of art, a unity of architecture and related crafts. Its industrial construction materials, concrete and glass, were employed without ornament, and circulation was clearly expressed in the layout.

Gropius also designed a series of seven dwelling units—one detached house and three duplex houses—for Bauhaus faculty. The duplex units are identical, yet by changing their orientations and making one the mirror image of the other Gropius obtained the effect of three different designs. Thus, standardization was combined with variety. Like the Bauhaus buildings, these houses are flat-roofed and were originally painted white with industrial-looking pipe-rail details on the balconies.

The Bauhaus in Dessau continued to emphasize design for industrial production and licensed a number of products to German manufacturers. Gropius began to offer specific architectural instruction to advanced workshop students, marking the first time building design had been taught in the curriculum. Bauhaus designs, whether for architecture, graphic design, or products, tended to favor primary geometric shapes and solids, coupled with linear elements, to achieve an appearance of simplicity. The forms of finished goods reflected both the nature of the material and the manufacturing process required for fabrication. Although Gropius always denied that there was a Bauhaus "style," there is a strong visual affinity among many of the student projects and faculty designs created there.

These designs became widely known through exhibitions and publications, gaining general acclaim for the school throughout Europe. The facilities in Dessau provided workspace superior to anything the Bauhaus had had in Weimar, and it seemed that the turmoil that had marked the school's early years was past. This was not to be, however. Financial problems, while greatly reduced, were not entirely solved, and the reactionary political forces accompanying the rise of Nazism were gaining strength in the provinces around Dessau. In hopes of diminishing criticism of the Bauhaus, criticism he interpreted as being directed at him personally, Gropius resigned as head of the school in April 1928 and returned to his private architectural practice.

A young architect, Hannes Meyer, was appointed to succeed Gropius. Meyer set about enlarging the architectural program, adding courses in mathematics and engineering and emphasizing through lectures and studio projects the social responsibilities of architects. The other workshops were urged to increase production, and more designs than ever were licensed to industry, bringing increasing royalties to the school. But Meyer also encouraged students to become active in politics, not the wisest counsel in the deteriorating political climate of the time, and in the summer of 1930 the authorities asked him to resign. His replacement was Mies van der Rohe, an architect long active in the Deutscher Werkbund, whose reputation was by then international.

Mies moved to stabilize the school by flatly prohibiting any political activity and insisting on the highest possible standards of work. More powerful political forces were gathering, however, and in 1932 the Nazis gained control of Dessau. One of their first acts was to move against the Bauhaus, which to them symbolized Communism, decadence, and subversion; in October 1932 they closed the school. Shortly afterward Mies managed to reopen the Bauhaus as a private institution in Berlin, but in April 1933 the building was raided by the Gestapo, and it finally closed its doors in July 1933.

LUDWIG MIES VAN DER ROHE

Ludwig Mies van der Rohe (1886–1969) was the son of a stonemason, and he received practical experience in construction from his father, later working as an apprentice in the office of furniture designer Bruno Paul. From 1908 to 1911, Mies worked in the office of Peter Behrens. His early designs as an independent architect show the influence of Schinkel, as can be seen in the projected house for Mrs. Kroller-Müller (1912), which was a symmetrical rectangular solid with a stripped classical colonnade across the front.

After World War I Mies worked on a series of projects that were to have an enormous impact on later architecture even though they were never constructed. The first was a competition entry for an office building above the Berlin Friedrichstrasse station (1919), a twenty-story skyscraper completely sheathed in glass. In 1920–21 Mies carried the concept of a transparent skyscraper a step further in a project for a thirty-story tower, again wrapped entirely in glass, with a highly irregular perimeter and two circular elevator-stair cores. Mies's idea was to capitalize on the varying reflections. The irregular curves of the walls were actually composed of short line segments, representing the width dimension of the curtain-wall panels, so the entire building was to be a highly faceted, shimmering shaft. Its internal structure was provided by reinforced concrete slabs, cantilevered to a thin edge at the outside wall. However, because material science and construction techniques in 1920 were inadequate to construct these designs, the first completely glazed office building was not built until 1950–52: Lever House on Park Avenue in New York City, designed by Gordon Bunshaft of Skidmore,

Owings, and Merrill. Its curtain-wall construction includes horizontal strips of plate glass with dark-green spandrel glass covering the floor construction, both set in stainless-steel frames.

Two other projects from the early 1920s show that Mies was thinking about materials other than glass. His project for a concrete office block (1922) has seven floors, each a great horizontal tray with cantilevers. The height of the tray edge was determined by the vertical dimension of filing cabinets; windows above ran in a continuous horizontal strip in a plane recessed from the outer edge of the concrete. If one recalls the Larkin Building, which had incorporated the same idea on its office floors, one can detect the influences of Wright's Wasmuth publications. The ideas of De Stijl and the free plans and flowing spaces of Wright's early Prairie houses also affected Mies's designs. His 1923 project for a brick country house, with its walls extending as vertical planes out into the landscape, seldom intersecting one another but effectively defining space, is an early example. Some of this freedom would reappear in his 1929 masterpiece, the Pavilion of the Deutscher Werkbund for the International Exposition in Barcelona.

THE BARCELONA PAVILION AND THE TUGENDHAT HOUSE

The Barcelona Pavilion (Figs. 15.63–15.64) has become one of the most celebrated architectural designs of the twentieth century, even though until recently it was known to most people only through photographs, since after the exposition was over, the building was dismantled and its materials sold at auction; a replica of the pavilion has recently been built on the original site. It is a small structure, and unlike most exhibition buildings, it contained no displays. Aside from the stainless-steel tables, stools, and chairs designed by Mies specifically for the building, the only object on view was a sculpture of a dancing girl by Georg Kolbe, carefully placed in a reflecting pool at one end of the building.

The influence of the Barcelona Pavilion derived not from what it contained but from the building itself. Mies intended that it should stand for quality design, materials, and craftsmanship. The design is at once simple and sophisticated. Raised on a low podium, as if to elevate it above the rabble of the fair, the pavilion was a one-story jewel box. Most of its ground plane was occupied by an exterior courtyard, dominated by the large reflecting pool lined with black glass. Eight cruciform columns supported a horizontal roof slab that appeared to hover, independent of the vertical walls (Fig. 15.65). The walls were not incorporated in or aligned with the column grid; in their way,

---

15.63 Ludwig Mies van der Rohe, Barcelona Pavilion, Barcelona, 1929 [1986].

Mies's building was dismantled at the end of the Barcelona exhibition. However, it has recently been rebuilt, using stone from the original quarries, so that Mies's ideas can be personally experienced once again. The image seen here is of the reconstruction of 1986.

15.64 Ludwig Mies van der Rohe, Plan of the Barcelona Pavilion, Barcelona.

Compare this plan to the early work of Frank Lloyd Wright or the dom-ino houses of Le Corbusier. All sought a new means of spatial expression, which was the most significant area of study among twentieth-century Modernists.

0   20 m

0   60 ft

Mies deliberately expressed a separation between structure and enclosure while conforming both to the same orthogonal geometry. The columns were shiny chromium-plated steel; the walls were polished book-matched marble in deep shades of green and red; the floors were Roman travertine; and the onyx and gray-tinted glass contributed to the feeling of taste and luxury. The Barcelona chairs and stools were chrome-plated steel with white kid upholstery. Mies's collaborator, Lilly Reich, shares credit with him for the interior design, particularly for the deep-red velvet curtain that hung over the front glass wall.

Sources for the pavilion's architecture can be identified: Schinkel for the podium and formality of the composition; Wright for the flowing spatial qualities and great horizontal sweep of the roof; and De Stijl for the almost

15.65 Ludwig Mies van der Rohe, Barcelona Pavilion interior, Barcelona, 1929.

While Mies was not a member of De Stijl, his spatial conceptions certainly corresponded to those of the movement. The materials he used were onyx for the floors, marble veneer for the partitions, and stainless steel for the columns.

15.66 Ludwig Mies van der Rohe, Plan of the Tugendhat House, Brno, 1930.

Mies's spatial experiments could be applied to day-to-day living conditions. The family space lies to the top in the plan and is only minimally subdivided. The service spaces are much more enclosed.

15.67 Ludwig Mies van der Rohe, Tugendhat House rear view, Brno, 1930.

The private terrace to the rear is surrounded by a retaining wall of rock-faced masonry. The glass walls offer unobstructed views out into the natural landscape.

abstract composition of solid, void, and line. The masterful integration of these diverse influences into a new architectural synthesis remains the great accomplishment of Mies van der Rohe.

Mies used his concepts from the Barcelona Pavilion in a residential commission of 1930, the Tugendhat House (Fig. 15.66) in Brno, Czech Republic. The same regular grid of chromium-steel cruciform columns supports the roof, and polished slabs of marble serve as walls to define interior spaces in an open plan. Because of the hilly site, the Tugendhat House is two stories, set firmly within a series of terraces cut into the slope; but thanks to its largely glass walls, the predominant view is out to the surrounding landscape (Fig. 15.67). Color on the interior is subdued, confined to the natural hues of the finish materials and a white linoleum floor, so that the changing light and colors of the outside world determine much of the color inside the house.

By the mid-1920s progressive architects in many European countries were working in a manner that reflected a new admiration for industrial materials and products, respect for rational, straightforward architectural expression devoid of applied ornament, and an accompanying interest in the purity of simply geometric forms and planar surfaces. For want of a better term, this is still called the "Modern Movement," although eventually we will need to develop a more descriptive label (perhaps even more than one) to reflect the diverse currents in architectural design since 1920.

THE WEISSENHOF SIEDLUNG AND THE INTERNATIONAL STYLE

In 1925 the Deutscher Werkbund proposed that an exhibition be held in 1927 to demonstrate the latest thinking about housing design, interior fittings, and construction technology. The City of Stuttgart and various materials suppliers contributed land and money for the construction of thirty-three permanent buildings on a hillside on the outskirts of the city. Mies, as vice-president of the Werkbund, was placed in charge of the enterprise; he developed the master plan and contributed the design of a block of flats. With characteristic generosity he invited participation by sixteen leading architects from across Europe, assigning them sites for detached houses, duplexes, or row houses. The permanent buildings became known as the Weissenhof Siedlung (or model housing estate at Weissenhof).

The concept behind the exhibition was to design modestly scaled, modern dwelling units suitable as prototypes for mass production. A variety of approaches were adopted by the individual designers, but it was the elements their designs had in common that were crucial in

15.68 Ludwig Mies van der Rohe, Weissenhof Siedlung blocks of flats, Stuttgart, 1927.

Mies developed the site plan for this exposition and built his apartment block on the highest ground. Notice the mass-produced windows and pipe-rail balconies like those used twenty years earlier by Adolf Loos.

the development of Modernism. All the buildings were painted white; they had "functional" windows that emphasized the horizontal; and almost all had flat roofs, some with garden terraces. Industrial character was expressed in the cylindrical pipe railings on balconies, the major decorative element on the exterior. Window trim was minimal, and there were no cornices. In a manner recalling the Cité Industrielle of Garnier, Mies had originally planned to keep cars on the perimeter, with only pedestrian access to the housing area; but the city authorities, who wanted to resell the units as individual dwellings after the exhibition, requested that the land be divided into plots with separate access. Mies was able to retain his basically sculptural conception of the overall form of the site, with the tallest and largest building, his own four-story block, set on the highest portion of the hill (Fig. 15.68).

Mies's building included standard elements—a kitchen-bathroom core, prefabricated partitions, and storage walls—that allowed each of the twenty-four units to be arranged differently in plan. Standardization and rational planning, together with a steel frame, made this flexibility possible. The roof terrace provided recreational facilities, and each apartment has a small balcony. Horizontal strip windows facilitated cross ventilation for each dwelling unit.

Walter Gropius built two detached houses, but neither remains. Continuing the approach being studied at the Bauhaus, he designed in close collaboration with several manufacturers, and both houses were constructed entirely of prefabricated panels. The module of the panels could readily be seen inside and out, and the interior was furnished with the products designed by Marcel Breuer and produced in the Bauhaus workshops. It is interesting to note that, after coming to the United States in 1937, Gropius continued his interest in prefabricated housing but failed to interest American manufacturers in the idea. When he built his own home at Lincoln, Massachusetts (1938), in collaboration with Breuer, Gropius turned instead to the building components already available in light-industrial construction and artfully incorporated them as the major elements of the house.

Le Corbusier also contributed two designs, one a single-family dwelling in reinforced concrete and the other a duplex with a steel frame (Fig. 15.69), a realization of the Citrohan concept. The latter was one of the most controversial structures at the exhibition, in part because of its unorthodox interior proportions. The main circulation spine is a corridor that runs the length of the house,

15.69 Le Corbusier, Weissenhof Siedlung housing unit, Stuttgart, 1927.

Le Corbusier composed his housing unit using by-now-familiar elements: supporting columns or pilotis, an unornamented façade, horizontal strip windows, and a roof garden.

with dimensions and windows that suggested a train more than a residence, particularly as some bedrooms were narrow, like the sleeping compartments of European trains. Le Corbusier was, in fact, fascinated by the functional designs of oceanliners and airplanes, so it is possible that railway cars also inspired his architecture.

The common thread of rational or functional design could be detected in all buildings at the Weissenhof Siedlung, and the projects of German architects were not dissimilar in appearance to those produced by designers from other countries. This esthetic affinity and a book, *Internationale Architektur* (1925) by Walter Gropius, led Alfred H. Barr of the Museum of Modern Art in New York to call the modern architecture of the late 1920s the International Style.

European architectural developments were a major focus of the MOMA show (mentioned at the beginning of this chapter) organized by Barr, Henry-Russell Hitchcock, and Philip Johnson in 1932. For the first time the American public and American architects were made aware of postwar advances in Germany, France, Holland, and Belgium, as works like Gerrit Rietveld's Schroeder House were displayed alongside early Wright designs such as the Winslow House, and the abstract rationalism of De Stijl appeared alongside the work of Mies, Gropius, and Le Corbusier.

According to the definition devised by Barr, the International Style was characterized by "emphasis upon volume—space enclosed by thin planes or surfaces as opposed to the suggestion of mass and solidity; regularity as opposed to symmetry or other kinds of obvious balance; and, lastly, dependence upon the intrinsic elegance of materials, perfection, and fine proportions, as opposed to applied ornament." Hitchcock later revised this statement to include the articulation of structure in the place of the point about ornament. Even allowing for this adjustment, it is apparent that the architecture of the Weissenhof Siedlung was succinctly described by Barr's definition.

As an indication of the strength of Beaux-Arts classicism and Art Deco in the United States in the 1920s, only a handful of American buildings were included in Hitchcock and Johnson's book, *The International Style*, which was based on material in the MOMA exhibition. The largest American International Style building included was the Philadelphia Saving Fund Society Building (1929–32) by George Howe (1886–1955) and William Lescaze (1896–1969) (Fig. 15.70). The entire Market Street façade was cantilevered beyond the column line, allowing the windows to wrap in a horizontal band around the corner to glorify the freedom from structural constraint. No towers quite so bold as this would be built in the United States for the next decade, in part because of the Great Depression and World War II. Smaller structures that were built according to the dictates of the International Style, or at least in imitation of it, were often seen as cheap because

15.70 George Howe and William Lescaze, Philadelphia Saving Fund Society Building, Philadelphia, Pennsylvania, 1929–32.

George Howe brought William Lescaze from Europe to inform his office about the new International Style. The vertical articulation masks horizontal strip windows and spandrels.

they lacked presumably expensive ornament or because they were simply bad imitations of the European originals.

LATER WORK OF MIES VAN DER ROHE

By making visible the modern architecture of Europe, the MOMA show did much to increase awareness of the International Style. The impact would be greater still when the leading architects of Germany, fleeing Nazi intolerance of their work (called "Arab" by Hitler), emigrated across the Atlantic. Walter Gropius arrived in 1937, after a period of professional practice in England, to direct the Department of Architecture at the Graduate School of Design at Harvard University; Marcel Breuer, a pupil and teacher at the Bauhaus, also taught under Gropius at Harvard; and Mies van der Rohe came to Chicago in 1938 to head the Architecture School at the Armour Institute of Technology (soon to merge with the Lewis Institute and become the Illinois Institute of Technology [I.I.T.]).

PLANNING AND BUILDING AT I.I.T.

In his twenty years at I.I.T. Mies had the opportunity to plan the new campus, design many of its buildings, and influence the architectural education of a whole generation of students. The curriculum laid down by him stressed clarity, rationality, intellectual order, and discipline, and progressed from building in wood to stone, brick, concrete, and finally steel. Once students understood the materials, they studied problems of design. The highest standards of draftsmanship and precision were expected at all levels, and the essence of architecture was reduced to skin and bones—the glass spandrel panels or brickwork (skin) set in the structural frame (the bones).

The master plan Mies made for I.I.T. reflects the order and rationality of the curriculum. A square grid subdivides the rectangular site, and the buildings are all conceived as rectangular masses conforming to the grid, creating a continuous series of interlocking courtyards and exterior walks. Mies saw that steel was the major American industrial building material (labor costs for formwork often made concrete less economical), so he set about designing the purest, most elegant steel expressions achieved up until that time. For the I.I.T. campus he designed Crown Hall (1956) (Fig. 15.71) to house the School of Architecture. It is a one-story building raised above a high basement. Four deep panel girders straddle the building, supporting the roof and leaving the entire interior free of columns. Except for the stairs and toilet rooms, which are fixed, the possible locations of subdividing walls are not hindered by the architectural container. As in his other projects, Mies was designing for flexibility and change, so that other, unforeseeable uses might easily be accommodated within the building at a later time.

In his office Mies designed a range of other projects. On a beautiful site in downtown Chicago overlooking Lake Michigan, he built a pair of apartment towers known by their address, 860 Lake Shore Drive (1949–51), the first glass-and-steel high-rise residential construction in the United States (Fig. 15.72). Twenty-six stories tall, they are the realization of the concept he first proposed in the glass-tower schemes of 1919-21. During the interval, technological capabilities had come up to the level required to construct a glass tower. The 860 Lake Shore Drive buildings are framed in steel, made fireproof by a masonry casing. Mies was able to express the actual

15.71 Ludwig Mies van der Rohe, Crown Hall, I.I.T. Chicago, Illinois, 1956.

"God is in the details," said Mies. At I.I.T. he demonstrated his mastery of detailing in steel, glass, and brick. The steel skeleton of Crown Hall is completely exposed, including the plate trusses that rise above the roof.

15.72 Ludwig Mies van der Rohe, 860 Lake Shore Drive, Chicago, Illinois, 1949–51.

Notice that Mies designed the blinds to be positioned up, down, or halfway between, and in no other positions. His reductivist mentality made accommodation of individual tastes impossible.

structural material only by welding additional non-structural steel to the exterior of the frames. To increase the vertical appearance of the buildings, thinner I-beams run continuously up the building as window mullions. This exterior steel serves no structural function, of course, but Mies judged it necessary to make the building "look right."

As early as 1946 Mies was at work designing an all-glass house for Dr. Edith Farnsworth, to be located on land near the Fox river in Plano, Illinois. Design and construction took six years, during which time Philip Johnson built a glass house for himself (1949) in New Canaan, Connecticut. The Farnsworth House (1950–52), raised off the ground because the Fox river occasionally flooded the site, sits as a simple white frame in the landscape, as elegant an expression of skin-and-bones architecture as could be imagined (Fig. 15.73). The glass walls can be screened with white curtains when privacy is desired, but the play of light as it reflects off the glass and the immediacy of the natural surroundings viewed through the walls are more effective unscreened. Thus, it is an expression of an architectural ideal rather than a model for everyday family living; it carries the concepts of the Tugendhat House to their logical conclusion, losing in the process a certain degree of practicality.

Mies evolved a thoroughly rational approach to architecture, designing "universal" spaces enclosed in rectangular containers, the most easily used of geometries. From the beginning, he designed with later modification and reuse in mind by making painstaking studies of the exterior architectural expression to ensure a timeless and elegant character. Mies used one of a selection of several steel-framing systems depending on the maximum clear span required. Short spans would use ordinary columns and beams, as in the Farnsworth House, 860 Lake Shore Drive, and the Seagram Building (1958) in New York City (Fig. 15.74); moderate spans would employ plate girders, as in Crown Hall; and the longest spans would have a steel space-frame, as in the Nationalgalerie in Berlin (completed 1968).

The previous discussion of Wright concluded with his design of the Imperial Hotel. While his architectural practice in the 1920s suffered because of his personal difficulties, he did manage to do some work, notably in California. There he built a series of so-called textile-block houses, which were not of cloth but of patterned concrete block, made to his own designs, laid in a stacked bond, and held together by internal steel reinforcing bars. One such house, built in Pasadena for Alice Millard (1923), illustrates the group. The use of concrete block imposed an orthogonal geometry on the design, although Wright, as usual, created an open and flowing plan, with balconies and terraces to link the house to its hillside site. The custom-designed pattern molded into each block contributes an overall texture to the exterior and reinforces the sense of surface integrity in both a structural and an artistic sense. As in Unity Temple and the Imperial Hotel, one can detect influence from Mayan art in the massing and ornamental detail.

Toward the end of the decade, Wright's chaotic private life became more orderly. He was still hounded by the press and pursued by creditors (his home at Spring Green, Wisconsin—Taliesin East—was almost forcibly sold for nonpayment of taxes), but in his third wife, Olgivanna Lazovich, he found a steadying influence. To rescue him from financial pressures, a group of loyal friends incorporated Wright and paid off the mortgages on Taliesin, counting on his future earnings to repay their investment. Wright formed the Taliesin Fellowship in 1932 for young men and women who wished to work under his tutelage, charging them a fee for the experience. It became a highly personal school of architecture, reflecting Wright's disdain for the formal trappings of educational enterprises. Students, called apprentices, participated in all aspects of life and work at Taliesin, from helping with farm and kitchen chores, to constructing the ever-expanding physical plant, to performing in musicals or theatrical events, and even to assisting Wright in the drafting room. With Olgivanna's encouragement, Wright also began to write; the first edition of his *Autobiography* dates from 1932.

BROADACRE CITY

Just as Wright was again becoming a productive architect, the national economy took a nosedive into the Great Depression. There was little work for anyone to do, so Wright and his apprentices turned their attention to a utopian scheme that Wright christened Broadacre City. It illustrated many of Wright's ideals about the proper manner of living in America. The single-family house, set in about one acre of land, was the basic dwelling unit. The urban center was rather small and dispersed, for Wright anticipated that efficient communications and high-speed transportation would largely eliminate the need for the congestion associated with city life and business. (Heavy industry seems to have been conveniently overlooked.) In some respects Broadacre City looked backward to the nineteenth century and to the small, largely agrarian towns that characterized much of the United States then. Small, self-sufficient communities clustered around cultural and recreational facilities conjure up romantic visions of a past that probably never existed. In other respects Wright's scheme was farsighted, for it seemed to incorporate enduring American attitudes: a mistrust of bigness, a love of the land and open air, and the opportunity for individual expression. The phenomenal suburban growth around American cities after 1945 reflects in part the popular interpretation of concepts embedded in Broadacre City.

All of Wright's later buildings were designed to fit into a setting like Broadacre City. For residences, Wright developed the Usonian House as an ideal, and he constructed many actual examples across the country from the mid-1930s until the late 1950s. Usonian houses differed from Prairie houses in several respects. They were generally smaller, reflecting the reduced size of the American family and middle-class budgets, and they were designed for families without household servants. Their designs provided easy access by automobile, and interior activities could be easily supervised from the kitchen, identified as the principal workstation of the housewife. The interior opens up to outdoor spaces away from the street, either to the side or the rear. Wright was a master of site planning, generally managing to locate the house so that it appeared to rise naturally (organically, as he would describe it) from the land.

As has already been mentioned, buildings by Wright were included in the 1932 MOMA show on modern architecture, although not in the book illustrating the International Style. Wright had scathing comments to make about the leading Internationalists and their designs, remarking with a characteristic lack of humility to Henry-Russell Hitchcock, "Not only do I fully intend to be the greatest architect who has yet lived, but the greatest who will ever live. Yes, I intend to be the greatest architect of all time." But by International Style standards, Wright's work in the 1920s was loaded down with fussy detail and excessive ornament. Seeing the 1932 exhibition in New York must have influenced him to a certain degree, for afterward he started to design in a much less ornate way, producing several masterpieces in the 1930s.

FALLINGWATER

One of the young men who came to Taliesin as an apprentice was Edgar Kaufmann, Jr., son of a wealthy Pittsburgh department-store owner. Hearing that his father was contemplating the construction of a vacation house in the mountains of western Pennsylvania, young Edgar

15.75 (above) Frank Lloyd Wright, Edgar Kaufmann House, "Fallingwater," Ohiopyle, Pennsylvania, 1935–37.

A stream runs under the house and the stratified stone walls appear to grow from the landscape as they support cantilevered balconies. Part of Wright's genius was to place the house atop the waterfall rather than situating it on adjacent ground with views to the falling waters.

15.76 (below) Frank Lloyd Wright, Plan of Fallingwater, Ohiopyle, Pennsylvania, 1935–37.

Wright had set out to "break the box" while at work in Oak Park forty years earlier. In this plan, the service spaces are more enclosed to the rear, while the living spaces in front break out dramatically onto the landscape. Compare it to Mies's Tugendhat House plan.

persuaded E.J. Kaufmann, Sr., to employ Wright as architect. The result was Fallingwater (1935–37), perhaps the most famous house not built for royalty anywhere in the world (Figs. 15.75–15.76). (Fallingwater is now open to the public under the trusteeship of the Western Pennsylvania Conservancy.) Wright took the major natural feature of the site, a rocky outcropping where a small stream falls over a series of ledges, and planted the house beside the stream, letting the reinforced concrete balconies cantilever dramatically out over the stream. In order to see the waterfall, one must go outside, below the house, where the falls and the house can be seen together in the classic view that Wright planned, and he did a rendering from just that point to measure the effect before construction.

Stone quarried on the site was laid in irregular horizontal courses to form the four great piers supporting the living room, the fireplace mass, and the remaining bearing walls. The balconies, which form the dominant and dramatic elements of the design, cantilever in two directions and are stiffened at their edges by the upturned parapet wall. Large expanses of glass float between slate floors and stuccoed ceilings, minimizing the distinction between interior and exterior. Fallingwater's planar treatment of surfaces and abstract fragmentation of volumes suggest a debt to the European Modernists. It is cultural historian Lewis Mumford's assessment that, in Fallingwater, Wright "created a dynamic multidimensional composition that made Le Corbusier's buildings seem flat cardboard

compositions." At age sixty-eight, Wright was just beginning his second great period of creativity.

THE JOHNSON WAX COMPANY

Close on the heels of the Kaufmann House came a commission from the Johnson Wax Company of Racine, Wisconsin, for an administration building (1936–39) (Figs. 15.77–15.78a), later completed by a research tower (1946–49) (Fig. 15.78b). Wright's growing interest in circular geometries materialized in this project. The brick walls sweep smoothly around radiused exterior corners, while the interior clerical area is covered by a skylit roof supported on tapering mushroom columns with flaring circular tops. (Skeptical building officials doubted the structural integrity of these columns and required Wright to demonstrate their strength by test-loading a sample before they would issue building permits.) The circular motif continues in balconies, door pulls, and even in the secretarial furniture designed by Wright for the building. Curtain walls in the research tower and connecting

15.77 Frank Lloyd Wright, Johnson Wax Company, Racine, Wisconsin, 1936–39; 1946–49.

This is the other project that propelled Wright's "second" career. His longstanding concern for horizontals is still apparent in this complex built for administration and research. The horizontal windows of the tower are made of Pyrex tubing.

Theater

Great
Workroom

Car parking
below

Tower
above

Lobby

Mezzanine floor

Ground floor

Automobile
entrance

0 ——————— 25 m

0 ——————— 75 ft

N

15.78a Frank Lloyd Wright, Plan of the Johnson Wax Company, Racine, Wisconsin, 1936–39; 1946–49.

Wright's mushroom-shaped columns appear as dotted circles in this plan. These columns are tallest in the grid to the right and create the roof of the main office area or great workroom.

15.78b Frank Lloyd Wright, Plan of and section through the research tower, Johnson Wax Company, Racine, Wisconsin, 1946–49.

The word organic has long been applied to Wright's architecture. This tower's similarity to a tree, with roots, trunk, and branches, is obvious.

0 ——————— 10 m

0 ——————— 30 ft

walkways to the administration building are glazed with glass tubing laid in parallel rows. The light quality achieved is stunning, even though neither the original nor modern sealants have been able to stop all the leaks.

THE GUGGENHEIM MUSEUM AND TALIESIN WEST

Wright continued to explore the possibilities of circular forms, especially those involving continuous ramps. A project for an observatory atop Sugar Loaf Mountain in Maryland (1925) may have first set his mind to the idea, and the concept reappeared in the V.C. Morris Gift Shop (1949) in San Francisco (Fig. 15.79), and in a car park proposed for Pittsburgh. The notion was brought to full realization in the Guggenheim Museum (1957–59) in New York City (Figs. 15.80–15.81), where a quarter-mile-long ramp spirals around a six-story interior sculpture court. The Guggenheim has extensive holdings of twentieth-century art, and it has been suggested that, by designing a museum with a continuously sloping floor and outward leaning, curving walls, Wright was expressing his scorn for modern art. Display possibilities are certainly restricted by the design, and no artist can single handedly compete with the strong three-dimensional spatial experience Wright has created on the interior.

As he grew older, Wright preferred the warm weather of the desert southwest to the cold, blustery Wisconsin

15.79 Frank Lloyd Wright, V.C. Morris Gift Shop, San Francisco, California, 1949.

The splayed entry arch of this one-time glass shop can be compared to the massive stone arches used by H.H. Richardson and to Richardson-influenced arches employed by Wright's mentor, Louis Sullivan.

15.80 Frank Lloyd Wright, Guggenheim Museum, New York City, 1957–59.

The Guggenheim is considered one of the great buildings of the twentieth century. Visitors can take the elevator to the top, then walk down the spiraling ramp; among the problems for art lovers are the limited viewing distance and the constant slope.

15.81 Frank Lloyd Wright, Guggenheim Museum interior, New York City, 1957–59.

This view shows clearly Wright's fascination with geometry; the art housed within the building was incidental. Such circular (as well as triangular, and polygonal) geometries dominated Wright's work in what was the third phase of his long career.

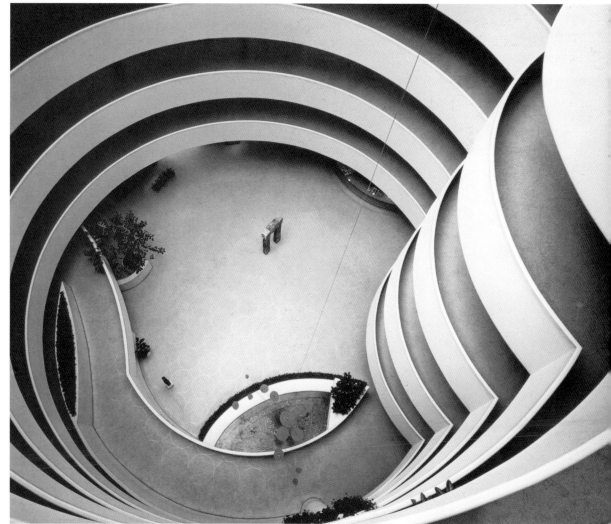

winters, so the Fellowship moved south to avoid the cold, returning to Wisconsin only in the spring. Near Phoenix, Arizona, Wright began construction of Taliesin West (1938 onward), a sprawling encampment set in the rugged spareness of the desert, to replace the wood-and-canvas Ocotillo desert camp dating from 1927. He used materials taken from the locale. He combined adobe and desert boulders, redwood beams, and canvas panels to create a shaded interior that moderated the sun's heat and glare.

LATER WORK OF LE CORBUSIER

Just as Wright designed his later works to fit into Broadacre City, Le Corbusier conceived of his later works as elements of an ideal city he called La Ville Radieuse (The Radiant City). His first opportunity to build an apartment block came after World War II, when the mayor of Marseille invited Le Corbusier to construct the first Unité d'Habitation or Unified Dwelling House (1946–52) (Figs. 15.82–15.83). Some critics consider the Unité a masterpiece, both for its bold sculptural forms and its novel approach to the problems of apartment living. The Unité block is set in a landscaped park and raised on pilotis. The apartments are ingeniously designed to have frontage on both the east and west sides of the building, making

possible cross-ventilation, a desirable trade-off for their long, narrow plans. Balconies, integrated into **brises-soleil** or sunscreens, give each side exterior living space. As a consequence of the apartment design, the elevator stops only on every third floor. The building originally featured a two-story shopping floor (grocery store, beauty shop, repair services, etc.) halfway up, and the roof levels were devoted to extensive recreational and health facilities: a gymnasium, running track, movie theater, health club, nursery school, sun terraces, and the like. The concrete work throughout is forceful. Patterns resulting from the carpentry formwork can be regarded as surface ornament disciplined by the fabrication process. Le Corbusier created the building's proportions using a system that he called "Le Modular," based upon the height of an average person repeatedly subdivided using the Golden Section ratio (approximately 5:8). Ship imagery characterizes the rooftop ventilation stacks, elevator housing, and recreational facilities, for here Le Corbusier could exercise his formal repertoire quite freely. Above all, the concept of sunlight, air, and green open space for all 1600 residents guided the design.

Le Corbusier's critics have pointed out that the scheme is essentially anti-urban, turning its back on the architectural and street patterns of Marseille. Even the provision of shops (which were a financial failure) was attacked,

15.82 Le Corbusier, Unité d'Habitation, Marseille, 1946–52.

Not visible here are the pilotis that support this ferroconcrete structure. The exterior walls are faced with *brises-soleil* that modulate light entering the apartments. The continuous vertical baffles about halfway up and toward the rear shield the ill-fated "shopping street" that was to provide for tenants' every need.

15.83 Le Corbusier, Section through and plans of the Unité d'Habitation, Marseille, 1946–52.

The apartments are obviously very narrow, particularly when they are divided into hall-like bedrooms. The section shows that each unit has a two-story living space with an overlooking balcony.

15.84 Le Corbusier, Axonometric view of Notre-Dame-du-Haut, Ronchamp, 1951–55.

Built as a pilgrimage site for worshipers, Ronchamp (near Belfort, France) has become as much a pilgrimage site for architects and architectural students. The tower lights an altar below. Services can be held inside or held outside on the concrete apron to the left.

because it meant the residents would have little need to associate with the commercial life of the town, and grocery shopping, done daily in France, is a great socializing opportunity. Rather than an affront to Marseille, however, the Unité must be seen as a design in harmony with Le Corbusier's idealized city, a world that was quite different from any existing urban setting.

RONCHAMP AND SAINTE-MARIE-DE-LA-TOURETTE

In the east of France, not far from the Swiss border, Le Corbusier designed a pilgrimage chapel of Notre-Dame-du-Haut at Ronchamp near Belfort, (1951–55) (Figs. 15.84–15.85), to replace a previous church destroyed by artillery fire during World War II. This small building allowed him to give maximum expression to the sculptural possibilities of architectural form. The rationalizations of earlier works were laid aside—no proportional system, no five points, no pilotis!—and a dramatic, highly symbolic design emerged. Even the structure is non-rational: a metal frame is made to look like massive masonry. The walls are rough-textured stucco painted white, and the roof is a great billowing sail of board-formed concrete that rolls over the east wall to provide protection for the exterior pulpit. Large crowds attend services out of doors, sitting on the lawn; the interior provides seats for only fifty people, although there is standing room for more. The spectacular south wall has exaggerated

thickness and an array of splayed windows inset with hand-painted colored glass. From the outside, they look like an irregular series of small apertures, but from the interior, the wall turns into a glowing light sculpture, as moving in its own way as the windows of Chartres

15.85 Le Corbusier, Notre-Dame-du-Haut, Ronchamp, 1951–55.

The chapel is built of brick covered with stucco. The random window openings contain glass decorated with Le Corbusier's painted images. The principal entry lies between this wall and the tower, with a secondary entry in the rear between the two smaller towers.

Cathedral. A very thin strip of clear glass intervenes between the walls and roof, which seems to float. Meditation chapels underneath the towers have top illumination from high clerestories on the wall behind the worshipers. The light from an unseen source spilling softly over the rough-textured red stucco powerfully conveys a sense of humanity's essential loneliness.

Southwest of Lyon is the small town of Eveux-sur-l'Arbrêsle, outside of which Le Corbusier was commissioned to design a Dominican monastery, Ste.-Marie-de-la-Tourette (1956–60) (Figs. 15.86–15.87). Here he accomplished a modern reworking of the medieval monastic program. The church, a simple rectangular solid with sculptural subsidiary chapels in the crypt, is located on the west side of an open courtyard, crisscrossed by enclosed passageways connecting the church to other parts of the monastery. The remaining monastic quarters are arranged in three wings: the refectory on the level of the church; the library, study rooms, and an oratory on the second level; and two floors of monks' cells around the upper levels.

All the work is in concrete. Le Corbusier returned to the use of pilotis and "regulating traces" of his proportioning system, although the sculptural freedom found at Ronchamp is present here, too. With a master's hand, he manipulated light in dozens of different ways to enrich the experience of the basically simple forms within the building simply by taking into account the movement of the sun from day to day and season to season. Window mullions vary according to a harmonic rhythm; scoops catch the light and direct it through colored conical sections to focus on altars in the crypt; long horizontal ribbons provide even illumination for the corridors on the dormitory floor; each monk's room has a virtual wall of glass looking out over the balcony *brise-soleil* to the distant horizon; and a truncated pyramidal roof with a skylight provides an ethereal glow for the oratory.

CHANDIGARH

Despite his numerous city-planning projects on paper, Le Corbusier was invited only once to design an actual town. In 1951 the government of India asked him to work on the

15.87 Le Corbusier, Ste.-Marie-de-la-Tourette, Eveux-sur-l'Arbrêsle, 1956–60.

Dormitory rooms rise above pilotis on this south façade (left in the plan). The rooms have sunscreens like those used in Fig. 15.82.

15.86 Le Corbusier, Plan of Ste.-Marie-de-la-Tourette, Eveux-sur-l'Arbrêsle, 1956–60.

Here, Le Corbusier transformed the traditional monastic plan. Ramps and a small chapel inhabit the traditional interior cloister, with the latter's functions moved to the roof. This arrangement was never found acceptable by the monks, who chose to meditate in the wooded areas nearby.

Governor's Palace   Monument of Martyrs   Open Hand   Palace of Justice

Parliament
Building

Secretariat
Building

Tower of
Shadows

N

0   50 m

0   150 ft

15.88 Le Corbusier, plan of Chandigarh, Punjab, 1951–59.

This master plan illustrates Le Corbusier's preference for large buildings set wide apart within a garden-like landscape.

15.89 Le Corbusier, Parliament Building, Chandigarh, Punjab, 1951–59.

Here Le Corbusier continued to explore ways to manipulate sunlight. The poured-in-place concrete structure is sculpted along one side and cut away sunscreen-fashion along the other. His goals were certainly in part environmental, but he also sought to celebrate the state by associating it with the sun

design of Chandigarh, the new capital of the state of Punjab in northern India (Figs. 15.88–15.89). Le Corbusier made a master plan, while the design of individual sectors and most buildings was left to others. However, Le Corbusier designed the symbolic governmental buildings, which he located on the highest ground at the head of the scheme with the majestic foothills of the Himalayas beyond, in a manner that recalls the Acropolis in Athens. He grouped four major buildings around a great ceremonial plaza: the palace of the governor (not built), the Secretariat Building (1951–57), the Parliament Building (1956–59), and the Palace of Justice (1951–56). All of these buildings blend the rational discipline so evident in his early works with the sculptural freedom of his later projects. The Parliament Building, for example, is almost square in plan, with stacked rows of offices around two sides. The legislative chamber is circular, located at the base of a truncated hyperbolic surface of revolution (a hyperbolic curve rotated about a central axis) equipped with monitors at the top to filter the intense Indian sun. Control of light was of great importance, for with shade comes coolness. The *brises-soleil* were designed to introduce indirect sunlight and to provide views. Concrete, Le Corbusier's favorite material, was well suited to the Indian context. It is labor-intensive but inexpensive to produce. Its mass also buffers climatic extremes.

THE DECLINE OF MODERNISM

While the quite divergent styles of Mies van der Rohe and Le Corbusier may have defined the limits of architectural production during the Modern period, it was the middle-ground designs of the International Style that inspired the largest body of imitators, particularly in the United States

after World War II. Schools of architecture adopted programs based on those of the Bauhaus, and the tenets of Modernism were reflected in the architectural work of the 1950s and '60s. At their best, the results were efficient and spacious buildings, well suited to their sites and purposes; at its worst, however, Modernism produced dreary, repetitive buildings that established the popular image of contemporary design as almost a parody of the real thing. While Wright's conception of Broadacre City struck a responsive chord in countless American suburbs, and office parks, corporate firms, and real-estate developers seized on the rationality and economy of curtain-wall high-rise construction to house downtown offices, the "triumph" of International Style architecture, particularly in business districts across the country, led to increasing banality, and both architects and laymen began to excoriate Modernism's effect on the cityscape.

CHAPTER 16

MODERNISMS IN THE MID- AND LATE TWENTIETH CENTURY

Most developments in architecture from 1945 through the 1980s have involved reactions of some kind to the International Style. Almost all architects came under the latter's influence, but some came to broaden or even reject it and took other design approaches. This chapter is an attempt to understand the recent past, as architecture has questioned the ideals of Modernism and grown in different directions. Which of these directions will prove of lasting value is hard to say when we are still so close to the events themselves; significant trends are more easily seen from a distance.

The International Style had a limited effect on three of the twentieth century's most distinguished architects: Alvar Aalto, Eero Saarinen, and Louis Kahn. Although each designed buildings that follow Modernist canons, all three eventually discarded orthodoxy to explore other approaches.

ALVAR AALTO

Alvar Aalto (1898–1976) was a native of Finland and spent most of his career there. He studied architecture at the Helsinki Polytechnic Institute; during his formative years, Finnish architects were seeking to develop a regional identity, experimenting with a Nordic version of Neo-Classicism and a nationalistic Romanticism associated with chauvinistic myths and respected local building traditions. Aalto developed, apparently independently, a functional approach that closely paralleled the Deutscher

Werkbund architects of the same period, but with overtones of both classicism and Romanticism. In 1927, he won the competition to create a municipal library for Viipuri (now Vyborg, Russia) (Figs. 16.1–16.2) with a design of such a thoroughly modern cast that conservative local forces delayed its construction until 1930–35. Its carefully proportioned form might be described as stripped classicism; but this apparent reductivism is tempered by a poetic sensitivity to both materials and humane conditions. For instance, the building includes an auditorium at ground level with an undulating wooden ceiling and custom-designed bentwood stools. Elsewhere, the reading-room walls are bathed in indirect lighting from deep skylights that minimize glare (Fig. 16.3).

Aalto's design for the Tuberculosis Sanatorium (1929–33) at Paimio brought him international acclaim, both for its overall planning and its attention to detail. Located on a hilltop surrounded by evergreens, the sanatorium rises dramatically in the landscape (Figs. 16.4–16.5). Like Walter Gropius at the Bauhaus, Aalto articulated each component. The block of patients' rooms, a long, thin, six-story wing, dominates the grouping, connecting via an entrance and circulation wing to the public rooms, kitchen and services building, garage, and boilerhouse. In order to conform to the topography, these units are not always related orthogonally (as at the Bauhaus), which introduces an expressive angularity to the site plan that is suggestive of Russian Constructivist work.

All the ward rooms face south to receive maximum sunlight; balancing artificial light comes in from behind the patients' heads, thereby reducing glare. Rooms are painted in soft tones and with dark ceilings to create a restful effect. Carefully positioned insulation absorbs sound; wall-hung cabinets ease floor-cleaning; windows can be opened without creating drafts; tilted washbowls control splashing; and the door handles are shaped to fit the hand. Aalto custom-designed all the furniture, including the sanitary fittings, specifically for hospital use.

Furniture design interested Aalto throughout his career. Finland's greatest natural resource is wood, and

Frank Gehry, Guggenheim Museum Bilbao atrium, Bilbao, 1997.

With its walls, glass, railings, and steel frame all twisting as they rise, the atrium offers an exhilarating sense of dynamic space. Inhabiting the structure makes manifest the previously impossible: entering and moving through a building-size piece of free-form sculpture.

Aalto used the material in innovative ways. Through experimentation, he developed a technique for bending and laminating thin wood veneers to form plywood sheets of any desired curvature. In 1932 he designed his first chair with a one-piece plywood seat and back supported on a tubular metal frame. Subsequent designs were fabricated entirely in wood, and many of these are still available on the commercial market.

In the 1930s Aalto's largest commission was for the Sunila Cellulose Factory (1936–39, with later expansion

16.2 Alvar Aalto, Plan of the Municipal Library, Viipuri, 1930–35.

This configuration, with one rectangle slid against another, was used frequently in the twentieth century. Two other notable examples are Frank Lloyd Wright's Robie House (see Figs. 15.11–15.12) and Mies van der Rohe's Farnsworth House (see Fig. 15.73).

16.1 Alvar Aalto, Municipal Library, Viipuri, 1930–35.

Early in his career, Aalto was strongly influenced by European Modernism. Even then, however, his work had moments of lyricism, such as this elegantly ascending stair, that set it apart from much of the International Style.

16.3 Alvar Aalto, Municipal Library interior, Viipuri, 1930–35.

Aalto consistently manipulated the ceiling plane in inventive ways. Here a field of skylights illuminates the main reading room. The ceiling of the theater in the adjacent rectangle is an undulating plane of matched boards that is both elegant and acoustically beneficial.

Reading room

Children's library

Entry lobby

Auditorium

Governor's Palace   Monument of Martyrs   Open Hand   Palace of Justice

Parliament
Building

Secretariat
Building

Tower of
Shadows

N ⊗   0 ———————— 50 m
0 ———————— 150 ft

15.88 Le Corbusier, plan of Chandigarh, Punjab, 1951–59.

This master plan illustrates Le Corbusier's preference for large buildings set wide apart within a garden-like landscape.

15.89 Le Corbusier, Parliament Building, Chandigarh, Punjab, 1951–59.

Here Le Corbusier continued to explore ways to manipulate sunlight. The poured-in-place concrete structure is sculpted along one side and cut away sunscreen-fashion along the other. His goals were certainly in part environmental, but he also sought to celebrate the state by associating it with the sun

design of Chandigarh, the new capital of the state of Punjab in northern India (Figs. 15.88–15.89). Le Corbusier made a master plan, while the design of individual sectors and most buildings was left to others. However, Le Corbusier designed the symbolic governmental buildings, which he located on the highest ground at the head of the scheme with the majestic foothills of the Himalayas beyond, in a manner that recalls the Acropolis in Athens. He grouped four major buildings around a great ceremonial plaza: the palace of the governor (not built), the Secretariat Building (1951–57), the Parliament Building (1956–59), and the Palace of Justice (1951–56). All of these buildings blend the rational discipline so evident in his early works with the sculptural freedom of his later projects. The Parliament Building, for example, is almost square in plan, with stacked rows of offices around two sides. The legislative chamber is circular, located at the base of a truncated hyperbolic surface of revolution (a hyperbolic curve rotated about a central axis) equipped with monitors at the top to filter the intense Indian sun. Control of light was of great importance, for with shade comes coolness. The *brises-soleil* were designed to introduce indirect sunlight and to provide views. Concrete, Le Corbusier's favorite material, was well suited to the Indian context. It is labor-intensive but inexpensive to produce. Its mass also buffers climatic extremes.

THE DECLINE OF MODERNISM

While the quite divergent styles of Mies van der Rohe and Le Corbusier may have defined the limits of architectural production during the Modern period, it was the middle-ground designs of the International Style that inspired the largest body of imitators, particularly in the United States

after World War II. Schools of architecture adopted programs based on those of the Bauhaus, and the tenets of Modernism were reflected in the architectural work of the 1950s and '60s. At their best, the results were efficient and spacious buildings, well suited to their sites and purposes; at its worst, however, Modernism produced dreary, repetitive buildings that established the popular image of contemporary design as almost a parody of the real thing. While Wright's conception of Broadacre City struck a responsive chord in countless American suburbs, and office parks, corporate firms, and real-estate developers seized on the rationality and economy of curtain-wall high-rise construction to house downtown offices, the "triumph" of International Style architecture, particularly in business districts across the country, led to increasing banality, and both architects and laymen began to excoriate Modernism's effect on the cityscape.

CHAPTER 16

MODERNISMS IN THE MID- AND LATE TWENTIETH CENTURY

Most developments in architecture from 1945 through the 1980s have involved reactions of some kind to the International Style. Almost all architects came under the latter's influence, but some came to broaden or even reject it and took other design approaches. This chapter is an attempt to understand the recent past, as architecture has questioned the ideals of Modernism and grown in different directions. Which of these directions will prove of lasting value is hard to say when we are still so close to the events themselves; significant trends are more easily seen from a distance.

The International Style had a limited effect on three of the twentieth century's most distinguished architects: Alvar Aalto, Eero Saarinen, and Louis Kahn. Although each designed buildings that follow Modernist canons, all three eventually discarded orthodoxy to explore other approaches.

ALVAR AALTO

Alvar Aalto (1898–1976) was a native of Finland and spent most of his career there. He studied architecture at the Helsinki Polytechnic Institute; during his formative years, Finnish architects were seeking to develop a regional identity, experimenting with a Nordic version of Neo-Classicism and a nationalistic Romanticism associated with chauvinistic myths and respected local building traditions. Aalto developed, apparently independently, a functional approach that closely paralleled the Deutscher

Werkbund architects of the same period, but with overtones of both classicism and Romanticism. In 1927, he won the competition to create a municipal library for Viipuri (now Vyborg, Russia) (Figs. 16.1–16.2) with a design of such a thoroughly modern cast that conservative local forces delayed its construction until 1930–35. Its carefully proportioned form might be described as stripped classicism; but this apparent reductivism is tempered by a poetic sensitivity to both materials and humane conditions. For instance, the building includes an auditorium at ground level with an undulating wooden ceiling and custom-designed bentwood stools. Elsewhere, the reading-room walls are bathed in indirect lighting from deep skylights that minimize glare (Fig. 16.3).

Aalto's design for the Tuberculosis Sanatorium (1929–33) at Paimio brought him international acclaim, both for its overall planning and its attention to detail. Located on a hilltop surrounded by evergreens, the sanatorium rises dramatically in the landscape (Figs. 16.4–16.5). Like Walter Gropius at the Bauhaus, Aalto articulated each component. The block of patients' rooms, a long, thin, six-story wing, dominates the grouping, connecting via an entrance and circulation wing to the public rooms, kitchen and services building, garage, and boiler-house. In order to conform to the topography, these units are not always related orthogonally (as at the Bauhaus), which introduces an expressive angularity to the site plan that is suggestive of Russian Constructivist work.

All the ward rooms face south to receive maximum sunlight; balancing artificial light comes in from behind the patients' heads, thereby reducing glare. Rooms are painted in soft tones and with dark ceilings to create a restful effect. Carefully positioned insulation absorbs sound; wall-hung cabinets ease floor-cleaning; windows can be opened without creating drafts; tilted washbowls control splashing; and the door handles are shaped to fit the hand. Aalto custom-designed all the furniture, including the sanitary fittings, specifically for hospital use.

Furniture design interested Aalto throughout his career. Finland's greatest natural resource is wood, and

Frank Gehry, Guggenheim Museum Bilbao atrium, Bilbao, 1997.

With its walls, glass, railings, and steel frame all twisting as they rise, the atrium offers an exhilarating sense of dynamic space. Inhabiting the structure makes manifest the previously impossible: entering and moving through a building-size piece of free-form sculpture.

Aalto used the material in innovative ways. Through experimentation, he developed a technique for bending and laminating thin wood veneers to form plywood sheets of any desired curvature. In 1932 he designed his first chair with a one-piece plywood seat and back supported on a tubular metal frame. Subsequent designs were fabricated entirely in wood, and many of these are still available on the commercial market.

In the 1930s Aalto's largest commission was for the Sunila Cellulose Factory (1936–39, with later expansion

16.1 Alvar Aalto, Municipal Library, Viipuri, 1930–35.

Early in his career, Aalto was strongly influenced by European Modernism. Even then, however, his work had moments of lyricism, such as this elegantly ascending stair, that set it apart from much of the International Style.

16.3 Alvar Aalto, Municipal Library interior, Viipuri, 1930–35.

Aalto consistently manipulated the ceiling plane in inventive ways. Here a field of skylights illuminates the main reading room. The ceiling of the theater in the adjacent rectangle is an undulating plane of matched boards that is both elegant and acoustically beneficial.

16.2 Alvar Aalto, Plan of the Municipal Library, Viipuri, 1930–35.

This configuration, with one rectangle slid against another, was used frequently in the twentieth century. Two other notable examples are Frank Lloyd Wright's Robie House (see Figs. 15.11–15.12) and Mies van der Rohe's Farnsworth House (see Fig. 15.73).

Reading room

Children's library

Entry lobby

Auditorium

16.4 Alvar Aalto, Tuberculosis Sanatorium, Paimio, 1929–33.

None of Aalto's commissions has been more celebrated as an International Style icon than this one. Notable features are the long strip windows and related spandrels and the extensive balconies for convalescing patients.

16.5 Alvar Aalto, Plan of the Tuberculosis Sanatorium, Paimio, 1929–33.

The plan appears at first glance to be randomly organized. However, its splayed distribution of components is a response to orientation toward the sun. As pure form, the composition can be compared to Russian Constructivist work of the 1910s and '20s.

Service wing

Dining wing

Doctor's wing

Patients' wing

N

0   50 m

0   150 ft

in 1951–57) at Karhula, including the design of workers' housing nearby. The factory is a carefully composed array of repetitive rectangular forms, animated by the diagonal lines of conveyors and the vertical thrust of a smokestack (Fig. 16.6). For employee housing situated well away from the factory's noxious fumes, Aalto built three-story blocks of apartments into the slope of a hill, so that each unit has its access at grade.

After World War II, Aalto's mature style moved away from the white rectangular solids and pipe railings of International Style architecture. Brick, timber, and copper became his favorite building materials, and he worked them into harmonious compositions that frequently included great curving walls, single-pitched roofs, and imaginative daylighting. During a teaching appointment at M.I.T. in the late 1940s, he designed Baker House (1947–49), a campus dormitory (Fig. 16.7). Located on a site parallel to the Charles river, the seven-story brick building has its riverfront plan arranged in a sinusoidal curve, permitting oblique views from

16.6 (above) Alvar Aalto, Cellulose Factory, Sunila, 1936–39.

This composition shows Aalto's moving away from the regimentation of the International Style and toward more romantic massing and the use of undulating forms as major exterior features. He was much impressed by the irregular silhouettes of the hilltowns in Italy and integrated his experiences there into his own design work.

16.7 (below) Alvar Aalto, Baker House, M.I.T., Cambridge, Massachusetts, 1947–49.

Aalto's only project in the United States faces the Charles river. He used the undulating plan here to gain views up and down the river. He placed support spaces in orthogonal rooms to the rear.

Council Chamber

Library with shops below

Offices

Courtyard

N

0   20 m

0   60 ft

16.8 Alvar Aalto, Roof-and courtyard-level plans of the Town Hall, Säynätsalo, 1951–52.

Aalto's plan *parti* also suggests the kind of spontaneous design found in Italian hilltowns. The C-shaped block has one of its sides slid away just far enough to allow a slightly deflected path through the complex. One stair is orthogonal, while the other cascades out of the plaza over grass-covered treads.

16.9 Alvar Aalto, Town Hall, Säynätsalo, 1951–52.

Aalto's complex has multiple scales. It is two stories on the outside, but only one story in the courtyard from which rises the tower of the council chamber. This view suggests that Aalto was still being influenced by his earlier travels to the Italian hilltowns.

the dormitory rooms up or down the river. As far as possible, Aalto placed service and common rooms at the rear on each floor, with the dining hall and lounge in a low wing at the front.

A more ambitious program was involved in the commission for a "Town Hall" for Säynätsalo (1951–52), designed as a group of buildings around a grassy courtyard (Figs. 16.8–16.9). In fact, it provides the entire civic center for this small community, housing the municipal offices, council chamber, public library, and retail shops, and announces a scheme that Aalto would repeat. Within a basically orthogonal layout, the brick volume of the council chamber dominates the ensemble, its sloped-roof profile reflecting a graceful wooden fan truss inside. The Town Hall is entered by a set of either brick or turf stairs; from both directions the sense of scale is exquisitely

controlled. The building, which seems monumental in photographs, is quite modest in size in reality.

In all his work Aalto took a humanistic approach to architecture that is perhaps unmatched in the twentieth century.

EERO SAARINEN

The works of Eero Saarinen (1910–1961) are eclectic, borrowing from a wider range of sources than those of Aalto. However, a constant in his work was a relentless, exploratory, inventive attitude toward new materials and technologies. Like Aalto, Saarinen was of Finnish ancestry; his architect father, Eliel, created the extraordinary campus at Cranbrook Academy outside Detroit, Michigan, after relocating the family to the United States in the 1920s. After studying sculpture in Paris and completing his architectural education at Yale in 1934, Eero practiced with his father until 1950. He considered architecture a fine art; it was the architect's role, he believed, to be a form-giver.

In the General Motors Technical Center (1948–56) at Warren, Michigan, Saarinen took an apparently Miesian approach, setting modular steel-and-glass-walled rectangular solids in a campus-like park; the orthogonal theme is broken only by a circular auditorium and a sculptural water tower that gives verticality to a composition of otherwise horizontal, seemingly mass-produced objects. Upon closer observation, however, the skins of his reductivist objects set in space are found to possess a sensuality unknown in Mies's work; one sees the hand of the fine artist leavening the mix of the technician.

For the Trans World Airlines Terminal (1956–62) at Kennedy Airport in New York City, Saarinen abandoned the General Motors esthetic in favor of a fluid, sculptural design expressive of flight (Fig. 16.10). Forsaking metal in favor of concrete, he created thin-shelled vaults with sculpted, poured-in-place concrete supporting piers. The

16.10 Eero Saarinen, TWA Terminal, Kennedy International Airport, New York City, 1956–62.

Saarinen died while still in his early 50s. He had not yet established a single direction for his architectural development. Here, he explored the potential of poured-in-place concrete to create dynamic shapes and spaces.

16.11 Eero Saarinen, Morse and Stiles colleges, Yale University, New Haven, Connecticut, 1958–62.

Like Aalto, Saarinen looked to medieval towns as an inspiration for these irregularly distributed dormitory units. The walls were formed of concrete poured among rubble stones inside slip forms.

terminal's billowing roof resembles a great bird alighting; it has also been compared to the swooping tail fins of 1959 Chevrolet automobiles, which Saarinen may have seen in developmental form at the General Motors Technical Center. Inside, the flow of space is dramatic but the interior is more intimate in scale than photographs suggest. Most fittings were custom-designed to match the spirit of the building, for ordinary furniture looks out of place in a space where curves dominate the walls and ceilings, and ramps generate motion in the floor plane. A later design for Dulles Airport (1958–62), outside Washington, D.C., drew its inspiration from early sketches done by the German Expressionist architect Erich Mendelsohn. Outward-leaning concrete pylons rise on the exterior to support the concrete-panel-covered cable-hung roof, which provides a clear-span interior. The effect of the building in the landscape is noble, but the interior is a disappointment, for the orthogonal clutter of partitions and a central roof drain that violates the untouched ceiling negate the curving geometries of the building's enclosure. In 1997, the firm of Skidmore, Owings, and Merrill doubled the length of the terminal by replicating Saarinen's profile of pylons and catenary cables.

Saarinen drew on yet another form language in his designs for Morse and Stiles colleges (1958–62) at Yale University (Fig. 16.11), finding inspiration for this commission in the irregular layouts and clustered massing of Italian hilltowns, particularly the medieval towers of San Gimignano. Although Yale's other residential colleges are generally based on the more orthogonal shapes of medieval-college quadrangles, Morse and Stiles merge smoothly into the circulation patterns of the campus and contribute a pleasant spatial variety to the academic setting.

LOUIS I. KAHN

The work of Louis I. Kahn (1901–1974) represents the fusion of seemingly contradictory sources. In 1905 Kahn immigrated to Philadelphia from the small Russian island of Saarama, in the Baltic Sea. He received a Beaux-Arts-influenced architectural education at the University of Pennsylvania, where he acquired the concept of served and servant spaces that would affect nearly all his buildings. Moreover, he crystallized an idea to create symmetrical, hierarchically arranged compositions, and to produce monumentality, even in everyday circumstances. In so doing, he was able to render the common uncommon, and the uncommon transcendent. Giving new life to a largely inert design tradition, he achieved timelessness where others had resorted to historicism.

Medieval vernacular forms from Italian hilltowns inspired Kahn in his design for the Richards Medical Research Building (1957–61) at the University of Pennsylvania (Fig. 16.12). In plan the building is a model of rationalism. The medical laboratories are square, open-plan, glass-walled spaces stacked into multi-floor units. Pairs of columns set on each side support the structural grid of each floor, while ducts, mechanical services, elevators, and stairs are set in shafts, articulated on the exterior as vertical brick towers. Thus, Kahn wedded straightforward functional planning with a picturesque massing to create one of the most influential architectural compositions of the 1960s. Purists note that one of the service shaft towers is a dummy, included for artistic effect rather than functional necessity, and scientists using the building have found the flexibility of the lab spaces to be less than the designer imagined and have been forced to install sun shades where glare and heat gain have been a problem.

In the Richards Medical Building the laboratories are the served spaces, and they are clearly distinguished in plan and reality from the servant functions of mechanical equipment and vertical circulation. But Kahn also absorbed principles of Modernism, particularly from the work of Le Corbusier; and he traveled in Europe, where Hadrian's Villa, vernacular townscapes, and the works of Brunelleschi created lasting impressions on him. The simple geometries of Neo-Classicism also influenced his architectural conceptions. Kahn admired the works of Boullée and Ledoux, considering them to have been as important to architecture as Johann Sebastian Bach was to music. Among Kahn's often poetic writings, one finds the following: "Spirit in will to express/ can make the great sun seem small./ The Sun is/ Thus the Universe./ Did we need Bach/ Bach is/ Thus music is./ Did we need Boullée/Boullée is/ Did we need Ledoux/ Ledoux is/ Thus

16.13 Louis Kahn, Library interior, Phillips Exeter Academy, Andover, New Hampshire, 1967–72.

Kahn admired imperial Roman architecture and here sought to capture both the period's monumentality and the rich layering seen in such complexes as Hadrian's Villa.

16.12 Louis Kahn, Plan of the Richards Medical Building, University of Pennsylvania, Philadelphia, 1951–61.

This plan illustrates Kahn's conception of servant and served spaces. The studio towers are served by the stairtowers and fume exhaust stacks, or plenums.

16.14 Louis Kahn, Kimbell Art Museum, Fort Worth, Texas, 1966–72.

Almost sepulchral in character, the apparently barrel-vaulted units house the museum galleries. Where necessary, Kahn opened them up, as in the external passage or porch in the foreground.

16.15 Louis Kahn, Kimbell Art Museum interior, Fort Worth, Texas, 1966–72.

Kahn's modular units are not really barrel-vaulted, as the summit of each intrados is a void into which a baffled skylight has been inserted. The structural system is actually repetitive double-cantilevered butterfly canopies.

16.16 Louis Kahn, Plan of the Kimbell Art Museum, Fort Worth, Texas, 1966–72.

One would hardly anticipate the spatial richness of Kahn's interiors from the simple geometry of his plan. This richness is amplified by the elegance of the building materials: silver-gray concrete, travertine, wood, and stainless steel.

Architecture is." Inspired by such poetic visions and by a high regard for rational construction, particularly the heavy vaulting of ancient Rome, Kahn imbued structural forms such as the arch and vault with a mystical, even sublime quality and allowed them to become metaphors for the human condition itself.

The influence of Neo-Classicism in general and Piranesi in particular is manifest in Kahn's designs for the National Assembly of Bangladesh in Dacca (1962–74).

The building is composed of ideal forms, circles and squares, expressed volumetrically as prisms, and its brick and concrete masonry features large circular openings for daylighting that recall buildings at Hadrian's Villa, while the interiors are as grand and somber as images in Piranesi's *Carceri* engravings. A similar treatment is found inside the library of Phillips Exeter Academy (1967–72) in Exeter, New Hampshire, where the essentially square building is dominated by a cubical volume at the center (Fig. 16.13). Huge circular cutouts provide vistas into the library stacks on the surrounding floors in a manner reminiscent of Piranesi's engravings of imaginary prisons. Individual study carrels surround the stacks on each floor, and the windows against which they fit provide a regular articulation for the brick exterior, which is treated rather like the nineteenth-century mill buildings of nearby Manchester, New Hampshire.

Kahn was never more successful than in his design for the Kimbell Art Museum in Fort Worth, Texas (1966–72). In his site plan, one enters into a court through a grove of trees, with reflecting pools to each side. He chose as his spatial and structural unit an apparently barrel-vaulted bay, which is actually covered by a pair of cantilevers meeting at a continuous skylight (Figs. 16.14–16.15). Kahn placed sixteen of these units side by side in three ranks (Fig. 16.16), combining many by replacing the load-bearing walls with longitudinal beams. As materials he chose poured-in-place concrete, travertine, oak, and stainless steel, all bathed in natural light, with much of it reflected by baffles beneath the skylights, so that the interiors have a consistent luminescence. The spaces are ancient Roman in their monumentality, gravity, and exquisite finishes. Yet their scale and general sense of humanity make them both neutral enough to serve as proper galleries and flexible enough to provide a rich spatial experience.

In contrast to his contemporaries, Kahn was a late bloomer, emerging as an original voice in American architecture only in the late 1950s. His buildings reflect Beaux-Arts principles, tenets of Modernism, and a respect for historical values in a highly original synthesis. Both his works and his teaching at the University of Pennsylvania encouraged a generation of younger architects to explore alternatives to the orthodoxies of the International Style. His preference for articulating individual rooms in plan, rather than employing the space-flow characteristics of much modern architecture, ties him to earlier eras, but his use of materials such as exposed concrete is modern in every way. Looking at his body of work, one can make the argument that he was the most original architect of the twentieth century. Among his students was Robert Venturi.

ROBERT VENTURI'S RADICAL COUNTER-PROPOSAL TO MODERNISM

The monolith of Modernism began to show hairline cracks after World War II. Aalto, Saarinen, and Kahn all sought new but related directions. Others surveyed the field and found the zeal, conviction, and utopian vision of the pioneering Modernists waning. Moreover, the despised eclecticism to which Modernists had reacted so vehemently thirty or forty years before now seemed less important, and to some even appeared to offer an opportunity for welcome diversity. Add to this mix an increasing concern for the environment and a related interest in more site-specific buildings, and the architectural stage was set for a radical change.

16.17 Robert Venturi and John K. Rauch, Guild House, Philadelphia, Pennsylvania, 1960–63.

The architects celebrated the ordinary in this housing unit for the elderly. From the mundane signage to the false, gold-anodized television antenna and aluminium window frames, the building presents itself as an unapologetic product of mass culture.

The 1960s saw the emergence of Post-Modernism, a way of thinking about architecture that is quite different from the approach of International Style designers. As did many earlier twentieth-century design movements, Post-Modernism began with a treatise, published in 1966 under the title *Complexity and Contradiction in Architecture* and hailed by Vincent Scully as "the most important writing on the making of architecture since Le Corbusier's *Vers une Architecture* of 1923." The author, Robert Venturi (born 1925), made the case for non-straightforward architecture. Using a style that echoed the phraseology of earlier manifestos, he observed:

> *Architects can no longer afford to be intimidated by the puritanically moral language of orthodox Modern architecture. I like elements which are hybrid rather than "pure," compromising rather than "clean," distorted rather than "straightforward," ambiguous rather than "articulated," perverse as well as impersonal, boring as well as "interesting," conventional rather than "designed," accommodating rather than excluding, redundant rather than simple, vestigial as well as innovating, inconsistent and equivocal rather than direct and clear. I am for messy vitality over obvious unity. I include the non sequitur and proclaim the duality.*

The book extolled the ambiguities, inconsistencies, and idiosyncracies of Palladio, Michelangelo, Hawksmoor, Soane, Aalto, and Le Corbusier, and glorified Mannerist and Baroque architecture generally. Venturi went on to equate the atmosphere, lighting effects, and theatrics of Las Vegas casinos with Counter-Reformation art. By celebrating the "ugly and ordinary" aspects of twentieth-century buildings, as exhibited in roadside strip developments, neon advertising signs, and billboards, Venturi discarded the orderly purity and pristine character of Modernism in favor of pluralistic, anonymously designed, and eminently practical populist work, dubbed by some detractors as the New Banality. Venturi restated the Miesian dictum "Less is more" as "Less is a bore." Roots for this shift in architectural thinking can be found in the cultural diversity manifested in political and social movements of the period; increased attention to vernacular architecture, stemming in part from Bernard Rudofsky's "Architecture Without Architects" exhibition at the MOMA in 1964; British "New Brutalism," which used large expanses of raw concrete as finish material in buildings; and the unique work of Venturi's mentor, Louis Kahn.

When *Complexity and Contradiction in Architecture* was published, Venturi had built very little, although he had placed well in architectural competitions. His largest completed commission was the ninety-one-unit Guild House (1960–63) (Fig. 16.17), an apartment block for the elderly in Philadelphia, in which common building elements were used in pragmatic yet unconventional ways. Double-hung windows were overscaled; a gold-anodized, roof-mounted, fake television antenna demarcated the central axis of the symmetrical façade; a single polished granite column denoted the entranceway and contrasted with the white glazed brick around the door, providing the building with an institutional character. Interiors were thoughtfully designed with the well-being of the tenants in mind. A majority of the apartments were oriented to the south and overlooked activity on the street, while the corridors were offset to avoid the institutional quality of long hallways.

More famous, perhaps, is Venturi's 1962 house for his mother, Vanna, in Chestnut Hill, Pennsylvania (Fig. 16.18). In this modest dwelling, Venturi combined simplicity of external form with complexity of interior layout, and conventional symbols and elements with contradictory arrangements. For example, the location of the central recess for the door is obvious, but the double-doors themselves are concealed and are much too grand for the cramped vestibule into which they open. Stairs to the second floor are set behind the chimney mass and compete with it for space; they widen as they ascend, then

16.18 Robert Venturi, Vanna Venturi House, Chestnut Hill, Pennsylvania, 1962.

Robert Venturi built this house for his mother. The modest building is loaded with allusions, from the arch-like molding above the entry to the split-pediment-like massing of the full block.

abruptly narrow to a minimum passage around the firebox. The fireplace and mantel are overscaled for the size of the living room, and the original furniture was of mixed ancestry rather than Bauhaus-inspired modern. On the outside the house presents a bold gable end to the street, in the manner of a Shingle Style house, yet its landlord-green color and stucco finish bear no resemblance to such buildings. While the Vanna Venturi House showed how his ideas could be translated into architectural form, Venturi's writings may ultimately prove more important than any of his buildings.

INTELLECTUAL INSPIRATIONS FOR POST-MODERNISM

Understanding the various ideas that led to Post-Modernism in architecture and understanding the meaning of Post-Modernism in society at large (and these are two quite different phenomena) requires a brief survey of twentieth-century methods of inquiry in both the humanities and sciences. At the turn of the century, the humanities still took exclusively the hermeneutic approach, that is, the interpretation of texts from the point of view of their authors; those critical of this method argue that it "privileges" or places far too much emphasis on these authors. At the same time, scientific inquiry was based on positivism, the view that science could address all questions about the world through the establishing of facts and the relationships between those facts. An alternative to these separate approaches was put forward by the philosopher Edmund Husserl (1859–1938). He created phenomenology, which he based upon a systematic investigation of human consciousness, as both a critique of and a means to combine humanistic and scientific endeavors. He proposed that every conscious act is based upon a meaningful object. In the mid-twentieth century, at a time when phenomenology was losing ground in other fields, architectural thinkers, disillusioned with what they considered to be the inhumane results of International Style principles, turned to it as a means of emphasizing people, values, belief systems, and motivations, and of privileging subjectivity over objectivity.

In the early twentieth century, however, it had been quantum physics in science and language in the humanities that had taken center stage. Physicists discovered a whole new world of subatomic particles that did not behave according to the laws of Newtonian mechanics. Einstein's theories of General and Special Relativity are the best-known results, but more important here are the uncertainties that these scientists uncovered and that, incidentally, Einstein never accepted. Werner Heisenberg's Uncertainty Principle says that it is impossible to know simultaneously both the position and velocity of a subatomic particle. It began to appear that ultimate truths about the natural world were ungraspable, and with this realization a sense of apprehension began to settle over not only the sciences but also the humanities. In the humanities, the philosopher Ludwig Wittgenstein (1889–1951) argued that language has limits and, therefore, that the task of philosophy is to "make us see what cannot be said, through clearly displaying the logic of propositions." In the 1920s and early 1930s, the so-called Logical Positivists in Vienna proposed that philosophy should focus its attention on why science works, ruling out esthetics entirely as a field of inquiry. Wittgenstein responded with the idea of linguistic analysis, whereby one could seek clarity through a critique of language and establish accurate means for analyzing information.

For those who found the empiricism of science inadequate for their needs, but who found phenomenology to be too mystical, linguistic analysis offered an alternative; the form of linguistic analysis known as Structuralism matured after World War I and reached its peak of influence in the mid-1960s. Created by individuals such as linguist Ferdinand de Saussure (1857–1913) and philosopher and anthropologist Claude Lévi-Strauss (born 1908), Structuralism looked at the world in terms of structures, that is, parts and the relationships between those parts within a system, with its goal being the discovery of universal principles that govern the human mind.

The line of Structuralist thinking that was most followed by architects and by architectural critics and theorists was semiotics. Semioticians saw the hermeneutic attempt to recover an author's intentions as impossible. They looked to the text, not the author, for meaning, specifically in the form of embedded signs and symbols. Buildings, they argued, carried layers of meaning too, and took on meanings never intended by their designers.

In the late 1960s Structuralism gave way to Post-Structuralism, whose developers included Jacques Derrida (born 1930) and Michel Foucault (1926–84). A loosely organized group, they argued that no philosophical system could arrange and explain man's knowledge and that there were no absolute standards in any field of inquiry, a kind of literary uncertainty principle. As a means of addressing the relativism they had created, the Post-Structuralists focused on the text as discourse. Discourses, they argued, contained within them their own criteria for judgment, but signs and symbols, they said, only pointed to other signs and symbols. One could deconstruct a text so that it spread out in a never-ending network of uncertainties. A text could be interpreted in any number of ways by any number of people; interpretations were relative.

With this intellectual background in mind, we can now return to a discussion of Post-Modernist architectural practice. The term Post-Modernist was created to identify new directions in architecture after Modernism. It did not describe what these directions were, only what they were not. Subsequent to its introduction in an architectural context, it has taken on a counter-meaning in the broader culture, suggesting a Post-Structuralist fragmentation and distrust of any attempt to build systems of thought on firm foundations. One strain of Post-Modernist architecture has connections to Structuralism, specifically to semiotics. Authors like Geoffrey Broadbent and particularly Charles Jencks have been interested in architecture as a language and have written about signs and symbols as a way of reading the buildings of such designers as Philip Johnson, Charles Moore, and particularly Michael Graves. Jencks set out this position in *The Language of Post-Modern Architecture* (1977). Here he speaks of "double-coding": creating forms that carry meaning for both the elite, as he says the Modernists did, and for the man on the street—the vernacular message. Jencks coined the terms "univalent" and "multivalent" architecture to describe the efforts of Post-Modernists to move beyond Modernist reductivism. Univalent means "an architecture created around one (or a few) simplified values." Multivalent means layers of values including historicism, revivalism, the vernacular, contextualism, and ecological issues, among others. The source for this coding has been a highly informed, some would say pedantic and esoteric, type of eclecticism with a high degree of relativity since, Jencks says, "all revivals are possible and each depends on an argument from *plausibility*, since it certainly can't be proved as necessary."

PHILIP JOHNSON

No twentieth-century architect has received more attention for his historicism than Philip Johnson, nor has any architect practiced or indeed lived longer than he (he was born in 1906), nor has any architect had a more varied or controversial career; Johnson has been dogged, for instance, by allegations that he was a Nazi sympathizer. When a twenty-six-year-old graduate of Harvard with a degree in philosophy, he co-authored *The International Style: Architecture Since 1922* (discussed in the previous chapter) to accompany the 1932 MOMA exhibition on the International Style. While the exhibition was only modestly successful at the time, it came to assume the stature of myth, foreshadowing the persona that Johnson would create for himself later in the century. In 1938 he entered the Harvard Graduate School of Design, then headed by Walter Gropius, and, once graduated, opened his own practice, with the most prominent result being his own Miesian house in New Canaan, Connecticut, mentioned in the previous chapter. By the late 1950s, however, he was moving away from his strongly Miesian, International Style tendencies, and producing a series of projects traceable to various sources, such as his Boissonas House in New Canaan (1956) (Fig. 16.19), which owes much to some of Louis Kahn's domestic work. His 1963 Museum for Pre-Columbian Art at Dumbarton Oaks in Washington, D.C. was overtly iconoclastic, with rooms defined by huge marble columns and covered by domes. But it was twenty-one years later, in 1984, that Johnson took the center of the Post-Modernist stage, with his American Telephone and Telegraph Headquarters in New York City (Fig. 16.20), designed in partnership with John Burgee. At its base is a giant Serliana, which has been compared by some

16.19 Philip Johnson, Boissonas House, New Canaan, Connecticut, 1956.

By the late 1950s, Johnson had begun to move away from the Miesian tendencies of his early work. Among his experiments was this house, which was influenced by the domestic projects of Louis Kahn.

16.20 Philip Johnson and John Burgee, American Telephone and Telegraph Headquarters, New York City, 1984.

With this building and its references to architectural styles of the past, Philip Johnson broke completely with the Miesian tradition. In fact, his client had said emphatically that the company did not want another glass box.

to the façade of Brunelleschi's Pazzi Chapel, and at its crown a broken pediment, which has been compared to a grandfather clock or eighteenth-century highboy. Johnson has received less than consistent critical acclaim. Rather than his ability as a designer, it often seems to have been his cleverness in garnering media attention and his role as a power broker in the awarding of commissions and the selection of participants in exhibitions that have ensured his fame.

CHARLES MOORE

Charles Moore (1925–1993) brought to Post-Modernism a gentle but studied playfulness that made his buildings immediately accessible to the public and professionals alike. Moore took pleasure in historical allusions, but with large doses of whimsy. His critics have called his work superficial and ephemeral; his supporters have called it refreshing and ironic. In 1963–65, at a time when he was practicing as a partner in Moore, Lyndon, Turnbull, and Whitaker (MLTW), he was a principal designer for Sea Ranch I (Fig. 16.21), a set of ten contiguous condominium units on the coast north of San Francisco. On the exterior, the complex combines the massing of Aalto's Villa Carré near Paris with the rough-hewn, redwood wall surfacing of the Bay Area vernacular to produce a serene early comment on regionalism and building in visual harmony with the environment. On the interior, each cubic unit is organized around an aedicula—four columns supporting a roof—that produces lighthearted and convivial, yet complex, spaces.

16.21 (above) Charles Moore et al, Sea Ranch condominiums, north of San Francisco, California, 1963–65.

Moore's living units are an early example of modern contextual design. The irregular massing reflects the topography and changing winds, and the redwood siding appears almost as camouflage.

16.22 (below) Charles Moore, Piazza d'Italia, New Orleans, Louisiana, 1975–79.

Moore's work took on an almost carnival aspect with projects like this one, a fountain with backdrop for a developing New Orleans public space. Here, the classical language has become a medium for wit and glibness, as in the Mannerist compositions of sixteenth-century Italy.

Moore's Piazza d'Italia (Fig. 16.22) in New Orleans (1975–79), done in collaboration with Perez Associates, consists of a flamboyant, wildly Neo-Classical, neon-outlined, scenographic backdrop for a contour map of Italy set in a pool of water that is demarcated by concentric rings of marble paving. It is as much spectacle as architecture, and its many details, such as the portrait of Moore's face in stainless steel spouting water like the fountain masks at the Villa d'Este near Rome, exhibit the wit that became his personal and professional trademark. The whole complex also seems to be an unintentional satire on Italian government, since its lights and fountains hardly ever work. Moore's academic appointments at Yale, U.C.L.A., and the University of Texas in Austin, as well as his indefatigable teaching and lecturing elsewhere, influenced myriad students from the 1960s onward.

MICHAEL GRAVES

No Post-Modernist architect has been more agreeable to semioticians than Michael Graves (born 1934). Graves describes his work as "figurative," with the figural elements traceable to "classical and anthropomorphic sources." His earliest projects, particularly house additions in Princeton, New Jersey, were neo-Corbusian, but he soon began to explore new ground. Grave's unbuilt Fargo-Moorhead Cultural Center Bridge (1977) (Fig. 16.23) contains broadcasting facilities and a concert hall on one bank and a history museum on the other, all linked by an art museum spanning from Fargo, North Dakota, to Moorhead, Minnesota, over the Red river. At the conceptual level, imagery for the bridge is traceable principally to Ledoux's design for the Inspector's House at the Source of the River Loue (see Fig. 13.13), but details such as **keystones** were transformed into windows and roof drains through a clever manipulation of the classical language. Graves's beautiful colored-pencil rendering of the bridge exhibits a lyricism that has become a constant in his work.

16.24 Michael Graves, Portland Building, Portland, Oregon, 1980.

It becomes almost a game with compositions such as this one to count all of the quasi-classical elements. Some of the appurtenances in Graves's published designs for the building, such as a flying figure and a roof-top village, were never realized.

The built Portland Building in Portland, Oregon (1980), is equally famous as a rendered elevation. It is replete with quotations from the classical language: the temples on the roof (never built), the giant keystone beneath them, the pair of fluted pilasters of indeterminate order, and the tiered stylobate at street level (Fig. 16.24). Graves was also a force in reintroducing color into twentieth-century architecture, as here with the green base, terra-cotta-colored columns, and tan flanking walls punctured

16.23 Michael Graves, Elevation of the Fargo-Moorhead Cultural Center Bridge, 1977.

Graves's projects and drawing style were influential long before he had constructed many buildings. Here he created his version of Claude-Nicolas Ledoux's eighteenth-century river-keeper's house (see Fig. 13.13).

16.25 Michael Graves, Swan Hotel, Disneyworld, Orlando, Florida, 1987.

Graves was certainly adept at fitting his brand of Post-Modernism into the Disney environment. Walking through this complex, one finds every manner of Graves-designed object, from placemats to light fixtures to scenographic room interiors.

by square windows. His Swan and Dolphin hotels (1987) at Disney World in Orlando, Florida demonstrate Graves's ability to design at all scales from building to flatware. He first developed a master plan for the area, then designed the hotels to be placed around a crescent-shaped lake. The mass of the Swan Hotel (Fig. 16.25) seems relatively

unimportant among the tent-lined approach causeway, palm trees, giant swan and clamshell sculptures, and even the hotel's own camouflage-like, wave-pattern paint scheme. Once inside, the visitor confronts more tents, a fountain, and wall murals, and Graves designed carpets, light fixtures, wallpapers, even placemats and plates. His style seems to fit perfectly the surreptitiously controlled environment of Disney World. The Dolphin Hotel has an equally diverse set of appurtenances in addition to its central Ledoux-having-fun triangular façade and Napoleonic-Empire-one-better tented rotunda lobby (Fig. 16.26). While only a pedant or an unreconstructed Modernist could fail to enjoy the place, one can question

16.26 Michael Graves, Dolphin Hotel, Disneyworld, Orlando, Florida, 1987.

Here Graves brings Boullée to a theme-park environment. While the rooms are modest, the designed context of water, causeways, cabanas, and palm-lined promenades makes for fun.

whether it has the staying power of the grand resort hotels of the late nineteenth and early twentieth centuries such as the Belleview-Biltmore in Belleair, Florida, or the Grand Hotel on Mackinac Island, Michigan.

ROBERT A.M. STERN

Graves's work conforms nicely to the attributes of Post-Modernism defined by the architect and architectural historian Robert A.M. Stern (born 1939): contextualism, allusionism, and ornamentalism. Contextualism refers to connections between the building and its setting as Post-Modernist architects attempt to link their buildings to established patterns, geometries, and possibilities for future growth, rather than conceiving each design as an isolated object in the landscape, as many would argue that Modernists did. As an architect, Stern has often quarried New England sources, producing for instance many convincing neo-Shingle Style houses. Less convincing but much-published at the time of its construction is his Lang House (1973–74) (Fig. 16.27) in Connecticut with its pencil-thin, classically motivated moldings applied almost like piping on the sleeve of a garment. His Newport Bay Club Hotel at Disneyland Resort Paris (1988–92) (Fig. 16.28) was successfully derived from classic resorts such as the Michigan Grand Hotel mentioned above. Stern has written at length about classicism, calling it the "fulcrum about which architectural discourse balances," and has built in a variety of traditional styles. Others who have done so include the Italian Aldo Rossi (1931–1997), who

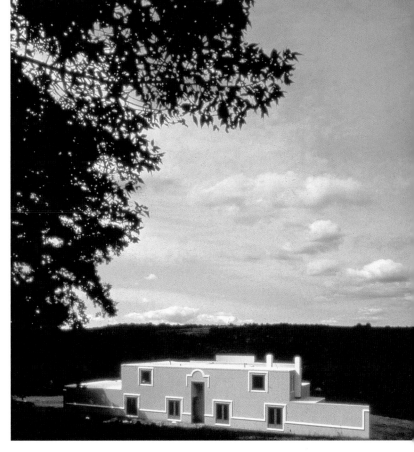

16.27 Robert Stern, Lang House, Washington, Connecticut, 1973–74.

This house in the country has a cowboy-storefront-like façade, over which extended **label moldings** have been piped on like cake icing. This is Stern's early brand of classical allusionism.

16.28 Robert Stern, Newport Bay Club Hotel, Disneyland Resort Paris, 1988–92.

This hotel near Paris is comparable to such North American resort buildings as the Grand Hotel on Mackinac Island, Michigan. It provides a symbolic gateway to the resort portion of Disneyland Resort Paris.

used classicism to analyze the city, Leon Krier (born 1936), who has concentrated on the making of public spaces, and Andres Duany and Elizabeth Plater-Zyberk, whose Florida new town called Seaside and subsequent planning work have been at the center of the "new urbanism," a term used to describe renewed interest in the townscape as civic art.

RICHARD MEIER

Not all architects of the Post-Modernist period have conformed to Stern's formula, however. Richard Meier (born 1934) has continued the early traditions of Modernism. While Meier's architecture owes an obvious debt to Le Corbusier's houses of the 1920s, as in his use of cubical massing relieved by gentle curves, he also claims to have been influenced by the spatial layering and light quality of Baroque interiors and by such works as Frank Lloyd Wright's Guggenheim Museum. Qualities abstracted from these and other sources include columnar systems of planning grids with a clearly expressed skin enclosing volumetric space; planar elements that slice through the building and penetrate one another; and impeccable white-panel exteriors comparable to the late works of Hoffman and Wagner.

The results of this approach can be seen in Meier's design for the Museum für Kunsthandwerk (Museum of Decorative Arts) in Frankfurt, which won a limited competition in 1980 and was completed in 1983 (Fig. 16.29). Although nominally an addition to an old villa containing the existing museum, Meier's building is nearly ten times larger than the Neo-Classical original, and, except for a second-floor glass-enclosed connector, it stands free of it in an L shape. The position of the villa and the angle of the frontage road paralleling the Main river prompted Meier to indulge in two overlapping grid systems set at an angle of 3.5 degrees to one another. While such a minor shift is imperceptible in reality (unless the museum-goer

16.29 Richard Meier, Axonometric drawing of the Museum für Kunsthandwerk, Frankfurt, 1980–83.

Meier graduated from Cornell University at a time when its design studios were dominated by the compositional manipulations celebrated in Colin Rowe and Fred Koetter's *Collage City*. This building seems to be ideally viewed in a bird's-eye axonometric drawing such as this one.

commonly notes slight misalignments in normally orthogonal building materials), the two grids are distinctly seen in the plan drawings, and their interaction obviously inspired Meier to play with room shapes that would otherwise have seemed arbitrary. Le Corbusier-style regulating traces were overlaid on elevation studies to show that both the villa and the new building have similar proportions; a module derived from the older building relates to basic quadrants in the addition. Panels cover the exterior and align with square mullions in the generously sized

16.30 Richard Meier, High Museum, Atlanta, Georgia, 1981–84.

This art museum stands along Peachtree Street. The ramp in the foreground takes visitors to the bulging entry vestibule, then into the three-story, switchback-ramped rotunda that gives access to the gallery floors.

windows. Interior circulation is organized by a system of switchback ramps linking axial corridors on all floors, while the exhibits are displayed in galleries created by partial-height walls set within the structural bays, establishing a domestic scale appropriate to the museum's collections. Despite the clashing geometries of the building's plan, spaces merge gracefully into one another, and abundant natural light reflecting off shiny white surfaces is welcome in the habitually overcast Frankfurt climate.

Meier employed a similar vocabulary in the High Museum (1981–84) in Atlanta, Georgia (Fig. 16.30). He disengaged the continuous ramp of the Guggenheim Museum and made it the dominant circulation path around the circumference of a quarter-cylinder glass-enclosed atrium, off which he arranged more conventional orthogonal galleries with artificial illumination. Whereas the ramp in the Frankfurt museum is immediately adjacent to gallery displays, in the Atlanta museum their separation isolates the art from the building's most interesting architectural feature. The conditions most curators demand for the display of paintings are in part responsible for this decision. Strong sunlight quickly deteriorates pigments, so works of art need to be kept in controlled lighting conditions.

Meier's billion-dollar Getty Museum (1984–97) in Malibu, north of Los Angeles, spreads out in the form and at the scale of a Modernist hilltown. For the outside walls, he combined his signature modular porcelin-enameled panels with equally modular but textured stone. A circular garden by Robert Irwin suggests the island enclosure at Hadrian's Villa.

Meier's work can also be interpreted as a response to new technologies, since the skins of the museums consist of glass and mass-produced metal panels. Such an esthetic can be traced back to the mid-nineteenth century and Joseph Paxton's Crystal Palace, discussed in Chapter 14. This rapidly erected iron-and-glass structure was one of the most important nineteenth-century buildings, both for its construction methods and its sweeping interior space, making it the common ancestor of two divergent architectural trends of the late twentieth century. In the first group are architects who employ industrial materials to shape buildings that create the sensation of being outdoors while being inside; in the second group are those who flaunt technological progress.

THE EXPLOITATION OF TECHNOLOGY BY JAMES STIRLING AND OTHERS

In the 1960s the English architect James Stirling (1926–1992) used the theme of industrial assemblage in his commissions for the Engineering Building at Leicester University (1964) and the History Faculty Building at Cambridge University (1968), both of which were

16.31 James Stirling, History Faculty Building, Cambridge University, Cambridge, England, 1968.

Stirling's use of dramatic, exposed structural elements can be compared to Russian Constructivist explorations of the early-twentieth century. Offices appear in the tower, with a library in the cascade of glass.

Galleries   Public footpath

Court

Gallery level

Exhibition Hall

Theater

Workshop

Lobby

Entrance level

0   50 m

0   150 ft

startling for their sculptural and unconcealed use of standard building materials. Aluminum-framed commercial greenhouse windows were set in the industrial brick walls of the Engineering Building's office tower and were also employed to wrap completely the walls and ceiling of its attached laboratory wing, where sawtooth skylights are treated as prismatic solids as they terminate at the edge of the building. In the History Faculty Building (Fig. 16.31), which contains a library on the lowest levels and faculty offices in the L-shaped block that rises on two sides, industrial glazing systems were used to cover the library and enclose the long exterior walls of the offices. A giant cascade of glass brings abundant light

16.32 James Stirling, Plan of the Staatsgalerie, Stuttgart, 1977–83.

By this stage of his career, Stirling had forsaken dramatic technology for an almost archaeological-dig historicism combined with spatial manipulations derived from the European Modernists.

16.33 James Stirling, Staasgalerie rotunda, Stuttgart, 1977–83.

Stirling presents this space almost as a ruin. Elsewhere, he left stone blocks strewn on the ground as though dislodged over time.

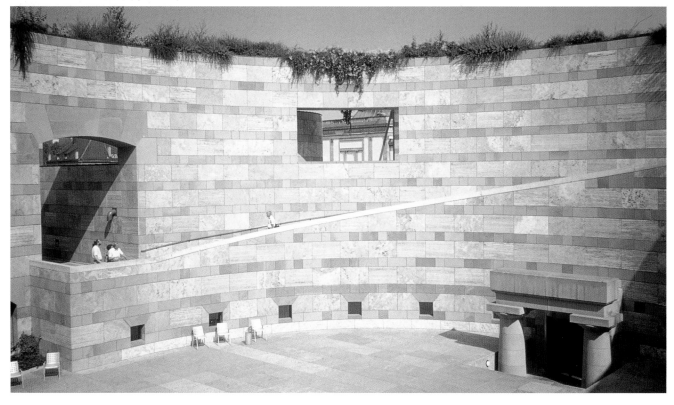

(and solar greenhouse-effect heat build-up in summer) to scholars working in the fan-shaped library. Stirling's Staatsgalerie (Fig. 16.32) in Stuttgart, Germany (1977–83), which owes much to Schinkel's Altesmuseum in Berlin (see Fig. 14.6), contains a host of historical allusions, and responds to its site in a fashion somewhere between the search for a *genius loci*, or peculiar character of a place, and literal deconstruction. The building contains galleries in a U shape around a central, open rotunda, hence the Schinkel connection. Stirling made the rotunda a sculpture garden and part of a public walkway designed in homage to an established pedestrian path through the site. As for the allusions, which range from Greek or Roman pediments to Egyptian **cavetto** cornices to displaced stonework like that used by the Mannerist Giulio Romano (Fig. 16.33), Stirling said that he was "sick and tired of the boring, meaningless, non-committed, faceless flexibility and open-endedness of the present architecture," meaning that he had moved on from his high-tech phase. At the interrupted side of the U in his plan, he set out a sculpture-like display of ramps, platforms, and a sinusoidal-curve lobby. The walls are laid up throughout in a striated coursing of variegated stone that gives the impression of an excavated classical site.

An effect of spaciousness similar to Stirling's History Faculty Building, but without the reliance on readymade components and their resulting economies, is manifested in the Ford Foundation Building (1963–68) (Fig. 16.34), designed by Kevin Roche (born 1922) and John Dinkeloo (1918–1981), successors to the firm founded by Eero Saarinen. Set between 42nd and 43rd streets on a nearly square site within a Manhattan block near the United Nations Building, the Ford Foundation's offices enframe an eleven-story greenhouse that occupies about half the ground floor. Additional planted terraces on the third, fourth, and fifth floors extend the greenery above the entrance level, and the office spaces either share the view into the court or have outside windows. The building's principal materials—weathering steel, granite, bronze, and glass—establish a neutral dark ground for the natural light and vegetation that characterize the interior. Richness and elegance, not cost-cutting, governed design decisions. The building's price, about $16 million for the 16,500 square feet of office space plus common areas and the great atrium, works out to over $200 per square foot in 1968 dollars.

Despite its extravagance, or perhaps because of it, the Ford Foundation headquarters became one of the most influential buildings of the third quarter of the twentieth century. Aside from providing a handsome working environment for the foundation's employees, it also created a pedestrian link through the long side of one of Manhattan's 200-by-400-foot blocks, and this idea of an enclosed walkway was taken up by the Office of Midtown Development as a solution to preserving pedestrian access within New York City. Zoning incentives encouraged developers to include ground-floor public passageways in new high-rise buildings. The idea was not new. The splendid nave of the Crystal Palace had inspired many glass-roofed commercial arcade buildings in Europe and the United States, of which the best-known example is the Galleria Vittorio Emanuele (1865–77) in Milan, Italy, designed by Giuseppe Mengoni (1829–1877) to connect the Piazza del Duomo to La Scala, the opera house a block away.

Major New York buildings that benefitted from these zoning incentives include the Citicorp Building (1974–77), set between 53rd and 54th streets on Lexington Avenue. Hugh Stubbins, the architect, designed a six-story podium for the building and dedicated it to retail shops opening off a central atrium and then placed the fifty-nine-floor office tower astride a sunken plaza at the Lexington Avenue end. The IBM Center by Edward Larrabee Barnes (1984) and Trump Tower by Der Scutt with Swanke, Hayden, and Connell (1984), both seen in

16.34 Kevin Roche and John Dinkeloo, Ford Foundation Building, New York City, 1963–68.

Various gestures toward urban amenity were made during the 1960s. Here Roche and Dinkeloo created a huge botanical-garden-like atrium inside one of the more expensive buildings of the period.

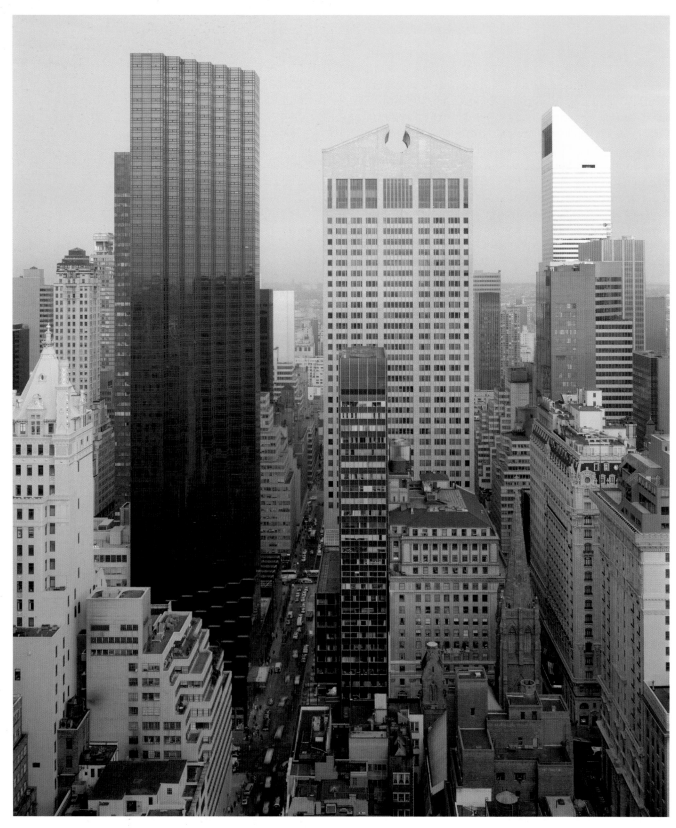

16.35 Manhattan looking along 56th Street, 1984.

Left to right, one sees Trump Tower by Der Scutt, Swanke, Hayden and Connell; the AT&T Building (now Sony Plaza) by Johnson/Burgee; and Citicorp by Hugh Stubbins Associates. This forest of skyscrapers is supported by the bedrock underlying Manhattan Island.

Figure 16.35, provide ground-level amenities with enclosed atrium spaces containing informal seating, food services, gallery displays, ornamental planting, and handsomely presented boutiques.

Industrial building technology was, of course, a contributing factor in the development of Modern architecture, becoming a hallmark of the International Style because it represented efficiency. Le Corbusier praised the uncluttered designs of oceanliners, while Mies considered glass-and-steel construction to be the significant architectural problem of the twentieth century. Walter Gropius's interest in prefabrication, developed during the Bauhaus years, continued into his tenure at Harvard, when he tried without much success to interest American manufacturers in systems building. In designing his own house in Lincoln, Massachusetts, in 1937, Gropius used windows, stairs, and other fittings from the catalogs of light-commercial building suppliers. After World War II, Charles and Ray Eames, known primarily as designers of furniture and graphics, built their house in California entirely from components available on the commercial market.

In the Post-Modern period this enchantment with using and expressing technology has been revived, particularly by European architects, and has led to designs in which the structural and mechanical aspects of buildings take precedence over formal issues. Unlike the atrium or galleria buildings of the Crystal Palace esthetic, which generally have sculptural form and internal spatial excitement, high-tech architecture concentrates on articulating and making visible all the building's components. An early example is the Pompidou Center (1976) in Paris (Fig. 16.36), designed by Renzo Piano and Richard Rogers in the Beaubourg area of Paris, not far from the former site of Les Halles. The principal architectural features hang on the outside of the building, where the white web of diagonally braced steel framing, bright blue air-handling ducts, red exhaust stacks, and exterior escalator snaking up the front façade encase a multi-story glass rectangular solid. The galleries contained inside are unremarkable when compared with the exterior, and the building's bristling mechanics are curiously out of place in its nineteenth-century neighborhood.

An even more spectacular tour de force is the international headquarters for the Hong Kong Bank (1986) by Norman Foster Associates (Fig. 16.37). Foster, a British architect, responded to a site which has splendid views of Hong Kong harbor (to the north) and Victoria Peak (to the south), by creating a forty-seven-story rectangular prism with its long sides oriented to the views while mechanical and service functions close off the short east and west elevations. The most public banking areas are housed in the third through twelfth floors, which are grouped around a central atrium lit by mirrors attached to a south-facing "sunscoop" (an adjustable apparatus with mirrors to track the sun's path) hung outside the building. Save for mechanical rooms, structure, and elevator lobbies, the ground level is devoted entirely to an open plaza from which paired escalators rise through a glass ceiling to the atrium above. Construction detail gives character to the exterior; eight steel-truss towers

16.36 Renzo Piano and Richard Rogers, Pompidou Center, Paris, 1976.

The innards of a building (structural skeleton, mechanical systems and piping, etc.) that had long been concealed or downplayed are allowed to become the building's principal expression. The site quickly became one of the most visited in Paris.

comprise the "legs" from which the floors are suspended in five modules of diminishing height. Thus a column-free interior is obtained with a structural system that acts like five superimposed bridges suspended from horizontal trusses. Each horizontal truss occupies a double-height story containing meeting rooms, recreation areas, and food services, and each has exterior terraces that serve as refuge areas in case of fire. The truss floors divide the building into zoned layers housing related functional units of the bank, and floors within each zone are linked with escalators rather than elevators to establish spatial

16.37 Norman Foster, Hong Kong Bank, Hong Kong, 1986. Like an insect, this high-rise bank has an exoskeleton. Its long sides orient to views, while mechanical and service functions close off the short east and west elevations.

CHAPTER 16 MODERNISMS IN THE MID- AND LATE TWENTIETH CENTURY

continuity. Setbacks at the upper levels conform to building codes, and a penthouse at the top provides space for the bank's officers with its roof serving as a helicopter landing pad.

DECONSTRUCTION

In contrast to these Constructivistic buildings, Post-Modernism has also included within it work described as Deconstructivist. In *Deconstructivist Architecture* (1988), which accompanied an exhibition at MOMA in New York City, the argument is made that, even though the terminology is the same, Deconstruction in architecture means something quite different from literary Post-Structuralist endeavors to deconstruct written texts in order to locate their hidden meanings:

> *A deconstructive architect is therefore not one who dismantles buildings, but one who locates the inherent dilemmas within buildings. The deconstructivist architect puts the pure forms of the architectural tradition on the couch and identifies the symptoms of a repressed impurity. The impurity is drawn to the surface by a combination of gentle coaxing and violent torture: the form is interrogated.*

16.38 Bernard Tschumi, *Folie*, Parc de la Villette, Paris, 1982–85.

The Parc de la Villette is intended to be an open-air cultural center with space for workshops, gymnasium and bath facilities, playgrounds, exhibitions, concerts, and more. Each *folie* is an undifferentiated, neutral object in the landscape where designated activities can take place.

The MOMA exhibition, assembled by the perceptive and wily Philip Johnson, was fraught with controversy even before it opened and was showered with constant criticism afterward because of the vagaries of Deconstruction's meaning and relevance.

Some practitioners, notably Bernard Tschumi (born 1944) and Peter Eisenman (born 1932), argue that their buildings are indeed Derridian; Tschumi says that his Parc de la Villette in Paris (1982–85) (Fig. 16.38) explores the disjunctures in culture, emphasizing fragmentation and dissociation rather than traditional unity and synthesis. Frank Gehry, on the other hand, has seemed quite content to "dismantle," beginning with the design for his own house in Los Angeles (see Fig. 16.41), and today has a thriving practice driven to a great extent by the ability of computer technology to make his irregular and often intersecting geometries understandable to builders. Charles Jencks sums up his view of Deconstruction this way, describing it as principally iconoclastic:

> *Deconstruction . . . always depends for its meaning on that which is previously constructed. It always posits an orthodoxy which it "subverts," a norm which it breaks, an assumption and ideology which it undermines. And the minute it loses this critical role, or becomes a dominant power itself (as in so many academies), it becomes a tyrannical bore. The same is true of Deconstructionist architecture: it works best as an exception within a strongly defined norm.*

Some have seen such arguments as erudite castles in the air made by professional designers envious of the intellectual depth found in the humanities. Others have supported these arguments, saying that they promote a serious and necessary criticism of unbridled consumer culture and media-driven hyper-reality.

PETER EISENMAN

The work of Peter Eisenman certainly fits Jencks's description. He is an architect who has reinvented himself more times than Philip Johnson, and like Johnson has exhibited a genius for self-promotion. In a career driven by an almost maniacal extraction of ideas from the then-current cultural milieu in fields as diverse as the linguistic investigations of Foucault and the potential geometries created by fractals, Eisenman has honed his image as a provocateur and man of intellect among lesser minds. Some criticize his work as contrived and opportunistic, while others see it as endlessly investigative and serious to the point of tragedy. He first became known for the series of houses, most of them unbuilt, that he designed in the late 1960s and early 1970s (Fig. 16.39). While they respond to complex programs based upon both individual and societal issues, they are outwardly formalistic experiments using colliding and interlocking geometries

M.C. ESCHER AND THE PARADOXICAL STAIRCASES OF POST-MODERNISM

by Robert M. Craig

16A M.C. Escher, *Relativity*, 1953. Lithograph.

Peter Eisenman's House VI, built in 1975 in Cornwall, Connecticut, contains a real stair, (painted green and functional), and a false stair (inverted overhead, painted red, and virtual). Elsewhere there are columns lacking structural purpose and walls positioned merely for compositional intent rather than to define usable space. As an alternative to orthodox Modernism, Eisenman's House VI was an architecture which positioned itself somewhere between the inverted logic of *Through the Looking-Glass*, or Alice's Wonderland, and the paradoxical strange loops of M.C. Escher's graphic art.

The urge to explore alternatives implies a rejection of convention. However, as new directions establish new models and in turn effect new displacements, then endorsements and rejections of convention begin to mirror one another in ironical and contradictory ways, evidencing virtues Robert Venturi proclaimed as admirable in his 1966 "gentle manifesto." In many ways, the development of twentieth-century architecture, as it dematerialized historic form only to return to it again as a model, was a journey up the paradoxical staircases of M.C. Escher's world, as shown in his lithographs *Relativity* (1953) (Fig. 16A) and *Concave and Convex* (1955).

Pre-modern, canonical academic architecture has valued "correctness" in the use of historical models. An architect's ability was demonstrated by his proper reflection of an ideal and his conformity to the rules of taste. After a long nineteenth century characterized by an eclectic reuse of past forms, Modernism displaced historic models, arguing that representational art was derivative and not reflective of the modern *Zeitgeist* based on technology. Moreover, if modern architecture at the hands of Mies or Le Corbusier remained classical, its historic substance was a "virtual reality," in which formal reality became abstract and was reduced to line, planar surface, and volume. Indeed, non-objectivity and functional space became the modern building's new reality: "I see nobody on the road," said Alice. "It's as much as I can do to see real people," said the King.

Beyond the modern masters, conventional Modernism disseminated a diluted, impersonal, and banal International Style worldwide, producing a minimalism and lack of visual and intellectual complexity that by the mid-1960s was considered "a bore." Just as the conventions of historical revivalism, considered to be the unoriginal work of copyists, had been displaced by a non-representational Modernism, so now alternatives to the conventions of Modernism were sought and a new complexity called for. The creative architect, considered as artistic genius rather than technocrat, would extend both traditional and modern models to produce an enriched, even distorted and perverse, but certainly innovative architecture. The paradox was that earlier historicist architects had been viewed as lacking in creative genius and unoriginal, and now conventional Modernists were considered authors of anonymous and univalent designs and were viewed as mere functionalists, producing work that lacked esthetic intellectual content. In the place of conventional Modernism, architects again began to reference and translate historic form, with no concern that they were mere copyists and convinced they were instead ingenious creators of "multivalent" forms. Thus, as Post-Modernists rediscovered history, by means of a kind of "strange loop" of Escherian logic, they employed historic form to create a contradictory architecture that was both derived *and* original; they began again to climb Escher's paradoxical staircase.

16.39 Peter Eisenman, House III, Lakeville, Connecticut, 1969–71.

In the 1960s, Peter Eisenman explored the abstract possibilities of rotated grids. Spaces became an effect caused by the manipulation of selected elements according to a set of rules.

16.40 Peter Eisenman, Model of Biocentrum, Frankfurt am Main, 1987.

Within this biotechnology research laboratory, Eisenman had to provide scientists and their staffs with a safe working environment free of cross-contamination, noxious odors, and the spread of toxic materials. Prominent on the exterior are the ventilation stacks that ensure a continuous cycling of clean, fresh air.

that seem only self-referential; Eisenman touted them as linguistic-architectural inquiries into the basic grammar and syntax of space. In his Biocentrum in Frankfurt am Main, Germany (1987) (Fig. 16.40), "DNA is used as a model of a logical sequence with infinite possibilities for expansion, change, and flexibility." Here, the collision of geometries remains, overlaid with biological metaphor, certainly more apparent to the designer than the casual passer-by.

FRANK GEHRY

Frank Gehry (born 1929) has succeeded in having a host of designs that would seem destined to remain as models or conceptual drawings actually built. He has been strongly influenced by artists, many of whom are his close friends. Early in his career he realized, as have many other architects, that he often preferred buildings in an incomplete state of construction to the finished products. While most would have left it at that, however, Gehry started to design new buildings, with an obvious kinship to Russian Constructivist work, that seem frozen in a state of becoming. His own much-published house in Santa Monica, California (1977–78) (Fig. 16.41) is a case in point. Its ribbed metal siding, chain-link fencing, and unpainted wood, all pouring forth from a seemingly confused early twentieth-century bungalow behind, make the composition look as much like an active construction site as an occupied structure. Afterward, Gehry began to explode buildings, breaking them up into discrete volumes in a way that, to some, reflects the fragmentation in modern society. His Winton Guest House in Wayzata, Minnesota (1983–86) (Fig. 16.42) stands adjacent to a main house designed in 1952 by Philip Johnson. Gehry somewhat awkwardly but powerfully arranged a set of very sculptural forms—one vault-like, one a shed-roofed box, the others boxes with flat roofs—around a central truncated pyramid. His objective, he said, was to create a building with a "certain amount of humor and mystery and fantasy." His Team Disneyland Administration Building in Anaheim, California (1996) can be compared organizationally to Aalto's Baker House. Seen from the freeway, its flat, quilted sheet-metal façade appears to be quite conventional, its regularity broken only by slight offsets in the stacking of windows and the mottled color scheme. To the rear (Fig. 16.43), however, the building's massing becomes curvilinear, warped, even delusional, as canary-yellow walls bend, lean forward, and lean back, their canopies equally disfigured, as if a result of a recent seismic event. On the interior, the same wildly sculptural unconventionality holds sway at the main stair, with its compound curves, and in the theater, where walls are formed by overlapping sheets of plywood shaped in response to acoustical requirements. Even more urbanistically aggressive is Gehry's Nationale Nederlander office building in Prague, in the Czech Republic, known locally as "Fred and Ginger" (1997) (Fig. 16.44). Here, within a historic context, Gehry took movement as his theme for a corner building that twists and projects in space with an energy expressive of the opening up of eastern Europe since the dissolution of the Soviet Union. Economic constraints called for one more floor than in neighboring buildings, but accommodated within the same cornice height. In order to resolve the conflict, Gehry lowered and camouflaged the floor levels by means of fishscale-like undulating layers of cement plaster and more displaced windows. The entrance tower of concrete columns bundled in glass seems to sway as if part of an urban choreography in step with the surrounding buildings and space, hence the "Fred and Ginger" nickname. The result, though idiosyncratic, is surprisingly contextual, acknowledging adjacent medieval towers and Baroque façades and domes.

Gehry's Guggenheim Museum Bilbao (opened 1997) in Bilbao, Spain (Fig. 16.45), has aroused a kind of popular and critical interest equalled by few other twentieth-century constructions. His exhilarating structure

16.41 Frank Gehry, Gehry House, Santa Monica, California, 1977–78.

Frank Gehry began modestly, making additions to his own bungalow that fall somewhere between sculpture and industrial residue. As with Peter Eisenman, Gehry eventually needed the computer to build fantastical structures that he could at first only imagine.

16.42 Frank Gehry, Winton Guest House, Wayzata, Minnesota, 1983–86. Model.

Gehry was always as interested in sculpture as architecture. Here simple, recognizable volumes collide. His sheathing materials are stone, Finnish plywood, and copper.

replaced dock facilities on a site adjacent to the Nervión river in a gritty manufacturing city. Out of a four-story mass blossom "pleated petals" of titanium attached to a steel frame. The museum acts as a mirror, reflecting and absorbing the city, reflecting and absorbing itself. Giving off a metallic luminescence, it hovers and shimmers at the end of hard-edged urban vistas (Fig. 16.46). Visitors have come to Bilbao in droves, more to see the building than its contents. They want to be in it and around it, and they want to touch it. In the complex first-floor plan, where the only orthogonal spaces house

mechanical systems, the loading dock, and storage and exhibition-preparation rooms, a towering central atrium connects to an auditorium and galleries, one of them a trapezoid, one L-shaped, and the largest one a long and narrow boat-like giant that passes beneath the Puente de

16.43 Frank Gehry, Team Disney Administration Building Computer rendering, Los Angeles, California, 1996.

Only computer technology made it possible to build such distorted forms. On the inside, Gehry's plans exhibit a much more conventional ordering.

16.44 (above) Frank Gehry, Nationale Nederlander ("Fred and Ginger"), Prague, 1997.

Taken out of context, this building perhaps appears shocking. However, it actually fits quite well among its neighbors. The nearby curving gables, spiky towers, and richly textured façades convey the same energy and urban liveliness as Gehry's intervention.

16.45 (below) Frank Gehry, Guggenheim Museum Bilbao, Bilbao, 1997.

No recent building has garnered more attention in the popular press or been a more popular site for architectural pilgrimages. Visitors love to touch its shiny skin of titanium.

Exam Review - History

1. Modern Architecture - why did it begin? prompted it?
2. Frank lloyd wright? Prarie house - characteristics?
3. Einstein tower - what did it represent? what kind of work?
4. Chryster building & Art deco - artistic view point?
5. red + blue chair modern design - what was desteele art movement about?
6. Eric boussier - 2nd most famous house - villa savoy - characteristics?
7. Beaux house - Germany - what was the purpose?
8. what is the mathematics of barcelona Pavillion?
9. International style - characteristics house?
10. Robert Van churry - most famous quotes "God is in the details"?
11. Most famous building. Frank lloyd wright "Falling water"?
12. Sculptural nature - Aerosterin design famous? besens Airport
13. Lowis Con inspiration for Kimmel art museum? where are lost?
14. Robert van curry - title of book?
15. "Less is more"? - "Less is a bore" - robert curry.
16. piazza italia - Charles moore - what architectural movement had a sense of humor?
17. Richard mayers - architecture?
18. High tech architecture - richard rogers - Pampanous Center? Paris.
19. Frank Gehrys - work? Guggenheim museum?
Fred + Ginger building - "Dancing house"?

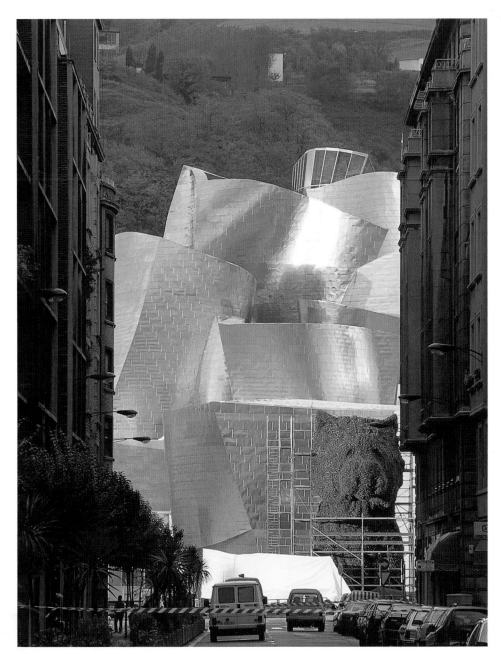

16.46 Frank Gehry, Guggenheim Museum Bilbao in its urban context, Bilbao, 1997.

The effect of the sculpted, quilted titanium surfaces at the end of the Calle de Iparragguirre is startling. The play of light on the facets of the metal causes the character of the building to change dramatically with the changing position of the sun and changing atmospheric conditions.

la Salve, the major road through Bilbao, as it reaches out to the east beside a free-form water garden. On the second and third floors, the plan becomes more regular, including a series of square galleries placed *en enfilade*. The space inside the atrium (page 532) is enormous, half as tall again as Wright's Guggenheim rotunda, with bowing steel, angular stone-faced walls, and undulating masses cut away to admit light; it is the fulfillment of a Baroque spatial dream made possible by modern building and computer technology.

GLENN MURCUTT

This chapter began with the work of Alvar Aalto, a designer who embraced Modernism early in his career then moved on to develop a personal idiom that acknowledged modern culture and technology but remained firmly grounded in the Nordic context with which he so obviously empathized; it will conclude with a designer in another hemisphere, but one who has followed a similarly successful and personal line of inquiry: the Australian architect Glenn Murcutt (born 1936).

Among the early influences on Murcutt were Mies van der Rohe, particularly his Farnsworth House, and Richard Neutra and Craig Ellwood in California, both of whom produced elegant post-and-beam frames like Mies. Murcutt was also imbued with a reverence for site by the so-called Sydney School of designers at work in Australia in the late 1950s and early 1960s. He became interested in lightweight, permeable structures, building upon his experiences with a father who exposed him to the Australian agricultural buildings of wood and corrugated metal and who sensitized him to the act of making. Murcutt tends to design units that are long and narrow, with their long sides facing north and south in order to assure proper ventilation, and respond to the path of the sun. He extrudes their cross sections, but gives them complex profiles responding

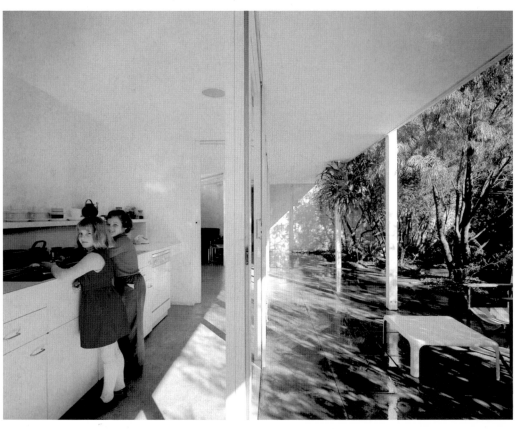

16.47 Glenn Murcutt, Douglas Murcutt House interior, Sydney, 1969–72.

Here is a subtle essay on interior and exterior space and the transition between the two. The structure is Farnsworth House-like, with thin, box columns supporting a hovering roof.

16.48 Glenn Murcutt, History Museum and Tourist Office, Kempsey, New South Wales, 1976, 1979–82, 1986–88.

Murcutt has drawn upon the local vernacular for many of his forms, but has reinterpreted them in terms of modern materials and methods of construction. The exhaust turbines on the roof become important formal elements.

16.49 Glenn, Murcutt, Local History Museum and Tourist Office interior, Kempsey, New South Wales, 1976, 1979–82, 1986–88.

Environmental control elements are important parts of the interior of every Murcutt design. Venetian blinds both alter light and provide scale-giving elements. Below them, wooden transoms can be opened for ventilation.

to sun and wind as well as to human habitation. He then details these skins to accept louvers and screens that both modulate climatic forces and articulate their surfaces. Subsequent to contact with the Mexican architect Luis Barragán, Murcutt has made pools of water a significant feature in many of his projects.

The Douglas Murcutt House in Sydney (1969–72) (Fig. 16.47) is Farnsworth House-like but lowered to the ground and merged with nature, in the form of a courtyard planted with native vegetation. The Ball-Eastaway House (1980–83), located northwest of Sydney, consists of a tubular-steel-frame pavilion, minimalist in its structure and minimal in its environmental impact. Sited in a forest of acacias, eucalyptuses, and banksias, it has a vaulted cross section with walls almost completely covered by louvers and a downspout system that is akin to sculpture. In Kempsey, New South Wales, Murcutt designed a Local History Museum and Tourist Office (1976, 1979–82, and 1986–88) (Fig. 16.48) that is equally subtle and overt in its responses to environmental forces. He placed non-bearing brick walls atop a brick base, insulated them, then covered them with zinc alloy panels; the corrugated metal roof is supported by a separate tubular-steel frame. Ventilation occurs in the seam between the systems (Fig. 16.49) and is enhanced and dramatized by roof monitors. The textures of the walls and ceiling, and the light qualities they allow, belie their straightforward construction origins. The Magney House at Bingi Point, New South Wales (1982–84) (Fig. 16.50) is a Miesian box no more. Its asymmetrical butterfly roof, metal cladding, louvers, and downspout system leading to subterranean cisterns come together in a metallic organism finetuned to its windswept environment and its purpose as a vacation house for clients who had long visited and admired the site.

16.50 Glenn Murcutt, Magney House, Bingi Point, New South Wales, 1982–84.

Beneath the slab of this house, Murcutt placed cisterns to collect rainwater. The apparently eccentric roof form actually responds both to the path of the sun and to prevailing winds.

16.51 Glenn Murcutt, Plan of the Minerals and Mining Museum, Broken Hill, New South Wales, 1987–89.

Many of Murcutt's plans are long and narrow, like this one, in order to take advantage of orientation and cross ventilation. The skin, separate from the structural grid, seems alive in its sensitivity to its context.

As a metaphor for Australian mining structures, Murcutt's unbuilt Minerals and Mining Museum in Broken Hill, New South Wales (1987–89) (Fig. 16.51) exaggerates both the frame and the skin, yielding something akin to but more explicable perhaps than the work of the Deconstructivists. Rammed-earth walls outfitted with wind traps of Egyptian inspiration keep the interior space ten degrees centigrade cooler than the outside air without the benefit of mechanical air-conditioning.

16.52 Glenn Murcutt, Simpson-Lee House, Mount Wilson, New South Wales, 1989–94.

This project combines a Spartan, mechanistic elegance with a sincere yet practical response to passive climate control. The result approaches art.

Finally, the Simpson-Lee House in Mount Wilson, New South Wales (1989–94) (Fig. 16.52) possesses an equipoise that results from the placement of each piece—frame-constructed pavilions, linear walkway, and pool of water—in a kind of environmental equilibrium. Movement along the walkway, past the studio, and alongside the pool and the living quarters is calculated to give the occupants a sense of gradual withdrawal into a private realm with almost monastic qualities.

Together these projects demonstrate Murcutt's synthesis of the Miesian version of European Modernism with what he had learned from Australian agricultural and industrial buildings and with the natural world and its expression in the local landscape. Given the increasing pressures of expanding populations and finite resources, Murcutt's design approach seems logical and even necessary in its generalities, if not its particulars. Such a conclusion for this chapter, begun with the humanity of Alvar Aalto and interrupted by the myriad, sometimes fractured and frantic design approaches of various Post-Modernists, offers some alternatives for thoughtful students.

GLOSSARY

Abacus On a classical column, the stone set directly over the capital.

Abbey A monastery governed by an abbot.

Acanthus A plant used as a model for decoration on Corinthian and Composite capitals.

Acropolis Literally "high city". In Greek city-states, the acropolis was the location of the most important temples and religious shrines.

Acroterion An upright ornament placed at the apex and eaves of gabled roofs in Greek architecture.

Agora In Greek cities, the term applied to the area of markets and city government.

Aisle In a basilican church, the portion set parallel to the nave, generally separated from it by columns or piers.

Allée A linear garden walk defined by trees on both sides.

Ambulatory The curving passageway behind the choir of a church, often used to connect the radiating chapels.

Amphitheater An arena with raked seating arranged around a circular or oval floor.

Apadana An audience hall in Persian palace architecture.

Appartements A suite of rooms (French).

Apse The termination of the nave of a basilica or the choir in a basilican church.

Aqueduct A pipe for conducting water under gravity flow. The term is often applied to the arched structure built to support the pipe across valleys.

Arcade A series of arches carried on columns or piers.

Arch A curved element that spans an opening and supports the structural loads above it. Most often, arches are made of small, wedge-shaped masonry elements called voussoirs. The profile of an arch may vary from semicircular to pointed to almost flat.

Architrave In classical architecture, the bottom portion of an entablature.

Arris The intersection of two curved surfaces, most commonly applied to the line formed when the flutes of a Doric column join.

Ashlar Smooth stone masonry laid so that the joints are visible.

Atrium The central space of a Roman house, open to the sky and serving as a source of light and fresh air. In Early Christian churches, the atrium was a large open courtyard, surrounded by covered galleries, which preceded the entrance to the church.

Attic The story built above the cornice of a building, sometimes used to conceal the roof.

Axis A line at the end of which movement terminates at a significant feature and thereby divides a composition into two equal parts.

Balcony A platform cantilevered from a wall, generally surrounded by a railing or balustrade.

Baldachin or **Baldacchino** An elaborate canopy erected over an altar.

Balloon framing A wooden framing system composed of vertical studs extended unbroken from bottom sill to top plate even in multistory construction.

Baptistery A building, generally octagonal, used for the Christian rite of baptism.

Barrel vault A semicircular vault over a rectangular space.

Base The lowest part of a column or pier, often broader than the sections above to spread the load to the foundation.

Basilica Literally, "king's hall". In Roman architecture, a hall used for public administration. The term generally refers to a rectangular building that has a central section with a higher roof (the nave if a church) flanked by lower aisles on both long sides. A semicircular projection, the apse, was often set at one or both of the shorter ends. Early Christians adapted the form as a basis for church design, replacing one apse with the main entrance and establishing a processional axis the length of the building. The altar was placed in the apse at the end.

Bastide A medieval new town founded both for defense and economic development of an unsettled region.

Bay A building module defined by the repetition of an element such as a column or pier.

Bazaar A covered market in Islamic cities.

Beam A horizontal element that carries structural loads between upright supports.

Bellcote A modest belfry located astride the ridge of a church roof or made as a narrowed extension upward of the principal gabled façade.

Belfry The tower or steeple in which bells are hung.

Beltcourse A projecting horizontal board or projecting course(s) of brick or stone that define a floor level on the inside.

Belvedere An elevated room or structure situated to afford a fine view or capture breezes.

Blind opening A framed element like a window applied to a wall but lacking an opening to the outside.

Bochki Reverse curve gables seen in Russian architecture.

Boiserie Interior wood paneling enriched by carving, gilding, painting, or inlay.

Bosco A dense grove of trees.

Bouleterion In classical Greek architecture, a building used for senate or council meetings.

Brise-soleil A screen attached to a building to shade windows from the sun.

Buttress Masonry reinforcement applied to a wall to provide additional strength.

Caisson An airtight box or chamber used for work on river bottoms.

Caldarium The hot or sweating bath chamber in Roman baths or thermae.

Campanile In Italy, the name given to a freestanding belltower.

Cantilever A beam firmly anchored on one end and unsupported at the other end.

Capital In classical architecture the termination of a column, generally given decorative carving.

Caravanserai Accommodation for traveling merchants, usually built around a large open court and provided with stables for animals, secure storage for cargo, and an inn for travelers.

Cardo In Etruscan and Roman cities, the principal north-south road.

Carolingian The term applied to buildings constructed under the influence of the emperor Charlemagne, who reigned from 792 to 814.

Cartouche A boldly decorated frame hung above doorways.

Caryatid A pier carved in the form of a standing woman and used in place of a column.

Castrum A Roman military camp or garrison (pl. *castra*).

Cathedral The church that serves as seat of a bishop. (The bishop's chair is called a cathedra.)

Cavetto A concave molding, usually a quadrant of a circle and often used for cornices.

Cella The shrine room in the center of a temple.

Cement The binding component of concrete. Natural cements occur in areas of former volcanic activity, as around Puteoli in Italy, where the Romans exploited deposits they called pozzolana. Artificial cements have been made since 1824, when Joseph Aspdin discovered a process for heating limestone, clay, and sand to a very high temperature and then grinding the results.

Cenotaph A monument erected in memory of someone who is not interred within it.

Centering The wooden scaffold or form required to support a masonry vault or arch while under construction.

Chaitya In India, a traditional village memorial erected over the grave of an honored person. A structure built to enclose such a memorial and permit circulation around it is known as a chaitya hall.

Chancel The east end of a church, in which the main altar is placed.

Chapter house An assembly room in a monastery, generally located off the cloister, where the monks and abbot gathered daily for reading a chapter of the Rule by which monastic life was governed.

Château The French word for castle. In Renaissance France, the term is generally applied to a large country residence without any military pretentions.

Chatra A triple-tiered umbrella form set atop a stupa, symbolic of the Bodhi tree under which Buddha gained enlightenment.

Chigi In Shinto architecture, upward extensions of bargeboards at gable ends of the shrine, forming an X-shape.

Choir The eastern end of a basilican church, where the divine service was sung.

Clerestory Windows placed high in a wall, generally above lower roof elements.

Cloister In a monastery, the covered walk surrounding a quadrangular court that connects the domestic buildings and the church.

Cloister vault A dome with groined surfaces rising from a square or octagonal base. Also known as a domical vault.

Coffers Ceiling recesses set in a geometric pattern.

Colonnade A linear series of columns with entablature.

Column In classical architecture, the upright structural element consisting of a base, shaft, and capital.

Composite A Roman order combining features of the Ionic and Corinthian.

Concrete A plastic building material consisting of sand, water, cement, and aggregate, which hardens to a stone-like consistency.

Console A bracket, generally decoratively curved, that supports a cornice or projecting element.

Coquille A seashell-like organic form.

Corbel Masonry that projects slightly from a wall and serves as a support.

Corbeled vault Construction, without true arching action, made by shifting opposing courses slightly and regularly inward until they meet.

Corinthian The order that features acanthus-leaf capitals atop a fluted shaft.

Cornice The uppermost element of an entablature, which projects beyond the plane of the exterior wall; more generally, the overhanging molding atop any building.

Corps-de-logis The main, freestanding unit in a French building complex.

Cortile In Italian architecture, the term applied to an open courtyard inside a building.

Crockets Decorative bud-like protrusions on the angles of Gothic stonework, especially on spires and towers.

Crossing In a basilican church, the space where transepts, nave, and choir intersect.

Cross-in-square Another name for the quincunx plan.

Cross vault The vault formed by two intersecting barrel vaults. Also known as a groin vault.

Crypt The basement level of a church, originally used for burial.

Cupola A dome. The term is also applied to the lantern on any roof structure, and is generally used to describe the structure over the oculus of a dome.

Curtain wall In medieval castles, a section of defensive walling between projecting towers. In modern construction, a nonstructural exterior surface hung from metal framing.

Cyclopean masonry Walls made of very large stones, only minimally shaped.

Decumanus In Etruscan and Roman cities, the principal east–west road.

Dentil A type of cornice molding composed of rectangular blocks set in a row like teeth; hence the name.

Dome A continuously curved roof over a polygonal or circular plan, generally having a semicircular or elliptical section.

Domical vault A dome with groined surfaces rising from a square or octagonal base. Also known as a cloister vault.

Domos The principal space in a megaron.

Doric The Greek order that has a fluted shaft, no base, and an echinus molding supporting the abacus. Roman Doric columns have a base.

Dormer A window that projects above the slope of a roof.

Drum The cylindrical volume supporting a dome.

Eave The edge of the roof plane that projects over the exterior wall of a building.

Echinus The curved cushion-like molding that, together with the abacus, forms the capital in the Doric order.

Eclecticism The selection and combination of architectural elements from a variety of styles.

Egg-and-Dart An egg-shaped ornament alternating with a dart-shaped one.

Enfilade The aligning of a series of doors through a series of adjacent rooms.

En suite A series of rooms arranged side by side.

Entablature In classical architecture, the horizontal elements supported by columns, consisting (in ascending sequence) of the architrave, frieze, and cornice.

Entasis The slight outward curve of a column, which then tapers toward the top of the shaft.

Exedra A semicircular niche, often used as a seat of honor or place for a statue.

Façade The exterior elevation of a building.

Fan vault In English Perpendicular Gothic buildings, vaults with ribs having the same curvature and radiating or fanning out from the springing of the vault.

Fascia Horizontal bands in the architrave of the Ionic and Corinthian orders; more generally, the end board of a roof at the eaves.

Ferroconcrete Concrete with embedded steel wire or rods. The combination takes advantage of the compressive strength of the former and the tensile strength of the latter.

Feng shui The Chinese art of adjusting a design to site-specific conditions so as to promote harmony in accordance with Daoist principles.

Fillet The flat vertical face between the flutings of a column shaft.

Fluting Vertical grooves incised in the shaft of a classical column.

Flying buttress In Gothic architecture, the combination of external buttress pier and slender arch, which attaches to a wall just below the springing of the vaulting in order to resist lateral thrust.

Forum In Roman towns, the open space near the center used for commerce and civic life.

Fresco A painting executed on wall surfaces by working pigments into wet plaster.

Frieze The horizontal element above the architrave and below the cornice in an entablature.

Frigidarium The cold-water baths in a Roman thermae.

Frontispiece An elaborated door surround at the front façade of a building.

Gable The pedimented end of a classical temple; more generally, the triangular space at the end of a double-pitched roof.

Galilee A porch or chapel at the west end of medieval churches.

Gallery The passage over the aisle in medieval churches.

Garbhagriha The "womb chamber" or shrine room at the heart of a Hindu temple.

Gargoyle A decorative rainwater spout, often carved to resemble a fanciful animal.

Gopura In Hindu architecture, a monumental gateway erected on axis with the temple.

Grand salon The major living space in a Venetian palace, usually extending from front to back of the house.

Greek-cross plan A plan in the form of a cross having arms of equal length.

Groin vault The vault formed by two intersecting barrel vaults. Also known as a cross vault.

Ha-ha A ditch used to control the movement of livestock, which is not visible in a planned landscape.

Half-timbering Wall construction with heavy-timber members carrying the structural load and made weather-tight with infill materials.

Hall church A basilican church where the nave and aisles are of similar height.

Hammerbeam A bracketed cantilevered beam used as support for a timber roof truss.

Haram Literally, "private" or "sacred". Used to describe the sanctuary in a mosque and the family living quarters in an Islamic house.

Harmika The square railing at the top of a stupa.

Hemicycle A semicircular room or recess.

Hipped roof A roof built with inclined gables on all four sides.

Hôtel A French urban domestic building.

Hypostyle hall A large hall composed of many columns placed close together to support the roof.

Iconostasis A screen in Byzantine churches that divides the nave from the chancel and that is used as a support for devotional images or icons.

Impluvium In Roman houses, the shallow pool that collected rainwater draining from the atrium roof.

Insula A Roman apartment house.

Intarsia Mosaic inlay in wood.

Intercolumniation The space between columns.

Ionic The order that features volutes in the capital; the shaft is usually fluted.

I-section A structural member with an I-shaped cross section; its horizontal members are called flanges and its vertical member a web.

Iwan Roofed or vaulted chamber open on one side, often facing the courtyard of a mosque.

Jetty A short wooden cantilever supporting an upper wall section, most commonly found on timber houses of the medieval period.

Jian A module used in Chinese wooden architecture, particularly houses, measuring about twelve by twenty feet.

Katsuogi Short horizontal elements set atop the ridge of Shinto shrines; probably used originally to hold down the thatch roof.

Keep The central enclosed tower of a medieval castle.

Keystone The central voussoir of an arch.

Ki A brush-and mud-covered domical structure built by indigenous tribes in the American southwest.

Kiva A ritual or assembly space in the Ancestral Pueblo culture, often circular, and usually sunken into the ground.

Kodo In Japanese Buddhist architecture, the name given to the lecture hall.

Külliye The Turkish word for a mosque and its related buildings, typically including educational, charitable, medical, and commercial facilities.

Label molding A molding that extends horizontally across an opening, then returns vertically for a short distance down each side.

Labyrinth A building with, or arrangement of, winding or confusing pathways.

Lantern A tower with windows rising above the roofline or above the oculus of a dome.

Lierne A decorative, nonstructural supplementary rib added to Gothic vaulting.

Lintel Any horizontal member that spans an opening.

Loggia An open porch, generally raised above the ground floor and covered by a roof.

Lombard bands Decorative wall detailing composed of corbeled arches and pilasters.

Long gallery A wide and long passageway in English and French Renaissance houses used for living purposes.

Lunette The semi-circular or crescent-shaped projection of a window opening into a vaulted ceiling.

Lustral basin A pool used for ritual purification.

Machicolation In medieval fortifications, a corbeled stone gallery projecting in front of a defensive wall, open at the bottom to allow materials to be dropped on those below.

Madrasa Islamic college for theological, legal, and literary studies.

Mandala The geometrical diagram based on a subdivided square that is used to generate proportions for Hindu temple designs.

Mandorla An almond-shaped frame surrounding the image of a saint, used to indicate divinity.

Maqsura In early mosques, an area in front of the mihrab reserved for officials and sometimes given extra ornamentation (unusual vaulting or a dome) or special screening for security.

Marché Movement along a defined architectural path.

Martyrium A building associated with a Christian martyr.

Masjid A district or neighborhood mosque.

Mastaba An Egyptian tomb with a flat top and sloping sides, built over a grave shaft.

Mausoleum An elaborate tomb, named after the tomb of King Mausoleus.

Medallion An ornamental plaque, frequently oval or square.

Megalith Large stones or boulders used in prehistoric architecture.

Megaron In Mycenaean architecture, a rectangular room having a central hearth and four columns supporting a roof with an atrium opening. More generally, the term applies to a single-cell house in the Aegean region.

Metope An element of the Doric frieze, set alternately with triglyphs. Metope panels contain low-relief carvings.

Mihrab A niche in the qibla wall indicating the direction of Mecca.

Minaret In Islamic architecture, the tower associated with a mosque from which the faithful are called to prayer.

Minbar In a mosque the pulpit from which the imam leads prayers.

Minka Wooden Japanese folk houses, typical of rural communities.

Moat A broad surrounding ditch, sometimes filled with water, constructed for defense.

Modillion Another word for console, sometimes applied to a series of ornamental brackets supporting a cornice.

Moment connection A connection between two elements, usually beam and column, that is capable of resisting a bending force.

Monastery A religious institution providing living accommodations and worship space for monks.

Mosaic A floor, wall, or ceiling decoration composed of small pieces of colored glass or stone that form designs.

Mosque An Islamic house of prayer.

Motte-and-bailey Medieval castle with a mound (motte) and yard (bailey) defined by a ditch and wall.

Muqarna Islamic vault treatment that fragments the surface into many concave segments. Muqarnas may be built in masonry or suspended as elements from an overhead structure.

Mutules A block beneath the soffit of a Doric cornice, usually decorated with cylindrical or truncated conical elements.

Naos The sanctuary of a Greek temple.

Narthex The entrance porch or chamber before the nave of a church.

Nave The western arm of a basilican church.

Newel The center post around which a circular stair winds or a straight stair turns.

Niche A wall recess.

Obelisk A stone monolith, square in plan, with sides tapering toward a pyramidal top.

Oculus The circular opening at the apex of a dome.

Opisthodomos The enclosed room at the back of a Greek temple, often used as a treasury.

Opus incertum Roman walls built of irregularly shaped stones facing a concrete core.

Opus listatum Roman walls constructed of stone and brick in alternate courses.

Opus quadratum A Roman wall built of squared masonry.

Opus reticulatum A Roman wall formed of pyramidal stones, their points set inward and their square heads set to form a diagonal grid.

Opus testaceum Roman walls constructed of brick facing on a concrete core.

Orangery A building used to protect ornamental shrubs and trees in cold weather.

Orchestra In a Greek theater, the circular floor used for dancing.

Orders The trabeated systems of architecture developed by the Greeks and extended by the Romans. The Greek orders—Doric, Ionic, and Corinthian—differ slightly from the Roman orders. The Romans developed the Tuscan and Composite orders.

Oriel window A corbeled bay window in English medieval architecture.

Pagoda A tapering tower with multiple roof levels, built by Buddhists particularly in China and Japan. The word derives from the Sanskrit dagoba, meaning stupa.

Palaestra A Roman building used for exercise; a gymnasium.

Palazzo A palace type; in the Italian Renaissance, a four-square block with central court or cortile and the main floor on the second or piano nobile level.

Palladian motif A central arched opening with lower trabeated openings to each side.

Parapet A low wall at the perimeter of a roof.

Parterre An ornamental, geometrical arrangement of flat, planted beds.

Pavilion A prominent feature in a façade composition, usually at the center or at the ends and typically set forward, raised higher, and capped with a distinctive roof form.

Pebble dash A stucco wall given a pitted texture by throwing pebbles against it.

Pediment The gable end of a temple, framed by cornices.

Pendant vaulting Vaults with suspended, decorative elements hanging from their ribs.

Pendentive A spherical triangle that transforms a square bay into a circle for the springing of a dome.

Peristyle A colonnaded court or garden.

Piano nobile The main living floor of a house, generally raised a story above ground level.

Piazza An open space surrounded by buildings; in nineteenth-century American architecture, the term is sometimes applied to a porch on a house.

Pier A structural element, square or rectangular in plan, that supports an arch.

Pilaster A rectangular column, engaged in a wall, which is sometimes articulated as an order.

Pilotis Freestanding posts or supports for an upper-level structure; the term was most commonly used by Le Corbusier.

Pit house A semi-subterranean structure with its one-room excavated space roofed by an earth-covered wood frame.

Plank house Similar to the shed house, a rectangular, post-and-lintel structure covered on its walls and roof with hand-split wood planks.

Pointed arch A two-centered arch, pointed at its apex.

Polis The ancient Greek city-state.

Polychromy The decorative use of colored stone, seen primarily in medieval architecture.

Pomochi In Russian wooden architecture, a series of stacked cantilevers.

Porte-cochère A projecting canopy or carriage porch.

Portico A colonnaded porch.

Post An upright structural member; a column.

Pronaos The vestibule or antechamber to the shrine room (naos) of a Greek temple.

Pueblo A communal house or group of houses built of adobe or stone.

Putti Representations of plump, naked, often winged young children in paintings or sculptures.

Pylon A massive entrance to an Egyptian temple, with sloping walls and a central opening.

Qasr An Arabic word for castle.

Qibla The direction of Mecca, indicated in a mosque by the mihrab; by extension, the wall in which the mihrab is placed.

Quincunx Five objects arranged in a square, with one in the center. Byzantine churches with a quincunx plan typically have five domes, the center one being balanced by four domes at the corners.

Quoin A brick or piece of stone used to give strength or visual prominence to an external corner.

Ramada A flat-roofed rectangular post-and-lintel structure roofed with brush.

Ratha A wheeled cart or chariot. In Hindu architecture, the stone building form carved or constructed to resemble such a chariot.

Rib A raised molding applied to the arris of a vault.

Rocaille Eighteenth-century scroll ornament based upon water-worn elements such as rocks and seashells.

Rustication Rough stonework with exposed joints.

Sahn An open courtyard in a mosque.

Salient A projecting element, particularly an arrowhead-shaped projection from the walls of a fort.

Serdab In Egyptian tombs, an above-ground chamber where offerings to the deceased were placed.

Serliana A central arched opening with lower trabeated openings to each side. Also sometimes called a Palladian or Serlian motif.

Shaft The vertical element above the base and below the capital in an architectural order.

Shatyor Tent-roof forms used on Russian churches.

Shed house Similar to the plank house, a flat- or gable-roofed, post-and-lintel structure covered with wood planks.

Shikhara The tall curving roof, often with a parabolic profile, that rises like an artificial mountain over the garbhagriha in a Hindu temple.

Sipapu A fist-sized depression in Ancestral Pueblo Kivas, perhaps intended as a portal to the spirit world.

Skene The backdrop building in a classical theater.

Spandrel A wall surface, ornamented or unornmented, between major architectural elements such as windows or arches.

Squinch A corbeled arch used to transform a square bay into an octagon for the springing of a dome.

Stave A tall post, generally a peeled tree-trunk, used in construction.

Stele An upright slab, often carrying images or inscriptions.

Stereotomy The art of carving stone in complex, three-dimensional forms.

Stoa In Greek architecture, a linear building with one or more rows of columns. Stoas could be used for shops, meetings, or exhibitions.

Stupa In Buddhist architecture, the mound of earth and stones erected over relics of the Buddha or, by extension, over the remains of a holy person.

Stylobate The base, usually having steps, on which a colonnaded temple sits.

Superimposed orders Orders placed atop one another.

Suq A street in an Islamic market.

Tablero The vertical, often ornamented, plane in Pre-Columbian pyramid construction, comparable to the frieze in ancient Greek architecture.

Tablinium In Roman atrium houses, a reception area, usually on axis with the entrance.

Talud The inclined plane in Pre-Columbian pyramid construction.

Tatami Mats woven of rice straw, approximately three by six feet, that establish the module for room dimensions in traditional Japanese houses.

Tepidarium The warm-water chamber in Roman baths or thermae.

Terracotta Unglazed fired clay, often used for ornamental purposes.

Thermae Roman baths, usually containing rooms for hot-, warm-, and cold-water bathing.

Tholos A dome over a circular-plan building, or more generally the building itself.

Totem pole The popular name for large cedar posts carved with effigies by Native Americans in the northwest.

Tierceron In Gothic vaulting, a secondary rib extending from the support to the crown of the vault.

Tokonoma In Japanese houses, an alcove in the vestibule of a house where treasured objects are displayed.

Torana An elaborate entrance gate into a Buddhist shrine.

Torii An elaborate post-and-lintel gateway into Buddhist shrines in Japan.

Tracery The stonework divisions in Gothic windows.

Transept The north and south arms of a basilican church.

Transfer beam A heavy beam that distributes (transfers) loads from the structure above to supports that are not directly aligned below.

Triclinium A dining room in Roman houses and palaces.

Triforium In Gothic churches, the narrow passage below the clerestory corresponding to the lean-to roof over the aisle.

Triglyph A channeled block set between metopes in a Doric frieze.

Trilithon Two upright stones supporting a lintel stone.

Triumphal arch In Roman architecture, a gateway structure, with one or three arched openings, built to celebrate the return of a conquering army.

Truss A structural frame composed of relatively short elements, typically configured into triangles, used to form a bridge or span a roof.

Tuscan An order based on Etruscan architecture, employing unfluted columns and simplified capitals.

Tympanum A panel, generally semicircular, over the lintel and under the arch of a doorway. Also, the central triangle of a pediment.

Vault An arched ceiling or roof of brick or stone.

Verdika Fence surrounding a stupa.

Vestibule An antechamber before a major space.

Vihara A Buddhist monastery.

Villa rustica A Roman agricultural establishment that included living quarters for family members and slaves as well as stalls, store rooms, etc.

Villa The Roman word for a farm. By extension, the term used during the Renaissance and afterward for a rural house, often of extensive size.

Volute A decorative spiral found in Ionic, Corinthian, and Composite capitals.

Voussoir A wedge-shaped masonry unit set to form an arch.

Westwerk The narthex, chapels, and towers set at the entrance end of churches of the Carolingian and later periods.

Ziggurat A stepped pyramid form used in ancient Mesopotamia as the platform for a religious building.

BIBLIOGRAPHY

Chapter 1

Arnold, Dieter. *Building in Egypt: Pharaonic Stone Masonry.* New York: Oxford University Press, 1991. A summary of what is known from archaeology about methods used in Egyptian monumental stonework, from quarrying to transport to erection.

Burenhult, G. (ed.) *Old World Civilizations: The Rise of Cities and States.* New York: Harper Collins, 1994. An illustrated overview of history and artifacts of the ancient world.

Fagan, Brian M. *The Seventy Great Mysteries of the Ancient World.* London: Thames and Hudson, 2001. For anyone curious about the unanswered questions surrounding early civilizations and peoples, this is a treat. Summaries of current knowledge are presented straightforwardly by international experts.

Gurney, Oliver Robert. *The Hittites.* Harmondsworth, England: Penguin, 1961.

Hawkes, Jacquetta. *The Atlas of Early Man.* New York: St. Martin's Press, 1993. In measured time frames, developments across the world are presented through text, maps, and drawings.

Hawkins, Gerald. S. *Stonehenge Decoded.* Garden City: Doubleday, 1965. This is the pioneering study that demonstrated how Stonehenge was used.

Isler, Martin. *Sticks, Stones and Shadows: Building the Egyptian Pyramids.* Norman, OK: University of Oklahoma Press, 2001. Isler looks at practical issues associated with cutting, moving, and placing very large stones, advancing the idea that staircases may have been used instead of ramps in constructing the great pyramids. Compare this book with Arnold's study.

Lerner, Mark. *The Complete Pyramids.* London: Thames and Hudson, 1997. Well-illustrated and concise text on all aspects of the pyramids, from religion to construction.

Lloyd, Seton, Hans Wolfgang Müller, and Roland Martin. *Ancient Architecture: Mesopotamia, Egypt, Crete, Greece.* New York: Abrams, 1973. Dry text but good illustrations, especially for reconstructions of now-ruined buildings.

Mellaart, James. *Catal Hüyük: A Neolithic Town in Anatolia.* New York: McGraw-Hill, 1967. Mellaart led the excavations at Catal Hüyük, and this book presents what he found there.

Renfrew, Colin. *Before Civilization.* Harmondsworth, England: Penguin, 1973.

Smith, Earl Baldwin. *Egyptian Architecture as Cultural Expression.* Watkins Glen: American Life Foundation, 1968. Somewhat dated text, but the line illustrations are well done.

Smith, W.S. *The Art and Architecture of Ancient Egypt.* Harmondsworth, England: Penguin, 1981.

Soffer, Olga. *The Upper Paleolithic of the Central Russian Plain.* Orlando, FL: Academic Press, 1985. One of the few sources in English on the prehistoric settlements in Ukraine.

Wilkinson, Richard H. *The Complete Temples of Ancient Egypt.* New York: Thames and Hudson, 2000. Covers not only the temples themselves, but also places these monuments in context of history, religion, and society. Excellent illustrations.

Chapter 2

Camp, John M. *The Athenian Agora: Excavations in the Heart of Classical Athens.* London: Thames and Hudson, 1986. Clear documentation of the Agora's development from earliest times through the Roman period, based on work undertaken by the American School of Classical Studies in Athens, with plans and reconstruction views for buildings no longer extant.

Coulton, J.J. *Ancient Greek Architects at Work.* Ithaca, NY: Cornell University Press, 1977.

Hoepfner, Wolfram and Ernst-Ludwig Schwandner. *Haus und Stadt im klassichen Griechland.* Munich: Deutscher Kunstverlag, 1994. Although written in German, this is still valuable for its extensive illustrations. It is the most recent book to report on field work at sites associated with the Classical city-states.

Lawrence, Arnold Walter. *Greek Architecture.* Harmondsworth, England: Penguin, 1983. Part of the generally excellent Pelican series on the history of art.

Marinatos, Nanno. *Minoan Religion: Ritual, Image, and Symbol.* Columbia, SC: University of South Carolina Press, 1993. Excellent study of Minoan religious practice, impeccably researched and clearly presented.

Rhodes, Robin Francis. *Architecture and Meaning on the Athenian Acropolis.* Cambridge, England: Cambridge University Press, 1995. A lively examination of the cultural references incorporated in the architecture on the Acropolis.

Robertson, Donald Struan. *A Handbook of Greek and Roman Architecture.* Cambridge, England: Cambridge University Press, 1969. Dry but thorough.

Scully, Vincent. *The Earth, the Temple, and the Gods.* New Haven, CT: Yale University Press, 1979. Studies the specific relationship of individual Greek temples to their settings.

Wycherley, Richard Ernest. *How the Greeks Built Cities.* London: Macmillan, 1973.

Chapter 3

Deva, Krishna. *Khajuraho.* New Delhi: Bribasi Printers, 1986. Well-illustrated account of the temples at Khajuraho, setting the monuments in cultural and historic perspective.

Grover, Satish. *The Architecture of India: Buddhist and Hindu.* New Delhi: Vikas Publishing House, 1980. A general text, written for Indian architecture students. Good diagrams and clear explanations of culture and terms.

Huntington, Susan L. *The Art of Ancient India: Buddhist, Hindu, Jain.* New York: Weatherhill, 1985. A summary text for art as well as architecture.

Michell, George. *The Hindu Temple: An Introduction to Its Meaning and Forms.* Chicago, IL: University of Chicago Press, 1988. Clearly written volume that provides religious and cultural background to understand Hindu temple design.

Miksic, John. *Borobudur: Golden Tales of the Buddhas.* London: Bamboo Publishing, 1990. Handsome illustrations and extensive narration of the architecture and iconography of the monument.

Rowland, Benjamin. *Art and Architecture of India: Buddhist, Hindu, Jain.* Harmondsworth, England: Penguin, 1953. One of the generally excellent volumes in the Pelican History of Art series.

Stierlin, Henri. *Hindu India: From Khajuraho to the Temple City of Madurai.* Cologne: Taschen, 1998. Part of a projected forty-volume set on world architecture, this book contains many color illustrations to support the text.

Tadgell, Christopher. *The History of Architecture in India: From the Dawn of Civilization to the End of the Raj.* London: Architecture Design and Technology Press, 1990. A more complex text than some, this book has good illustrations.

Chapter 4

Boyd, Andrew. *Chinese Architecture and Town Planning, 1500 BC—AD 1911.* Chicago, IL: University of Chicago Press, 1962. This volume is older than most, but its text is still worth reading closely. As "a very small book on a very large subject," it carries off the presentation exceptionally well.

Chinese Academy of Architecture. *Ancient Chinese Architecture.* Hong Kong: Joint Publishing Company and Beijing: China Building Industry Press, 1982. Remarkable for demonstrating how the writing of history can also be a political statement. Good color photographs are juxtaposed with a collectively written text intended for English-speaking audiences. Among other things, readers are informed that "[t]he Great Wall is a masterpiece of ancient China. It manifests the tough, determined, and unwavering spirit of the Chinese, and the brightness of the wisdom of the working people."

Chinese Academy of Sciences, Institute of the History of Natural Sciences. *History and Development of Ancient Chinese Architecture*. Beijing: Science Press, 1986. A massive book, methodically treating the subject with concise text, clear illustrations, and a minimum of political commentary. It includes separate coverage of buildings by China's ethnic minorities.

Frankfort, Henri. *The Art and Architecture of the Ancient Orient*. Harmondsworth, England: Penguin, 1970.

Isozaki, Arata. *Katsura Villa: Space and Form*. New York: Rizzoli, 1987. A thoughtful text with extensive and beautiful photography.

Kawashima, Chuji. *Minka: Traditional Houses of Rural Japan*. Tokyo: Kodansha International, 1986. Clearly written and handsomely illustrated study of the great variety of minka, with particular attention to construction techniques and design features.

Liu, Laurence G. *Chinese Architecture*. New York: Rizzoli, 1989. A well-written account supplemented with clear photographs and plans.

Nishi, Kazuo and Kazuo Hozumi. *What Is Japanese Architecture?* Tokyo: Kodansha International, 1985. A concise text illustrated with line drawings to illustrate the basic characteristics of traditional Japanese buildings.

Suzuki, Kakichi. *Early Buddhist Architecture in Japan*. New York: Kodansha International, 1980.

Tange, Kenzo and Noboru Kawazoe. *Ise: Prototype of Japanese Architecture*. Cambridge, MA: M.I.T. Press, 1965. Features beautiful photographs by Yoshio Watanabe taken after the 1953 rebuilding of the shrines offering views not normally available. Separate essays by Tange and Kawazoe cover architecture and cultural context.

Chapter 5

Grant, Michael. *Cities of Vesuvius*. Harmondsworth, England: Penguin, 1976.

MacDonald, William L. *The Architecture of the Roman Empire*. New Haven, CT: Yale University Press, 1982.

—— *The Pantheon: Design, Meaning, and Progeny*. Cambridge, MA: Harvard University Press, 1976.

—— and John A. Pinto. *Hadrian's Villa and Its Legacy*. New Haven, CT: Yale University Press, 1995. This is a very readable account of the villa and its place in architectural history.

Packer, James E. *The Forum of Trajan in Rome: A Study of the Monuments*. Berkeley, CA: University of California Press, 1997. A truly monumental, three-volume study of this forum, including new restoration drawings based on excavations.

Richardson, Lawrence. *Pompeii: An Architectural History*. Baltimore, MD: Johns Hopkins University Press, 1988.

Sear, Frank. *Roman Architecture*. Ithaca, NY: Cornell University Press, 1992. A useful text with good illustrations, this book includes substantial coverage of Roman works outside Italy, in Africa, the Middle East, and Europe.

Vitruvius, M. *The Ten Books on Architecture*. New York: Dover, 1960. English translation of the only complete surviving architectural treatise from antiquity.

Ward-Perkins, John B. *Roman Imperial Architecture*. Harmondsworth, England: Penguin, 1981.

Chapter 6

Brumfield, William Craft. *A History of Russian Architecture*. Cambridge, England: Cambridge University Press, 1993. Text and photographs covering all aspects of Russian architecture, including the churches considered here.

Krautheimer, Richard. *Early Christian and Byzantine Architecture*. Harmondsworth: Penguin, 1986. Part of the generally excellent Pelican History of Art series.

—— *Rome: Profile of a City, 312–1308*. Princeton, NJ: Princeton University Press, 1980. A fascinating account of Rome from the Early Christian period through the medieval period.

Lowden, John. *Early Christian and Byzantine Art*. London: Phaidon Press, 1997. A beautifully illustrated and lucid book that covers selected monuments in detail, placing them firmly in their historical context.

Mainstone, Rowland J. *Hagia Sophia: Architecture, Structure, and Liturgy of Justinian's Great Church*. London: Thames and Hudson, 1988. A detailed examination of this masterpiece church. Clear text and ample illustrations.

Opolovnikov, Alexander and Yelena Opolovnikova. *The Wooden Architecture of Russia: Houses, Fortifications, Churches*. New York: Abrams, 1989. The best available source in English for information about wooden buildings in Russia, which vastly outnumber structures in masonry.

Chapter 8

Braunfels, Wolfgang. *Monasteries of Western Europe: The Architecture of the Orders*. Princeton, NJ: University Press, 1972. Clear explanation of Western monasticism and its architectural manifestations.

Calkins, Robert. *Medieval Architecture in Western Europe*. New York: Oxford University Press, 1998. A readable and comprehensive guide to architecture from 330 to 1500.

Conant, Kenneth John. *Carolingian and Romanesque Architecture, 800–1200*. Harmondsworth, England: Penguin, 1974. A basic guide to this period, part of the excellent Pelican History of Art series.

—— *Cluny: Les églises et la maison du chef d'ordre*. Macon: Imprimerie Protat Freres, 1968. The culmination of a lifetime's scholarly investigation. Although the text is in French, the extensive illustrations are universally understandable.

Horn, Walter, and Ernest Born. *The Plan of St. Gall*. Berkeley, CA: University of California Press, 1979. A model of research and scholarship, this beautiful three-volume work traces the impact of antique building on Carolingian architecture and the influence of the Plan of St. Gall on later buildings.

Kubach, Hans Erich. *Romanesque Architecture*. New York: Abrams, 1975. An extensive review of Romanesque architecture.

Male, Emile. *Religious Art in France: The Twelfth Century*. Princeton, NJ: Princeton University Press, 1978. An excellent guide to understanding the medieval mind and religious symbolism captured in Romanesque sculpture.

Shaver-Crandell, Annie and Paula Gerson. *The Pilgrim's Guide to Santiago de Compostela: A Gazetteer*. London: Harvey Miller, 1995. Includes a translation of the twelfth-century "Pilgrim's Guide" and an alphabetical guide to the sites as they would have appeared to a contemporary traveler.

Stalley, Roger. *Early Medieval Architecture*. New York: Oxford University Press, 1999. Lucid text, good photographs: highly recommended.

Chapter 9

Beresford, Maurice and John Hurst. *Wharram Percy: Deserted Medieval Village*. New Haven, CT: Yale University Press, 1991. For anyone interested in the ordinary buildings of the medieval period, this book serves as a readable introduction to the complex and tentative nature of our knowledge of non-monumental architectural history.

Bony, Jean. *French Gothic Architecture of the Twelfth and Thirteenth Centuries*. Berkeley, CA: University of California Press, 1983. Notable for its thorough treatment of Gothic churches in France, together with clear photographs and many building plans.

Coldstream, Nicola. *Medieval Craftsmen: Masons and Sculptors*. London: British Museum Press, 1991. A concise summary of the builders and building processes of medieval times.

Erlande-Brandenburg, Alain. *Cathedrals and Castles: Building in the Middle Ages*. New York: Harry N. Abrams, 1995. Well-illustrated account of the entire medieval building process, including translations of selected historic documents related to building sites and construction matters.

James, John. *Chartres: The Masons Who Built a Legend*. London: Routledge and Kegan Paul, 1982. James's detailed studies of the physical fabric of Chartres lead him to conclude that eight teams of master masons worked simultaneously on different parts of the cathedral. His thesis is not universally accepted, but his book provokes thought.

Mark, Robert. *Experiments in Gothic Structure*. Cambridge, MA: M.I.T. Press, 1982. The author considers engineering problems posed by Gothic buildings through analysis of models using polarized light.

Taylor, Arnold. *The Welsh Castles of Edward I*. London: Hambledon Press, 1986. A concise account from documentary sources of the construction of seventeen castles in Wales, this book gives an indication of what surviving records tell about the process of castle-building.

White, John. *Art and Architecture in Italy, 1250 to 1400*. Baltimore, MD: Penguin Books, 1966. Part of the excellent Pelican series in the History of Art, this volume is particularly interesting for its extended summary of the debates over the design of Milan Cathedral.

Wilson, Christopher. *The Gothic Cathedral: The Architecture of the Great Church, 1130–1530*. New York: Thames and Hudson, 1990. Discusses cathedrals and large churches across Europe, including lesser-known examples.

Chapter 10

Andrews, G.F. *Maya Cities: Placemaking and Urbanization*. Norman, OK: University of Oklahoma Press, 1975. Contains an introductory section on city components, then a city-by-city survey.

Driver, H.E. *Indians of North-America*, 2nd revised edition. Chicago, IL: University of Chicago Press, 1969. Broad discussion of Indian cultures.

Gasparini, G. and L. Margolis. *Inca Architecture*. Bloomington, IN: Indiana University Press, 1980. A good place to begin when doing research on Incas. Abundant images accompany the text.

Heyden, D. and P. Gendrop. *Pre-Columbian Architecture of Meso-America*. New York: Abrams, 1975. Part of the Abrams series on Western architecture. It covers Mexico and Central America and is filled with black-and-white photographs and drawings.

Kosok, P. *Life, Land and Water in Ancient Peru*. New York: Long Island University Press, 1965. This book emphasizes the Inca manipulation of the land, especially their extraordinary systems of irrigation. It includes material culture as well as architecture.

Morgan, W.N. *Ancient Architecture of the Southwest*. Austin, TX: University of Texas Press, 1994. Covers Native American sites in Utah, Colorado, Arizona, and New Mexico. Maps and some drawings, but no photographs.

Nabokov, P. and R. Easton. *Native American Architecture*. New York: Oxford, 1989. An excellent survey with plenty of photographs and drawings. This is the first book to look at for an introduction to Native American building in North America.

Robertson, D. *Pre-Columbian Architecture*. New York: Braziller, 1963. A short but very useful look at ancient building practices from Mexico to Peru.

Various editors. *Handbook of North American Indians*. 17 vols. Washington, D.C.: Smithsonian Institution, 1978. Offers in-depth information on Native-American cultures. Volumes 4–9, 11, and 17 have so far appeared.

Chapter 11

Ackerman, J.S. *Palladio*. Baltimore: Penguin, 1966. A very readable account by the foremost American scholar on Palladio.

——— *The Architecture of Michelangelo*. Baltimore: Penguin, 1971. A thoroughly illustrated account of Michelangelo's building designs.

Alberti, L.B. *On the Art of Building in Ten Books*. Cambridge, MA: M.I.T. Press, 1988. Alberti's fifteenth-century treatise expressing his ideas and theories about architecture.

Bruschi, Arnaldo. *Bramante*. London: Thames and Hudson: 1977. A focused, understandable and well-illustrated study. The line drawings are particularly useful.

Burckhardt, J. *The Architecture of the Italian Renaissance*. London: John Murray, 1985. A classic text first published in 1860. Much of the information has been superseded, but a comparison with later works provides insights into changing attitudes about the period.

Heydenreich, L.H. and W. Lotz. *Architecture in Italy, 1400 to 1600*. Harmondsworth, England: Penguin, 1974. Another volume in the useful and workmanlike, if slightly dry, Penguin series.

Howard, D. *The Architectural History of Venice*. London: Batsford, 1980. A readable account of the broader architectural trends in a city that participated in Eastern as well as Western traditions.

Murray, P. *Renaissance Architecture*. New York: Abrams, 1971. Peter Murray offers the best general survey of Renaissance buildings. The text is accessible to the undergraduate and is supported by ample illustrations.

Norberg-Schulz, C. *Intentions in Architecture*. Cambridge, MA: M.I.T. Press, 1965. Architectural history written from the existential point of view.

Palladio, A. *The Four Books of Architecture*. New York: Dover, 1965. Palladio's highly influential treatise with illustrations of his own work.

Saalman, H. *Filippo Brunelleschi: The Buildings*. University Park, PA: Pennsylvania State University Press, 1993. Saalman wrote extensively on Brunelleshi throughout his career, eventually yielding this thorough account.

Serlio, S. *The Five Books of Architecture*. New York: Dover, 1982. The first Renaissance treatise to contain a significant number of illustrations.

Shepherd, J.C. and G.A. Jellicoe. *Italian Gardens of the Renaissance*. Princeton, NJ: Princeton Architectural Press, 1986. The beautiful watercolor plans and sections alone make this book worth thumbing through.

Summerson, J. *Inigo Jones*. Harmondsworth, England: Penguin, 1966. The literature on Jones is almost uniformly dull. Much of this can be traced to inadequate knowledge of his life. Summerson's account is the most readable.

Wittkower, R. *Architectural principles in the Age of Humanism*. London: Tiranti, 1962. Theories of proportion from Alberti to Palladio. A strong influence on twentieth-century archiecture.

Chapter 12

Blunt, A. *Art and Architecture in France, 1500–1700*. Harmondsworth, England: Penguin, 1957. Sir Anthony Blunt is equally known as an architectural historian, as director of the Courtauld Institute of Art, and as a Communist spy. All of the volumes in this Penguin series (two more below) were written by leading scholars in their fields. All are readable if a little dense.

——— *Borromini*. Harmondsworth, England: Penguin, 1979. A good place to begin on Borromini for whom much of the literature has not been translated from the Italian.

Braham, A. *François Mansart*. London: Zwemmer, 1973. While Braham's separating of this work into a volume of text and a volume of illustrations makes using them slightly inconvenient, they are well researched and well written.

Hibbard, H. *Bernini*. Harmondsworth, England: Penguin, 1965. A short but useful text.

Meek, H. A. *Guarino Guarini and His Architecture*. New Haven, CT: Yale University Press, 1988. A relatively brief and to the point study of this architect-engineer.

Norberg-Schulz, C. *Baroque Architecture*. New York: Abrams, 1971.

——— C. *Late Baroque and Rococo Architecture*. New York: Abrams, 1971. These volumes cover all aspects of Baroque architecture throughout Europe. The two offer the best starting point for undergraduate research on the subject.

Pommer, R. *Eighteenth-Century Architecture in Piedmont*. New York: New York University Press, 1967. Pommer treats Guarini, Vittone, and Juvarra in their development of Late Baroque architecture in Italy.

Portoghesi, P. *Rome of Borromini; Architecture as Language*. New York: Braziller, 1967. Portoghesi is not the most readable source on Borromini, but the illustrations, especially Borromini's drawings, are splendid.

Summerson, J. *Architecture in Britain 1530–1830*. Harmondsworth, England: Penguin, 1977. Sir John Summerson wrote particularly well. All of his books, article and essays are worth spending some time with.

Walton, G. *Louis XIV's Versailles*. Chicago, IL: University of Chicago Press, 1986. Just as there are monographs on individual architects, there are works dedicated to individual buildings. Intended for the non-specialist, this book tries to explain why Versailles took the form that it did.

Wittkower, R. *Art and Architcture in Italy, 1600–1750*. Harmondsworth, England: Penguin, 1958. Another volume in the comprehensive Penguin series. Wittkower was one of the most eminent European scholars to emigrate to America as a result of events leading to World War II.

Chapter 13

Braham, A. *The Architecture of the French Enlightenment*. Berkeley, CA: University of California Press, 1980. The most comprehensive and up-to-date source for French Neo-Classicism in the eighteenth century.

Honour, H. *Neo-Classicism*. Harmondsworth, England: Penguin, 1968. Honour emphasizes painting and sculpture, but includes architecture in which he intended as a study of "all manifestations of the Neoclassical style."

Kalnein, W.G. and M. Levy. *Art and Architecture in Eighteenth-Century France*. Harmondsworth, England: Penguin, 1972. Penguin's effort to deal with the eighteenth century offers significant doses of painting, sculpture, and architecture.

Kaufmann, E. *Architecture in the Age of Reason: Baroque and Post-Baroque in England, Italy, and France*. New York: Dover, 1968. Kaufmann was the first scholar to write comprehensively on the period. Others have superseded him in many areas, but his book is still worth studying.

Chapter 14

Clark, K. *The Gothic Revival: An Essay in the History of Taste*. London: Constable, 1950.

Condit, C. *American Building Art—The Nineteenth Century*. New York: Oxford University Press, 1960. A survey of developments in wood framing, iron framing, iron bridge construction, and concrete.

——— *The Chicago School of Architecture: A History of Commercial and Public Building in the Chicago Area, 1875–1925*. Chicago, IL: University of Chicago Press, 1964. A place to start in understanding the development of the Chicago School skyscraper.

Drexler, A. (ed.). *The Architecutre of the Ecole des Beaux-Arts*. Cambridge, MA: M.I.T. Press, 1977. Published to coincide with an exhibition at the Museum of Modern Art in New York City, this volume includes a series of essays and reproductions of many drawings made by the Ecole's students.

Hitchcock, H.R. *Architecture: Nineteenth and Twentieth Centuries*. Harmondsworth, England: Penguin, 1977. An encyclopaedic survey, long on description and short on analysis. Many photographs.

Middleton, R. and D. Watkin. *Neoclassicism and 19th-Century Architecture*. New York: Abrams, 1980. The best place to begin for a survey of Neo-Classicism throughout Europe.

Scully, V. *The Shingle Style and the Stick Style*. New Haven, CT: Yale University Press, 1971. Written as Scully's doctoral dissertation, this lively volume sheds much light on the complex architectural developments in late nineteenth-century America. It deals primarily with domestic buildings.

Stanton, P. *Pugin*. New York: Viking, 1971. Some have traced the roots of Modernism to the kind of passionate search for truth or at least honesty promoted by Gothic Revivalist Augustus Welby Northmore Pugin.

Twombly, R. *Louis Sullivan: His Life and Work*. New York: Viking, 1986. One of many monographs on the man that Frank Lloyd Wright called his master.

Chapter 15

Banham, R. *Theory and Design in the First Machine Age*. Cambridge, MA: M.I.T. Press, 1960. Early revisionist writing on Modernism, challenging the arguments made by such scholars as Pevsner and Giedion.

Benevolo, L. *History of Modern Architecture*. Cambridge, MA: M.I.T. Press, 1971. Comprehensive history by an author who emphasizes city planning and urban development.

Boesiger, W. (ed.). *Le Corbusier and Pierre Jeanneret: Oeuvre Complète*. Zurich: Girsberger, 1935–65. These volumes provide the opportunity to view the life's work by one of the principal European Modernists.

Collins, P. *Changing Ideals in Modern Architecture*. London: Faber, 1965. A book about ideas that have influenced modern architecture and about architectural ideas rather than forms, so few illustrations.

Frampton, K. *Modern Architecture: A Critical History*, 3rd edition. London: Thames and Hudson, 1992. A thoughtful, comprehensive survey, but a little dense for anyone just beginning a study of the period.

Giedion, S. *Space, Time, and Architecture*. Cambridge, MA: Harvard University Press, 1941. A classic of polemical work that purports to examine the roots of Modernism. Giedeon hobnobbed with many of the great architectural talents of the mid-twentieth century and was an unabashed proponent of European Modernism.

Gropius, Walter. *The New Architecture and the Bauhaus*. New York: Museum of Modern Art, 1937. Gropius relates the radical experiment in design education at the Bauhaus to the "new architecture" then being produced in Europe.

Hitchcock, H.R. *In the Nature of Materials: The Buildings of Frank Lloyd Wright, 1887–1941*. New York: Duell, Sloan, and Pierce, 1942. The literature on Wright is almost endless. This book, by a scholar who wrote on a broad variety of architectural-history topics, accompanied an exhibition on Wright at the Museum of Modern Art in 1940.

——— and P. Johnson. *The International Style: Architecture Since 1922*. New York: Norton, 1932. This small book accompanied the exhibition of European and American Modernism mounted at the Museum of Modern Art in New York City.

Jordy, W.H. *American Buildings and Their Architects: The Impact of European Modernism in the Twentieth Century*. New York: Doubleday, 1972. A readable author's interpretation of Modernism in America through the close study of six seminal buildings.

Le Corbusier. *Towards a New Architecture*. New York: Praeger, 1972. Le Corbusier's ideas about architecture, first published in 1923.

Pevsner, H. *Pioneers of the Modern Movement* (originally *Pioneers of Modern Design: From William Morris to Walter Gropius* [1936]). Harmondsworth, England: Penguin, 1975. Pevsner was among the first to look for the sources of European Modernism. While he later admitted that he should have been more inclusive, his small book does illuminate many of the principles that Modernists held dear.

Schulze, F. *Mies van der Rohe: A Critical Biography*. Chicago, IL: University of Chicago Press, 1985. A thorough study but with limited illustrations.

Sharp, D. *Modern Architecture and Expressionism*. New York: Braziller, 1966. The first work to focus on a large part of twentieth-century architectural production that was not intensely "rational" and so at odds with the fundamental tenets of Modernism.

Tafuri, M. and F. Dal Co. *Modern Architecture*. New York: Rizzoli, 1986. Modernism interpreted from the Marxist perspective.

Wingler, H. *Bauhaus: Weimar, Dessau, Berlin, Chicago*. Cambridge, MA: M.I.T. Press, 1969. A history of the Bauhaus in its various manifestations. Large format with abundant illustrations.

Wright, F.L. *Modern Architecture*. Princeton, NJ: Princeton University Press, 1931. Some of Wright's ideas about architecture and his answer to the polemics of Le Corbusier.

Chapter 16

Curtis, W.J.R. *Modern Architecture Since 1900*. Englewood Cliffs, NJ: Prentice-Hall, 1987. An excellent, very readable, well-illustrated survey with many color images.

Drexler, A. (ed.). *Five Architects: Eisenman, Graves, Gwathmey, Hejduk, Meier*. New York: Oxford University Press, 1975. This thin, overtly promotional publication advanced five careers and gave the false impression that their work was alike.

Jencks, C. *Modern Movements in Architecture*. New York: Doubleday, 1973. Charles Jencks explores the demise of Modernism and the then-emerging pluralism that he saw as taking its place.

——— *Late-Modern Architecture*. New York: Rizzoli, 1980. Jencks's first effort to pull together his ideas about the 'end' of Modernism.

——— *The Language of Post-Modern Architecture*. New York: Rizzoli, 1981. One among many volumes by the high priest of Post-Modernism. Like Sigfried Giedion for Modernism, Jencks has been a tireless promotor as well as a reporter and analyst.

Klotz, H. *The History of Post-Modern Architecture*. Cambridge, MA: M.I.T. Press, 1984. The most complete survey of the various architectural directions that have been lumped into the category of Post-Modernism.

Venturi, R. *Complexity and Contradiction in Architecture*. New York: Museum of Modern Art, 1977. Robert Venturi's iconoclastic work announced the crumbling of the edifice of Modernism.

Wigley, M. and P. Johnson. *Deconstructivist Architecture*. Boston, MA: Little, Brown, 1988. Published by the Museum of Modern Art in New York City to accompany an exhibition of the same name.

PICTURE CREDITS

The authors and Laurence King Publishing Ltd thank the sources of photographs for supplying and granting permission to reproduce them. Every effort has been made to contact all copyright holders, but should there be any errors or omissions Laurence King Publishing Ltd would be pleased to insert the appropriate acknowledgment in any subsequent printing of this publication.

p.ii © Paul M.R. Maeyaert; 0.1, 0.3, 0.4, 0.6, 0.7, 0.9, 0.10 Marian Moffett; 0.2 Ronald Scott; 0.5 R. Bruce Moffett; **p.8**, 1.21, 1.36, 1.40 Robert Harding Picture Library; 1.4, 1.7, 1.8 Marian Moffett; 1.5 Corbis; 1.13 Hirmer Fotoarchiv; 1.19 Pergamon Museum, Berlin; 1.22 R. Bruce Moffett; 1A Michael Fazio; 1.24 © Paul M.R. Maeyaert; 1.27 Spectrum Colour Library; 1.29 Raiford Scott; 1.32 AKG London; 1.34 Ancient Art & Architecture; 1.37 C. Murray Smart, Jr; **p.38** Robert Harding Picture Library; 2.2 Rachel McCann; 2.3, 2.33 AKG London; 2.4 Ancient Art & Architecture; 2.5, 2.12, 2.13 Marian Moffett; 2.7, 2.29 Craig & Marie Mauzy, Athens mauzy@otenet.gr; 2.9 TAP; 2.10, 2.26 Hirmer Fotoarchiv; 2.17 J. William Rudd; 2.18 Kenneth Moffett; 2.20, 2.21 Michael Fazio; 2.22 Sonia Halliday Photographs; 2.25 Alison Frantz Archive, American School, Athens; 2.31 J. Allan Cash, Ltd, London; 2.33 Michael Fazio; 2.36 BPK, Berlin; **p.66**, 3.4, 3.6, 3.17, 3.19 A.F. Kersting, London; 3.2, 3.21, 3.22 Robert Harding Picture Library; 3.7, 3.14 Lawrence Wodehouse; 3A, 3.18 AKG London; 3.12, 3.13 Dinodia; 3.16 Ancient Art & Architecture; 3.23 C. Murray Smart; 3.25, 3.26 Gerald Anderson; **p.86**, 4.30 AKG London; 4.2 Spectrum Colour Library; 4.3, 4.22, 4.24, 4.29, 4.36 Gerald Anderson; 4.4, 4.5 Orientphoto; 4.8, 4.9, 4.11 Chinapix; 4.15 Robert Harding Picture Library; 4A, 4.18 Robert Craig; 4.20 Japan Information and Cultural Center; 4.21 Ancient Art & Architecture; 4.23, 4.35 Japan Information & Cultural Centre, London; 4.26 Courtesy Jingu Administration Office; 4.32, 4.33 Lawrence Wodehouse; **p.110**, 5.16 © Paul M.R. Maeyaert; 5.3, 5.31 Alinari; 5.4 Ancient Art & Architecture; 5.6, 5.8, 5.14, 5.15, 5.17, 5.28, 5.34, 5.39 © Vincenzo Pirozzi, Rome; 5.11, 5.12 Scala; 5.13, 5A Fototeca Unione; 5.18 Bridgeman Art Library; 5.20 Michael Fazio; 5.22 AKG London; 5.27, 5.35 Lawrence Wodehouse; 5.32, 5.33 Robert Harding Picture Library; 5.40 Corbis; 5.41 Peter Clayton; **p.140**, 6.29, 6.33 AKG London; 6.1, 6.2, 6.5, 6.6, 6.11, 6.12, 6.26, 6.27, 6.31, 6.34, 6.35 Marian Moffett; 6.7 Lawrence Wodehouse; 6.8 © Vincenzo Pirozzi, Rome; 6A Mary Evans Picture Library; 6.9 Peter Clayton; 6.10, 6.20 Scala; 6.13 Turkish Tourist Office; 6.15 Kenneth Moffett; 6.17 Art Archive; 6.18, 6.21 A.F. Kersting, London; 6.19 Alinari; 6.23 Marvin Trachtenberg, New York; **p.164**, 7.3, 7.14, 7.33 Robert Harding Picture Library; 7.1, 7.8, 7.19, 7.20, 7.21 A.F. Kersting, London; 7.5 BPK; 7.9, 7.10, 7.11 Lawrence Wodehouse; 7.13, 7.15 R. Bruce Moffett; 7.18, 7.23 Ancient Art & Architecture; 7.24, 7.27 Sonia Halliday Photographs; 7.26 Art Resource; 7.29 Foto Marburg; 7.35, 7.36 © Paul M.R. Maeyaert; 7.37 Spectrum Colour Library; **p.190**, 8.3, 8.7, 8.20, 8.25, 8.50, 8.51, 8.52, 8.54, 8.55, 8.57, 8.58, 8.61 © Paul M.R. Maeyaert; 8.2, 8.13, 8.15 AKG London; 8.4, 8.12, 8.18, 8.22, 8.36, 8.37, 8.38, 8.39, 8A, 8.43, 8.44, 8.48, 8.59, 8.63, 8.65 Marian Moffett; 8.5 Michael Fazio; 8.10, 8.11 Lawrence Wodehouse; 8.16 J. Allan Cash, London; 8.24, 8.29, 8.30, 8.64 A.F. Kersting, London; 8.26, 8.60 Bildarchiv Foto Marburg; 8.27 © Studio Fotografico Quattrone, Florence; 8.31, 8.32 Giancarlo Costa; 8.34 Serge Chirol, Paris; 8.45, 8.46, 8.53 Robert Craig; **p.228**, 9.4, 9.5, 9.14, 9.18, 9.21, 9.28 © Paul M.R. Maeyaert; 9.2, 9.7, 9.25, 9.30, 9.31, 9.32, 9.34, 9.35, 9.38, 9.49 A.F. Kersting, London; 9.6, 9.10, 9.17, 9.22, 9A, 9.36, 9.40, 9.43, 9.44, 9.47, 9.48, 9.49, 9.51, 9.58, 9.60, 9.62, 9.70, 9.74 Marian Moffett; 9.9 Art Resource; 9.11 © Museum of Notre Dame de Paris; 9.12, 9.20, 9.33 © Angelo Hornak; 9.16 James Austin; 9.23 Photo Zodiaque; 9.24 Sonia Halliday Photographs; 9.41, 9.57, 9.68 Corbis; 9.42, 9.71 AKG London; 9.46 Alinari; 9.52 Lauros-Giraudon, Paris; 9.64, 9.66 Kenneth Moffett; 9.73 Cameraphoto Arte, Venice; **p.274** A.F. Kersting, London; 10.2, 10.3, 10.10 Smithsonian Institution; 10A Smithsonian Institute; 10.4, 10.11, 10.17, 10.18, 10.19, 10.21, 10.22, 10.23, 10.24, 10.25, 10.26, 10.30, 10.32 Michael Fazio; 10.5 Corbis; 10.9 Jamen Berk; 10.14 © Tony Morrison/South American Pictures; 10.15 Robert Harding Picture Library; 10.27, 10.28 Ronald Scott; 10.29 Justin Kerr, New York; **p.294**, 11.24 AKG London; 11.2, 11.10, 11.41 © Studio Fotografico Quattrone, Florence; 11.3, 11.7, 11.29, 11.38, 11.61, 11.74 A.F. Kersting, London; 11.5, 11.12, 11.14, 11.15, 11.46, 11.51 Alinari; 11.16, 11.77 Lawrence Wodehouse; 11.17 © Ralph Lieberman and Laurence King archive; 11.20 Hutchison Picture Library; 11.22 James Austin; 11.23 © Guglielmo Chiolini; 11.26, 11.54, 11.58 Marian Moffett; 11.31, 11.44, 11.66 © Vincenzo Pirozzi, Rome; 11.36, 11.39, 11.50, 11.55, 11.59, 11.78 Michael Fazio; 11.47 © James Morris, London; 11.52 Ancient Art & Architecture; 11.62, 11.63 Cameraphoto Arte, Venice; 11.68, 11.69, 11.71, 11.73 © Paul M.R. Maeyaert; 11.70 Spectrum Colour Library; 11.76 Country Life Picture Library; 11.80 RCHM; 11.82 Robert Harding Picture Library; **p.352**, 12.30, 12.32, 12.39, 12.46 © Paul M.R. Maeyaert; 12.1, 12.3, 12.15, 12.16, 12.18, 12.20, 12.21, 12.22, 12.24 Vincenzo Pirozzi, Rome; 12.5 Spectrum Colour Library; 12.8 Scala; 12.11, 12.36 Michael Fazio; 12.13 © Araldo De Luca, Rome; 12A, 12.27, 12.33 AKG London; 12.21, 12.29 Alinari; 12.23 © Peter Kent; 12.28 Lawrence Wodehouse; 12.34, 12.35, 12.38, 12.51, 12.52, 12.57, 12.59, 12.62 A.F. Kersting, London; 12.41, 12.45 Pamela Scott; 12.47 Private Collection; 12.48 Roger-Viollet; 12.49 J. William Rudd; 12.55 © Angelo Hornak, London; 12.58 RCHM; **p.396**, 13.2 A.F. Kersting, London; 13.4 Lawrence Wodehouse; 13A Private Collection; 13.9 © Peter Kent; 13.16, 13.17 Pamela Scott; 13.21, 13.22 Roger-Viollet; 13.26 Ronald Scott; 13.27 J. William Rudd; **p.418**, 14.38, 14.59, 14.71, 14.72 © Paul M.R. Maeyaert; 14.3, 14.4, 14.5 AKG London; 14.8, 14.9 Courtesy John Soane Museum; 14.10, 14.36, 14.42 A.F. Kersting, London; 14.11, 14.87 Wayne Andrews; 14.12 G.E. Kidder Smith; 14.13, 14.14, 14.18, 14.19, 14.51, 14.62, 14.64, 14.73 Michael Fazio; 14.15 The Library of Virginia; 14.17, 14.34, 14.44, 14.45, 14.63, 14.67, 14.74, 14.79 Marian Moffett; 14.24 Lawrence Wodehouse; 14.25 Leo Sorel; 14.27, 14.31 J. William Rudd; 14.28 Used with permission from Biltmore Estate, Asheville, North Carolina; 14.29, 14.48, 14.76 Chicago Historical Society; 14.30 New York Historical Society; 14.33, 14A Science and Society Picture Library; 14.35 Hulton Getty; 14.39, 14.40 James Austin; 14.47 Library of Congress; 14.53, 14.54 RCHM; 14.57, 14.58 Bastin & Evrard; 14.60 © Inigo Bujedo Aguirre, London; 14.61, 14.85, 14.89 © Ralph Lieberman and Laurence King Publishing archives; 14.65 © Glasgow School of Art; 14.69 RCHM; 14.70 Foto Marburg; 14.77, 14.88 J. William Rudd; 14.80, 14.81, 14.82, 14.84 Esto/Wayne Andrews; 14.86 RIBA; **p.474** Esto; 15.5, 15.8, 15.31, 15.46, 15.49, 15.51, 15.68, 15.77 Michael Fazio; 15.6 Pamela Scott; 15.9, 15.10, 15.12, 15.13 a,b,c, 15.15, 15.16, 15.17, 15.76, 15.78 a,b © ARS, NY and DACS, London 2003; 15.11, 15.44, 15.47, 15.59, 15.61, 15.69, 15.85 Marian Moffett; 15.14 Wayne Andrews; 15.18 Courtesy AEG; 15.21, 15.22, 15.46, 15.48, 15.64, 15.65, 15.66 © DACS 2003; 15.23 Musée des Arts Décoratifs; 15.24 Canadian Center for Architecture, Montreal; 15.25, 15.63, 15.65 AKG London; 15.26 Courtesy Beurs van Berlage, photo Jan Derwig, Amsterdam; 15.27 Jeff Elder; 15.28 Netherlands Architecture Institute; 15.29, 15.30 Foto Marburg; 15.32 J. William Rudd; 15.33 BPK; 15.34 Plansammlung, Technische Universitätsbibliothek, Berlin; 15.35, 15.37 Peter Mauss/Esto; 15.36 Ezra Stoller/Esto; 15.38 Courtesy The Rockefeller Group; 15.39, 15.43 Peter Aaron/Esto; 15.40 Museum of the City of New York; 15.41 Robert Craig; 15.42 Courtesy of the Coca-Cola Company; 15.48 Courtesy Centraal Museum, Utrecht/© DACS 2003; 15.50 © Paul M.R. Maeyaert; 15.52 Kenneth Moffett; 15.55, 15.56, 15.57, 15.58, 15.83, 15.84, 15.86, 15.88 © FLC/ADAGP, Paris and DACS, London 2003; 15.60 Peter Kent, London; 15A ADAGP, Paris and DACS, London 2003/RMN; 15.62, 15.67, 15.71, 15.80 J. William Rudd; 15.70 G.E. Kidder Smith, New York; 15.72 Chicago Historical Society; 15.73 Lawrence Wodehouse; 15.74, 15.75 Esto; 15.79 Wayne Andrews/Esto; 15.81 © ARS, NY and DACS, London 2003; 15.82 Anderson & Low, London; 15.87 RIBA; 15.89 Mark DeKay; **p.532** © FMGB Guggenheim Bilbao Museoa/Erika Barahona Ede; 16.1, 16.3, 16.4, 16.6 Courtesy Alvar Aalto Museum; 16.7 photo by Donna Coveney, MIT; 16.9 Kenneth Moffett; 16.10, 16.14, 16.30, 16.34 J. William Rudd; 16.11, 16.18, 16.38 Marian Moffett; 16.13 © Steve Rosenthal; 16.15 Kimbell Art Museum, Fort Worth, Texas; 16.17 Robert Craig; 16.19, 16.21 Ezra Stoller/Esto; 16.20 Peter Mauss/Esto; 16.22, 16.25, 16.26, 16.33, 16.41 Michael Fazio; 16.27 Ed Stocklein; 16.28 Used by permission from Disney Enterprises, Inc., photo Peter Aaron/Esto; 16.31 © John Donat; 16.35, 16.43 © Timothy Hursley; 16.36 A.F. Kersting, London; 16.37 Ian Lambot; 16.39, 16.40 Eisenman Architects; 16.42, 16.44 Frank Gehry; 16.45 © The Solomon R. Guggenheim Foundation, New York, photo David Heald; 16.46 Richard Bryant/Arcaid; 16.47, 16.48, 16.49, 16.50 Max Dupain; 16.52 Anthony Browell.

INDEX

Page numbers in **bold** refer to illustrations and captions.

Aachen (Germany)
    Charlemagne's palace 192, **192**
    Palatine Chapel 192, **192**, **193**, 194
Aalto, Alvar 533–7, 560, 563
abacus 49
Abbas I, Shah **184**, 185, 186
abbeys
    Carolingian *see* St. Gall
    Early Gothic *see* St. Denis
    Norman 224
    Romanesque/early medieval 202, 209, 219, 221–4
    see also monasteries; *and by name*
Abu Simbel (Egypt), temples 36, 37, **37**
Acropolis *see under* Athens
acroteria 403
Adam, Robert 401, 402–4, **403**, **404**, 405
Adena culture 277
Adler, Dankmar 467–9, **468–70**, 472–3, 480, **480**, **481**
adobe structures 281, 292–3
Agora *see under* Athens
aircraft hangars (Nervi) 505
airports (Saarinen) 537–8
airship hangars (Freyssinet) 505
Ajanta (India), cave temples 73, 75
Akbar, Mughal emperor 174, 176
Akbar al-Isfahani, Ali 174
Akhenaten (Amenophis IV), pharaoh 33–4, 35
Akhetaten (Tell-el-Amarna) (Egypt) 34, 35, **35**, 39
Akkadians 16, 18
Alberti, Leon Battista 303–8
    churches 303–8
    ideal city 308
    Palazzo Rucellai, Florence **304**, 305
    S. Andrea, Mantua 121, 306, **306**, 308, 354–5
    S. Francesco, Rimini 5, 305, **305**, 306, 436
    S. Maria Novella, Florence 305–6, **305**, 323, 355, **355**
    S. Sebastiano, Mantua 308
    St. Peter's, Rome 317
    writings 303–4
alée 339
Alen, William Van 496, **496**
Aleuts, Alaska 279
Alexander the Great 21–2, **22**, 24, 57, 61, 62, 64, 69
Alfeld-an-der-Leine (Germany), Fagus Shoe-Last Factory (Gropius and Meyer) 511, **512**
Alhambra palace, Granada (Spain) 186–9, 339
Amenemhet III, pharaoh 40
Amenophis IV *see* Akhenaten
American Telephone and Telegraph Headquarters (Johnson and Burgee), New York 544–5, **545**
Americas, Pre-Columbian 275–93
Ames estate, gate lodge (Richardson), North Easton, Mass. 465, **466**
Amiens Cathedral (France) 240, 241, 432

Amorite Dynasty 18
amphitheaters, Roman 113, 117, **117**, 126, 130–1, **130**
Amsterdam (Holland)
    De Dageraad housing project (de Klerk) 491, **492**
    Eigen Haard housing project (de Klerk) 491, **492**
    Henrietta Ronnerplein (de Klerk) 491
    Stock Exchange (Berlage) 490, **490**
Anasazi *see* Ancestral Pueblo
Anatolia (modern Turkey) 18, 39, 57
    Islamic domed prayer hall designs 180–4
    mosques 170
    see also Catal Hüyük
Ancestral Pueblo (Anasazi) 281–2
Ancy-le-Franc (France), château (Serlio) 344
Andover, New Hampshire *see* Phillips Exeter Academy
andron (men's room) 63, **64**
Angkor Wat (Cambodia) 74, 83–5, **83**
Anglo-Saxon, English churches 198–9, 224
Angoulême (France), Cathedral of St. Pierre **218**, 219, **219**, 229
Animal Style 199, 200, 452
Ankhesenamun, Queen 19
Anthemius of Tralles, architect 149, 151
Antoine, Jacques-Denis 411, **411**, **412**
apadanas (audience halls) 168, 169, 172
Apollodoros of Damascus, architect 120
appartements 346
aqueducts, Roman **110**, 113, 115, 170, 295, 465
Aquitaine, William, Duke of 213
Aquitaine (France), Romanesque churches 217–20
Arch of Augustus
    Perugia 112, **113**
    Rimini 305, 436
Arch of Constantine, Rome 121, **121**, 194
arch-and-column motifs **194**, **207**
Archaic period *see under* Greece
arches 3–4, **3**
    Carolingian, horseshoe 194, 195, **195**
    centering **3**, 114
    cusped 171, 311
    diaphragm **205**, 205, 207
    Gothic *see* pointed arches
    horseshoe, Islamic **3**, 170, **171**, **194**, 195
    Indian temples, true arch 77
    Islamic pointed arches 4, 167–8, **176**, 189
    lobed 171, **171**
    profiles 3–4, **3**
    Roman (semicircular) **3**, **110**, 112, **113**, 114, 115, 125, **125**, 130, **130**, 202, 204, 300
    Romanesque 202, 204, **205**
    true arch 77, 114
    see also domes; pointed arches; triple-arched structures; triumphal arches; vaults; voussoirs
architects 2, 5, 114, 303
Arctic tribes **276**, 279–80
Arles (France), St. Trophîme 221, **221**
Arnolfo di Cambio 296
arris 49
Art Deco 293, 495–501

Art Nouveau 452–60, 469, 475, 476
Artaxerxes 21
Arts and Crafts Movement 448–52, 476, 480
Asam brothers 378
ashlar 40, 115
Asklepios, Sanctuary of *see* Epidauros
Asoka, Indian emperor 69, 71
Asoka columns 71, 72
Aspdin, Joseph 448
Assyria and Assyrians 19–20, **21**, 111
Aswan (Egypt), obelisk **23**
Athens 50–6, 57, 116, 462
    Acropolis 50–6, **50**, **51**, 57, 60, **61**, 64, 531
    Agora 53, 54, 60–2, **61**
    bouleterion 61
    Caryatid maidens **55**, 56
    Choragic Monument of Lysikrates 58, 59, 426
    Delian League treasury 50, 51
    Erechtheion 49, 51, **55**, 56, **56**
    Great Panathenaic Procession 54
    Hephaisteion temple 60–1, 62
    Metroon 61, 62
    Older Parthenon 51, 56
    Panathenaic Way 53, 60, **61**, 62
    Parthenon 49, 50, 51–3, **51**, **52**, 56, 122
    Propylaea 50, **51**, 53, **53**, 54, 55, **55**, 56, 408
    Royal Stoa 60, 61
    stoas 61, **61**, 62, **62**, 118
    Temple of Athena Nike 50, **51**, 53, 54, 55–6
    Temple of Athena Polias 55, **55**, 56
    Theater of Dionysos 59
Atlanta, Georgia, High Museum (Meier) **550**, 551
atria
    Early Christian 142, 143
    Etruscan temples **112**
    New York **553**, 554
    Roman 132–4, **132**, **133**, 135, **135**, 136, 506
Attalos of Pergamon **62**
Attica 56
Atwood, Charles B. 434
audience halls, Sassanian 168, 169, 172
Austin, Henry 419
Australia *see* Murcutt, Glenn
Austria *see* Vienna; Viennese Secession
Autun (France), St. Lazare 217, **217**
axonometric drawings 7, **7**
Aztecs 291, 292

Baalbek (Lebanon), Temple of Venus 126, **126**, 395
Babylon 18, 19, 20, **20**, 122
    Ishtar Gate 20, **20**, **21**
    ziggurat 20, **20**
Babylonia and Babylonians 111, 287
Bacon, Edmund 357
Badger, Daniel 446
Baghdad (Iraq), Islamic houses **184**
Bagnaia (Italy), Villa Lante (Vignola) 339, **340**
baldachin, Greece 58
ballcourts 285, **286**, 288, 292
balloon frame 448, **448**

Baltimore, Mass., Roman Catholic cathedral (Latrobe) 424, **425**
bamboo structures
  India 72, 73, 77
  Japan 103, 106
Bamiyan (Afghanistan), colossal Buddha 74
Banham, Reyner 476, 496
Bank of England (Soane), London 423, **423**
Bank of Pennsylvania (Latrobe), Philadelphia 424
banks 423, **423**, 424, 426, **426**, 460–1, 473, **473**, 506, **506**
  Renaissance 311
Banpo (China), Neolithic houses 87, **88**
Banqueting House (Inigo Jones), London 350–1, **350**, 392
baptisteries, Christian 141, 143, **145**, 152, 191
barabara, Aleuts 279
Barbaro, Daniele and Marcantonio 331
Barcelona (Spain)
  Barcelona Pavilion (Mies van der Rohe) 516–18, **516**, **517**
  Casa Milá (Gaudí) 456, **456**
  Church of the Sagrada Familia (Gaudí) 455–6, **455**
  Parc Güell (Gaudí) 456–7, **456**, **457**
Barma, architect **156**, 162–3, **163**
Barnes, Edward Larrabee 553
Baroque architecture 139, 163, 328, 353–95, 452
  Central Europe 373–81
  France 381–8
  Italy 126, 171, 353–72, 373
  London churches 389–92
  urban open spaces in Rome 365–70
Barozzi da Vignola, Giacomo see Vignola, Giacomo Barozzi da
Barr, Alfred 476, 520
barrel-vaults
  Baroque 354–5
  Byzantine basilicas and churches 149, 151, 153
  Carolingian 194
  Early Christian, Ravenna 147, 148
  Islamic 167, 168, **168**
  Kahn's buildings 540, **540**, 541
  Late Renaissance/Mannerism 322, 332, 333, 336
  Neo-Classical 405
  Renaissance 306, 308, 314–15, **315**
  Roman **114**, 115, 120, 127, **127**, 130
  Romanesque 211, 214, **218**, 219, **219**, 223, **223**
Barry, Charles 429, **430**
Bartholdi, Auguste **445**
basilicas
  Byzantine 148–52
  Early Christian 142–3, 191, 207, **207**, 357
  Roman 126–7, 198, 205, 306, **306**, 308, 390
Bassai, Temple of Apollo Epicurius 48, 57–8, **57**
bastides 269, **270**
Bath (England) 127
Baths of Diocletian, Rome **128**, 129, 317, 336
baths (thermae), Roman 113, 117, **117**, 118, **118**, 122, 126, 127–9, **129**, 168, 308, 336, 404, 437
Baudot, Anatole de 448
Bauhaus 451, 480, 511, 512–15, 531
Bavaria, church of Die Wies (Zimmerman) 376, **377**

bazaars, Islamic 185–6, **185**
Beauvais (France), St. Pierre Cathedral **237**, 240, 241, **242**, 243, **243**, 245, 259, 432
Behrens, Peter 451, 460, 480, 487–8, 508, 515
Beijing (China) 94, 95–6, **95**, 96, **96**, 98
  Fragrant Hills Hotel (Pei) 97
bellcote 431
Belper (England), West Mill (Strutt) 415, **415**
belt courses 322
belvedere 318; see also Rome
Benedict of Nursia, St. 197
Benedictines 250; see also St. Gall (Plan of St. Gall); St. Gallen
Beni Hasan (Egypt), rock-cut tombs 30–1, **30**, 36
Berlage, H.P. 490–1, **491**, 501
Berlin (Germany)
  AEG Turbine Factory (Behrens) 487–8, **487**
  Altesmuseum (Schinkel) 421, **422**, 553
  Friedrichstrasse station (Mies van der Rohe) 515
  Nationalgalerie 522
  Neue Wache (Schinkel) 420, **420**
  Pergamon Museum 20, **21**, 65
  Schauspielhaus (Schinkel) 421, **421**
Bernard of Clairvaux, St. 221, 223, 224, 230, 258
Bernini, Gianlorenzo 358–62, 368, 374, 381
  Piazza Navona, Rome 365, **365**, 367
  Piazza of St. Peter's, Rome 360–1, 368
  S. Andrea al Quirinale, Rome 361–2, **361**
  St. Peter's 358–61, Baldacchino 359, **359**, 362, Chair of St. Peter 360
  Scala Regia, Rome 360, **360**
Bessemer, Henry 438
Bethlehem, Church of the Nativity 143, **144**, 205
Bhitargaon (India), Vishnu Temple 77, **77**
Bhubaneshwar (India), temples 78, **78**
Bibliothèque Ste.-Geneviève see Paris
Bilbao (Spain) see Guggenheim Museum Bilbao
Biltmore (Hunt), Asheville (USA) 433, **433**
Bingi Point (Australia) see Magney House
Biondo, Flavio 307
Biskupin (Poland), prehistoric village and houses 13–14, **14**
bitumen, Mesopotamia 16, **16**
Blenheim Palace (Vanbrugh), Oxfordshire (England) 394, **394**, 397
  grounds (Brown) 416, 417
Blois château (France) 341, **342**, 343, 384
Blondel, J.F. **404**, 405, 409, 413, **417**
Boboli Gardens (Tribolo), Florence 340–1, **341**, 357
bochki gables, Russia 161, **162**, 163
Boffrand, Germain 397
Bogardus, James 446
Bohier, Thomas 343
boiserie 397
Boissonas House (Johnson), New Canaan 544, **544**
Borgund (Norway), stave church **201**, 202, **202**
Borobudur (Java), stupa shrine 74, 75–6, **75**
Borromini, Francesco 362–5, 374, 375
  Piazza Navona 365, **365**
  S. Agnese, Rome **366**, 390, 392
  S. Carlo alle Quattro Fontane, Rome 362–3, **362**, **363**

  S. Ivo della Sapienza 363–5, **363**, **364**, 370, 372
bosco 339
Boston, Mass.
  Boston Public Library (McKim, Mead, and White) 5, 305, 436, **436**
  Trinity Church (Richardson) 462–3, **463**
bouleterion, Athens 61
Boullée, Etienne-Louis 405, **406**, 416, 539
Bourges (France), St. Etienne Cathedral **237**, 239–41, **240**, **241**, 259, **261**
Boyle, Richard see Burlington, third Earl of
Bramante, Donato 311, 314–19, 331, 343, 344
  Belvedere Courtyard, Rome 318, **318**, 319, 339
  House of Raphael, Rome 318–19, **319**
  Milan Cathedral crossing 314
  S. Maria della Consolazione, Todi 313, **314**
  S. Maria delle Grazie, Milan 314, **314**, 317
  S. Maria presso S. Satiro, Milan 314–15, **315**
  St. Peter's, Rome 315, 317, **317**, 326, 327, 387, 390, 392
  Tempietto, Rome 316–17, **316**, 408
The Breakers (Hunt), Newport, Rhode Island 433, **433**
Bremerhaven (Germany), medieval longhouse (**263**)
Breuer, Marcel 519, 521
brick 2
  Byzantine 150, **151**, 152, 155
  China 90, 98
  Early Christian **142**, 143, **145**, 147, **147**
  Egypt, sun-dried 24, **24**
  Etruscan, unbaked 112
  Greece, mud-brick 47
  Hattusas, sun-dried 18
  Hindu temples 77, **77**
  Indus Valley, fired 67
  Mesopotamia, kiln-fired and sun-baked 15, 16, **16**, 17, 122
  Moscow, Renaissance 313
  Roman 115–16, **117**, 120, 135
bridges
  concrete 503–4, **503**, 505
  iron and steel 4, 414, **414**, 415, 437–40, 444
  Post-Modernist (Graves) 547, **547**
  Renaissance France 344, 346
  Roman 4, 437
  suspension 4, 5, **437**, 438, **438**, 440, **440**
  trusses 4, 437–8
Brihedesvara Temple, Tanjore 80, **81**
brises-soleil 528, 530, 531
Britannia Bridge (Stephenson), Menai Straits **437**, 438
Brno (Czech Republic), Tugendhat House (Mies van der Rohe) 518, **518**
Broadacre City 523, 531
Broadleys (Voysey), Cumbria (England) 451, **452**
Brooklyn Bridge (Roebling), New York 438, 440, **440**
Brosse, Salomon de 346, 382
Brown, Joseph 395
Brown, Lancelot (Capability) 416–17, **416**
Brunelleschi, Filippo 296–301, 539
  Florence Cathedral dome 5, 126, 296–9, 328
  Foundling Hospital, Florence 299, **299**, 302, 346

S. Croce, Pazzi Chapel, Florence **294**, 300–1, **301**, 545
S. Lorenzo, Florence 299, 300, **300**, 323
S. Maria degli Angeli, Florence 301, **301**
S. Spirito, Florence 299, 300, **300**, 315
Brussels (Belgium)
   Hotel Van Eetvelde (Horta) 454, **454**
   Maison du Peuple (Horta) 454
   Tassel House (Horta) 453–4, **453**
Buddhism
   China 74, 89
   India 69–70, 75, 76, 83, 84
   Japan 99
Buddhist monasteries
   India 70, 71–2, 74
   Japan 100
Buddhist shrines, India 69, 70–6, 176
Buddhist temple halls, China 91–2
Buddhist temples, Japan 99–102
Buildwas, Shropshire (England), bridge (Telford) 415
Bullant, Jean, architect **343**, 344
Bunshaft, Gordon 515
Burgee, John 544, **545**, **554**
Burghley House, Northants. (England) 349
Burgundy (France) 191, 213, 221, 223
Burlington, Richard Boyle, third Earl of, architect 398, 399–400, **399**
Burlington House, London 398
Burne-Jones, Edward 463
Burnham, Daniel H. 447, **447**
Burr, Theodore 437
Burton, Decimus 441, **441**
Byzantine architecture 148–63
   basilicas 148–52, 195
   centrally-planned churches 148, 152–5, 166, 180, 209
   churches in Russia 155–63

cables 4–5
Cades Cove, Tennessee, barn **3**
Caen (France), abbey church of St. Etienne 224, **224**, **225**, 226, 227, 229, 233
Caernarvon Castle (Wales) 266–8, **267**
Cahokia, Illinois 279
caissons 440
caldarium
   Islamic 168
   Roman 129, **129**
California (northern), tribes **276**, 280–1
Cambodia, Khmer architecture 83, 84, 85; *see also* Angkor Wat
Cambridge, Cambs. (England)
   History Faculty Building (Stirling), University 551–3, **551**
   King's College Chapel 248, 249, 254, **254**, 346
   Pembroke College Chapel (Wren) 389
Cambridge, Mass. (USA)
   M.I.T., Baker House (Aalto) 535, **536**, 537
   Stoughton House (Richardson) 466–7, **467**
Campbell, Colen 398–9, **398**, 426
Canadian Inuit (Eskimos) 279–80, **280**
Candela, Felix 505, 506
Canigou *see* St. Martin at Canigou
Canterbury Cathedral, Kent (England) 247, **248**
cantilever construction 3, **3**, 5
   Baroque church **371**
   by van t'Hoff 501
   China 90, 90, 92
   English Gothic 253
   Japan 100, 101, **101**

medieval half-timbering **264**
Nervi's stadium 505
Wright's buildings 486, **524**, 525
capitals, Romanesque 215, **215**, 217, **217**
caravanserai 181
Carcassonne 268, **268**, **269**, 432
cardo 111, 118
Carnac (France) *see* Er-Mané
Carolingian architecture 191–8, 204, 205
   horseshoe arches 194, 195, **195**
   masonry construction 192–5
   monasteries 195–8
   westwerk and towers 194, 207
Carthusian monastery 311–12
caryatids **55**, 56
Castle Acre Castle, Norfolk (England) 266
Castle Howard (Vanbrugh), Yorks. (England) 393–4, **393**
castles
   Japan, timber 106–7
   medieval 265–8
   Norman 224
   wooden 265
castra (military camps), Roman 111, 118, 169, 267, **267**
catacombs, Rome 141
Catal Hüyük (Anatolia), prehistoric settlement 9–10, **10**
cathedra 142, 143
cathedrals 142–3
   early Gothic 232–6
   English Gothic 247–53
   High Gothic 236–45
   Italian Renaissance 296–9
   Moscow, Renaissance 312–13
   Neo-Classicism 424
   Norman 224–7
   Romanesque 205–7, 219, 229
   see also by name and location
Caux, Isaac de 351
cave-temples
   China 89, 90
   India 73, **73**, 75, 79, 80, 89, 174
   see also rock-cut temples
cavetto 553
Cawston, Norfolk (England), St. Agnes's church 246, **246**
Cecil, William 349
cellas
   Greece 50, 52, 53, 333
   Roman 123, 125, 126
centering *see under* arches
Certosa monastery, Pavia (Italy) 311–12, **311**, 341
Cerveteri (Italy), tombs 112
Chaco Canyon 281, 282, **282**
chaitya halls, India 70, 72, 73, **73**, 75, 80, 158
Chambers, William 401, 404–5, **404**, **405**
Chambord (France), château (Cortona) 342, 343, 346
Chan Chan (Peru) 292–3
Chandigarh (India), town (Le Corbusier) 530–1, **531**
Chandragupta 69
Chang'an (modern Xian) (China) 93–5, **94**, 104
Charlemagne (Charles the Great) 191, 192, 194, 195, 196, 197, 198, 212
Charleston, S. Carolina, St. Michael's (Harrison) 395
Charlottenhof (Schinkel), Potsdam 421, **422**
Charlottesville, Virginia
   Monticello (Jefferson) 426–7, **427**

   University of Virginia (Jefferson) 428, **428**
Charnley House (Adler and Sullivan), Chicago 480, **480**, 481
Chartres (France), Notre-Dame Cathedral **228**, **236**, 237–9, **237–9**, 240, 241
châteaux
   Baroque 382, **383**, 384–7
   Renaissance, Loire valley 341–3, **433**
chatra 71, **71**
Chatsworth House (England), Conservatory (Burton and Paxton) 441
Chaux (Ledoux) 406–7, **407**, 408, 508
Chelles, Jean de 234
Chenonceau (France), château (Orme and Bullant) 343, **343**, 344
Cheops *see* Khufu
Chephren *see* Khafre
Chestnut Hill, Penn., Vanna Venturi House (Venturi) 542–3, **542**
Chiasso (Italy), customs warehouse (Maillart) 504
Chicago, Illinois
   Auditorium Building (Adler and Sullivan) 467–8, **468**
   Carson Pirie Scott Department Store (formerly Schlesinger and Mayer Store) (Sullivan) 471–2, **472**
   Charnley House (Adler and Sullivan) 480, **480**, 481
   Crown Hall, I.I.T. (Mies van der Rohe) 521, **521**
   Glessner House (Richardson) 465, **465**
   Home Insurance Building (Jenney) 446–7, **446**
   860 Lake Shore Drive (Mies van der Rohe) 521–2, **521**
   Marshall Field Wholesale Store (Richardson) **464**, 465, 467, 468
   Monadnock Building (Burnham and Root) 447, **447**
   Rand McNally Building (Burnham and Root) 447
   Reliance Building (Burnham and Root) 447, **447**
   Robie House (Wright) 483–4, **483**
   skyscrapers 446–8, 521–2
   Tribune Building (Loos) 479
   World's Columbian Exposition (Hunt) 433–4, **434**, 467
Chicago School 447, 466
Chichen-Itzá (Mexico) 290–1
chickee, Native American 279
chigi 103, **103**
Chimú Empire 292–3
China 87–99
   architectural principles 90–3
   brick structures 90, 98
   Buddhism 70, 74, 89, 91–2
   cantilever construction 90, **90**, 92
   cave temples 89, 90
   city planning 88, 93–6, **94**, **104**
   color schemes 91, 102
   courtyard plans 90, 91, **91**, 93, 96, 98, **98**
   fibers for tension structures 4, 438
   garden design 88, 97, 98–9, **98**, 416
   Great Wall 87–8, **88**
   Hellenistic art 89
   houses 90, 96–8, **98**
   and India 74, 75, 89
   Islamic pavilion designs for mosques 165, 170, 179–80
   and Japan 99, 100, **100**, 101, **101**, 102
   jian (modular unit) 90, **90**
   Neolithic houses at Banpo 87, **88**

pagodas 75, 89–90, **89**, **90**
palaces 93, 94, **94**, 95, 98
religions 88–9
Song Dynasty 101, **101**, 107
Tang Dynasty 94–5, 99, 103
temples 91–3, **91**, 96
watchtowers 89, 90
Chishti, Salim, tomb of 176
Chiswick House (Lord Burlington), London 399–400, **399**
Choragic Monument of Lysikrates, Athens **58**, 59, 426
Chorleywood (England), The Orchard (Voysey) 450–1
Christian architecture *see* Early Christian architecture
Christianity 141, 191, 198, 202
  in Russia 155–6
Chrysler Building (Van Alen), New York 470, 496, **496**
churches 142–3
  Alberti's plans 303–4
  America 395
  Anglo-Saxon, English 198–9, **198**, **199**
  Baroque 353–5, 361–5, 370–2, 373–81, 382
  Baroque London 389–92, 394–5
  Byzantine **150**, 152–63, 166, 180, 209
  Carolingian 194, 204, 197
  Central Europe, Baroque 373–81
  centrally-planned, Byzantine 148, 152–5, 166, 209, by Leonardo 313, **313**
  Christian, converted to mosques **151**, 169, 170
  Early Christian 127, 143, 194, 198
  Ecclesiological Movement 430–2
  Egypt style (Strickland) 419–20
  France, Baroque 382
  Gothic Revival 429, 430, **430**
  Italian Gothic 257–61
  Jesuit 353–5, 361
  Late Renaissance/Mannerist 336
  medieval 4, 159, 210–13
  by Michelangelo 323, 326–8, 329–30
  Mozarabic 195
  Norman 224, 233, **248**
  Norwegian stave 199–202
  Palladian 335–6
  on pilgrimage routes 210–13, 220, 229
  Renaissance 299–301, 303–8, 311–15, 317
  Romanesque/early medieval 115, 153, 202–20
  Russia, Byzantine 155–63, Moscow 312–13
  wall-pillar 373–4, 375, 376, **376**, 378, 379
  see also basilicas; Gothic architecture; hall churches
Cistercian monasteries 221–4, 249, 258
Citeaux monastery (France) 221, 224
cities, medieval 268–73, 429, **429**; *see also* city planning; ideal towns and cities
Citrohan houses (Le Corbusier) 44, **508**, 509, 519
city planning
  Athens 60–2
  China 88, 93–6, **94**, **104**
  Egypt 34–5, **35**, **36**
  Etruscan 111
  Futurist, "Città Nuova" (Sant'Elia) 488, **489**
  Greek 47, 60–5, 111
  Hellenistic 62–5
  Islamic 184, 185–6

Japan 103–4
Le Corbusier 511
medieval 268–73
Paris, Renaissance 345–6, **345**
Poland 308
Renaissance 308–9
Roman 116–21
see also ideal towns and cities
Classical period *see under* Greece
Clement VII (Giulio de' Medici), pope 320, 323
Clérisseau, Charles-Louis 402
Cloaca Maxima, Etruscan/Roman sewer 112, 115, 118
Cluniacs (Cluny Order) 213–17, 220, 221
Cluny (France), medieval house **265**
Cluny II-III monastery (France) 213–14, **213**, **214**, **216**, 217, 229, 239, **248**, 249, **261**
Coalbrookdale Bridge (Darby III and Pritchard), Shropshire (England) 414, **414**, 415
Coca-Cola Bottling Plant (Derrah), Los Angeles 499, **500**
Cockerell, Samuel Pepys and Charles 419, **419**
Coducci, Mauro 336
Cola da Caprarola 313, **314**
Coleshill (Pratt), Berks. (England) 392, **392**
Cologne (Germany), Glass Pavilion (Taut) 492, **493**
colonial houses, America 6–7, **6**, **7**, 467
colonnaded or arcaded space, Athens 62
color schemes
  China 91, 102
  Graves's 547–8
  Japan 102
  Oud's 501
Colosseum *see* Rome
column and beam construction *see* post-and-lintel construction
Composite order 113, 345
Compostela (Spain), St. James's shrine 210, **210**, 213
compression, of structural materials 2, 3, 114–15
concrete 2, 448, 476
  concrete block (textile-block) 523
  poured (poured-in-place) **485**, 486, **531**, 537, **538**, 541
  pre-stressed and post-tensioned 505
  reinforced 2, 3, 503–6, 508, 514, 519
  Roman 115–16, 120, **121**, 123, 125, 131, 136
  Wright's use of 523–31
Confucius and Confucian 88–9, 91, 93, **94**, 95, 98, 402
Connecticut, colonial houses 6–7, **6**, **7**
Conques (France), St. Foy 210, **210**, 211, **211**, 212, **212**, 213
Constantine, emperor 141, 142, 143, 146, 153, 165, 359
Constantinople 148, 155, 165, 180
  Chalki Gate 170
  Church of the Holy Apostles 181, 218
  Hagia Sophia (Anthemius and Isidorus) 149–52, 156, **156**, 157, 180, **181**, 183, 211, 230, 375
  relics from 245
  S. Irene 149, **149**, 155
  Sinan's work in 180–3 (*and see* Istanbul)
  SS. Sergius and Bacchus **150**, 152, **152**
  Venetian connections 295, 336
  Viking contacts 199

walls 266, 267
see also Istanbul
Constructivism 488, **489**, 490, **490**, 496, 533, 560
Copán (Honduras) 288–9, **289**
corbeled construction 3, 114
  Egypt 26, 27, 44
  Hattusas, vaults 18
  Indian temples 77
  Mayan arches and vaults **2**, **3**, 288, **289**, 290
  medieval machicolations 266
  megalith tombs 10, **10**
  Mycenae 43, 44, **44**, **45**
  Romanesque arches 204, 207, **209**, 211
  Tiryns, galleries 46, **46**
Corbett **498**
Córdoba (Spain), Great Mosque **169**, 170–2, **171**, **172**, 173, 370, **371**
Corinthian order
  Baroque 381, 389, 394, 395
  Carolingian 194
  Greece 48, **48**, 56, 57, 58, **58**, 59
  Late Renaissance/Mannerist 325, 335, 336, 338, 345, 351, 361, 366
  Neo-Classical, France 410
  Renaissance 299, 300, 301, **304**, 305, 306, **306**, 318
  Roman 113, 123, 125, 131, 170, 220, at Nimes 123, **123**, 426
  Romanesque 209, 220
Cornwall, Connecticut, House VI (Eisenman) 558
corps-de-logis 346
cortile 310
Cortona, Domenico da **342**, 343
Cortona, Pietro da 366, **366**, 368, 392
country houses
  Elizabethan 347–9
  Neo-Palladian 398
courtyard plans
  China 90, 91, **91**, 93, 96, 98, **98**
  India, Islamic mosques 174–9
  Indus Valley 67, 72
  Islamic houses 184, **184**
  Islamic mosques **164**, 170, 173
  Mesopotamian houses **17**, 18
  Minoan 39, **40**, 41–2
  Renaissance Italy 299, 302–3
  viharas, India 72
Crete 39; *see also* Minoans
cross-domed plans, Byzantine 153
cross-in-square plans *see* quincunx plans
Crusades, castles 266
Crystal Palace (Paxton), London 441–2, **442**, 551, 553
Cuipers, P.J.H. 490
Cuthbert, St. 224
cutting plane 5, 6
Cuvillés, Françoise 397
Cuzco (Peru) 293, **293**
cyclopean construction 42, **47**, **466**
  Inca 293, **293**
Cyclopes 42

Dacca (India), National Assembly of Bangladesh (Kahn) 540–1
Dahshur (Egypt), pyramid 26–7, **26**
Damascus (Syria), Great Mosque 169–70, **169**, 173
Daniell, Thomas 402
Daoism 88–9, 91, 97, 98, **99**
Darby, Abraham 414
Darby III, Abraham 414, **414**, 415

Darius 20, 50
Darmstadt (Germany) 459–60, 461
    Wedding Tower (Olbrich) 461, **462**
De Klerk, Michael 491, **492**
De Stijl 476, 495, 501–2, 516, 517, 520
dead loads 2, 229
Deconstructivist architecture 557
Decorated period *see* English Gothic
decumanus 111, 118
Deir-el-Bahari (Egypt)
    Hatshepsut's mortuary temple 31, 32, **32**,
        33, 47
    Mentuhotep's tomb and temple 30, **30**, 32
Deir el-Medina (Egypt) 34, **36**
Delhi (India), tomb of Humayun 176–7,
    177
Delian League 50, 51, 56
Dengfeng (China), Songyue Pagoda 90
Denon, Dominique Vivant 402
dentil course 303
Der Scutt 553, **554**
Derrah, Robert 499, **500**
Dessau (Germany), Bauhaus (Gropius)
    514–15, **514**
Deutscher Werkbund 487–8, 492, 518, 533
diaphragm arches *see* arches
Dientzenhofer, Christoph 375–6, **376**
Dientzenhofer brothers 375, **376**
Dinkeloo, John 553, **553**
Disney World, Swan and Dolphin hotels
    (Graves), Orlando, Florida 548, **548**
Djoser, pharaoh 24–6
Doesburg, Theo Van 501, 502
Dom-ino House (Le Corbusier) 508, **508**
Dome of the Rock, Jerusalem 165–7, **166**,
    170, 183
Domenico da Cortona *see* Cortona,
    Domenico da
domes 3–4, 5, 114, 126
    Baalbek, Roman temple 126
    Baroque 171
    Byzantine basilicas and churches 148,
        149–55, 166
    Carolingian 194
    Early Christian mausoleum, Rome 143–4,
        144
    Islamic 4, 165, 166, 168, 171, 172–3,
        172, 181, 183–4
    onion-shaped **154**, 158–9, 163, 308
    "pumpkin vault" 152, **152**
    Renaissance 5, 296–9, 328
    Roman, Pantheon 125–6, **125**
    Romanesque churches in Aquitaine
        218–19, **218**, **219**
    Russian churches **154**, 157, 158–9, 161,
        163
    see also Florence, Cathedral; London; St.
        Paul's; Rome, St. Peter's
Dominicans 258, **258**, 259, 530
domos, Mycenaean 44, 45, 46, 47
domus, Roman 351
Dorians 47
Doric order
    Greece 47–50, **48**, **49**, 51, **52**, 53, 55, 56,
        57, 58, 61, 111, 112, 117
    Late Renaissance/Mannerism 322, 331,
        332, 338
    Loos's buildings 479
    Modernism 480
    Neo-Classicism 420
    proto-Doric, Egypt 32, **33**
    Renaissance **304**, 305, 308, 317, 318, 344,
        348
    Roman 130, 131

Dornach (Germany), Goetheanums
    (Steiner) 494, **494**
drawings (plans, elevations, sections) 5–7
Duany, Andres 550
Duban, Félix 413
Dulles Airport (Saarinen), Washington D.C.
    538
Durham (England), St. Cuthbert's Cathedral
    224, **225**, 226–7, **226**, **227**, 229
Dutch Expressionism (Wendigen) 490–1

Eads Bridge (Eads), St. Louis 438, 440
Eads, James B. 438, 440
Eames, Charles and Ray 555
Eanna, Sumer, temples 15
Earl's Barton, Northants. (England), All
    Saints Church 199, **199**
Early Christian architecture 141–8, 191, 192
    churches 127, 194
    shrines 166
    see also baptisteries; basilicas; martyria;
        mausolea
Early English *see* English Gothic
earth lodges, Plains tribes 276
earth mounds, Native American 277, 278,
    278, 279, **279**
eave 3
Ecclesiological Movement 430–2
Ecole des Beaux-Arts 404, 413, 431–7, 462,
    464, 467, 476, 506
Edirne (Turkey), Selimiye Mosque (Sinan)
    183–4, **183**
Edward I 266, **267**, 268, 269
Eesteren, Cor Van 501, 502
egg-and-dart moldings 303
Egret's Castle, Himeji (Japan) 106–7, **106**
Egypt 14, 15, 20–1, **21**, 22–37, 39, 44, 57
    building materials 27, 29, 122, 127
    Christian hermits 197
    corbeled construction 26, 27, 44
    Hittites and 19, 36
    pylon gates 36
    see also hypostyle halls; pyramids;
        temples; tombs
Egyptian style (Revival) 419–20, **419**
Eiffel, Gustave **418**, 444–5, **445**
Einstein Tower (Mendelsohn), Potsdam
    494–5, **494**
Eisenman, Peter 557, 558, 559, **559**
El-Lahun (Egypt) 34, **36**
El Lissitzky 501
Elder Brother Rock 97
Elementarism 502
elevations 5, 6, **6**, 7
Elgin, Lord 53
Ellet, Charles 438
Ellwood, Craig 563
Ely Cathedral (England) **252**, 253, **253**
Empire State Building (Shreve, Lamb, and
    Harmon), New York 470, 499, **499**
en suite 303
Enfant, Pierre L' 357, **386**
England
    Anglo-Saxon churches 198–9, 224
    Art Deco 496
    Baroque 388–95
    Medieval castles 265–6
    Neo-Classicism 423–4
    Renaissance 346–51
English Gothic 245–54, 346
    Decorated period 245, 247, **247**, 250–4,
        431
    Early English 245, 247–50, **247**
    Perpendicular 247, **247**, 249, 250–4, 346

entablature 47
entasis 49, 51, 92
Ephesus, Temple of Artemis 47
Ephesus (Greece) **2**, 60
Epidauros
    Sanctuary of Asklepios tholos 58–9, **58**
    theater **59**, 60, **60**, 130
Er-Mané, Carnac (France), megalith tomb
    10, **10**, 44
Eridu, Sumer, temple 15
Ernst Ludwig, Grand Duke of Hesse 459,
    460, 461
Escher, M.C. 558, **558**
Eskimos *see* Canadian Inuit
Etruscans 111–13, 116, 123, 129
Euro Disney (France), Newport Bay Club
    Hotel (Stern) 549, **549**
Eusebius of Caesarea, bishop 146, **146**
Evans, Sir Arthur 40, 42, 44
Eveux-sur-l'Arbrèsle (France), Ste.-Marie-de-
    la-Tourette (Le Corbusier) 530, **530**
exedrae 126, 136
Exposition des Arts Décoratifs, Paris 490,
    490, 496, 501, **502**

Fagus Shoe-Last Factory (Gropius and
    Meyer), Alfeld-an-der-Leine 511, **512**
Fairfield (USA) *see* Ogden House
Fallingwater *see* Wright, Frank Lloyd
fan vaults, English Gothic 247, 249, 254, **254**
Fargo-Moorhead Cultural Center Bridge
    (Graves) 547, **547**
Farnsworth House (Mies van der Rohe),
    Plano 522, **522**, 563, **564**, 565
Fatehpur Sikri (India) 174–6
    Friday mosque 175, **175**, 176, **176**, 177
    palace 175, **175**
Feng shui 91
ferro-cemento 505–6, **505**
ferroconcrete 448
fibers, for tension structures 4, 438
Fiesole (Italy), Medici Villa (Michelozzo)
    339, **339**
Il Filarete (Antonio Avertino) 308, 311
Fillmore, Lavius 395
Findley, James 438
Finland *see* Aalto, Alvar
Fioravanti, Aristotele 312–13, **312**
Fischer von Erlach, Johann Bernhard 374–5,
    374, **375**
Florence (Italy) 295
    baptistery 297, 299
    Boboli Gardens (Tribolo) 340–1, **341**, 357
    Cathedral (Brunelleschi), dome 5, 126,
        296–9, 328, (Michelangelo) 5
    Foundling Hospital (Brunelleschi) 299,
        299, 302, 346
    Laurentian Library (Michelangelo) **300**,
        323–5, **324**, 326
    Municipal Stadium (Nervi) 505
    Palazzo Medici (Michelozzo) 302–3, **302**
    Palazzo Pitti 340
    Palazzo Rucellai (Alberti) **304**, 305
    Piazza S. Annunziata 346
    S. Croce, Pazzi Chapel (Brunelleschi) **294**,
        300–1, **301**, 545
    S. Lorenzo, (Brunelleschi) 299, 300, **300**,
        323, Medici Chapel (Michelangelo)
        323
    S. Maria degli Angeli (Brunelleschi) 301,
        301
    S. Maria Novella 258–9, **258**, (Alberti)
        305–6, **305**, 323, 355, **355**, (Masaccio
        fresco) 296, **297**

S. Miniato al Monte 207, **207**, 299
S. Spirito (Brunelleschi) 299, 300, **300**, 315
Uffizi (Vasari) 321–2, **321**
flying buttresses, Gothic 229–30, **230**, 232–3, 234, 236, 237, 238, 239, **240**, 250, 431
Fogong Temple, Yingxian (China) **89**, 90, **90**
Foguang Temple, Shaanxi (China) 92, **92**
follies 417
Fontana, Domenico 357, 358, 365, 368
Fontenay abbey (France) **222**, 223, **223**
Ford Foundation Building (Roche and Dinkeloo), New York 553, **553**
Fort Worth, Texas *see* Kimbell Art Museum
forums, Roman 116, **116**, 117, **117**, 118, **118**
Foster, Norman 555–7, **556**
Fouiloux **498**, 499
Fouquet, Nicolas 384
France
    architects and the aggrandizement of the state 409–13
    Baroque 381–8
    Carolingian architecture 191
    concrete buildings 504–5
    Gothic Revival 431–2
    l'art moderne (Art Deco) 496
    medieval cities 268–9, **270**
    Neo-Classicism 397, 405–8
    Renaissance 341–6, **433**
    Rococo 397
    Romanesque churches 153, 217–20
    see also châteaux
Francis I of France 341, **342**, 343, 344
Franciscans 258, 259
Frankfort Bridge, Erie Canal (USA) 437
Frankfurt am Main (Germany), Biocentrum (Eisenman) 559, **559**
Frankfurt (Germany), Museum für Kunsthandwerk (Meier) 550–1, **550**
Franks 191
Freyssinet, Eugène 505
frigidarium 129, **129**
Frith, W.P. 439, **439**
Futurism 476, 488, **488**, 496

Gabriel, Ange-Jacques 410, **410**, 411
Gale, Elizabeth 483
Gandhara (India), cave-temples 89
Gandy, J.M. **423**, 424
Garabit Viaduct (Eiffel) 444, **445**
garbhagriha (womb-chamber) **76**, 77, **77**, 80, 81, 84
Garches (France), Villa Stein (Le Corbusier) 509, **509**
gardens and designers 338–41
    Baroque châteaux 384, 385, **386**
    in China 88, 97, 98–9, **98**, 416
    English designers 416–17
    Islamic *see* Alhambra palace
    Late Renaissance/Mannerism 321, 322
Garnier, Tony 480, 506–8
Gaudí, Antonio 454–7
Gehry, Frank **532**, 557, 560–3
General Motors Technical Center (Saarinen), Warren 537
geometry
    Baroque 363, **363**, 370, 372
    descriptive 414
    Eisenman's use of 557, 559
    French Neo-Classical 405, 406, 539
    Islamic 166, **166**, 168–9, **180**, 181
    medieval 263
    Renaissance 295–6, **301**, 313

sacred 76, 77
Teotihuacán 285, **285**
German Expressionism 490, 491–5
Germany
    Arts and Crafts Movement 451
    Deutscher Werkbund 487
    Gothic hall churches 255–7
    Gothic work 158, **158**
    Jugendstil 452, 459–60
    medieval longhouse 263
    Neo-Classicism 420–1, **422**
    Romanesque (Ottonian) architecture 205–7
Germigny-des-Près (France), Oratory 194–5, **194**, **195**
Getty Museum (Meier), Malibu 551
Ghiyath, Mirak Sayid 176–7
Giacomo della Porta 328, 354, **354**, **355**, 358, **358**, 363, **363**
Gibbons, Grinling 389, 392
Gibbs, James 395, **395**
Giedion, Sigfried 453, 476
Gilbert, Cass 496
Giorgio, Francesco di, engineer 310
Gislebertus, sculptor **217**
Giza (Egypt)
    Khafre's (Chephren's) Pyramid and mortuary temple **26**, 27, **28**, 29, **29**
    Khufu's (Cheop's) Pyramid **26**, 27, **28**, 29
    Menkaure's (Mycerinus's) Pyramid **26**, 27, **28**
    pyramids 26, **26**, 27–9, 31, 37
    Sphinx 27, **29**, 36
Glasgow (Scotland)
    School of Art (Mackintosh) 457–8, **457**, **458**
    Scotland Street School (Mackintosh) 458
glass
    German Expressionism 491, 492, **493**
    Mies van der Rohe 515, 518, 521–2, 555
glass-and-iron structures 441–2, 454, **454**; *see also* Crystal Palace
Glessner House (Richardson), Chicago 465, **465**
Goetheanums (Steiner) 492, 494, **494**
Goharshad Mosque, Mashhad (Iran) **4**
Gol (Norway), stave church **202**
Gondoin, Jacques 411, **412**
Gonzaga family 306, 322
gopuras (gateways) **81**, 82, **82**
Gothic architecture 191, 203, 229–73, 311, 312, 417
    early Gothic cathedrals 232–6
    English 245–54, 346
    in Germany 255–7
    High Gothic 236–45
    in Italy 257–61
    Neo-Classical interest in 429, 430, 432
    quadripartite vaults 237, **237**, 243
    see also flying buttresses; pointed arches; rib vaults; window tracery
Gothic Revival 273, 429–32, 450, 462
"Gothick" 417
Granada (Spain), Alhambra palace 186–9, 339
granaries **68**
    Japan 102–3
grass houses, Plains tribes 275–6
Graves, Michael 544, 547–9
Great Buddha style, Japan 101, **101**
Great Lakes and Plains tribes 275–6
Great Wall of China 87–8, **88**
Greece 39, 47–65, 420
    Archaic period 47–50, 60

building materials 2, 47, 49
city/town planning 47, 60–5, 111
Classical period 50–6, 57, 60, 61, **61**
colonial cities 64–5, 116, **117**
Hellenistic period 57–60, 61–5, 75, 89, 285
painted buildings 59
tholoi 58, **58**, 123
see also Athens; stoas; temples; theaters
Greek Revival Style 58, 426, 462
Greek-cross plans 144, 152, 153, **154**
    Baroque 362, 365
    Carolingian 194
    Renaissance 308, 327
    Romanesque churches 218
    Russian church 161, **162**
    St. Peter's (Bramante), Rome 317
Greensted (England), St. Andrew's church, Anglo-Saxon 198, **198**, 200
Greyfriars (Voysey), Surrey (England) 450–1
Grignasco (Italy), church (Vittone) 372, **372**
groin-vaults
    Byzantine basilicas and churches 150, 155
    Carolingian 194
    Gothic 229
    Islamic 168
    Moscow Cathedral 313
    Norman 224
    Renaissance 308, 330, **330**, 331
    Roman 120, **121**, 127, **127**, **128**, 129, 227
    Romanesque 209, **209**, **211**, 217, 219
Gropius, Walter 475, 479, 480, 488, 511–15, **512**, **514**, 520–1
    home in Lincoln, Mass. 519, 555
    Weissenhof Siedlung 519
Guaranty Building (Adler and Sullivan), New York 470, **470**
Guarini, Guarino 171, 370–2, 375
    Cappella della SS. Sindone, Turin 370, **370**
    S. Lorenzo, Turin 370, **371**, 372
Guatemala *see* Maya, the; Tikal
Guggenheim Museum Bilbao (Gehry), Bilbao **532**, 560–1, **562**, 563, **563**
Guggenheim Museum (Wright), New York City 526, **527**, 550
Guimard, Hector 454, **454**
Gunzo, architect of Cluny 214
Guti, the 16

Hadrian, emperor 5, 120, 124, 136, 137
Hadrian's Villa, Tivoli 136–9, **320**, **364**, 539, 541, 551
Hagia Sophia *see* Constantinople
Hagley Park, Worcs. (England), sham ruin (Miller) 417
ha-ha 416
half-timber construction 264, **264**
hall churches 255, 376
    German Gothic 255–7
    Italy 259, **259**
Halladie Building (Polk), San Francisco 470, **471**
hammerbeam roofs 246, 253, **254**, 346, **348**
Hammurabi, king 18
Hampton Court Palace (England) 346, 392
haram (covered prayer hall) 170, 172, 184
Harappa 67
Harappan culture 67, 69
Hardwick Hall (Smythson), Derbyshire (England) 348–9, **348**
harmika 71, **71**
Harmon, Arthur 499, **499**
Harrison, Peter 395

Harrison, Wallace K. 498
Harvard University, Sever Hall and Austin
    Hall (Richardson) 464
Hastings castle (England) 265
Hatshepsut, Queen 30, **31**, 32, **32**, **33**, 39, 47
Hattusas (Turkey) 18, **18**
Haussmann, Baron Eugène Georges 357
Haviland, John **419**
Hawara (Egypt), mortuary temple 40
Hawksmoor, Nicholas 393, **394–5**, **394**
Heian capital, now Kyoto (Japan) 104, **104**
Heijo (Japan) 104
Helensburgh (Scotland) *see* Hill House
Heliopolis, temple 24
Hellenistic period 57–60, 89, 285
    cities 62–5
hemicycles 120, 318
Hennebique, François 448
Henry IV of France 345–6, 351
Henry VIII 346, 349
Herodotus 23
Hézelon, architect 214
Highland Park, Illinois, Ward Willits House
    (Wright) 481, **482**
Hildesheim (Germany), St. Michael **204**,
    204, **206**
Hill House (Mackintosh), Helensburgh 458,
    459
Himeji (Japan), Egret's Castle 106–7, **106**
Hindu temples 76–85, **76**, **89**, 90, 176
Hinduism, in India 69, 70, 75, 76, 83, 85
Hippodamus of Miletus 62, **64**
Historic American Buildings Survey 6, **7**
Hitchcock, Henry-Russell 476, 520, 523
Hittites 18–19, 21, 35, 36, **44**, 111
t'Hoff, Rob van 501
Hofmeister 498
hogans, Navajo 282, **282**
Hohokam, the 281
Holkham Hall, Norfolk (England) 400, **400**,
    416
Holland *see* De Stijl; Dutch Expressionism;
    strapwork decoration
Holy Roman Empire 205–9
Home Insurance Building (Jenney), Chicago
    446–7, **446**
Hong Kong Bank (Foster) 555–7, **556**
Hood, Raymond 497, **497**, **498**, 499
Hook of Holland housing project (Oud),
    Rotterdam 501, **501**
horseshoe arches *see* arches
Horta, Victor 453–4, **453**, **454**
Horyuji Temple (Japan) 100, **100**
Hosios Loukas (Greece), monastery
    churches **150**, 153, 155, **155**, 159
hospitals and sanatoriums, Renaissance 299,
    299; *see also* Paimio
Hôtel Amelot (Boffrand) 397
hôtels 346, 403, 426
House of the Prophet, Medina 169, **169**
houses
    China **90**, 96–8, **98**
    Inca 293
    Islamic 184–5
    Japan 104, **105**
    medieval 263–4
    medieval town houses 264, **265**
    Roman 132–5, 136
Howe, George 520, **520**
Hubbard, Elbert 450
Huis ter Heide (Holland) 501
Humayun, tomb of, in Delhi 176–7, **177**
Hunt, Richard Morris 433–4, **433**, **434**, 445
Hurley, William 253

Husserl, Edmund 543
huts, prehistoric 9, 409
    Banpo, Neolithic 87
hydraulic cement 115
"hydraulic" civilizations 23
Hyksos, the 31
hypostyle halls
    Egyptian **8**, 21, 30, **30**, 32–3, **34**, 291
    Nashville (Strickland) 420
    Persepolis 21

I-sections 415
iconostasis (screen) 159, **160**
icons, Russian 158, 159, 162
ideal towns and cities
    city plans 308
    Garnier's industrial city 506–8
    Le Corbusier's La Ville Radieuse 528, 529
    Ledoux's plan 406, 508 (*and see* Chaux)
iglu, Inuit 279–80, **280**
Iktinos, architect 51, 57
Illinois Institute of Technology (I.I.T.) 521–2
Imhotep, architect 24, **25**
impluvium 132, **132**
Incas 292–3
India 57, 67
    bamboo structures 72, 73, 77
    Buddhism 69–70, 75, 76, 83, 84
    Buddhist shrines 69, 70–6, 176
    cave-temples 73, **73**, 75, 79, 80, 89, 174
    chaitya halls 70, 72, 73, **73**, 75, 80, 158
    and China 74, 75, 89
    Hellenistic art 65
    Hindu temples 76–85, **76**, **89**, 90, 176
    Hinduism 69, 70, 75, 76, 83, 85
    mosques and courtyard designs, Islamic
        83, 165, 170, 174–9
    Persian craftsmen 21–2
    religions 69–70
    shikhara roofs 77, 78, **78**, **89**, 90
    shrines 69, 70–5
    stupas 70–6, **70**, 89, **89**, 90, 158
    see also Chandigarh
Indonesia 75–6, 170
Indus Valley 67, 72
industrial city 506–8
Industrial Revolution 397, 413–15, **432**, 448
Inspector's House (Ledoux) 406, **407**
insulae (apartment blocks), Roman **134**,
    135, 318, **319**, 411
intarsia 311
interlace ornament, Romanesque 199
International Style 497, 511, 520, 523, 531,
    533, 543, 554, 558
Inuit 279–80, **280**
Ionians 47
Ionic order
    Baroque 361
    Etruscans 112
    Greece 48, **48**, 49, 51, 55, 56, **56**, 57, 58,
        61, 62,
    Neo-Classicism 421, 424, 426
    Neo-Palladian 398
    Renaissance 318, 331, 338
    Roman temple 123, **123**, 130, 131
Iowa, Mason City Hotel 512
Iran 14, 16, 69, 165
    mosques 170, 172, 176, **177**
    see also Persepolis
Iraq 14, 165
Ireland, megalith tombs 10–11
iron 2, 431, 437–48
    bridges 4, 414, **414**, 415, 437–40, 444
    Industrial Revolution 414, 415, **432**

Ise Shrine, Uji-Yamada (Japan) 102–3, **103**
Isfahan
    bazaar 185–6, **185**
    city planning **184**, 185–6
    Friday Mosque **164**, 172–4, **172**, **184**,
        186
    Masjid-i-shah **172**, **173**, 174, **174**, **184**,
        186
Isidorus of Miletus 149, 151
Islamic architecture 165–89
    Alhambra palace and garden 186–9, 339
    arches 4, 167–8, 170, **171**, **176**, 189, **194**,
        195, 229
    bazaars 185, **185**
    castles in Syria 266
    city planning 184, 185–6
    houses 184–5
    India 83, 170, 174–9
    mosques 169–84, 185, 370, **371**
    palaces 167–9
    polychromy 167, 170, **171**, 189, 194
    shrines 165–7
    tombs 176–9, 181, 183
    see also Spain
Istanbul (Turkey)
    Mosque of Süleyman the Magnificent
        (Sinan) 181, **182**, 183
    Shehzade Mosque (Sinan) 180, 181, **181**
    see also Constantinople
Italy
    Baroque 126, 353–72, 373
    Futurism 488, **488**
    Gothic style 257–61
    medieval houses 264, **265**
    medieval towns and cities 271–3
    Renaissance 295–338
    Romanesque churches 205, 207–9
    see also Etruscans
Itten, Johannes 512
Ivan III, Tsar of Russia 312
iwans **164**, 170, 172–4, **172**, **173**

Jahan, Shah 178
Jainism 69, 70
James of St. George, Master 266
Japan 99–109
    Buddhist temples 99–102
    cantilever construction 100, 101, **101**
    castles 106–7
    city planning 103–4
    color schemes 102
    granaries 102–3
    Great Buddha style 101, **101**
    houses 104, **105**
    minka (wooden folk houses) 104, **105**,
        106
    monasteries 100–1
    pagodas 75, 100, **100**, **101**
    palaces 103, 104, **104**
    Pure Land Buddhism 101–2
    raised-floor structures 102–3, 104, **105**,
        106, 109
    Shinto shrines 99, 102–3, 109
    tatami **105**, 106, **108**, 109
    tea houses **108**, 109, **109**
    temples 99–103, 104
    thatch roofs 103, **105**, 106
    torii (gateway) 102
    wooden structures 99–100
Jefferson, Thomas 123, 126, 424, 426–8,
    427, **428**, 462
Jencks, Charles 544, 557
Jenney, William Le Baron 446–7, **446**, 467
Jericho (Israel), prehistoric settlement 9

Jerusalem
    Church of the Holy Sepulcher 165–6
    Dome of the Rock 165–7, **166**, 170, 183
    pilgrimages 210
    Temple of Solomon 143, 188, 230, 359, **359**
Jesuits 353–4, 355, 361
jetty (of a building) 3
jian (modular unit), China 90, **90**
Jinci temple complex, Taiyuan (China) 92–3, **93**
Jizodo of Shofukuji (Japan), Zen temple 107
John Graves House, Madison **6**
Johnson, Philip 476, 520, 522, 544–5, **544**, **545**, **554**, 557, 560
Johnson Wax Company (Wright), Racine 525–6, **525**, **526**
Jones, Inigo 331, 349–51, 398, 399, 416
    Banqueting House, Whitehall, London 350–1, **350**, 392
    Covent Garden, London 351, **351**
    Queen's House, Greenwich 349–50, **349**, **350**
    St. Paul's, London 351, **351**
    Whitehall Palace, London 351
Jordan, Mshatta Palace 168–9, **168**
Jugendstil 452, 459–60
Julius II, pope 317, 318, 339, 356
Justinian, emperor 148, 152, 153, 181
Juvarra, Filippo 372, **373**

Kabah (Mexico), arch **2**
Kahn, Ely Jacques **474**, 496–7
Kahn, Louis I. 533, 538–41, 542, 544
Kairatos (Crete) 39
Kallikrates, architect 51, 56
Kanchipuram (India), Satiangam Temple **82**
Kandariya Mahadeva Temple, Khajuraho **66**, **79**
Kandinsky, Wassily 514, **514**
Karli (India), cave-temple 73, **73**, 75
Karnak (Egypt)
    Great Temple of Amun 8, 32–3, **33**, **34**, **35**, 36, 122
    pylon gates 36
Kassites 19
katsuogi 103, **103**
Katsura Imperial Villa, Kyoto (Japan) 107, **108**, 109, **109**
Kaufmann House, "Fallingwater" (Wright), Ohiopyle 483, 523, **524**, 525
Kelly, William, ironmonger 438
Kempsey (Australia), History Museum and Tourist Office (Murcutt) **564**, 565, **565**
Kent, William 398, 399, 400, **400**, 416
Kew Gardens, London, Palm House (Burton and Turner) 441, **441**
keystones 547
Khafre (Chephren), pharaoh, pyramid and temple 26, 27, **28**, 29, **29**
Khajuraho (India) **66**, 78–9, **78**, **79**
Khan, 'Abd al-Karim Ma'mur 178
Khan, Makramat 178
Khmer architecture 83, 84, 85
Khorsabad (Assyria), palace and ziggurat 19–20, **19**
Khufu (Cheops), pharaoh, pyramid 26, 27, **28**, 29
ki, southwest tribes 281
Kiesler, Friedrich 501, **502**
Kiev (Russia)
    Cathedral of the Dormition of the Virgin (Church of the Virgin of the Tithe) 156, **156**

St. Sophia 156–8, **156**, **157**, 161
Kimbell Art Museum (Kahn), Fort Worth, Texas **540**, 541
Kirby Hall, Northants. (England) 349
kivas 281–2
Kizhi (Russia)
    Church of the Raising of Lazarus, from Muromansky monastery 159, 160, **160**
    Church of the Transfiguration 161–2, **162**, **163**
Knossos (Crete), palace/temple 38, 39–42, 43
    Queen's Megaron 42, 44
Knoxville, Tennessee, railroad bridge **4**
Korea 99
Kraków (Poland) 271, **271**
Kramer, Piet 491, **492**
Krier, Leon 550
Kroller-Müller, Mrs. 515
Kutná Hora, Bohemia, St. Barbara 255, **256**, 257, **257**
Kyoto (Japan), Heian capital 104, **104**; *see also* Katsura Imperial Villa

La Venta, Tabasco (Mexico) 283, **283**
Labrouste, Henri 5, 436, **436**, 442, **443**, 444, **444**, 448
labyrinth 39, 40
Ladkhan Temple, Aihole **76**, 77, 79–80
LaFarge, John 463
Lahawri, Ahmad 178
Lakeville, Connecticut, House III (Eisenman) **559**
Lakshmana Temple, Khajuraho 78–9, **79**
Lamb, William 499, **499**
landscaped urban spaces, Renaissance 318, 339
landscapes, Romantic 416–17
Lang House (Stern), Washington, Connecticut 549, **549**
lantern 407
Laon (France), Notre-Dame Cathedral **231**, 232–3, **233**, 238, **238**
Larkin Building (Wright), Buffalo, New York 484–5, **484**, 512, 516
Latrobe, Benjamin Henry 413, 419, 424, **425**, 426, 428
Latrobe, John H.B. **425**
Laugier, Marc-Antoine 409, 410
Laurana, Luciano 308, 310
Le Corbusier 139, 475, 476, 479–80, 496, 505, 508–11, 528–31, 539, 554
    Chandigarh, India 530–1, **531**
    Cité Universitaire, Swiss Pavilion 511
    Citrohan houses 44, **508**, 509, 519
    Dom-ino House 508, **508**
    "Five Points" 511
    garden terraces/roof gardens 508, 511
    La Ville Radieuse 528
    Notre-Dame-du-Haut, Ronchamp 529–30, **529**, **530**
    Ste.-Marie-de-la-Tourette 530, **530**
    Unité d'Habitation, Marseille 528–9, **528**, **529**
    Villa Savoye, Poissy 509, **510**, 511
    Villa Stein, Garches 509, **509**
    Weissenhof Siedlung housing unit 519–20, **519**
Le Nôtre, André 384, **385**, **386**, 387
Le Raincy (France), Notre Dame (Perret) 504, **504**
Le Vau, Louis 381, **382**, 384, 385, **385**, **386**, 387, 397
Lebrun, Charles 381, **382**, 384, **385**, 387

Ledoux, Claude-Nicolas 405, 406–8, **407**, **408**, 508, 539, 547, **547**
Leicester University (England), Engineering Building (Stirling) 551–2
Lemercier, Jacques **344**, 345, 381, 382, **383**
Leonardo da Vinci 296, **296**, **301**, 311, 313–14, 317, 343
Leoni, Giacomo 398
Leptis Magna, Hunting Baths 129
Lescaze, William 520, **520**
Lescot, Pierre 344–5, **344**, 349
Leyswood (Sussex) 450, **450**
Library of Celsus, Ephesus **2**
lierne vaults 247, **251**
Ligorio, Pirro 339–40, **340**, 363
Limoges (France), church of St. Martial 210
Lincoln Cathedral, Lincs. (England) **248**, 250, **251**, 253
Lincoln, Mass., Gropius's home 519, 555
linear perspective 296, **297**, 315
Lingaraja Temple, Bhubaneshwar 78, **78**
lintels 3
live loads 2
loads 2–3, 4–5
log construction
    American log cabins 159–60
    Anglo-Saxon, upright logs 198, **198**
    Navajo 282, **282**
    Norwegian stave churches (Viking) 199–200, **201**
    Russia, horizontal 159–61
loggias
    Late Renaissance 320, 321, 333, 336
    Renaissance 339, **339**, 350
    Renaissance France 343
Loire valley (France), châteaux 341–3
Lombard bands **145**, 204, **206**, **209**
Lombard masons 204
Lombardo, Martino and Tullio 336
Lombards and Lombardy 191, 192, 207, 209
London (England)
    Adelphi scheme (Adam) 403
    Bank of England (Soane) 423, **423**
    Banqueting House, Whitehall (Jones) 350–1, **350**, 392
    Baroque churches 389–92
    Burlington House 398
    Christ Church, Spitalfields (Hawksmoor) 394–5, **394**
    Covent Garden (Jones) 351, **351**
    Crystal Palace (Paxton) 441–2, **442**, 551, 553
    Frederick Leyland's mansion 453
    Houses of Parliament (Barry and Pugin) 429, **430**
    New Zealand Chambers (Shaw) 450, **451**
    old St. Paul's Cathedral 417
    Paddington Station 439, **439**
    Palm House (Burton and Turner), Kew Gardens 441, **441**
    Queen's House, Greenwich 349–50, **349**, **350**
    St. Bride's, Fleet Street (Wren) 389
    St. Dunstan-in-the-East (Wren) 389
    St. Martin-in-the-Fields (Gibbs) 395, **395**
    St. Mary-le-Bow (Wren) 389
    St. Paul's Cathedral, (Hawksmoor) towers 393, (Jones) 351, **351**, (Wren) 5, 388, 389, 390, **390**, **391**, 392
    St. Stephen Walbrook (Wren) 389, **389**, 390
    Soane's Museum, Lincoln's Inn Fields 423–4, **424**

Somerset House (Chambers) 401, 404, 405, **405**
Tower of London (White Tower) 265–6, **266**
Westminster Abbey 346, 417
Westminster Hall 253, **254**
Whitehall Palace (Jones) 351
Williams-Wynn House (Adam), St. James's Square 403, **403**
Wren's replanning 388, 389
longhouses
    Iroquois 277
    medieval 263–4, **263**
Longhua Pagoda, Shanghai 90
Loos, Adolf 453, 454, 476, 477–80, 496
Lorsch (Germany), abbey gatehouse 194, **194**, **121**
Los Angeles, Calif.
    Art Deco 499, **500**
    Coca-Cola Bottling Plant (Derrah) 499, **500**
    Gehry House (Gehry), Santa Monica 557, 560, **560**
    Pantages Theater (Priteca) 499, **500**
    Team Disneyland Administration Building (Gehry), Anaheim 560, **561**
    Wiltern Theater 499
Luckenwalde (Germany), hat factory (Mendelsohn) 494–5
lunettes 148
lustral-basins, Knossos 41, 42
Luton Hoo (Adam), Bedfordshire (England) 403–4, **404**
Lysikrates, and monument **58**, 59, 426

machicolations 266
Machu Picchu (Peru) **274**, 293
McKim, Charles Follen 435, 436–7, **443**
McKim, Mead, and White 5, 305, 434–7
Mackintosh, Charles Rennie 457–60, **457**, 461
Mackmurdo, Arthur 453, **453**
Maderno, Carlo 328, 355, **355**, 358, **358**, 360, 362
Madison *see* John Graves House
madrasas 174
Magney House (Murcutt), Bingi Point (Australia) 565, **566**
Mahabalipuram (India), temples (rathas) 80, **80**
Maillart, Robert 503–4, **503**
Maison Carrée *see* Nimes
Maisons-sur-Seine (France), château (Mansart) 382, **383**, 384, 409
Malatesta, Sigismondo 305
Malcontenta (Italy), Villa Foscari (Palladio) 333, **334**
mammoth bones, in prehistoric hut construction 9
Mannerism (Late Renaissance) 319–23
    garden design 339, 340
manor houses, medieval 264, **264**
Mansart, François 5, 382–4, 409
Mansart, Jules-Hardouin 385, **386**, 409
Mantua (Italy)
    Palazzo del Te (Romano) 322–3, **322**
    Romano's house 322
    S. Andrea (Alberti) **121**, 306, **306**, 308, 354–5
    S. Sebastiano (Alberti) 308
maqsura 170, 171, 172–3
Marinetti, Filippo 488
Marseille (France), Unité d'Habitation (Le Corbusier) 528–9, **528**, **529**

Marshall Field Wholesale Store (Richardson), Chicago 464, 465, 467, 468
Martel, Charles 165, 191
martyria, Early Christian 143, **144**, 205, 317
Marzabotto (Italy) 111, **112**
Masaccio 296, **297**, 303
Maser (Italy), Villa Barbaro (Palladio) 331–3, **333**
Mashhad (Iran), Goharshad Mosque 4
Mason City Hotel, Iowa (USA) 512
mass-production of buildings 496, 508, 509, 514, 519, 551, 555
mastaba tombs, Egypt 24, **24**, 25, **28**
master builders, medieval 262, 263
mausolea, Early Christian 143–4, **145**, 147–8, **147**, 152
Maya, the 2, 286–91, 523
Mead, William Rutherford 434–5
Mecca 165, 169, 170, **172**, 173, **173**, 174, 179, 186
    Ka'ba 167
Medes 20
Medical College of Virginia (Steward), Richmond 419
Medici Chapel *see* Florence
Medici family 302, 308, 311, 323, 340–1
Medici Palace (Palazzo Medici) *see* Florence
Medici Villa (Michelozzo), Fiesole 339, **339**
medieval architecture 191–227, 429–30
    castles 265–8
    cities 268–73, 429, **429**
    construction 262–3
    gardens 339
    housing 263–4
    see also Carolingian architecture; Gothic architecture; Norman architecture; Vikings
Medina, House of the Prophet 169, **169**
megalith constructions 10–13, 44
    tombs 10–11, **10**, **11**, 13
    see also Stonehenge
megarons 333
    Athens 55
    Miletus 62
    Minoan, at Knossos 42, 44
    Mycenaean 42, **43**, 44, 45, 46–7, **46**
    Priene 63, **64**
Meidum (Egypt), pyramid 26, **26**
Meier, Richard 550–1
Meissonier, J.A. 397
Meledo (Italy), Villa Trissino (Palladio) 335, **335**
Melk abbey (Austria) 375, **376**
Melnikov, Konstantin 490, **490**
Memphis (Egypt) 24, 25, 30
Menai Bridge (Telford), Menai Straits 438, **438**
Mendelsohn, Erich 494–5, **494**, 538
Menes, king of Egypt 24, 30
Mengoni, Giuseppe 553
Menier Chocolate Factory (Saulnier) 445, **445**
Menkaure (Mycerinus), pharaoh, pyramid at Giza 26, 27, **28**
Mentuhotep II, tomb and temple 30, **30**, 32, **32**
Mereworth Castle (Campbell), Kent (England) 398–9, **398**
Mesa Verde, Colorado 281, **281**, 282
Mesopotamia (Iraq) 14–22, 39, 43, 50
    ziggurats **16**, 17–18, **17**, 293
metopes 48, 49

Métro station entrances, Paris (Guimard) 454, **454**
Mexico, Pre-Columbian 283–6, **283**, 288–92, 293
Meyer, Adolf 488, 511, **512**, 514
Meyer, Hannes 515
Miami Beach, Florida, The Breakwater (Skislewicz) 499, **500**
Michelangelo Buonarroti 319, 323–30
    Campidoglio, Rome 325–6, **325**, **326**, 331, 361
    Laurentian Library, Florence **300**, 323–5, **324**, 326
    Medici Chapel, S. Lorenzo, Florence 323
    Palazzo Farnese, Rome 326, **327**
    Porta Pia, Rome 328–9, **329**, 356, **356**
    S. Maria degli Angeli, Rome **128**, 129
    St. Peter's, Rome 5, 326–8, **327**, **328**, 357, **358**, 359, 387, 392, tomb for Julius II 317
    Sforza Chapel, S. Maria Maggiore, Rome 329–30, **330**
Michelozzo di Bartolomeo
    Banco Mediceo, Milan 311
    Medici Villa, Fiesole 339, **339**
    Palazzo Medici, Florence 302–3, **302**
Mies van der Rohe, Ludwig 106, 255, 476, 479–80, 515–18, 520–2, 531, 555, 563
    Barcelona Pavilion 516–18, **516**, **517**
    Crown Hall, I.I.T. 521, **521**
    Farnsworth House, Plano 522, **522**
    860 Lake Shore Drive, Chicago 521–2, **521**
    Seagram Building, New York City 522, **522**
    Tugendhat House, Brno 518, **518**
    Weissenhof Siedlung block of flats 518–19, **519**
mihrabs 170, 171, 179
Milan (Italy) 311–12, 341
    Banco Mediceo (Michelozzo) 311
    Cathedral, Gothic 241, **258**, 259, 261, **261**, 262
    Cathedral crossing (Leonardo and Bramante) 314
    Galleria Vittorio Emanuele (Mengoni) 553
    S. Ambrogio abbey church **207**, 209, **209**
    S. Maria delle Grazie (Bramante) 314, **314**, 317
    S. Maria presso S. Satiro (Bramante) 314–15, **315**
Miletus (Asia Minor) 62
mill buildings
    English textile mills 414–15, **415**
    Manchester, New Hampshire 541
Miller, Sanderson 417
minarets **151**, 170, 179, 180, **180**, 181, 183, **183**, 184
minbar 170
Minerals and Mining Museum (Murcutt), Broken Hill (Australia) 566, **566**
minka (wooden folk houses), Japan 104, **105**, 106
Minneapolis, Johnson-Borey Building 503
Minoan columns 38, 40, 41
Minoans 39–42, 111; *see also* Knossos
mints *see* Paris, Hôtel de Monnaies; Venice, La Zecca
Mique, Richard 417, **417**
Mirande (France), bastide 269, **270**
Mississippi River basin, tribes 277–9
M.I.T. School of Architecture 432; *see also* Cambridge, Mass.

Mitanni 19
Mitla, Oaxaca (Mexico) 286, **286**
Mixtecs 286, 289
Mnesikles, architect 53, 55
Modern Movement 518
Modernism 454, 461, 475–531, 533, 539, 558
modillions 303
Mogollan culture 281
Mohenjo-Daro (Indus Valley) **17**, 67, **68**
moment connections 503
Monadnock Building (Burnham and Root), Chicago 447, **447**
monasteries
    Benedictine *see* St. Gall; St. Gallen
    Carolingian 195–8
    Carthusian 311–12
    Cistercian 221–4, 249, 258
    Cluniac 213–17, 220 (*see also* Cluny II-III)
    Dominican 530
    India, Buddhist (viharas) 70, 71–2, **73**, 74
    Japan 100–1
    Norman 224
    pilgrims 210
    Romanesque 202
    Zen 107
    see also Hosios Loukas; St. Gall; St. Martin at Canigou
Mondrian, Piet 501, 502, **503**
Monpazier (France), bastide 269, **270**
Monte Albán (Mexico) 285, **286**, 291
Montefeltro, Federigo da 310
Monticello (Jefferson), Charlottesville 426–7, **427**
Montreuil, Pierre de 234
Moore, Charles 544, 545, **546**, 547
Moosbrugger, Caspar 376–8
Moosbrugger, Johann 376
Morando, Bernardo 308–9
Morris, William 449–50, 453, 463, 476, 487, 514
mortuary temples, Egyptian 27–9, 30, **30**, **31**, 32, **32**, **33**, 40, 47
Moscow (Russia) 162
    Cathedral of the Dormition of the Virgin 312–13, **312**
    churches 162
    Kremlin 162
    Pravda Newspaper Building (Vesnin) 488, **489**, 490
    Rusakov Workers' Club (Melnikov) 490, **490**
    St. Basil the Blessed (Barma and Posnik) **156**, 162–3, **163**
mosques 4, 169–84, 185, 370
    columnar hall designs 170–2
    courtyard designs in India 170, 174–9
    domed prayer hall designs in Anatolia 180–4
    pavilion designs in China 170, 179–80
    triple-arched entry 170
motte and bailey castles 265, **266**
mounds *see* earth mounds
Moundville, Alabama 279, **279**
Mount Wilson (Australia), Simpson-Lee House (Murcutt) 567, **567**
Mozarabic churches 195
Mshatta Palace (Jordan) 168–9, **168**
mud-over-timber-frame buildings, Native American 279
muqarnas vaults **164**, **173**, 174, **174**, 188
Murcutt, Glenn 563, **564**, 565–7
Muromansky monastery *see* Kizhi

Museum for Pre-Columbian Art (Johnson), Dumbarton Oaks 544
Museum für Kunsthandwerk (Meier), Frankfurt 550–1, **550**
museums 433, 544, 550–1, **550**; *see also* Berlin; Guggenheim Museum Bilbao; Guggenheim Museum
Muthesius, Herman 451, 476, 487
mutules 329
Mycenae 42–7, **43**
    houses and megaron layouts 45–6, **46**
    Lion Gate 43, **43**, 44
    palace and megarons 42, **43**, 44, **46**
    tombs (tholoi) 44–5, **44**
    Treasury of the Atreus 44–5, **44**, **45**
Mycenaeans 19, 39, 40, 42–7, 111
Mycerinus *see* Menkaure

Nanchan Temple, Shaanxi (China) 91–2, **91**
Nanih Waiya mound, Mississippi 278, **278**
Nash, John 419
Nashville, Tennessee
    First Presbyterian Church (Strickland) 419–20
    Tennessee State Capitol (Strickland) 59, 426, **426**
Nasrid Dynasty 186
National Assembly of Bangladesh (Kahn), Dacca 540–1
National Farmers' Bank (Sullivan), Owatonna 473, **473**
Native Americans 275–9, 280–1
Navajo nation 282, **282**
Nebuchadnezzar II 20, **20**
Neo-Babylonian Empire 20
Neo-Classicism 397, 400, 401, 402, 405–8, 461, 467, 539, 540
Neo-Palladians 335, **335**, 398–400, 415, 416
Neo-Sumerian period 16–17
Neolithic
    Banpo, houses 87, **88**
    Knossos settlements 39
Nervi, Pier Luigi 505–6, **505**
Neumann, Johann Balthasar 379–81
Neutra, Richard 563
New Canaan, Connecticut
    Boissonas House (Johnson) 544, **544**
    glass house (Johnson) 522, 544
New Haven (USA), cemetery gates 419
New Orleans, Louisiana, Piazza d'Italia (Moore) **546**, 547
New York
    American Telephone and Telegraph Headquarters (Johnson and Burgee) 544–5, **545**
    AT&T Building (now Sony Plaza) (Johnson and Burgee) 554
    Brooklyn Bridge (Roebling) 438, 440, **440**
    Chrysler Building (Van Alen) 470, 496, **496**
    Citicorp Building (Stubbins) 553, **554**
    City Prison (Haviland) 419
    Empire State Building (Shreve, Lamb, and Harmon) 470, 499, **499**
    Fifth Avenue (Hunt) 433
    Ford Foundation Building (Roche and Dinkeloo) 553, **553**
    Guaranty Building (Adler and Sullivan), Buffalo 470, **470**
    Guggenheim Museum (Wright) 526, **527**
    IBM Center (Barnes) 553
    Larkin Building (Wright), Buffalo 484–5, **484**, 512, 516

Lever House, Park Avenue (Bunshaft) 515–16
New York Daily News Building (Hood) 497, **497**
Number Two Park Avenue (E.J. Kahn) **474**, 497
Pennsylvania Station (McKim, Mead, and White) **436**, 437
Radio City Music Hall (Harrison) **498**, 499
Rockefeller Center **498**, 499
Seagram Building (Mies van der Rohe) 470, 522, **522**
skyscrapers 445–6, 470, **554**
Statue of Liberty (Eiffel, Bartholdi, and Hunt) 433, 445, **445**
Trinity Church (Upjohn) 431, **431**
Trump Tower 553, **554**
TWA Terminal (Saarinen), Kennedy Airport 537–8, **538**
Villard Houses (McKim, Mead, and White) 435, **435**
Woolworth Building (Gilbert) 496
newel 349
Newgrange, Co. Meath (Ireland), passage grave 10–11, **11**, 44
Newport Bay Club Hotel (Stern), Euro Disney (France) 549, **549**
Newport, Rhode Island
    The Breakers (Hunt) 433, **433**
    Watts Sherman House (Richardson) 466, **466**
Newton, Sir Isaac, cenotaph (Boullée) 405, **406**
Nicholas V, pope 356
Nimes (France) 220
    amphitheater 130
    Maison Carrée 123, **123**, 426
    Pont du Gard aqueduct **110**, 115
    Temple of Diana **114**, 115
Nimrud 19
Nineveh 19
Nördlingen (Germany), St. George Church 255, **255**, 257
Norman architecture 224–7, 233, 247, **248**, 250, **252**, 253
    castle 265–6
Normandy 224
North Easton, Mass. *see* Ames estate
northwestern and northeastern tribes, North America 276–7, **276**, 280–1, **281**
Norway, stave churches 199–202
Novgorod (Russia)
    Church of the Nativity of the Virgin 160–1, **161**, 162
    Church of the Transfiguration of the Savior 158, **158**
Nymphenburg Castle (Germany) 397

Oak Park, Illinois *see* Unity Temple
Oaxaca (Mexico) 285–6, **286**
obelisks
    Egypt **23**, 24, 32, 122
    in Rome 357, 368, **368**
    Vatican Obelisk (Egyptian) 357, 358, 360, **360**, 365
observatories
    Mayan (Caracol) 290–1, **291**
    Sugar Loaf Mountain (Wright) 526
Odo of Metz 192, **192**, **193**, 194
Ogden House, Fairfield, Connecticut 7, **7**
Ohiopyle, Penn. *see* Fallingwater *under* Wright, Frank Lloyd
Olbrich, Joseph Maria 460, 461, **462**, 495

Olmecs 283, **283**
Olmsted, Frederick Law 434, **435**
Olympia, Temple of Hera 47, **48**
onion domes *see* domes
open-plan buildings 503
opisthodomos (back room) 51
opus reticulatum 115, 194, **304**, 305
orangery 382
Order of Citeaux *see* Cistercian monasteries
orders of architecture 47–9, 303,344, 381–2
oriel windows 450
Orlando, Florida *see* Disney World
Orly (France), airship hangars (Freyssinet) 505
Orme, Philibert de l' 343, **343**, 344
orthographic projections 5, 6, **6**
Ostia, insula **134**, 135
Otis, Elisha Graves 445
Ottonian architecture 205–7
Oud, J.J.P. 501, **501**
Owatonna, Minnesota, National Farmers' Bank (Sullivan) 473, **473**
Oxford (England), Sheldonian Theater (Wren) **388**, 389

Paestum 62, **63**, 400, 409, 424
    Temple of Hera **48**, 49–50, **50**, 51
pagodas
    China 75, 89–90, **89**, **90**
    Japan 75, 100, **100**, **101**
Paimio (Finland), Tuberculosis Sanatorium (Aalto) 533–4, **535**
palaces
    Baroque 372, 379–80
    Carolingian 192
    China 93, 94, **94**, 95, 98
    Egyptian 25
    Hattusas 18, **18**
    India 175, **175**
    Islamic 167–9, 186–9
    Japan 103, 104, **104**
    Khorsabad 19–20, **19**
    Persia 21, **21**, 22, **22**, 173
    Renaissance/Mannerism (palazzi) 302–3, **304**, 305, 310–11, 319, 322–3, **322**, 326, 331, 338
    Roman, urban 135–9, 331, **435**
    see also Alhambra; châteaux; Knossos; Mycenae; Rome
Palatine Chapel *see* Aachen
Palenque (Mexico) 288, 289, **289**
Palladio, Andrea **290**, 319, 330–6, **388**, 437
    churches in Venice 335–6
    and the English Renaissance 349–50, 351
    and the Neo-Palladians 398, 399
    Palazzo Chiericati, Vicenza 331, **332**, 349–50
    Palazzo Valmarana 331
    S. Francesca della Vigne, Venice 335
    S. Giorgio Maggiore, Venice 335–6, **335**
    Teatro Olimpico, Vicenza 336, **336**
    Vicenza basilica 331, **331**
    Villa Barbaro, Maser 331–3, **333**
    villa designs in the Veneto 331–5
    Villa Foscari, Malcontenta 333, **334**
    Villa Rotonda (Villa Americo-Capra), Vicenza 333, **334**, 398, 399, 408
    Villa Trissino, Meledo 335, **335**
Palmanova (Italy) 308
Panini, Giovanni Paolo **125**, 367
Pantheon *see under* Rome
Paris (France)
    Arc du Triomphe 121
    Barrière de la Villette (Ledoux) 408

Bibliothèque Nationale (Labrouste) 442, 444, **444**
Bibliothèque Ste.-Geneviève (Labrouste) 5, 436, **436**, 442, **443**
Castel Béranger (Guimard) 454
Cité Universitaire, Swiss Pavilion (Le Corbusier) 511
Comédie-Française (Peyre and Wailly) 411, **411**
Ecole de Chirurgie (Gondoin) 411, **412**, 413
Eiffel Tower (Eiffel) **418**, 444–5
Exposition des Arts Décoratifs 490, **490**, 496, 501, **502**
Haussmann's boulevards 357
Hôtel de Thelluson (Ledoux) 407, **408**
Hôtel des Monnaies (Antoine), royal mint 411, **411**, **412**
Ile-de-France 230, 232
Louvre, (Bernini) 381, (Lemercier) **344**, 345, (Lescot) 344–5, **344**, 349, (Perrault, Lebrun and Le Vau) 381–2, **382**, 392
Luxembourg Palace (Brosse) 346
Métro entrance (Guimard) 454, **454**
Notre-Dame Cathedral 233–6, **234**, **235**, 239, 432
Panthéon (Ste.-Geneviève) (Soufflot) 409, **409**, 414
Parc de la Villette (Tschumi) 557, **557**
Place Dauphine 346
Place Royale 345–6, **345**, 351
Pompidou Center (Piano and Rogers) 555, **555**
Pont Neuf 346
Renaissance town planning 345–6, **345**
Roman baths, Cluny Museum 129
Rue Franklin apartment house (Perret) 504–5, **504**
St.-Jean de Montmarte (Baudot) 448
St. Louis-des-Invalides (J.-H. Mansart) 387–8, **387**, 391, 392
Ste. Marie de la Visitation (Mansart) 382, **382**, **383**, 384
Sainte-Chapelle **244**, 245, **245**, 432
Soviet Pavilion (Melnikov) 490, **490**
tollgates (Ledoux) 407–8
Val-de-Grâce (Mansart) 5, 382, **383**
Parler, Johann 255
parterre 321
Parthenon *see under* Athens
Pasadena, house for Alice Millard (Wright) 523
Pasti, Matteo de' 305
Pataliputta (Patna) (India) 22
Paul III, pope 325, 326–7, 356
Pavia (Italy), Certosa monastery 311–12, **311**, 341
pavilion designs, for mosques 170, 179–80
Paxton, Joseph 441–2, 442, 551
pebble dash 458
Pei, I.M. 97
pendant vaulting 417
pendentives
    Christian 147, **149**, 153
    Renaissance 313, 314, 317, 323
    Romanesque churches 209, 211–12, 218, **218**, 219, **219**
Pennsylvania Station (McKim, Mead, and White), New York **436**, 437
Pergamon 63–4, **65**
Périgueux (France), St. Front 218–19, **218**
peristyle **132**, 133, **133**, 134, 135, **135**, 136
Perpendicular *see* English Gothic

Perrault, Claude 381–2, **382**, 392
Perret, Auguste 480, 504–5, **504**, 508
Persepolis, Persia (Iran) 20–1, **21**, 22, **22**
Persia, Persians (Persian Empire) 20–2, 50, 51, 56, 62, 89
    masons in India 69, 71, 174
    Parthian palaces 173
    Sassanian audience halls 168, 169, 172
perspective, linear 296, **297**, 315
perspective drawings 6–7, **6**
Peru 4, 283, 438; *see also* Incas
Perugia (Etruscan Perusia), Arch of Augustus 112, **113**
Peter the Great of Russia 161, 163
Pevsner, Nikolaus 450, 476
Peyre, Marie-Joseph 401, 411, **411**
Phidias, sculptor 52
Philadelphia, Penn.
    Bacon's redevelopment 357
    Bank of Pennsylvania (Latrobe) 424
    Guild House (Venturi and Rauch) 541, 542
    Philadelphia Exchange (Strickland) 59, 426
    Philadelphia Saving Fund Society Building (Howe and Lescaze) 520, **520**
    Richards Medical Research Building (Kahn), University of Pennsylvania 539, **539**
    St. James-the-Less 431, **431**
    Second Bank of the United States (Latrobe) 426, **426**
Philip of Macedon 57
Phillips Exeter Academy (Kahn), New Hampshire 539, 541
Piano, Renzo 555, **555**
piano nobile 303
piazzas, Baroque Rome 365–70
Picturesque 416, 417
Pienza (Italy) 307, **307**, 325, 343
Pietro da Cortona *see* Cortona, Pietro da
pilgrimage routes, churches 210–13, 220, 229, 237
pilgrims 215, 247, 378
    Early Christian 143, **144**
    to Mecca 165, 167
    Rome 357, **368**
    Ronchamp church (Le Corbusier) 529–30, **529**, **530**
pilotis 509, 530
Piranesi, Giovanni Battista 401, **401**, 402, **402**, **405**, 411, 415, 423, 465, 540, 541
Pisa (Italy), Campanile (Leaning Tower) and Cathedral **207**, **208**, 209
pit houses 280, 281, **281**
Pius II, pope 307
Placidia, Galla 144; mausoleum *see* Ravenna
Plan of St. Gall (manuscript) *see* St. Gall
plank houses, northwestern tribes 280
Plano (Ill., USA) *see* Farnsworth House
plans 5–6, **6**, **7**
Plater-Zyberk, Elizabeth 550
Platz, Gustav 475
Pliny the Elder 122, 303
Pliny the Younger 318
Poelzig, Hans 451, 495, **495**
pointed arches 3
    Gothic 229, 230, 233, 431
    Islamic 4, 167–8, **176**, 189, 229
    Norman 227
    Renaissance 295, 297, **298**, 311
    Romanesque churches 214, **214**, 219, 229
Poissy (France), Villa Savoye (Le Corbusier) 509, **510**, 511

Poland, city planning 308–9, **309**
Polk, W.J. 470, **471**
polychromy (polychrome)
    Carolingian 194
    Islamic 167, 170, **171**, 189, 194
    by Richardson 462–3
    Romanesque 205, **206**, 209, 217
Polykleitos, architect 58, 60
pomochi 161
Pompeii (Italy) 400, 402, 403
    amphitheater 117, **117**, 130, **130**
    basilica 118, 126, 127
    baths 117, **117**, 127, 129, **129**, 168
    Capitolium 117, 123
    forum 116, **116**, 117–18, **117**
    houses 132–5, 136
    planning 116–18, **116**, **117**
    streets 134, **134**
    temples 117, 118
    theaters 117, **117**
    Triumphal arch 121, **121**
    Villa of the Mysteries 135, **135**
    wall paintings 134–5
Pope, Thomas 438
Porta, Giacomo della *see* Giacomo della
    Porta
porte-cochère 349, 481
Portland Building (Graves), Portland
    (Oregon, USA) 547, **547**
Portland cement 448
Poseidonia *see* Paestum
Posen (Germany), water tower (Poelzig)
    495, **495**
Posnik, architect 156, 163, **163**
post-and-beam construction
    China, wooden buildings 90
    concrete 503
post-and-lintel (column-and-beam)
    construction 2, 3, 114
    Catal Hüyük 9–10
    earth lodges 276
    hogans 282
    Indian temples 77
    Japan 100
Post-Modernism 139, 476, 542–4
Post-Structuralism 543
potlatches 280
Potsdam (Germany), Einstein Tower
    (Mendelsohn) 494–5, **494**
Poverty Point site, Louisiana 279
pozzolana 115, 122
Praeneste (Palestrina), Sanctuary of Fortuna
    Primigenia 318, **319**
Prague (Czech Republic)
    Nationale Nederlander office (Gehry)
        560, **562**
    St. Nicholas on the Lesser Side 376, **376**
Prairie houses (Wright) 480–4, 516
Prandtauer, Jacob 375, **376**
Pratt, Roger 392, **392**
Pravda Newspaper Building (Vesnin),
    Moscow 488, **489**, 490
prayer hall designs, Islamic, in Anatolia
    180–4
Pre-Columbian Americas 275–93, **497**
prefabrication *see* mass production
prehistoric huts 9, 87, 409
prehistoric settlements 9–10, 13–14
Priene
    house (megaron) **46**
    houses 17, 63, **64**
    Temple of Athena 62, 63
    theater 60
    town plan 62–3, **64**

Pritchard, Thomas 414, **414**, 415
Priteca, B. Marcus **500**
Provence (France) 220–1, 463
Providence, Rhode Island, Baptist church
    (Brown) 395
Pueblo *see* Ancestral Pueblo
pueblos 282, **282**, 293
Pugin, A.W.N. 429–30, **429**, 431, 448, 450,
    467, 483
"pumpkin vaults" 152, **152**, 364
putti 338
Putún culture 290
pyramids
    Aztec 292
    Egyptian 23, 24–9, 31, 293
    Inca, adobe 292
    Khmer, stepped 84
    Mayan 287, 288, **288**, 289, 291
    Olmec, earthen stepped 283, **283**
    Palenque 289
    Toltecs 291–2
    Zapotecs, stepped 285, 286
Pythagoras 295
Pytheos, architect 62

qibla 169, 170, 171, 173, 174
Queen Anne style 450, **451**, 466
Queen's House (Jones), Greenwich 349–50,
    349, 350
quincunx plans (cross-in-square)
    Byzantine 153
    Moscow, Renaissance 313
    Russian churches, Byzantine 156, **156**,
        157, 158, 194
Quirin, Egid 378
Qusayr Amra, palace 167–8, **167**, 168

Rabirius, architect 135
Racine, Wisconsin, Johnson Wax Company
    (Wright) 525–6, **525**, **526**
Radio City Music Hall (Harrison), New York
    498, 499
Raganatha Temple, Shrirangam 81–3, **82**
railroad bridge, Warren trusses 4
railroads 438, 439
Rainaldi, Carlo 365, **366**, 368
Rainaldi, Girolamo 365
raised-floor structures, Japan 102–3, 104,
    105, 106, 109
ramada, southwest tribes 281
Ramesses II 19, 32, **35**, 36, **37**
Ramsgate (Kent), St. Augustine's chapel and
    The Grange (Pugin) 429–30, **430**, 467
Rand McNally Building (Burnham and
    Root), Chicago 447
Ransome, Ernest 448
Raphael 308, 319, 326, 403
    House of Raphael (Bramante), Rome
        318–19, **319**
    Villa Madama, Rome 320–1, **320**, 339
rathas (temples) 80
Rauch, John K. **541**
Ravenna (Italy)
    Baptistery of the Orthodox 143, **145**
    church of Apollinare Nuovo **142**, 143,
        144, 148, 170
    Justinian's palace 170
    Mausoleum of Galla Placidia 144, 147–8,
        147, 204
    Palace of the Exarchs 194
    S. Apollinare in Classe **144**, 148, **148**, **149**
    S. Vitale **150**, 152–3, **153**, 192, **193**, 194
    Tomb of Theodoric 5, 305, 436
Red House (Webb), Bexleyheath 449, **449**

reeds
    Egypt 24
    Sumerian roofs 15
Reims Cathedral (France) 240, 241, **262**,
    263, 432
reinforced concrete *see* concrete
Reinhard 498
Rejsek, Matej 255
Reliance Building (Burnham and Root),
    Chicago 447, **447**
Renaissance architecture 139, 295–351
    city planning 308–9, 345–6, **345**
    in England 346–51
    in France 341–6
    gardens and landscapes 318, 339
    ideal city 308
    Moscow 312–13
retrochoir, Lincoln Cathedral Angel Choir
    251, 253
Revel (France), bastide 269, **270**
Revett, Nicholas 400
Rhodes, street **3**
rib vaults
    Gothic 229, 230, **230**, 231, 233, **235**, 431
    Norman 224, **225**, 226, **226**, 227
Richardson, Henry Hobson 430, 435, 436,
    462–7, 483, **526**
Richmond, Virginia
    cast-iron façade 446
    Medical College of Virginia (Steward) 419
    State Capitol of Virginia (Jefferson) 123,
        426, **427**
Ried, Benedikt 255, 257
Rietveld, Gerrit 501, 502, **502**, 503, 520
Rimini (Italy)
    Arch of Augustus 305, 436
    S. Francesco (Alberti) 5, 305, **305**, 306,
        436
River Forest, Illinois *see* Winslow House
Robie House (Wright), Chicago 483–4, **483**
Roche, Kevin 553, **553**
rock-cut temples 77, 79; *see also* cave-
    temples
rock-cut tombs, Egyptian 30–1, **30**, 36
Rockefeller Center, New York 498, 499
Rococo 397, 417, 452
Roebling, John Augustus 438, 440, **440**
Roebling, Washington Augustus 438, 440,
    440
Rogers, Richard 555, **555**
Roman architecture 111, 113–39, 299, 300,
    301, 330
    bridges 4, 437
    building materials 115–16, 122, 125
    building techniques 2, 114–16
    and Carolingian architecture 192, 194,
        194, 195, 196
    city planning 116–21
    domus 351
    influence on Provence Romanesque
        churches 220–1, **220**, 221
    public buildings 126–31
    residences 132–9
    ruins 307, 322, **322**, 397
    thermae *see* baths, Roman
    triple-arched structures 121, **121**, 194,
        220, **220**
    triumphal arches 118, 121, **121**, 169, 194,
        194, 220, **220**, **221**
    urban housing 132–5
    urban palaces 135–9
    see also amphitheaters; aqueducts; arches;
        basilicas; baths; castra; insulae; temples;
        theaters; vaults; villas

Romanesque architecture 115, 153, 458, 463–4, 466
  Early Romanesque 202–5
  in Germany 205–7
  Holy Roman Empire 205–9
  Italian churches 205, 207–9
Romano, Giulio 319, 338, 403, 553
  Mantua house 322
  Palazzo del Te, Mantua 322–3, **322**
  Villa Madama loggia **320**, 321
Romanticism 397, 401, 415–16, 421, 429, 440, 467, 533
Rome (Italy) 65, 116, 191, 299, 330
  Arch of Constantine 121, **121**, 194
  Arch of Septimus Severus 119, 121
  Baroque replanning 355–7
  Baroque urban open spaces 365–70
  Basilica of Constantine 306, 308, 321, 322
  Basilica Nova 127, **127**
  Basilica Ulpia **119**, 120, 126–7
  basilicas (Christian) 142, 357
  baths 129
  Baths of Diocletian **128**, 129, 317, 336
  Belvedere Courtyard (Bramante) 318, **318**, **319**, 339
  Campidoglio (Michelangelo) 325–6, **325**, **326**, 331, 361, 401
  Castel Sant'Angelo 356, 357
  catacombs 141
  Cloaca Maxima, sewer 112, 115, 118
  Colosseum (amphitheater) 121, 131, **131**, **304**, 307, 318, 321, 357, 401
  Early Christian basilicas 357
  Forum Romanum 118, **119**, 121, 401
  Forum of Trajan (Apollodorus of Damascus) **119**, 120
  forums 118, **119**, 120, 123, **123**
  founding of 112
  gardens 339
  House of Raphael (Bramante) 318–19, **319**
  Il Gesù (Vignola and Giacomo della Porta) 353–5, **354**, **355**, 373, 375
  Lateran Palace 142, 192
  Nero's Golden House **320**, 321, 403
  obelisks 357, 368, **368**
  Old St. Peter's (martyrium) 143, **144**, 194, 211
  palaces of Domitian (Rabirius) 135–6, **136**
  Palazzetto dello Sport (Nervi) **505**, 506
  Palazzo Farnese (Michelangelo and Sangallo the Younger) 326, **327**
  Pantheon 5, 124–6, **124**, **125**, 139, 152, 297, 317, 335, 359, 375, 413, 421, 428
  Piazza del Popolo **356**, 357, 368–70, 385
  Piazza dell'Esedra 129
  Piazza Navona (Bernini and Borromini) 365–8, **365**
  Piazza of St. Peter's (Bernini) 360–1, 368
  pilgrims 210, 357, **368**
  Piranesi's views of 401, **401**, 402, **402**, **405**
  Porta del Popolo 357
  Porta Pia (Michelangelo) 328–9, **329**, 356, **356**
  Portico of Octavia 307
  Roman city planning 118–21, **119**
  Roman ruins 307, 397, 401, 402, **402**
  S. Agnese in Agone (Borromini and Rainaldi) 365, **366**, 374, **390**, 392
  S. Andrea al Quirinale (Bernini) 361–2, **361**
  S. Bernardo 129
  S. Carlo alle Quattro Fontane (Borromini) 362–3, **362**, **363**

S. Costanza's church (Constantia's mausoleum) 143, **144**, **145**, 152
S. Ivo della Sapienza (Borromini and Giacomo della Porta) 363–5, **363**, **364**, 370, 372
St. John Lateran 142
S. Maria degli Angeli (Michelangelo) **128**, 129
S. Maria dei Miracoli (Rainaldi and Bernini) 368, **368**
S. Maria della Pace (Cortona) 366, **366**, 368, 392
S. Maria Maggiore, Sforza Chapel (Michelangelo) 329–30, **330**
S. Maria in Montesanto (Rainaldi and Bernini) 368, **368**
St. Peter's 5, 307, (Alberti) 317, Baroque dome 357, 358, (Bernini) 358–61, (Bramante) 315, 317, **317**, 326, 327, 387, 390, 392, (Giacomo della Porta) 328, 358, **358**, (Maderno) 328, 358, **358**, 360, (Michelangelo) 5, 326–8, **327**, **328**, 357, **358**, 359, 387, 392, (Sangallo the Younger) 326, 327
S. Susanna (Maderno) 355, **355**
Scala Regia (Bernini) 360, **360**
Spanish Steps (Francesco de Sanctis) 368, **369**
Stadium of Domitian *see* Piazza Navona
Strada Felice 356, 357
Strada Pia 356, **356**
Tempietto (Bramante) 316–17, **316**, 408
Temple of Fortuna Virilis 123, **123**
temples **119**, 120, 123, **123**, 124–6
Theater of Marcellus 129–30, **130**, 131, 336, 389
Trajan's Column **119**, 120, 375
Trajan's markets 120, **120**, 121
Vatican Obelisk 357, 358, 360, **360**, 365
Via della Conciliazione 357
Villa Madama (Raphael) 320–1, **320**, 339
warehouse (Nervi) 505
water supply 115
Ronchamp (France), Notre-Dame-du-Haut (Le Corbusier) 529–30, **529**, **530**
roofs
  bracketing systems, China 90, 91, **91**, **92**
  "hidden" structure, Japan 107
  hip, China 92
  Japan 100–7
  stave church trusses **202**
  see also hammerbeam roofs; shatyor; shikhara roofs
Root, John Welborn 447, **447**
Rossellino, Bernardo **307**, 317, 325
Rossi, Aldo 549–50
Rotterdam (Holland), Hook of Holland housing project (Oud) 501, **501**
Roycrofters Workshop 450
Rurik 155, 199
Ruskin, John 435, 448–9, 450, 454, 475
Russia
  bochki gables 161, **162**, **163**
  Byzantine churches, masonry and timber 155–63, 194
  horizontal log construction 159–61
  icons 158, 159, 162
  onion domes **154**, 158–9, 163
  see also Constructivism; shatyor
rustication
  Baroque 381
  Renaissance 303, 318, 319, 322, 333, 338, 344, 351

Saarinen, Eero 537–8
sahns 169, 170, 172, 181, 183
St. Basil the Blessed *see* Moscow
St. Denis abbey church (France) 230–2, **231**, **232**, 237, 239, **239**, 432
St. Gall, Benedictine monastery (Plan of St. Gall) **196**, 197–8, **197**, 205, **222**, 223, 379
St. Gallen abbey church (Beer) 378–9, **378**
S. Gimignano (Italy) 264, **265**
St. Gilles-du-Gard, Provence (France) 220–1, **220**, 463, **463**
St. Louis, Missouri, Wainwright Building (Adler and Sullivan) 468–70, **469**
St. Luke's in Smithfield, Virginia 273
S. Marco *see* Venice
St. Martin at Canigou, monastery 202, **203**, 204, 214
St. Martin at Tours 210
St. Michael Longstanton, Cambs. (England) 431
St. Paul's Cathedral *see* London
St. Peter's *see* Rome
St. Petersburg (Russia) 381
St. Savin-sur-Gartempe, hall church **218**, 219–20, **219**, **220**, 255
St. Sophia *see* Kiev
Saint-Gaudens, Augustus 463
Salamanca (Spain), Old Cathedral 463
Salginatobel Bridge (Maillart) (Switzerland) 503, **503**
salients 308, **309**
Salisbury, Wilts. (England)
  cathedral **248**, 249–50, **249**, **250**
  houses in cathedral close 392
saltbox houses 6, 7, **7**
saltworks (Ledoux) 406–7, **407**
Samuel Daggett House, Connecticut 6
San Francisco, Calif.
  Halladie Building (Polk) 470, **471**
  Sea Ranch I (Moore) 545, **546**
  V.C. Morris Gift Shop (Wright) 526, **526**
Sanchi (India)
  fence and torana gate 71, **72**
  Great Stupa 71–2, **71**
  temples 72, 73, **73**, 77
Sanctis, Francesco de 368, **369**
Sangallo the Younger, Antonio da 326, 327, **327**
Sanmichele, Michele 338, **338**
Sansovino, Jacopo 331, 336, **337**, 338, **338**, 411
Santa Monica, Calif. *see* Los Angeles
Sant'Elia, Antonio 488, **488**, **489**
Santiago de Compostela *see* Compostela
Saqqara (Egypt)
  Djoser's funerary complex 25–6, **25**
  pyramid 24–6, **25**, **26**
Sargon II, Assyrian ruler 19, 20
Sassanian, audience halls 168, 169, 172
Satiangam Temple, Kanchipuram **82**
Saulnier, Jules 445, **445**
Sayid Ghiyath, Mirak *see* Ghiyath, Mirak Sayid
Sayid, Muhammad, architect 176–7
Säynätsalo (Finland), Town Hall (Aalto) 537, **537**
Scamozzi, Vincenzo 336, **336**, 346, 349, 351, 400
Scheerbart, Paul 491–2, **493**
Schinkel, Karl Friedrich 420–1, **420–2**, 479, 480, 515, 553
Schliemann, Heinrich 42, 44

Schroeder House (Rietveld), Utrecht 502, **502**, **503**, 520
Schwandbach Bridge (Maillart) 503–4
Scythians 20, 199
Sea Ranch I (Moore), San Francisco 545, **546**
Seagram Building (Mies van der Rohe), New York City 470, 522, **522**
Seaside, Florida 550
sections 5, 6, **6**
Segovia (Spain), Roman aqueduct 465
seismic loads 2
    Wright's hotel 486
Seleucids 57
Selimiye Mosque (Sinan), Edirne 183–4, **183**
Semper, Gottfried 490
Senmut, architect 32
Sens Cathedral (France) 229, 247, **247**
Serliana **306**, 331, 370, 382, 395, 400, **406**, 408, 480, 544
Serlio, Sebastiano 331, 343–4, 345, 346, 348, 389
Sezincote (Cockerell), Glos. (England) 419, **419**
Sforza family 308, 311, 313–14, 341
Sha-ji-ki-Dheri, Mahastupa 75
Shanghai (China), Longhua Pagoda 90
Sharp, Dennis 476
shatyor (tent roof) 161, **161**, 163
Shaw, Richard Norman 430, 450, **450**, **451**, 466
shed houses, northwestern tribes 280, **280**
shikhara roofs, India 77, 78, **78**, **89**, 90
Shingle Style 450, 466–7, **467**, 543
shingles, Russian churches 161, **162**, 163
Shinto shrines 99, 102–3, 109
Shreve, Richmond 499, **499**
Shrewsbury, Shropshire (England), flax mill 415
shrines
    Buddhist, in India 69, 70–6
    Canterbury, St. Thomas à Becket 247, **248**
    Catal Hüyük 10, **10**
    Christian 166
    India 69, 70–5
    Islamic 165–7
    Shinto, Japan 99, 102–3, 109
    Sumerian 15
Shrirangam, Raganatha Temple 81–3, **82**
Siena (Italy) 272, **272**, 295
Simone da Orsenigo, master builder 259
Simpson-Lee House (Murcutt), Mount Wilson 567, **567**
Sinan, Koca 180–4
    Mosque of Süleyman the Magnificent 181, **182**, 183
    Selimiye Mosque, Edirne 183–4, **183**
    Shehzade Mosque, Istanbul **180**, 181, **181**
sipapu 282
Sixtus IV, pope 356
Sixtus V, pope 355–7, **356**, 362, 365, 368, **368**
skeletal construction, concrete and wood 448
Skidmore, Owings, and Merrill 515–16, 538
skin-coverings
    prehistoric huts 9
    subarctic tupik 280
Skislewicz, Anton **500**
skyscrapers 445–8, 469–70, 496–9, **554**
Smeaton, John 448
Smythson, Robert 347–9, **347**, **348**
Sneferu, pharaoh 26–7

Soane, Sir John 423–4, **423**, **424**
Solari, Guiniforte **311**, 312
Songyue Pagoda, Dengfeng 90
Soufflot, Jacques-Gabriel 409–10, **409**
southwestern and southeastern tribes, North America **276**, 281–2
Spain
    Art Nouveau see Gaudí, Antonio
    Islamic architecture 165, 186–9, **194**, 195, 202
    mosques with columnar hall designs, Islamic 170–2
Specchi, Alessandro 368, **369**
Speyer Cathedral (Germany) **204**, 205, 206
Sphinx, Giza 27, **28**, **29**, 36
squinches 209, 211–12, **212**
stairs
    Baroque 372
    France, Renaissance 343
    monumental, Renaissance 318
State Capitol of Virginia see Richmond
Statue of Liberty (Eiffel, Bartholdi, and Hunt) 433, 445, **445**
Ste.-Marie-de-la-Tourette (Le Corbusier), Eveux-sur-l'Arbrèsle 530, **530**
steel 2, 3, 4, 438, 440, 444, 445, 447, 448, 469, 483, 521–2
Steiner, Rudolf 492, 494, **494**
stelae, Mayan 288, **289**
Stephenson, Robert **437**, 438
stereotomy 382, **384**
Stern, Robert A.M. 549–50
Steward, Thomas S. 419
Stirling, James 551–3, **551**, **552**
stoas
    Greek 60, 61, **61**, 62, **62**, 63, 118, 126
    Neo-Classical 421
Stock Exchange (Berlage), Amsterdam 490, **490**
stone (masonry) construction
    arches and vaults 114–15
    Byzantine churches in Russia 155–9
    Carolingian revival 192–5
    Egypt 26, 122
    Greek transition to 47
    Roman 115, 122
    in tension 3, 114
Stonehenge, Wilts. (England) 11–13, **12**, **13**
Stornoloco, Gabrielle 259
Stoughton House (Richardson), Cambridge (Mass.) 466–7, **467**
strapwork decoration 347, **348**
Strawberry Hill (Walpole), Twickenham **396**, 417
Streamline Modern 499, **500**
Street, George Edmund 450
Strickland, William 59, 419, 426, **426**
structural design 413–14
structural systems, classification 3
Structuralism 543, 544
Strutt, William 414–15, **415**
Stuart, James 400
Stubbins, Hugh 553, **554**
stupas, India 70–6, **70**, 89, **89**, 90, 158
Stupinigi (Italy), royal hunting lodge (Juvarra) 372, **373**
Sturgis, Russell 435
Stuttgart (Germany)
    Staatsgalerie (Stirling) **552**, 553
    Weissenhof Siedlung 518–20
stylobate 51
subarctic tribes **276**, 280
subway system stations see Paris; Vienna

Sugar Loaf Mountain, Maryland, observatory (Wright) 526
Suger, Abbot 230–2, 237, 238, 239, 245
Süleyman the Magnificent, mosque and tomb (Sinan), Istanbul 181, **182**, 183
Sullivan, Louis Henri 434, 467–73, 477, 479, 480, **480**, **481**, **526**
Sumerians 14, 15–16, 19, 39
Sunila (Finland), Cellulose Factory (Aalto) 534–5, **536**
suspension bridges 4, **5**, 438, **438**, 440, **440**
Suzhou (China), garden 97, **97**, **98**, 99, **99**
Swanke, Hayden, and Connell 553, **554**
Sydney (Australia)
    Ball-Eastaway House (Murcutt) 565
    Douglas Murcutt House (Murcutt) **564**, 565
Syria and Syrians 18, 19, 165, 170, 266
    pointed arches 167–8, 229
    see also Damascus

tablero motifs see talud and tablero motifs
tablinum 132, **132**, 135
Taihu rocks 97
Taj Mahal, Agra (India) 177–9, **178**
Talenti, Francesco 296
Talman, William 392, 393, **393**
talud and tablero motifs 283, 285, **285**, 286, **286**, 288, **290**, 292
Tanjore (India), Brihedesvara Temple 80, **81**
Taos Pueblo, near Santa Fe 293
tatami, Japan **105**, 106, **108**, 109
Tatlin, Vladimir 488, **489**
Taut, Bruno 492, **493**
Tavanasa Bridge (Maillart) 503
tea houses, Japan **108**, 109, **109**
Team Disneyland Administration Building (Gehry), Los Angeles 560, **561**
Teatro Olimpico (Palladio and Scamozzi), Vicenza 336, **336**
Telford, Thomas 415, 438
Temple of Apollo Epicurius, Bassai 48, 57–8, **57**
Temple of Artemis, Ephesos 47
Temple of Athena see Priene
Temple of Athena Nike see Athens
Temple of Athena Polias see Athens
Temple of Hera see Olympia; Paestum
    Olympia 47, **48**
    Paestum 48, 49–50, **50**, 51
Temple of Solomon see Jerusalem
temples
    Babylon 18
    Buddhist, in India 89, in Japan 99–102
    China 89, 90, 91–3, **91**, 96
    Egyptian, mortuary and valley 27–9, 30, **30**, **31**, 32–4, **32**, **33**, 35, 36, 37, 40, 47
    Etruscan 111–12, **112**, 123
    Greek 47, 49–50, 92, 111, 112, **112**, 123, 333, 400
    Hattusas 18, **18**
    Heliopolis 24
    Hindu, in India 76–85, **76**, **89**, 90
    India 69, 70–85, 89, **89**, 90
    Jain 70
    Japan 99–103, **104**, 107
    Khmer 83, 84, 85
    Mayan 287, 288, **288**, 289, **289**
    Neo-Sumerian 16–17, **16**
    Palenque 289, **289**
    rathas 80
    Roman 113, **114**, 115, 118, **119**, 120, 122, 123–6, **123**, 142, 152, 170, 375
    Sumerian 15, **15**, **16**

Zapotecs 286
Zen Buddhist, in Japan 107
see also Athens; cave-temples; Knossos; Rome; shrines
Tennessee State Capitol (Strickland), Nashville 59, 426, **426**
Tenochtitlán (Mexico) 292, **292**
tension, of structural materials 2, 3, 4–5, **5**
Teotihuacán (Mexico) 283, **284**, 285, **285**, 291
Tepe Gawra, Sumer (Iraq), temple 15, **15**
tepidarium
    Islamic 168
    Roman 129, **129**
terracotta
    America 469–70, 473
    Etruscan 112
    molded details 49
textile mills 414–15, **415**
thatch/thatch roofs
    bamboo structures 77
    China 87, **88**
    Egypt 24
    Greece 47
    Japan 103, **105**, 106
    medieval 263, 264
    Native American 279
Theater of Marcellus *see* Rome
theaters
    Art Deco 499, **500**
    French Neo-Classical 410–11, **411**
    Greek 59–60, **59**, **60**, 126, 129, 130
    Renaissance stage-sets 329
    Roman 117, **117**, 118, **118**, 126, 129–31, 336
Thebes (Egypt) 30, 34, 35–6
Theodoric, tomb in Ravenna 5, 305, 436
Theophanes the Greek 158
thermae *see* baths, Roman
tholoi
    Greek 58, **58**, 123
    Mycenaean tombs 44–5, **44**
Thomas of Hoo 249
Thornton, William 428
Thorpe, John 349
Thumb, Peter 379
tiercon vaults 247, **251**, 253
Tijou, Jean, ironmonger 392
Tikal (Guatemala) 287–8, **287**, **288**
Timgad (Algeria), Roman city 118, **118**, 121
Timur the Lame 174, 176
tipi 275, **276**
Tiryns, palace megarons, gates and citadel 43, 46–7, **46**, **47**
Tivoli (Italy) 115
    Hadrian's Villa 136–9, **320**, 364, 539, 541, 551
    Temple of the Sibyl 123
    Villa d'Este garden (Ligorio) 339–40, **340**, 547
Todaiji, Nara (Japan), monastery 100–1
    Great South Gate 101, **101**
Todi (Italy)
    S. Fortunato 259, **259**
    S. Maria della Consolazione (Cola da Caprarola and Bramante) 313, **314**
tokonoma 109
Tokyo (Japan), Imperial Hotel (Wright) 486, **486**
tollgates (Ledoux), Paris 407–8
Toltecs 286, 290, 291–2
tombs
    Egyptian 30–2, mastaba 24, **24**, 25, **28**, rock-cut 30–1, **30**, 36

English Renaissance 346
Etruscan 112
Islamic 176–9, 181, 183
Mayan 289
megalithic, chambered and passage 10–11, **10**, **11**, 13
Mycenaean (tholoi) 44–5, **44**
Renaissance 305, 323
Theodoric, in Ravenna 5, 305, 436
toranas (entrance gates) 71, 72, **72**
torii (gateway), Japan 102
totem poles 280, 288
Toulouse (France), St. Sernin **190**, 210–11, **210**, **211**, 213, 214, 432
Tournus (France), St. Philibert, monastic church 204–5, **204**, **205**, 210, 223
tower houses, medieval 264, **265**
Town, Ithiel 437
town walls
    medieval 268, **268**, **269**
    Renaissance 308
trabeated systems 3, 384, **426**
Trans World Airlines Terminal (Saarinen), Kennedy Airport, New York 537–8, **538**
tree cult 43
Tribolo, Niccolò 340–1, **341**
triclinium (dining room) 134, 136, 141
Trinity Church *see* Boston
triple-arched structures
    American 463, **463**
    Islamic palace 169
    Roman 121, **121**, 194, 220, **220**
    Romanesque 463
    see also mosques
triumphal arches
    Neo-Classical 407, 408, 413
    Renaissance 305, 306, **306**, 346, 349
    Roman 118, 121, **121**, 169, 194, **194**, 220, **220**, **221**
trusses 3, 4, **4**, 437–8
Tschumi, Bernard 557, **557**
Tula (Mexico), pyramid and temple 291–2, **291**
Tun-Huang caves (China) 74
Tuni, Badi' al-Zaman 174
tupik, subarctic region 280
Turin (Italy)
    Cappella della SS. Sindone (Guarini) 370, **370**
    Palazzo Madama (Juvarra) 372
    S. Lorenzo (Guarini) 370, **371**, 372
Turner, Claude A.P. 503
Turner, Richard 441, **441**
Tuscan order 111, 351, **351**, 361, 368, 407, 408, 411
Tutankhamun, pharaoh 36
tympanums 212–13, **212**, 217, **217**
Tyre, basilica 146

Al Ubaid people 15
Udaigiri, rock-cut temples 77
Udine, Giovanni da 321
Uffizi (Vasari), Florence 321–2, **321**
Uji-Yamada (Japan), Ise Shrine 102–3, **103**
Ukraine, prehistoric huts 9
Umayyad Dynasty 167, 170
underground structures *see* barabara; catacombs; iglu
United States of America
    American style 462–73
    architectural university education 432–7
    Art Deco 496–501
    Arts and Crafts Movement 448
    Baroque church prototypes 395, **395**

Blois château **342**
bridges 437
Ecclesiological Movement 431
Georgian houses 335, **335**, 392, **392**, **393**
International Style 520
log construction 159–60, 282
Neo-Classicism 424–8
railroads 439
Renaissance prototypes **319**
tribes, Native American 275–82
urban design 356
Venetian palazzi models 338
Unity Temple (Wright), Oak Park 293, 484, 485–6, **485**
University of Pennsylvania, Philadelphia, Richards Medical Research Building (Kahn) 539, **539**
University of Virginia (Jefferson), Charlottesville 126, 428, **428**
Upjohn, Richard 430, 431
Uppark (Talman), Sussex (England) 392, **393**
Ur, Mesopotamia (Iraq), houses and ziggurat 16, 17–18, **17**
Urban VIII, pope 359, 364
Urbino (Italy) 308, 310–11, **310**
Urnes (Norway)
    carved portal 200, **200**, **201**
    stave churches 199–200, **200**, **201**
Uruk, Sumer, White Temple 15, **16**
U.S. Capitol
    dome (Walter) 5
    (Latrobe) 413, 419, 424
Usonian houses 523
Utrecht (Holland), Schroeder House (Rietveld) 502, **502**, **503**, 520
Uxmal (Mexico) 289–90, **290**

Valadier, Giuseppe 368, **369**
Valinotto (Italy), Santa Maria della Visitazione (Vittone) 372
Van de Velde, Henri 492, 494, 495
Vanbrugh, Sir John 393–4, **393**, **394**, 395
Vasari, Giorgio 299, 319, 321–2, **321**, 326
vaults 3
    Baroque 370
    Hattusas, corbeled 18
    net vaulting **256**, 257
    Norman rib 224, **225**, 226, **226**, 227
    pendant 417
    quadripartite 229, 237, **237**, 243, 245, 249
    Roman 112, 114, **114**, 115, 120, **121**, 122, 125, 126–30, **127**, **128**
    sexpartite 237, **237**, 239, **241**, 243, **243**
    see also barrel-vaults; fan vaults; groin-vaults; lierne vaults; muqarnas vaults; "pumpkin" vaults; tiercon vaults
Vaux-le-Vicomte (France), château (Le Vau) 384, **385**
vegetable fibers 4, 438
Veneto, villa designs by Palladio 331–5
Venice (Italy) 295, 336–8
    Ca' d'Oro 272–3, **273**
    Doge's Palace 272, **273**, 336
    La Zecca (Sansovino), mint 338, **338**, 411
    Library of S. Marco (Sansovino) 331, 336, **337**, 338
    Lido villa (Loos) 479, **479**
    medieval 272
    Palazzo Grimani (Sanmichele) 338, **338**
    Palazzo Vendramini-Calergi (Coducci) 336
    Palladian churches 335–6

Piazza S. Marco 336, **337**
Renaissance 336–8
S. Francesca della Vigne (Palladio) 335
S. Giorgio Maggiore (Palladio) 335–6, **335**
S. Marco **140**, **150**, 153, **154**, 218, **218**, 313
Scuola di S. Marco 336
SS. Giovanni e Paolo (or S. Zanipolo) 259, **260**
Venturi, Robert 476, 541–3, **541**, 558
verdika (stone fence) 72, **72**
Versailles (France)
  château 384–5, **386**, 397
  hamlet (Mique) 417, **417**
  Petit Trianon (Gabriel) 410, **410**
Vesnin, Viktor and Alexandr 488, **489**, 490
Vézelay (France)
  Mystic Mill capital 215, **215**
  Ste. Madeleine abbey **216**, 217, 432
Vicenza (Italy) 349
  basilica (Palladio) 331, **331**
  Palazzo Chiericati (Palladio) 331, **332**, 349–50
  Palazzo Valmarana (Palladio) 331
  Teatro Olimpico (Palladio and Scamozzi) 336, **336**
  Villa Rotonda (Villa Americo-Capra) (Palladio) 333, **334**, 398, 399
Vienna (Austria)
  Goldman and Salatsch Store (Loos) 479, **479**
  Karlskirche 374–5, **374**, **375**
  Moller House (Loos) 478–9, **478**
  Postal Savings Bank (Wagner) 460–1, **460**, **461**
  Secession Hall (Olbrich) 461, **462**
  Stadtbahn (subway system) stations (Wagner) 460
  Steiner House (Loos) **477**, 478, 479
Viennese Secession 460–1, 477
Vierzehnheiligen (Germany), church (Neumann) 380–1, **380**, 397
Vignola, Giacomo Barozzi da 339, **340**, 346, 354–5, **354**, **355**
viharas 70, 72, **73**
Viipuri (Russia), Municipal Library (Aalto) **532**, 533
Vikings 155, 197, 199, 200, 224; see also Norway, stave churches
Villa d'Este garden (Ligorio), Tivoli 339–40, **340**, 547
Villa Giulia 339
Villa Lante (Vignola), Bagnaia 339, **340**
Villa Madama (Raphael), Rome 320–1, **320**, 339
Villa Rotonda, Vicenza see Palladio, Andrea
Villa Savoye (Le Corbusier), Poissy 509, **510**, 511
Villard, Henry 435, **435**
Villard de Honnecourt 233, 262–3, **262**
villas
  Japan 107, **108**, 109, **109**
  Neo-Classical **422**
  Renaissance 320–1, **320**, 331–5
  Roman 135–9, 318, 320

Villefranche-de-Rouergue (France), bastide 269, **270**
Vincent, St. 147, **147**
Viollet-le-Duc, Eugène-Emmanuel 234, 431–2, **432**, 448, 453, 490
Virgin Mary 232, 237
Virginia State Capitol see Richmond
Vishnu Temple, Bhitargaon 77, **77**
Vitruvius (Marcus Vitruvius Pollio) 1, 47, 49, 56, 62, 115, 296, 317, 381, 398, 400, 402, 403, 414
  basilica 350, 390
  education of architects 114
  Etruscan temples 112
  Renaissance 331, 332–3, 335, 336
  The Ten Books of Architecture 114, 296, 303, 304
Vittone, Bernardo 372, **372**
Vladimir, Prince of Kiev 155–6
volutes (scrolls), Ionic 48, **49**
voussoirs 3, **3**
Voysey, Charles Francis Annesley 450–1, **452**
Vries, Hans Vredman de 347, 348

Wagner, Otto 460–1, **460**, **461**, 550
Wailly, Charles de 401, 411, **411**
Wainwright Building (Adler and Sullivan), St. Louis 468–70, **469**
al-Walid I, Caliph 167, 170
wall-pillar churches see churches
Walpole, Horace **396**, 417
Walter, Thomas U. 5
Ward Willits House (Wright), Highland Park 481, **482**
Ware, Isaac **330**
Warren, Michigan, General Motors Technical Center (Saarinen) 537
Warren trusses 4, **4**, 437
Washington, Connecticut see Lang House
Washington D.C. 357, **386**, 544
Wastell, John 249, 254
watchtowers, China 89, 90
water tower (Poelzig), Posen 495, **495**
Watts Sherman House (Richardson), Newport, Rhode Island 466, **466**
Wayzata, Minnesota, Winton Guest House (Gehry) 560, **561**
Webb, Philip 449, **449**
Weimar (Germany) see Bauhaus
Weissenhof Siedlung 518–20
Wendigen 490–1
westwerks
  Carolingian 194, 204
  Early Romanesque 204, 205
Whistler, James MacNeill 453
White, Stanford 435, **466**, 479
wigwams 277, **277**
wikiup 275
William the Englishman 247, **248**
William of Sens 247, **248**
wind-eyes 199, **201**
wind loads 2, **256**, 257
window tracery, Gothic (plate and bar) 230, 238, 243, 245, 247, **247**

Windyhill (Mackintosh), Kilmacolm 458
Winslow House (Wright), River Forest 481, **481**, **482**, 514, 520
Winton Guest House (Gehry), Wayzata 560, **561**
Wittgenstein, Ludwig 543
Wollaton Hall (Smythson), Notts. (England) 347–8, **347**, **348**
Wood, Robert 402
wooden structures 2
  bridge trusses 4
  China 90, 91, 96, 98
  Indian temples and shrines 80, **80**
  Japan 99–109
  North America 279, 280–1, **281**
  Russian churches 159–63
  see also log construction
wool churches 246
World's Columbian Exposition, Chicago 433–4, **434**, 467
Wren, Christopher 388–92, 393, 395
  London replanning 388, 389
  St. Paul's Cathedral, London 5, 388, 389, 390, **390**, **391**, 392, 409
  St. Stephen Walbrook, London 389, **389**, **390**
  Sheldonian Theater, Oxford **388**, 389
Wright, Frank Lloyd 97, 106, 430, 450, 473, 475, 479, 480–7, 501, 512, 523–8
  Broadacre City 523, 531
  early public buildings 484–6
  Fallingwater (Kaufmann House), Ohiopyle 483, 523, **524**, 525
  Guggenheim Museum 526, **527**, 550
  Johnson Wax Company, Racine 525–6, **525**, **526**
  Prairie houses 480–4, 516
  Taliesin West 528
  Unity Temple 293, 484, 485–6, **485**
  Usonian houses 523
  V.C. Morris Gift Shop, San Francisco 526, **526**
Würzburg Residenz (Neumann) (Germany) **352**, 379, **379**, 397

Xian (China), Great Mosque 179–80, **179**; see also Chang'an

Yale University, Connecticut, Morse and Stiles colleges (Saarinen) 538, **538**
Yingxian (China), Fogong Temple **89**, 90, **90**
Yoshimura House, near Osaka (Japan) **105**

Zamość (Poland) 308–9, **309**
Zamoyski, Jan 308
Zapotecs 285–6
Zen Buddhism, architecture 107–9
Zig-Zag Moderne 499
ziggurats
  Khorsabad 19, **19**
  Mesopotamia 16–18, **16**, **17**, 293
Zimmerman, Dominikus 376, **377**
Zimmerman, Johann Baptist 376, 397
Zurich (Switzerland), warehouse 503